TAIYO MATSUMOTO

No.5

2

CONTENT5

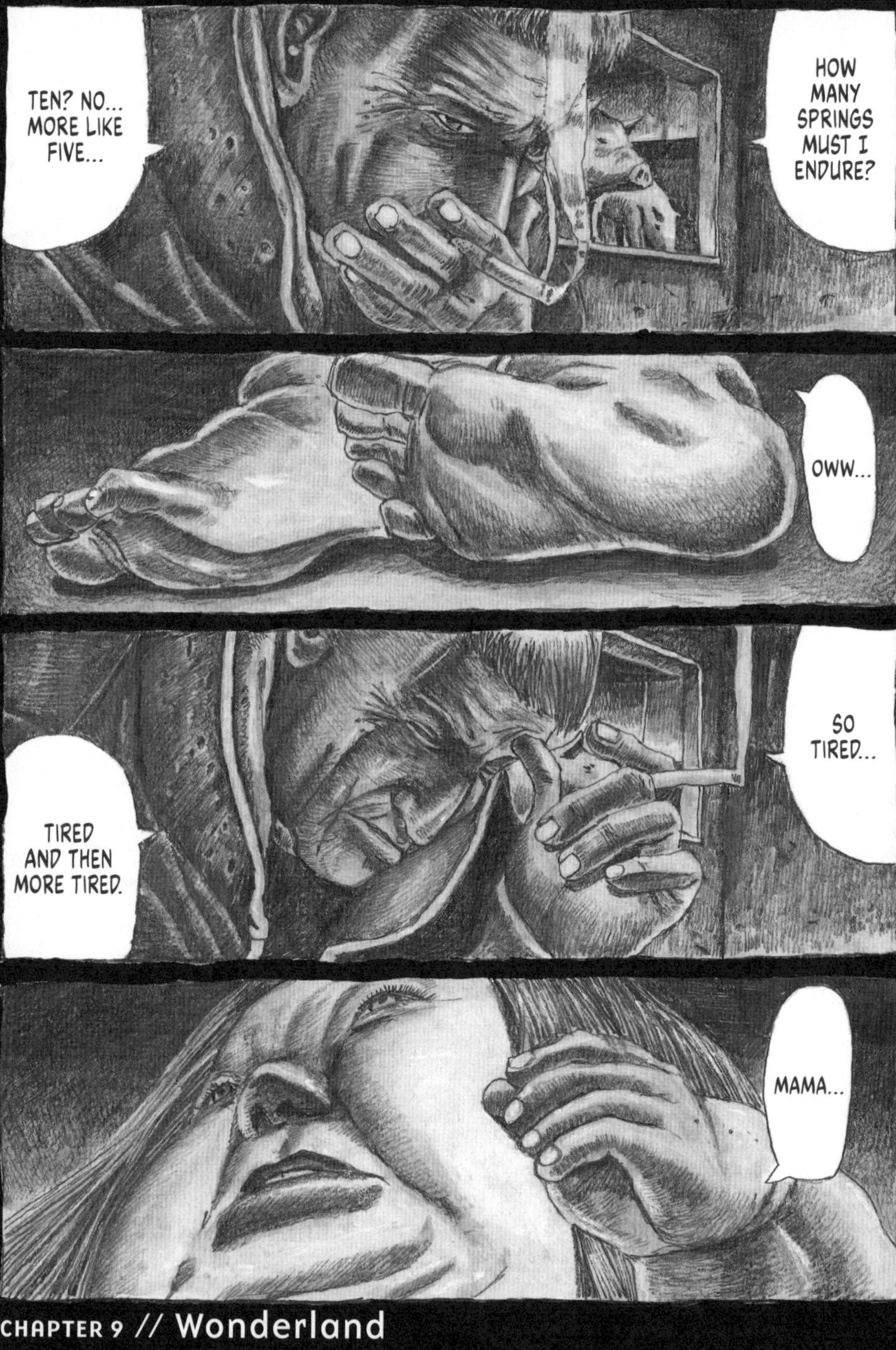
HOW MANY SPRINGS MUST I ENDURE?
TEN? NO... MORE LIKE FIVE...
OWW...
SO TIRED...
TIRED AND THEN MORE TIRED.
MAMA...

CHAPTER 9 // Wonderland

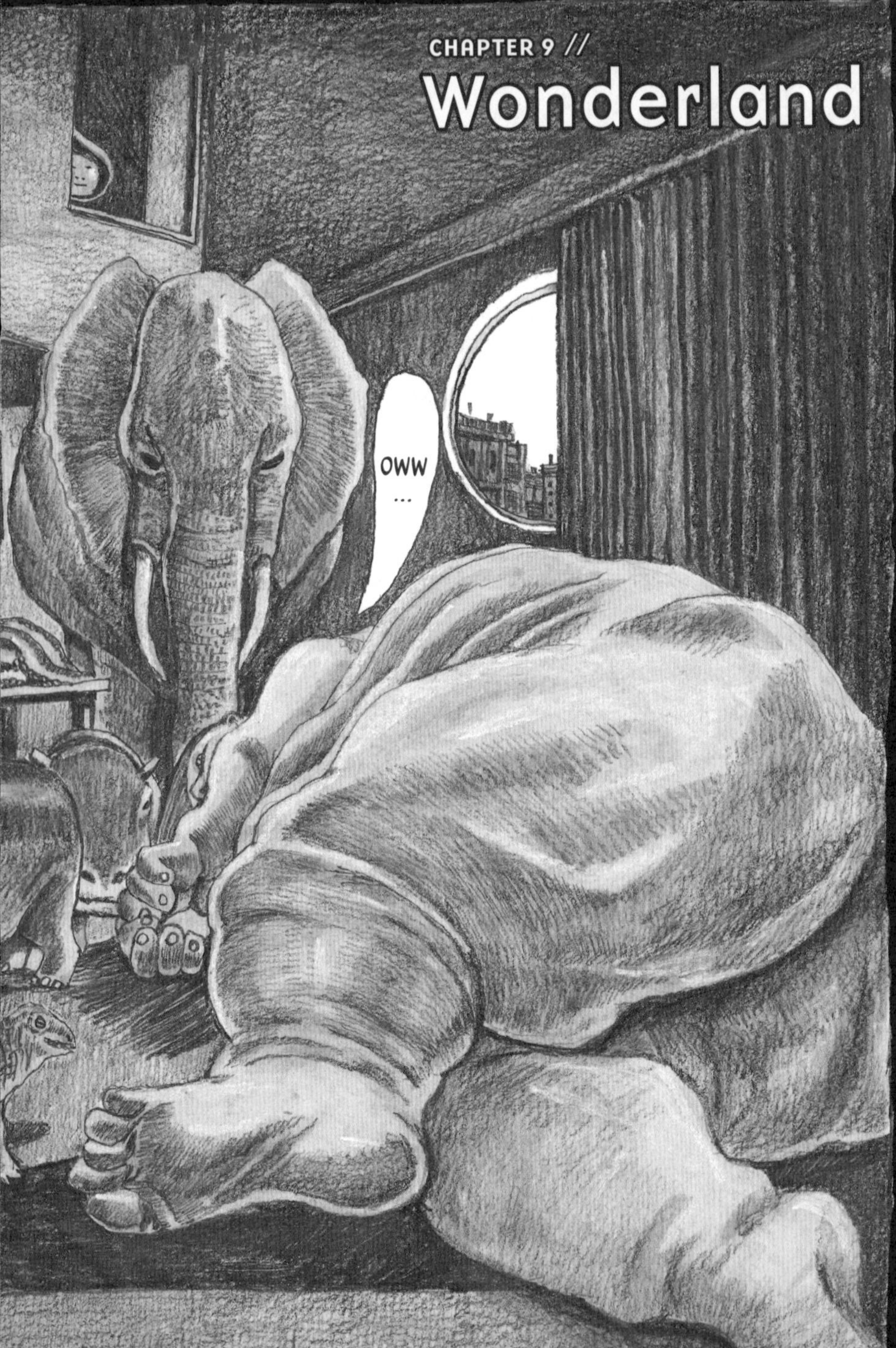
CHAPTER 9 //
Wonderland
OWW ...

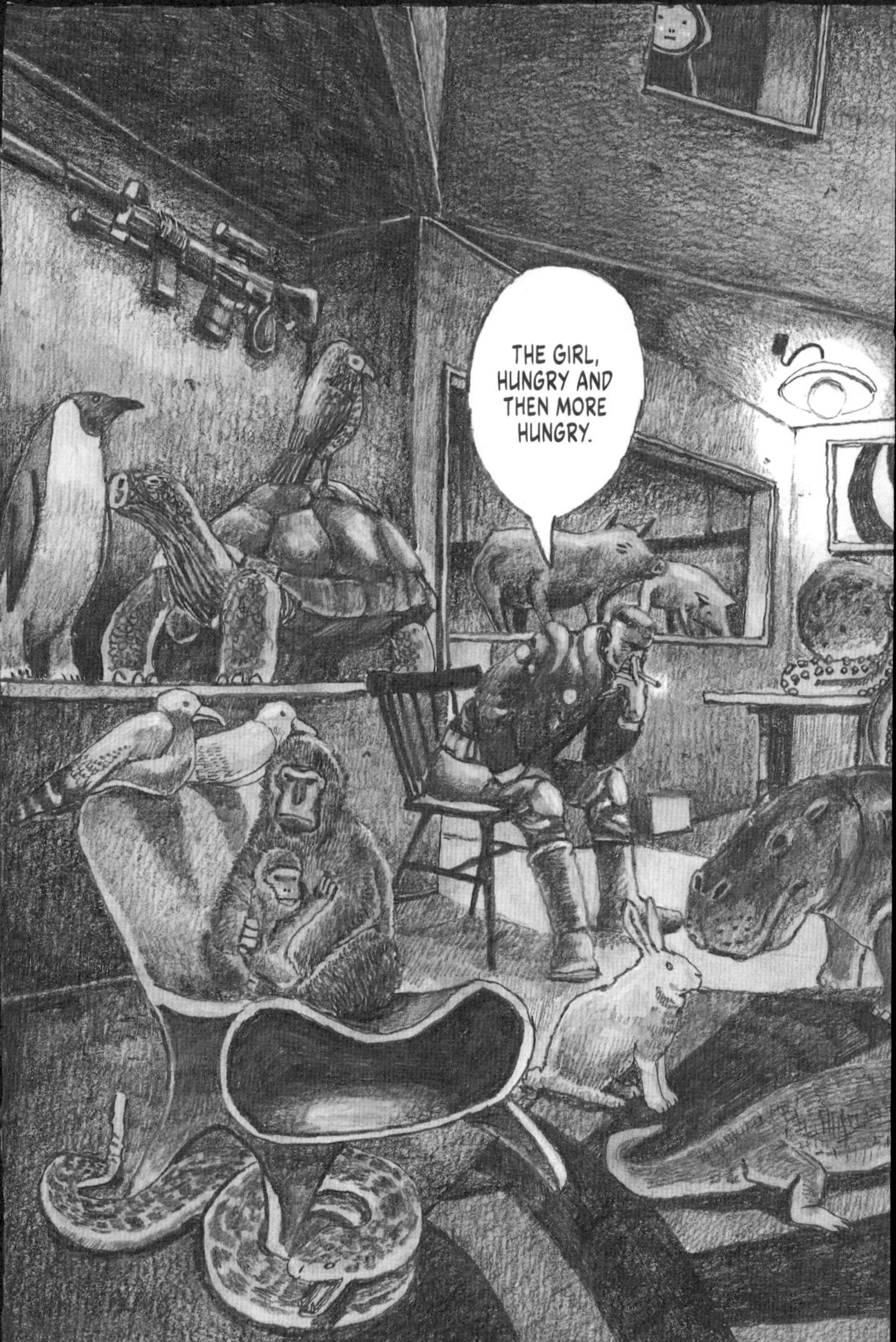
THE GIRL, HUNGRY AND THEN MORE HUNGRY.

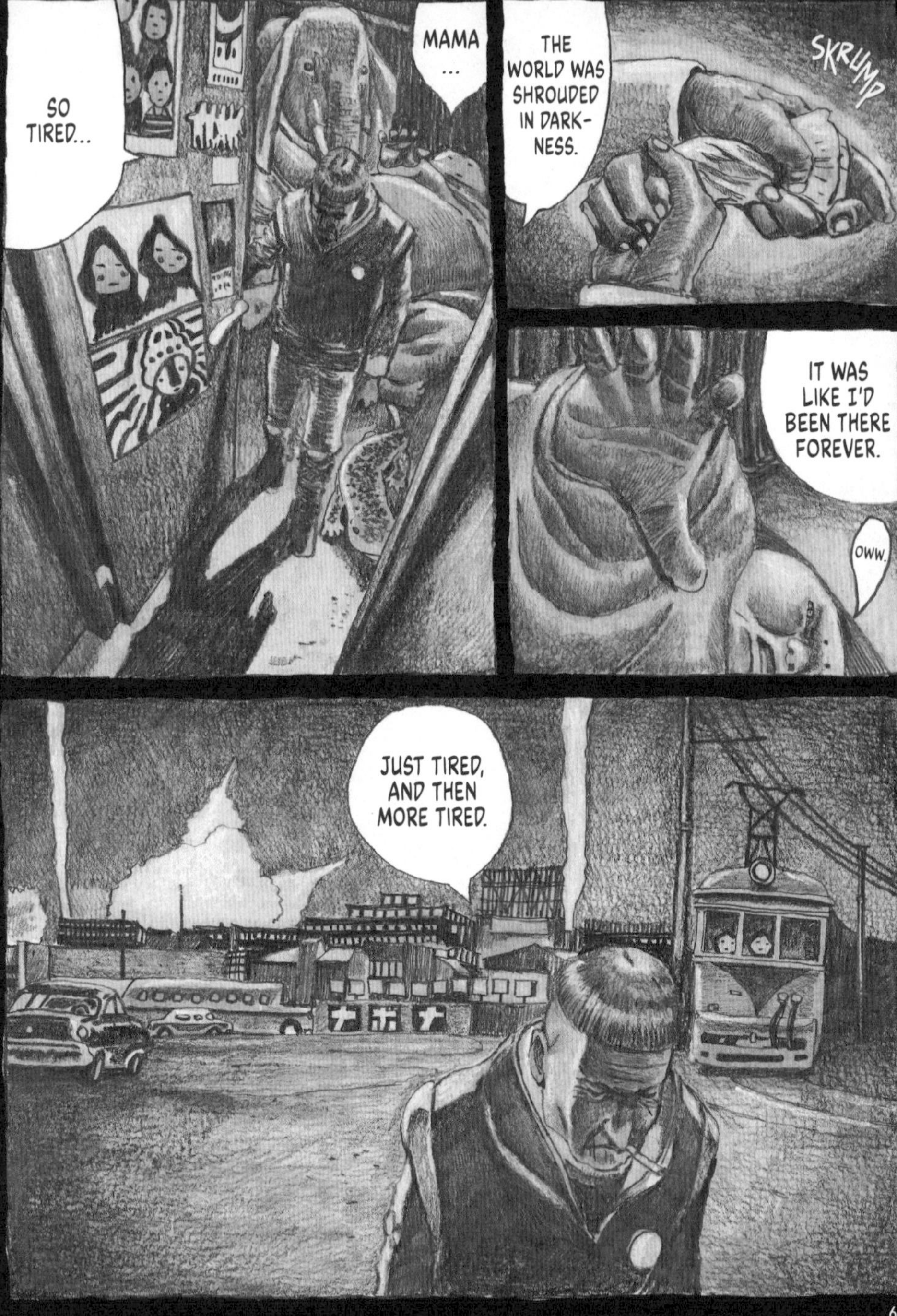
THE WORLD WAS SHROUDED IN DARKNESS.
SKRUMP
IT WAS LIKE I'D BEEN THERE FOREVER.
OWW.
MAMA ...
SO TIRED...
JUST TIRED, AND THEN MORE TIRED.

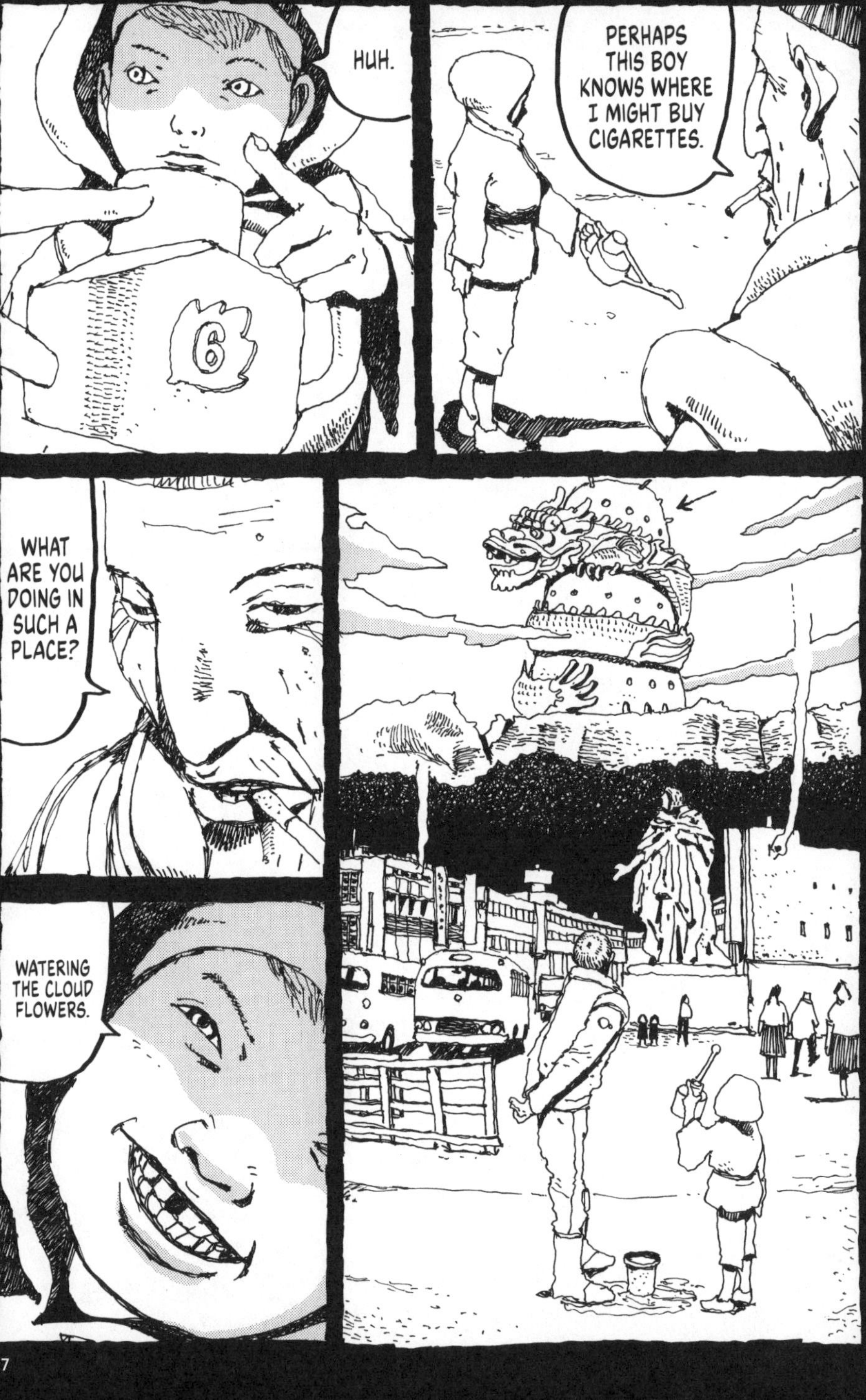
PERHAPS THIS BOY KNOWS WHERE I MIGHT BUY CIGARETTES.
HUH.
WHAT ARE YOU DOING IN SUCH A PLACE?
WATERING THE CLOUD FLOWERS.

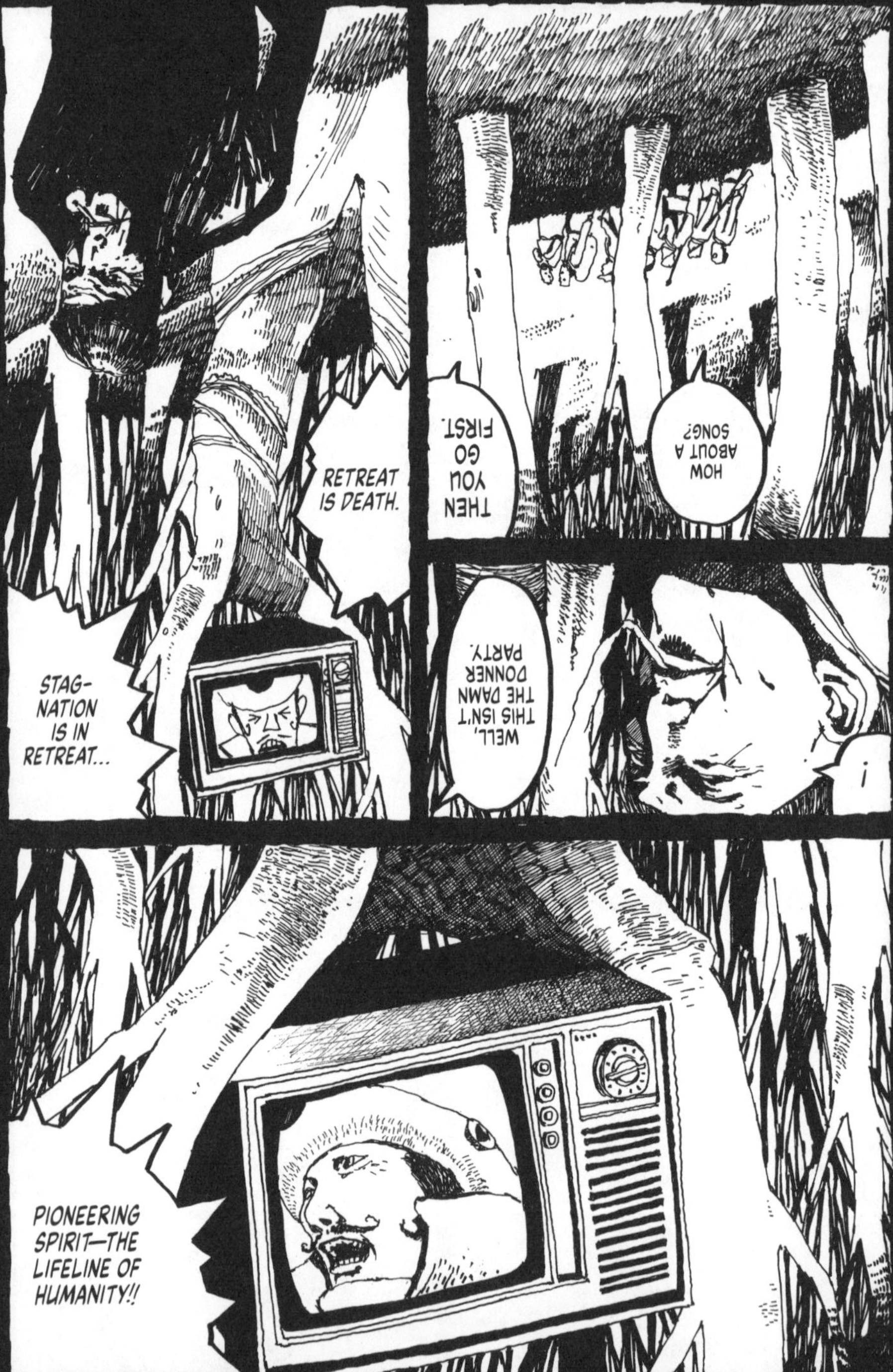
HOW ABOUT A SONG?
THEN YOU GO FIRST.
!
WELL, THIS ISN'T THE DAMN DONNER PARTY.
RETREAT IS DEATH.
STAG-NATION IS IN RETREAT...
PIONEERING SPIRIT—THE LIFELINE OF HUMANITY!!

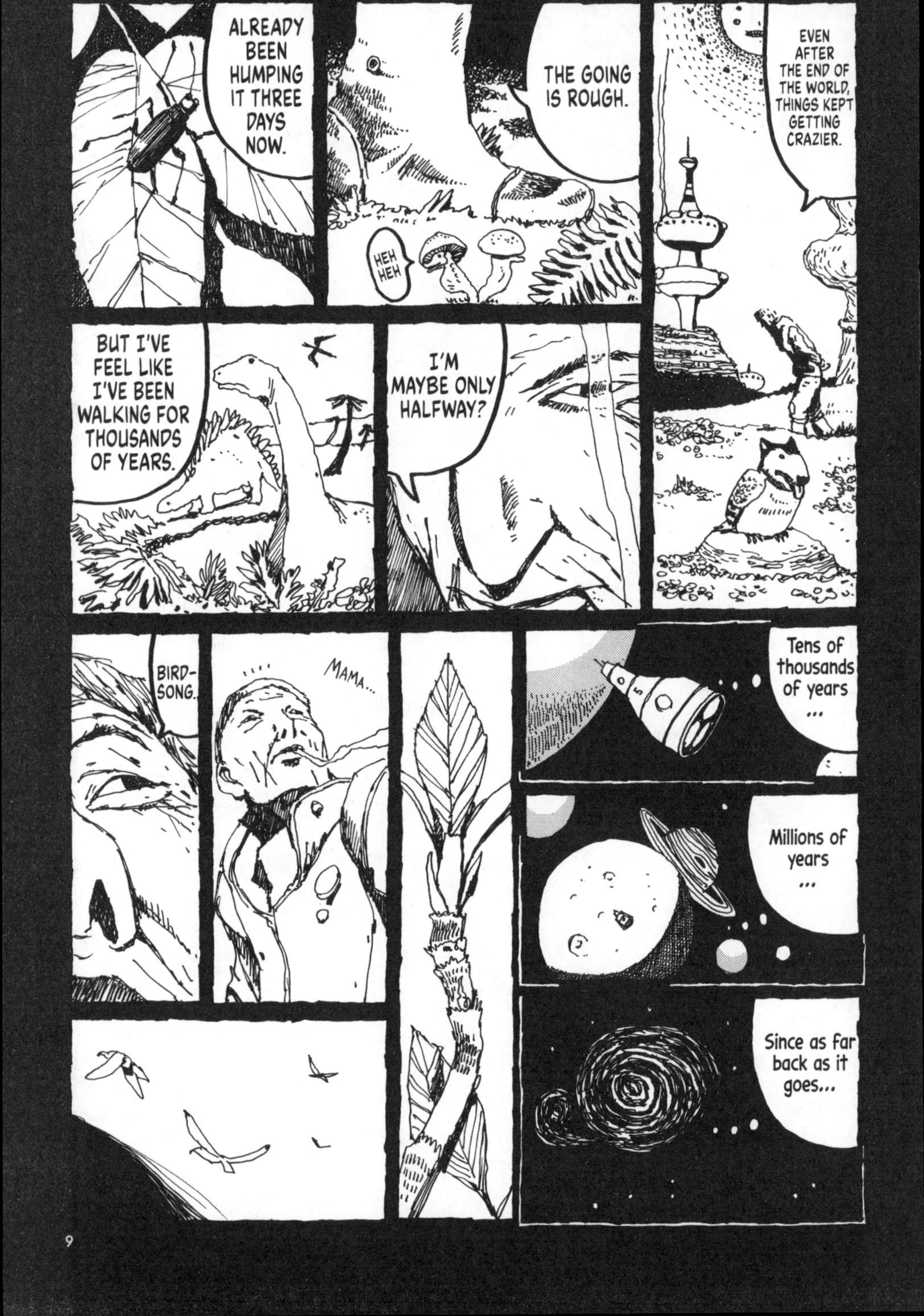
EVEN AFTER THE END OF THE WORLD, THINGS KEPT GETTING CRAZIER.
THE GOING IS ROUGH.
HEH HEH
ALREADY BEEN HUMPING IT THREE DAYS NOW.
I'M MAYBE ONLY HALFWAY?
BUT I'VE FEEL LIKE I'VE BEEN WALKING FOR THOUSANDS OF YEARS.
Tens of thousands of years ...
Millions of years ...
Since as far back as it goes...
MAMA...
BIRD-SONG.

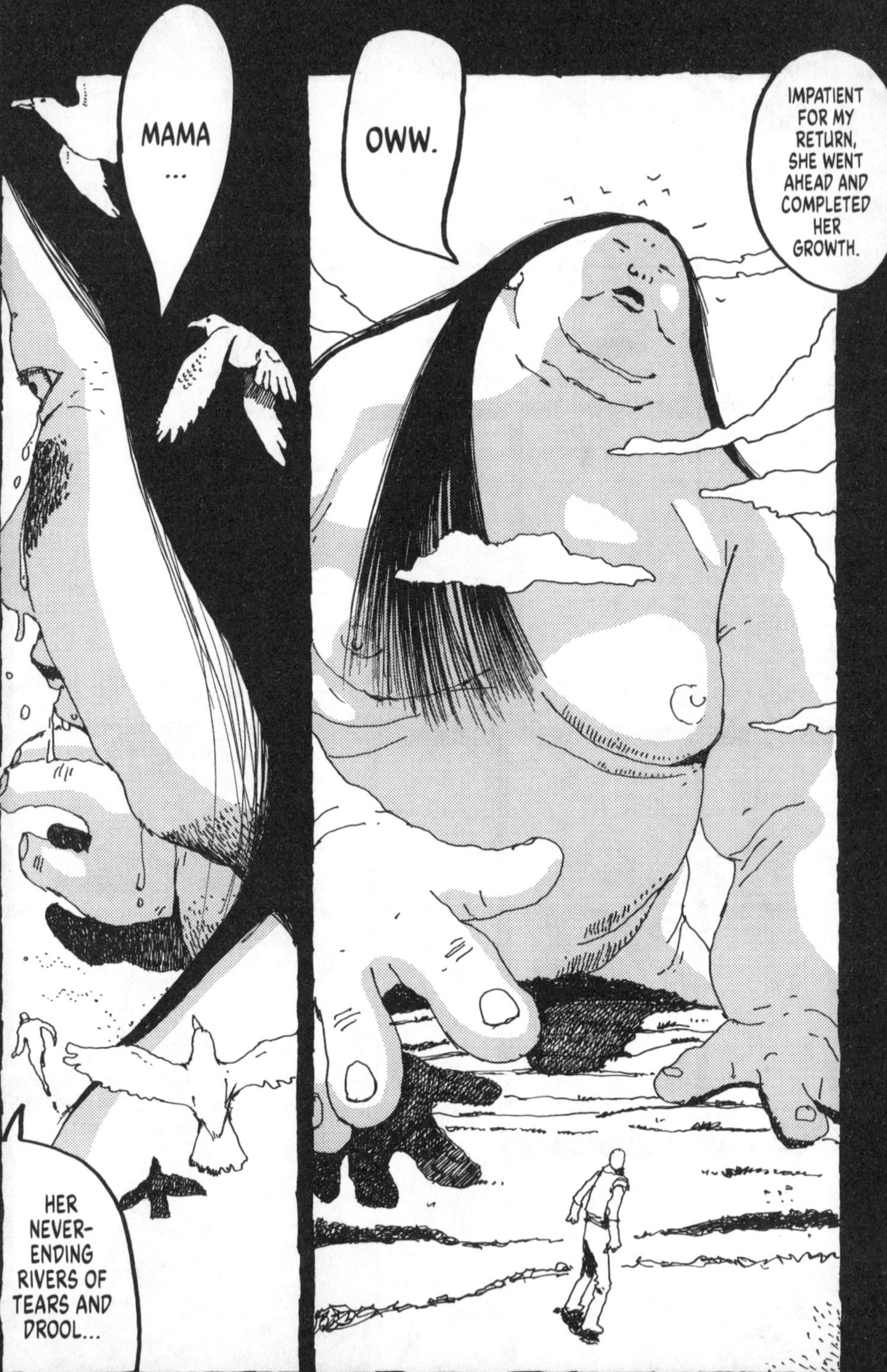
IMPATIENT FOR MY RETURN, SHE WENT AHEAD AND COMPLETED HER GROWTH.
OWW.
MAMA ...
HER NEVER-ENDING RIVERS OF TEARS AND DROOL...

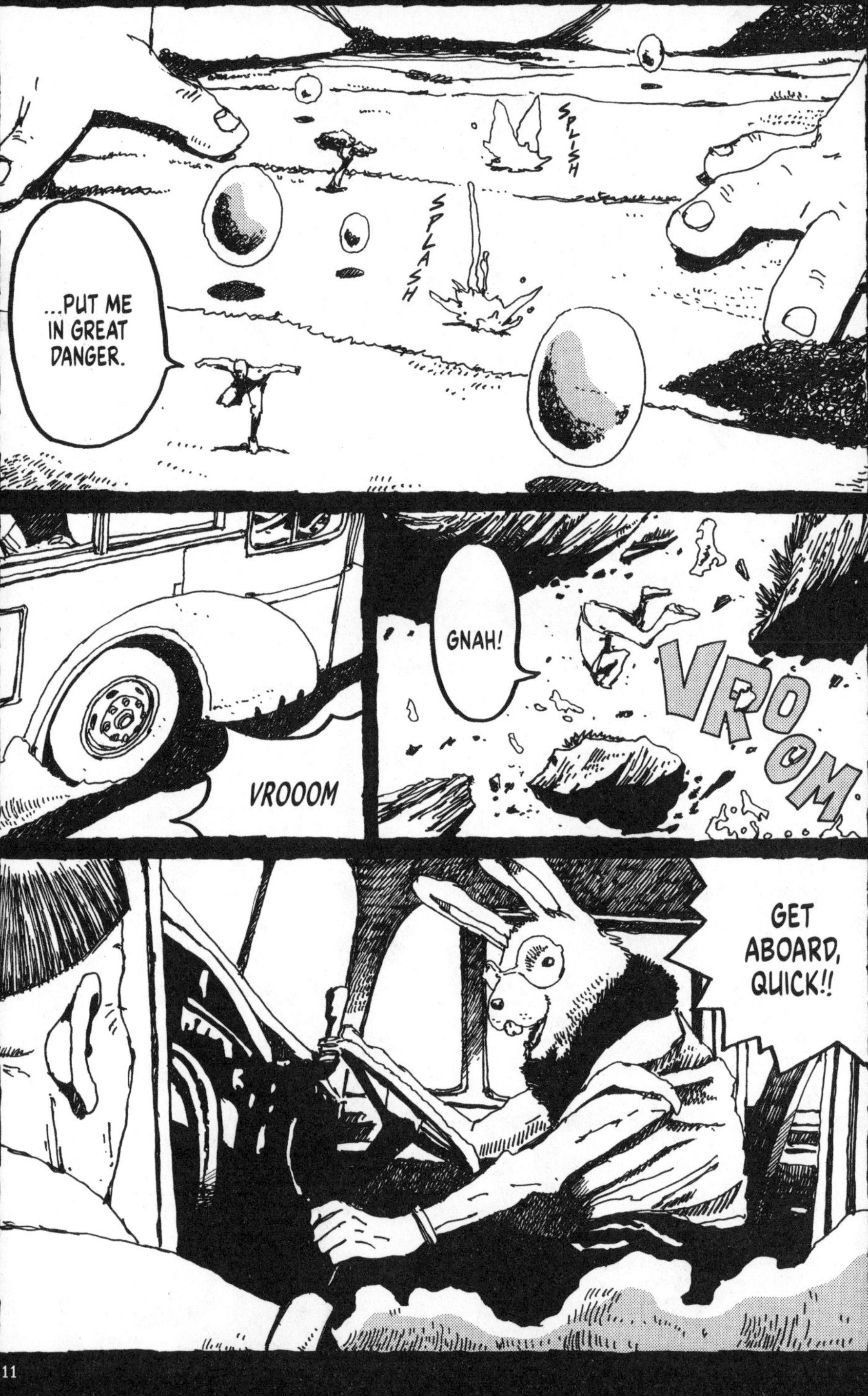
SPLISH
SPLASH
...PUT ME IN GREAT DANGER.
GNAH!
VROOM
VROOOM
GET ABOARD, QUICK!!

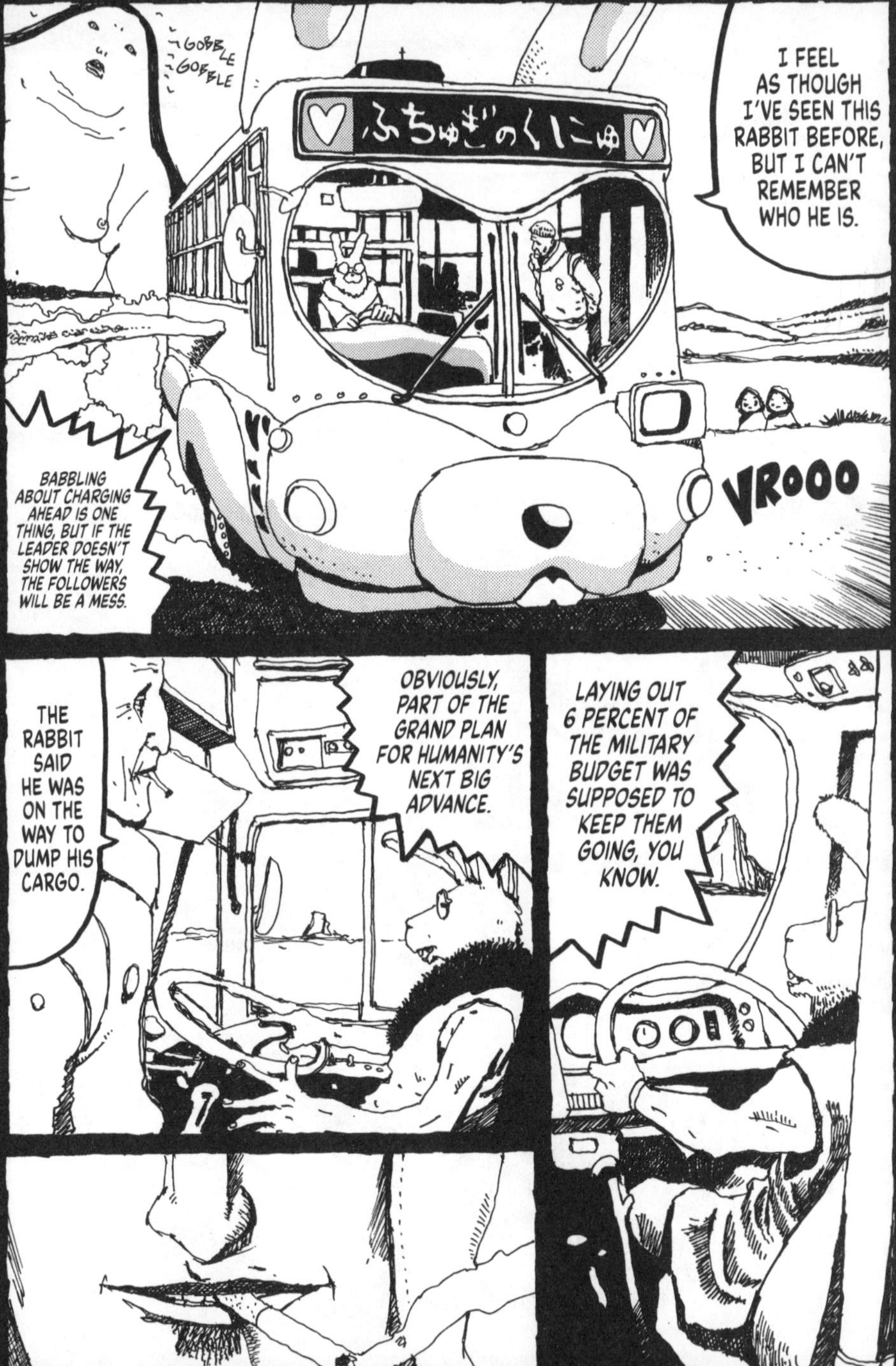
I FEEL AS THOUGH I'VE SEEN THIS RABBIT BEFORE, BUT I CAN'T REMEMBER WHO HE IS.
ふちゅぎのくにゅ
GOBBLE GOBBLE
VROOO
BABBLING ABOUT CHARGING AHEAD IS ONE THING, BUT IF THE LEADER DOESN'T SHOW THE WAY, THE FOLLOWERS WILL BE A MESS.
LAYING OUT 6 PERCENT OF THE MILITARY BUDGET WAS SUPPOSED TO KEEP THEM GOING, YOU KNOW.
OBVIOUSLY, PART OF THE GRAND PLAN FOR HUMANITY'S NEXT BIG ADVANCE.
THE RABBIT SAID HE WAS ON THE WAY TO DUMP HIS CARGO.

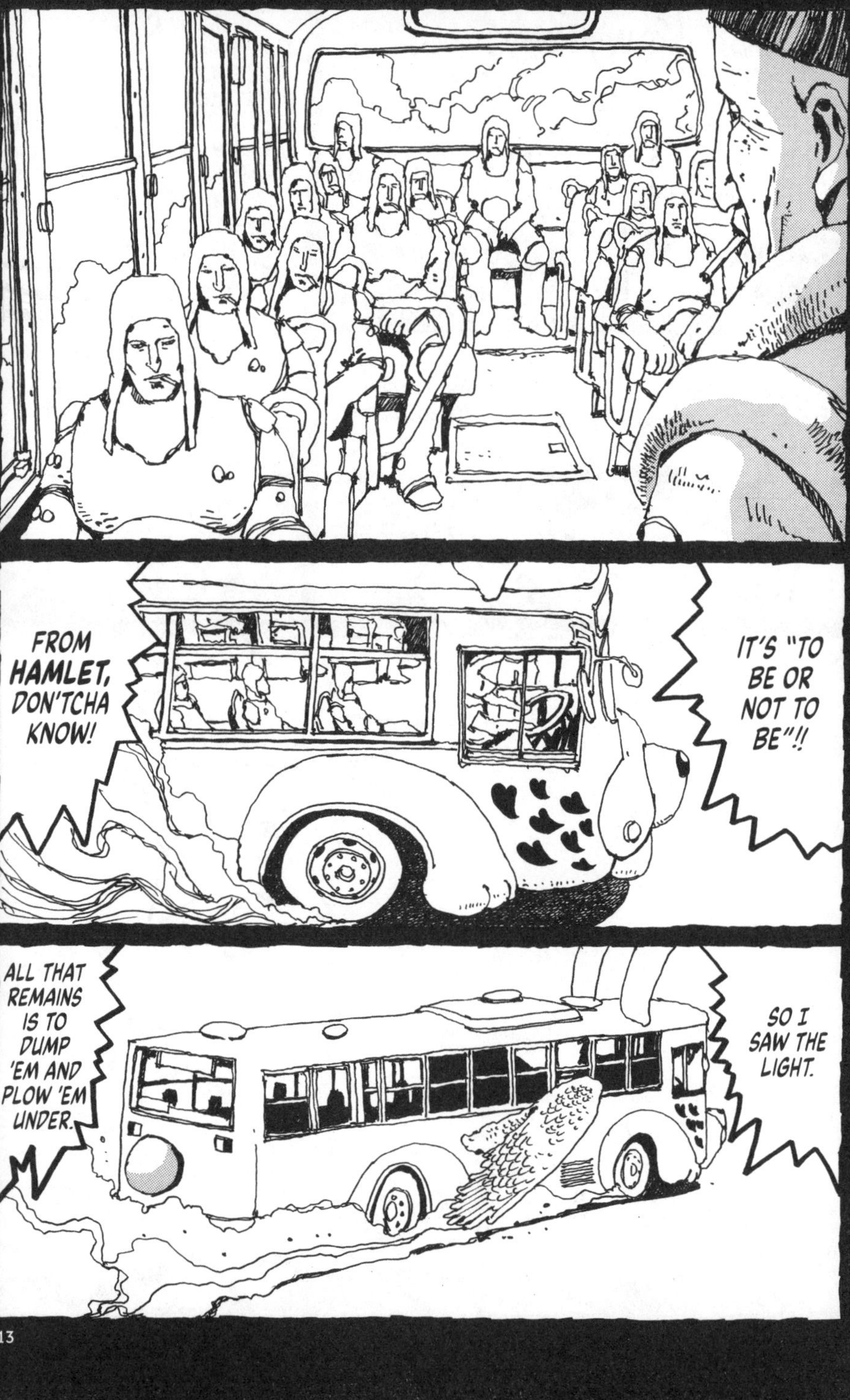
IT'S "TO BE OR NOT TO BE"!!
FROM HAMLET, DON'TCHA KNOW!
SO I SAW THE LIGHT.
ALL THAT REMAINS IS TO DUMP 'EM AND PLOW 'EM UNDER.

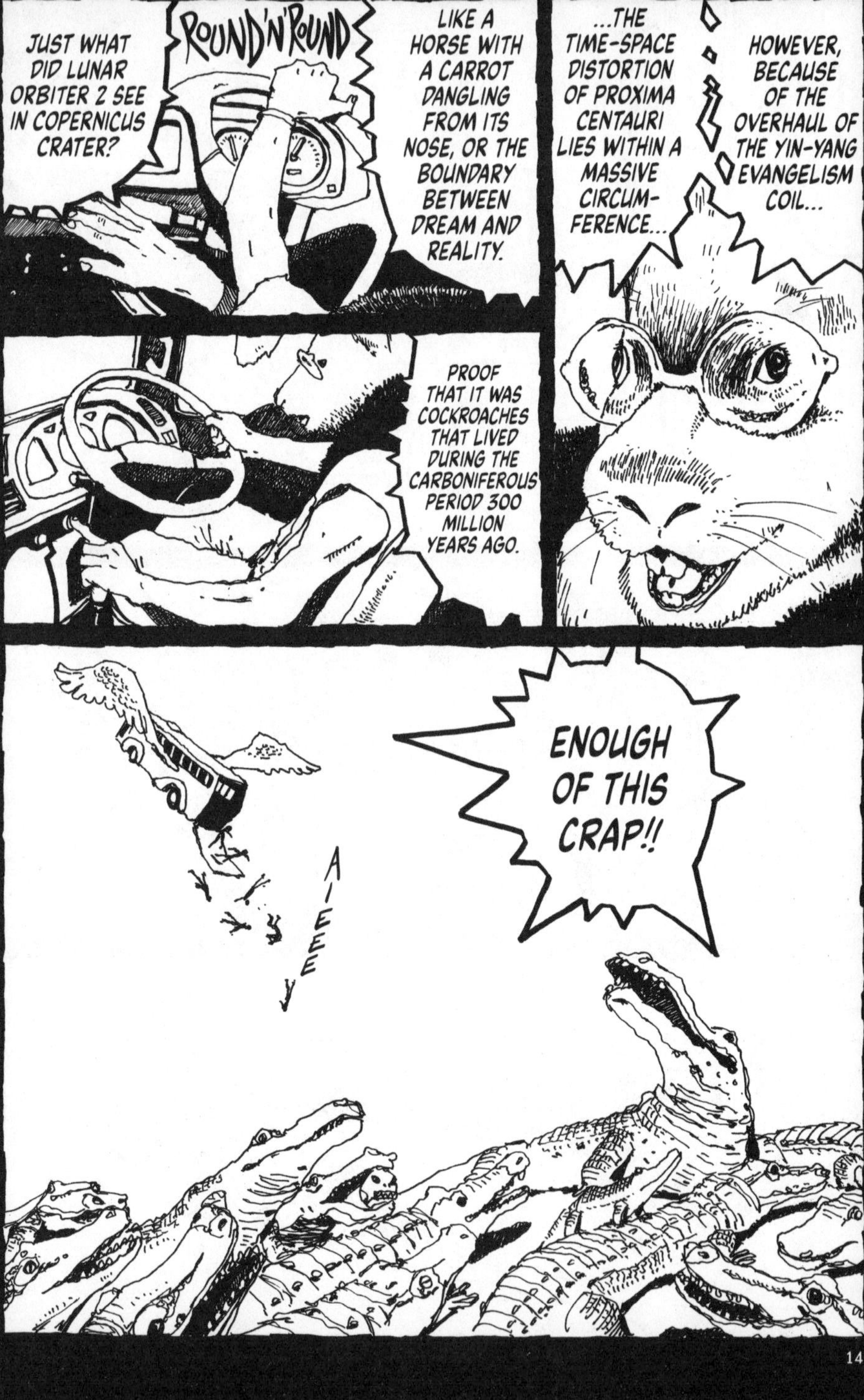
HOWEVER, BECAUSE OF THE OVERHAUL OF THE YIN-YANG EVANGELISM COIL...
...THE TIME-SPACE DISTORTION OF PROXIMA CENTAURI LIES WITHIN A MASSIVE CIRCUM-FERENCE...
LIKE A HORSE WITH A CARROT DANGLING FROM ITS NOSE, OR THE BOUNDARY BETWEEN DREAM AND REALITY.
ROUND'N'ROUND
JUST WHAT DID LUNAR ORBITER 2 SEE IN COPERNICUS CRATER?
PROOF THAT IT WAS COCKROACHES THAT LIVED DURING THE CARBONIFEROUS PERIOD 300 MILLION YEARS AGO.
ENOUGH OF THIS CRAP!!
AIEEE

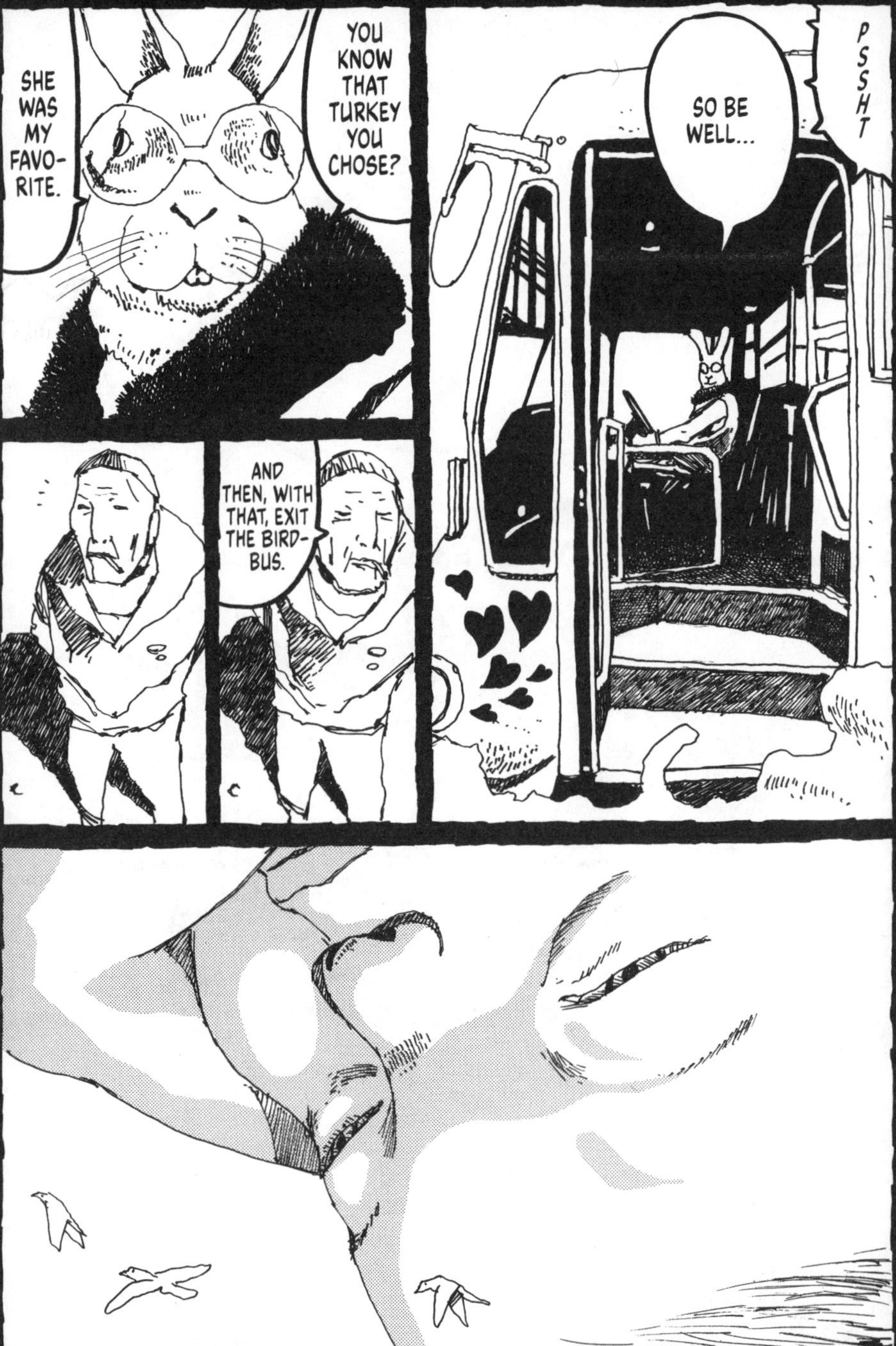
PSSHT
SO BE WELL...
YOU KNOW THAT TURKEY YOU CHOSE?
SHE WAS MY FAVORITE.
AND THEN, WITH THAT, EXIT THE BIRD-BUS.

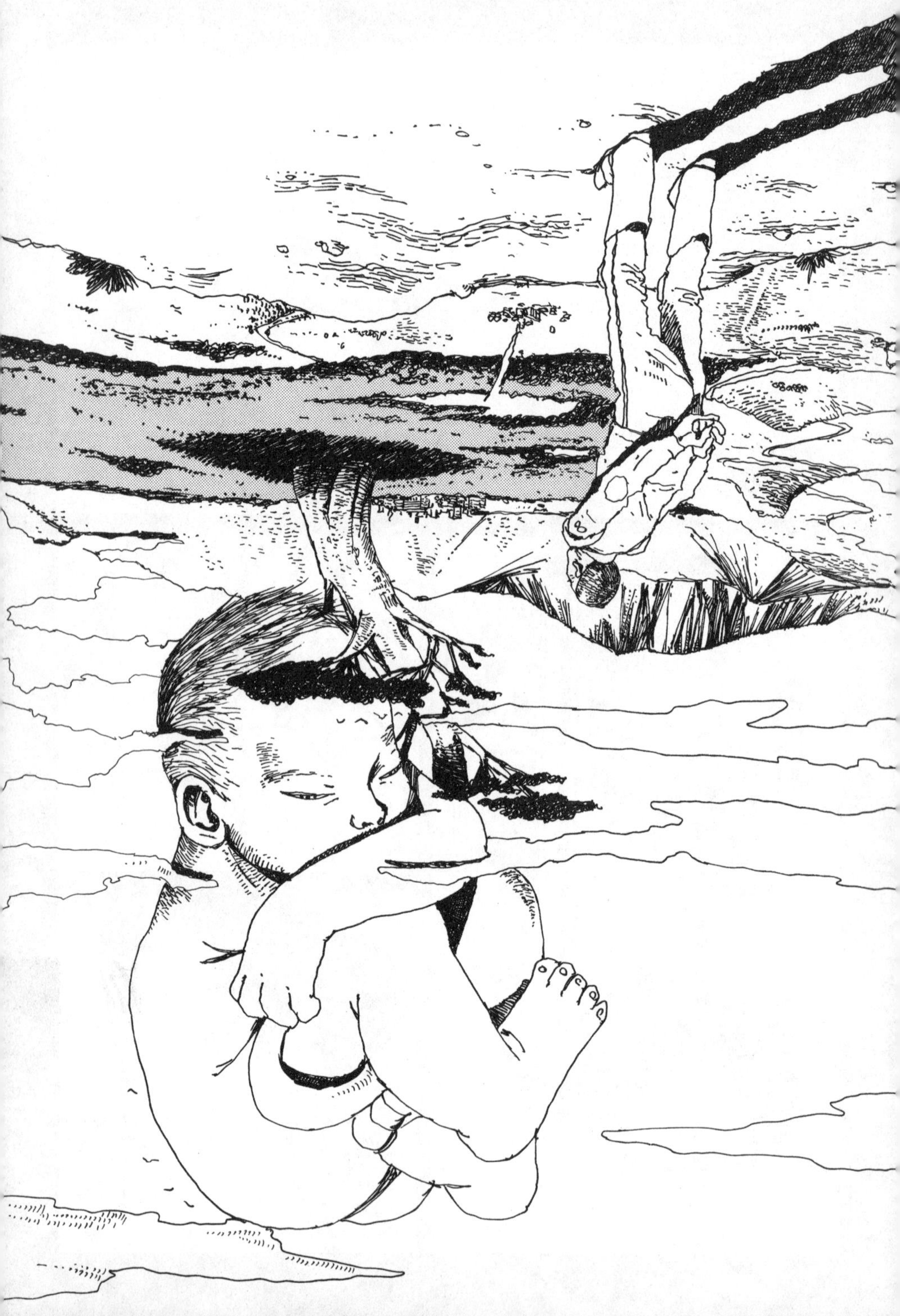

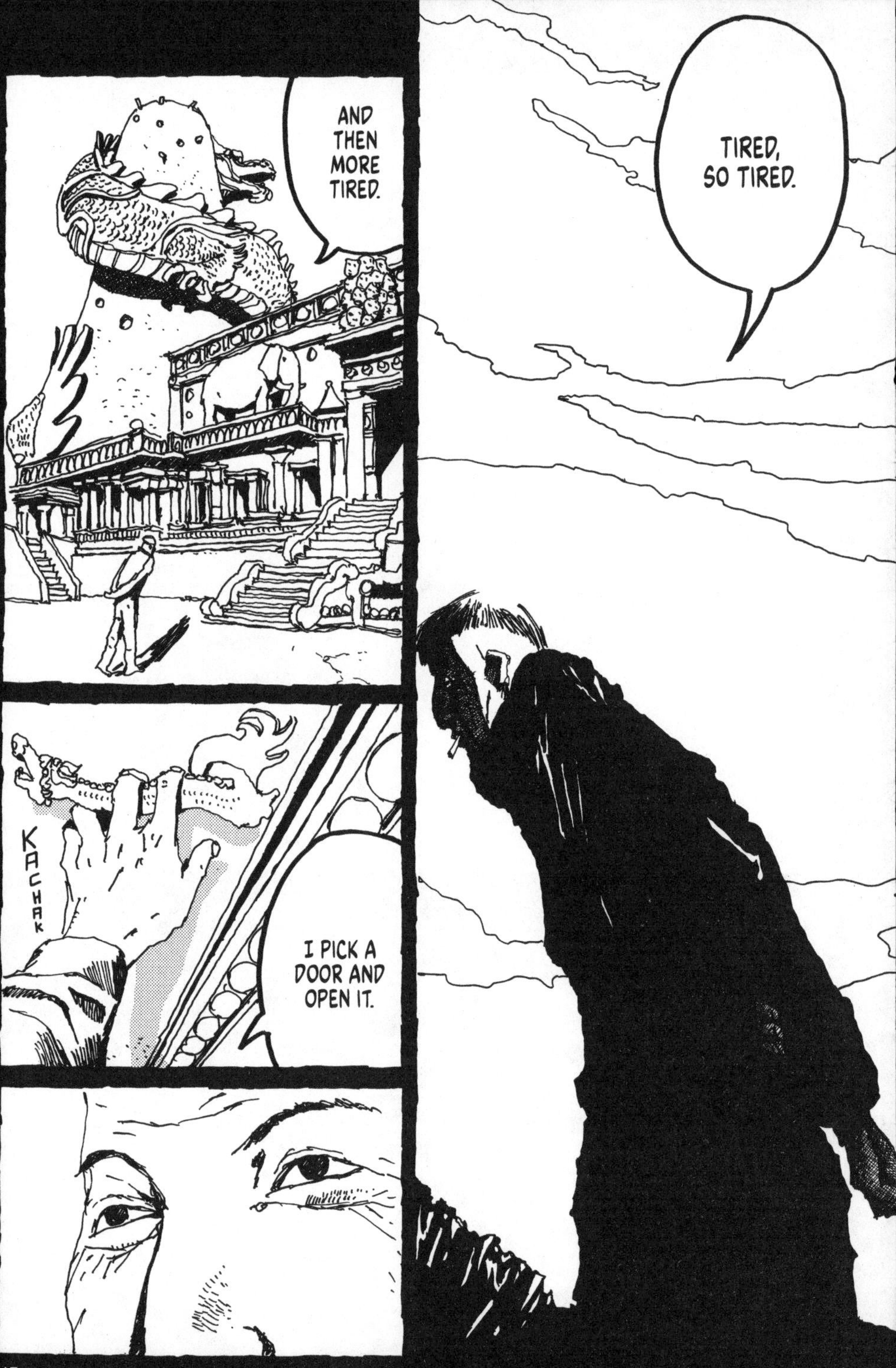
TIRED, SO TIRED.
AND THEN MORE TIRED.
KACHAK
I PICK A DOOR AND OPEN IT.

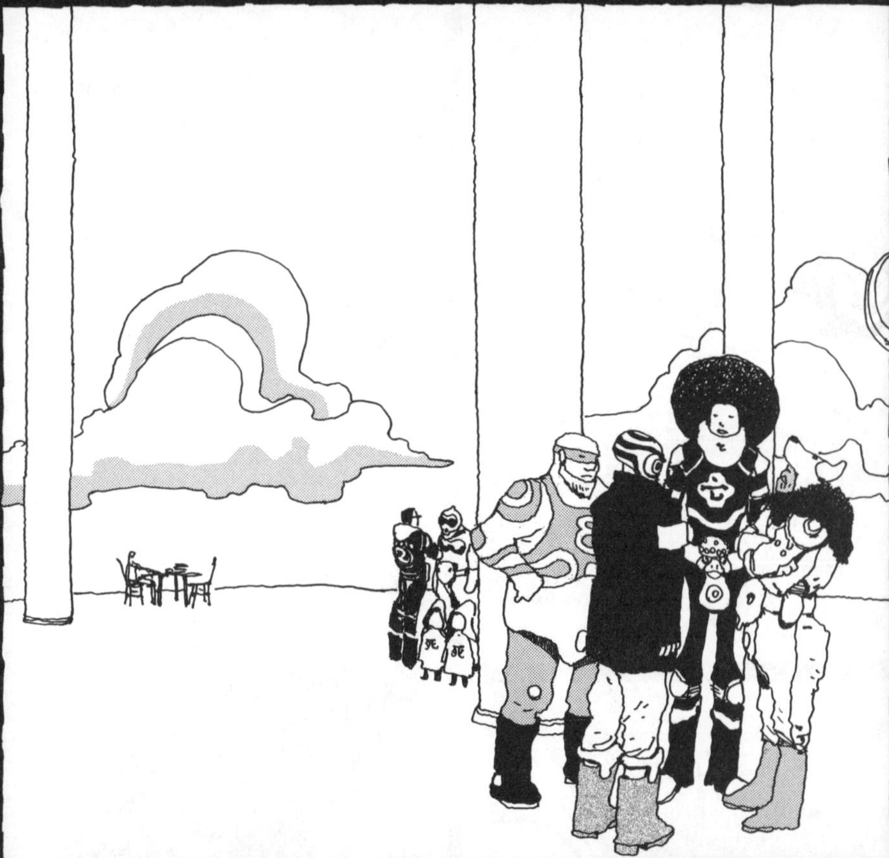

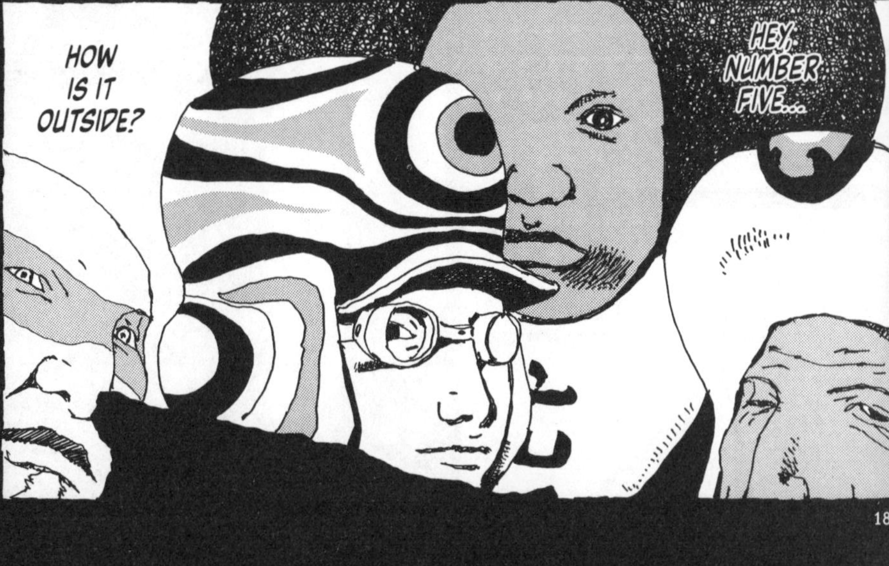
HEY, NUMBER FIVE...
HOW IS IT OUTSIDE?

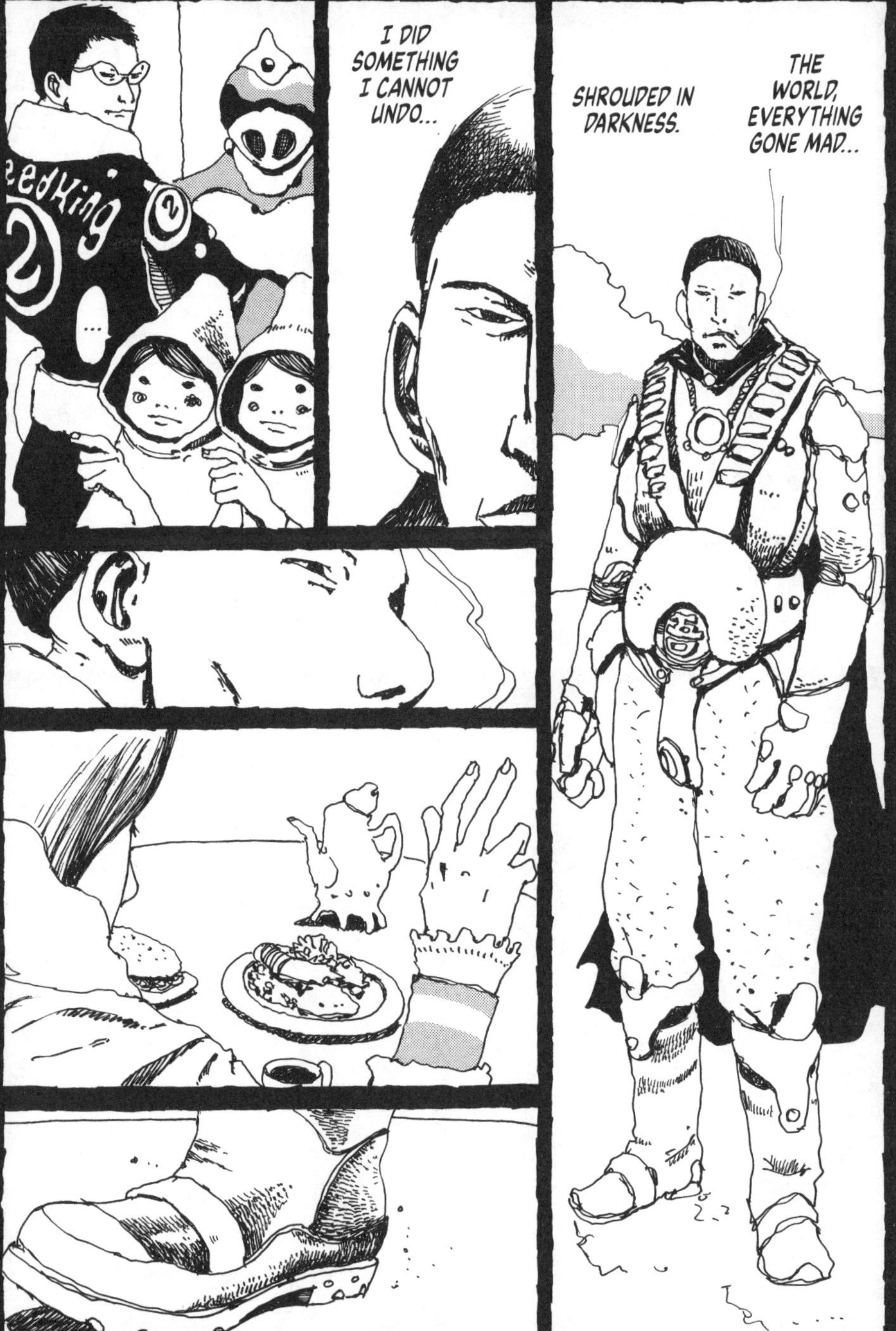
THE WORLD, EVERYTHING GONE MAD...
SHROUDED IN DARKNESS.
I DID SOMETHING I CANNOT UNDO...
...
eedKing

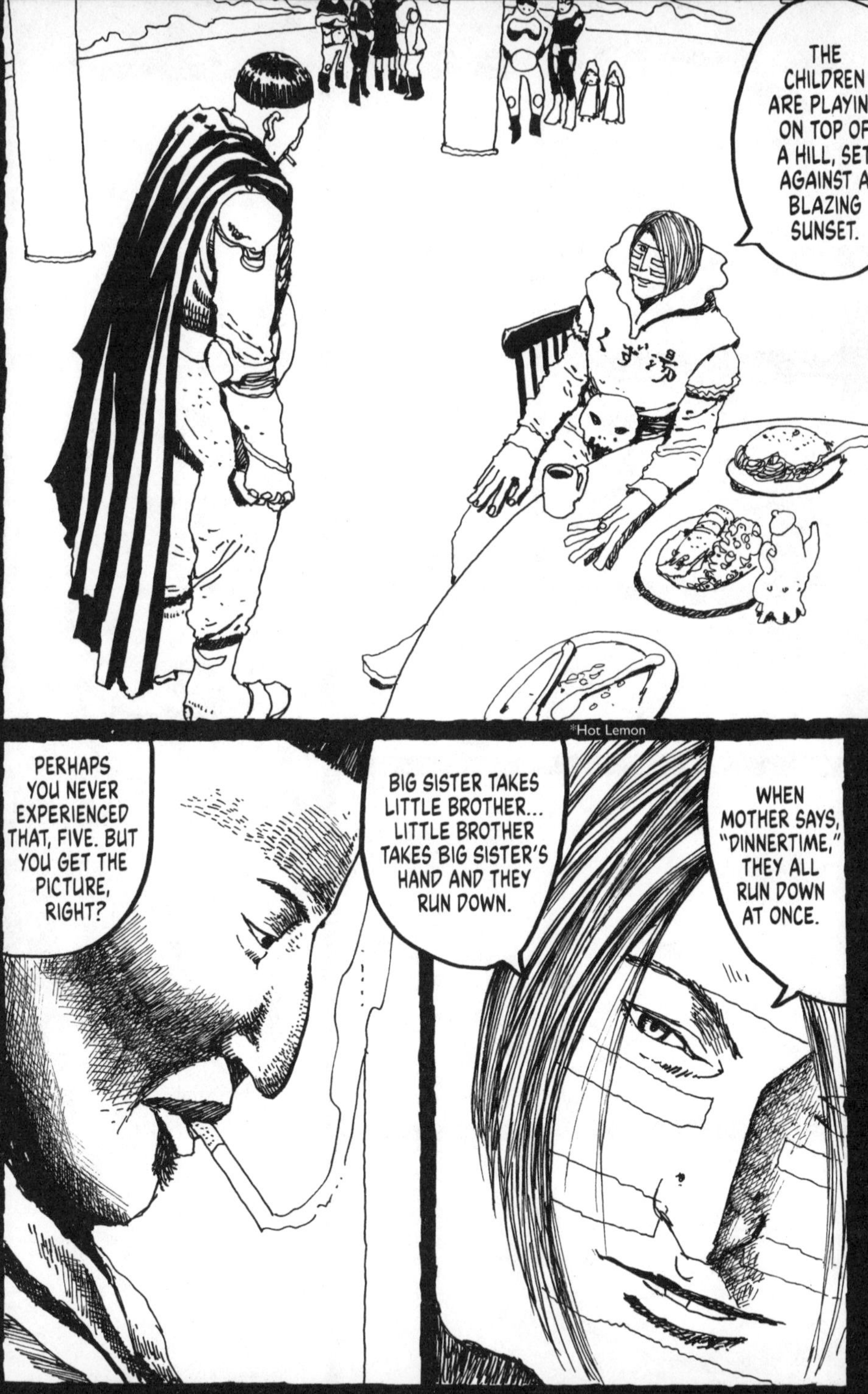
THE CHILDREN ARE PLAYING ON TOP OF A HILL, SET AGAINST A BLAZING SUNSET.
*Hot Lemon
WHEN MOTHER SAYS, "DINNERTIME," THEY ALL RUN DOWN AT ONCE.
BIG SISTER TAKES LITTLE BROTHER... LITTLE BROTHER TAKES BIG SISTER'S HAND AND THEY RUN DOWN.
PERHAPS YOU NEVER EXPERIENCED THAT, FIVE. BUT YOU GET THE PICTURE, RIGHT?

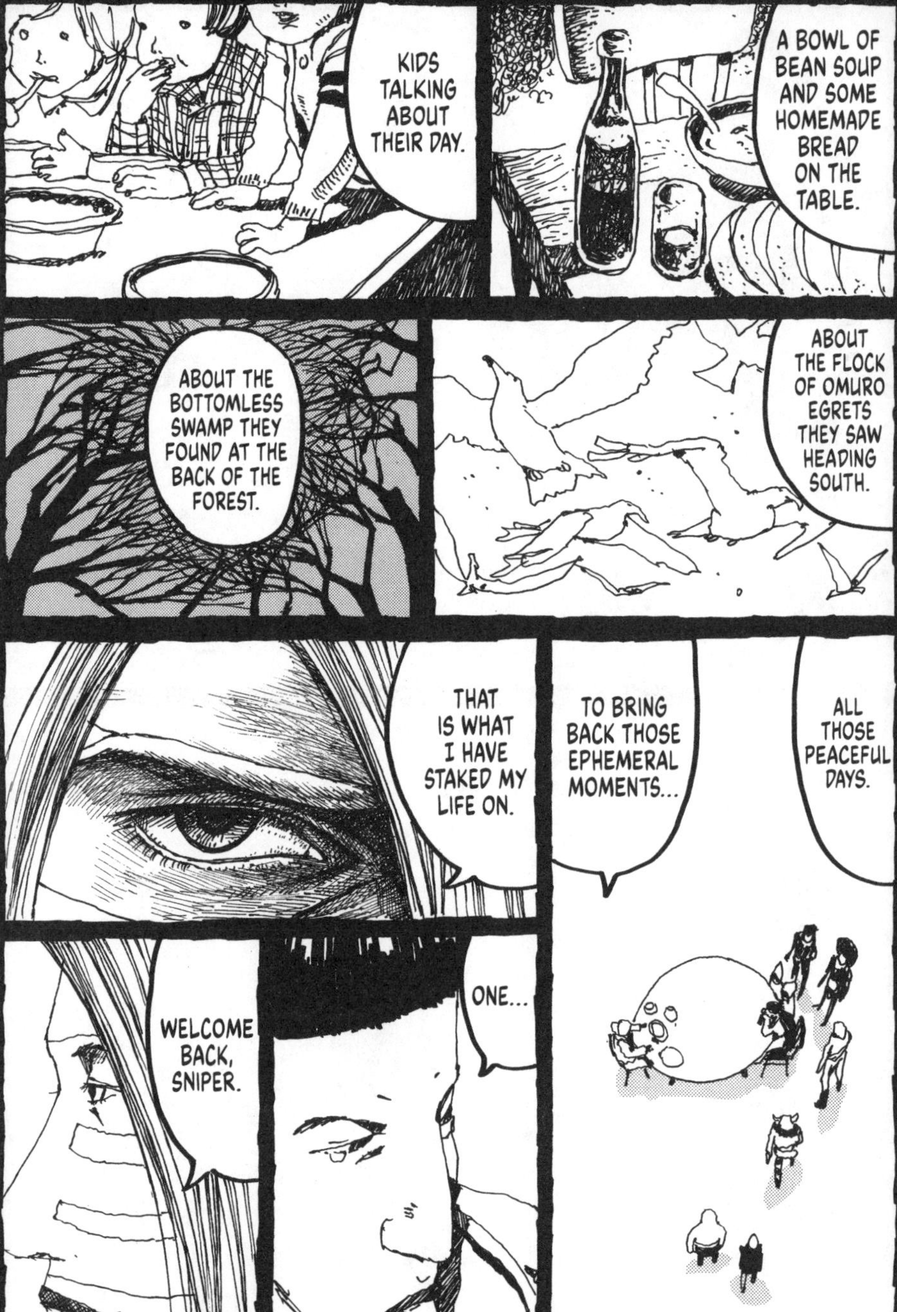
A BOWL OF BEAN SOUP AND SOME HOMEMADE BREAD ON THE TABLE.
KIDS TALKING ABOUT THEIR DAY.
ABOUT THE FLOCK OF OMURO EGRETS THEY SAW HEADING SOUTH.
ABOUT THE BOTTOMLESS SWAMP THEY FOUND AT THE BACK OF THE FOREST.
ALL THOSE PEACEFUL DAYS.
TO BRING BACK THOSE EPHEMERAL MOMENTS...
THAT IS WHAT I HAVE STAKED MY LIFE ON.
ONE...
WELCOME BACK, SNIPER.

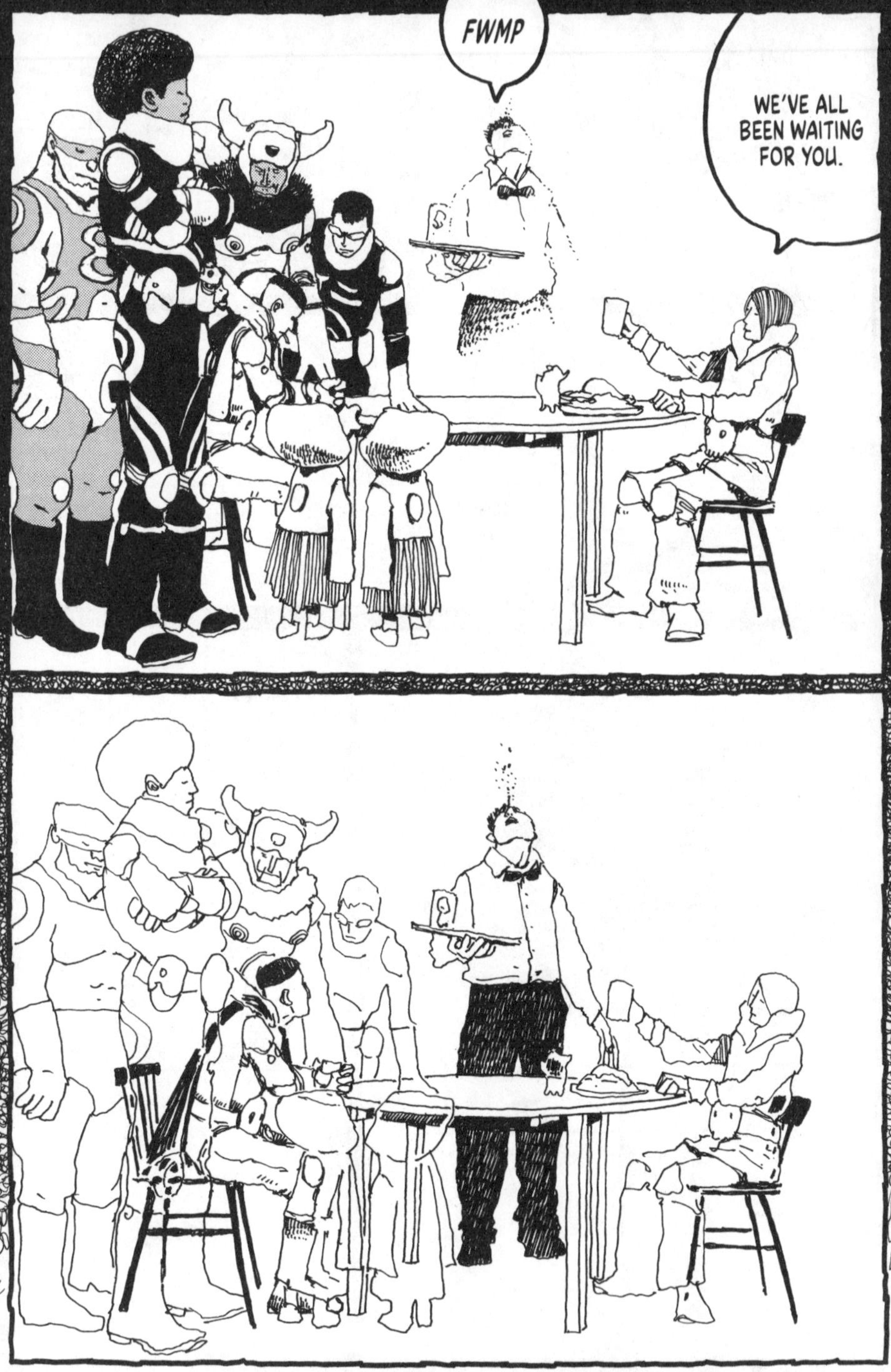
WE'VE ALL BEEN WAITING FOR YOU.
FWMP

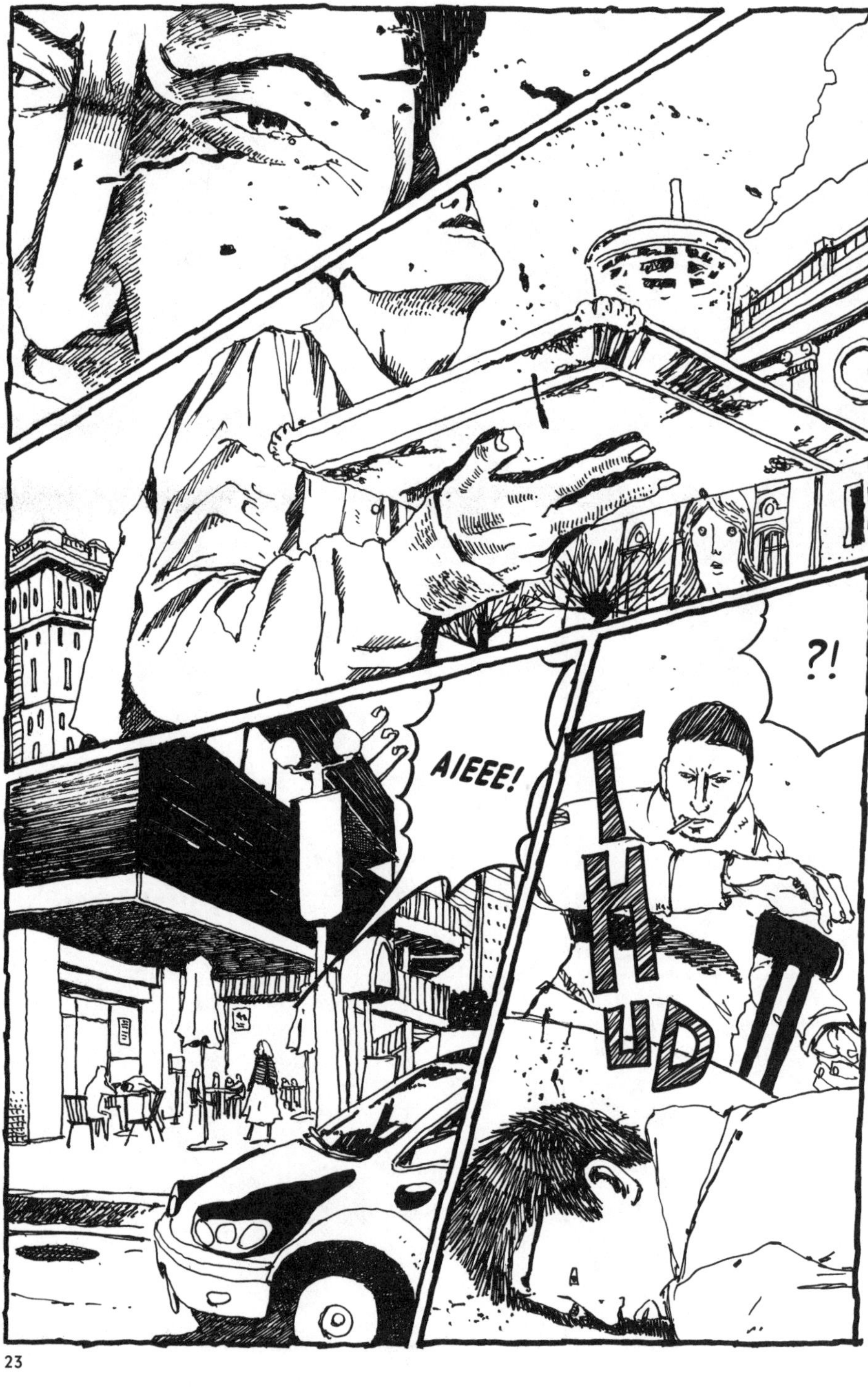
?!
THUD
AIEEE!

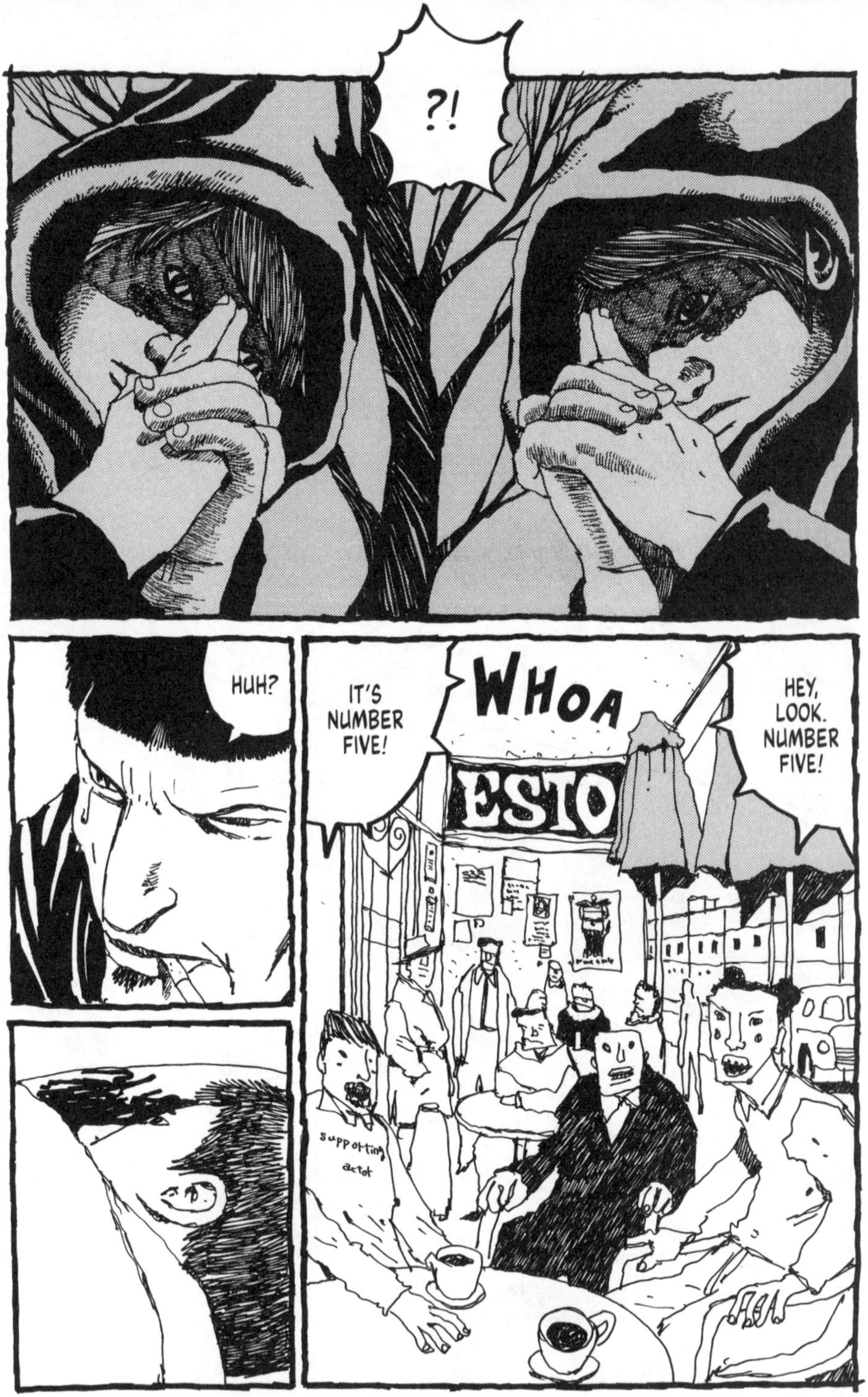
?!
HEY, LOOK. NUMBER FIVE!
WHOA
IT'S NUMBER FIVE!
ESTO
supporting actor
HUH?

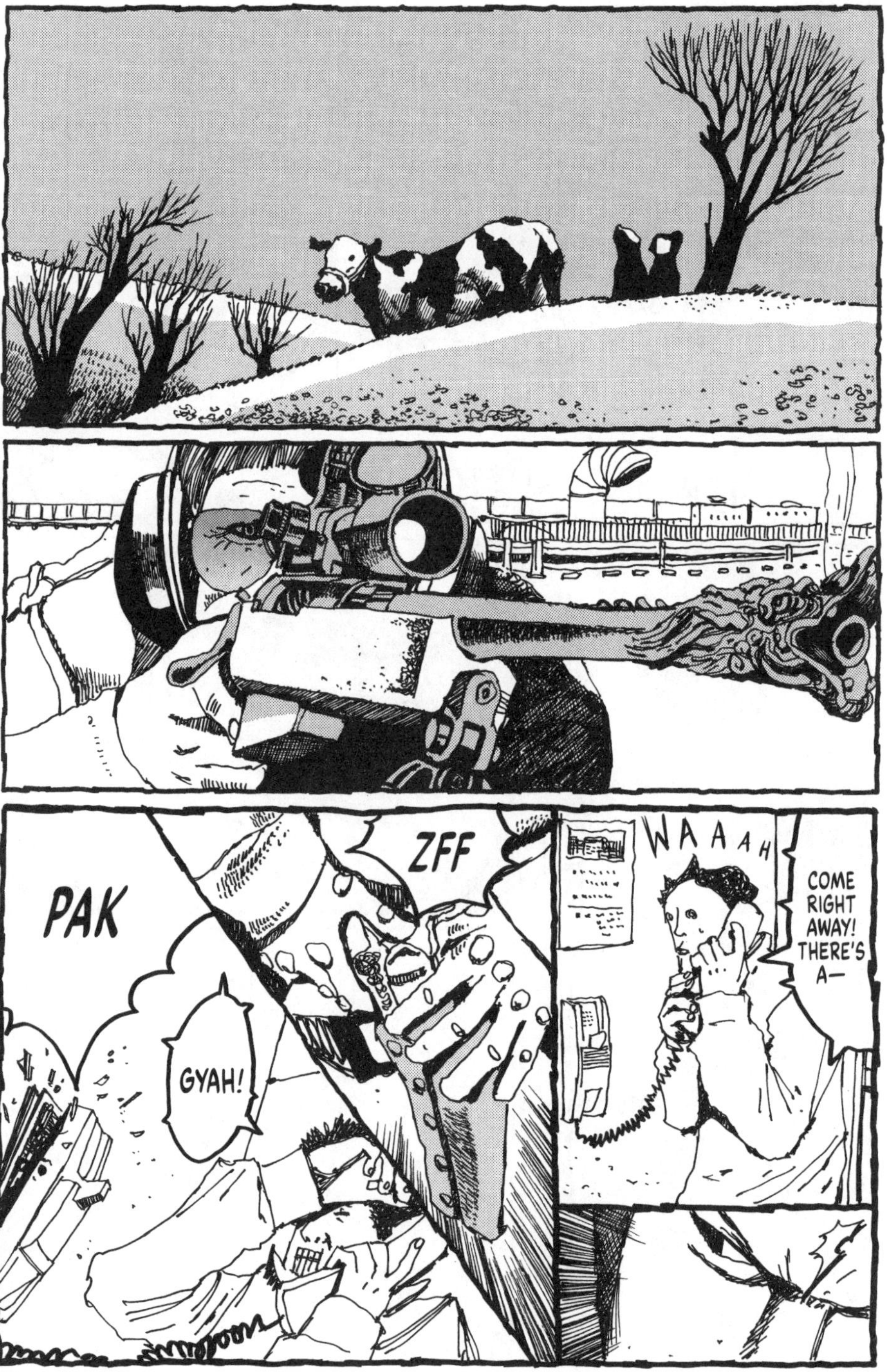
WAAAH
COME RIGHT AWAY! THERE'S A—
ZFF
PAK
GYAH!

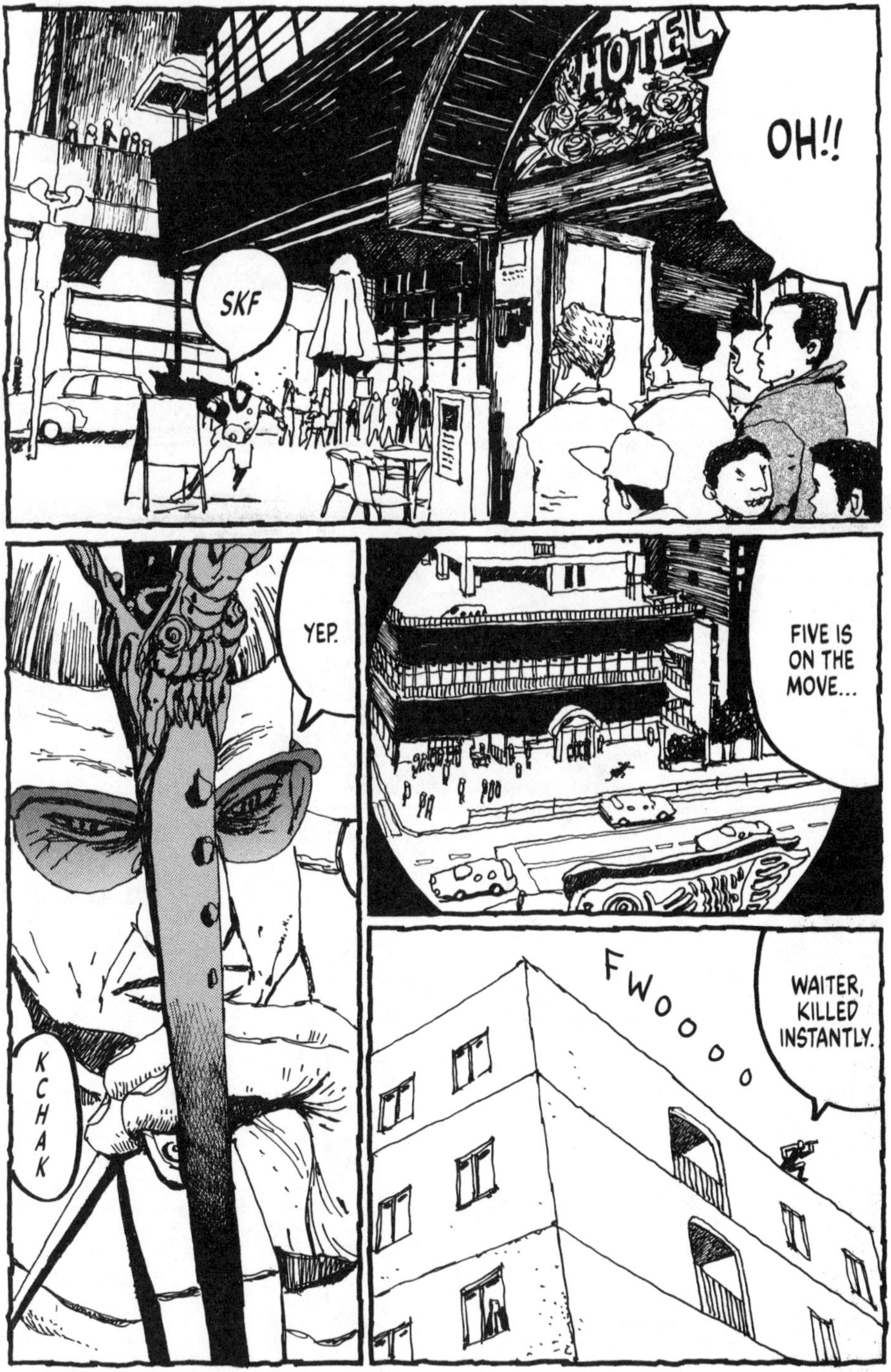

OH!!
HOTEL
SKF
FIVE IS ON THE MOVE...
WAITER, KILLED INSTANTLY.
FWOOOOO
YEP.
KCHAK

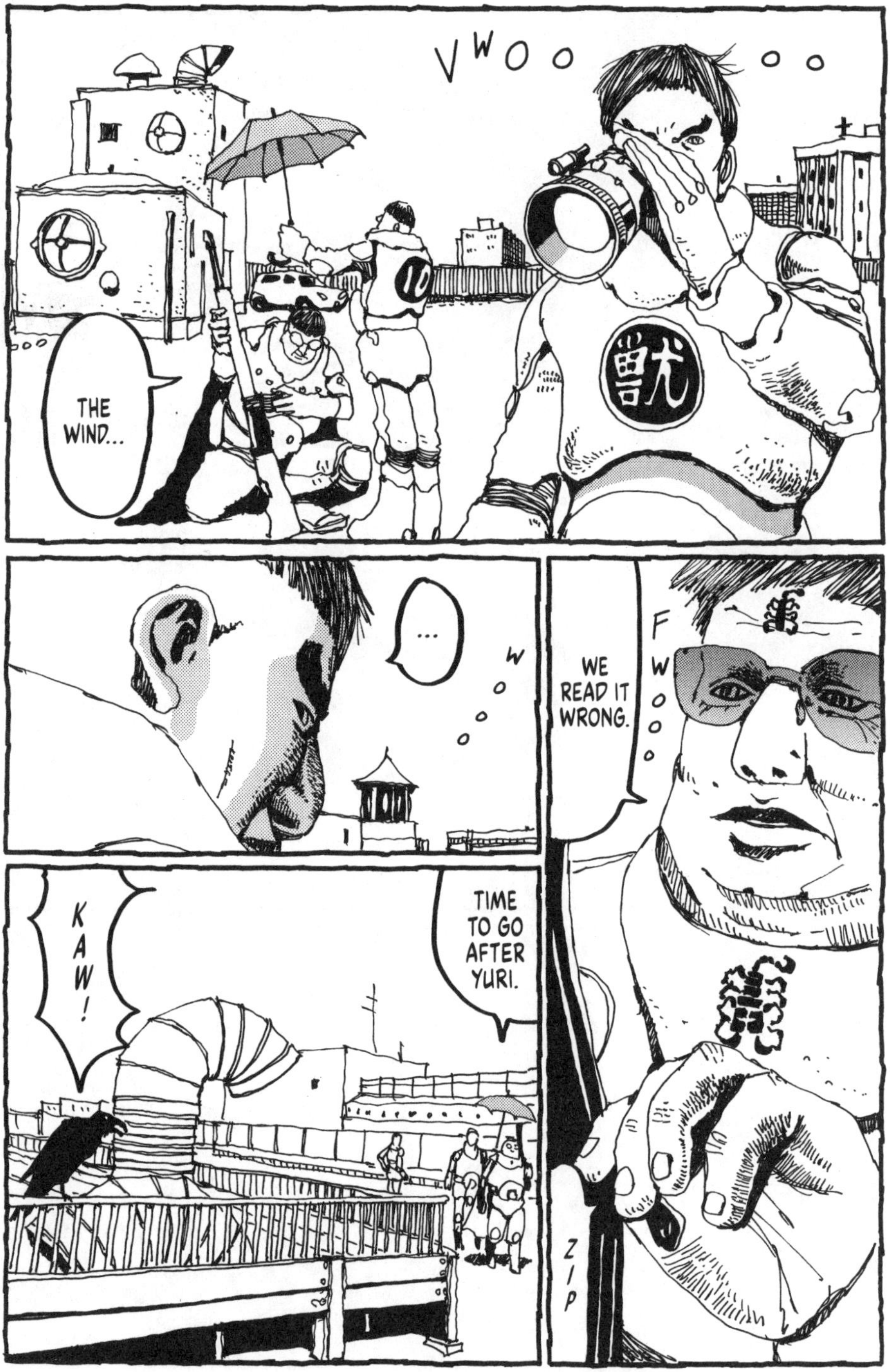
VWOO OO
THE WIND...
FWOOO
WE READ IT WRONG.
ZIP
WOOO
...
TIME TO GO AFTER YURI.
KAW!

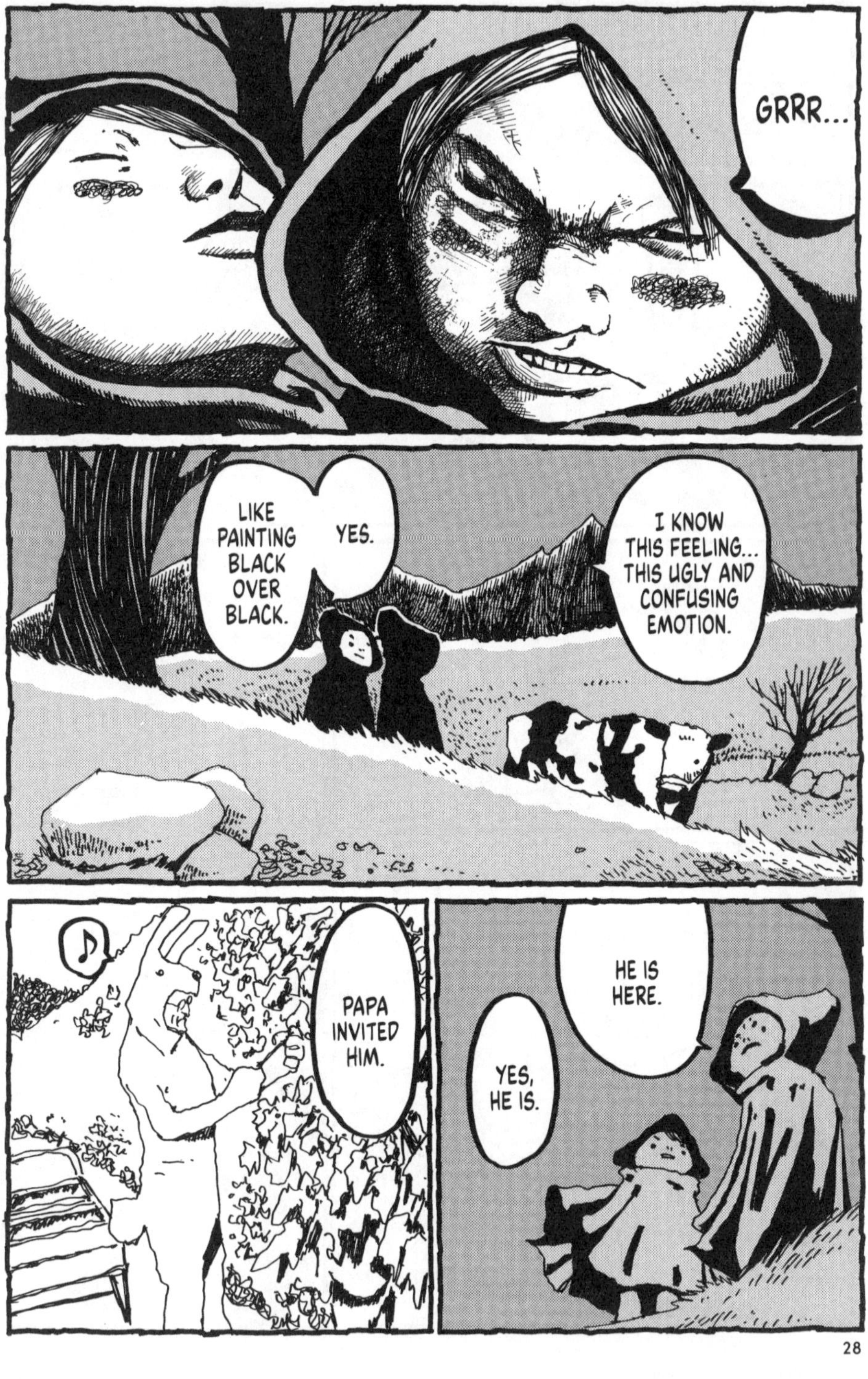
GRRR...
I KNOW THIS FEELING... THIS UGLY AND CONFUSING EMOTION.
YES.
LIKE PAINTING BLACK OVER BLACK.
HE IS HERE.
YES, HE IS.
PAPA INVITED HIM.
♪

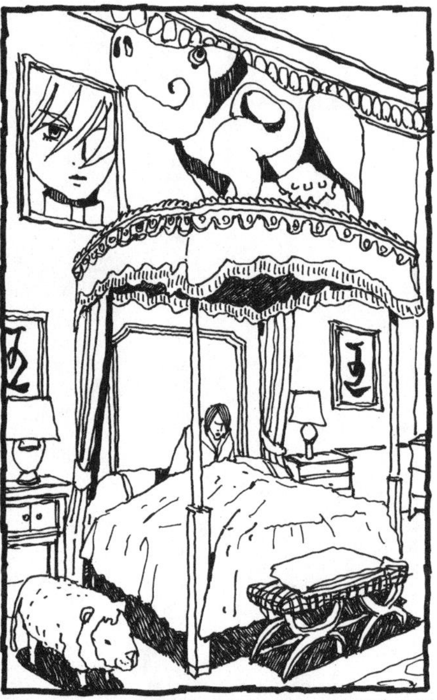

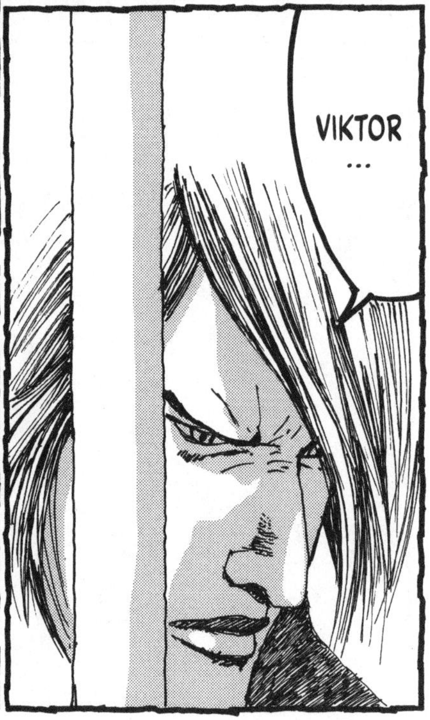
VIKTOR
...

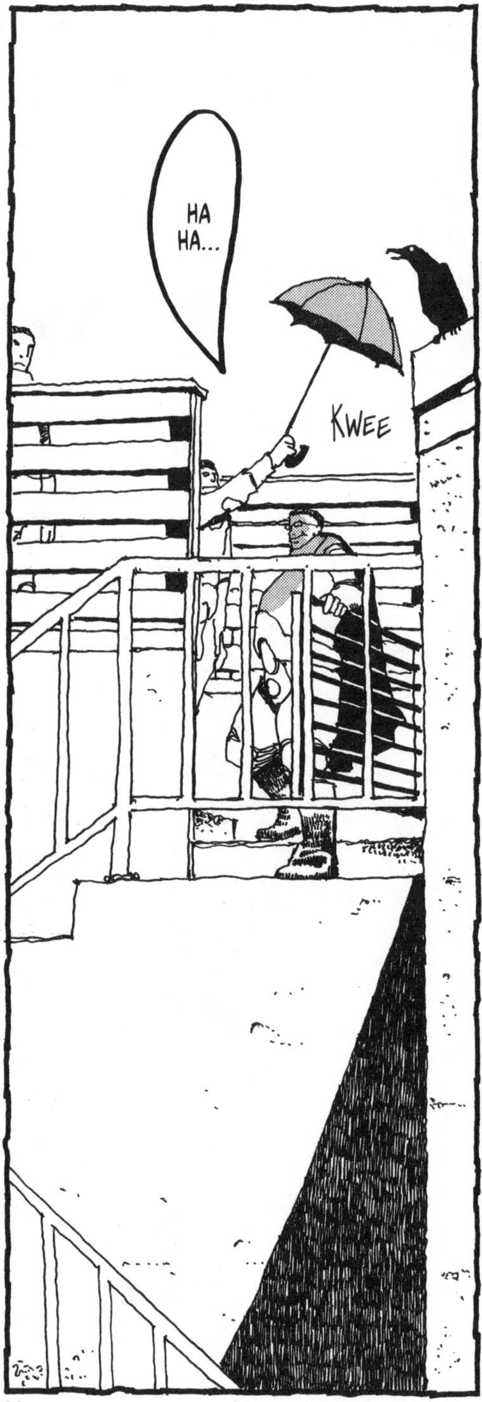
HA
HA...
KWEE

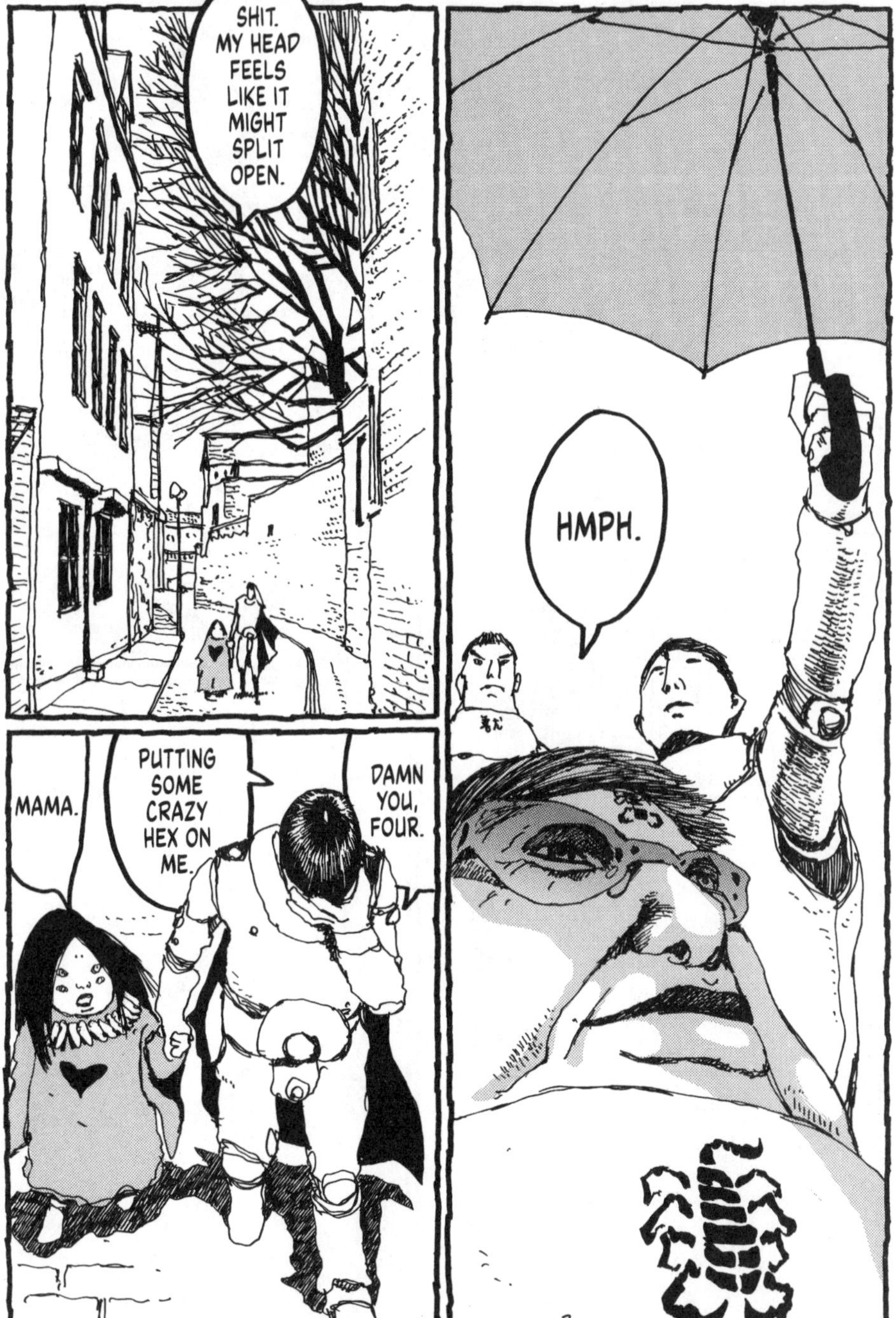
HMPH.
SHIT. MY HEAD FEELS LIKE IT MIGHT SPLIT OPEN.
DAMN YOU, FOUR.
PUTTING SOME CRAZY HEX ON ME.
MAMA.

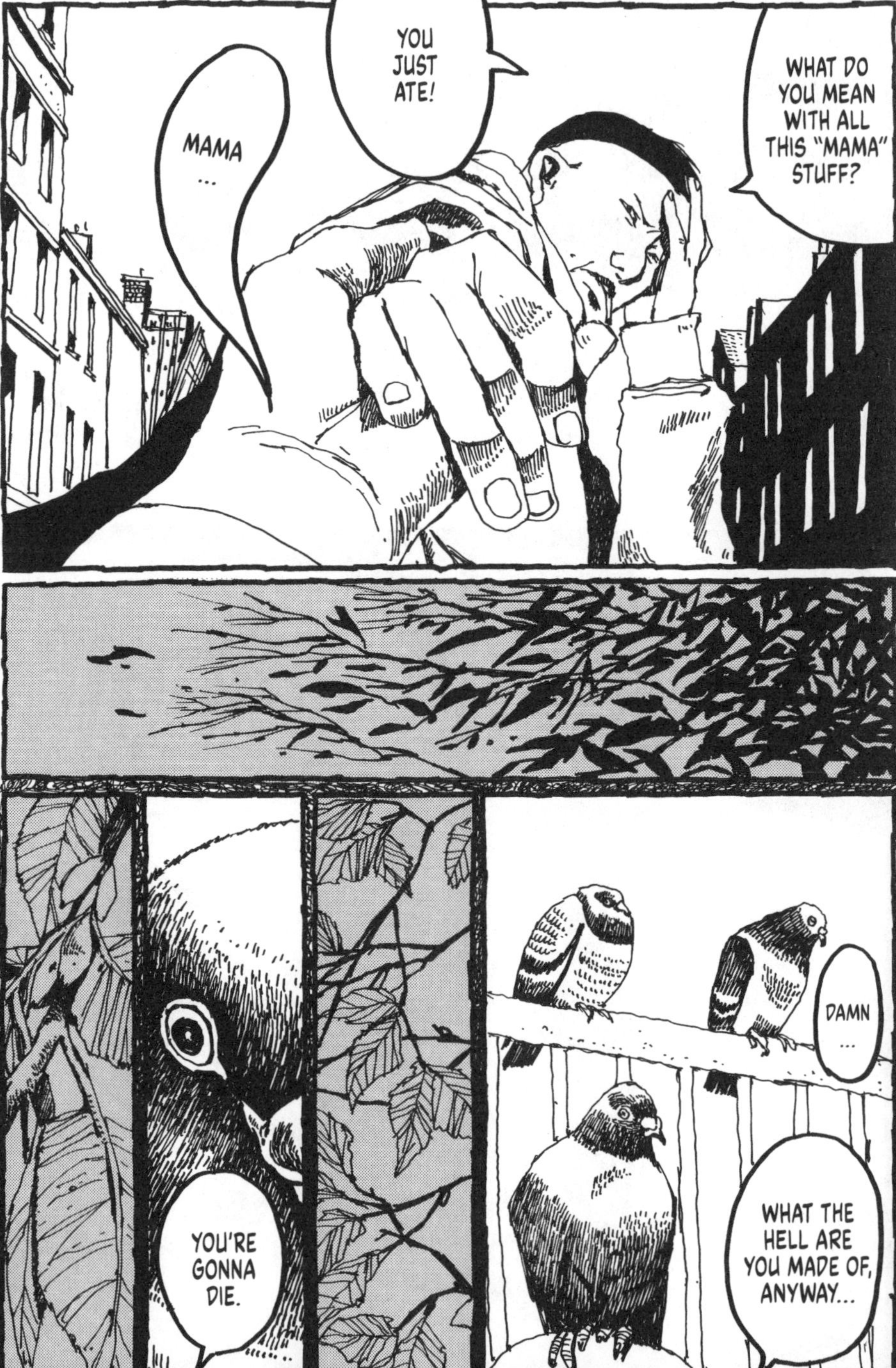
WHAT DO YOU MEAN WITH ALL THIS "MAMA" STUFF?
YOU JUST ATE!
MAMA ...
DAMN ...
WHAT THE HELL ARE YOU MADE OF, ANYWAY...
YOU'RE GONNA DIE.

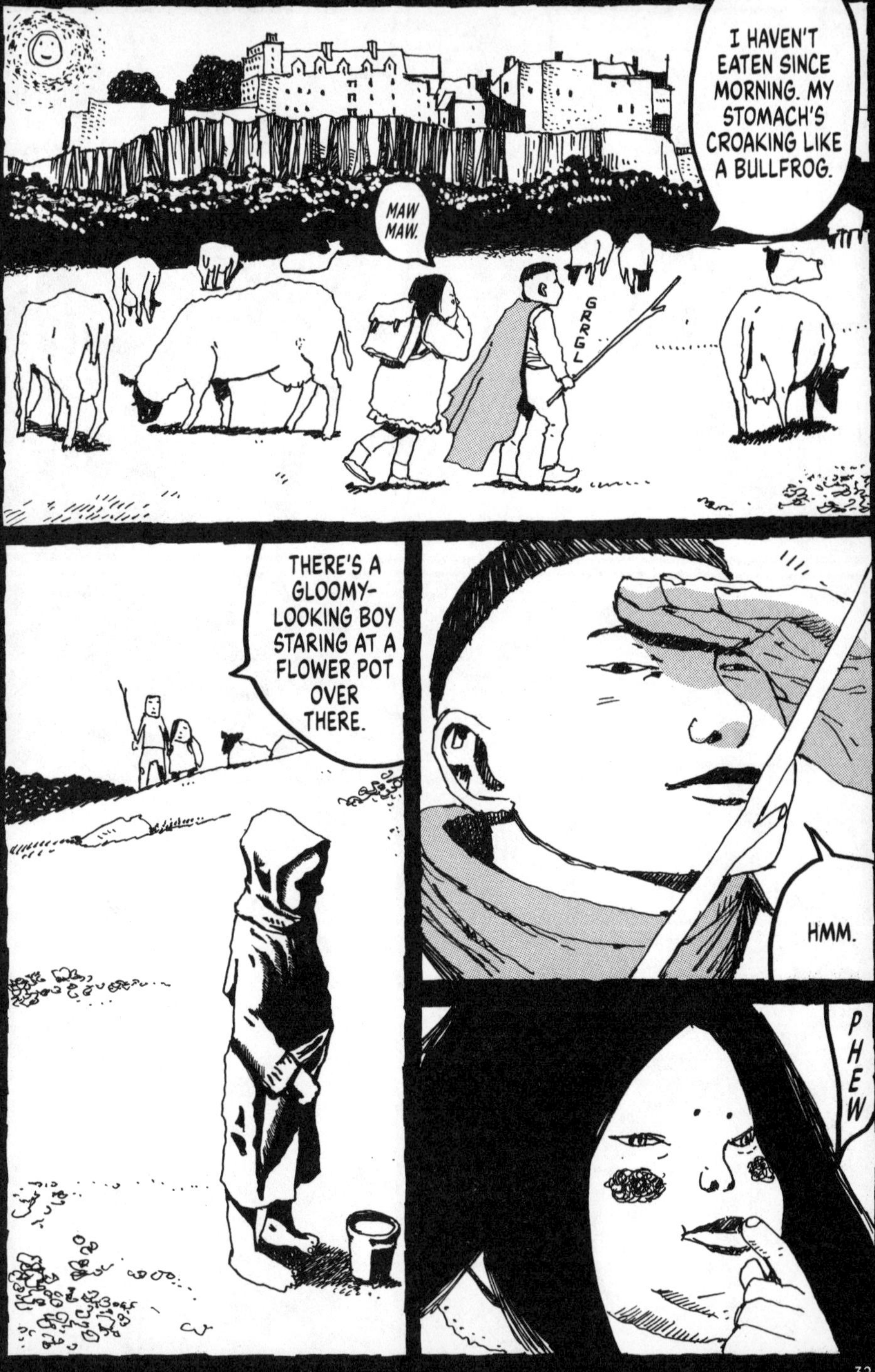
I HAVEN'T EATEN SINCE MORNING. MY STOMACH'S CROAKING LIKE A BULLFROG.
MAW MAW.
GRRGL
HMM.
PHEW
THERE'S A GLOOMY-LOOKING BOY STARING AT A FLOWER POT OVER THERE.

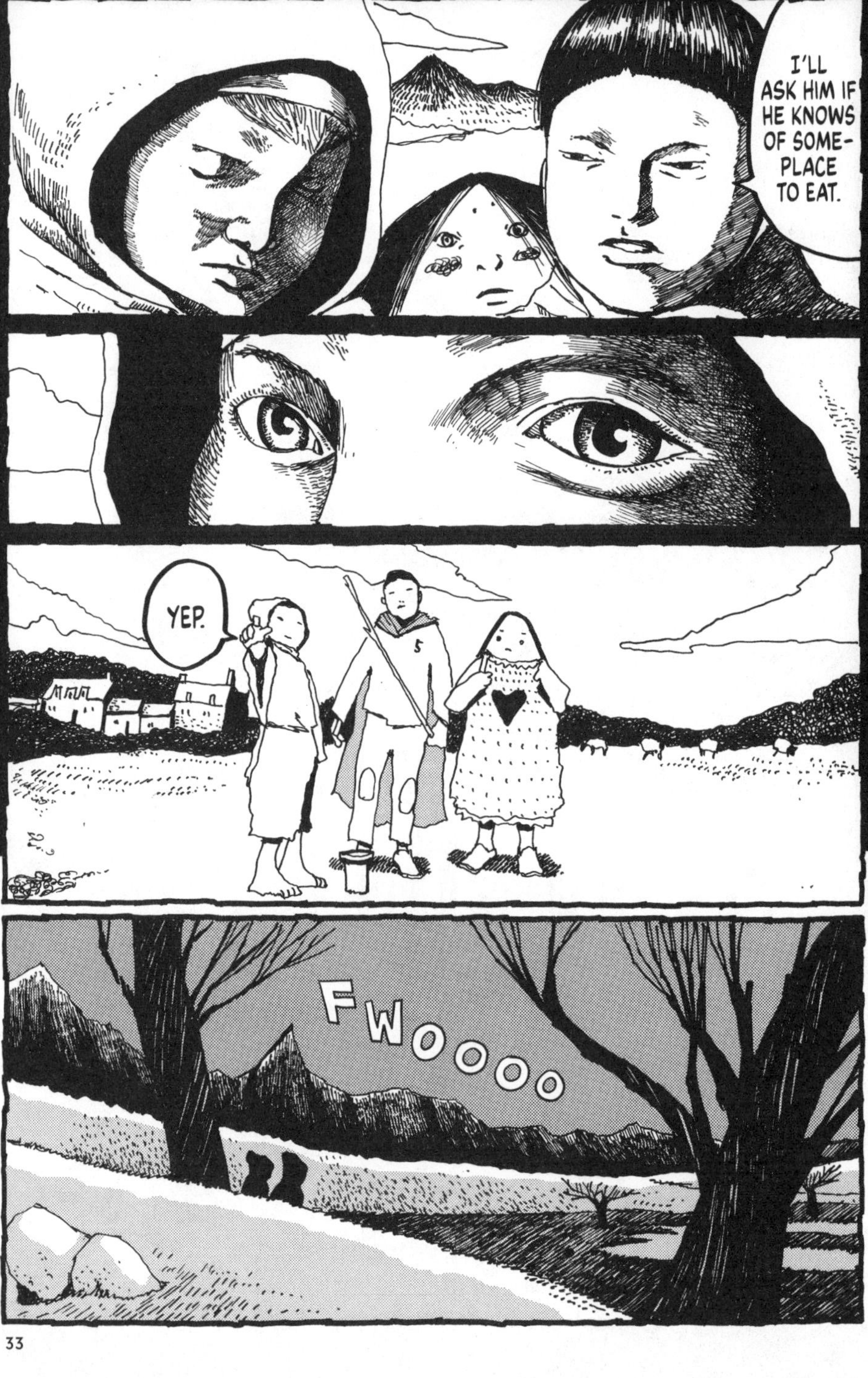
I'LL ASK HIM IF HE KNOWS OF SOME-PLACE TO EAT.
YEP.
FWOOOO

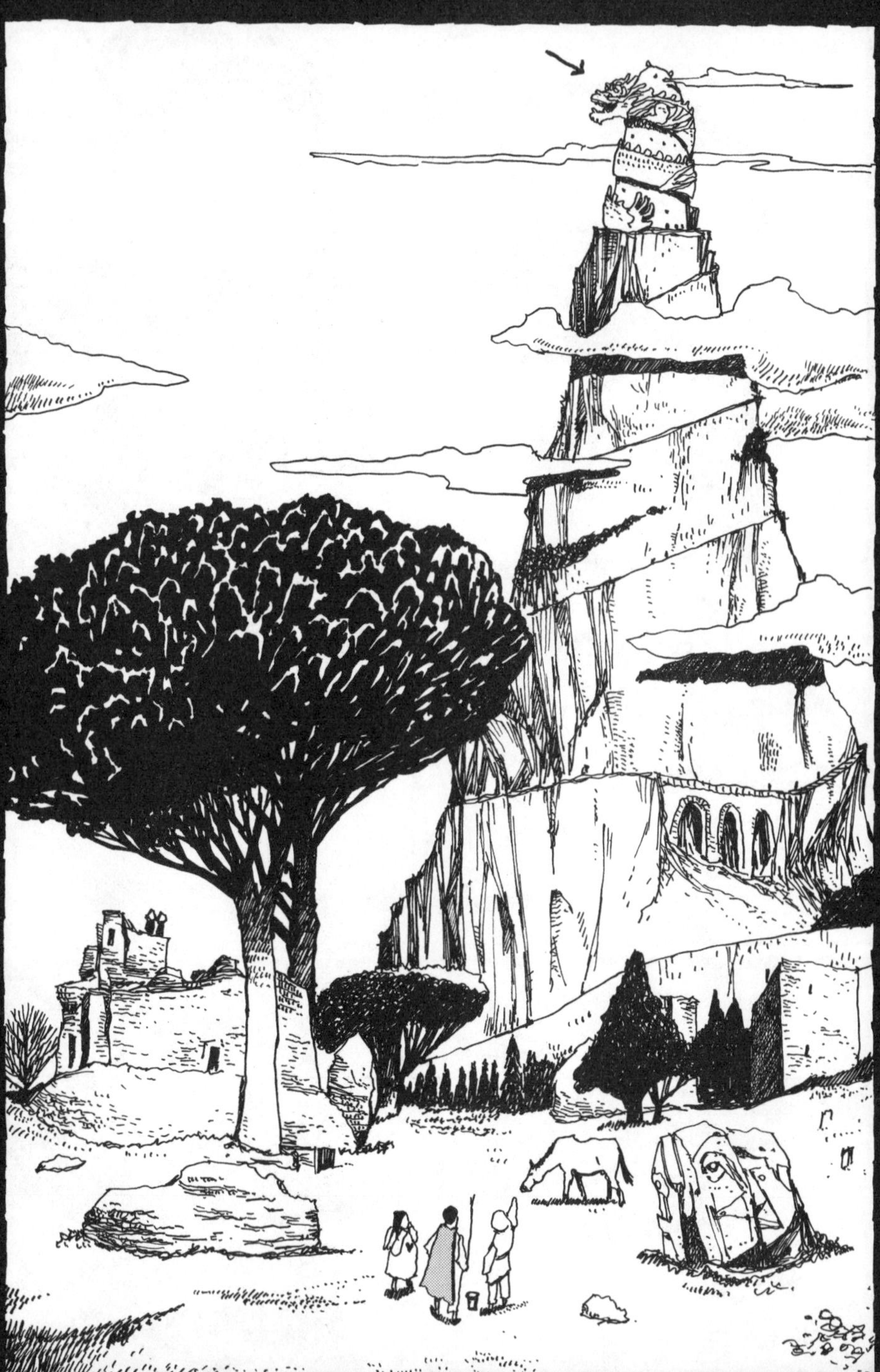

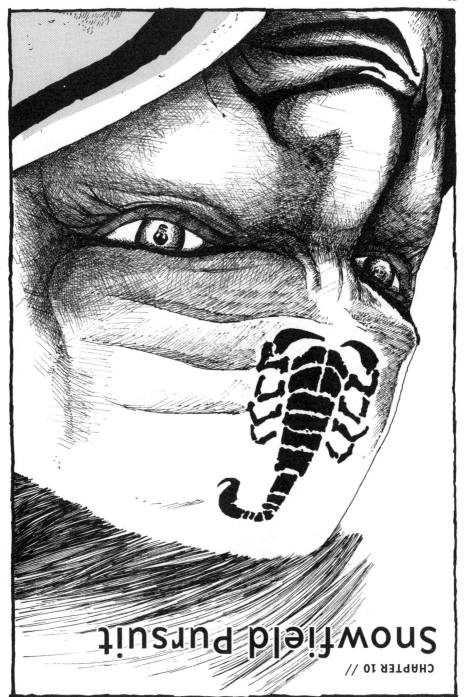

CHAPTER 10 //
Snowfield Pursuit

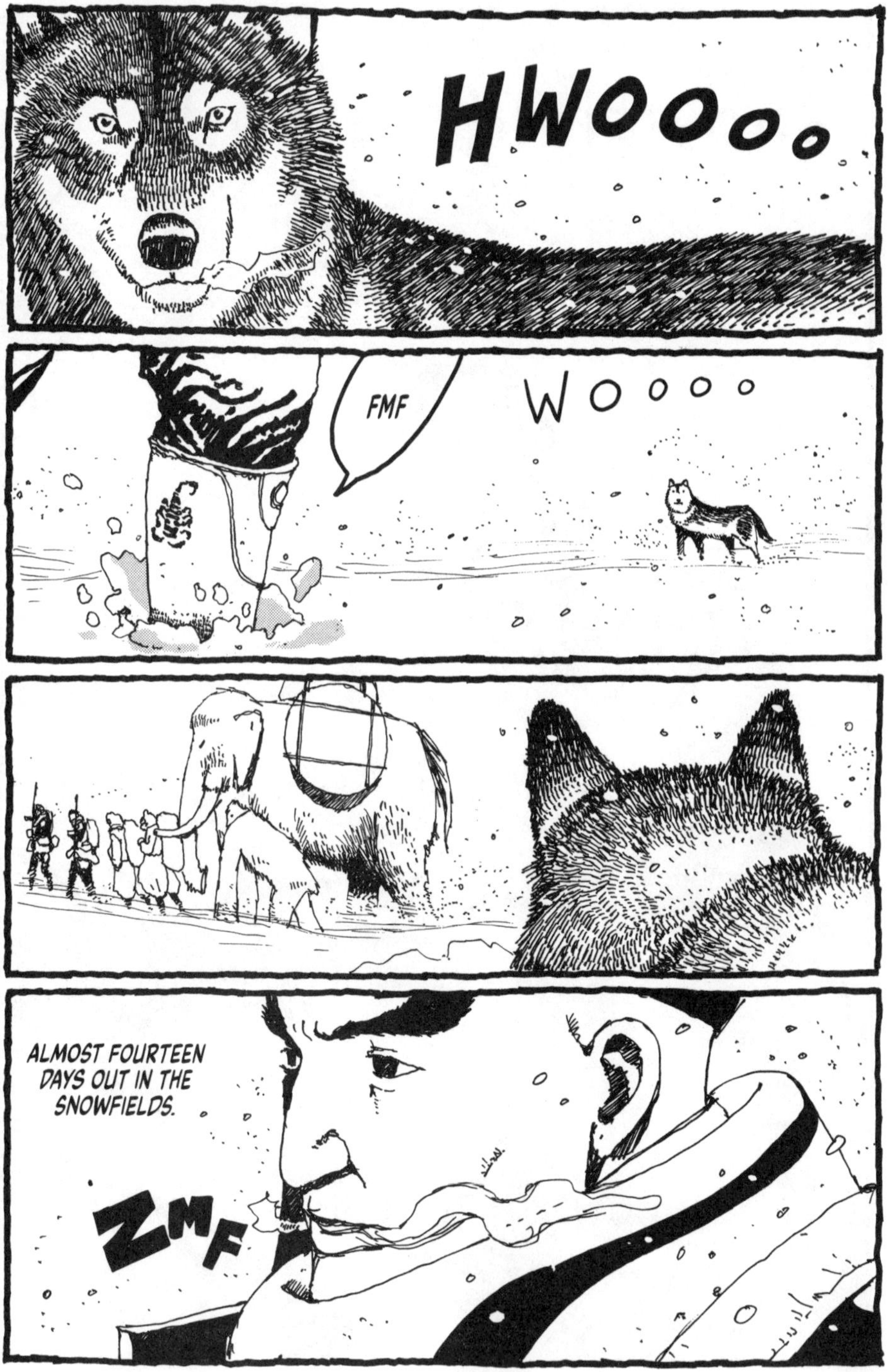
HWOOOO
FMF
WOOOO
ALMOST FOURTEEN DAYS OUT IN THE SNOWFIELDS.
ZMF

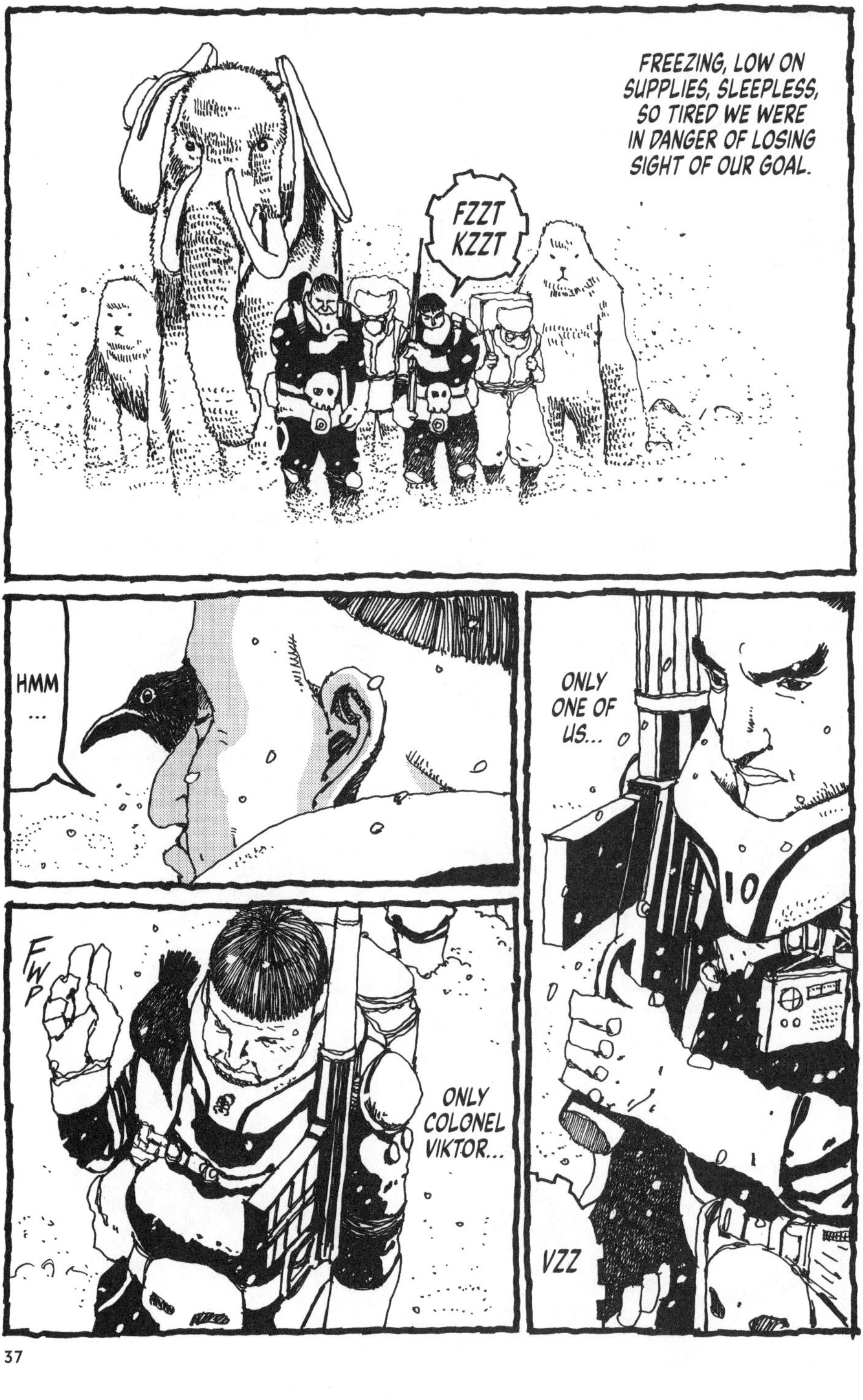
FREEZING, LOW ON SUPPLIES, SLEEPLESS, SO TIRED WE WERE IN DANGER OF LOSING SIGHT OF OUR GOAL.
FZZT KZZT
ONLY ONE OF US...
VZZ
HMM ...
FWP
ONLY COLONEL VIKTOR...

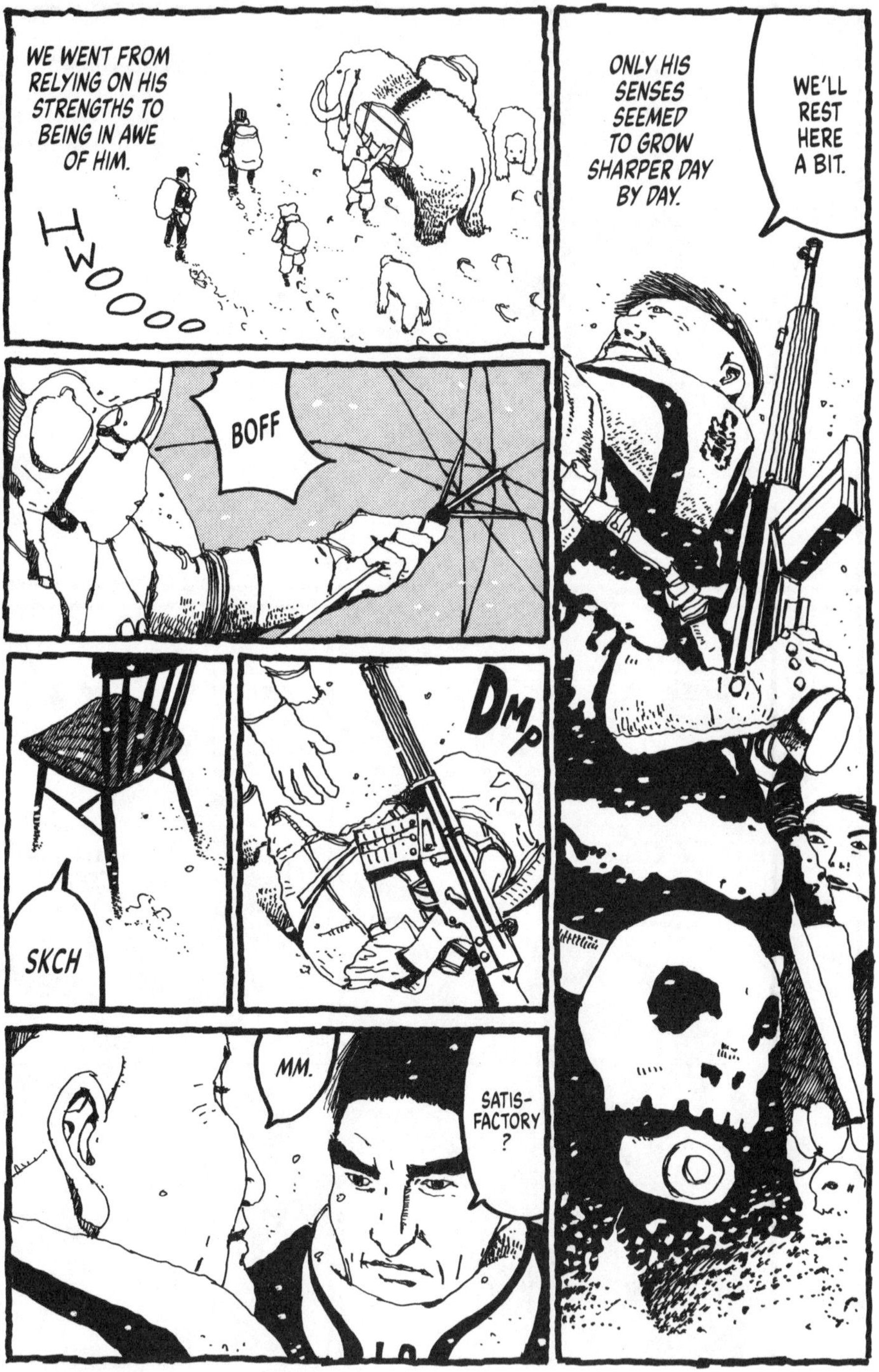
ONLY HIS SENSES SEEMED TO GROW SHARPER DAY BY DAY.
WE'LL REST HERE A BIT.
WE WENT FROM RELYING ON HIS STRENGTHS TO BEING IN AWE OF HIM.
HWOOOOO
BOFF
DMP
SKCH
SATIS-FACTORY?
MM.

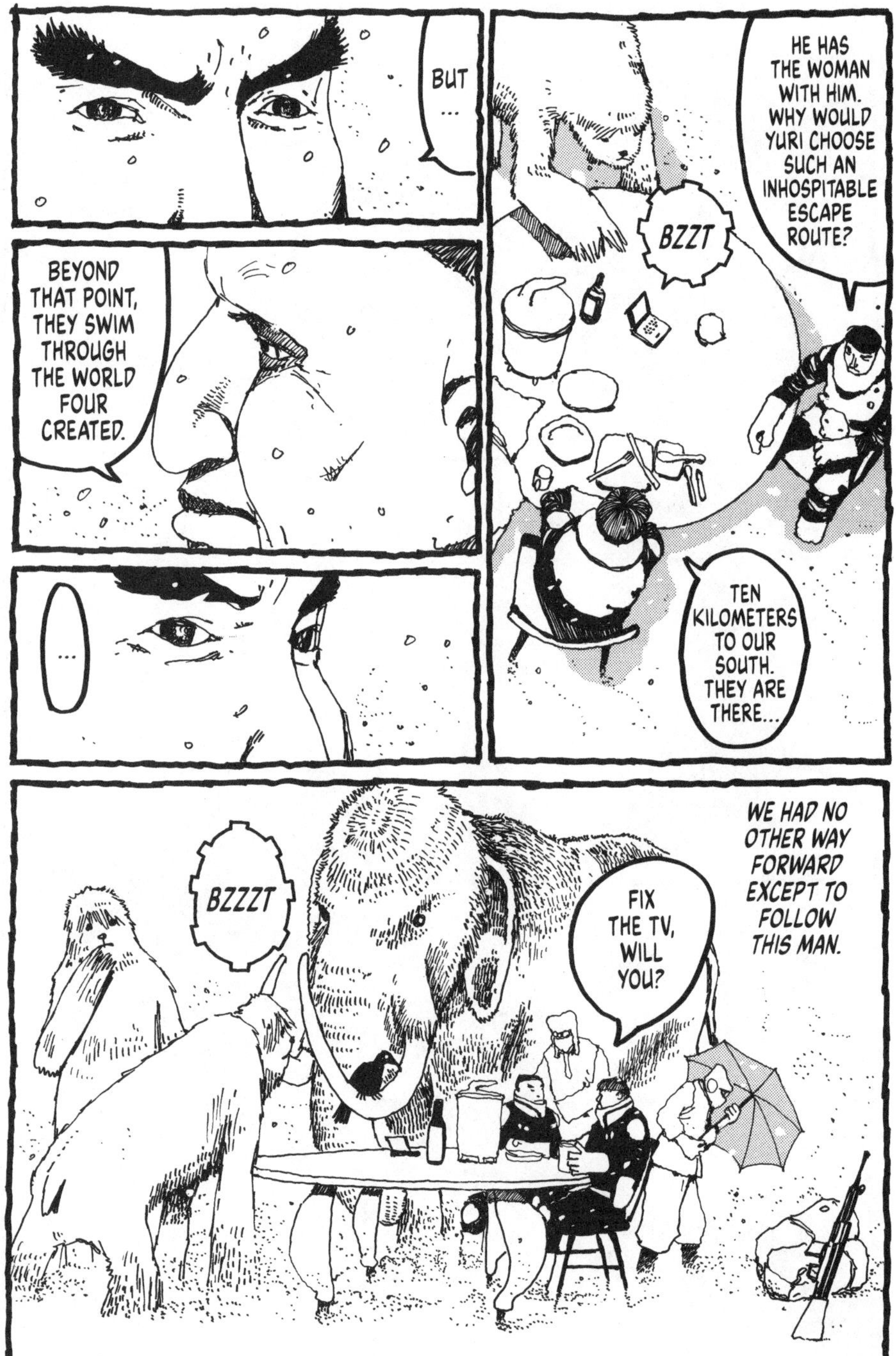
HE HAS THE WOMAN WITH HIM. WHY WOULD YURI CHOOSE SUCH AN INHOSPITABLE ESCAPE ROUTE?
BZZT
TEN KILOMETERS TO OUR SOUTH. THEY ARE THERE...
BUT ...
BEYOND THAT POINT, THEY SWIM THROUGH THE WORLD FOUR CREATED.
...
WE HAD NO OTHER WAY FORWARD EXCEPT TO FOLLOW THIS MAN.
FIX THE TV, WILL YOU?
BZZZT

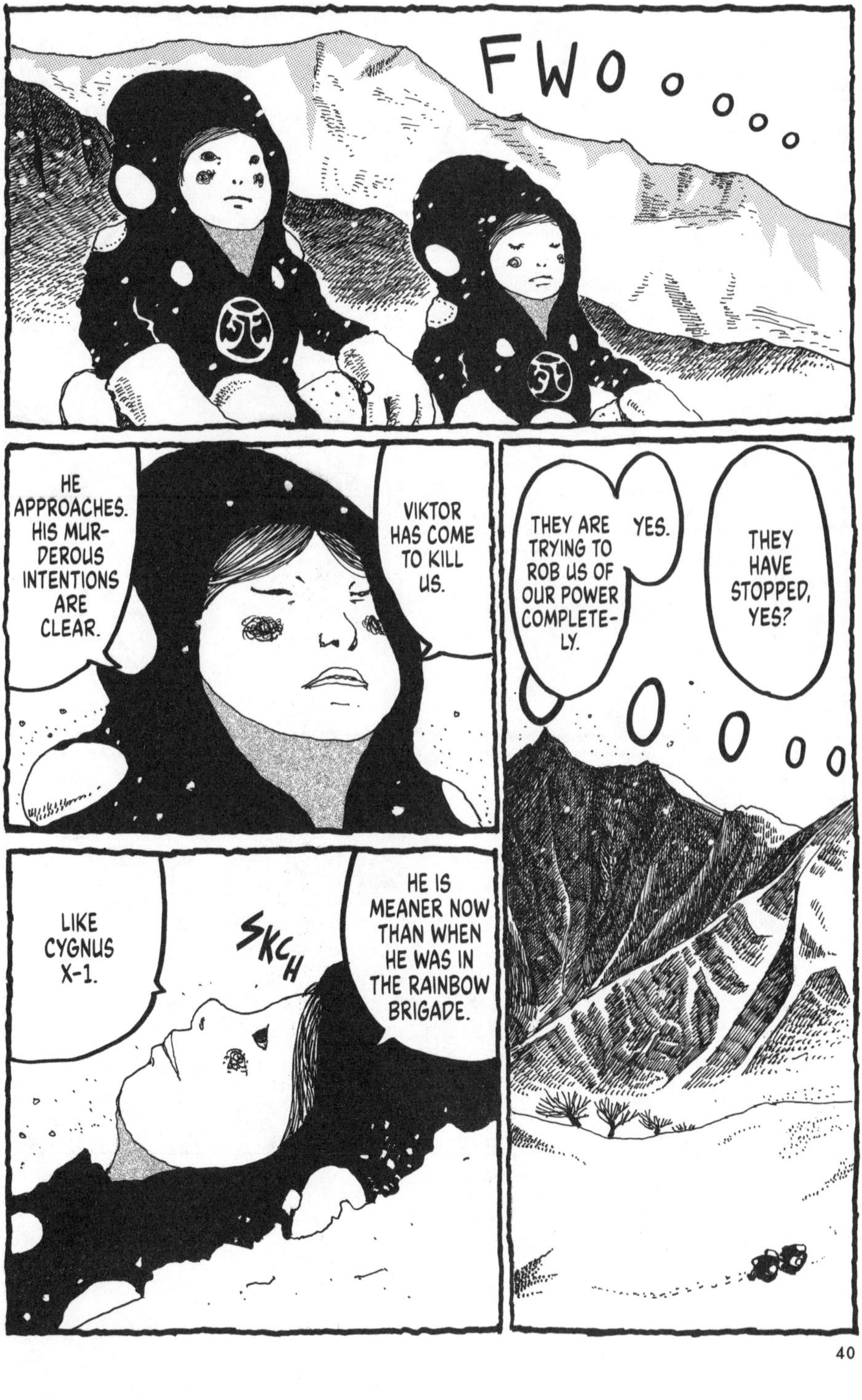
FWOoooo
THEY HAVE STOPPED, YES?
YES.
THEY ARE TRYING TO ROB US OF OUR POWER COMPLETE-LY.
OOOO
VIKTOR HAS COME TO KILL US.
HE APPROACHES. HIS MUR-DEROUS INTENTIONS ARE CLEAR.
HE IS MEANER NOW THAN WHEN HE WAS IN THE RAINBOW BRIGADE.
SKCH
LIKE CYGNUS X-1.

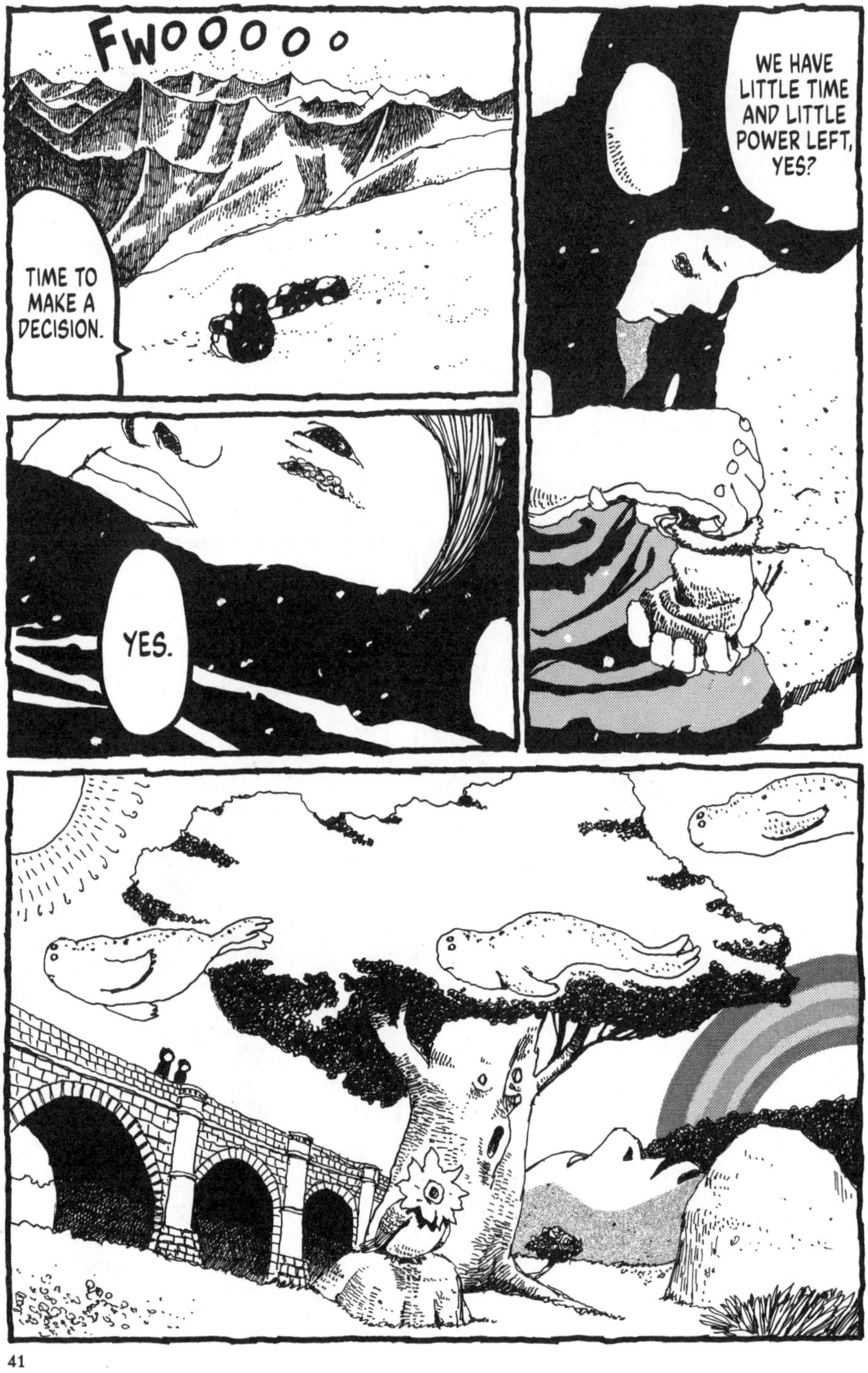
WE HAVE LITTLE TIME AND LITTLE POWER LEFT, YES?
FWOOOOO
TIME TO MAKE A DECISION.
YES.

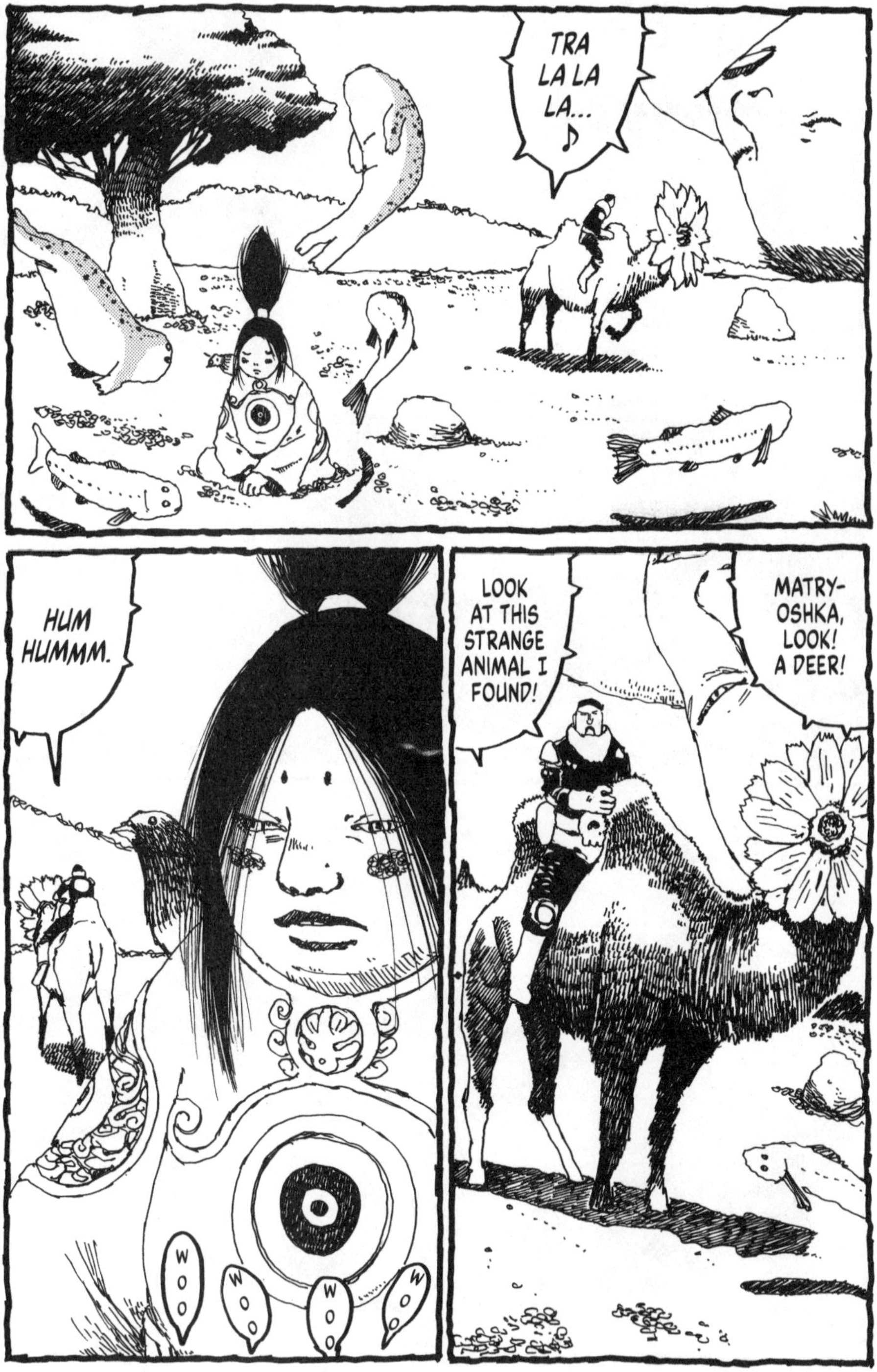
TRA LA LA LA... ♪
MATRY-OSHKA, LOOK! A DEER!
LOOK AT THIS STRANGE ANIMAL I FOUND!
HUM HUMMM.
WOO
WOO
WOO
WOO

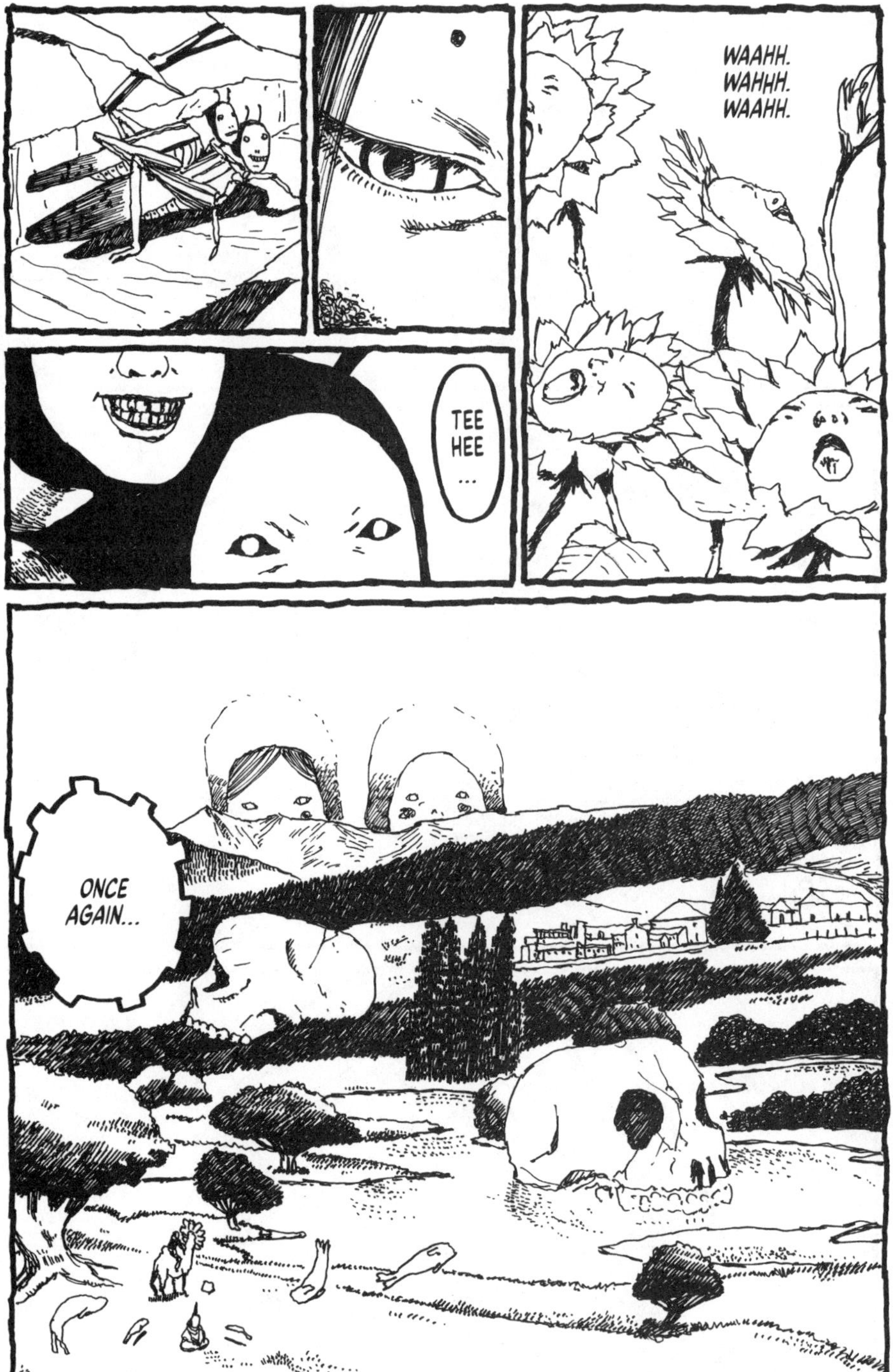
WAAHH.
WAHHH.
WAAHH.
TEE HEE ...
ONCE AGAIN...

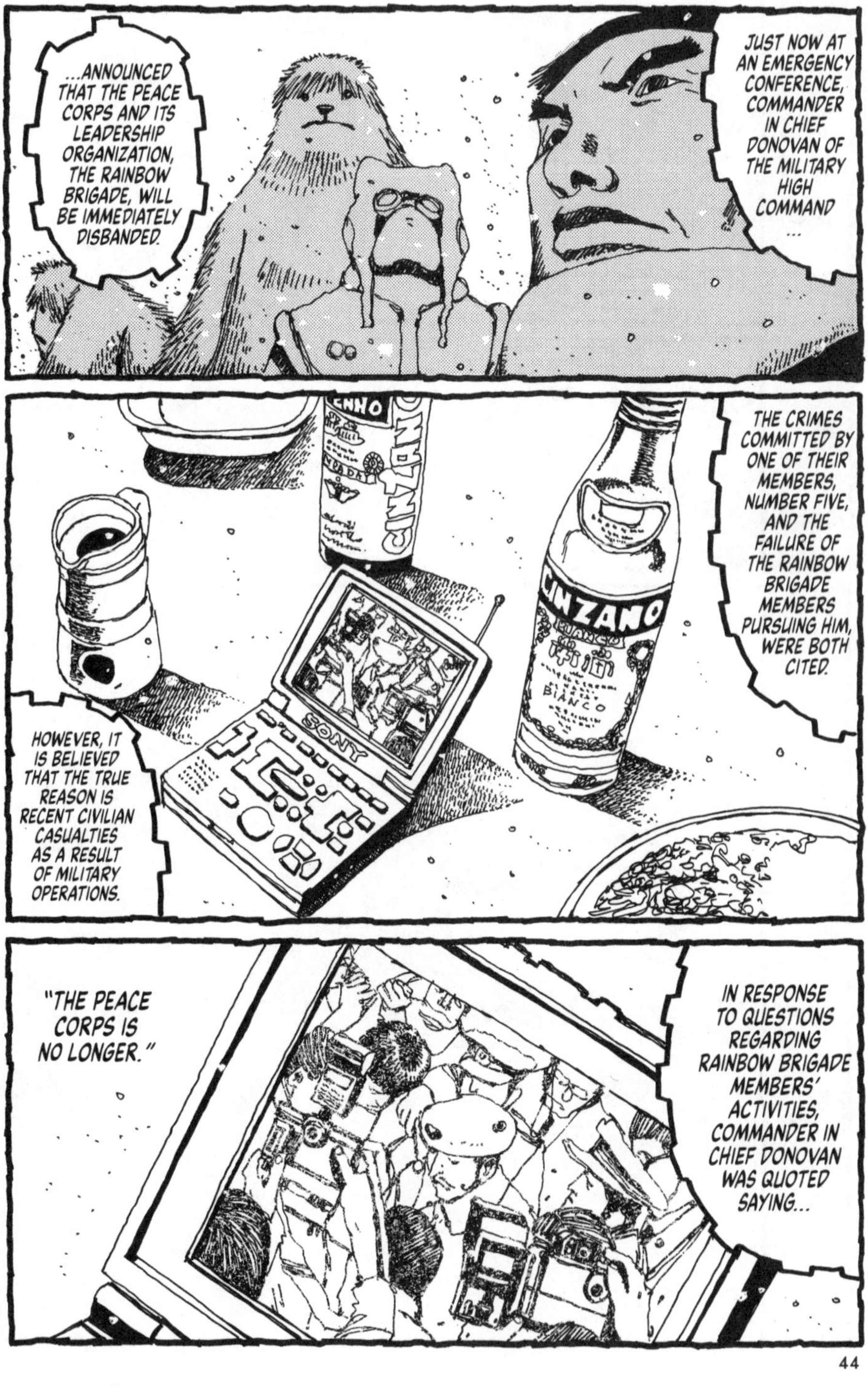
JUST NOW AT AN EMERGENCY CONFERENCE, COMMANDER IN CHIEF DONOVAN OF THE MILITARY HIGH COMMAND ...
...ANNOUNCED THAT THE PEACE CORPS AND ITS LEADERSHIP ORGANIZATION, THE RAINBOW BRIGADE, WILL BE IMMEDIATELY DISBANDED.
THE CRIMES COMMITTED BY ONE OF THEIR MEMBERS, NUMBER FIVE, AND THE FAILURE OF THE RAINBOW BRIGADE MEMBERS PURSUING HIM, WERE BOTH CITED.
CINZANO
BIANCO
SONY
HOWEVER, IT IS BELIEVED THAT THE TRUE REASON IS RECENT CIVILIAN CASUALTIES AS A RESULT OF MILITARY OPERATIONS.
IN RESPONSE TO QUESTIONS REGARDING RAINBOW BRIGADE MEMBERS' ACTIVITIES, COMMANDER IN CHIEF DONOVAN WAS QUOTED SAYING...
"THE PEACE CORPS IS NO LONGER."

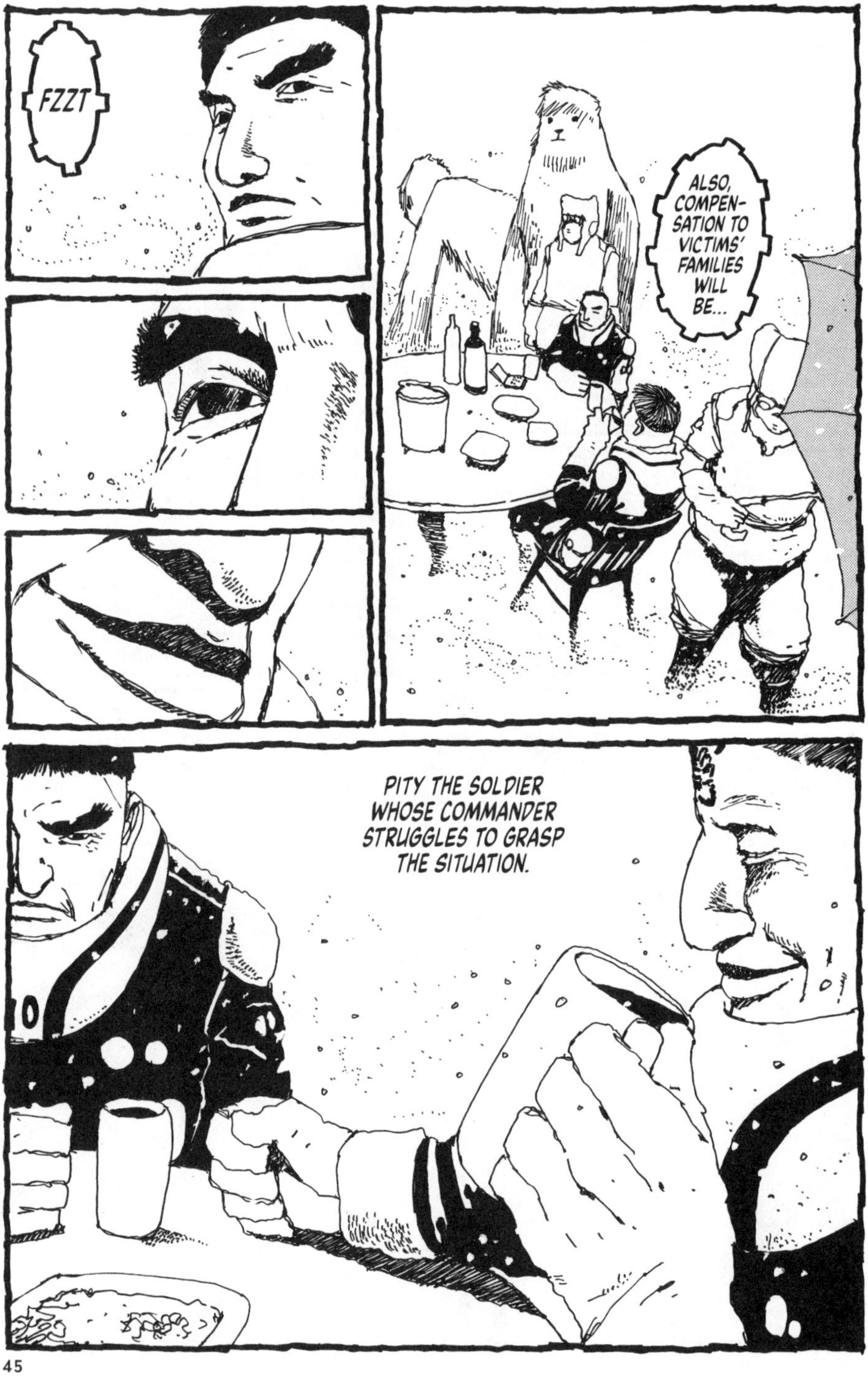
ALSO, COMPEN-SATION TO VICTIMS' FAMILIES WILL BE...
FZZT
PITY THE SOLDIER WHOSE COMMANDER STRUGGLES TO GRASP THE SITUATION.

*Fresh

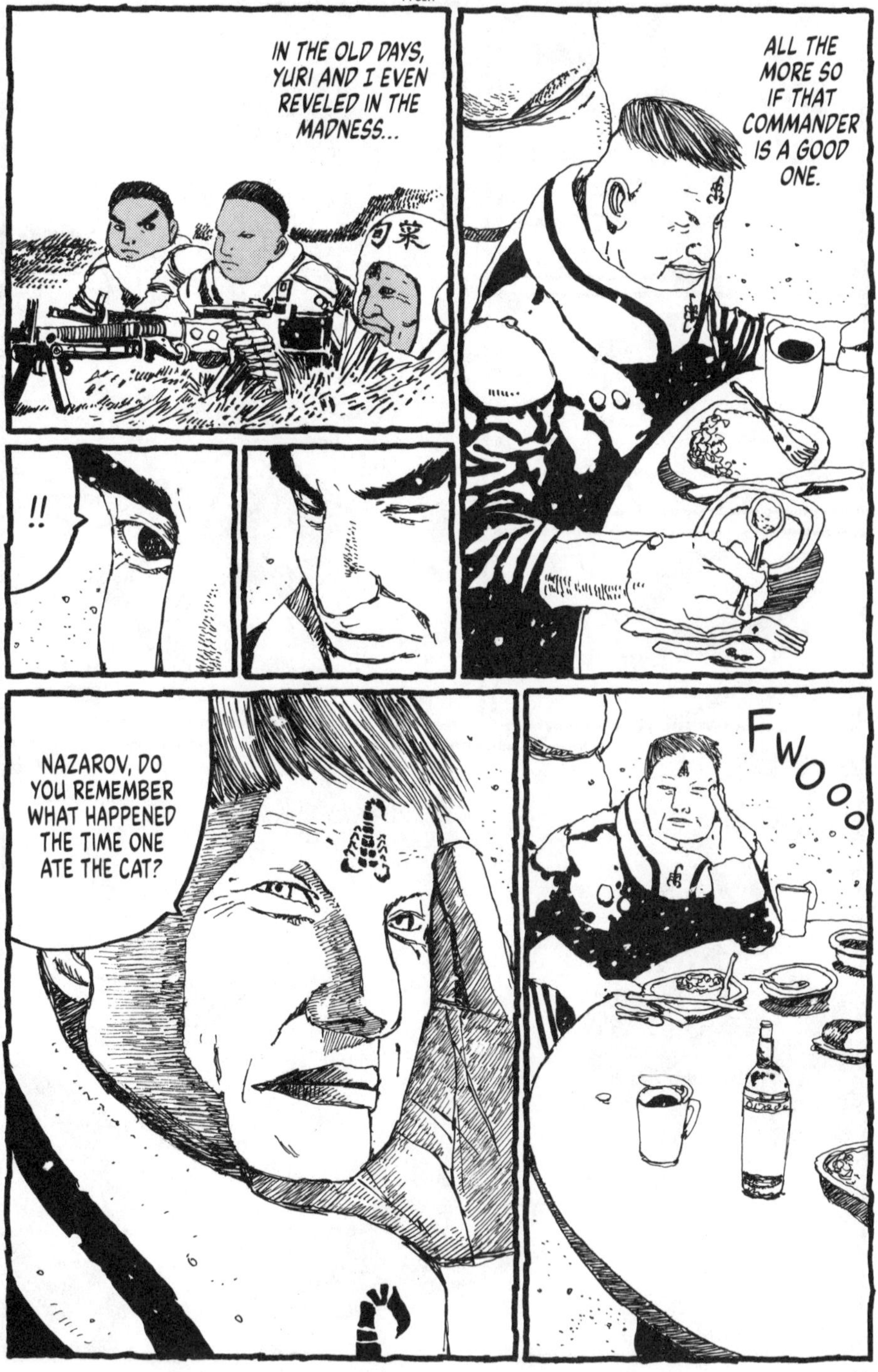
ALL THE MORE SO IF THAT COMMANDER IS A GOOD ONE.
IN THE OLD DAYS, YURI AND I EVEN REVELED IN THE MADNESS...
!!
FWOOOO
NAZAROV, DO YOU REMEMBER WHAT HAPPENED THE TIME ONE ATE THE CAT?

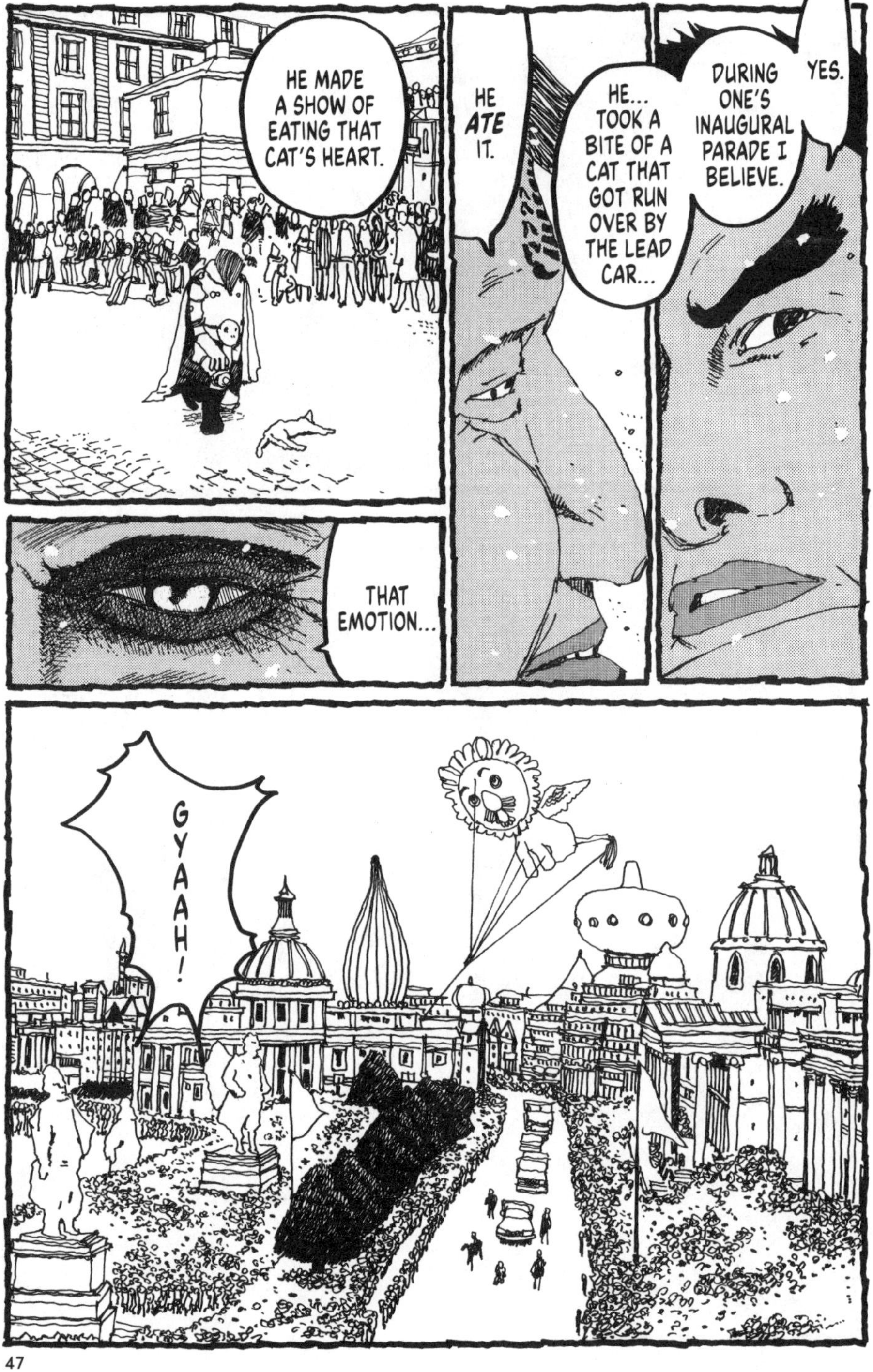
YES.
DURING ONE'S INAUGURAL PARADE I BELIEVE.
HE... TOOK A BITE OF A CAT THAT GOT RUN OVER BY THE LEAD CAR...
HE *ATE* IT.
HE MADE A SHOW OF EATING THAT CAT'S HEART.
THAT EMOTION...
GYAAAH!

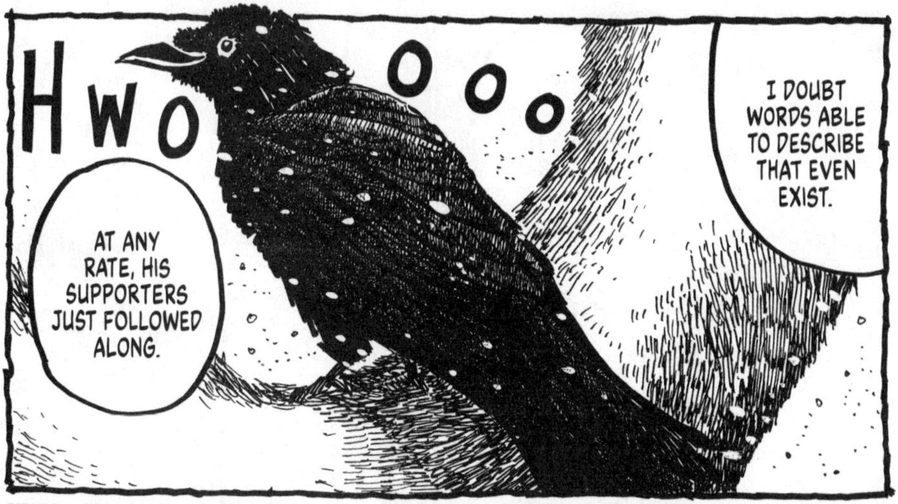
I DOUBT WORDS ABLE TO DESCRIBE THAT EVEN EXIST.
HWOOOO
AT ANY RATE, HIS SUPPORTERS JUST FOLLOWED ALONG.
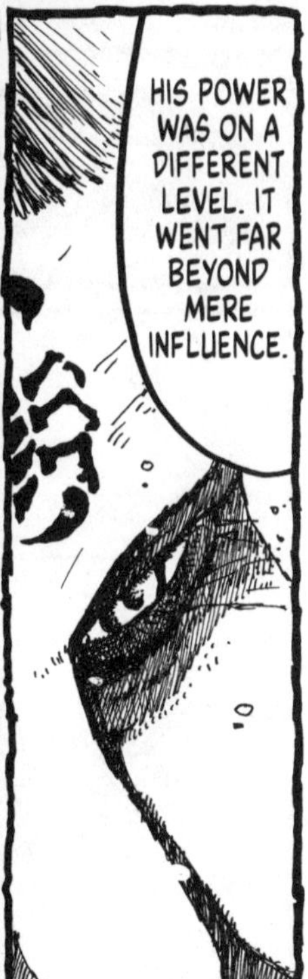
HIS POWER WAS ON A DIFFERENT LEVEL. IT WENT FAR BEYOND MERE INFLUENCE.
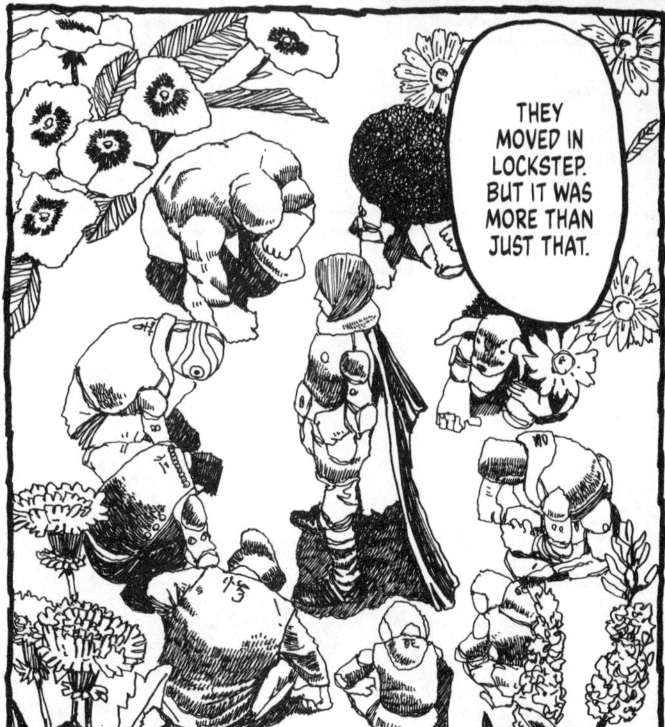
THEY MOVED IN LOCKSTEP. BUT IT WAS MORE THAN JUST THAT.

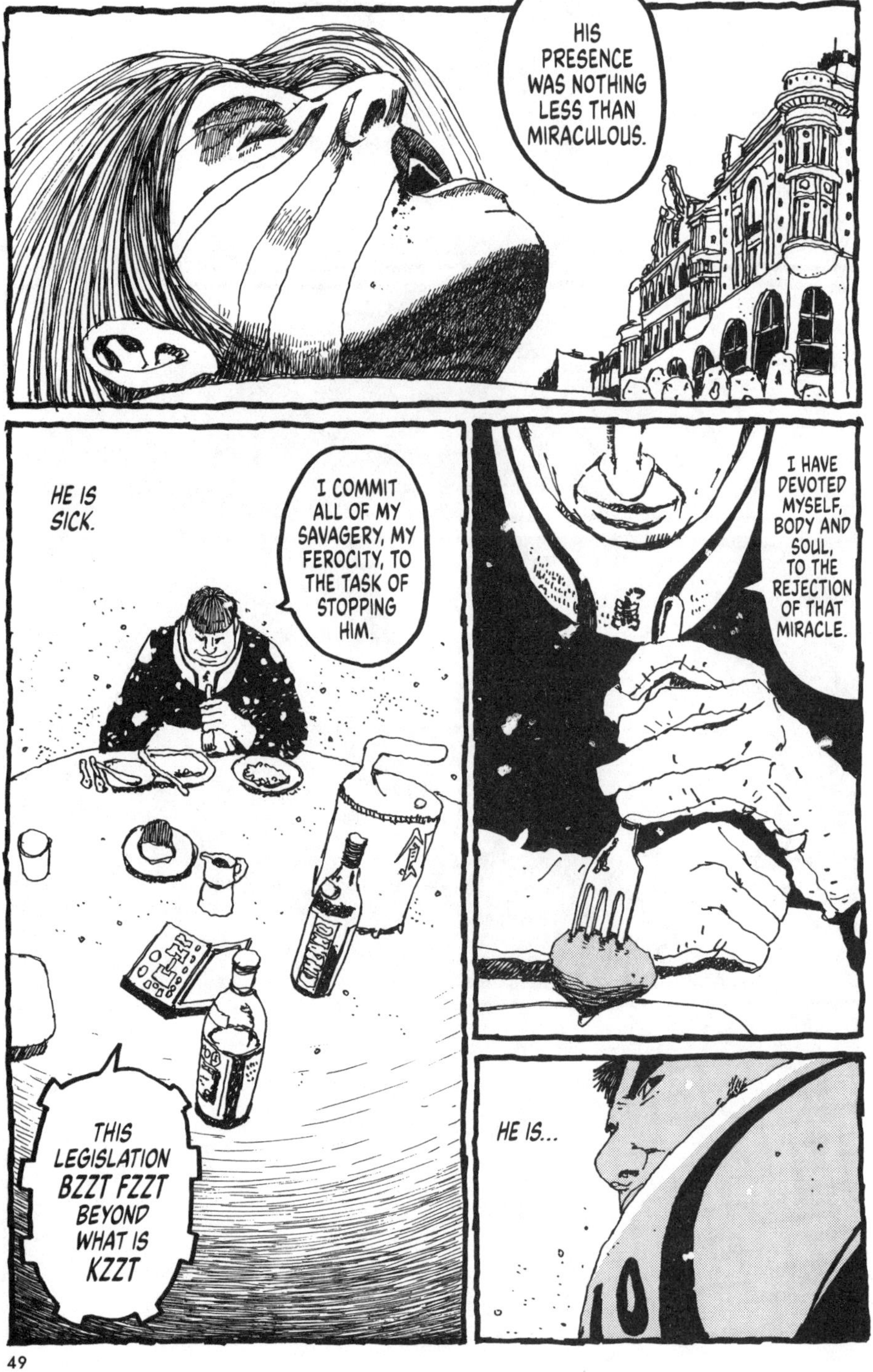
HIS PRESENCE WAS NOTHING LESS THAN MIRACULOUS.
I HAVE DEVOTED MYSELF, BODY AND SOUL, TO THE REJECTION OF THAT MIRACLE.
HE IS...
HE IS SICK.
I COMMIT ALL OF MY SAVAGERY, MY FEROCITY, TO THE TASK OF STOPPING HIM.
THIS LEGISLATION BZZT FZZT BEYOND WHAT IS KZZT

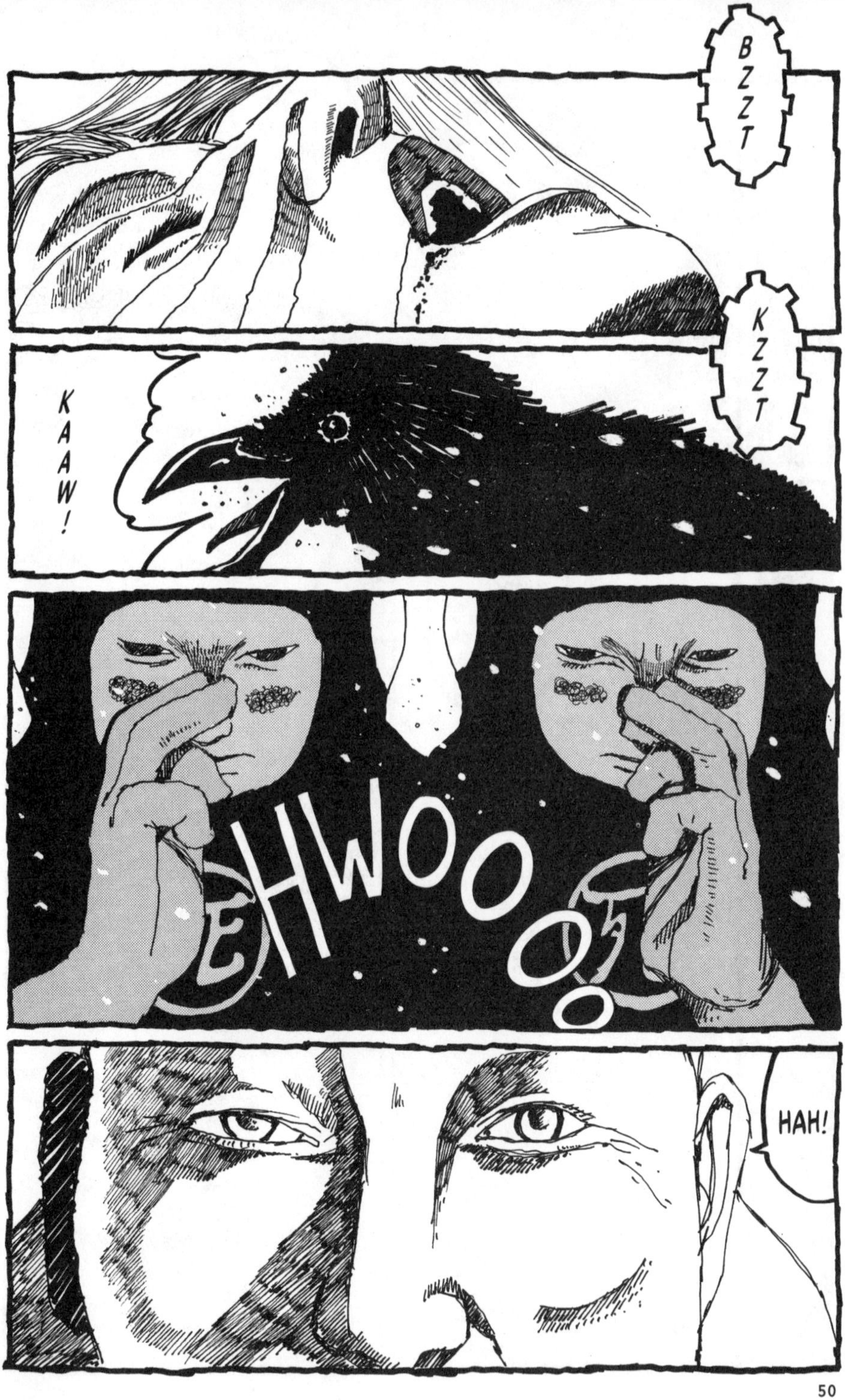
BZZT
KZZT
KAAAW!
EHWOOOO
HAH!

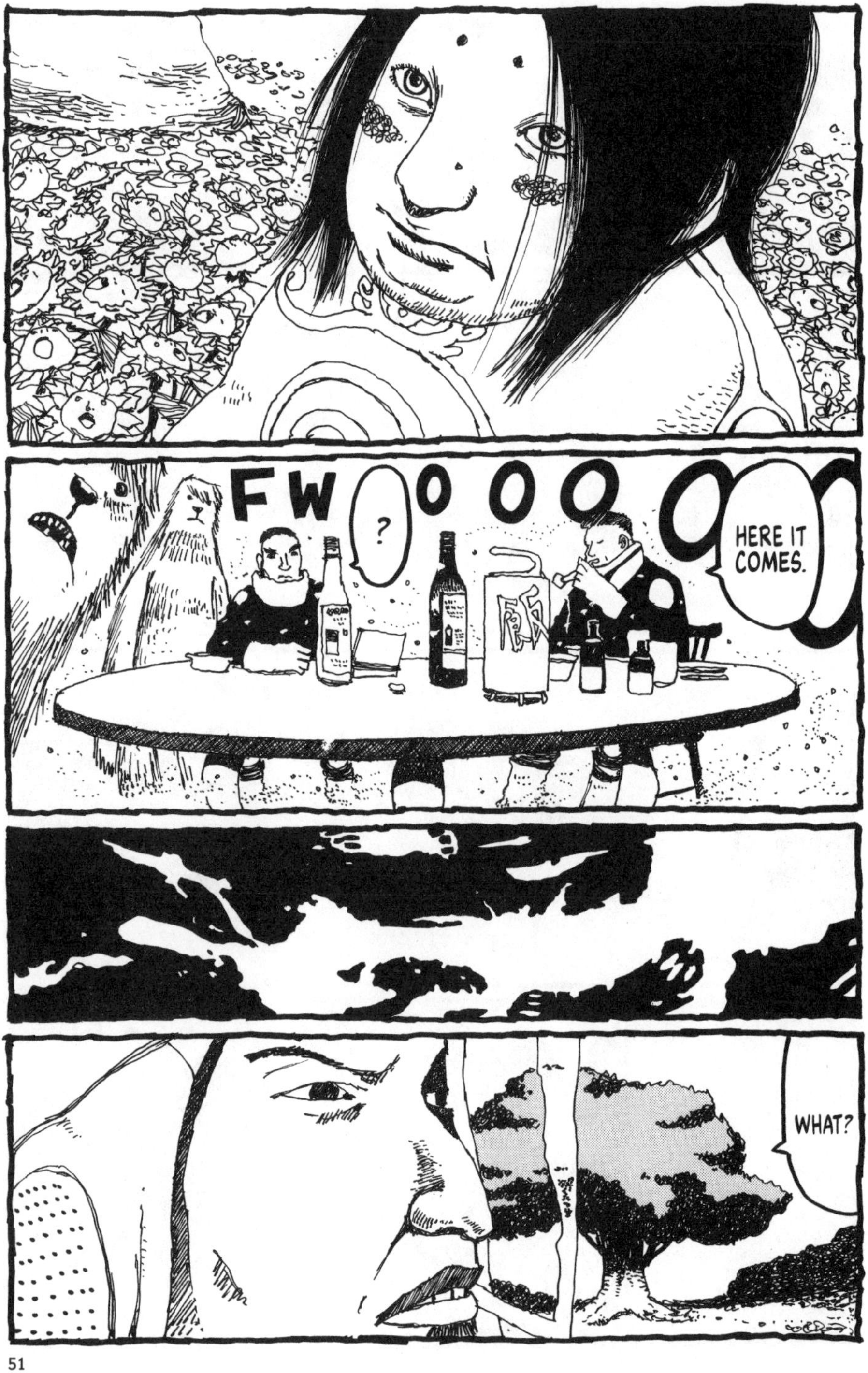
HERE IT COMES.
FWOOOOO
?
WHAT?

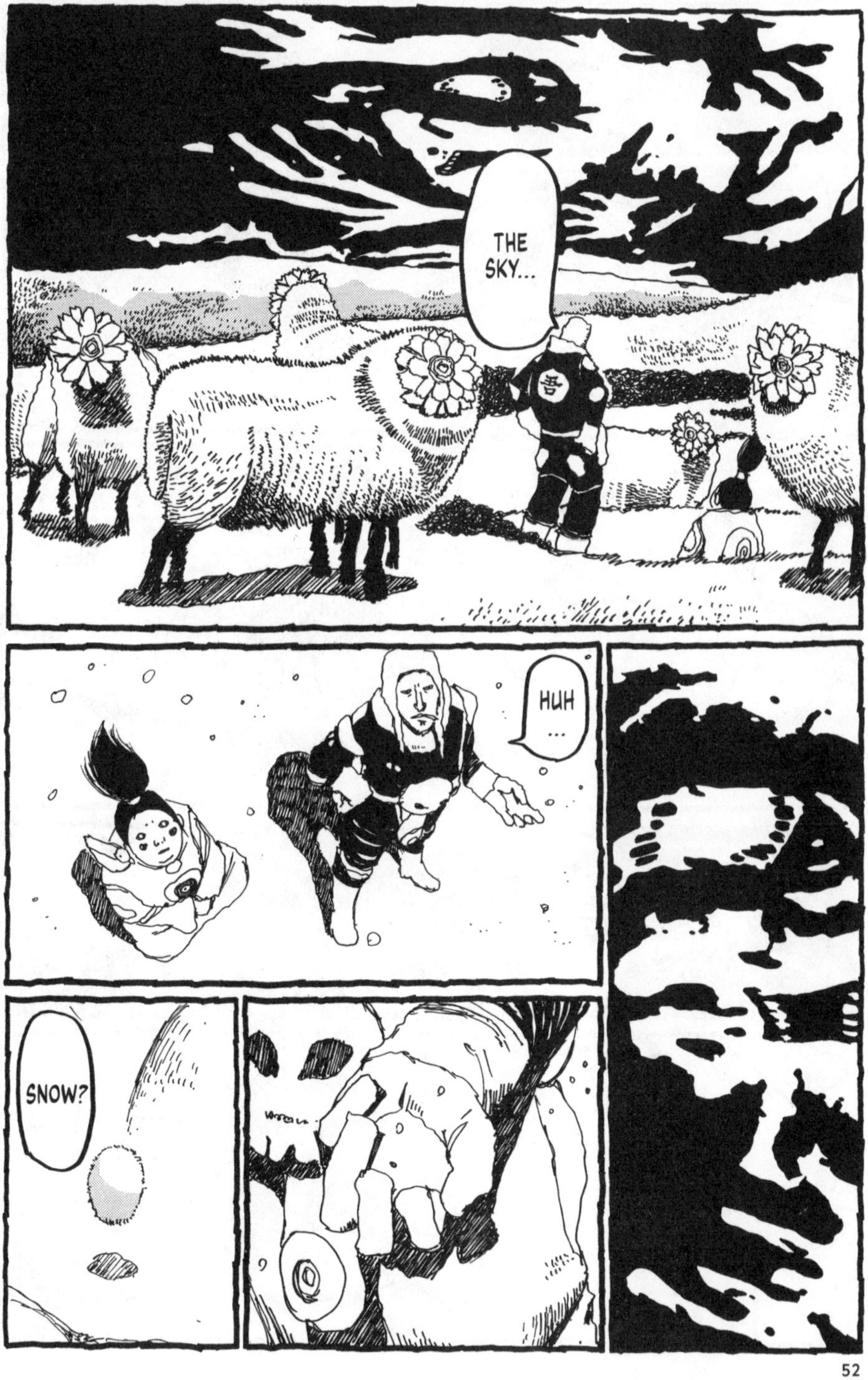
THE SKY...
HUH
...
SNOW?

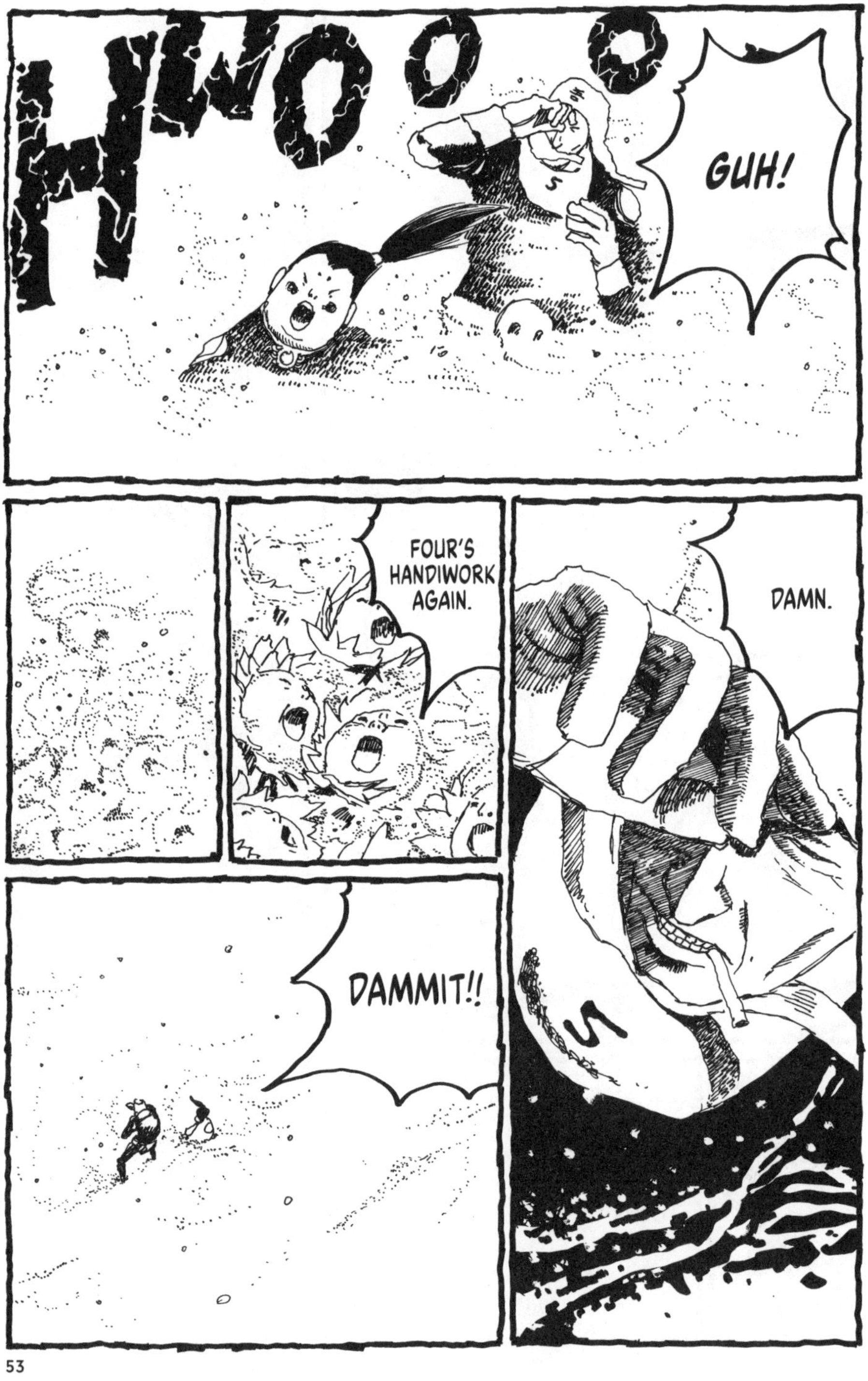
GUH!
HWO O O
DAMN.
FOUR'S HANDIWORK AGAIN.
DAMMIT!!

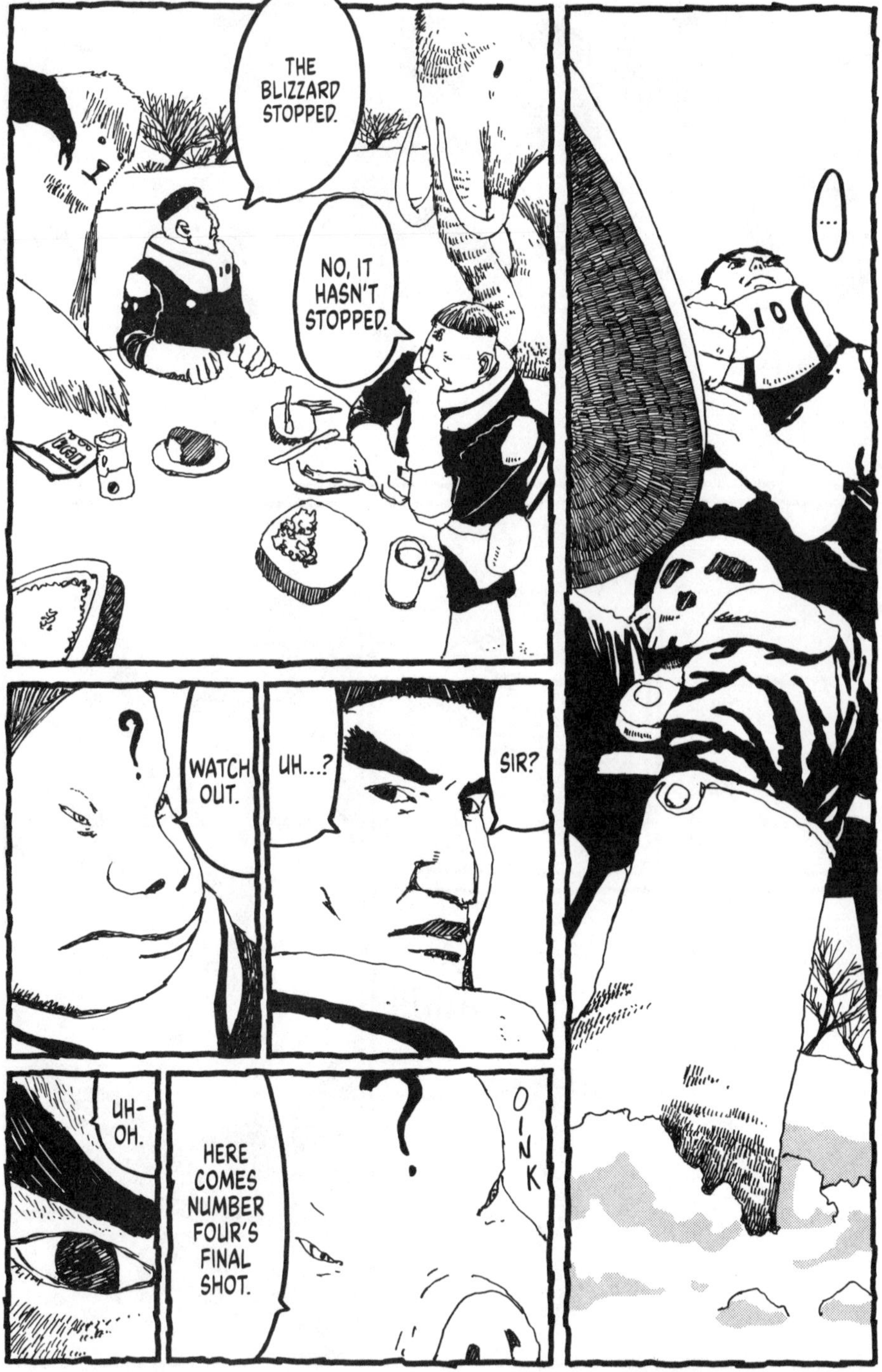
...
THE BLIZZARD STOPPED.
NO, IT HASN'T STOPPED.
SIR?
UH...?
WATCH OUT.
OINK
HERE COMES NUMBER FOUR'S FINAL SHOT.
UH-OH.

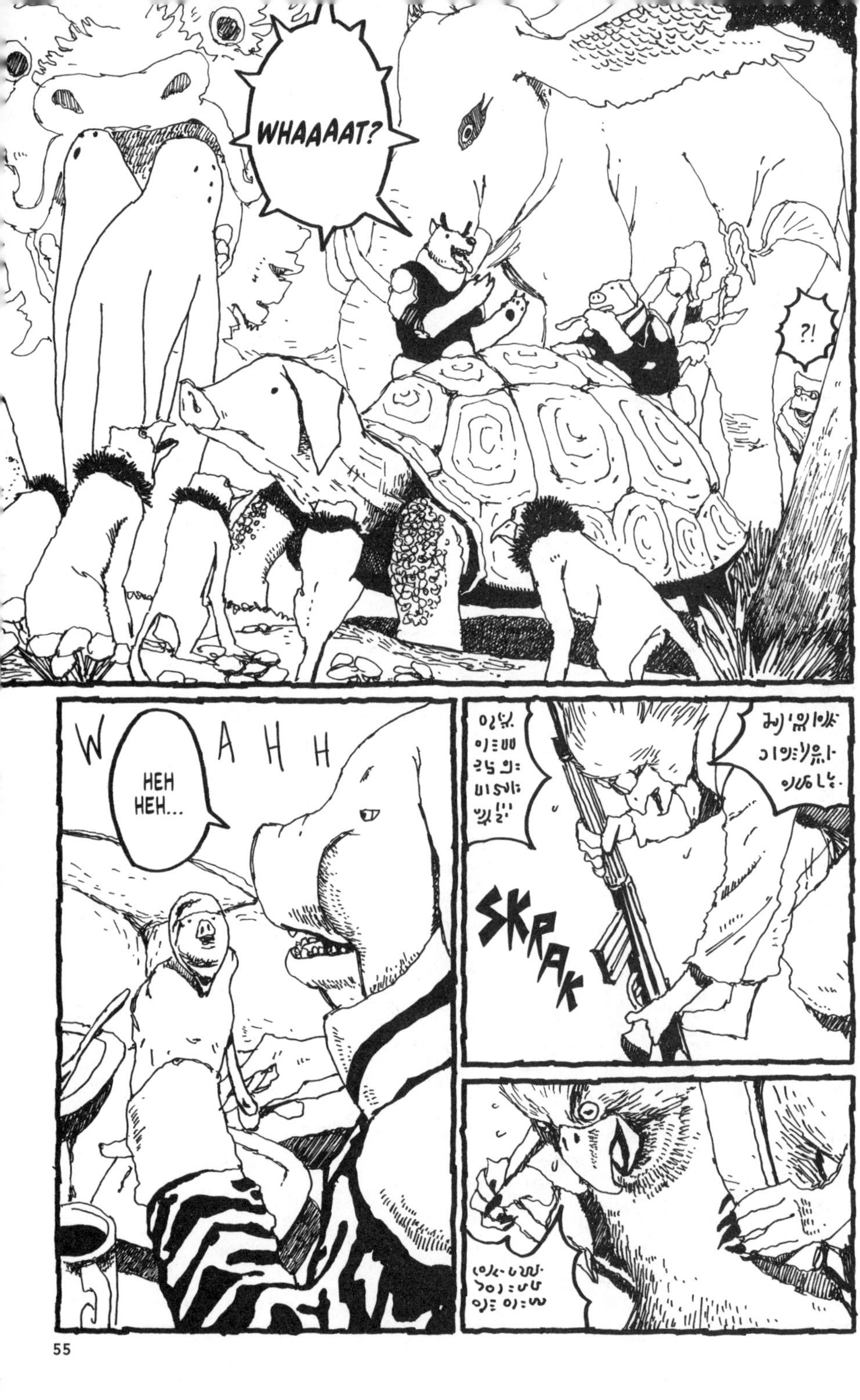
WHAAAAT?
?!
SKRAK
WAHH
HEH HEH...

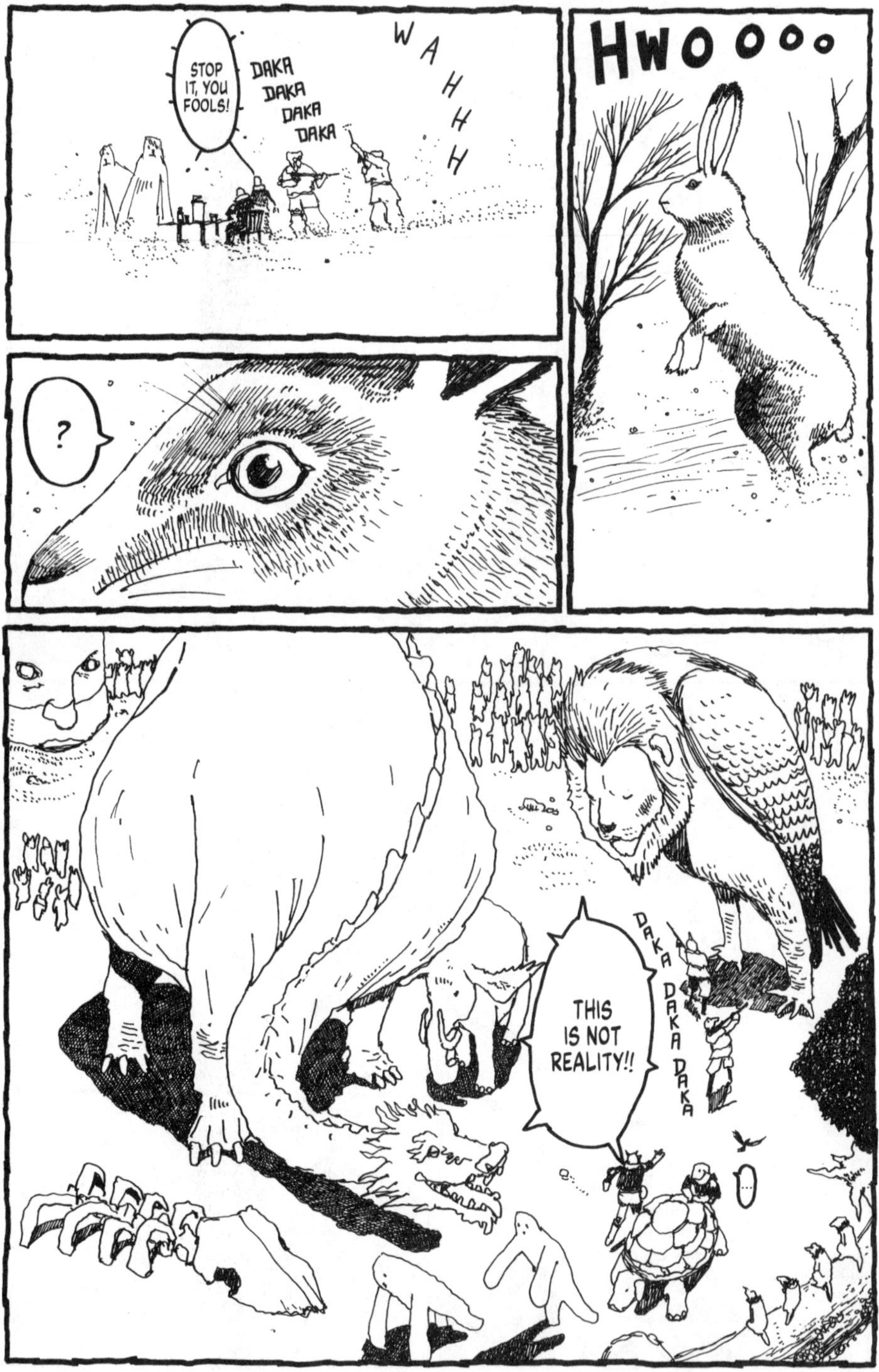
HWOOOOO
WAHHHH
STOP IT, YOU FOOLS!
DAKA DAKA DAKA DAKA
?
...
DAKA DAKA DAKA
THIS IS NOT REALITY!!

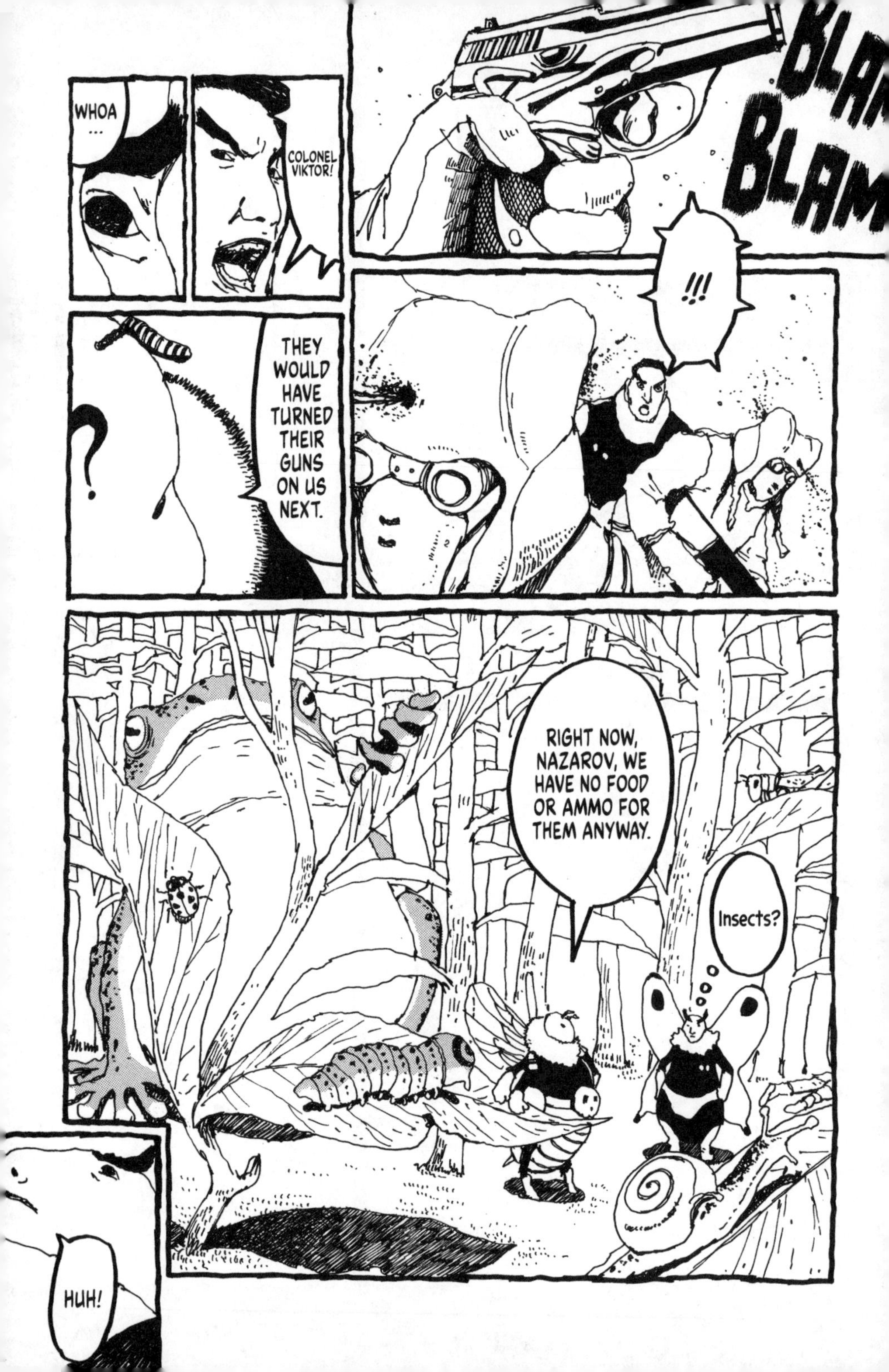
BLAM BLAM
COLONEL VIKTOR!
WHOA ...
!!!
THEY WOULD HAVE TURNED THEIR GUNS ON US NEXT.
RIGHT NOW, NAZAROV, WE HAVE NO FOOD OR AMMO FOR THEM ANYWAY.
Insects?
HUH!

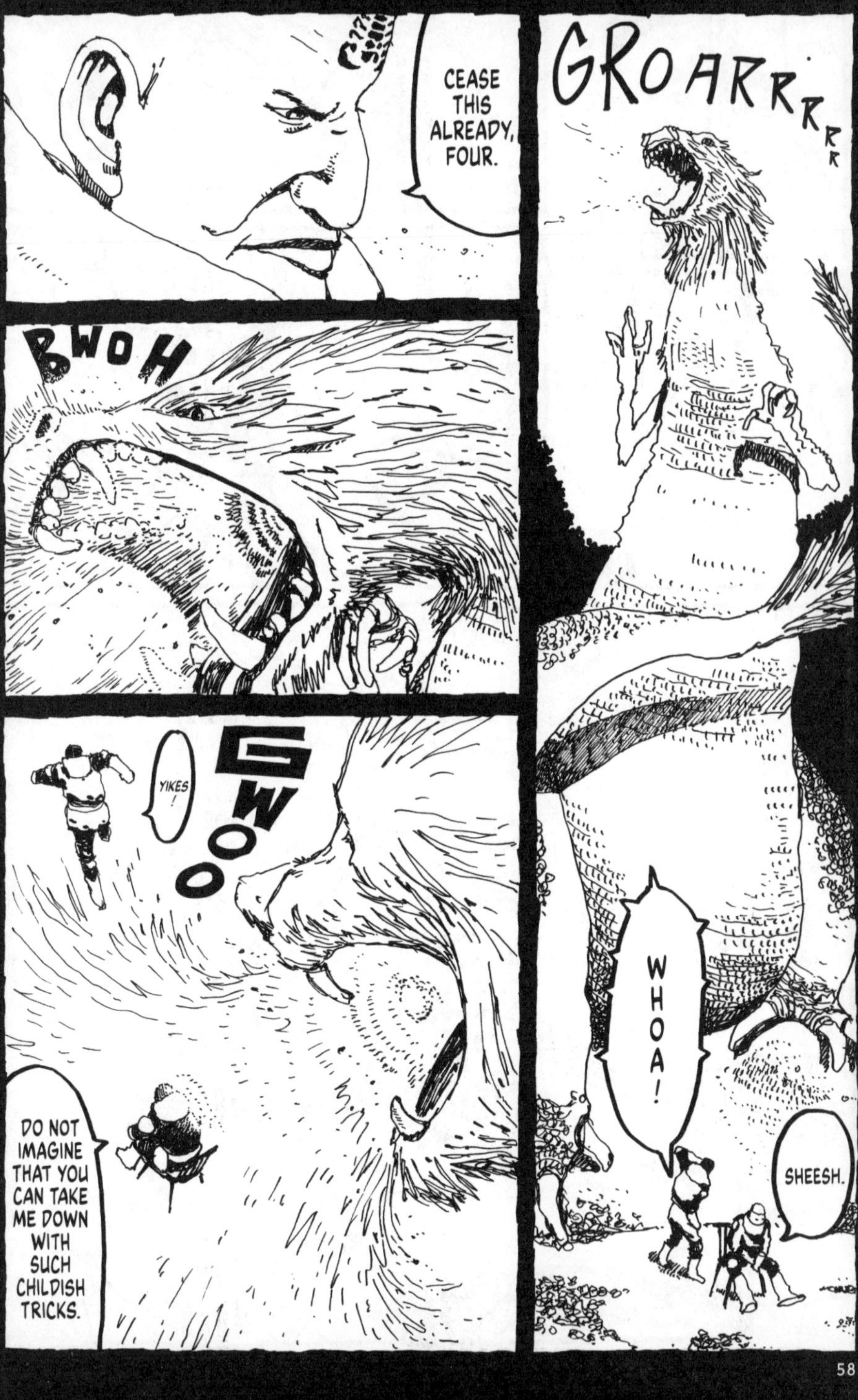
GROARRRRR
WHOA!
SHEESH.
CEASE THIS ALREADY, FOUR.
BWOH
GWOOO
YIKES!
DO NOT IMAGINE THAT YOU CAN TAKE ME DOWN WITH SUCH CHILDISH TRICKS.

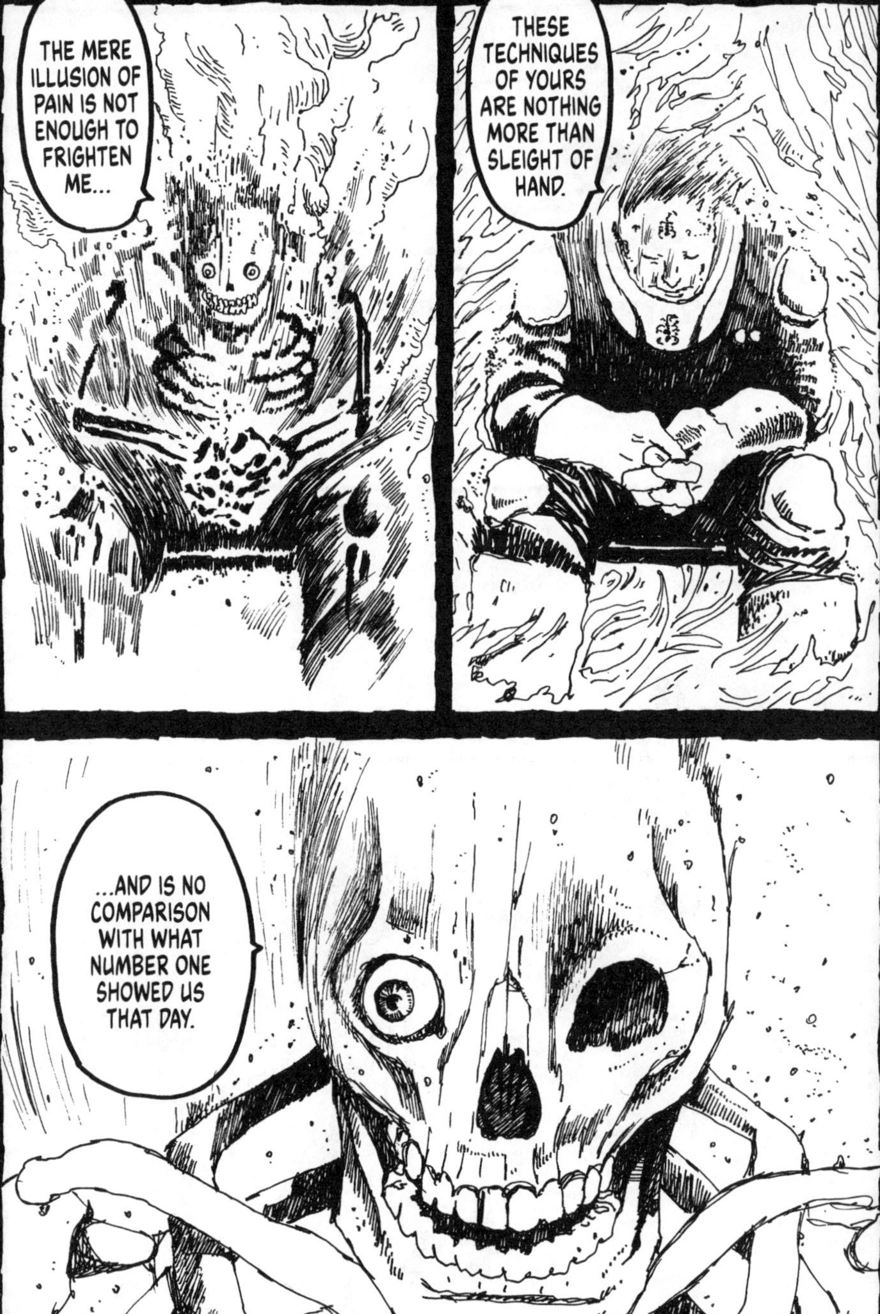
THESE TECHNIQUES OF YOURS ARE NOTHING MORE THAN SLEIGHT OF HAND.
THE MERE ILLUSION OF PAIN IS NOT ENOUGH TO FRIGHTEN ME...
...AND IS NO COMPARISON WITH WHAT NUMBER ONE SHOWED US THAT DAY.

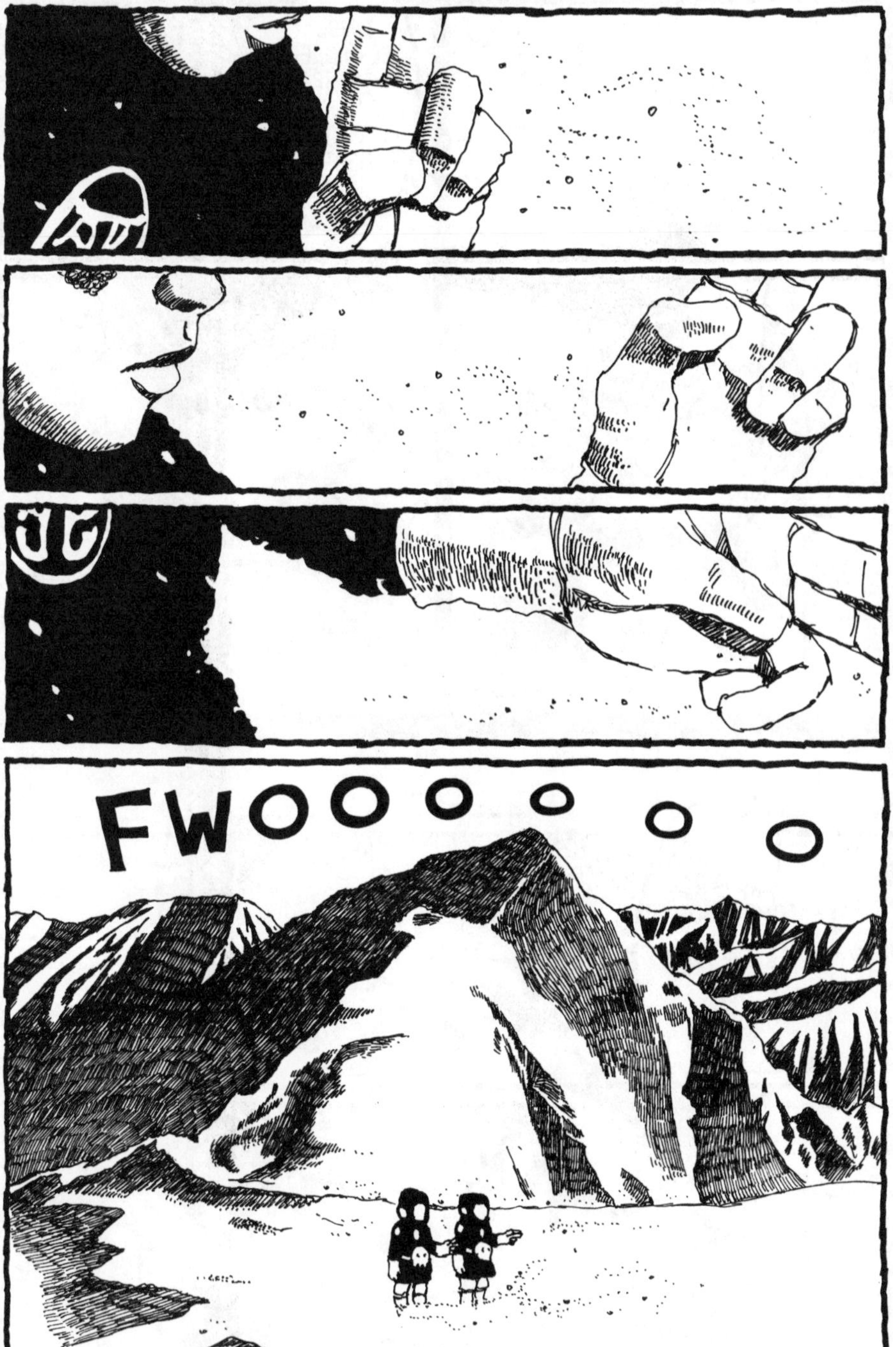
FWOOOOOOO

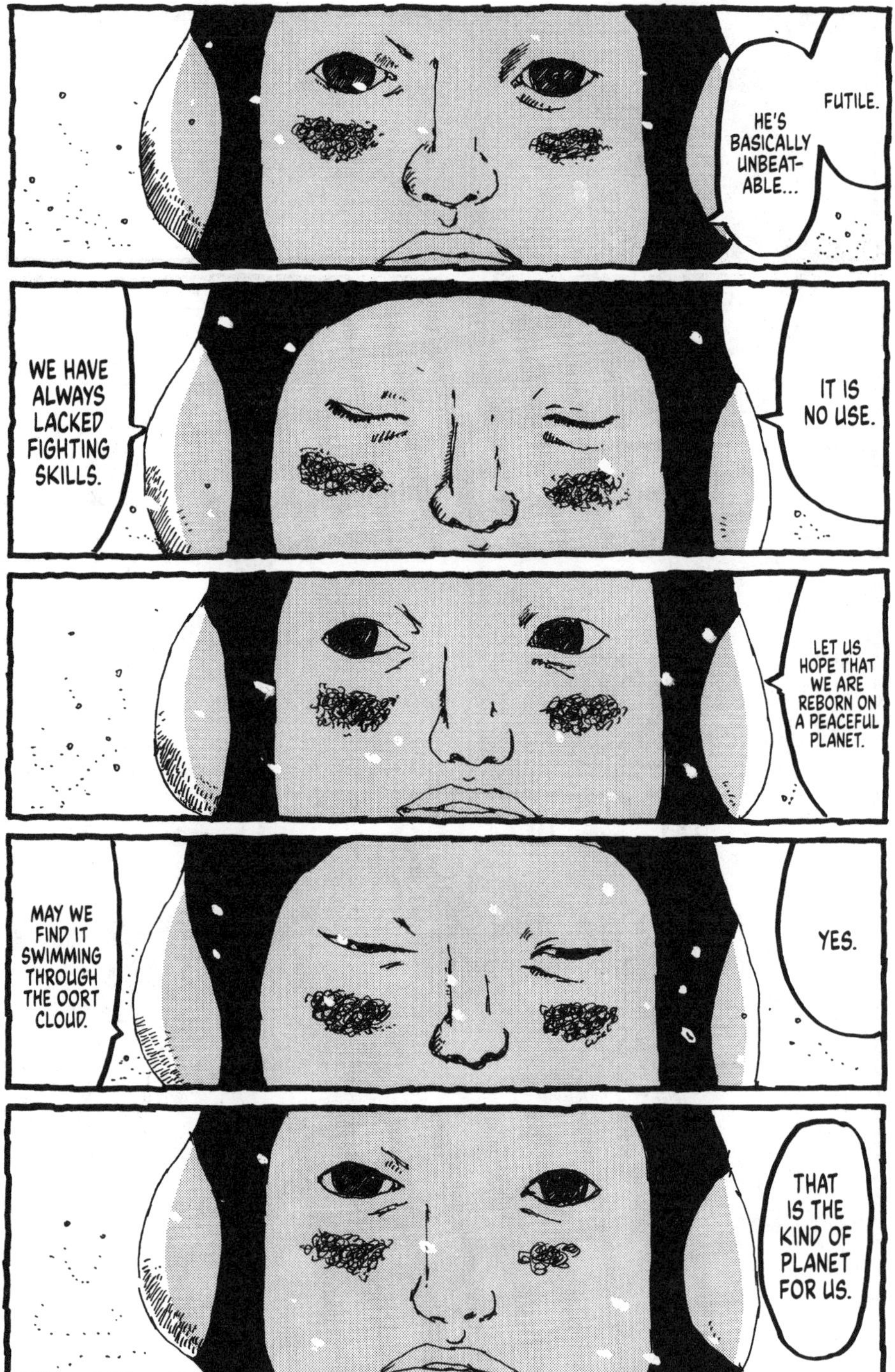
FUTILE.
HE'S BASICALLY UNBEAT-ABLE...
IT IS NO USE.
WE HAVE ALWAYS LACKED FIGHTING SKILLS.
LET US HOPE THAT WE ARE REBORN ON A PEACEFUL PLANET.
YES.
MAY WE FIND IT SWIMMING THROUGH THE OORT CLOUD.
THAT IS THE KIND OF PLANET FOR US.

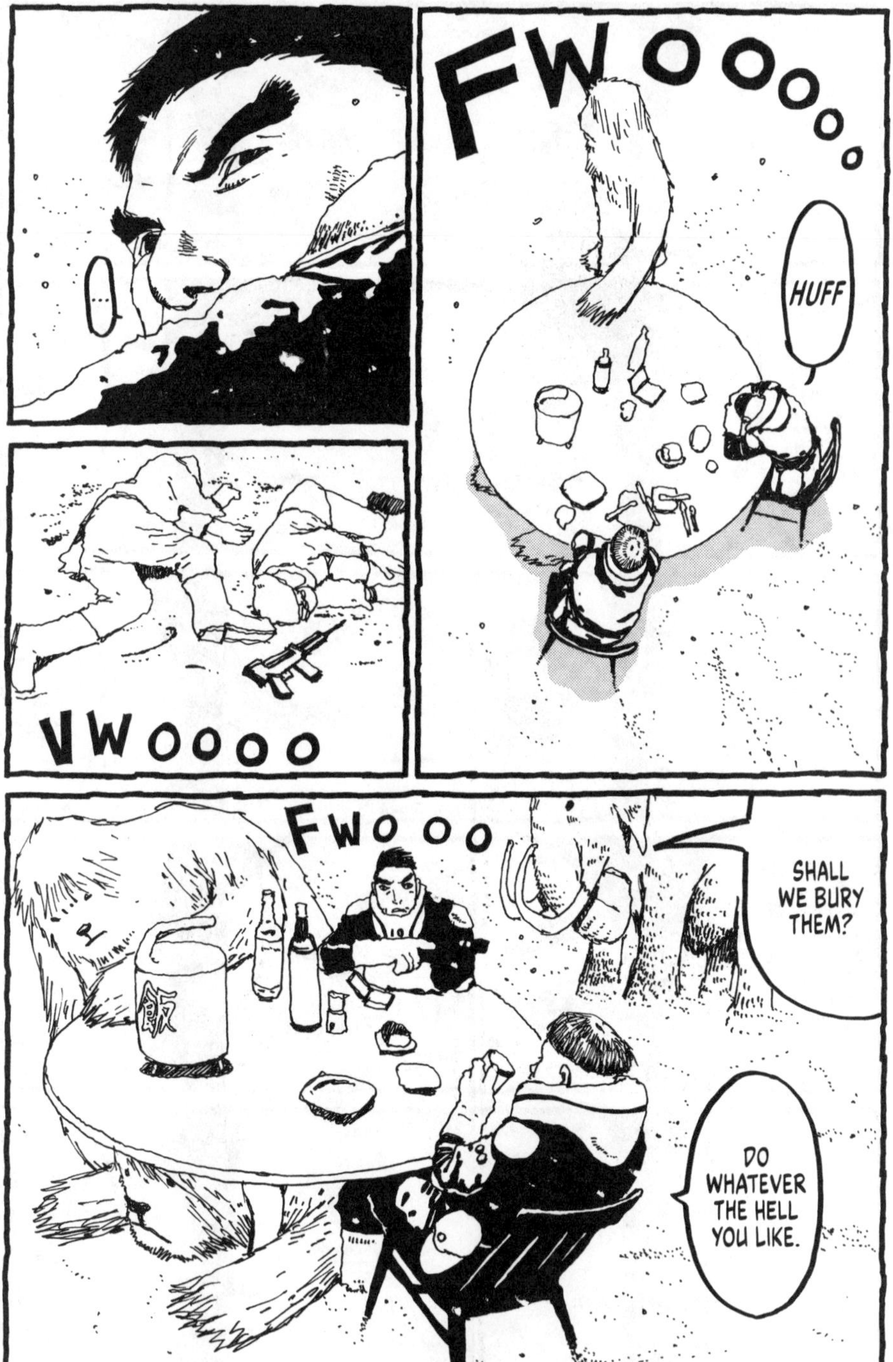
FWOOOOo
HUFF
...
VWOOOO
FWOOO
SHALL WE BURY THEM?
DO WHATEVER THE HELL YOU LIKE.

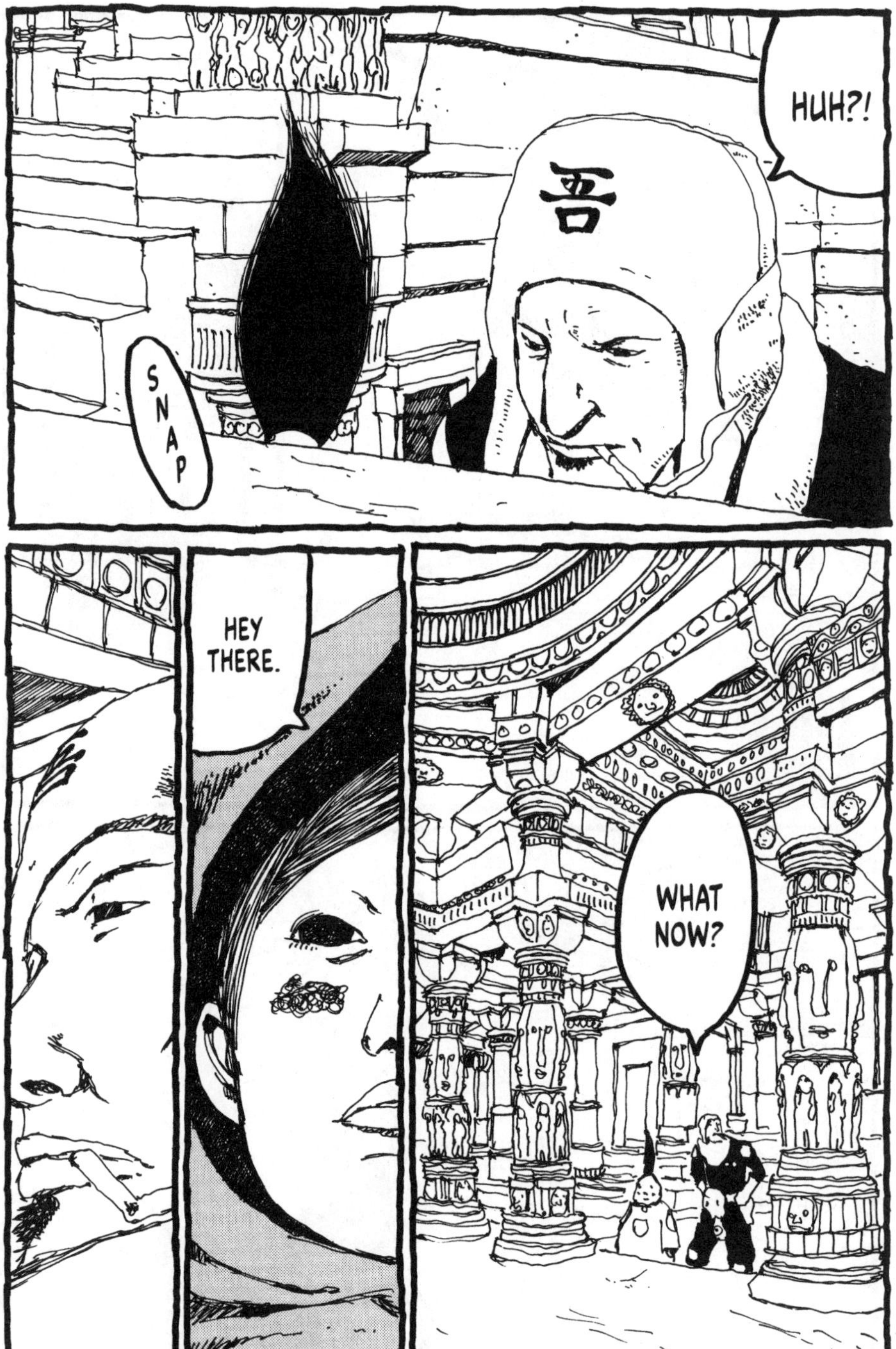
HUH?!
吾
SNAP
WHAT NOW?
HEY THERE.

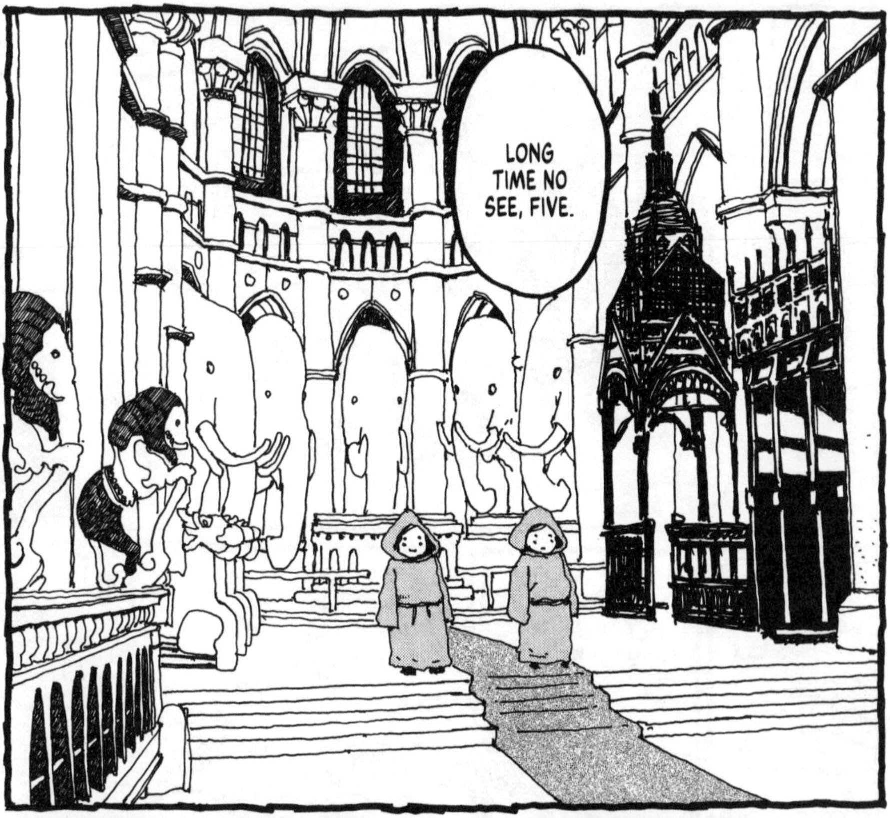
LONG TIME NO SEE, FIVE.

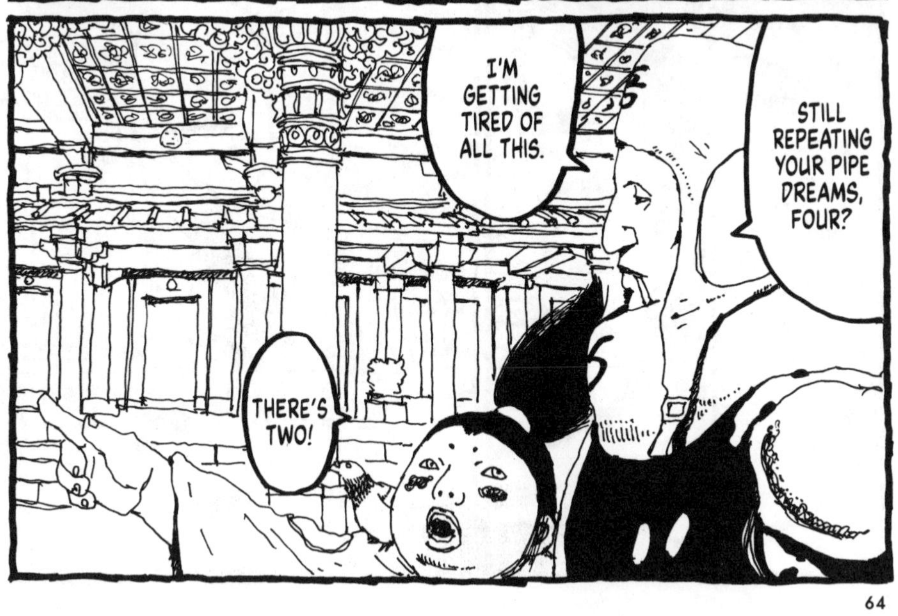
STILL REPEATING YOUR PIPE DREAMS, FOUR?
I'M GETTING TIRED OF ALL THIS.
THERE'S TWO!

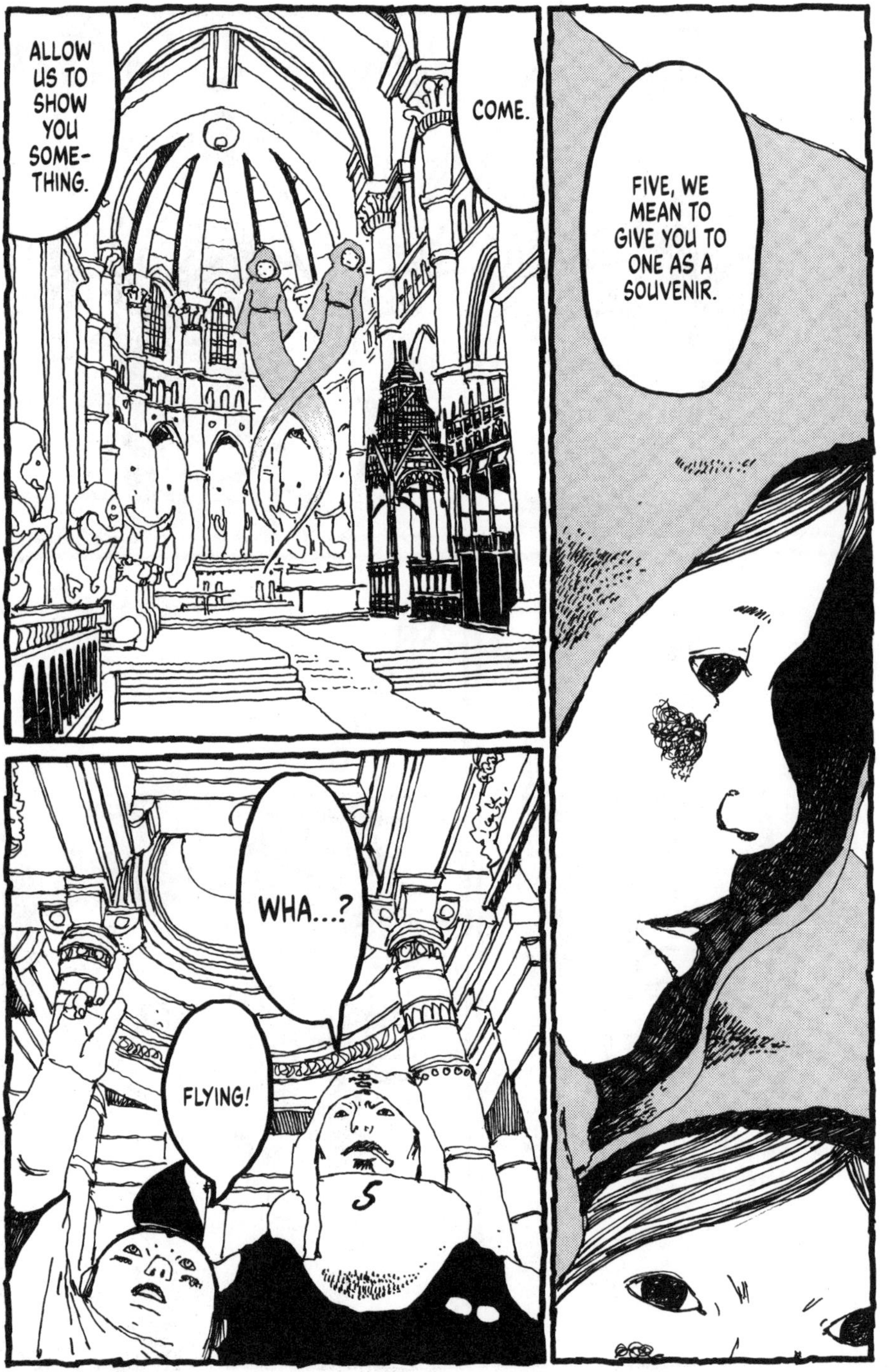
FIVE, WE MEAN TO GIVE YOU TO ONE AS A SOUVENIR.
COME.
ALLOW US TO SHOW YOU SOME-THING.
WHA...?
FLYING!

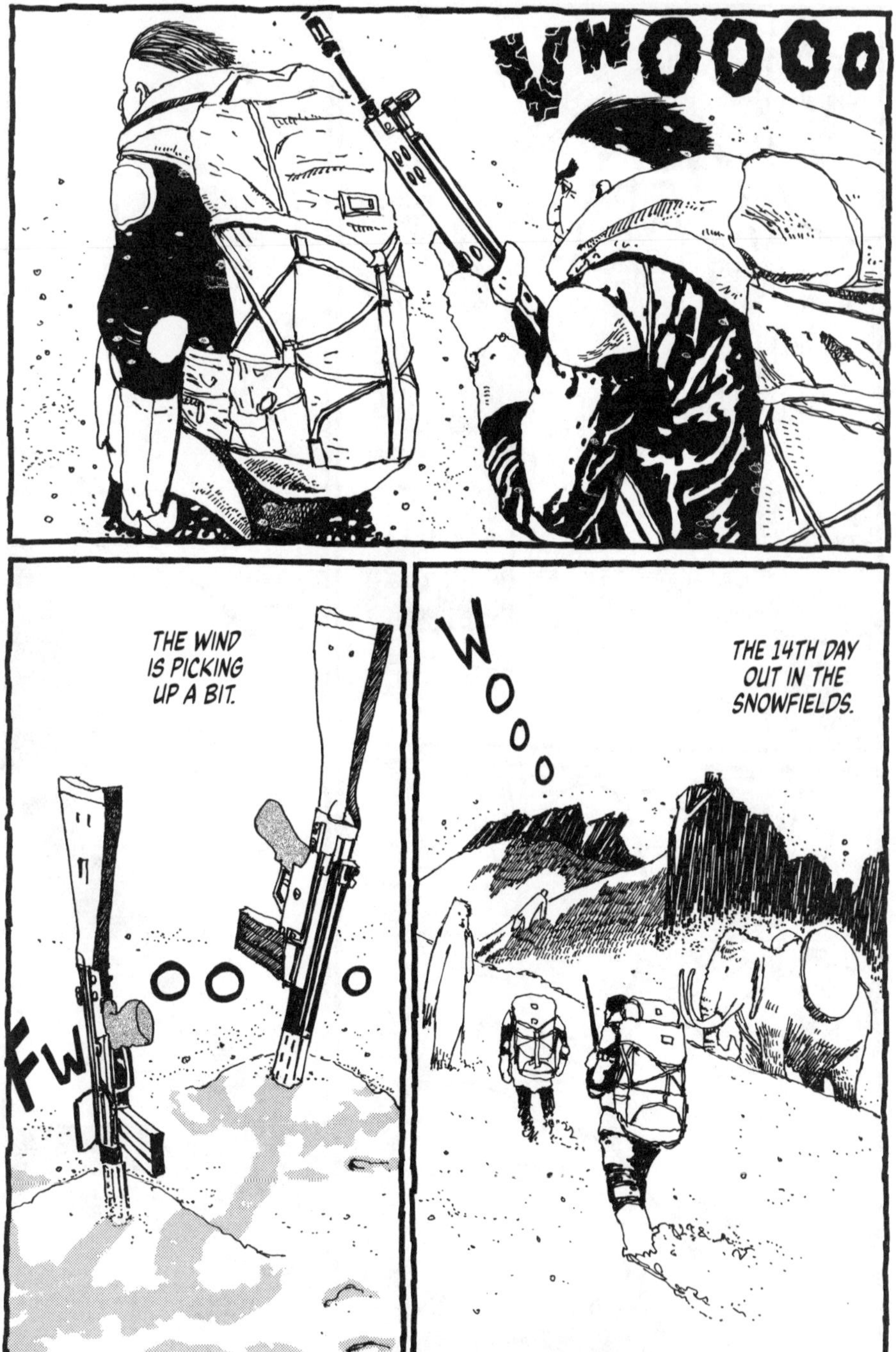
VWOOOO
THE 14TH DAY OUT IN THE SNOWFIELDS.
WOOO
THE WIND IS PICKING UP A BIT.
FWOOO

CHAPTER 11 //
Vision

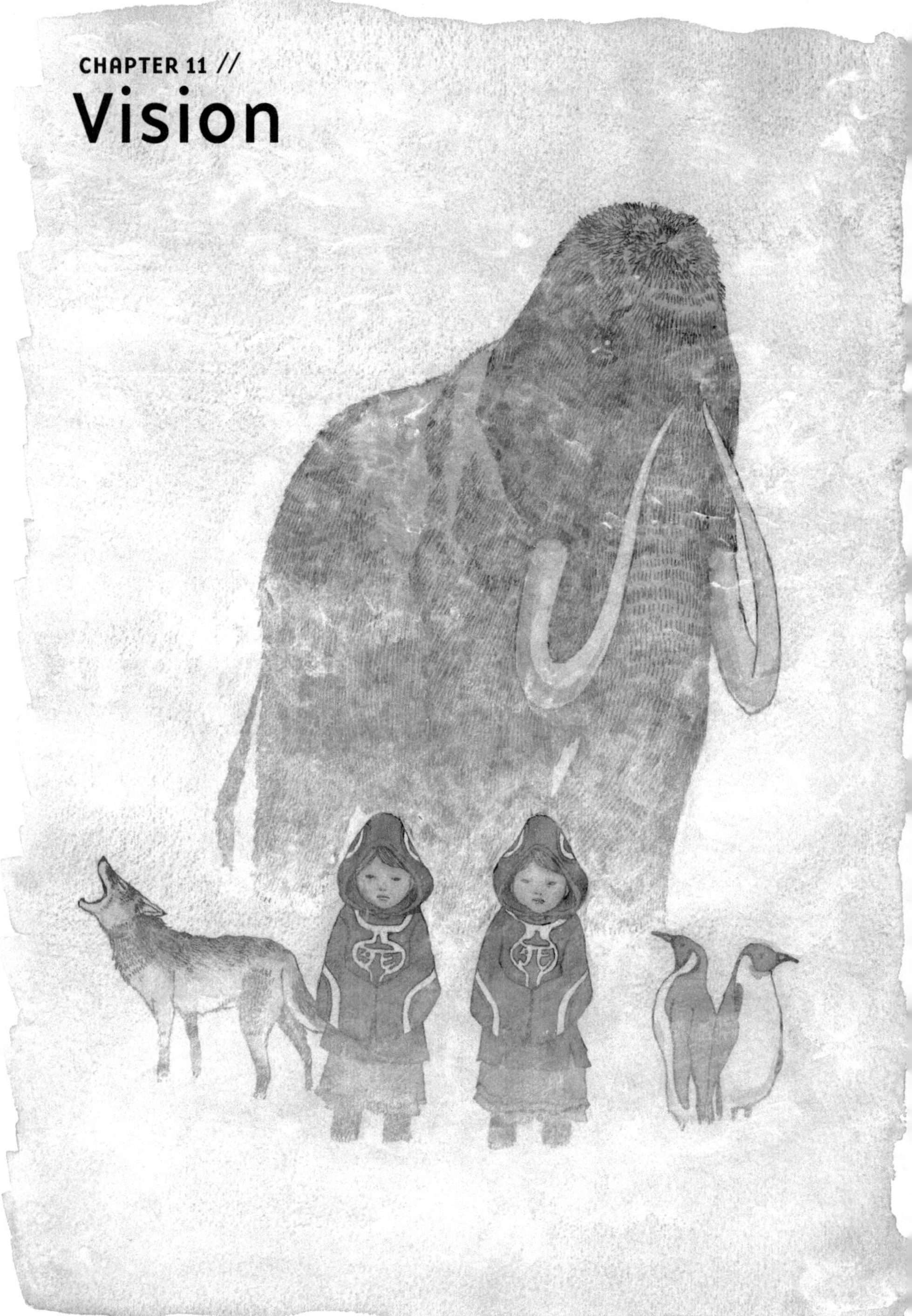

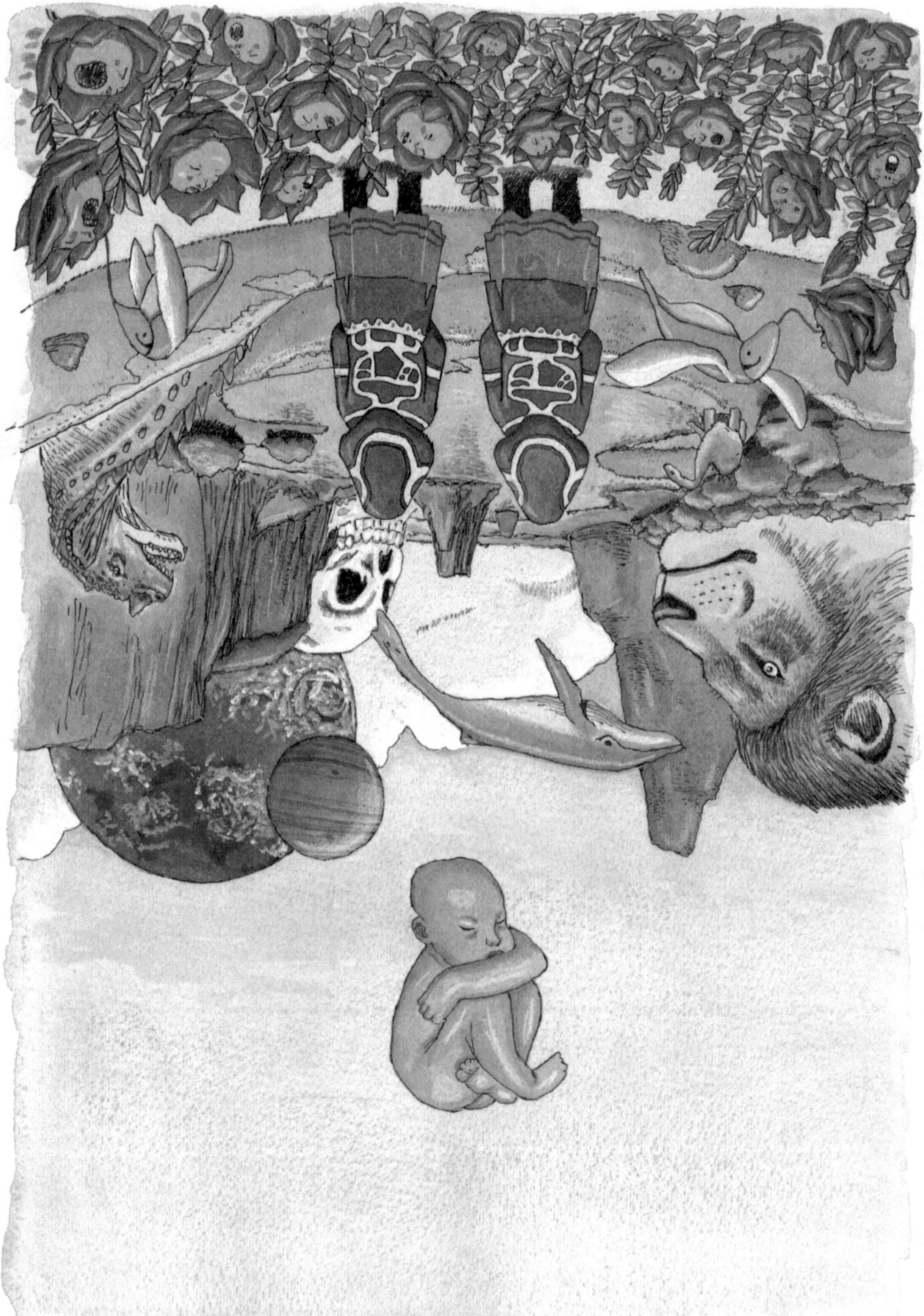

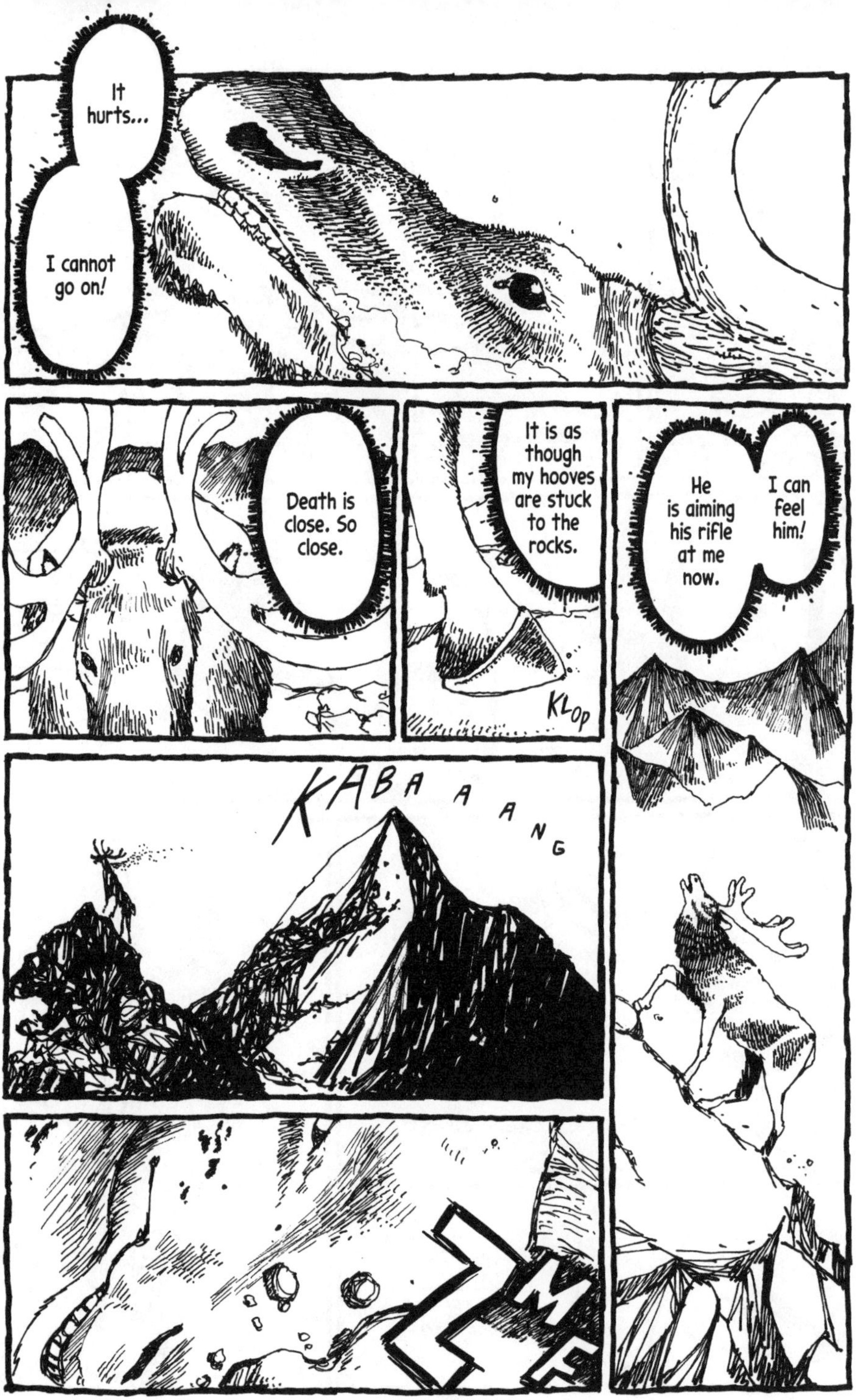
It hurts...
I cannot go on!
He is aiming his rifle at me now.
I can feel him!
It is as though my hooves are stuck to the rocks.
KLop
Death is close. So close.
KABAAANG
MF

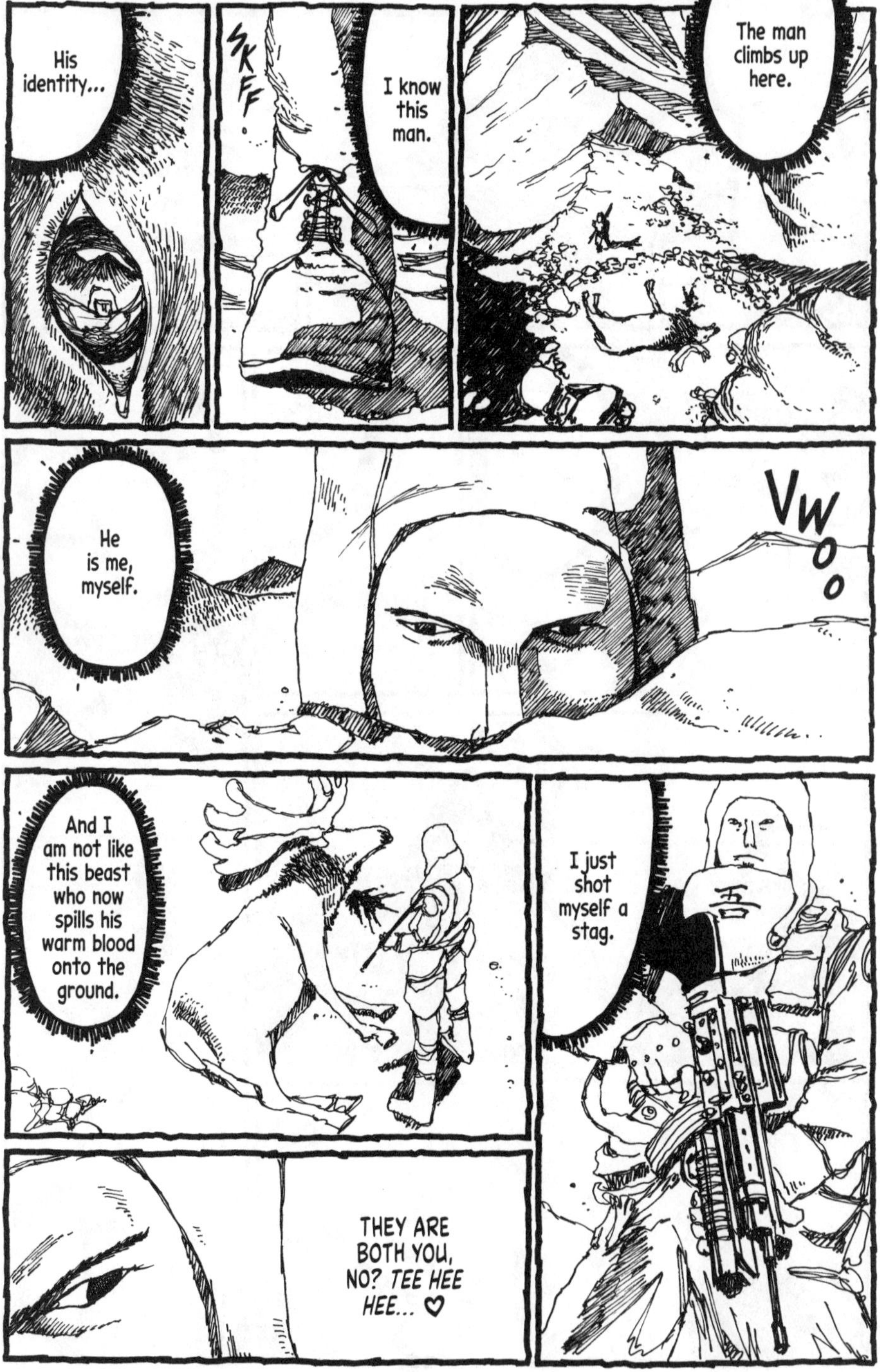
The man climbs up here.
I know this man.
SKFF
His identity...
VWOO
He is me, myself.
I just shot myself a stag.
吾
And I am not like this beast who now spills his warm blood onto the ground.
THEY ARE BOTH YOU, NO? TEE HEE HEE... ♡

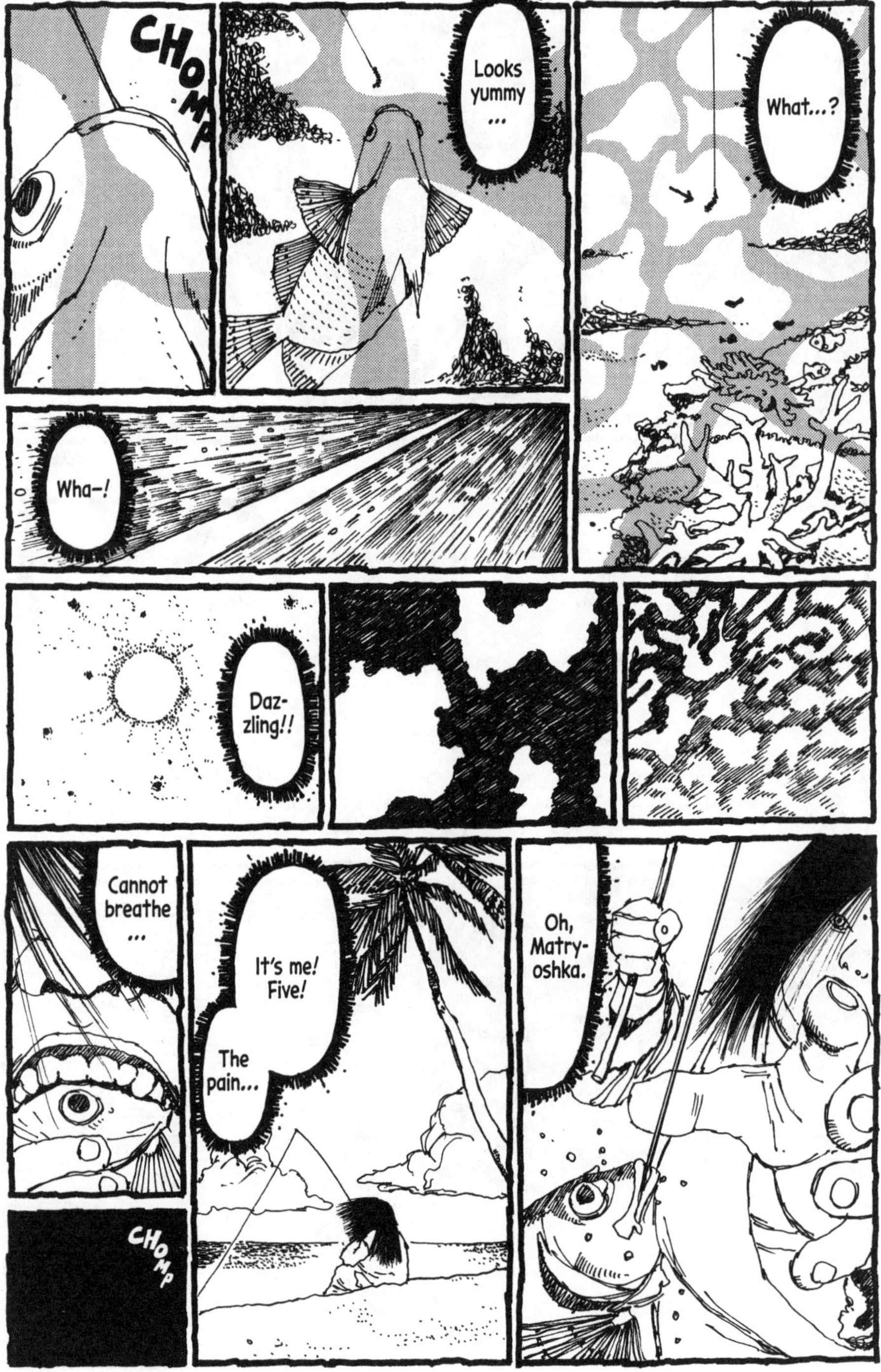
What...?
Looks yummy ...
CHOMP
Wha–!
Daz-zling!!
Oh, Matry-oshka.
It's me! Five!
The pain...
Cannot breathe ...
CHOMP

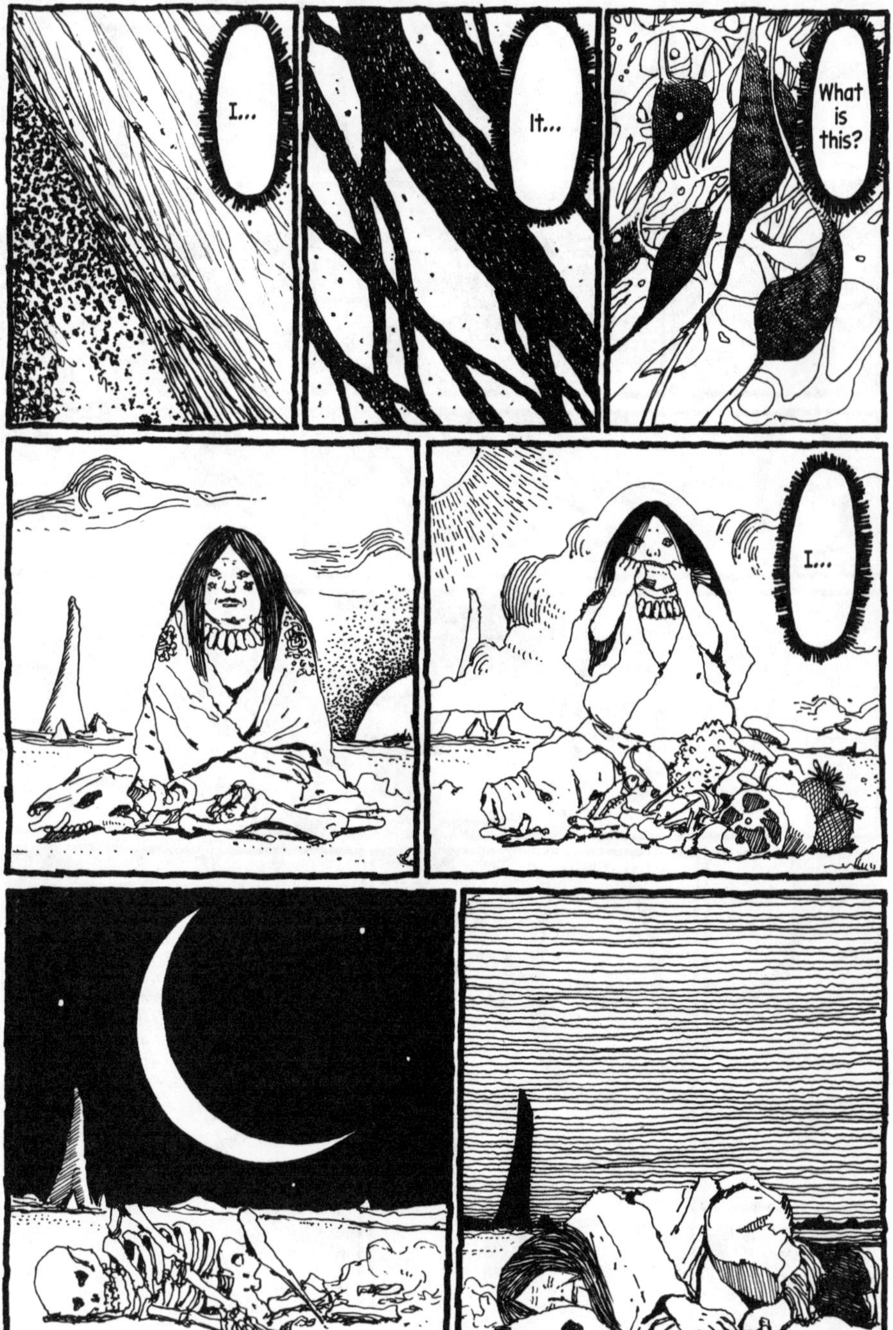
What is this?
It...
I...
I...

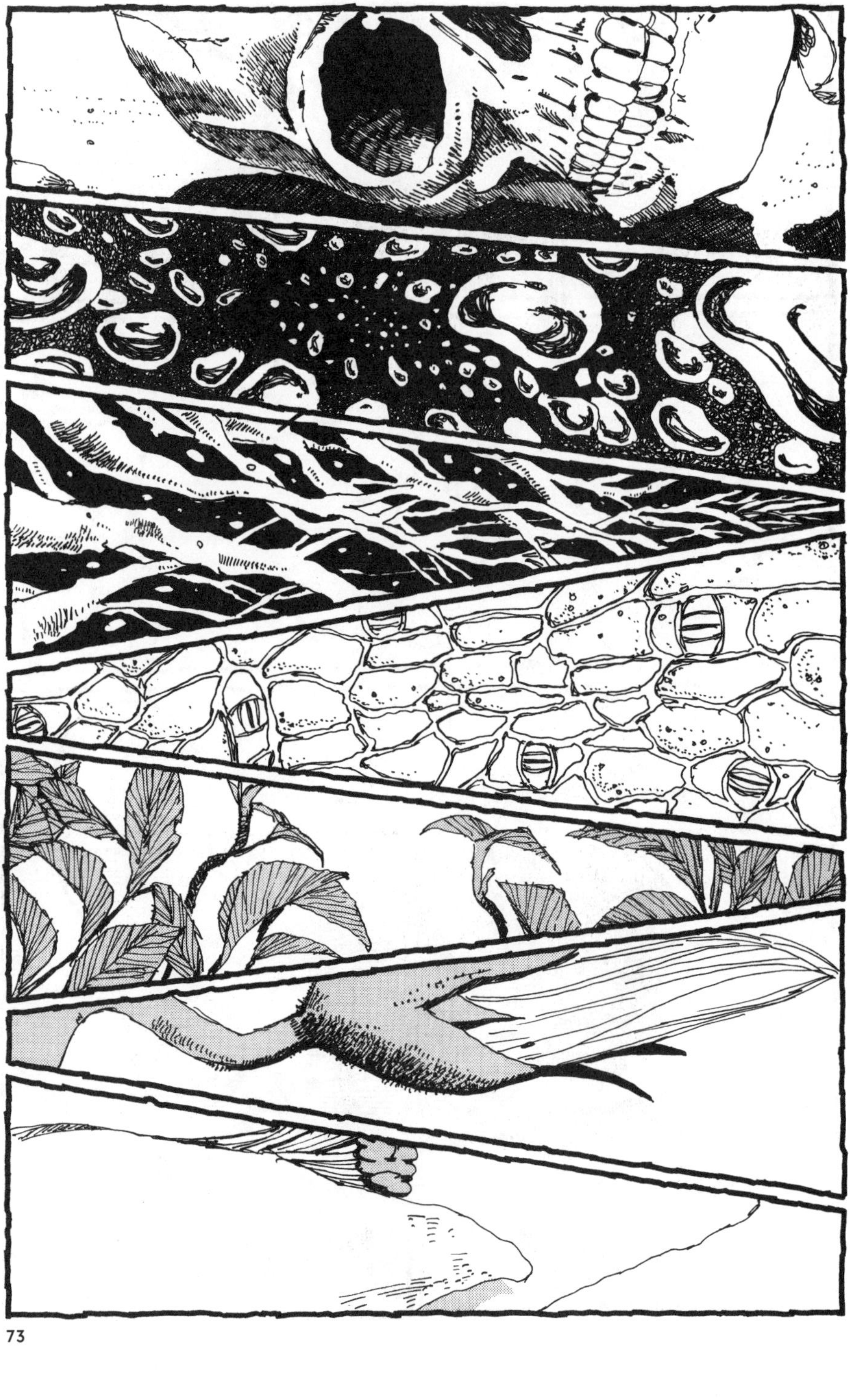

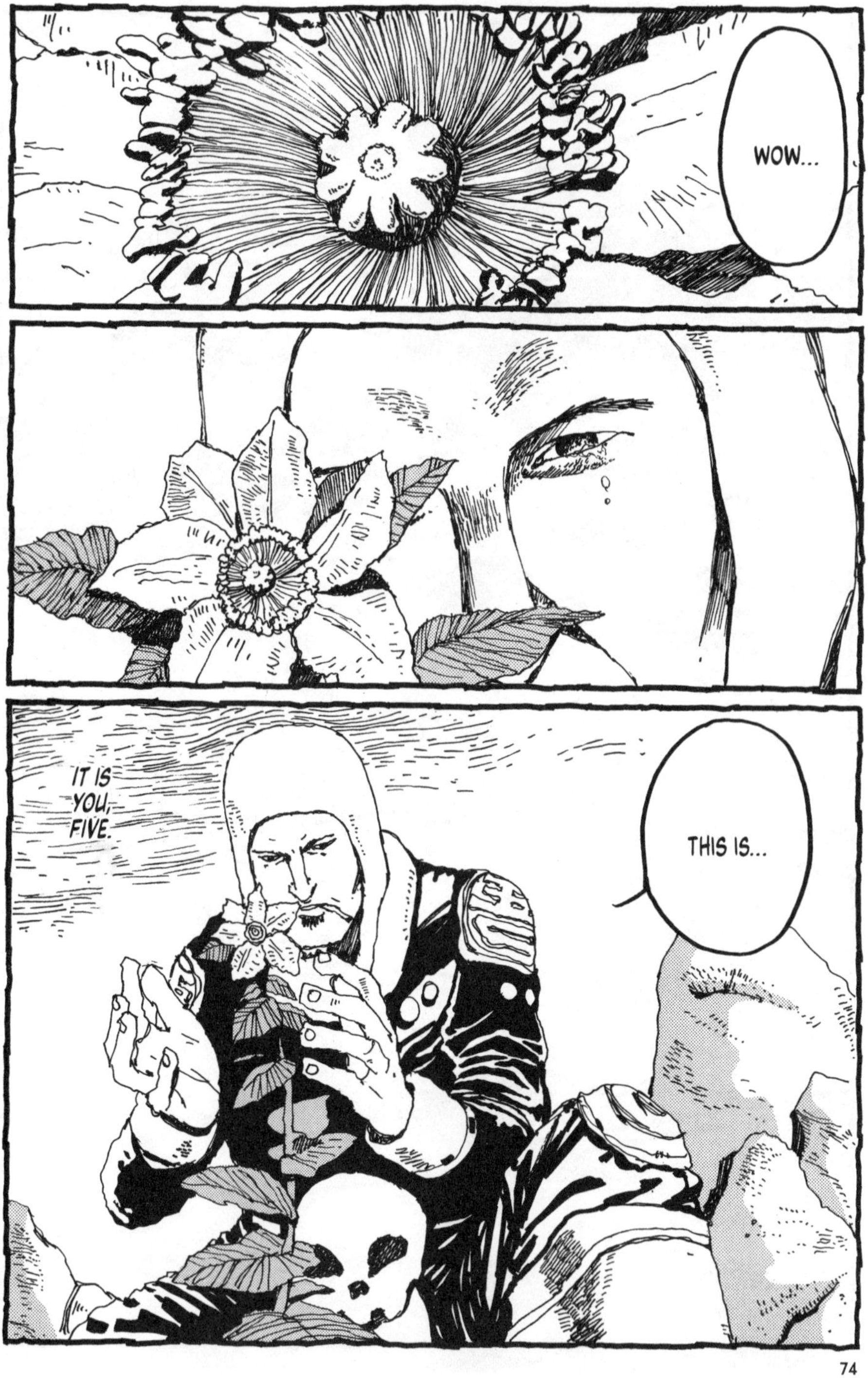
WOW...
THIS IS...
IT IS YOU, FIVE.

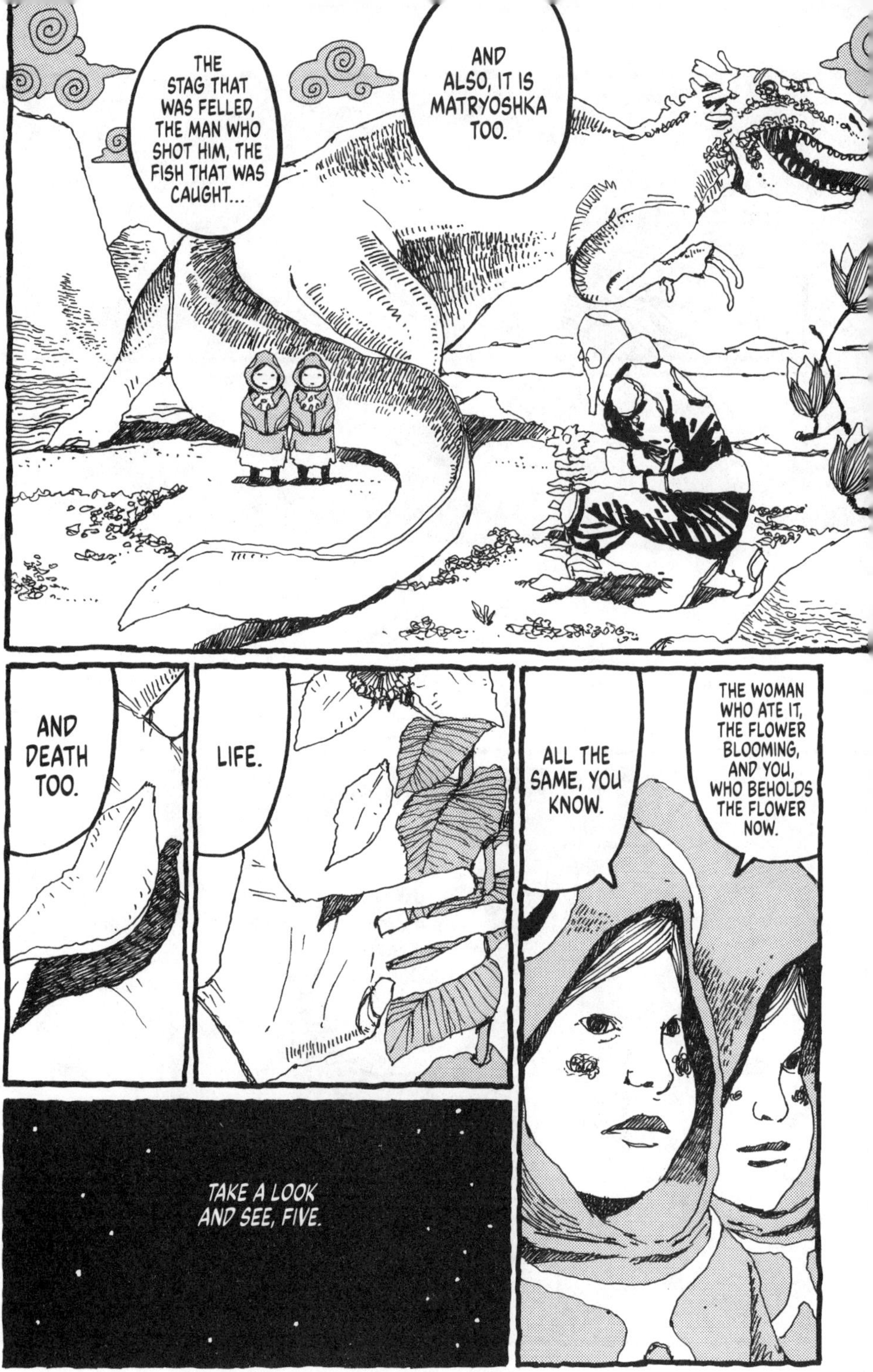
AND ALSO, IT IS MATRYOSHKA TOO.
THE STAG THAT WAS FELLED, THE MAN WHO SHOT HIM, THE FISH THAT WAS CAUGHT...
THE WOMAN WHO ATE IT, THE FLOWER BLOOMING, AND YOU, WHO BEHOLDS THE FLOWER NOW.
ALL THE SAME, YOU KNOW.
LIFE.
AND DEATH TOO.
TAKE A LOOK AND SEE, FIVE.

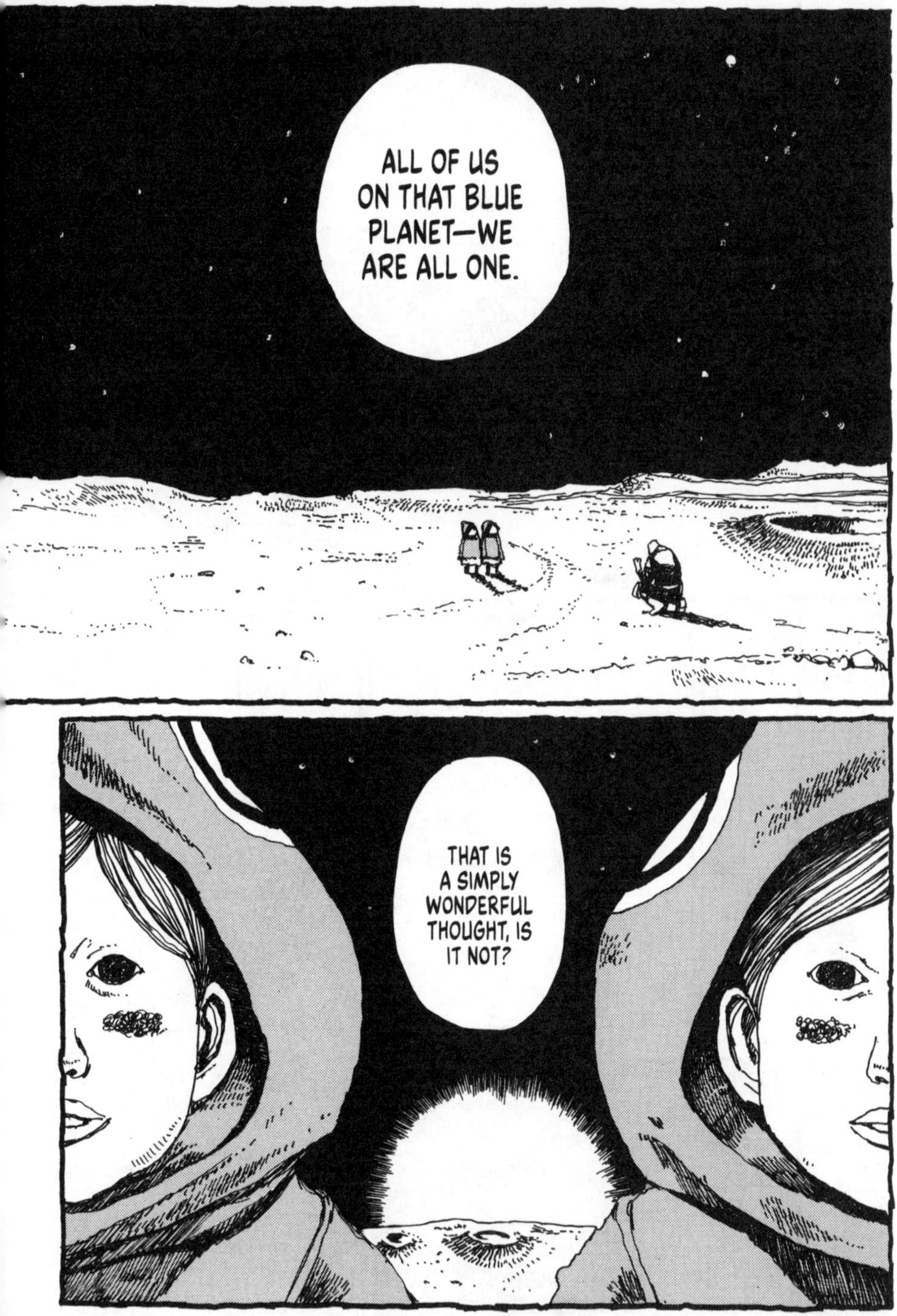
ALL OF US ON THAT BLUE PLANET—WE ARE ALL ONE.
THAT IS A SIMPLY WONDERFUL THOUGHT, IS IT NOT?

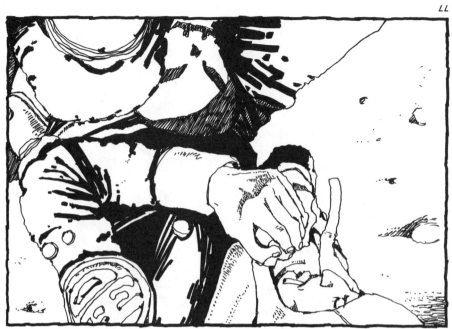

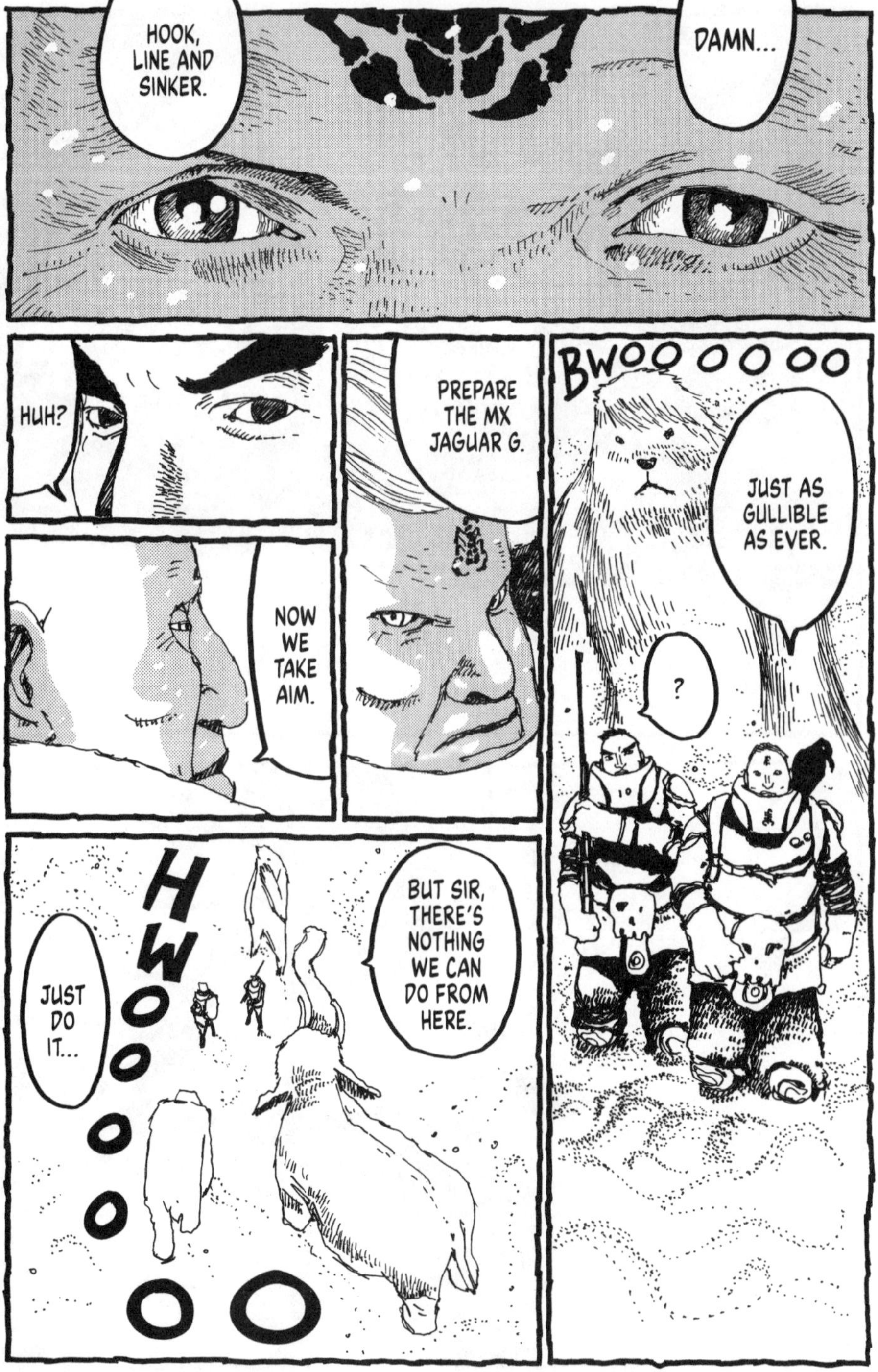
DAMN...
HOOK, LINE AND SINKER.
BWOO O O O OO
JUST AS GULLIBLE AS EVER.
?
PREPARE THE MX JAGUAR G.
HUH?
NOW WE TAKE AIM.
BUT SIR, THERE'S NOTHING WE CAN DO FROM HERE.
HWOOOOOOO
JUST DO IT...

*Science

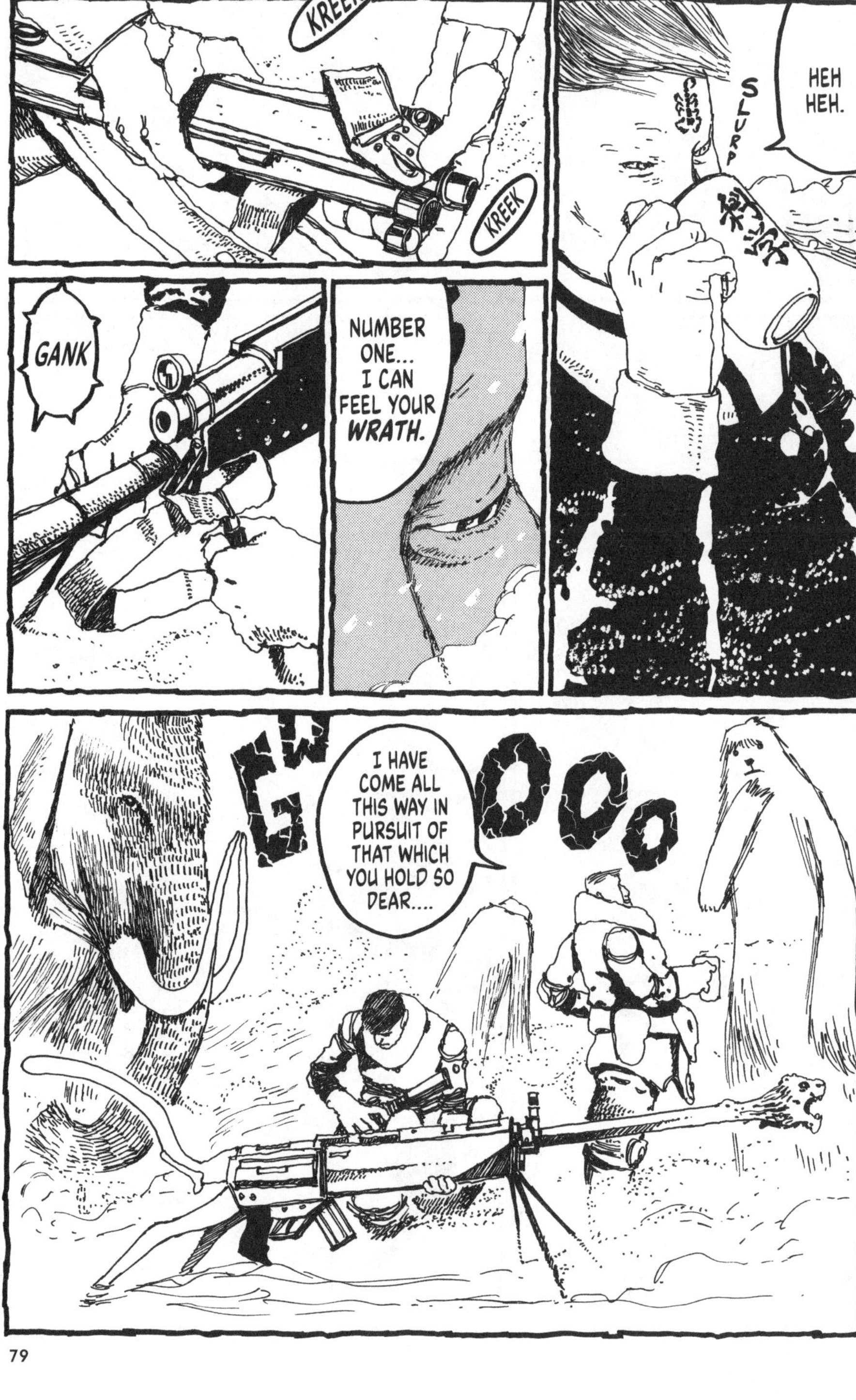

HEH HEH.
SLURP
科学
KREEK
KREEK
NUMBER ONE... I CAN FEEL YOUR *WRATH.*
GANK
GWOOO
I HAVE COME ALL THIS WAY IN PURSUIT OF THAT WHICH YOU HOLD SO DEAR....

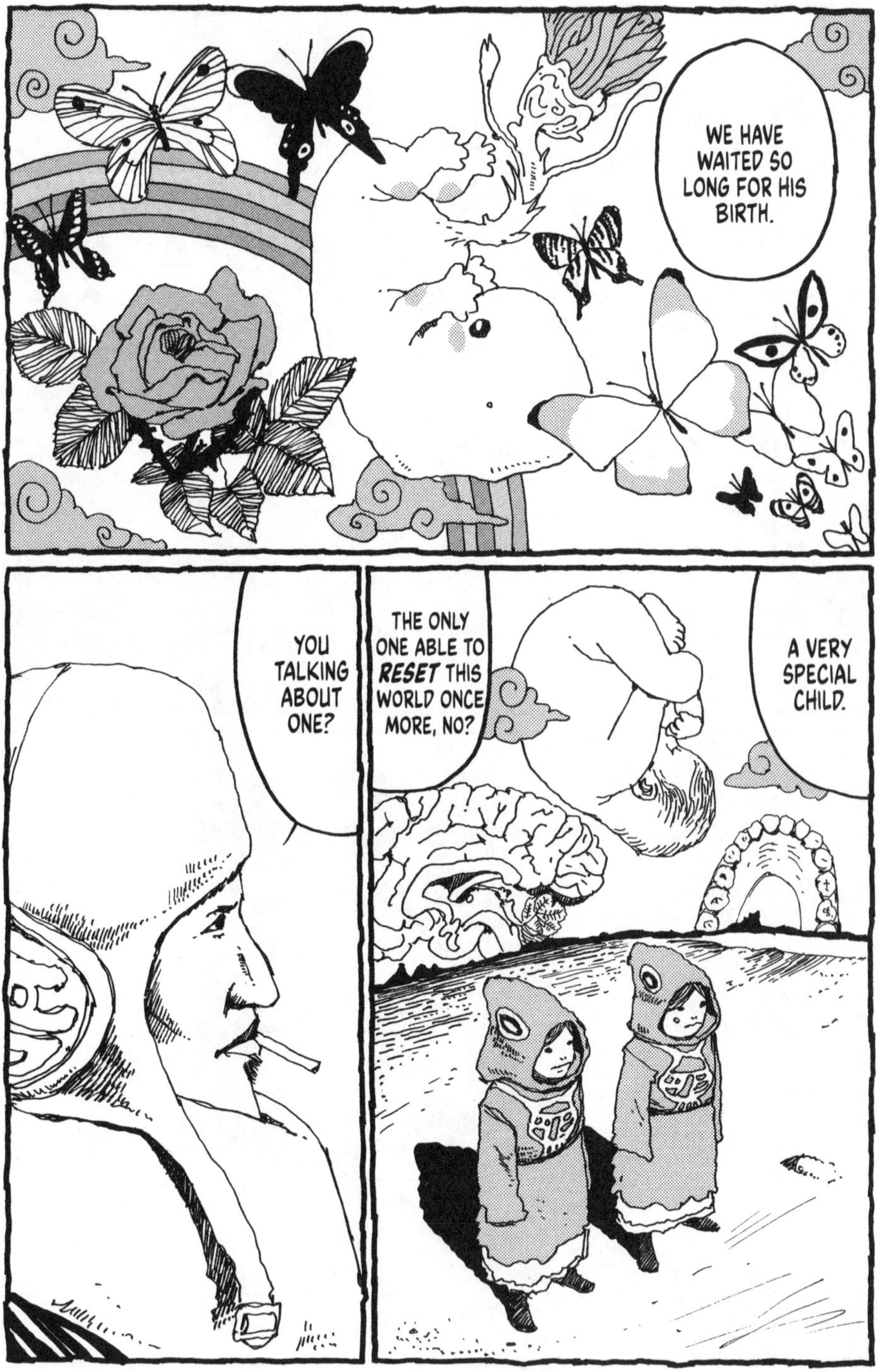
WE HAVE WAITED SO LONG FOR HIS BIRTH.
A VERY SPECIAL CHILD.
THE ONLY ONE ABLE TO **RESET** THIS WORLD ONCE MORE, NO?
YOU TALKING ABOUT ONE?

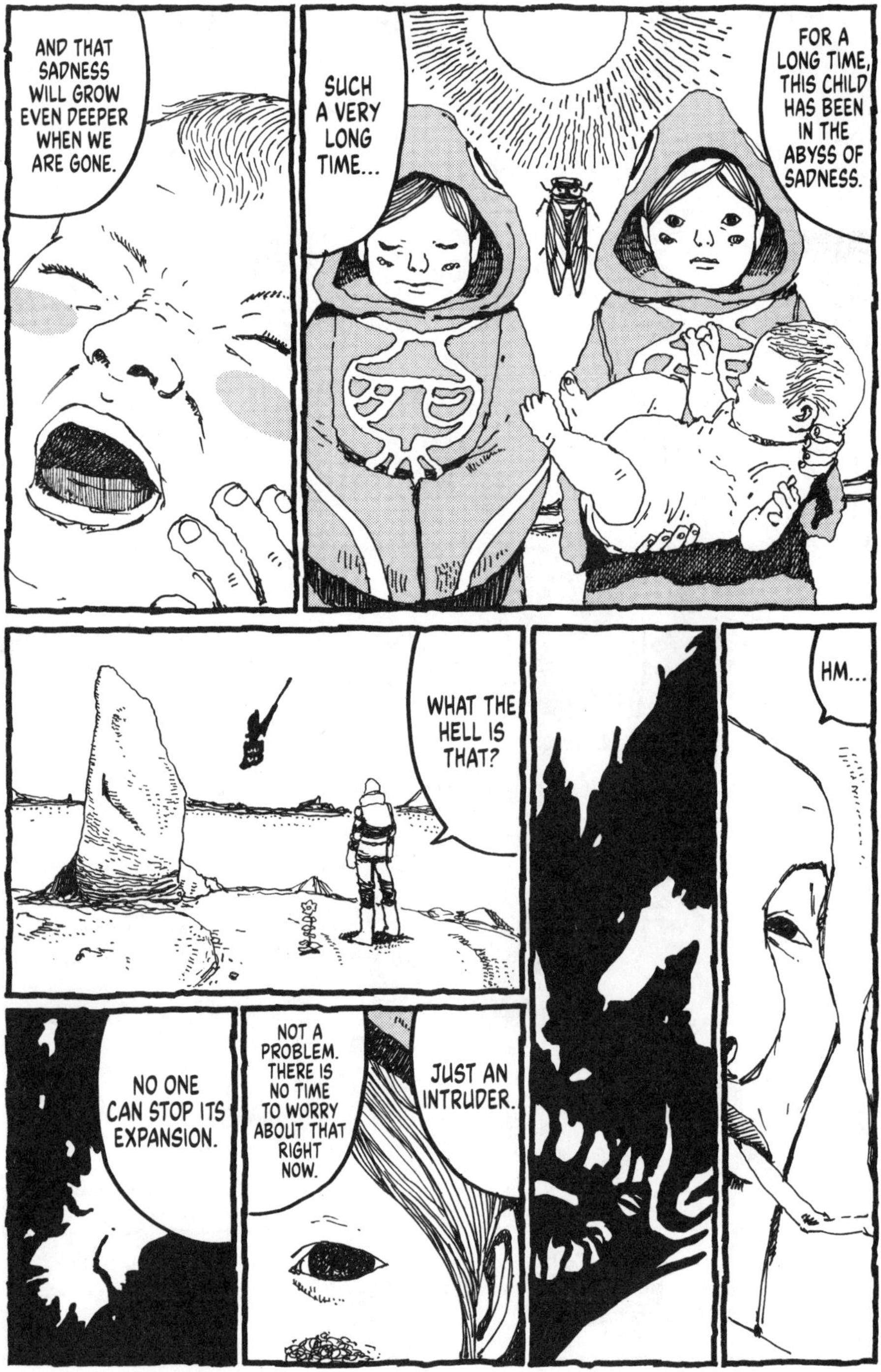
FOR A LONG TIME, THIS CHILD HAS BEEN IN THE ABYSS OF SADNESS.
SUCH A VERY LONG TIME...
AND THAT SADNESS WILL GROW EVEN DEEPER WHEN WE ARE GONE.
HM...
WHAT THE HELL IS THAT?
JUST AN INTRUDER.
NOT A PROBLEM. THERE IS NO TIME TO WORRY ABOUT THAT RIGHT NOW.
NO ONE CAN STOP ITS EXPANSION.

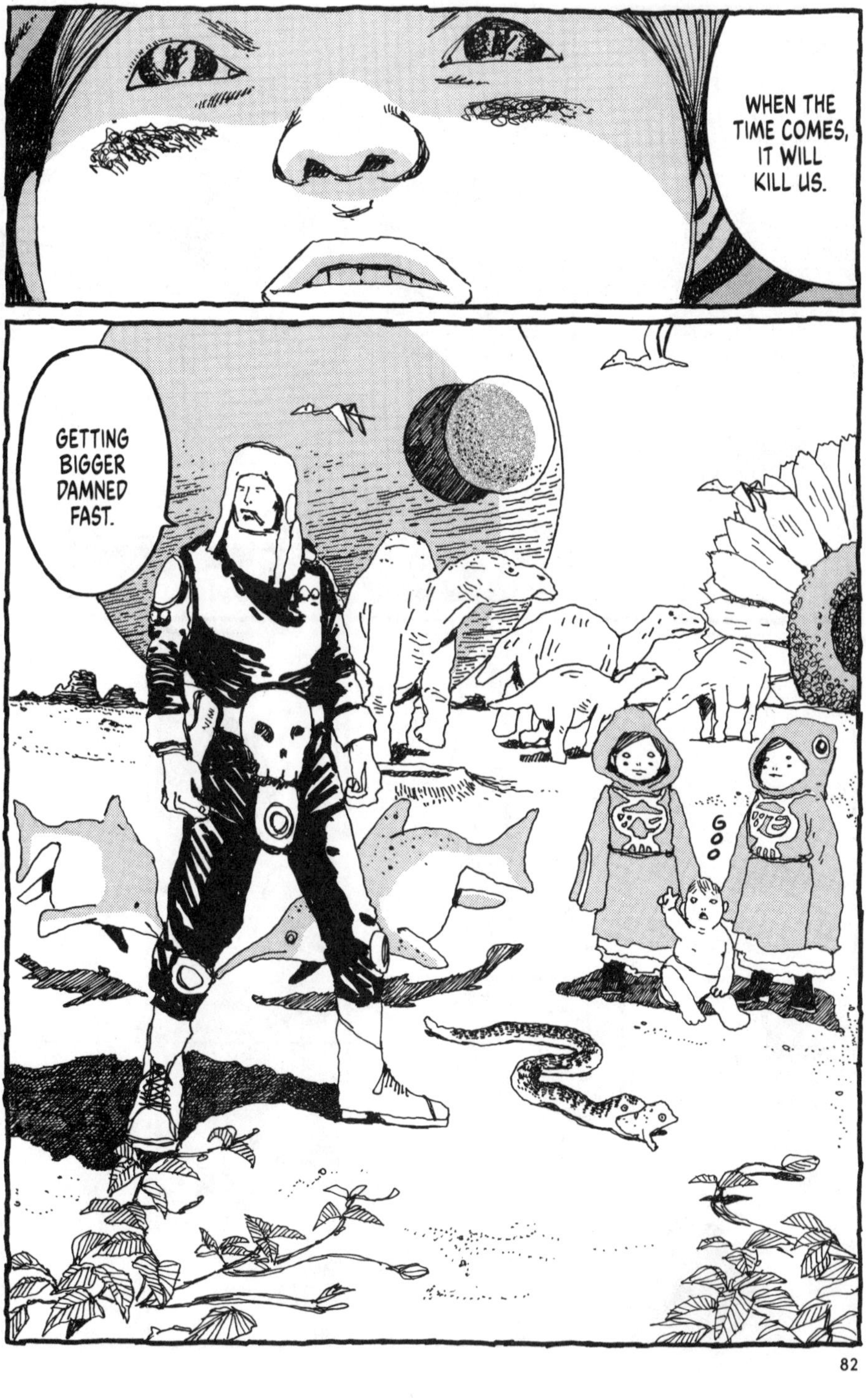
WHEN THE TIME COMES, IT WILL KILL US.
GETTING BIGGER DAMNED FAST.
GOO

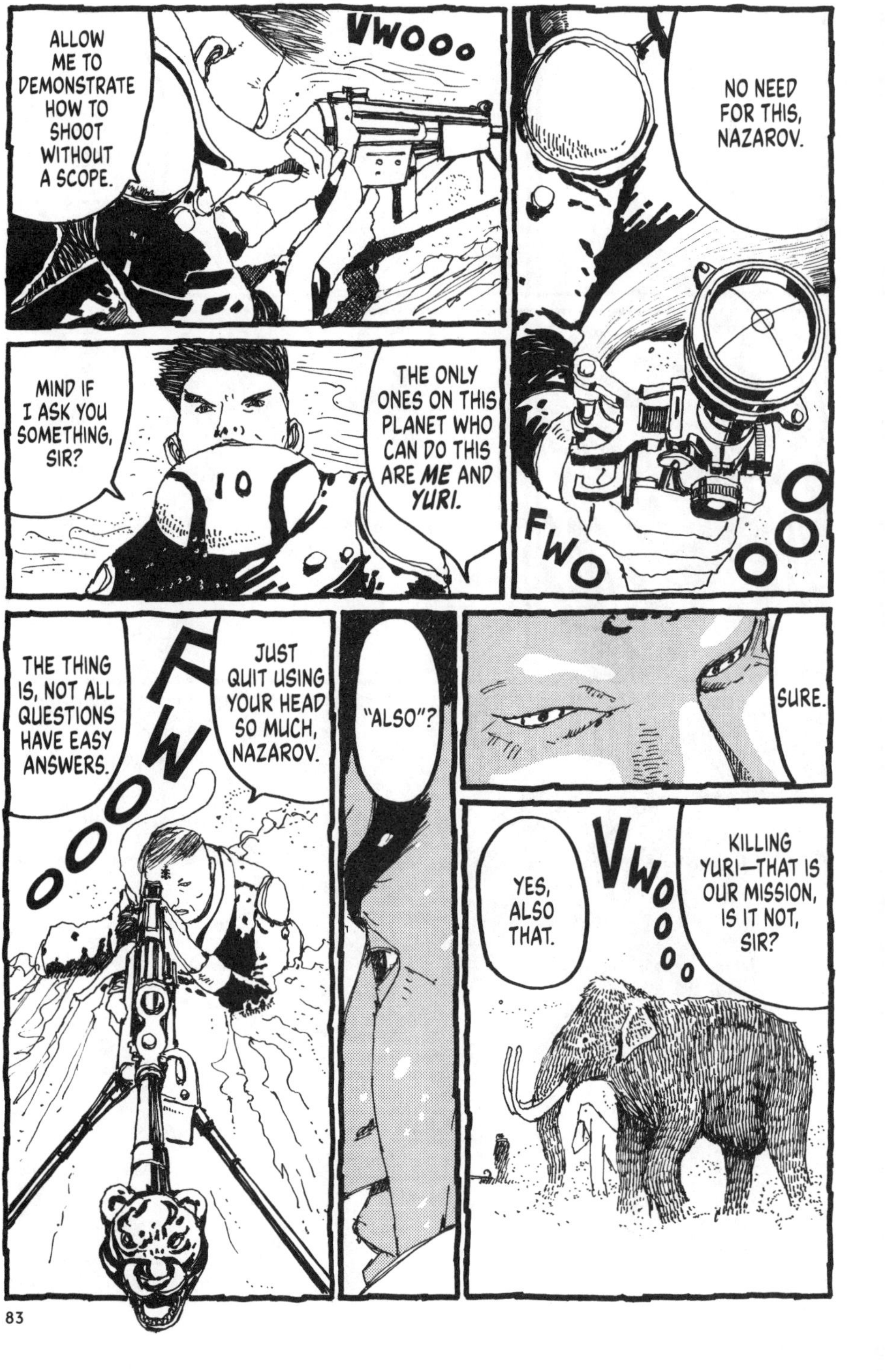
NO NEED FOR THIS, NAZAROV.
FWOOOO
ALLOW ME TO DEMONSTRATE HOW TO SHOOT WITHOUT A SCOPE.
VWOOOO
THE ONLY ONES ON THIS PLANET WHO CAN DO THIS ARE *ME* AND *YURI.*
MIND IF I ASK YOU SOMETHING, SIR?
SURE.
KILLING YURI—THAT IS OUR MISSION, IS IT NOT, SIR?
VWOOOOO
YES, ALSO THAT.
"ALSO"?
JUST QUIT USING YOUR HEAD SO MUCH, NAZAROV.
FWOOOO
THE THING IS, NOT ALL QUESTIONS HAVE EASY ANSWERS.

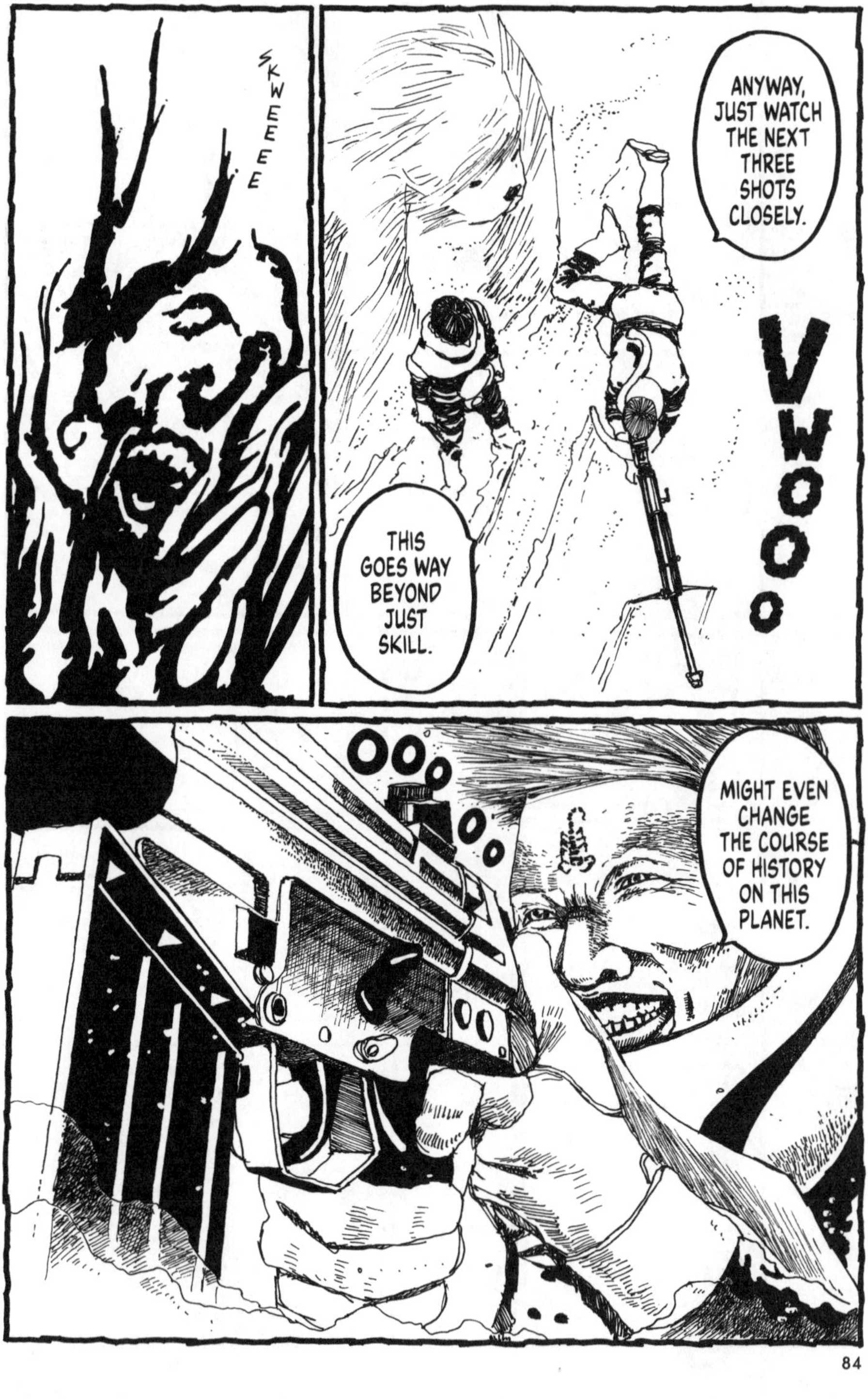
ANYWAY, JUST WATCH THE NEXT THREE SHOTS CLOSELY.
VWOOOO
THIS GOES WAY BEYOND JUST SKILL.
SKWEEEEE
OOOOOO
MIGHT EVEN CHANGE THE COURSE OF HISTORY ON THIS PLANET.

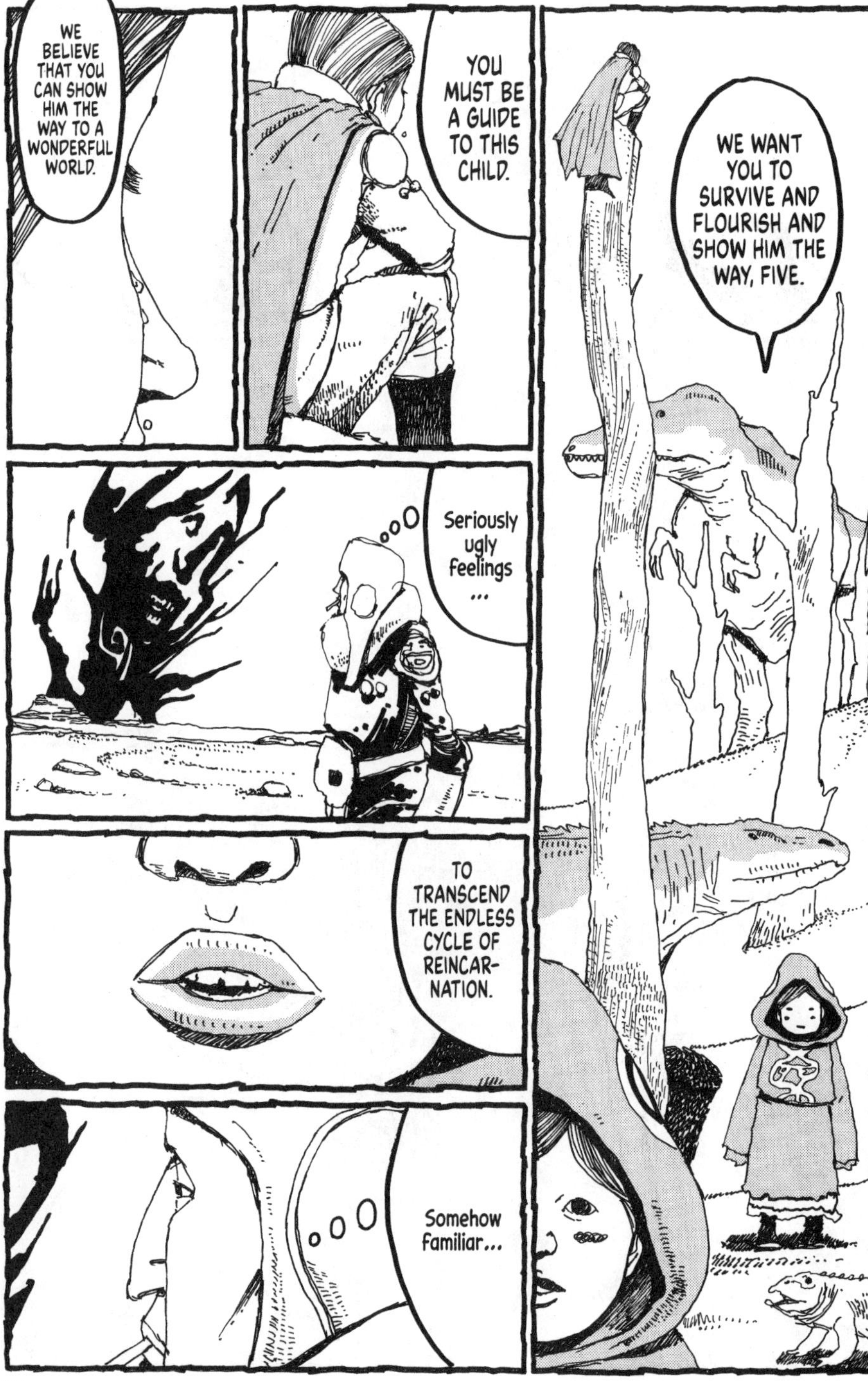
WE WANT YOU TO SURVIVE AND FLOURISH AND SHOW HIM THE WAY, FIVE.
YOU MUST BE A GUIDE TO THIS CHILD.
WE BELIEVE THAT YOU CAN SHOW HIM THE WAY TO A WONDERFUL WORLD.
Seriously ugly feelings ...
TO TRANSCEND THE ENDLESS CYCLE OF REINCAR-NATION.
Somehow familiar...

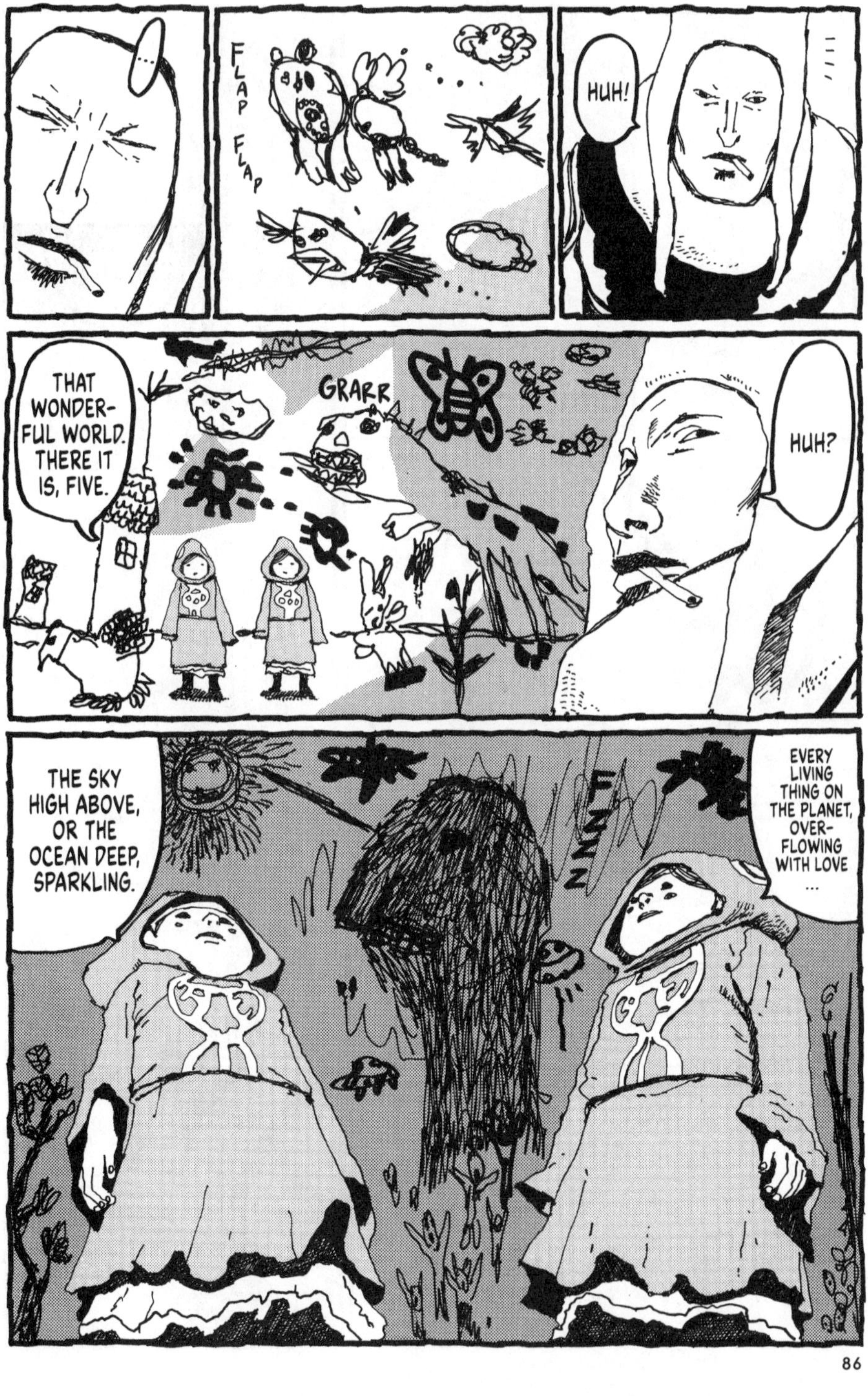
HUH!
FLAP FLAP
...
HUH?
GRARR
THAT WONDER-FUL WORLD. THERE IT IS, FIVE.
EVERY LIVING THING ON THE PLANET, OVER-FLOWING WITH LOVE ...
FZZZ
THE SKY HIGH ABOVE, OR THE OCEAN DEEP, SPARKLING.

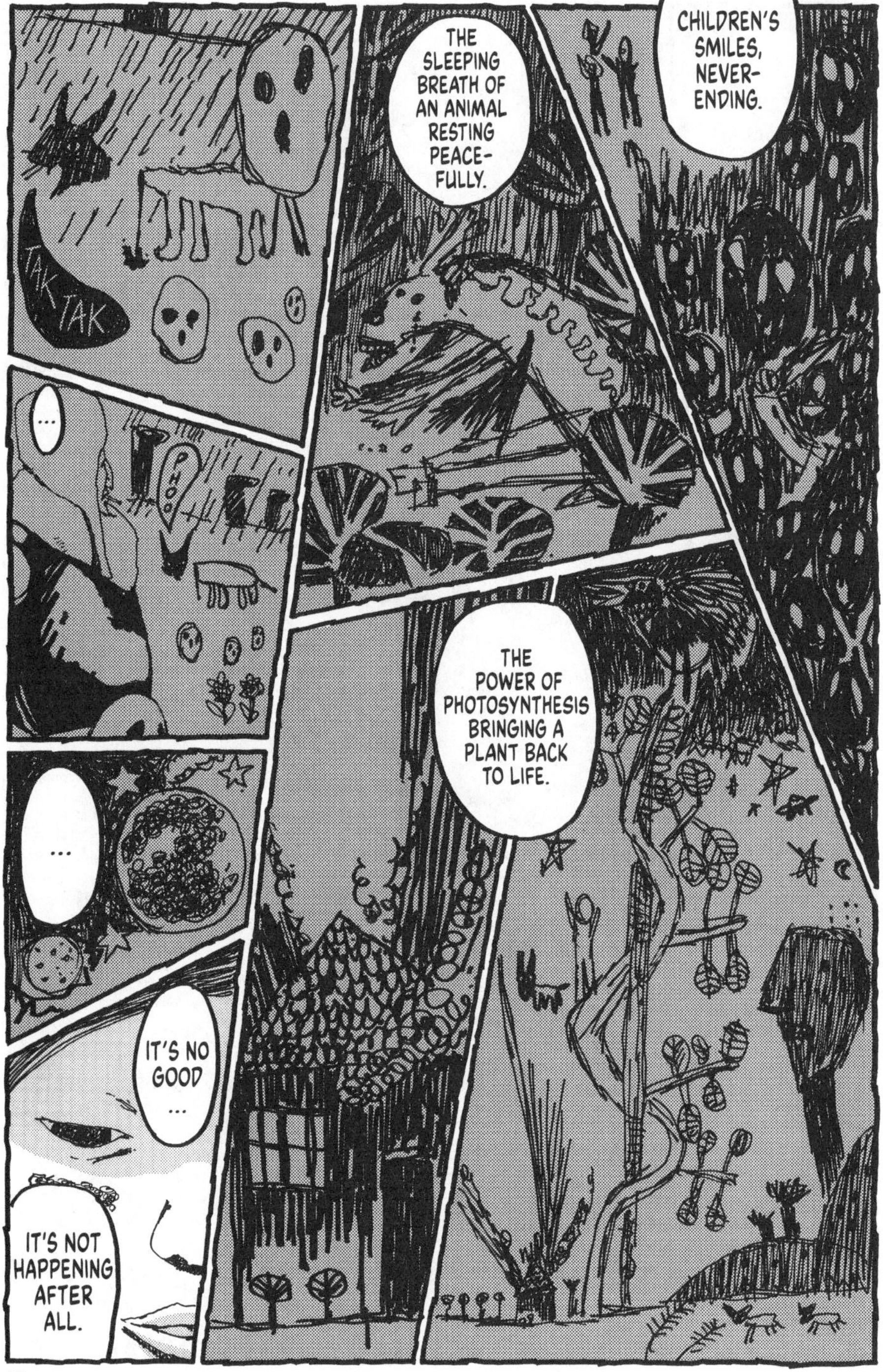
CHILDREN'S SMILES, NEVER-ENDING.
THE SLEEPING BREATH OF AN ANIMAL RESTING PEACE-FULLY.
TAK TAK
THE POWER OF PHOTOSYNTHESIS BRINGING A PLANT BACK TO LIFE.
...
PHOO
...
IT'S NO GOOD ...
IT'S NOT HAPPENING AFTER ALL.

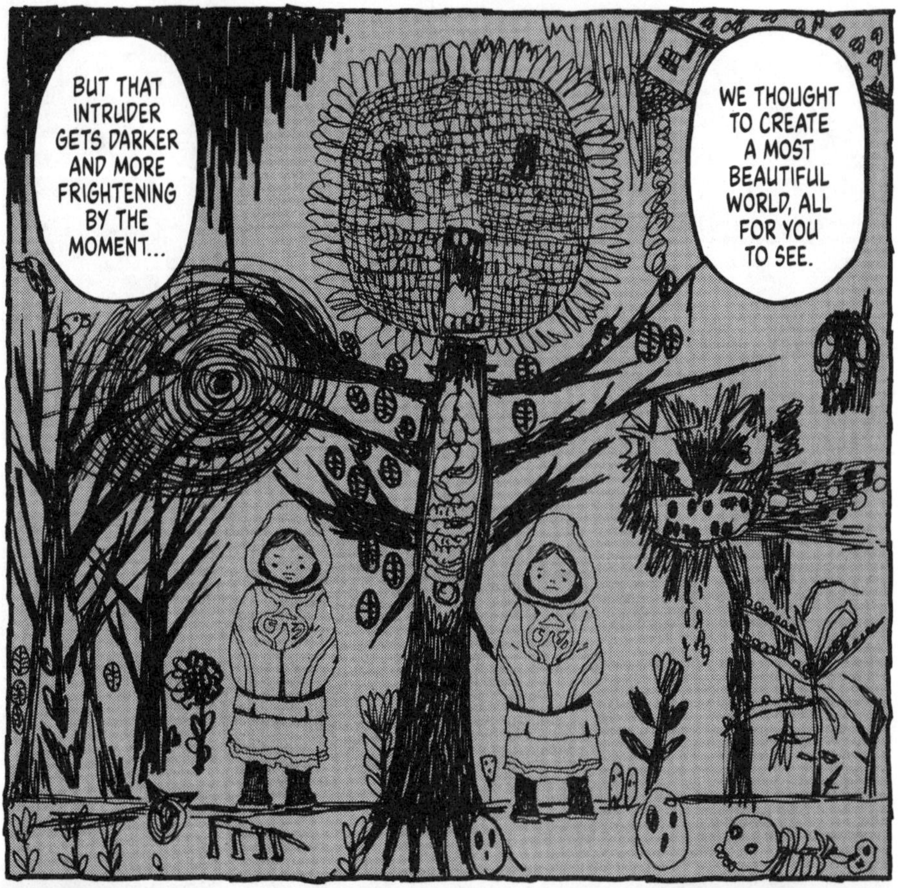
WE THOUGHT TO CREATE A MOST BEAUTIFUL WORLD, ALL FOR YOU TO SEE.
BUT THAT INTRUDER GETS DARKER AND MORE FRIGHTENING BY THE MOMENT...

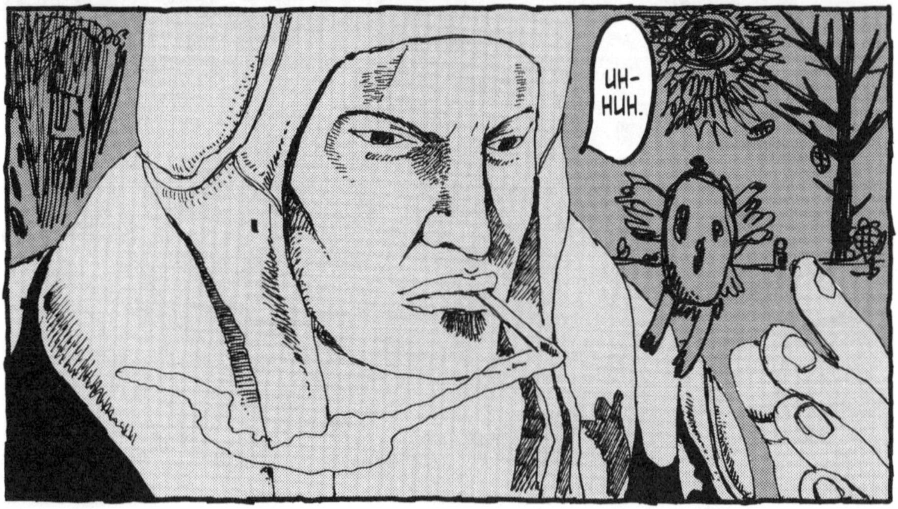
UH-HUH.

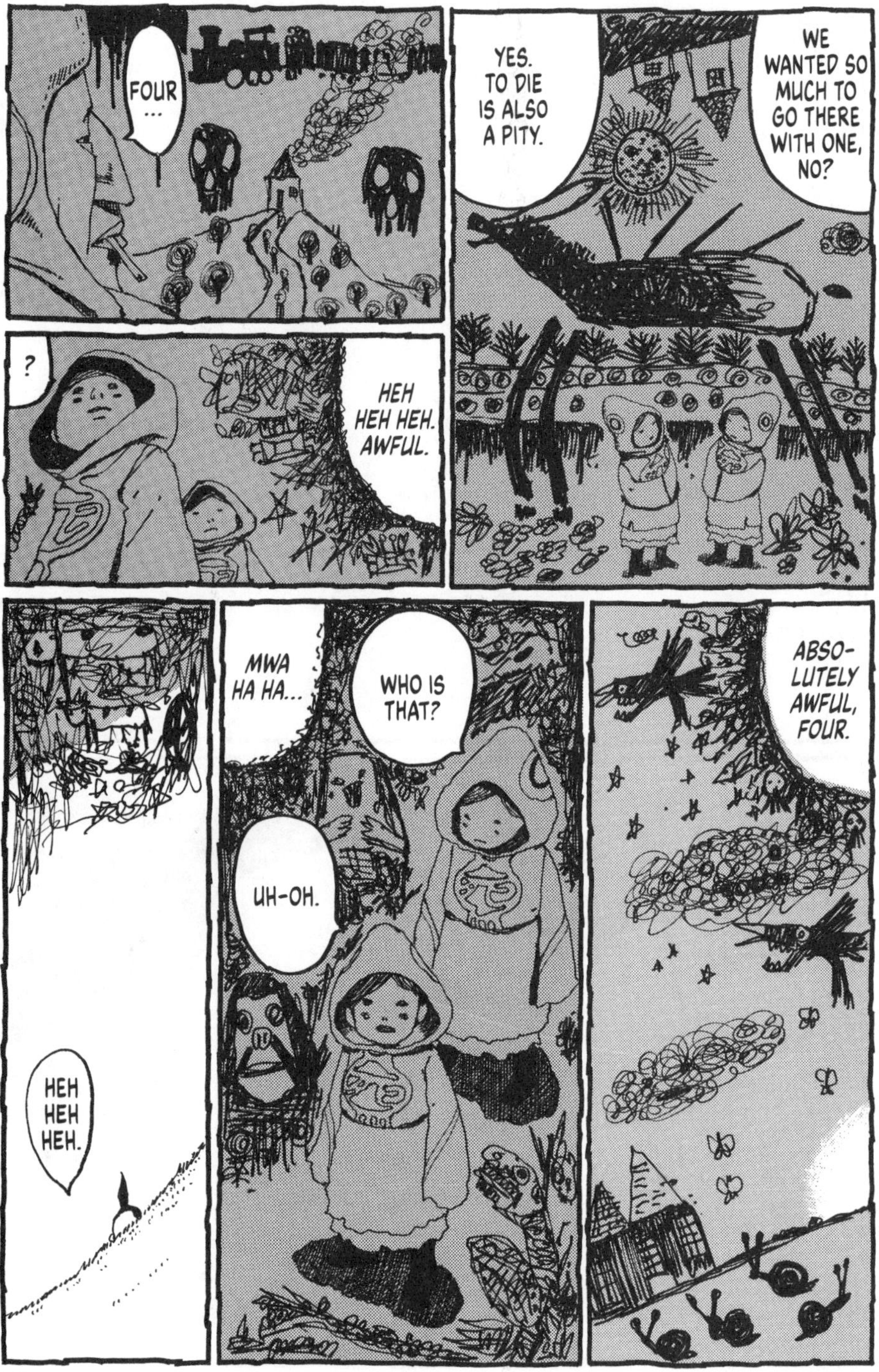
WE WANTED SO MUCH TO GO THERE WITH ONE, NO?
YES. TO DIE IS ALSO A PITY.
FOUR ...
?
HEH HEH HEH. AWFUL.
ABSO-LUTELY AWFUL, FOUR.
WHO IS THAT?
MWA HA HA...
UH-OH.
HEH HEH HEH.

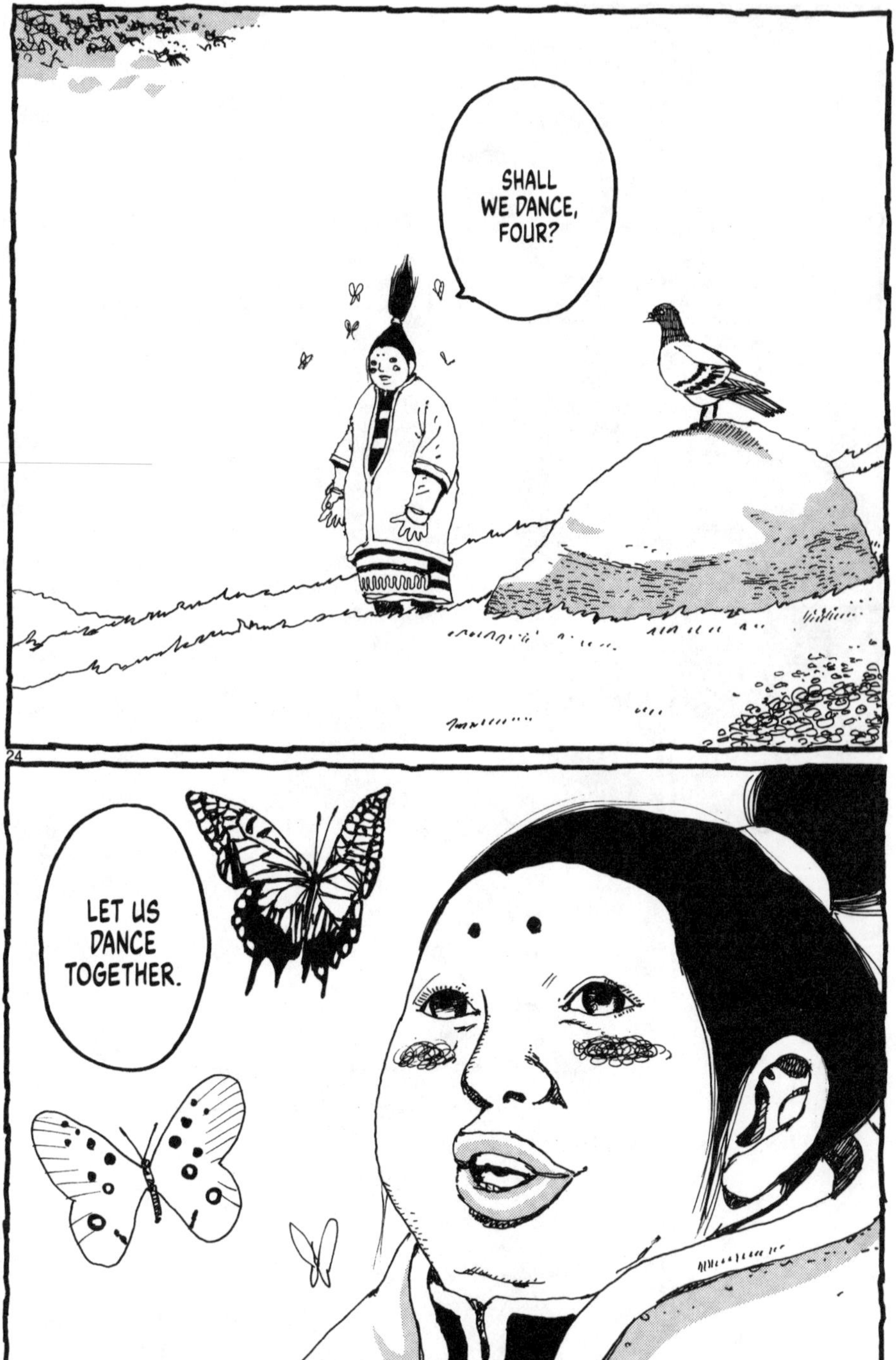
SHALL WE DANCE, FOUR?
24
LET US DANCE TOGETHER.

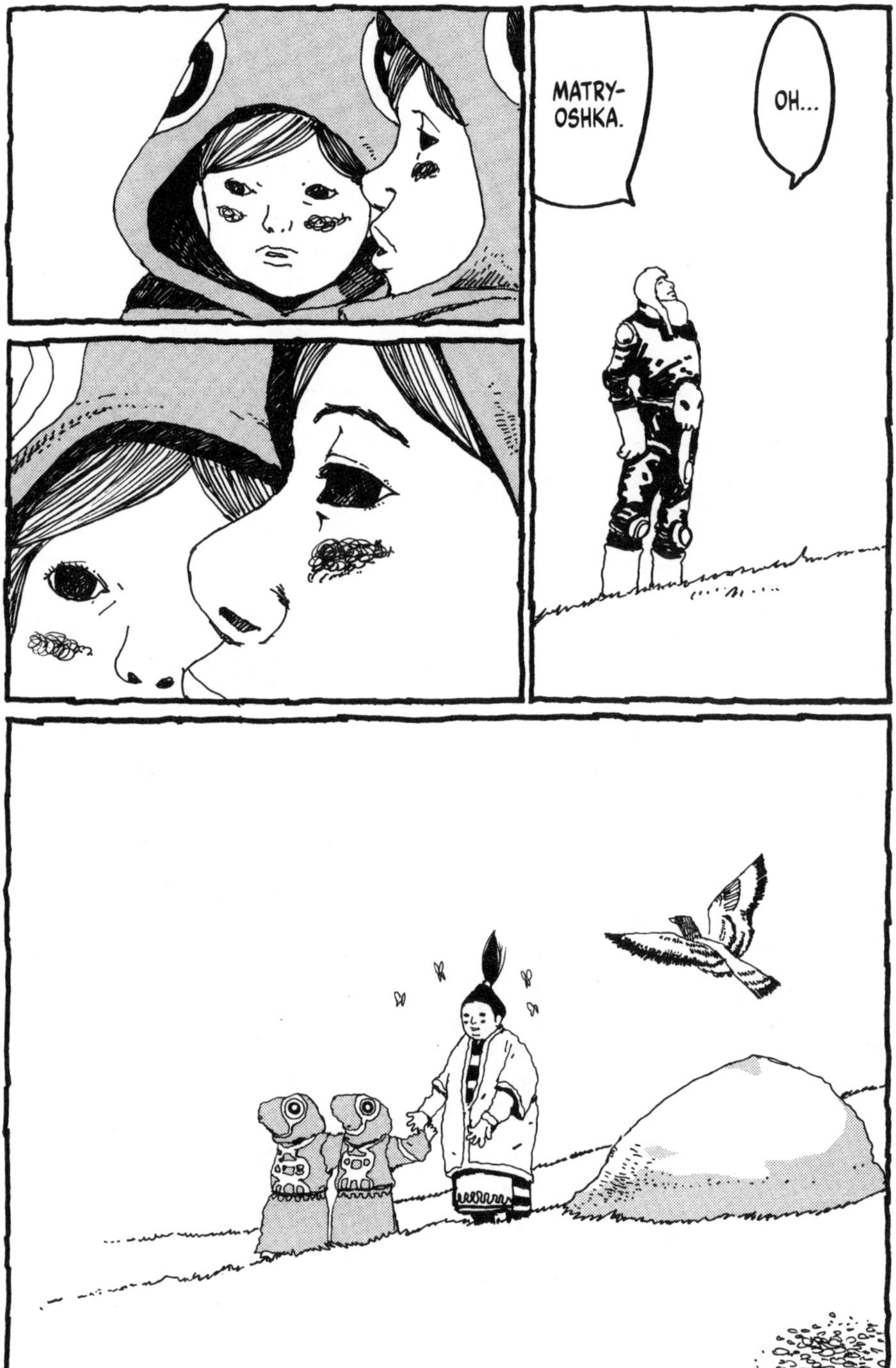
OH...
MATRY-
OSHKA.

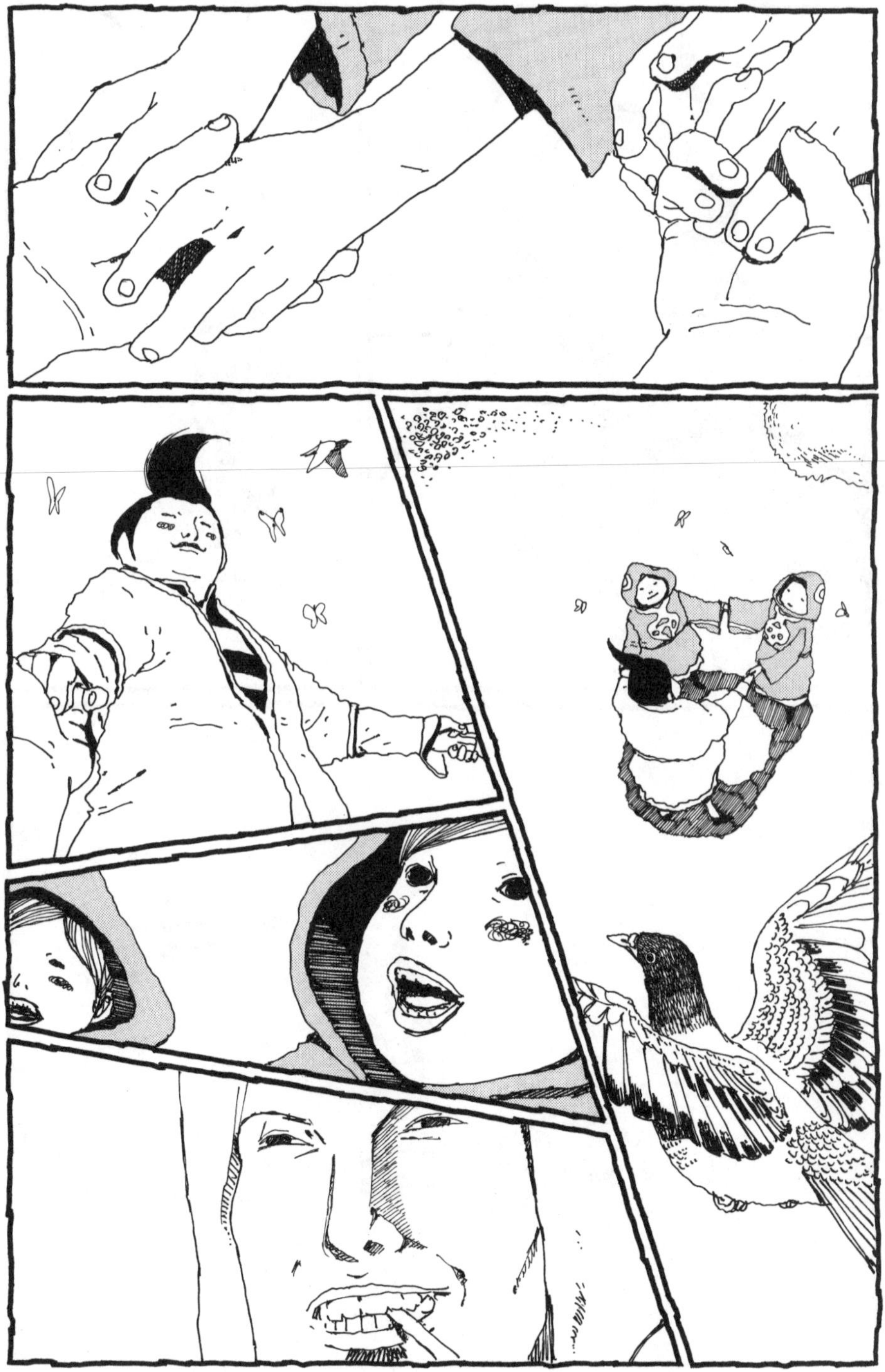

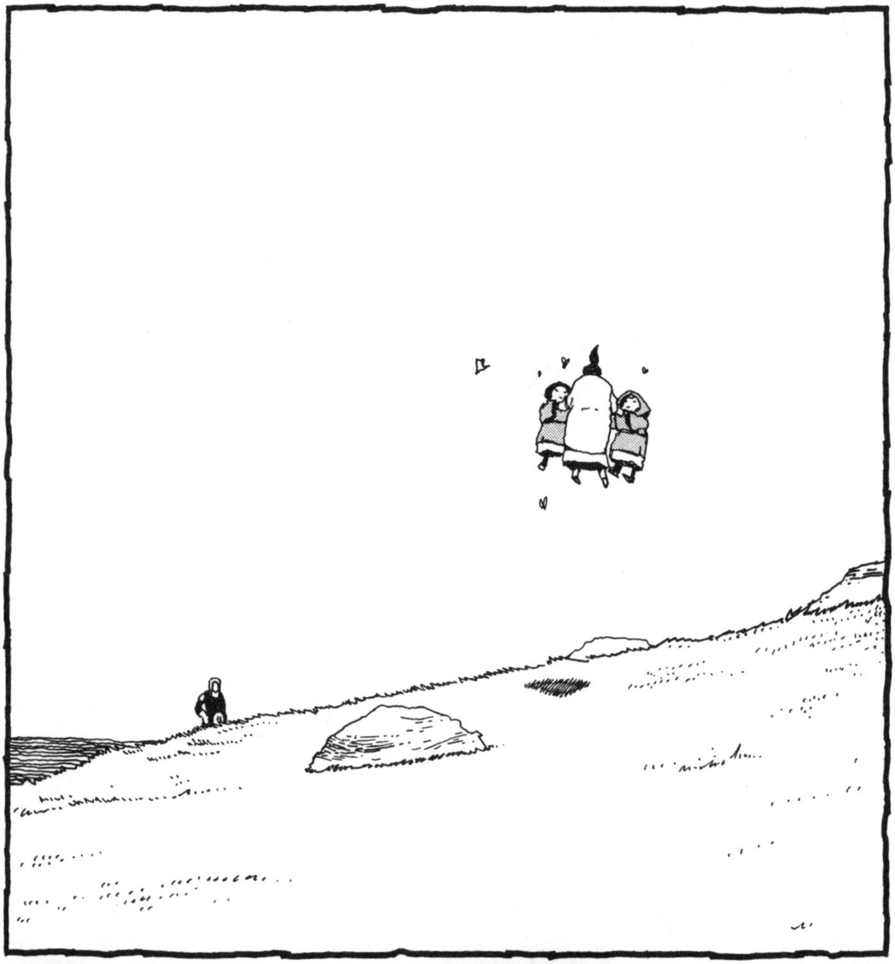

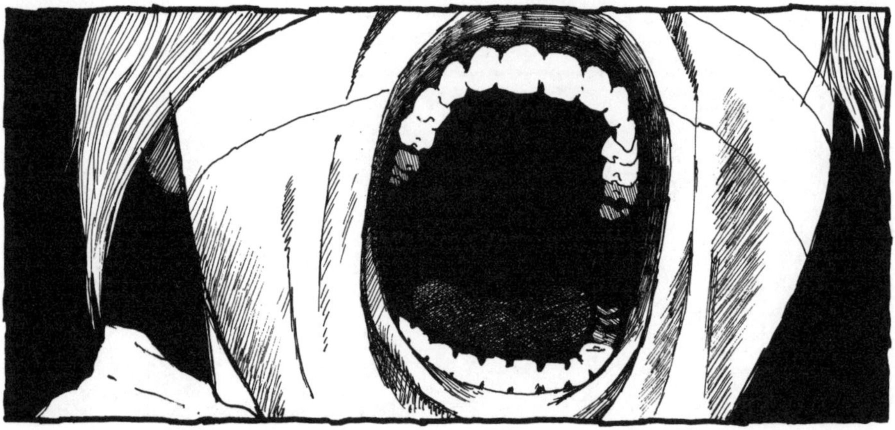

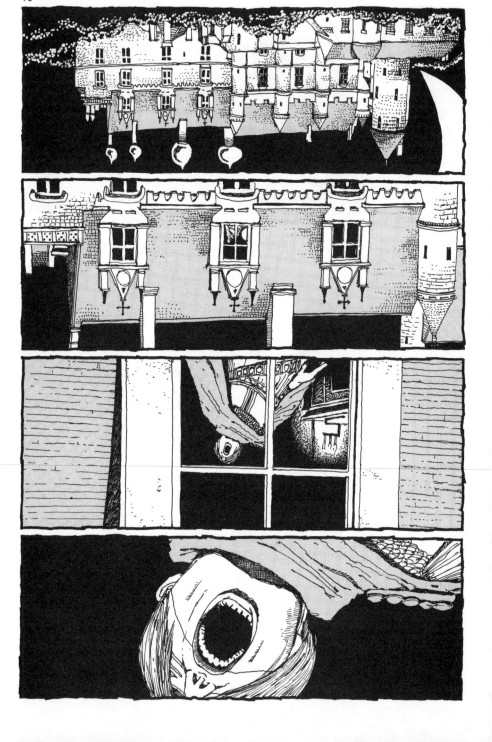

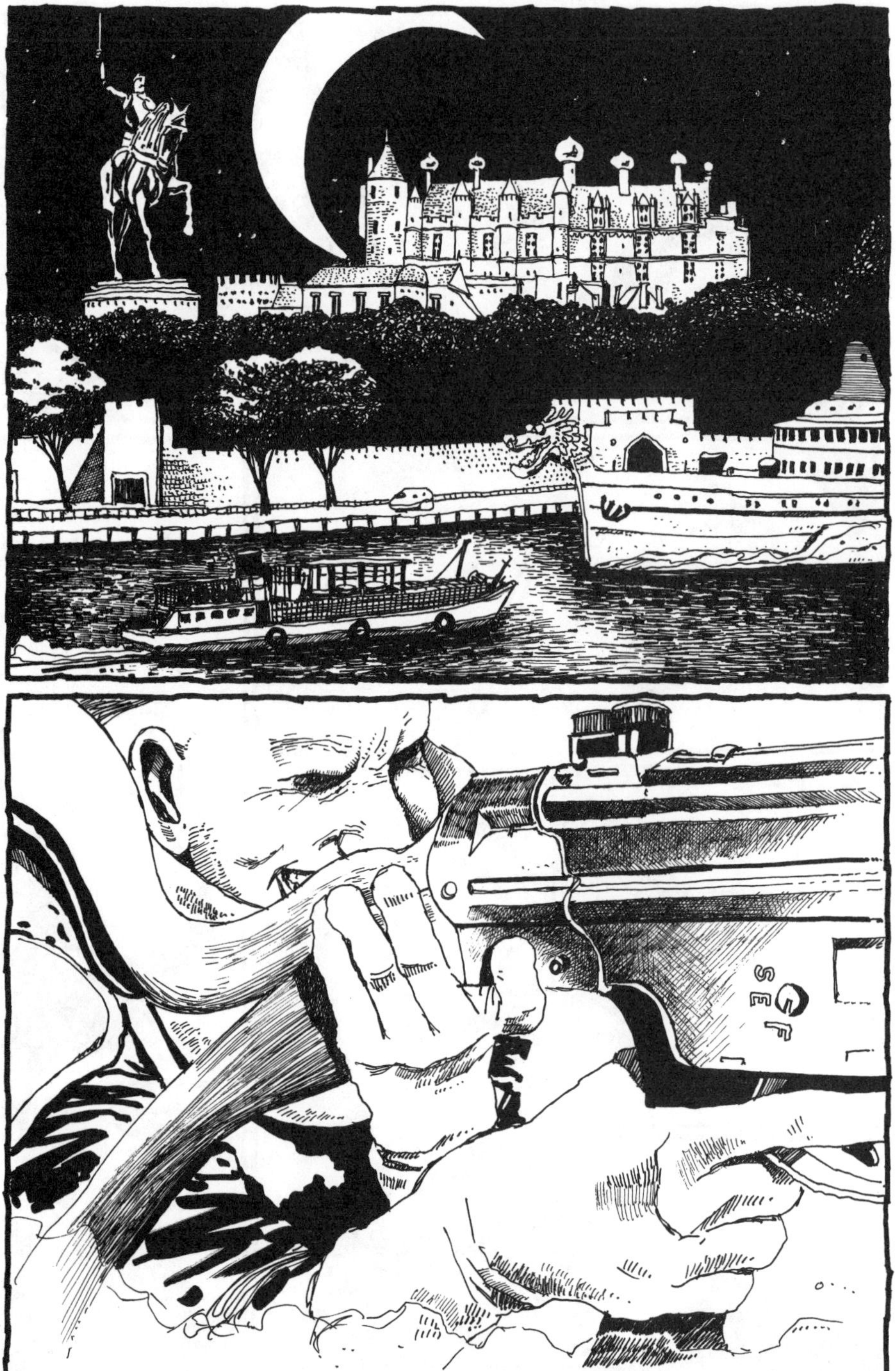
S E F

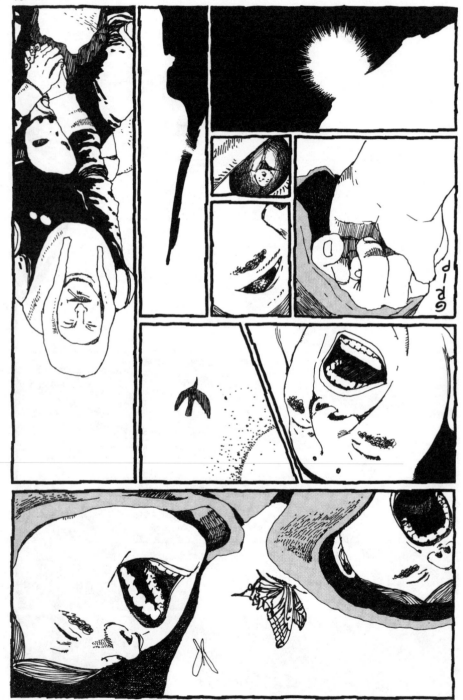

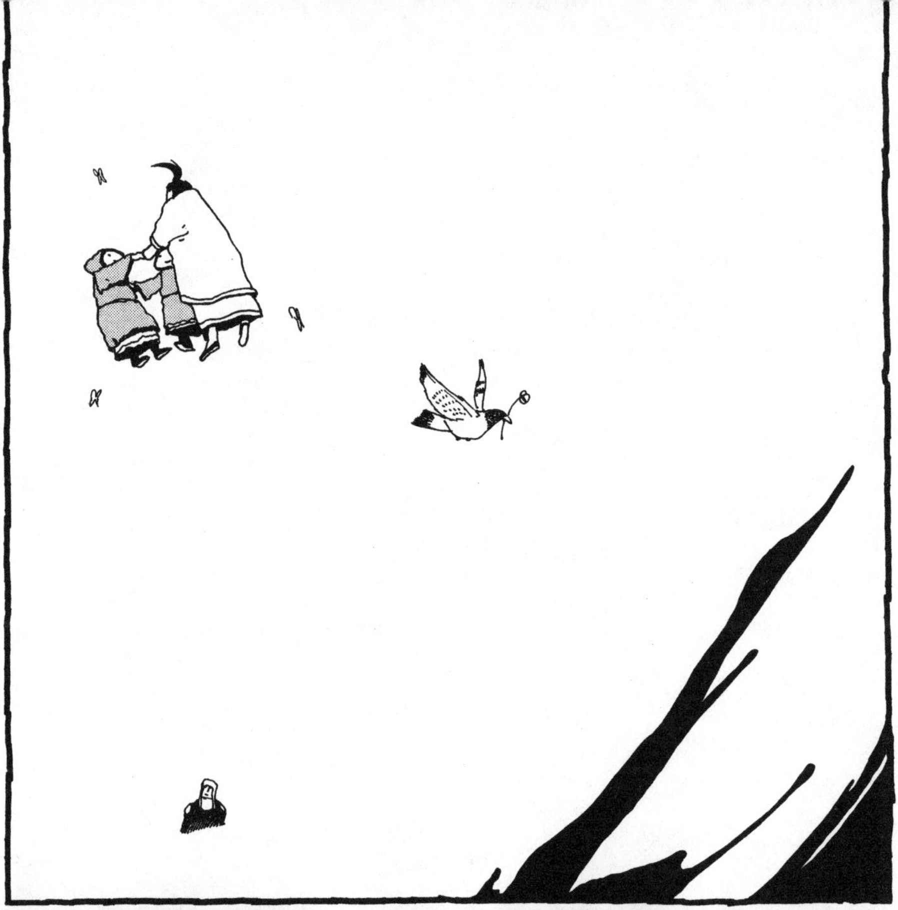

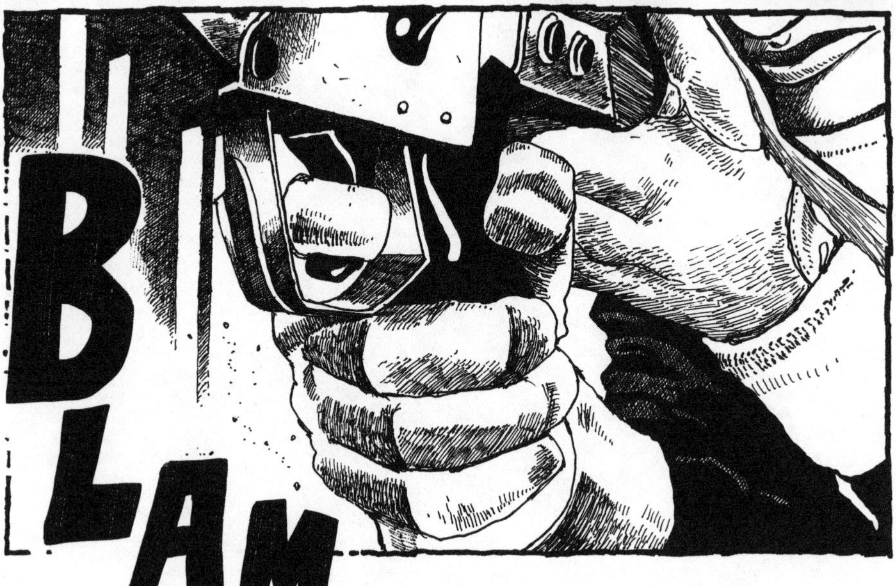
BLAM

CHAPTER 12 //

Everywhere on This Planet

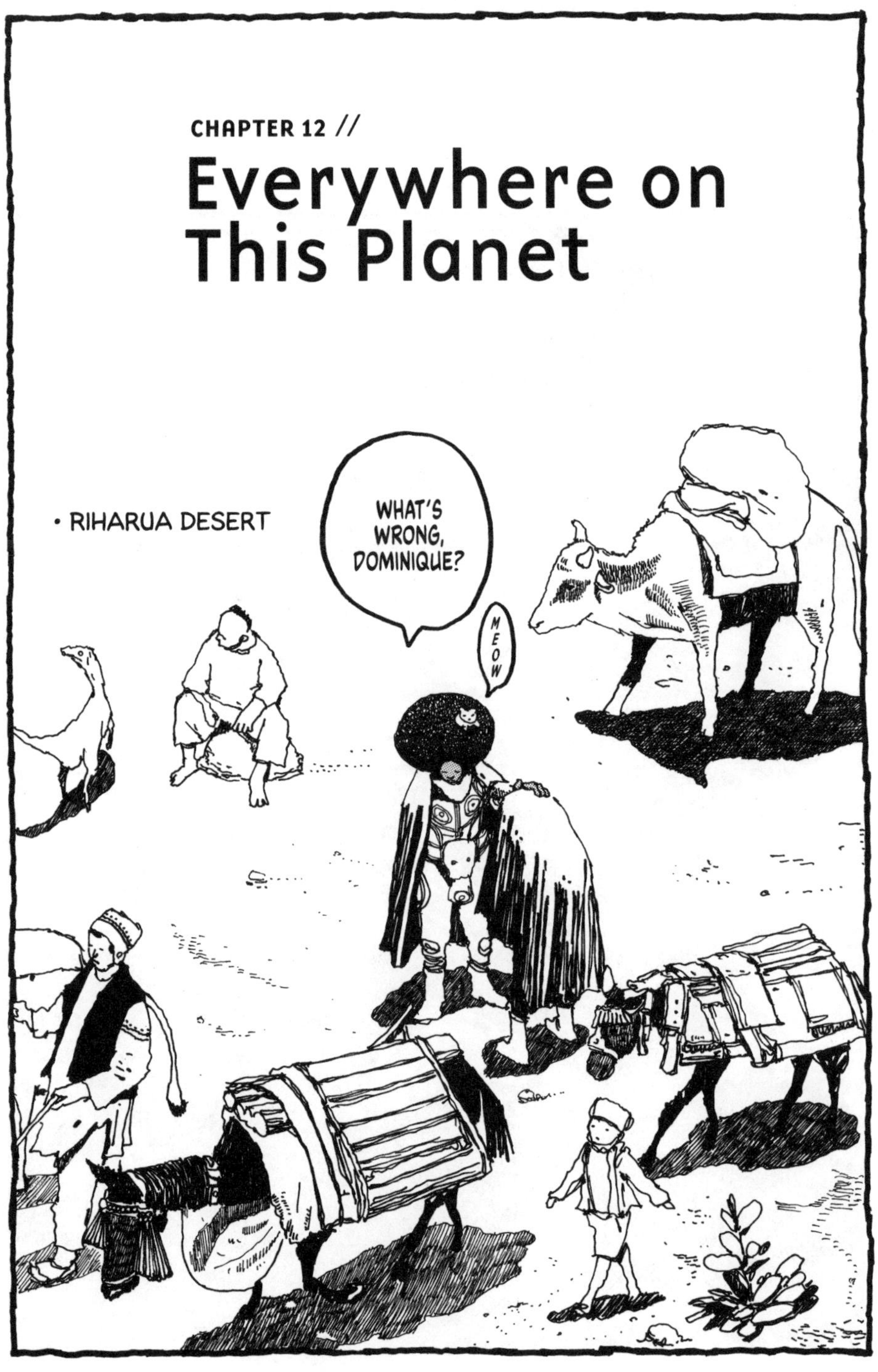
• RIHARUA DESERT
WHAT'S WRONG, DOMINIQUE?
MEOW

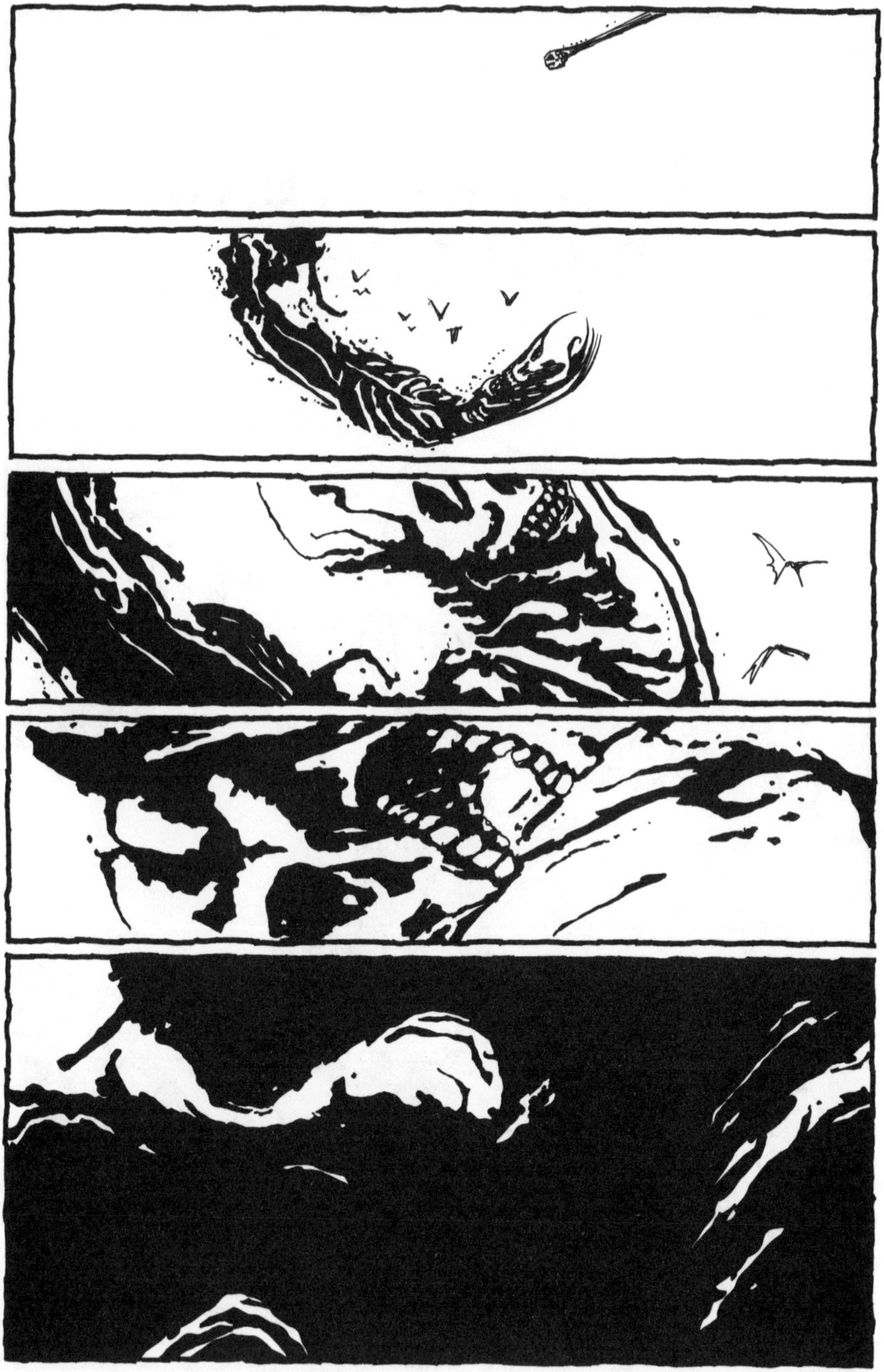

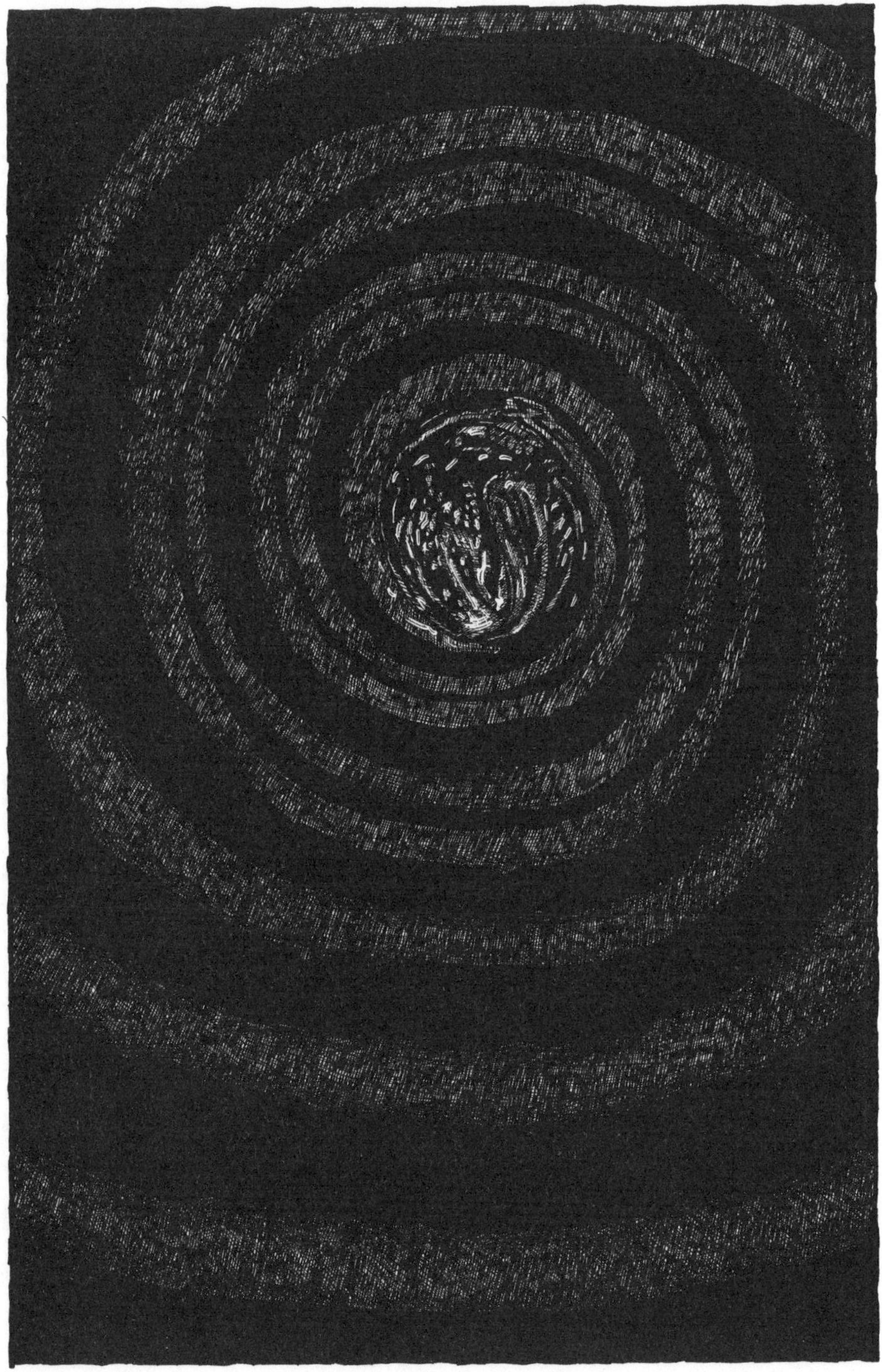

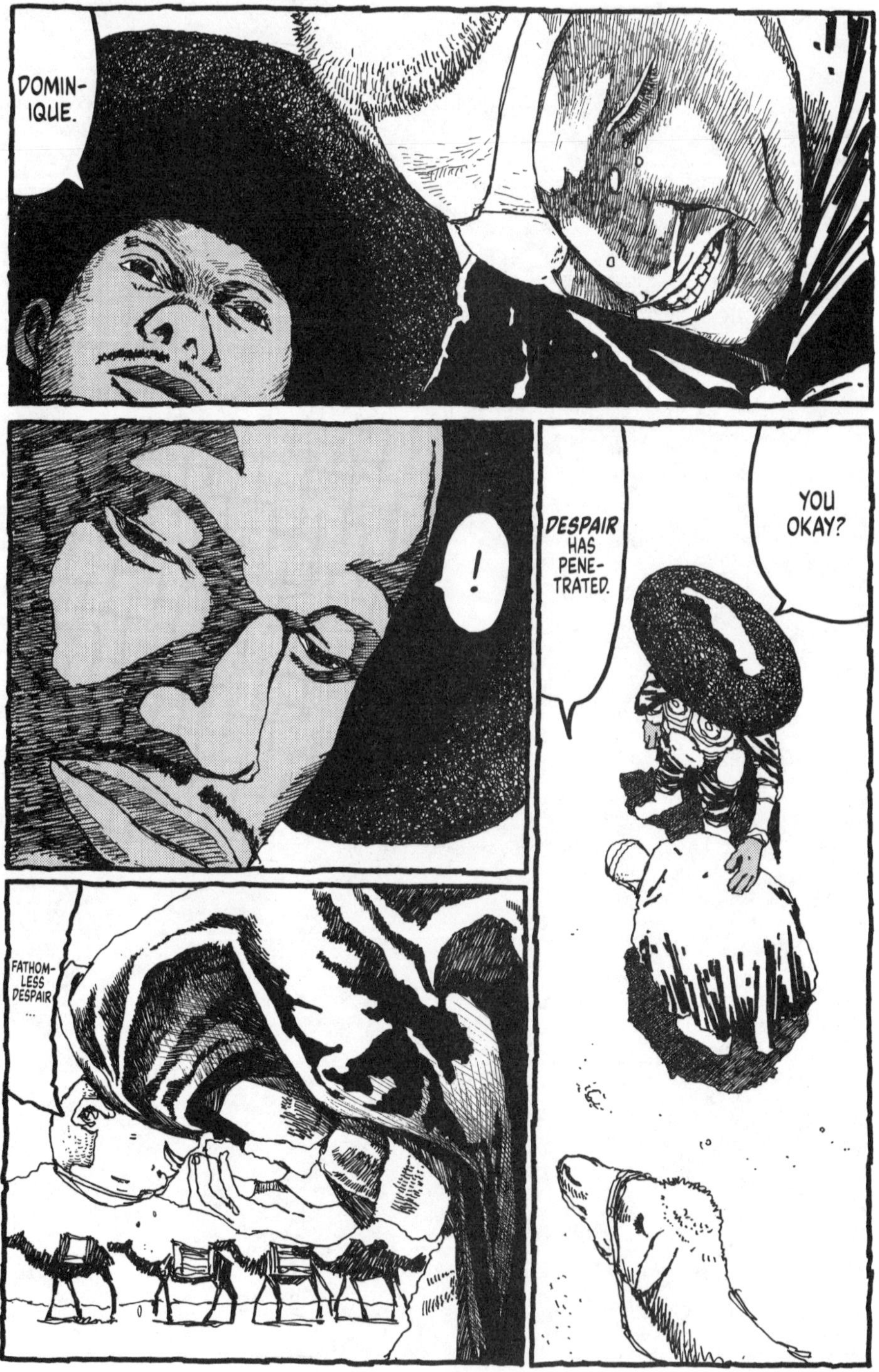
DOMINIQUE.
YOU OKAY?
DESPAIR HAS PENETRATED.
!
FATHOMLESS DESPAIR...

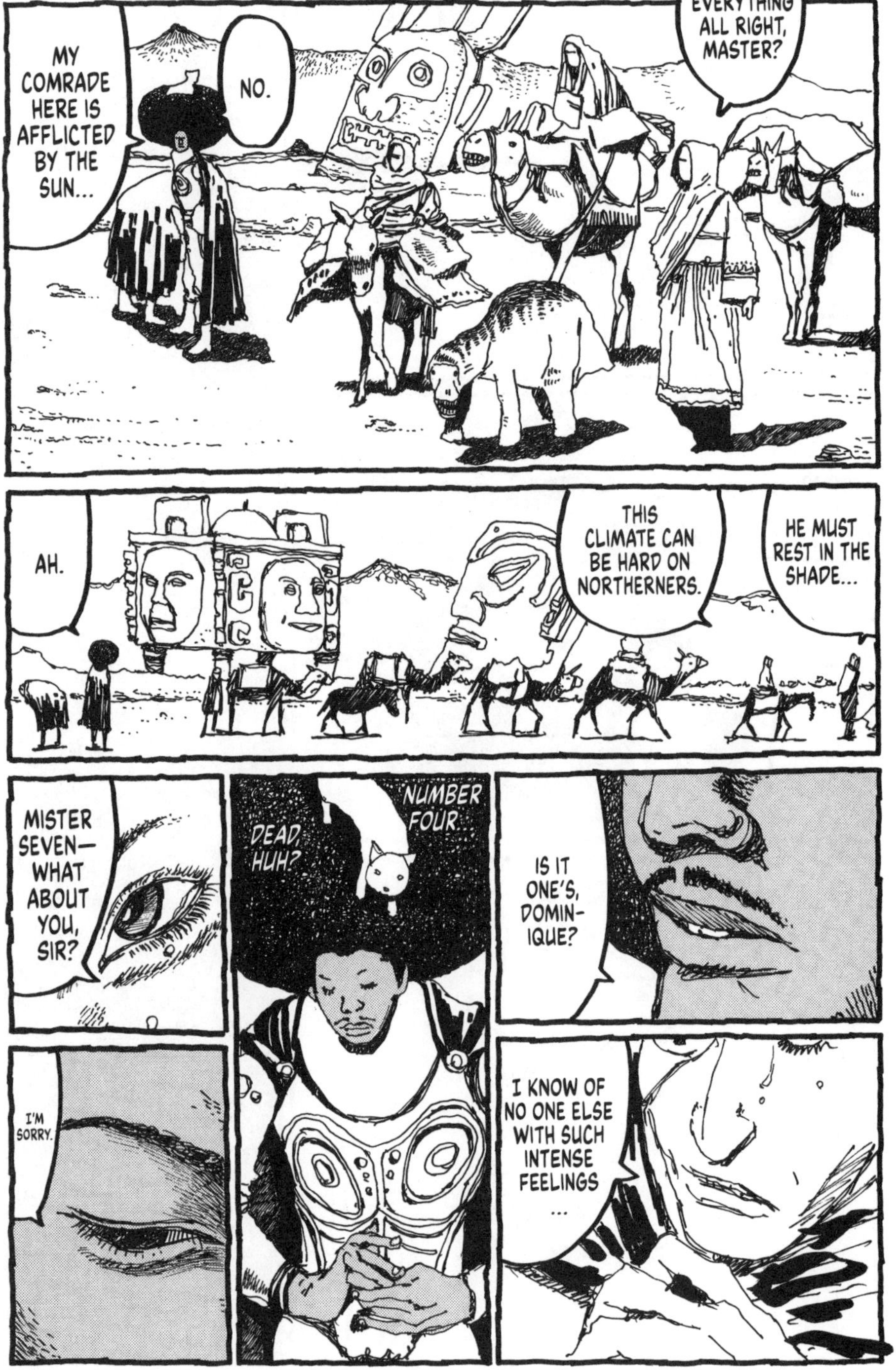
IS EVERYTHING ALL RIGHT, MASTER?
NO.
MY COMRADE HERE IS AFFLICTED BY THE SUN...
HE MUST REST IN THE SHADE...
THIS CLIMATE CAN BE HARD ON NORTHERNERS.
AH.
IS IT ONE'S, DOMINIQUE?
I KNOW OF NO ONE ELSE WITH SUCH INTENSE FEELINGS ...
NUMBER FOUR...
DEAD, HUH?
MISTER SEVEN— WHAT ABOUT YOU, SIR?
I'M SORRY.

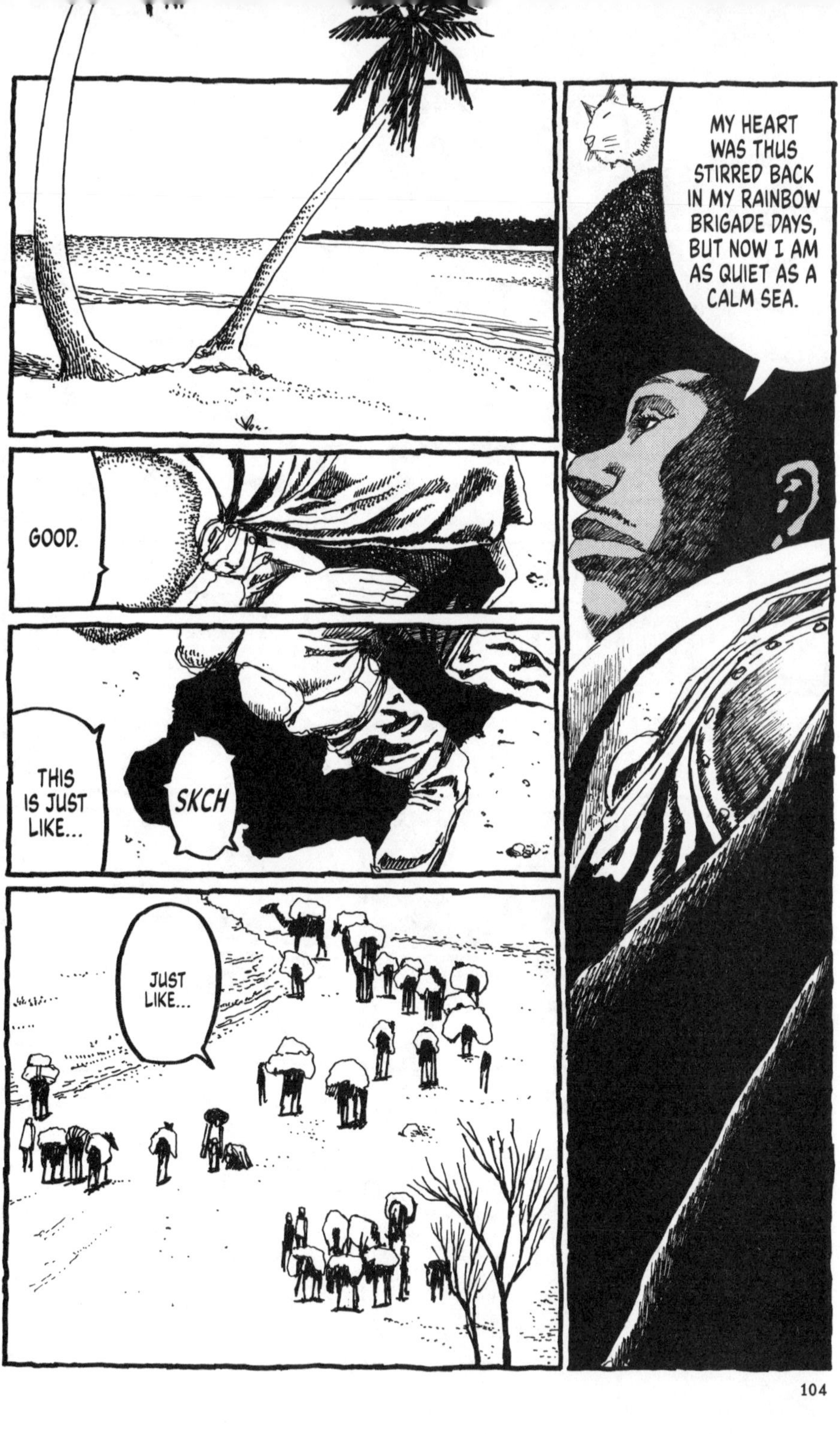
MY HEART WAS THUS STIRRED BACK IN MY RAINBOW BRIGADE DAYS, BUT NOW I AM AS QUIET AS A CALM SEA.
GOOD.
THIS IS JUST LIKE...
SKCH
JUST LIKE...

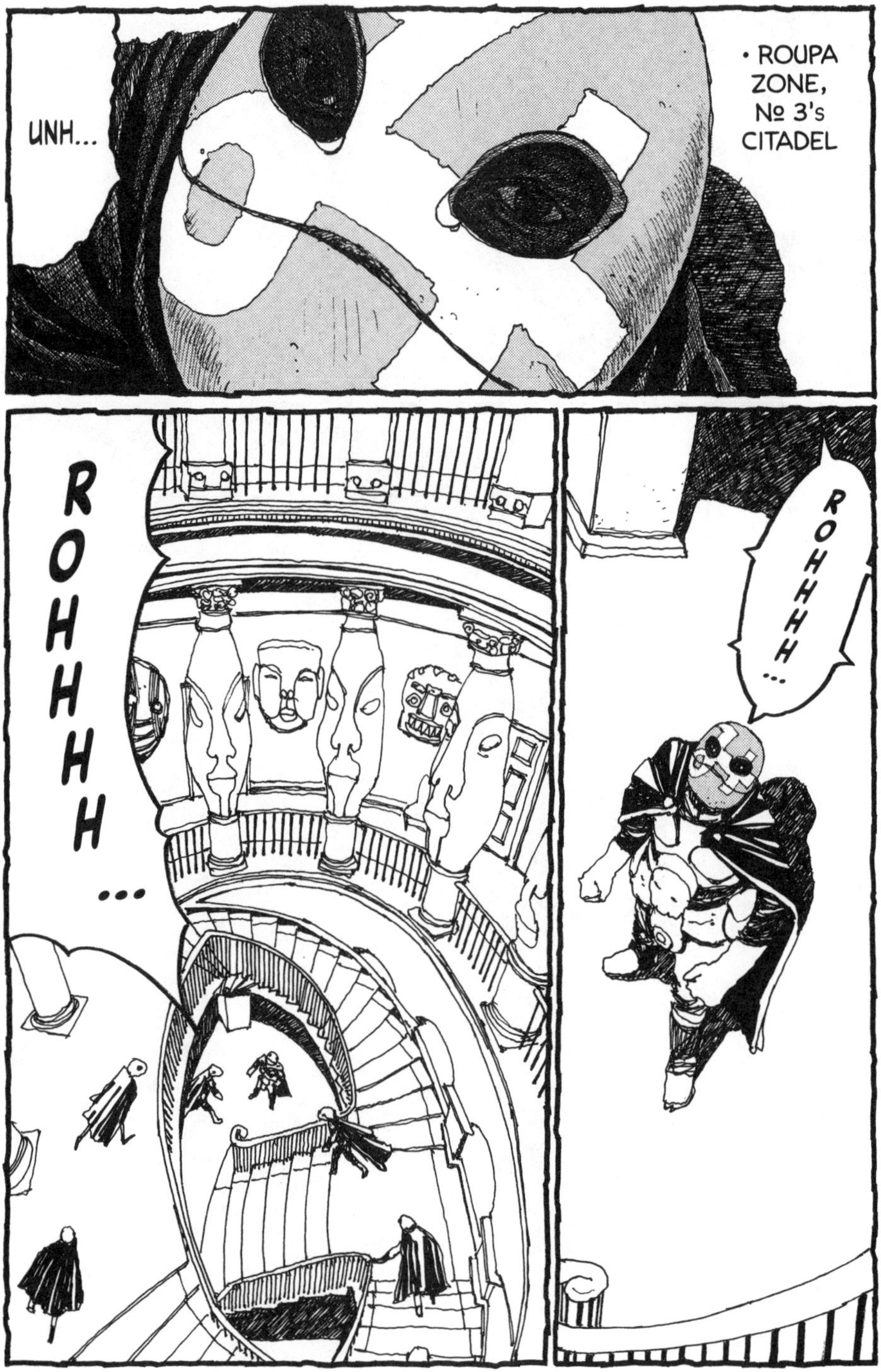
• ROUPA ZONE, № 3's CITADEL
UNH...
ROHHHH...
ROHHHHH...

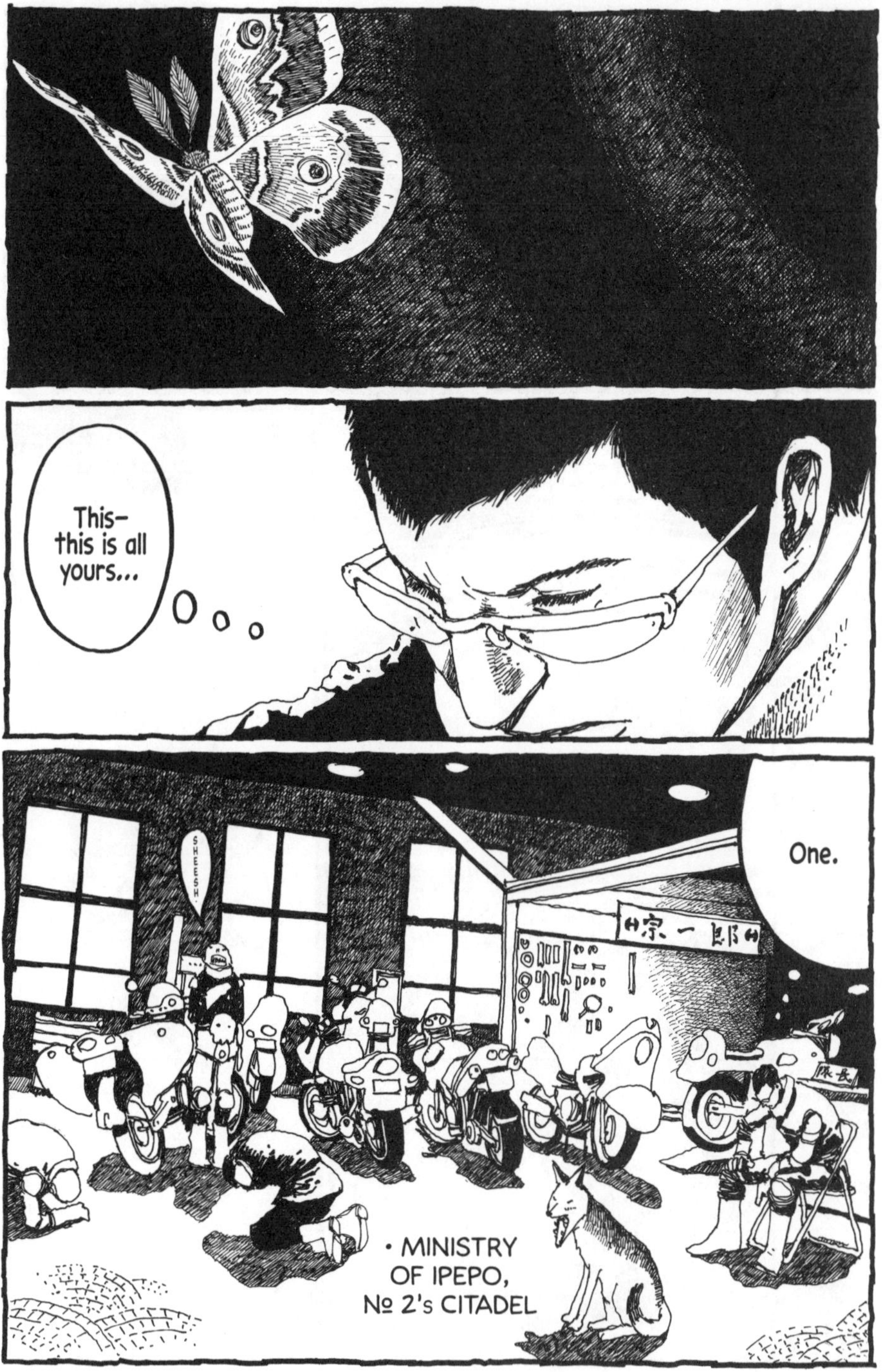
This-
this is all
yours...
One.
宗一郎
SHEESH.
• MINISTRY
OF IPEPO,
№ 2's CITADEL

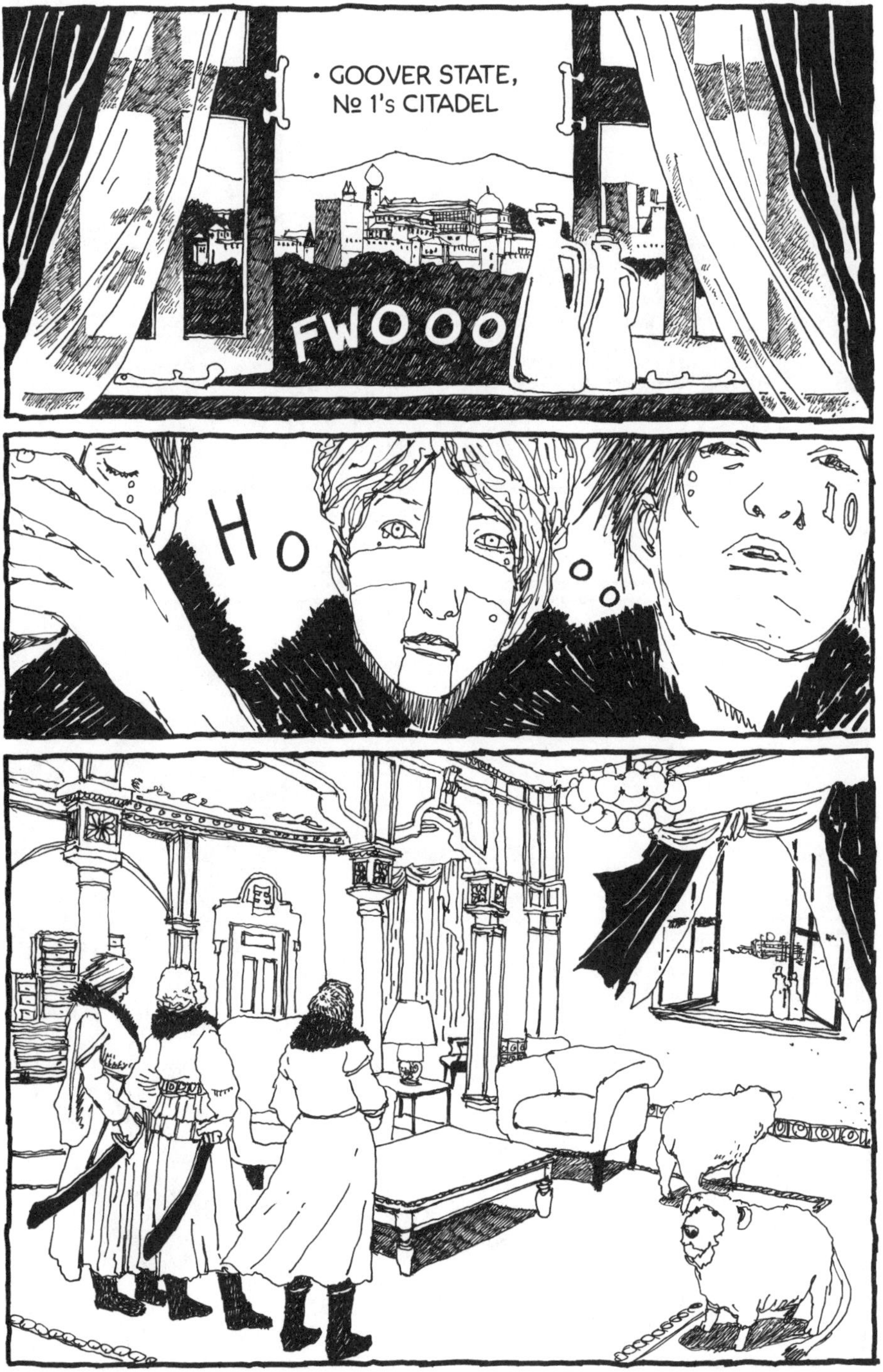
• GOOVER STATE,
№ 1's CITADEL
FWOOO
HO
OO
10

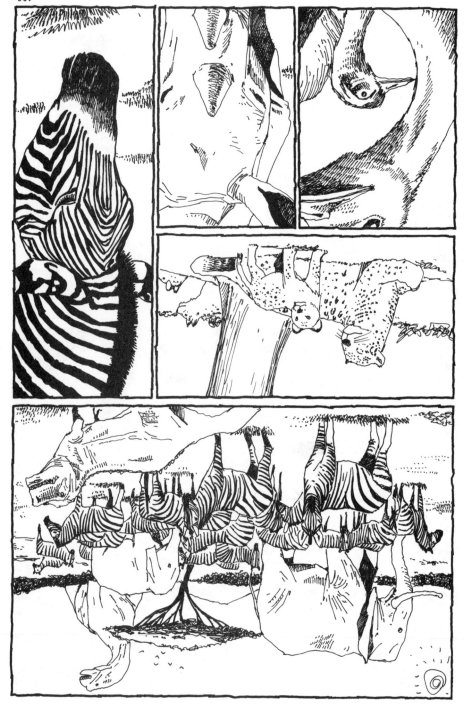

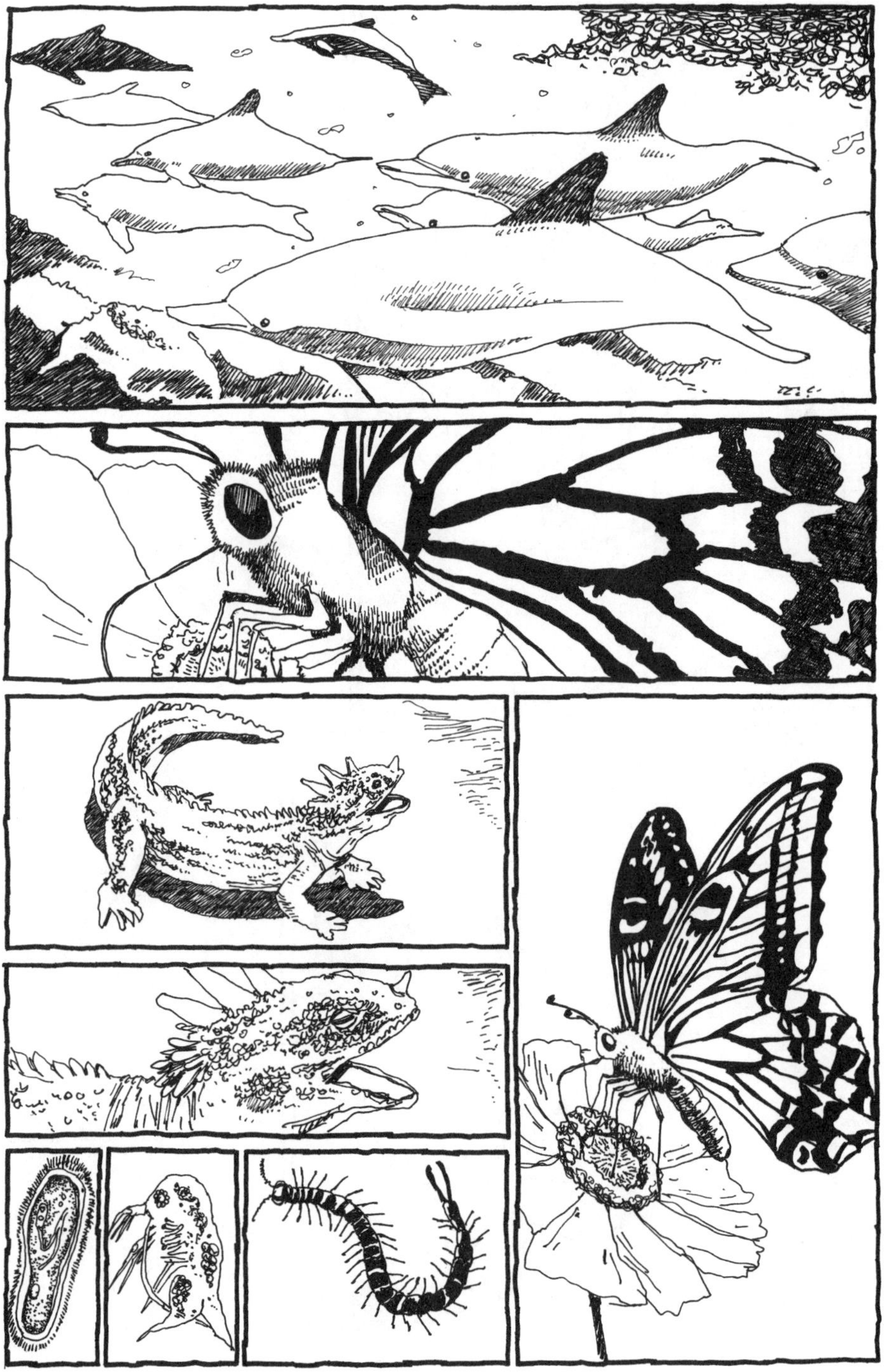

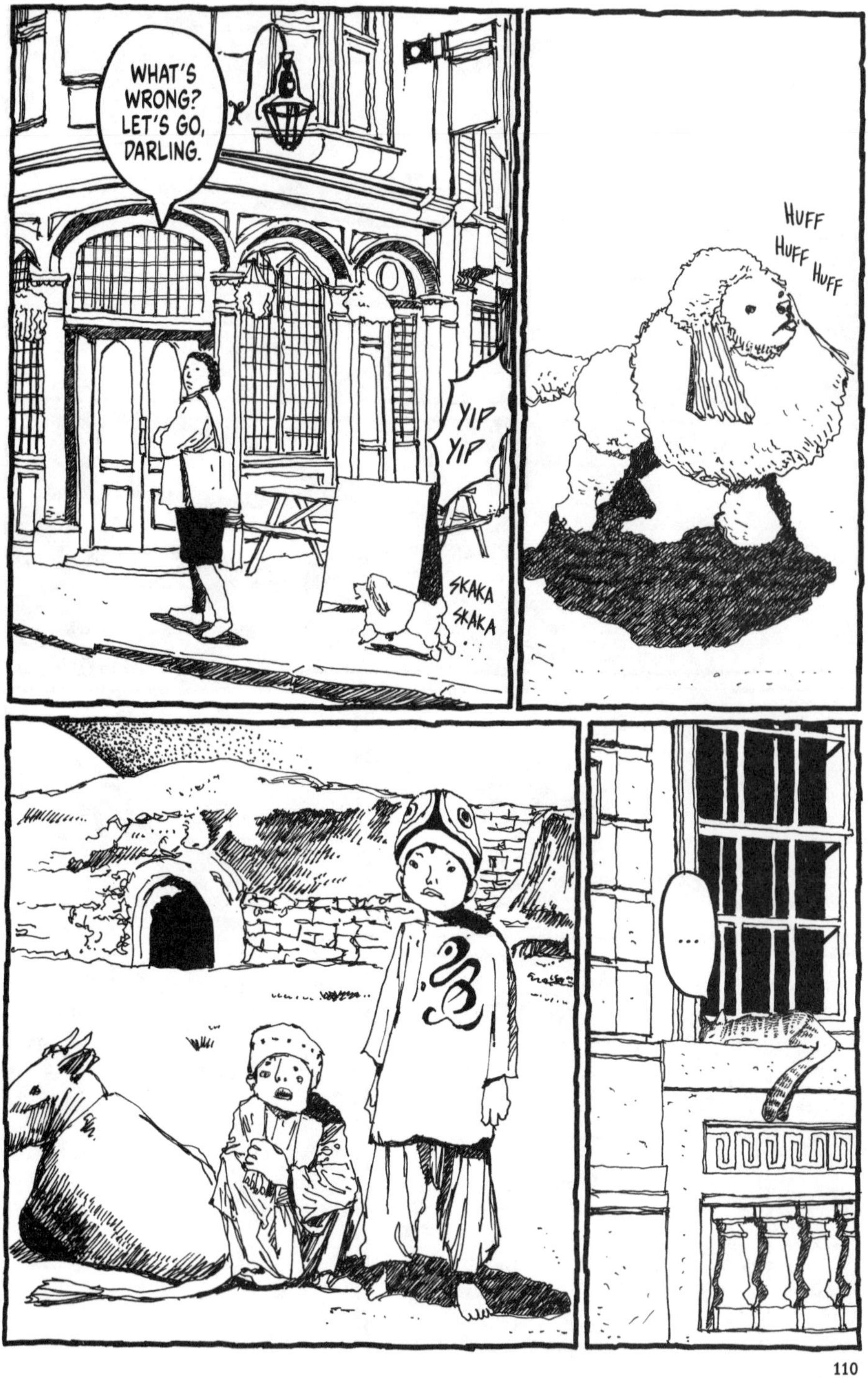
HUFF
HUFF HUFF
WHAT'S WRONG? LET'S GO, DARLING.
YIP YIP
SKAKA SKAKA
...

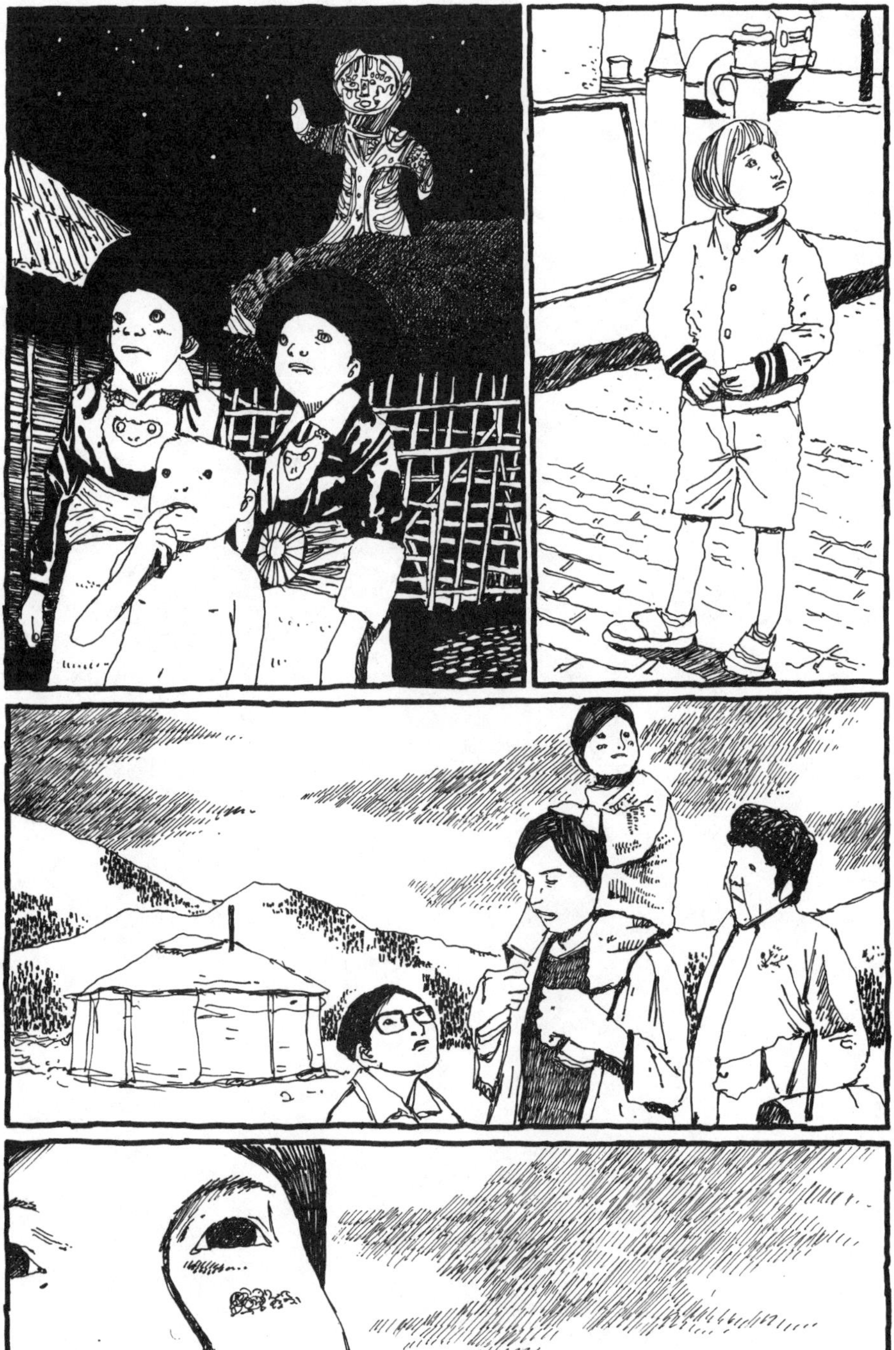

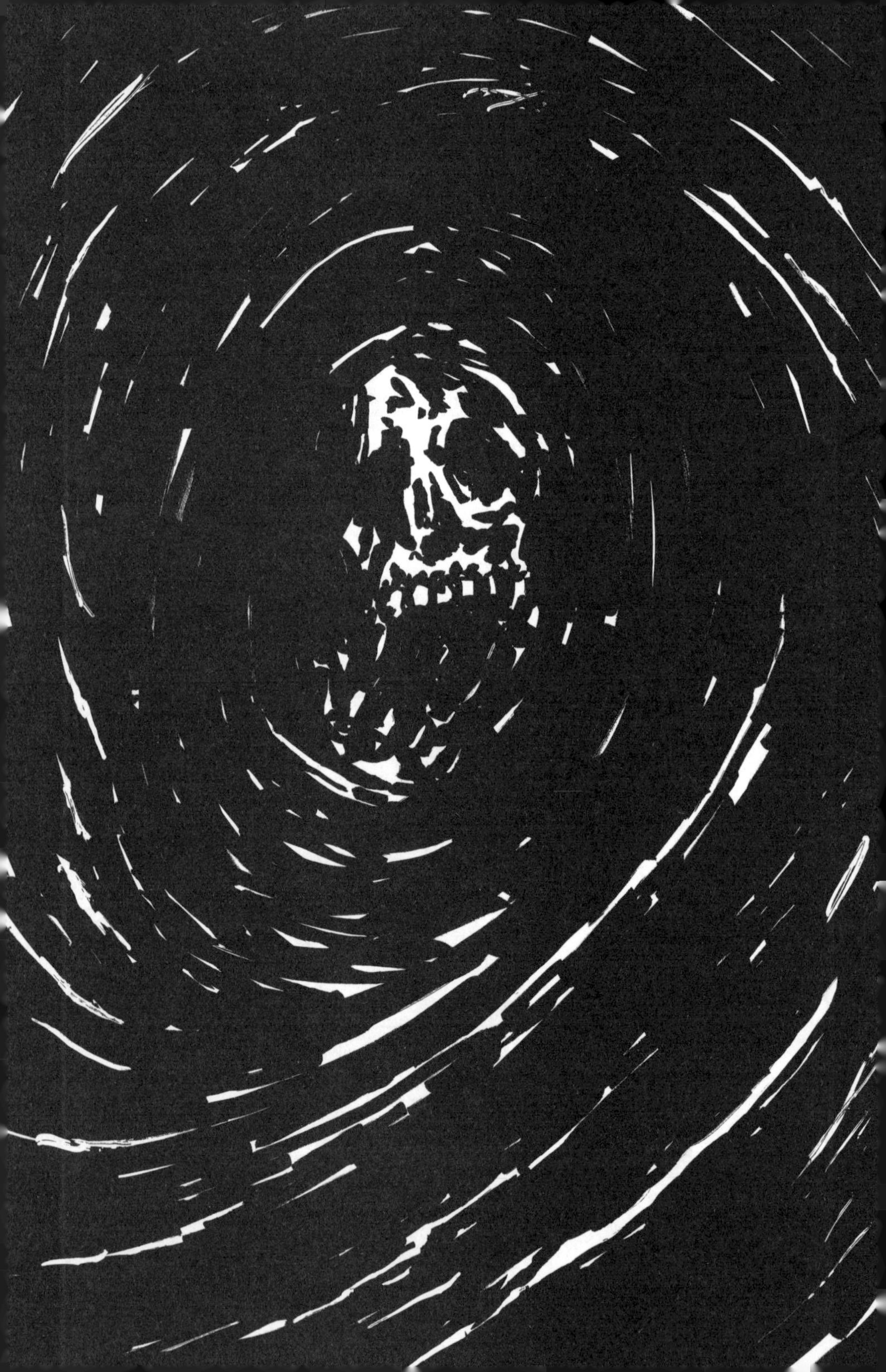

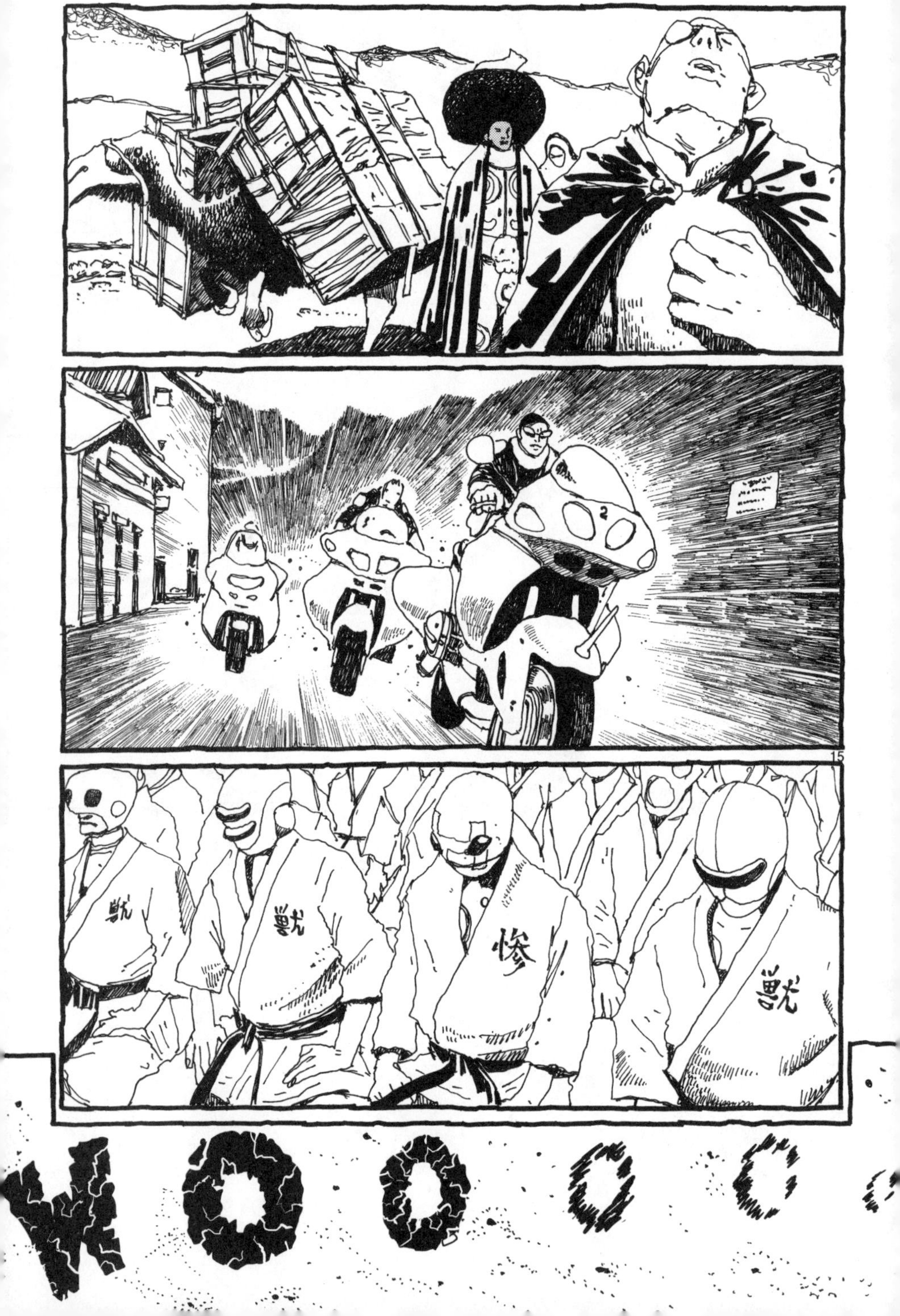
獣
惨
獣
獣
WOOOO

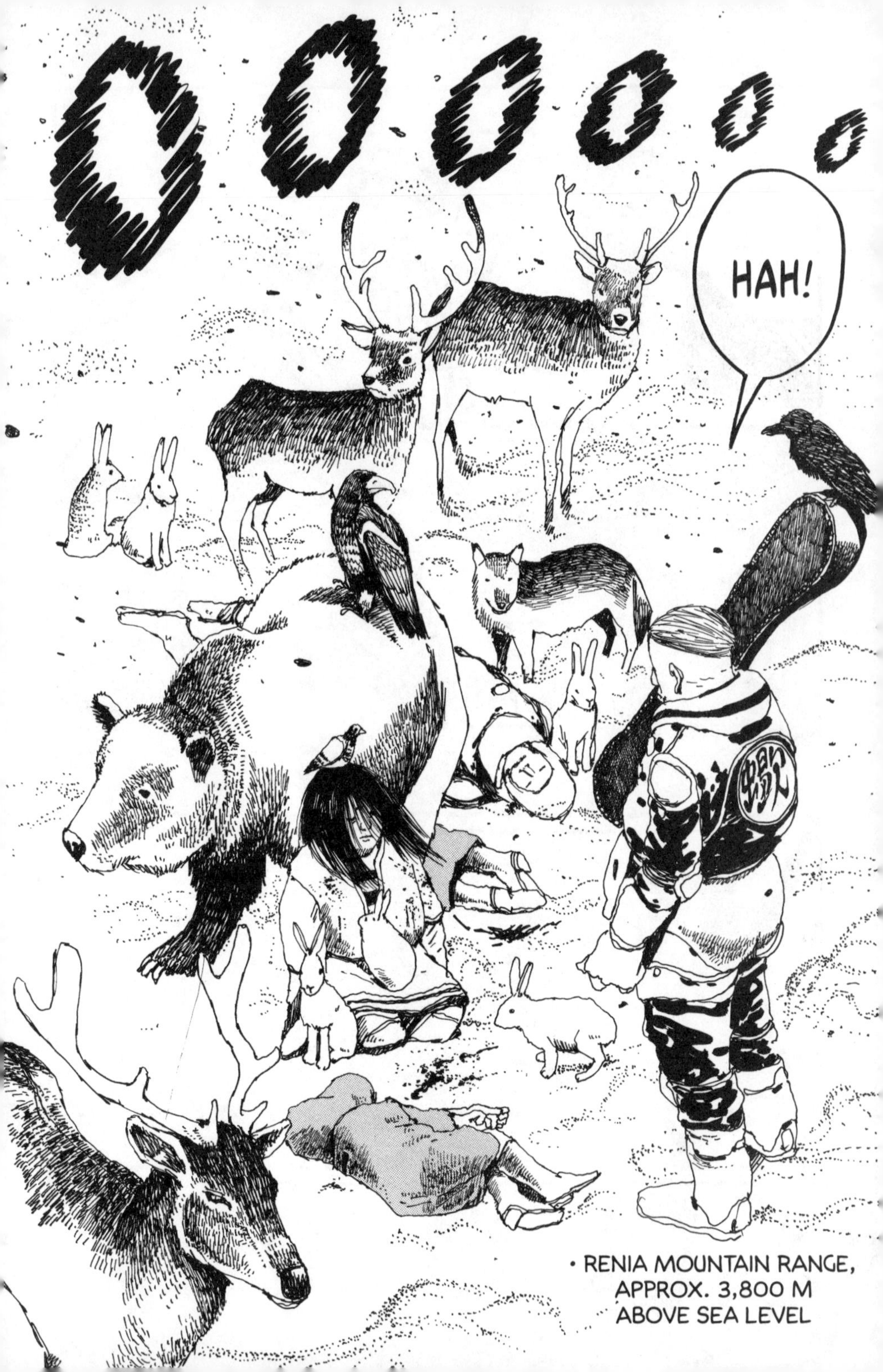
OOOOOO
HAH!
• RENIA MOUNTAIN RANGE, APPROX. 3,800 M ABOVE SEA LEVEL

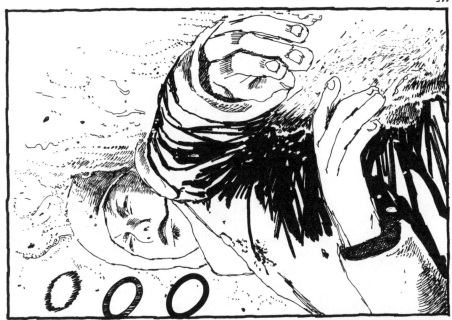

WELL, WELL.
YOU CERTAINLY
HAVE QUITE AN
ENTOURAGE,
MATRYOSHKA.

YOU
MUST HAVE
INVITED THEM
ALONG WITH
YOU, NO?

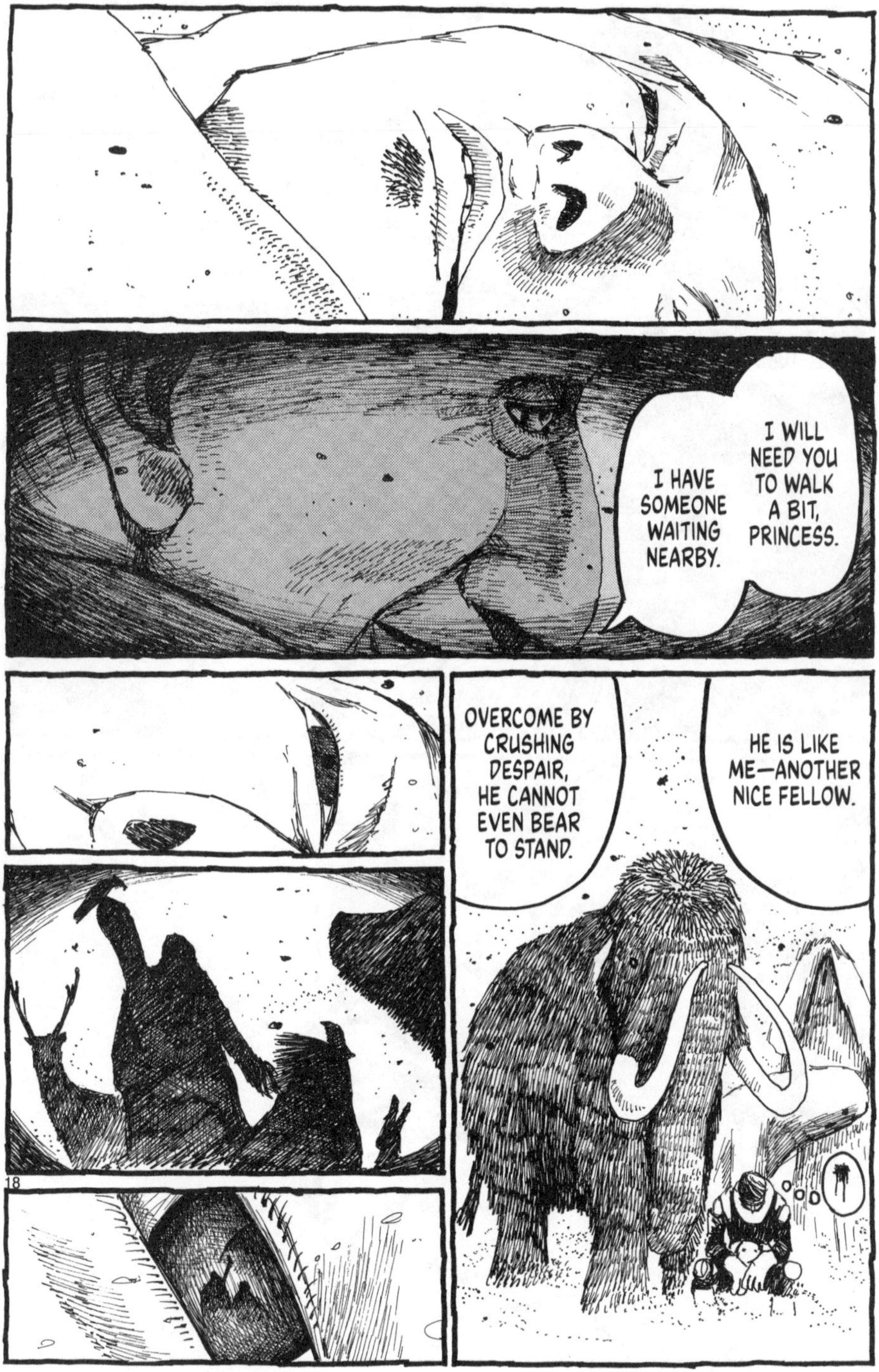

I WILL NEED YOU TO WALK A BIT, PRINCESS.
I HAVE SOMEONE WAITING NEARBY.
HE IS LIKE ME—ANOTHER NICE FELLOW.
OVERCOME BY CRUSHING DESPAIR, HE CANNOT EVEN BEAR TO STAND.

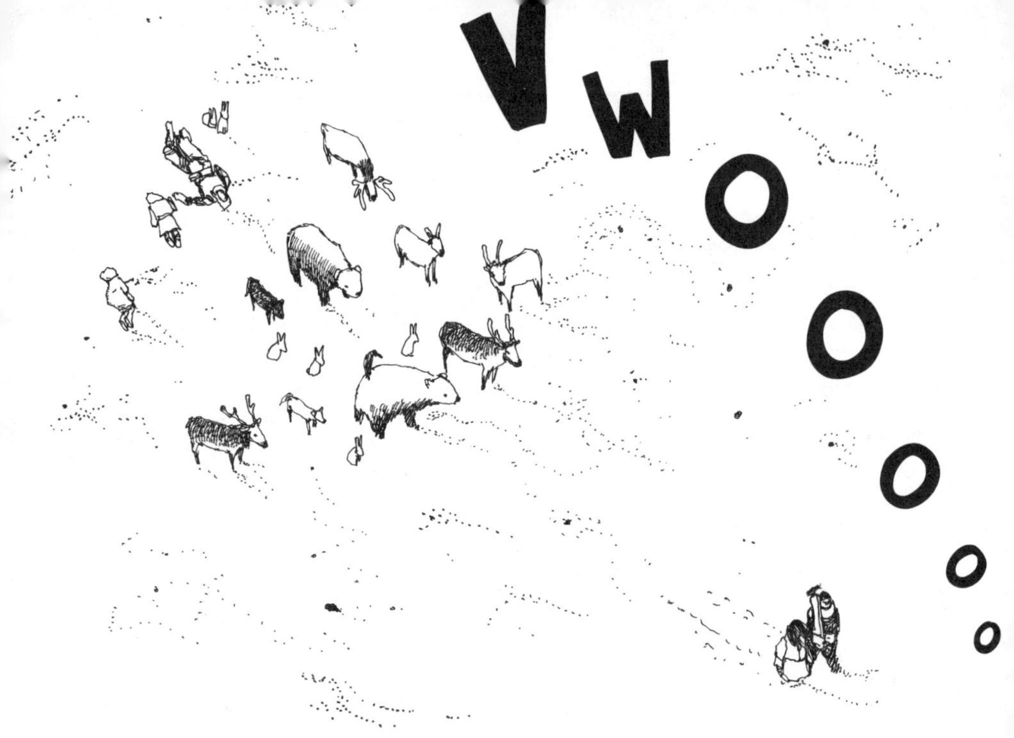
VWOOOOOo
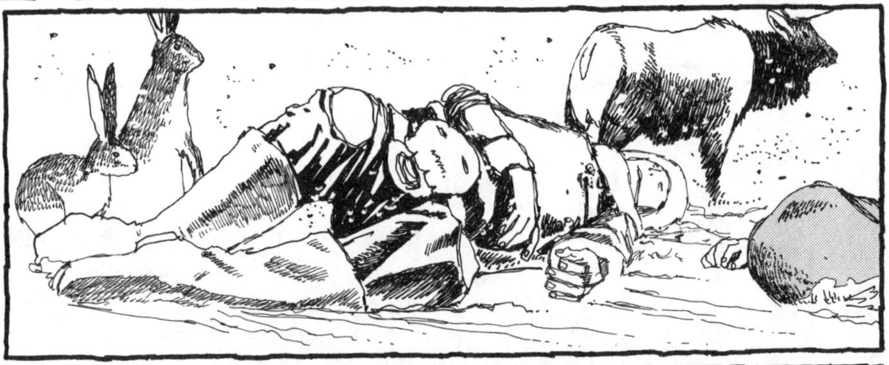
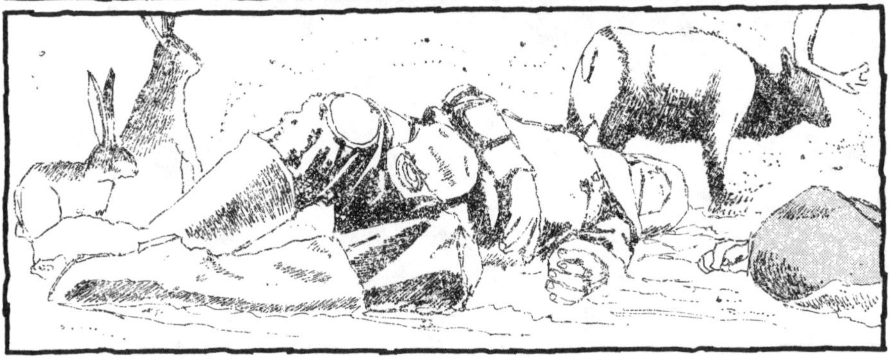

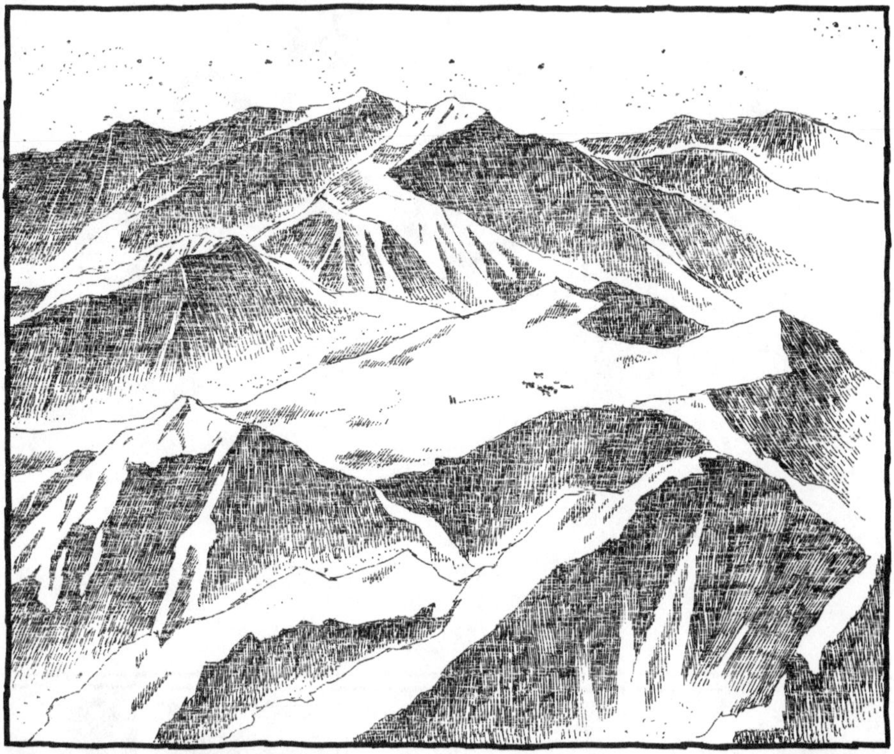

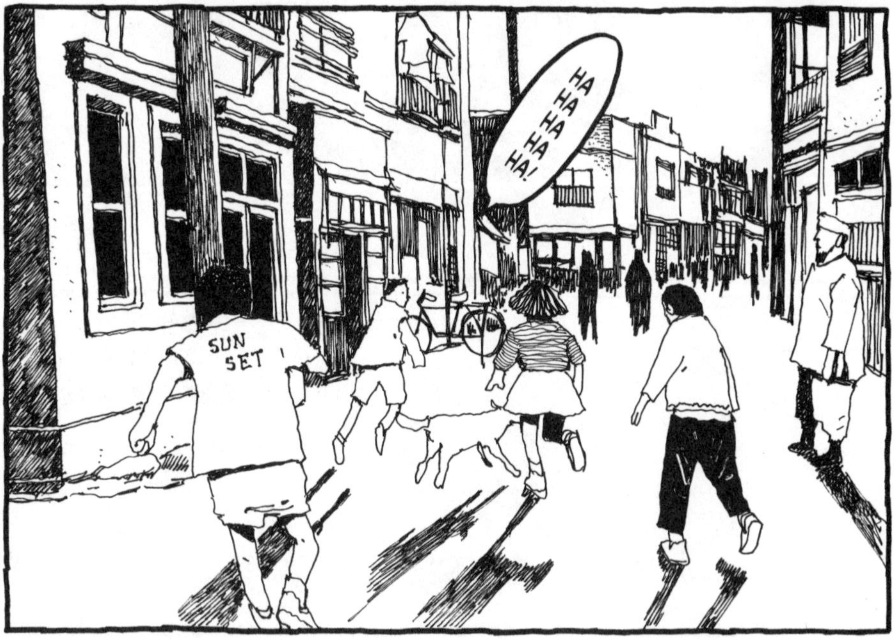
HA HA HA HA HA!
SUN SET

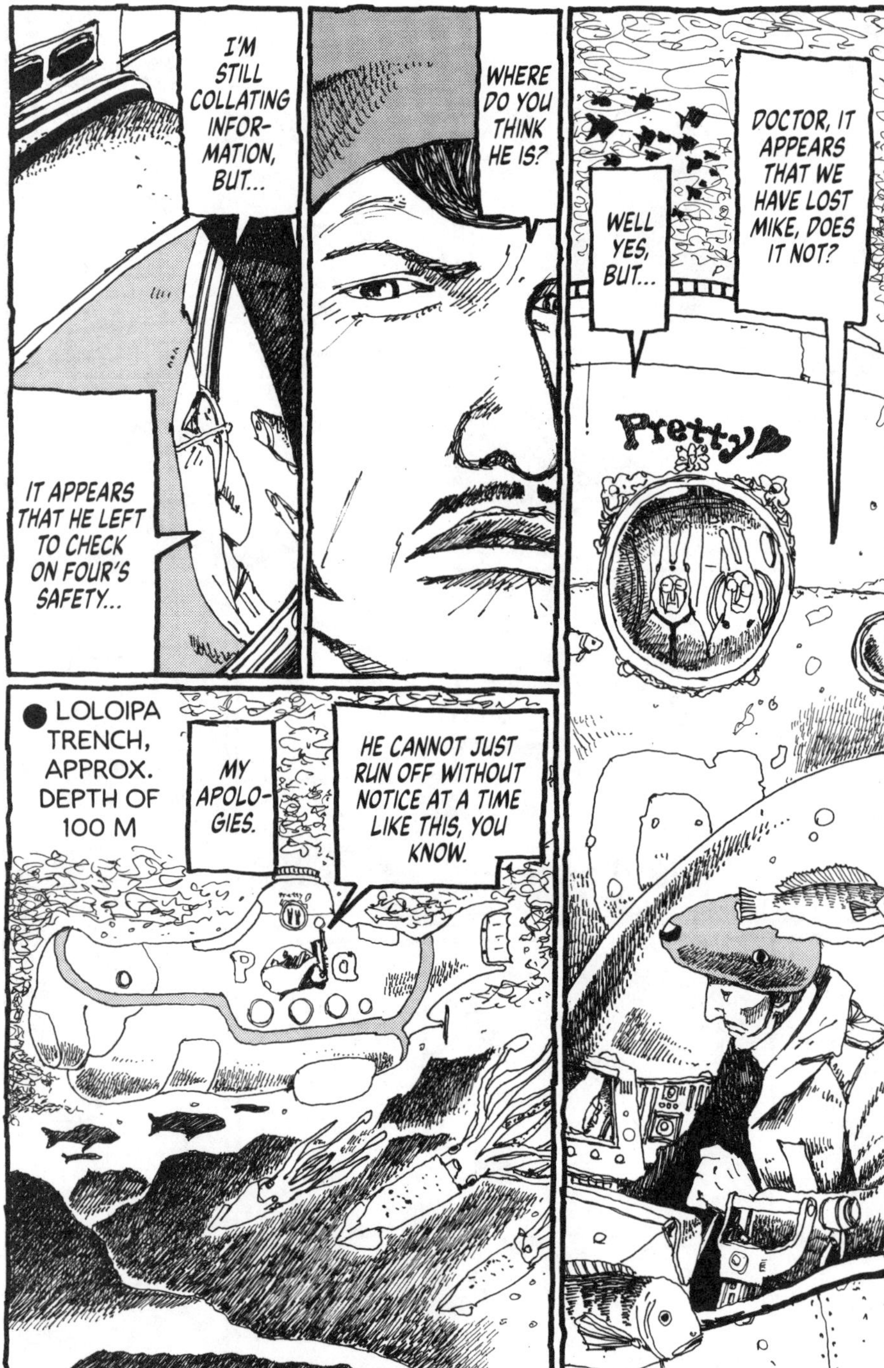
DOCTOR, IT APPEARS THAT WE HAVE LOST MIKE, DOES IT NOT?
WELL YES, BUT...
Pretty
WHERE DO YOU THINK HE IS?
I'M STILL COLLATING INFORMATION, BUT...
IT APPEARS THAT HE LEFT TO CHECK ON FOUR'S SAFETY...
HE CANNOT JUST RUN OFF WITHOUT NOTICE AT A TIME LIKE THIS, YOU KNOW.
MY APOLOGIES.
LOLOIPA TRENCH, APPROX. DEPTH OF 100 M

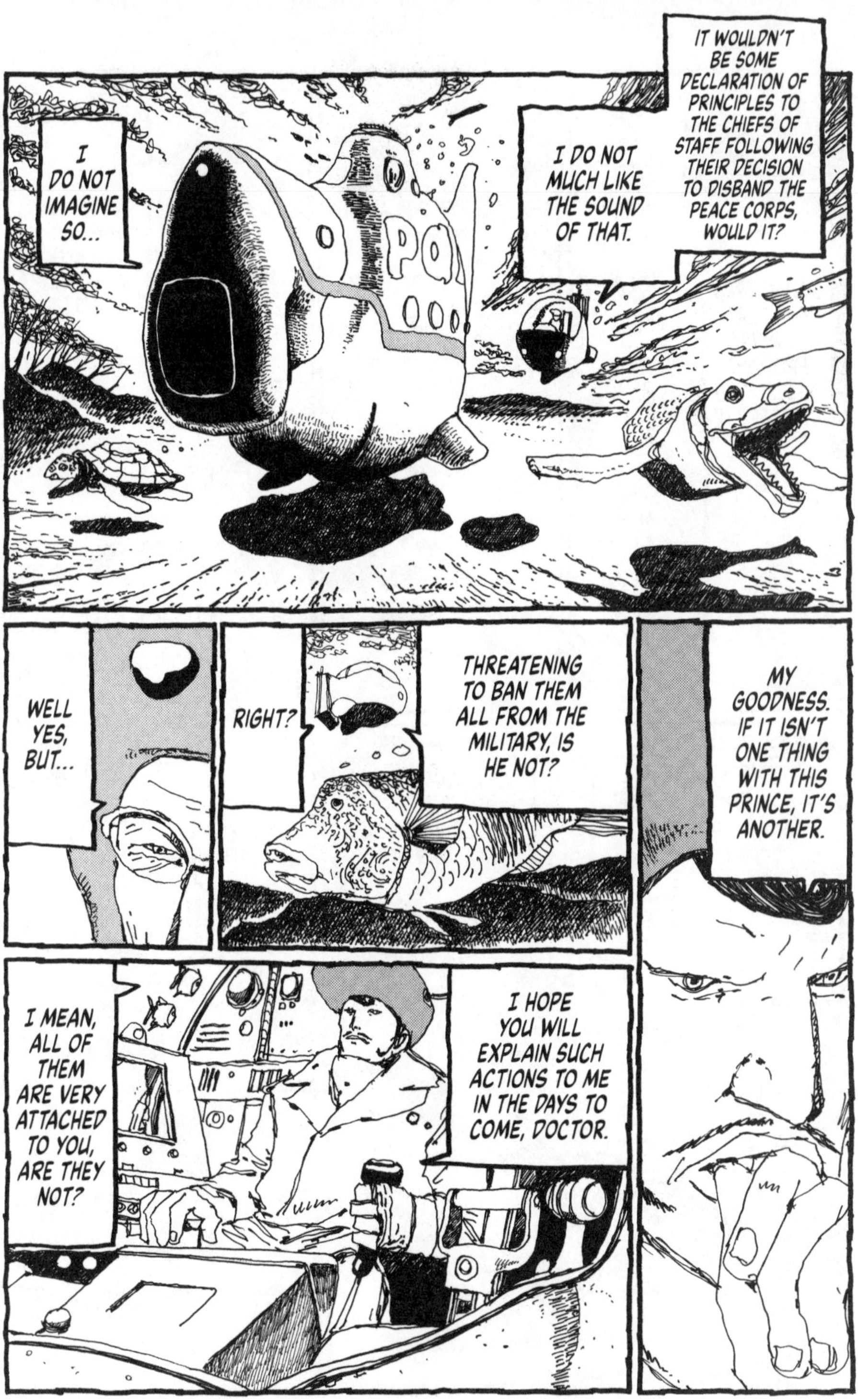
IT WOULDN'T BE SOME DECLARATION OF PRINCIPLES TO THE CHIEFS OF STAFF FOLLOWING THEIR DECISION TO DISBAND THE PEACE CORPS, WOULD IT?
I DO NOT MUCH LIKE THE SOUND OF THAT.
I DO NOT IMAGINE SO...
MY GOODNESS. IF IT ISN'T ONE THING WITH THIS PRINCE, IT'S ANOTHER.
THREATENING TO BAN THEM ALL FROM THE MILITARY, IS HE NOT?
RIGHT?
WELL YES, BUT...
I HOPE YOU WILL EXPLAIN SUCH ACTIONS TO ME IN THE DAYS TO COME, DOCTOR.
I MEAN, ALL OF THEM ARE VERY ATTACHED TO YOU, ARE THEY NOT?

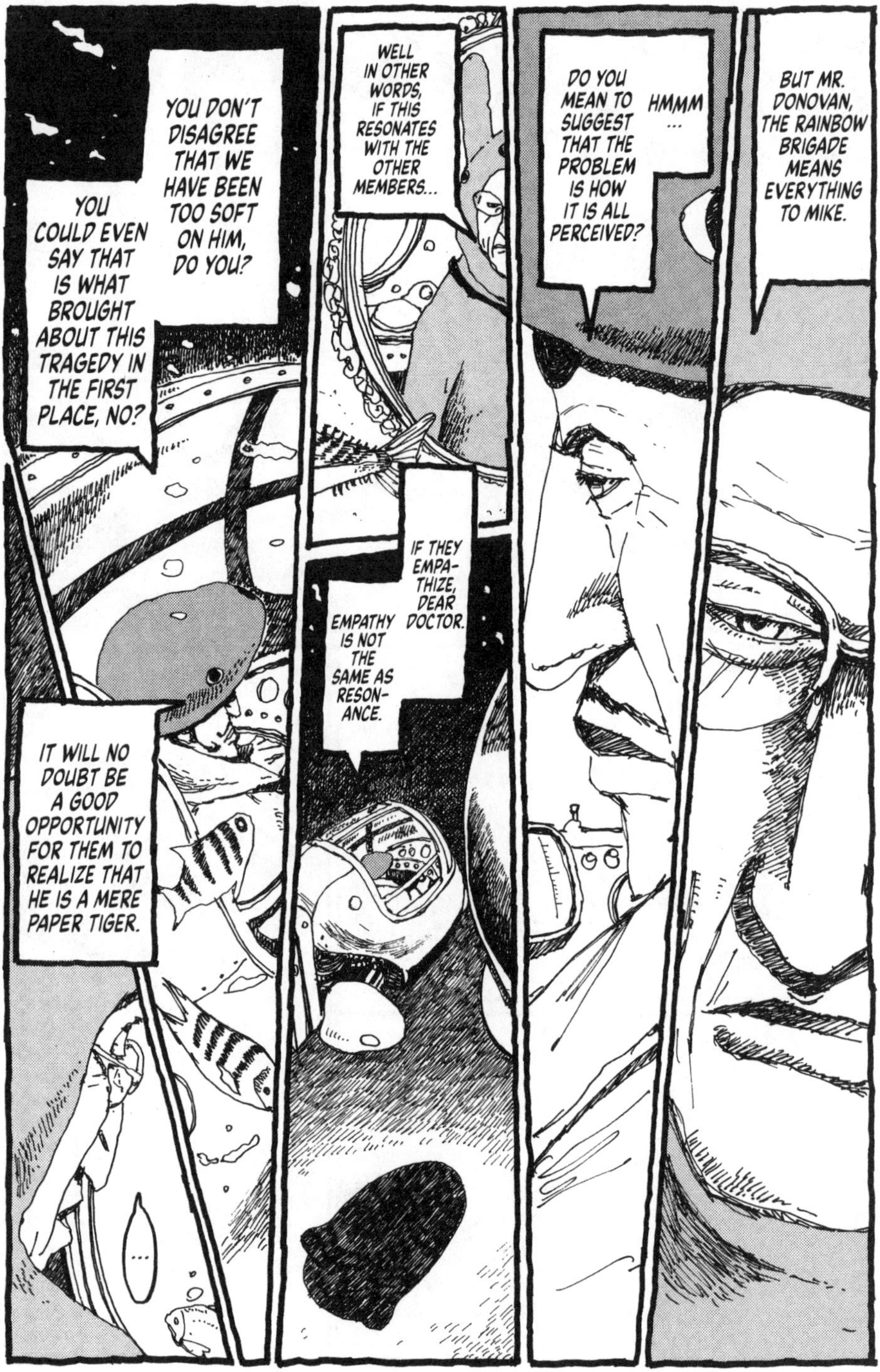
BUT MR. DONOVAN, THE RAINBOW BRIGADE MEANS EVERYTHING TO MIKE.
HMMM ...
DO YOU MEAN TO SUGGEST THAT THE PROBLEM IS HOW IT IS ALL PERCEIVED?
WELL IN OTHER WORDS, IF THIS RESONATES WITH THE OTHER MEMBERS...
IF THEY EMPATHIZE, DEAR DOCTOR.
EMPATHY IS NOT THE SAME AS RESONANCE.
YOU DON'T DISAGREE THAT WE HAVE BEEN TOO SOFT ON HIM, DO YOU?
YOU COULD EVEN SAY THAT IS WHAT BROUGHT ABOUT THIS TRAGEDY IN THE FIRST PLACE, NO?
IT WILL NO DOUBT BE A GOOD OPPORTUNITY FOR THEM TO REALIZE THAT HE IS A MERE PAPER TIGER.
...

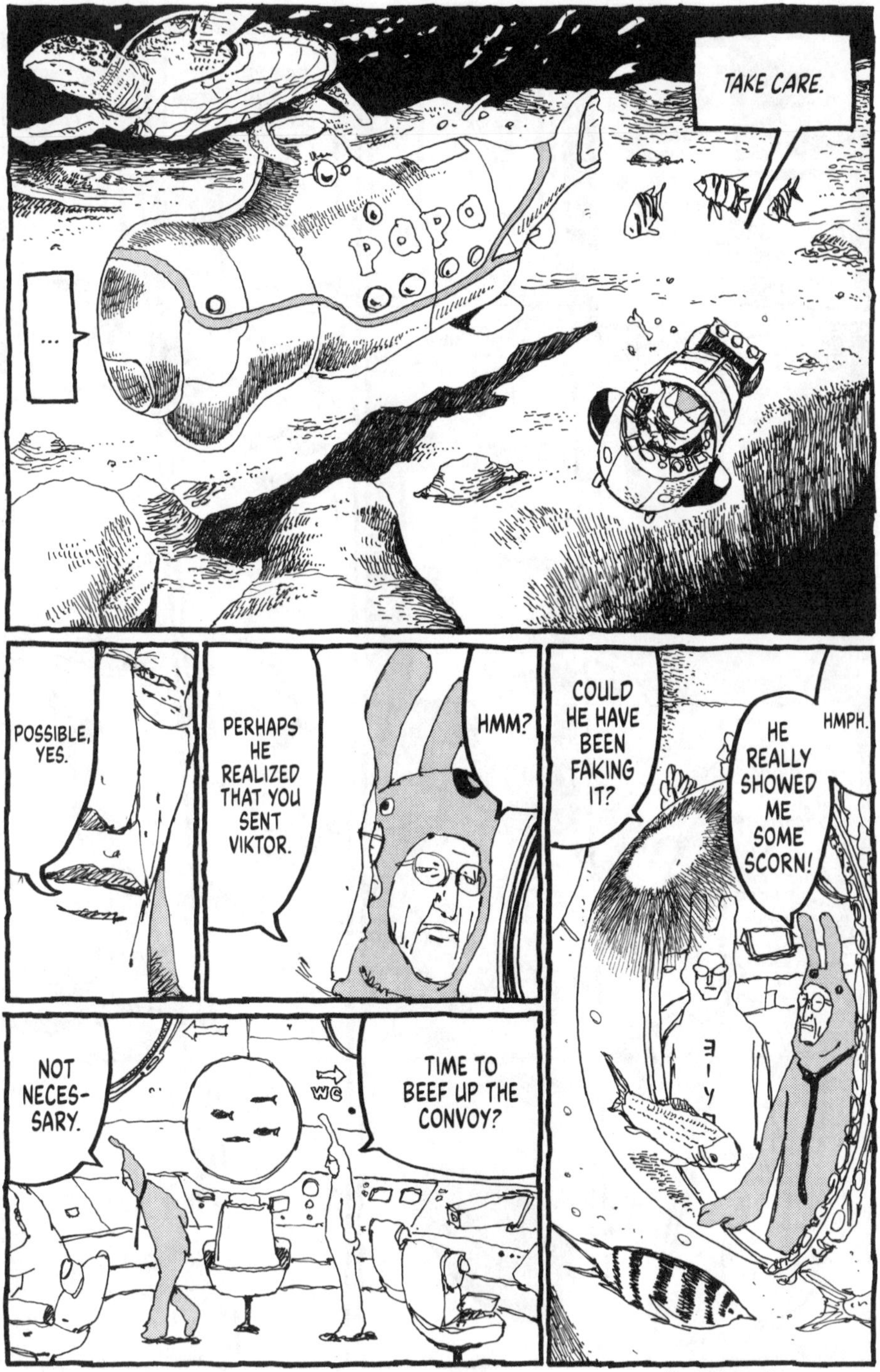
TAKE CARE.
...
HMPH.
HE REALLY SHOWED ME SOME SCORN!
COULD HE HAVE BEEN FAKING IT?
ヨーソロ
HMM?
PERHAPS HE REALIZED THAT YOU SENT VIKTOR.
POSSIBLE, YES.
TIME TO BEEF UP THE CONVOY?
WC
NOT NECES-SARY.

*Steady As She Goes

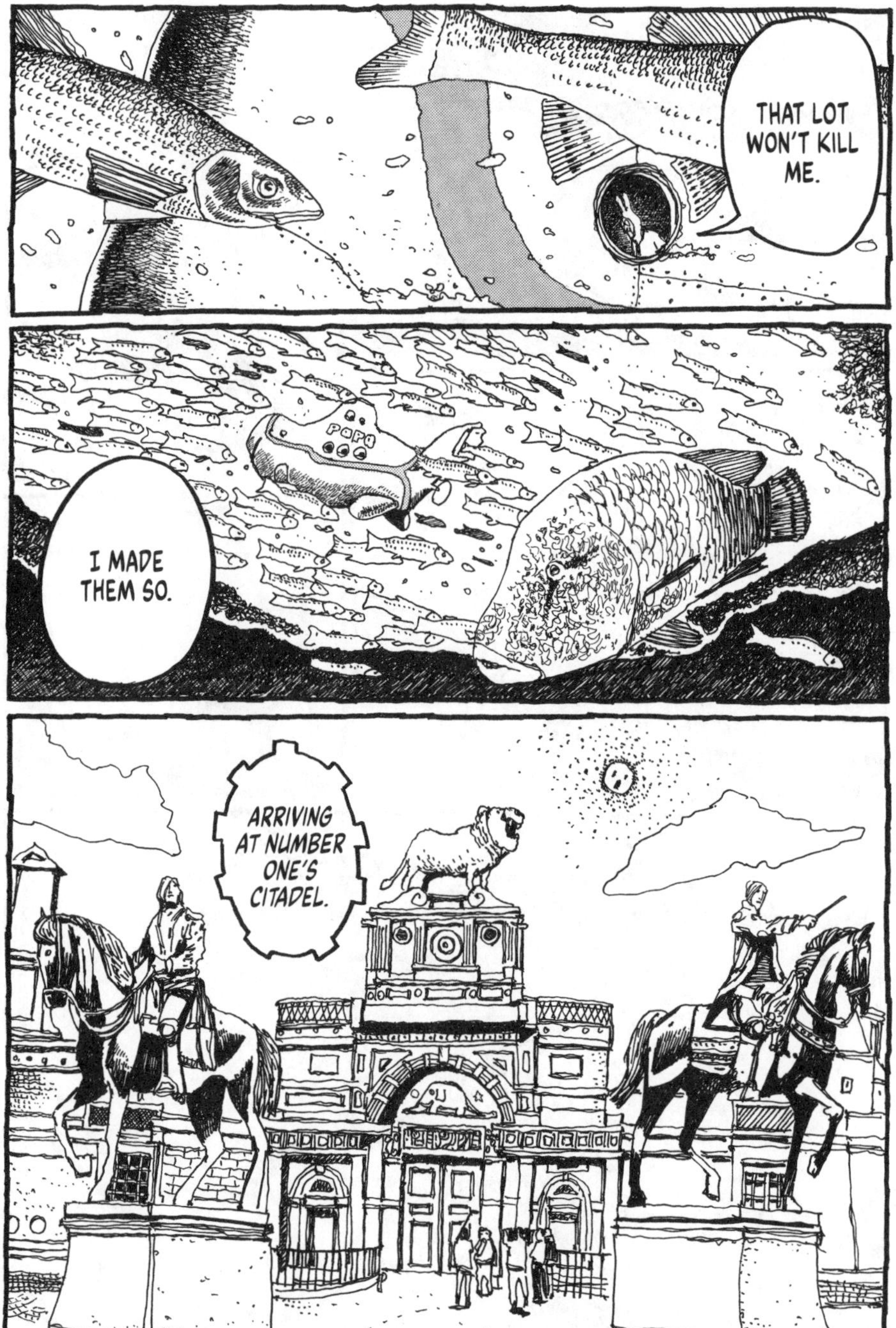
THAT LOT WON'T KILL ME.
I MADE THEM SO.
POPO
ARRIVING AT NUMBER ONE'S CITADEL.

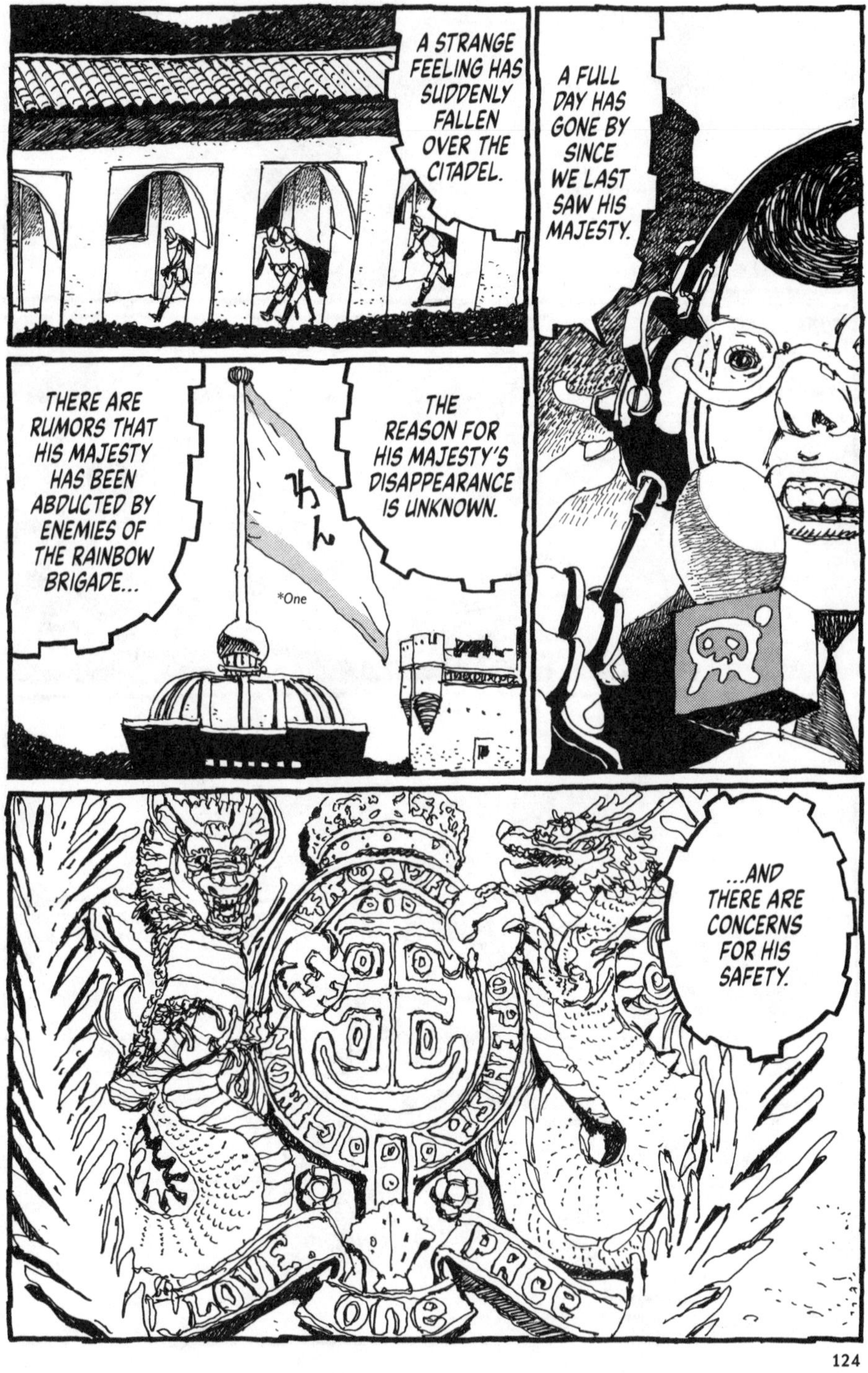
A FULL DAY HAS GONE BY SINCE WE LAST SAW HIS MAJESTY.
A STRANGE FEELING HAS SUDDENLY FALLEN OVER THE CITADEL.
THE REASON FOR HIS MAJESTY'S DISAPPEARANCE IS UNKNOWN.
わん
*One
THERE ARE RUMORS THAT HIS MAJESTY HAS BEEN ABDUCTED BY ENEMIES OF THE RAINBOW BRIGADE...
...AND THERE ARE CONCERNS FOR HIS SAFETY.
LOVE
one
PACE

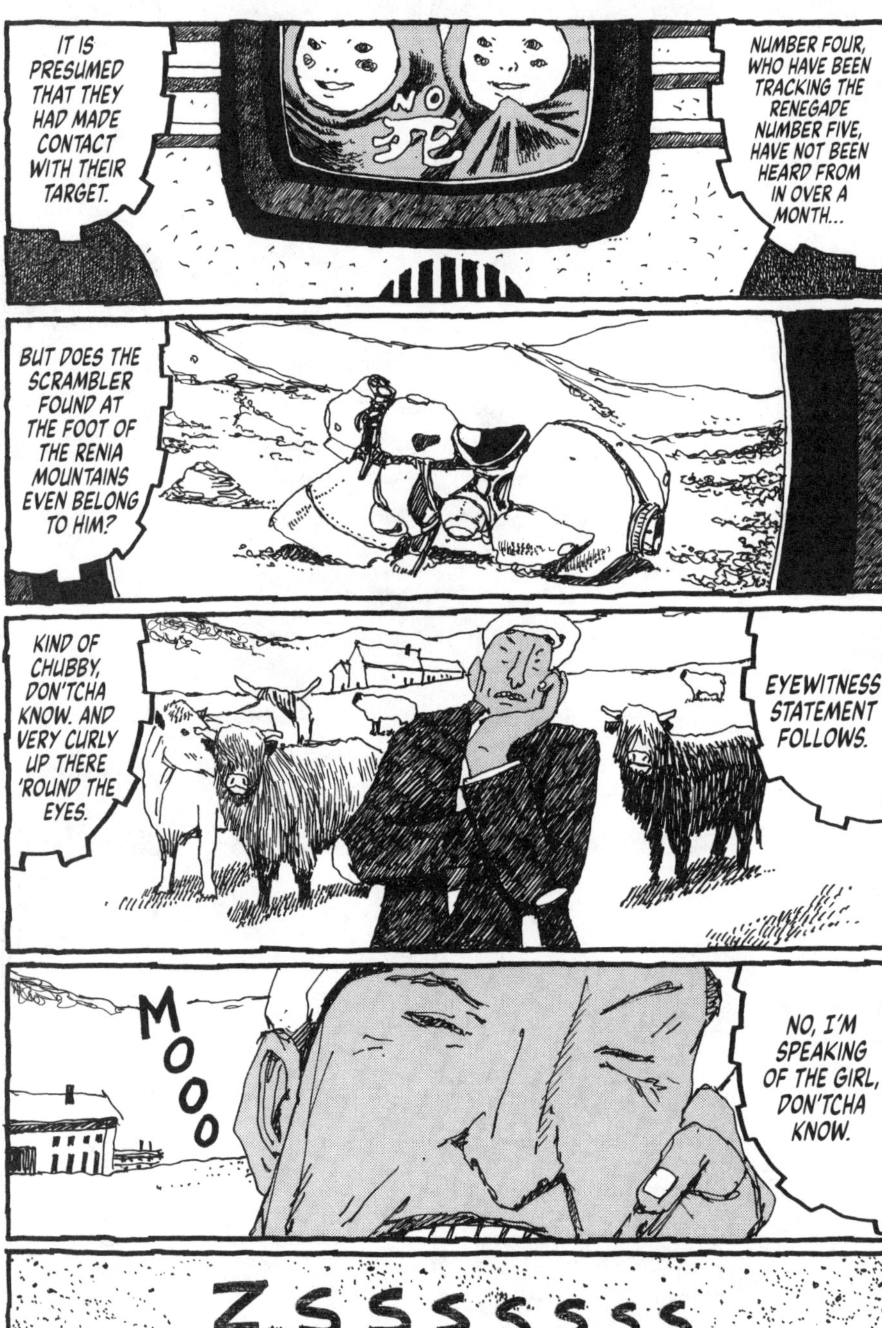
NUMBER FOUR, WHO HAVE BEEN TRACKING THE RENEGADE NUMBER FIVE, HAVE NOT BEEN HEARD FROM IN OVER A MONTH...
NO
IT IS PRESUMED THAT THEY HAD MADE CONTACT WITH THEIR TARGET.
BUT DOES THE SCRAMBLER FOUND AT THE FOOT OF THE RENIA MOUNTAINS EVEN BELONG TO HIM?
EYEWITNESS STATEMENT FOLLOWS.
KIND OF CHUBBY, DON'TCHA KNOW. AND VERY CURLY UP THERE 'ROUND THE EYES.
NO, I'M SPEAKING OF THE GIRL, DON'TCHA KNOW.
MOOO
ZSSSSSSS

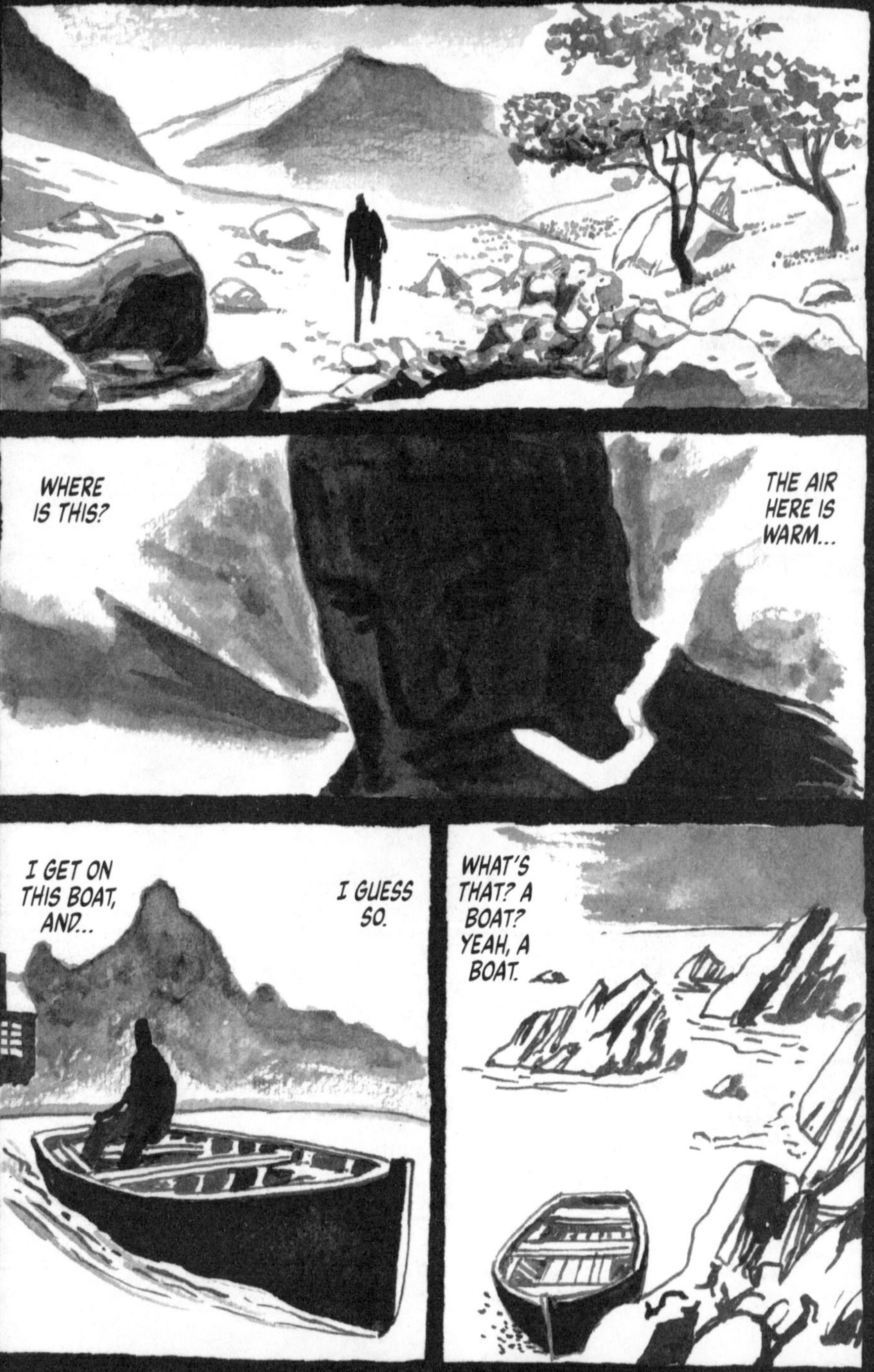
THE AIR HERE IS WARM...
WHERE IS THIS?
WHAT'S THAT? A BOAT? YEAH, A BOAT.
I GUESS SO.
I GET ON THIS BOAT, AND...

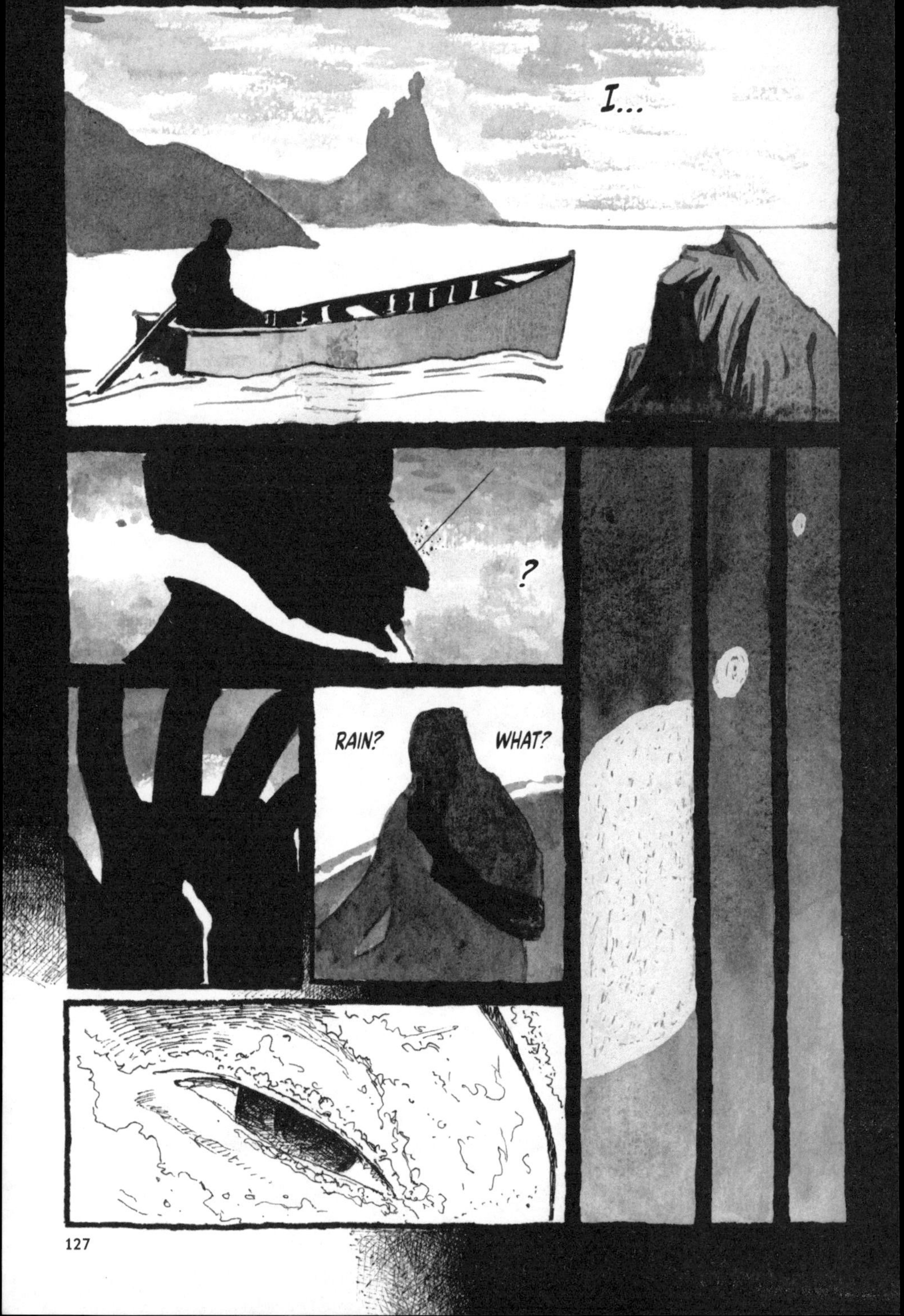
I...
?
WHAT?
RAIN?

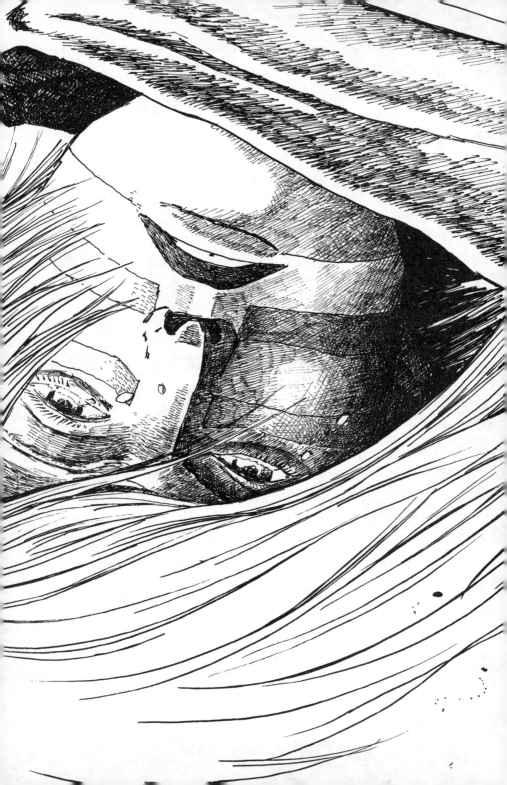

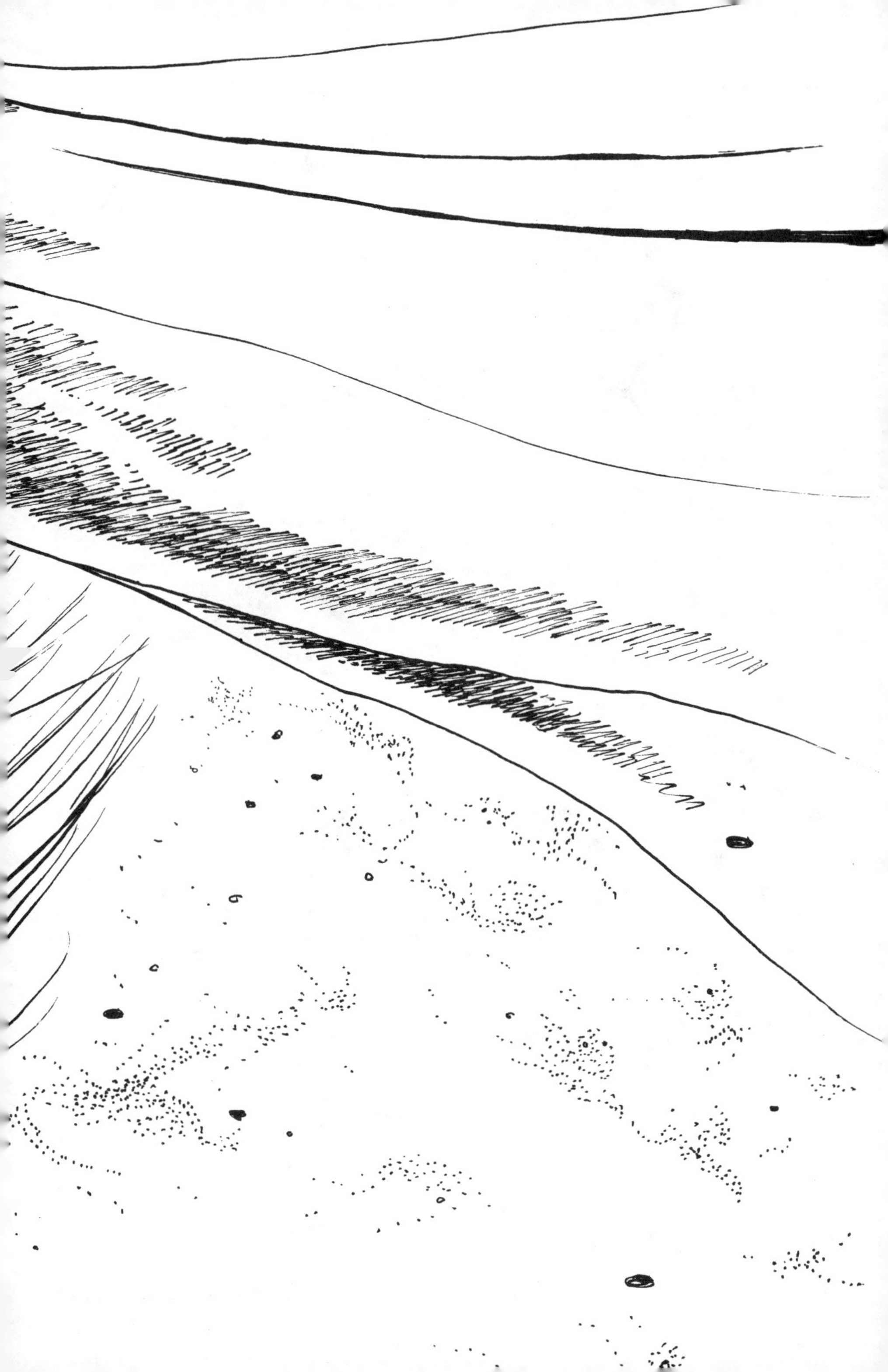

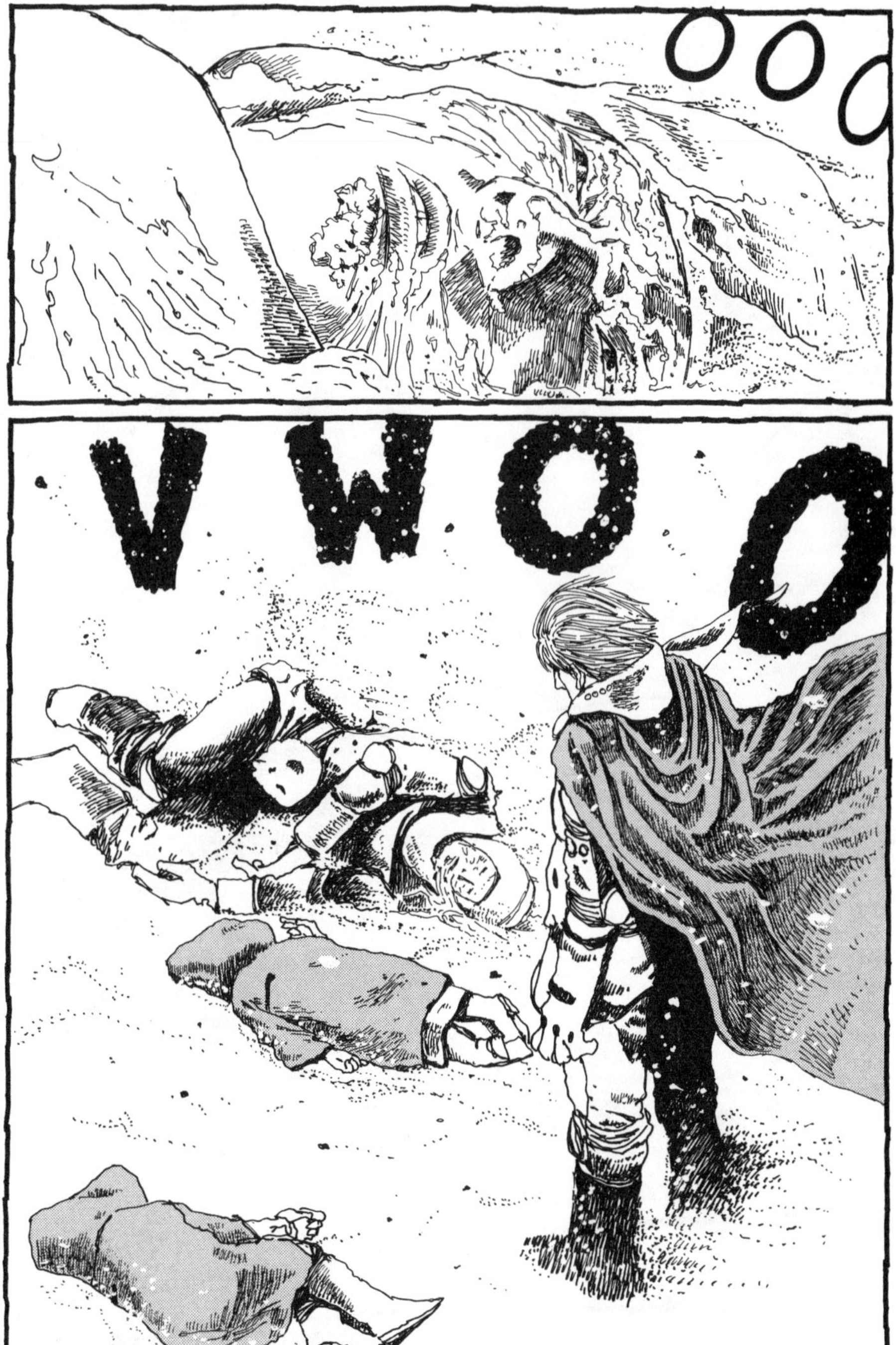
VWOOOOO

CHAPTER 13 //

Fifteen Years Ago

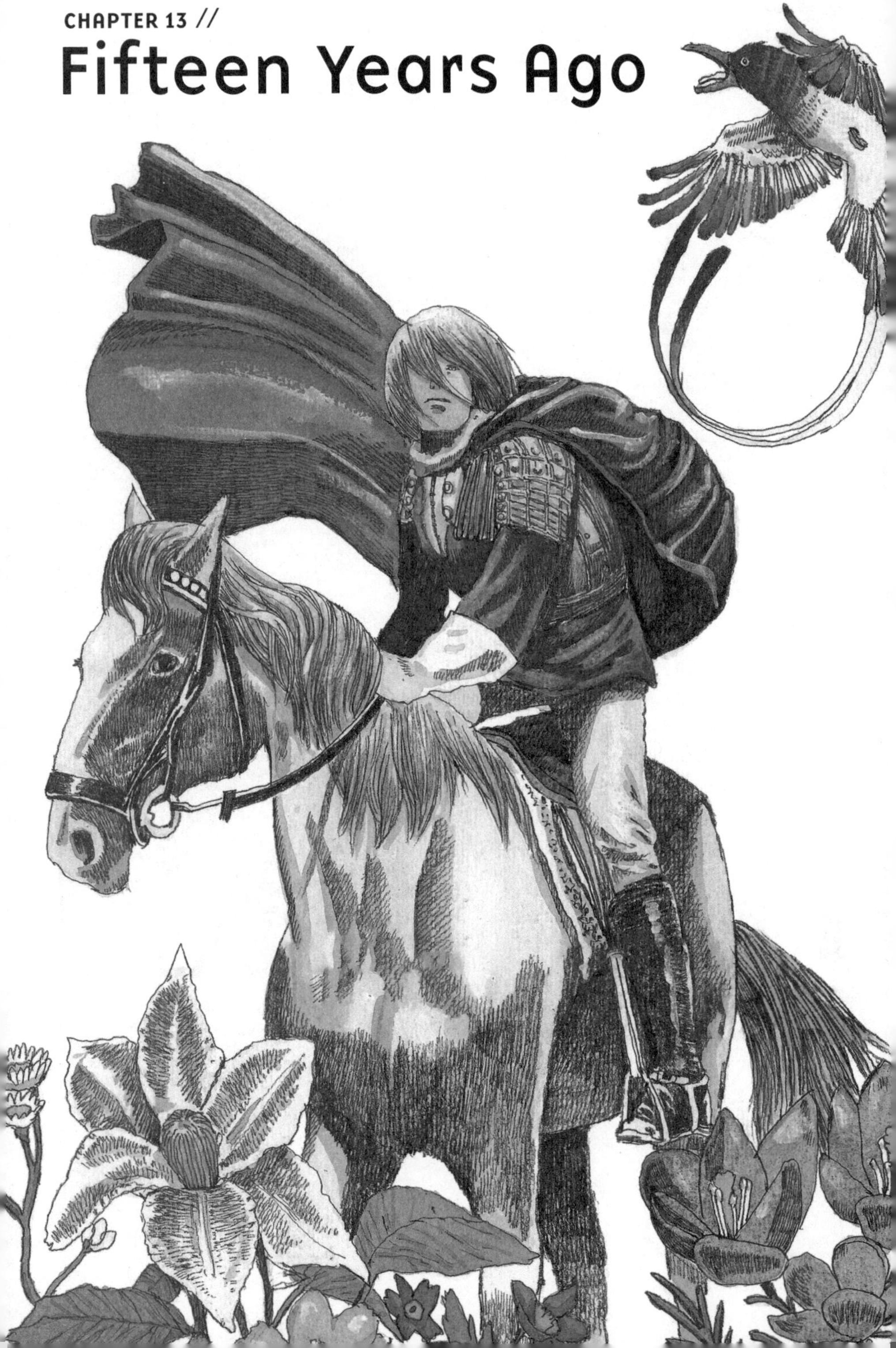

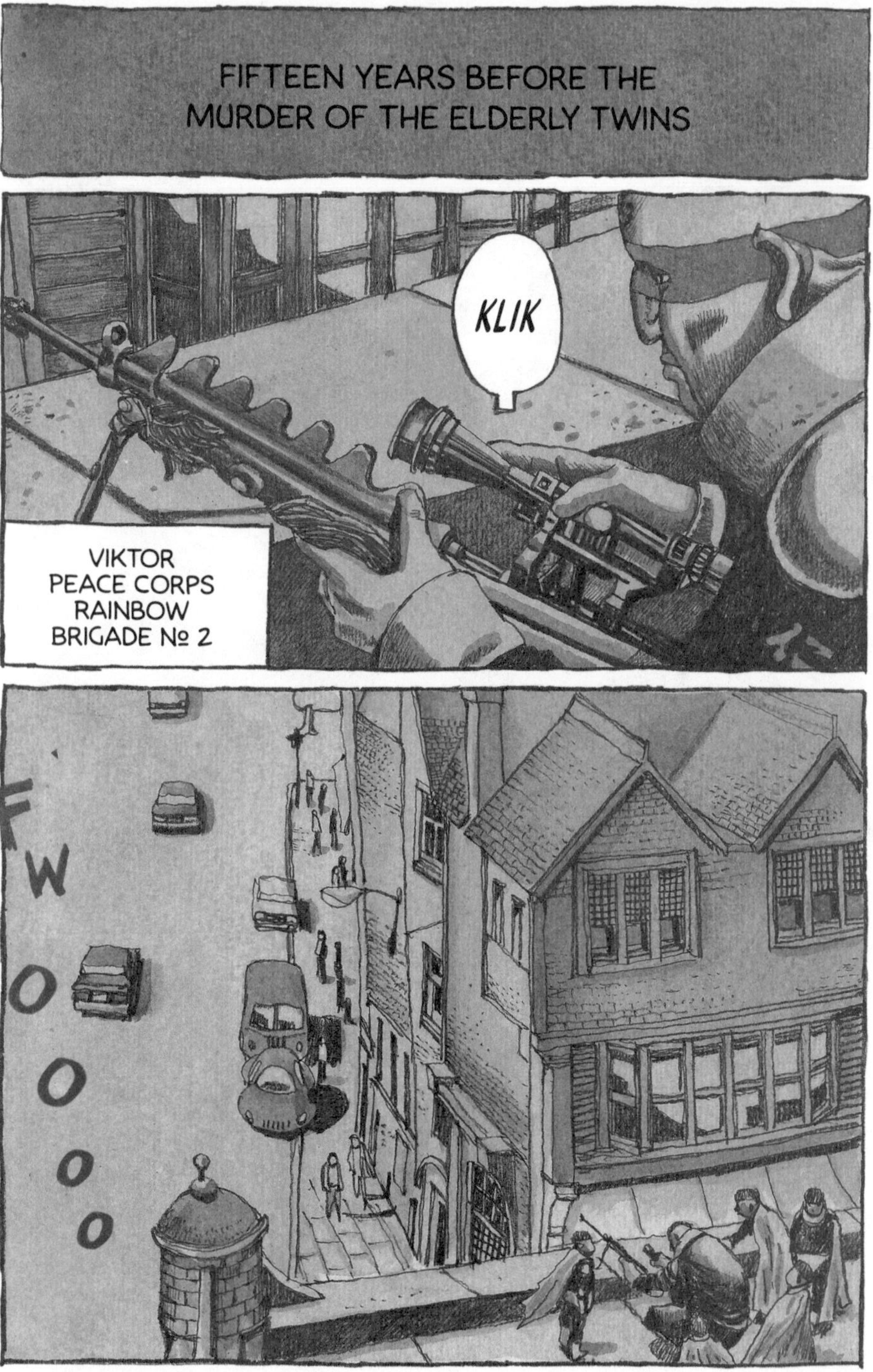
FIFTEEN YEARS BEFORE THE
MURDER OF THE ELDERLY TWINS
KLIK
VIKTOR
PEACE CORPS
RAINBOW
BRIGADE № 2
FWOOOOO

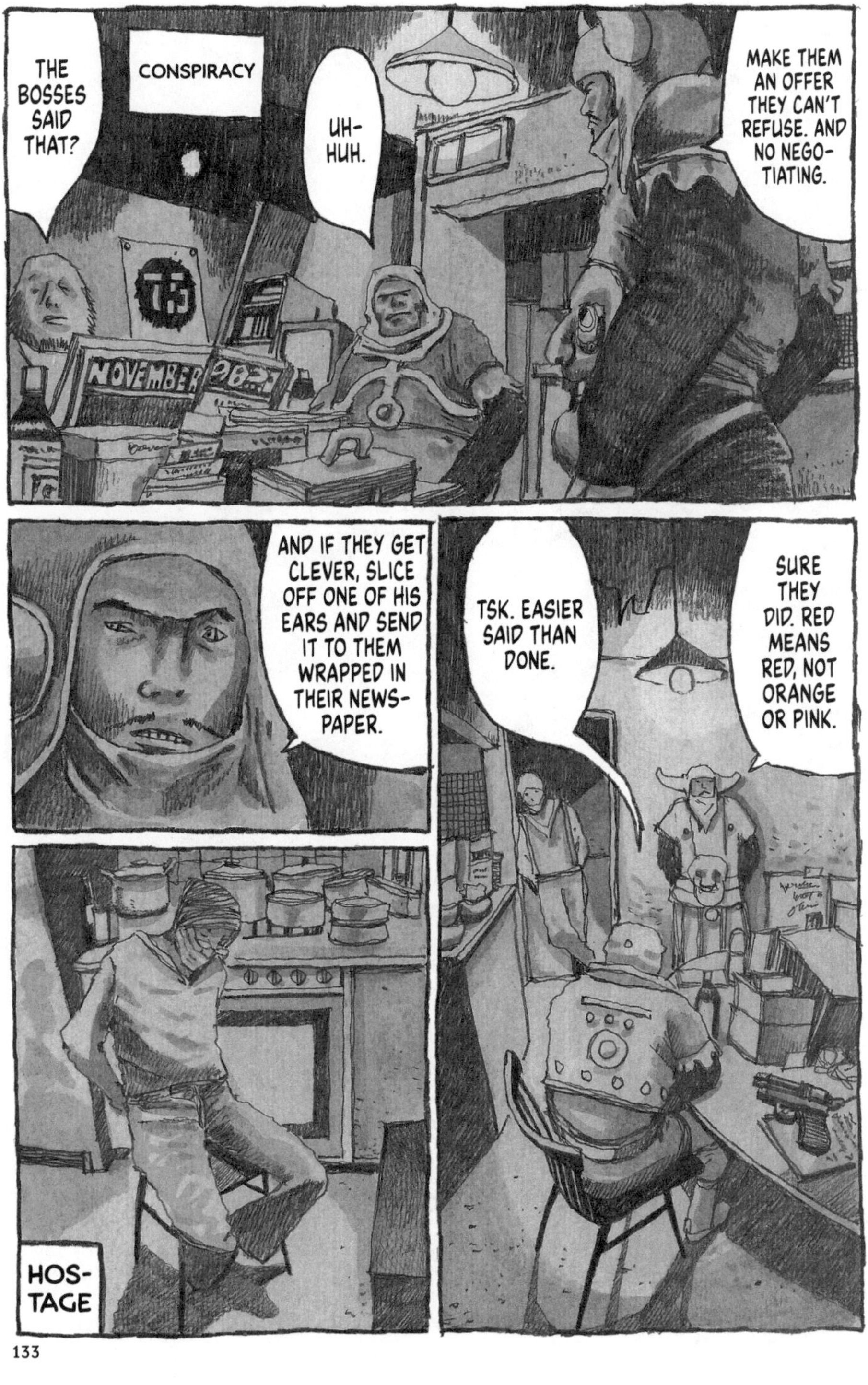
MAKE THEM AN OFFER THEY CAN'T REFUSE. AND NO NEGO-TIATING.
UH-HUH.
CONSPIRACY
THE BOSSES SAID THAT?
NOVEMBER
SURE THEY DID. RED MEANS RED, NOT ORANGE OR PINK.
TSK. EASIER SAID THAN DONE.
AND IF THEY GET CLEVER, SLICE OFF ONE OF HIS EARS AND SEND IT TO THEM WRAPPED IN THEIR NEWS-PAPER.
HOS-TAGE

YOU'RE MAKING NOISE LIKE A HERD OF ELE-PHANTS.
LT. COLONEL YURI (LATER KNOWN AS №5) PEACE CORPS 2ND DIVISION
THEY CAN HEAR YOU COMING FROM TWO BLOCKS AWAY.
獣
I WANNA LIVE DOWN SOUTH. GO SOUTH, BUY A HOUSE...
TOO HOT DOWN THERE...
LOOKOUTS
SMASH

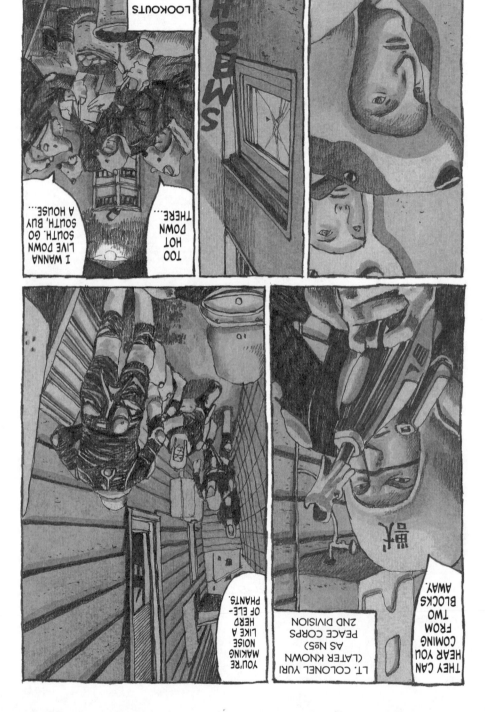

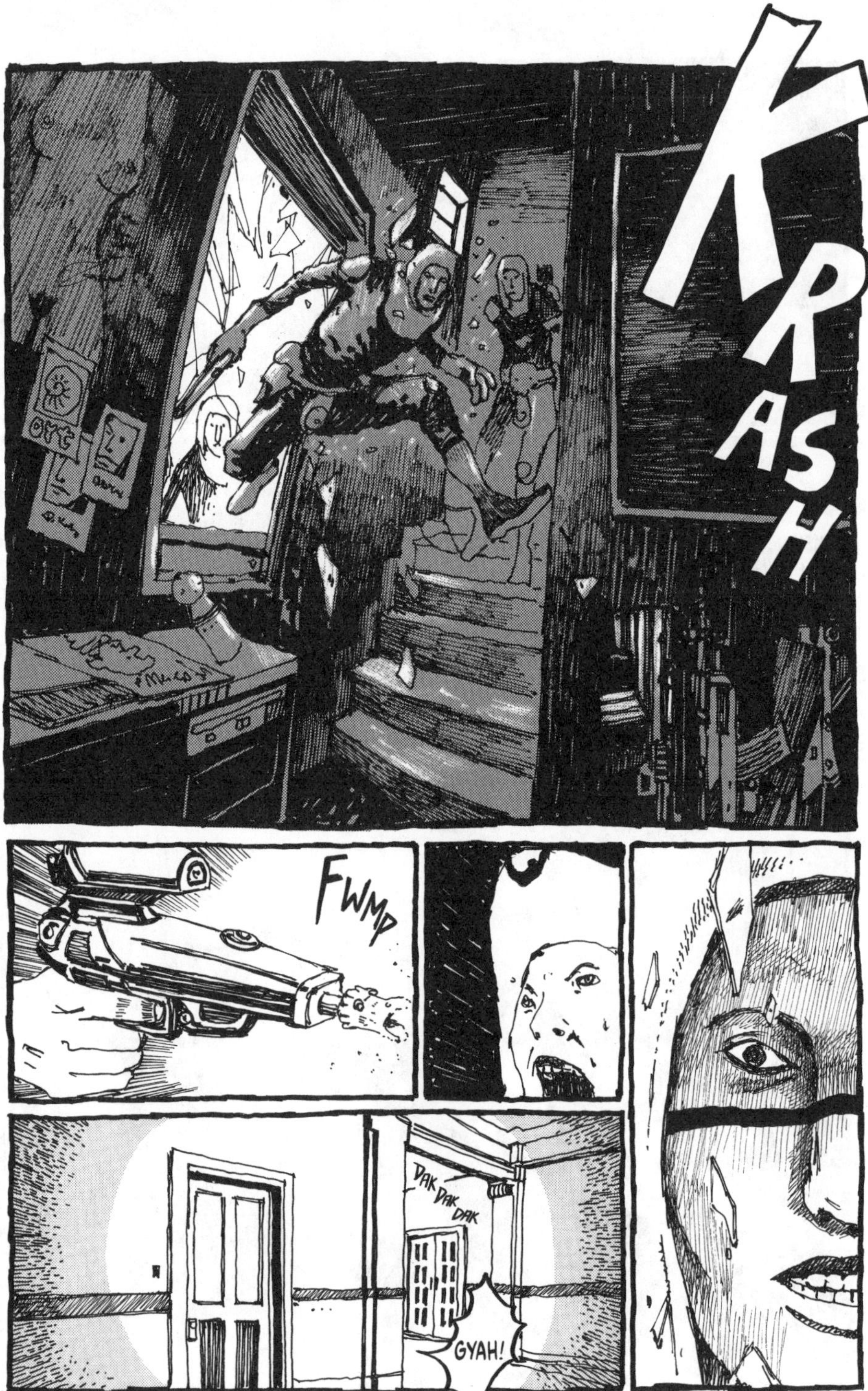
KRASH
FWMP
DAK DAK DAK
GYAH!

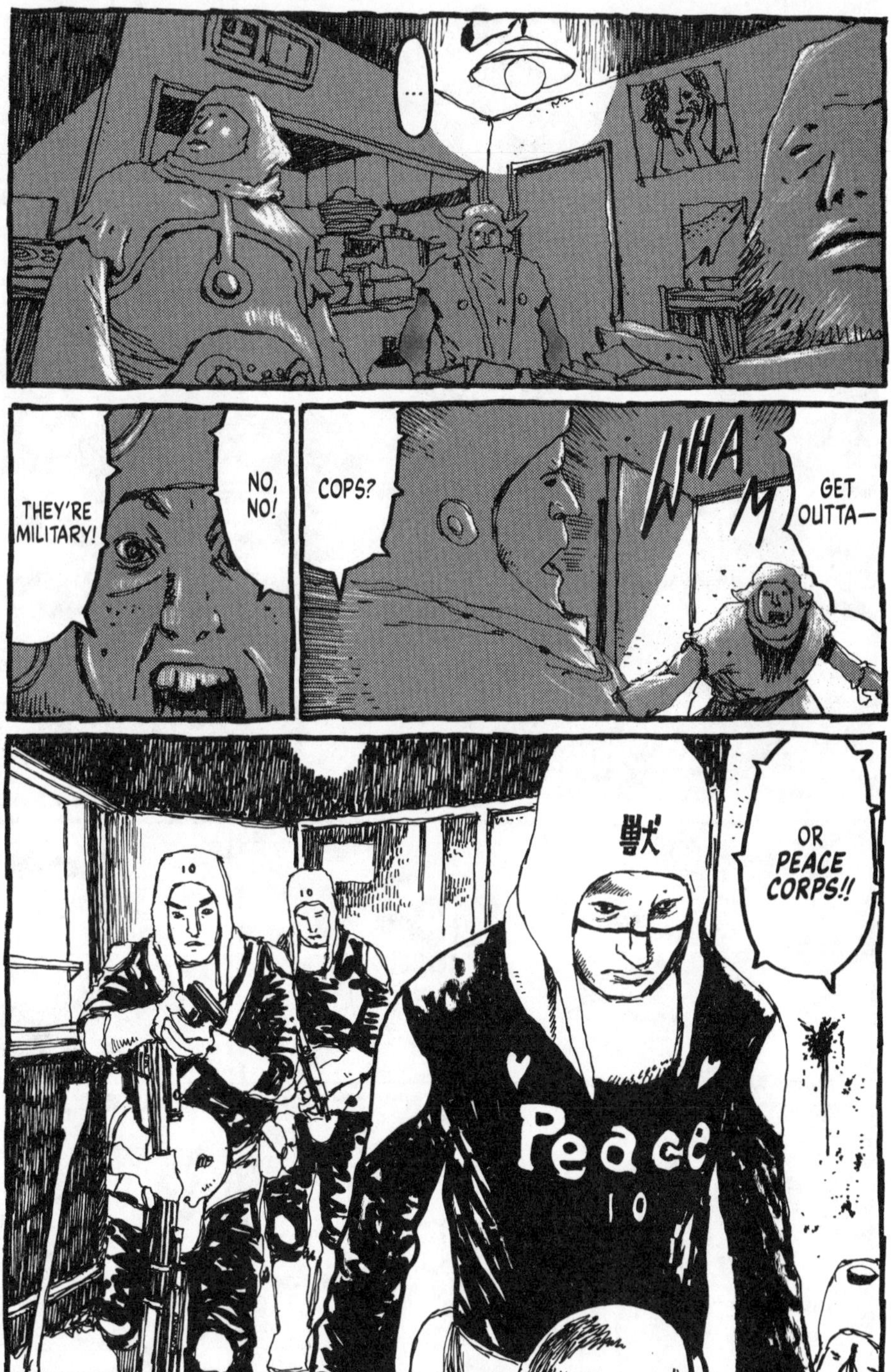
...
GET OUTTA—
WHAM
COPS?
NO, NO!
THEY'RE MILITARY!
OR PEACE CORPS!!
獣
Peace
10

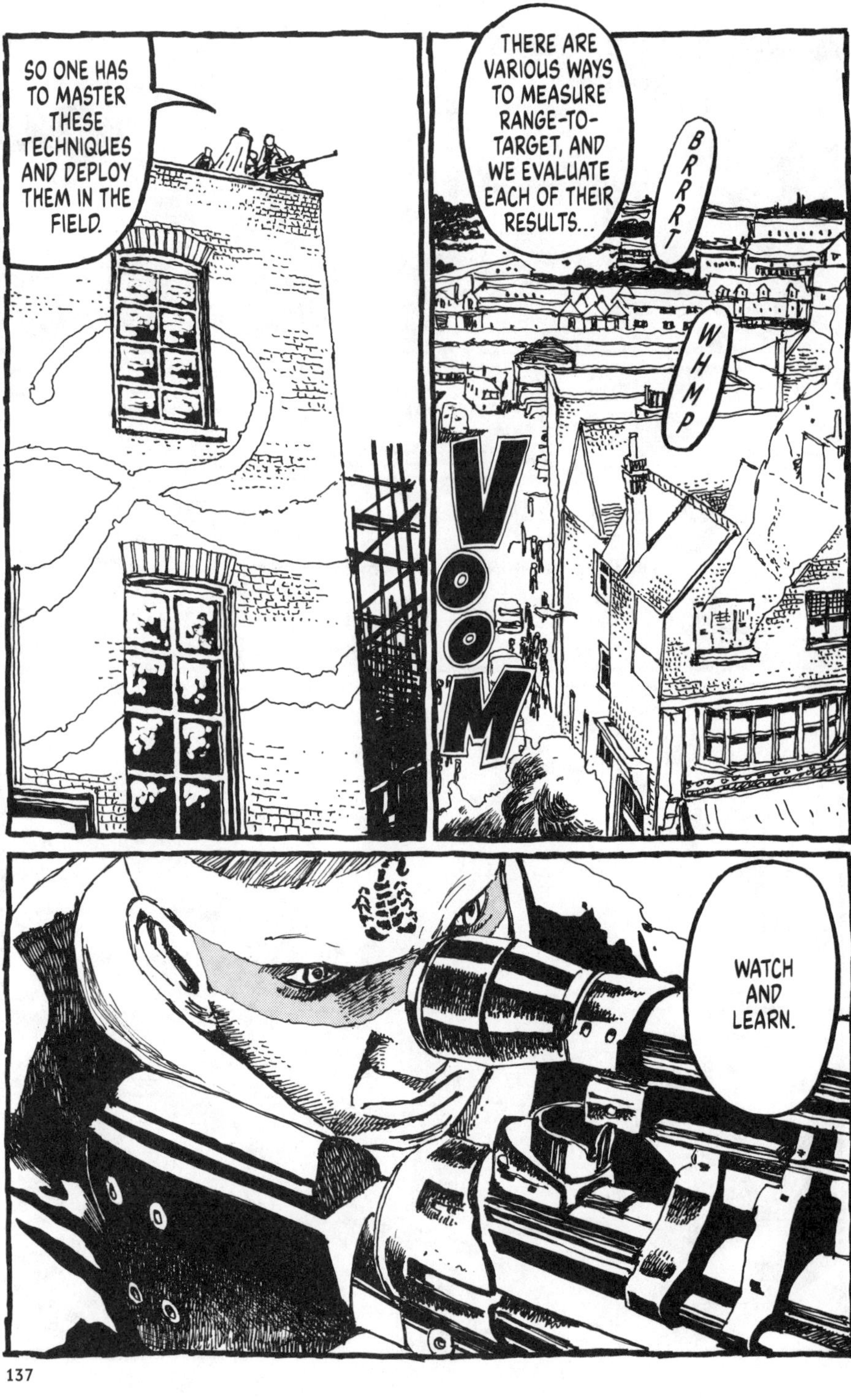
THERE ARE VARIOUS WAYS TO MEASURE RANGE-TO-TARGET, AND WE EVALUATE EACH OF THEIR RESULTS...
BRRRT
WHMP
VOOM
SO ONE HAS TO MASTER THESE TECHNIQUES AND DEPLOY THEM IN THE FIELD.
WATCH AND LEARN.

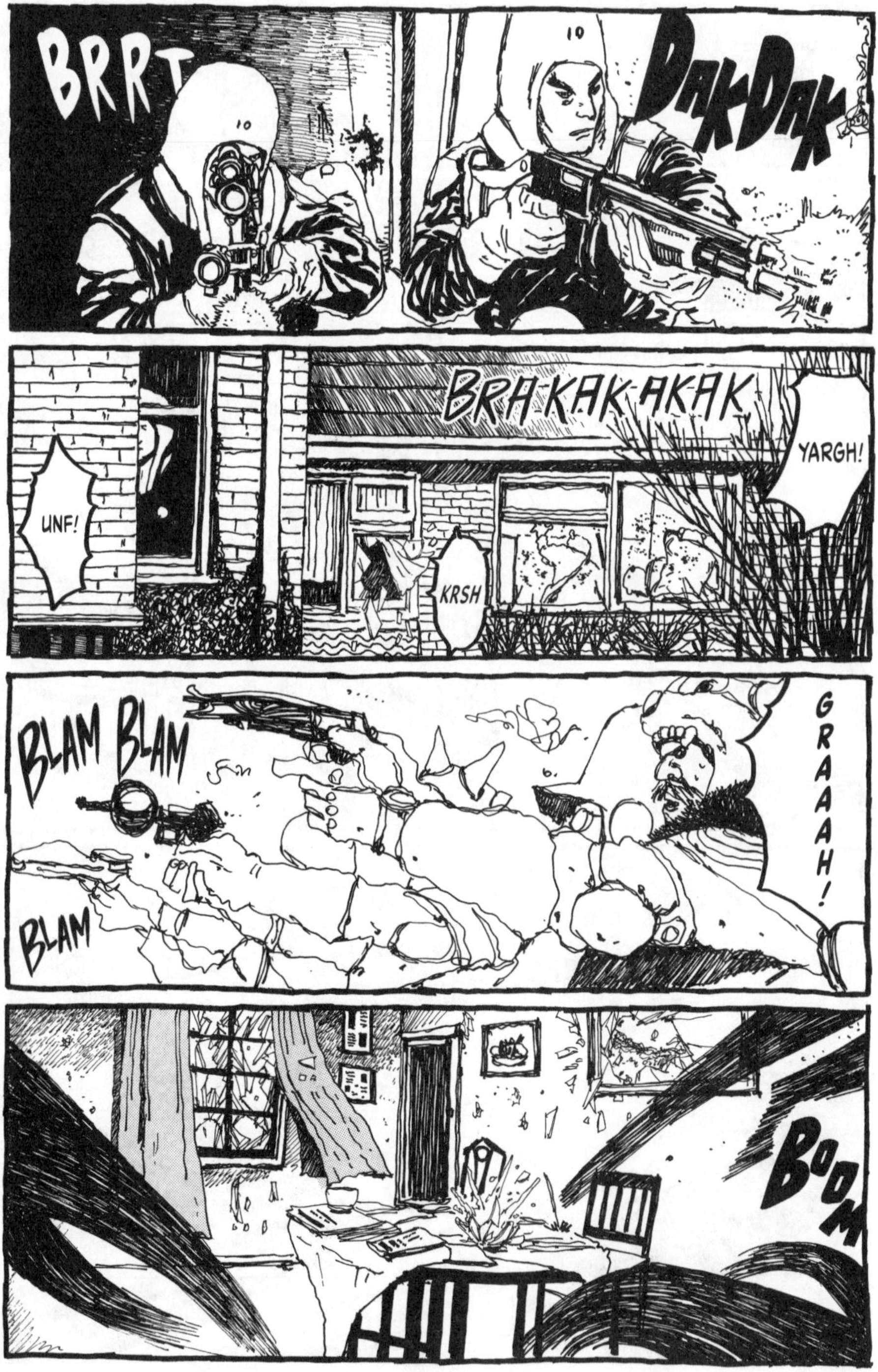
DAK DAK
BRRT
YARGH!
BRA-KAK-AKAK
KRSH
UNF!
GRAAAAH!
BLAM BLAM
BLAM
BOOM

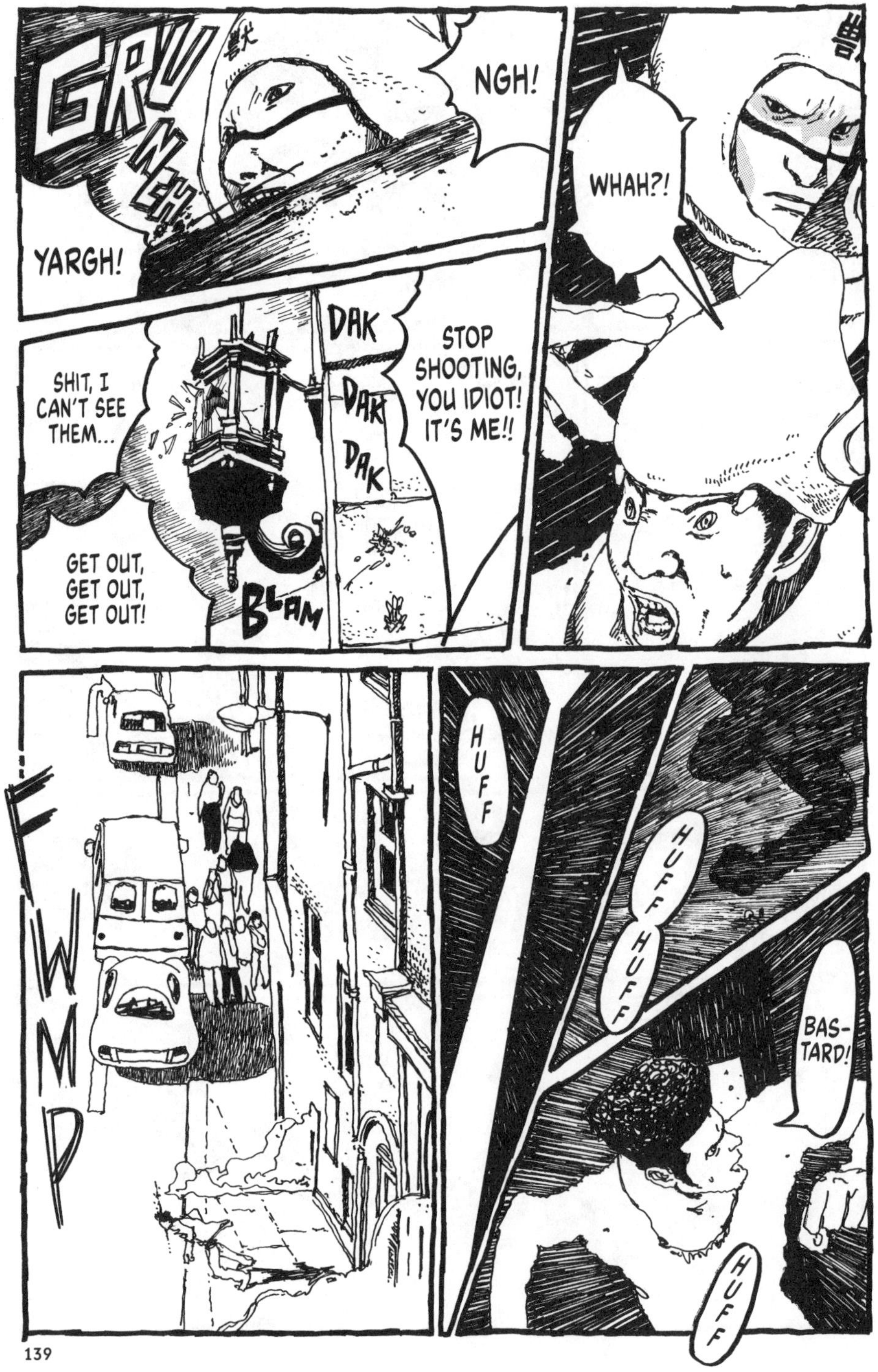
WHAH?!
NGH!
GRUNCH
YARGH!
STOP SHOOTING, YOU IDIOT! IT'S ME!!
DAK
DAK
DAK
SHIT, I CAN'T SEE THEM...
GET OUT, GET OUT, GET OUT!
BLAM
BASTARD!
HUFF
HUFF HUFF
HUFF HUFF
HUFF
FWMP

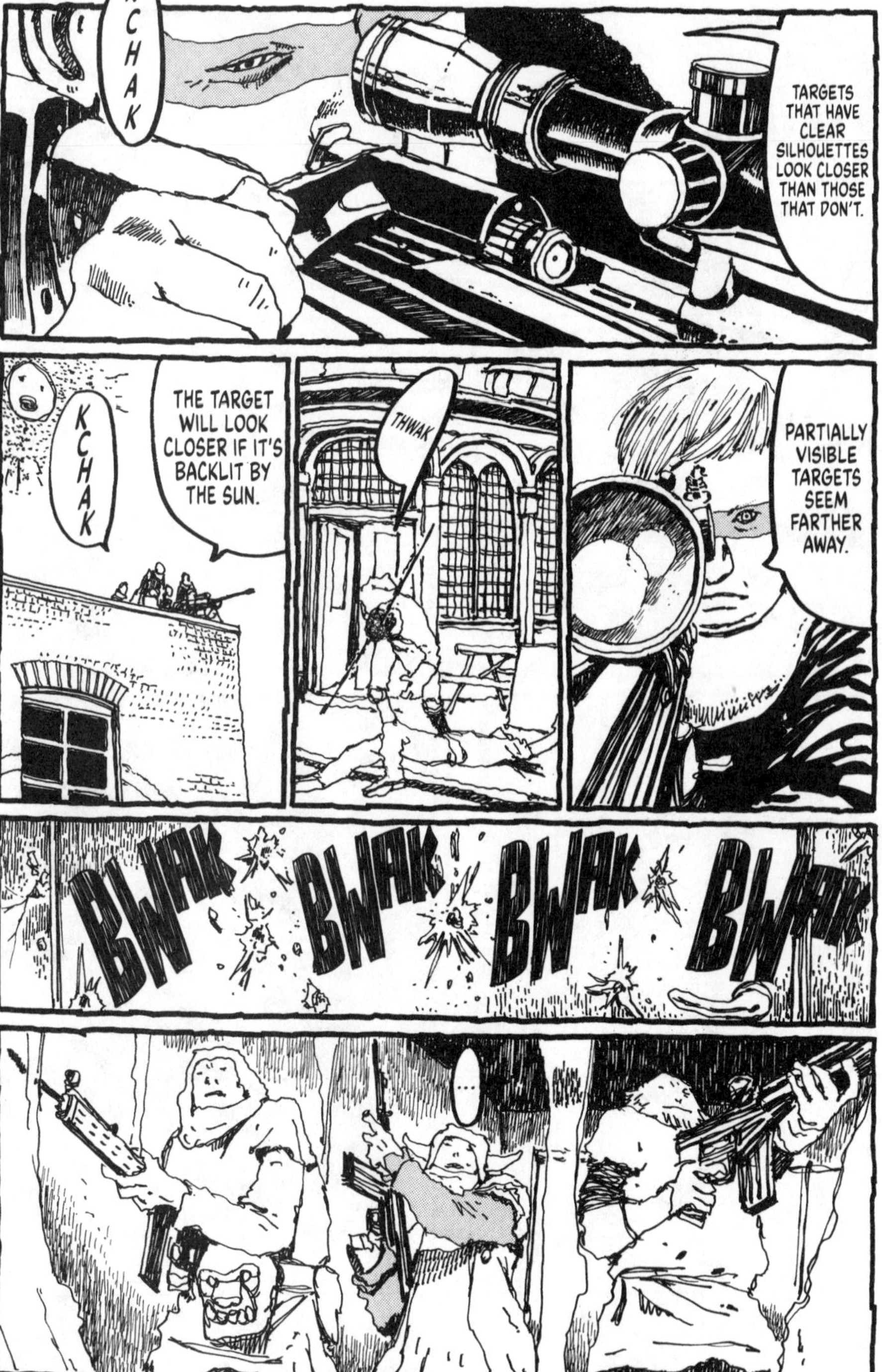
TARGETS THAT HAVE CLEAR SILHOUETTES LOOK CLOSER THAN THOSE THAT DON'T.
KCHAK
PARTIALLY VISIBLE TARGETS SEEM FARTHER AWAY.
THWAK
THE TARGET WILL LOOK CLOSER IF IT'S BACKLIT BY THE SUN.
KCHAK
BWAK
BWAK
BWAK
BWAK
...

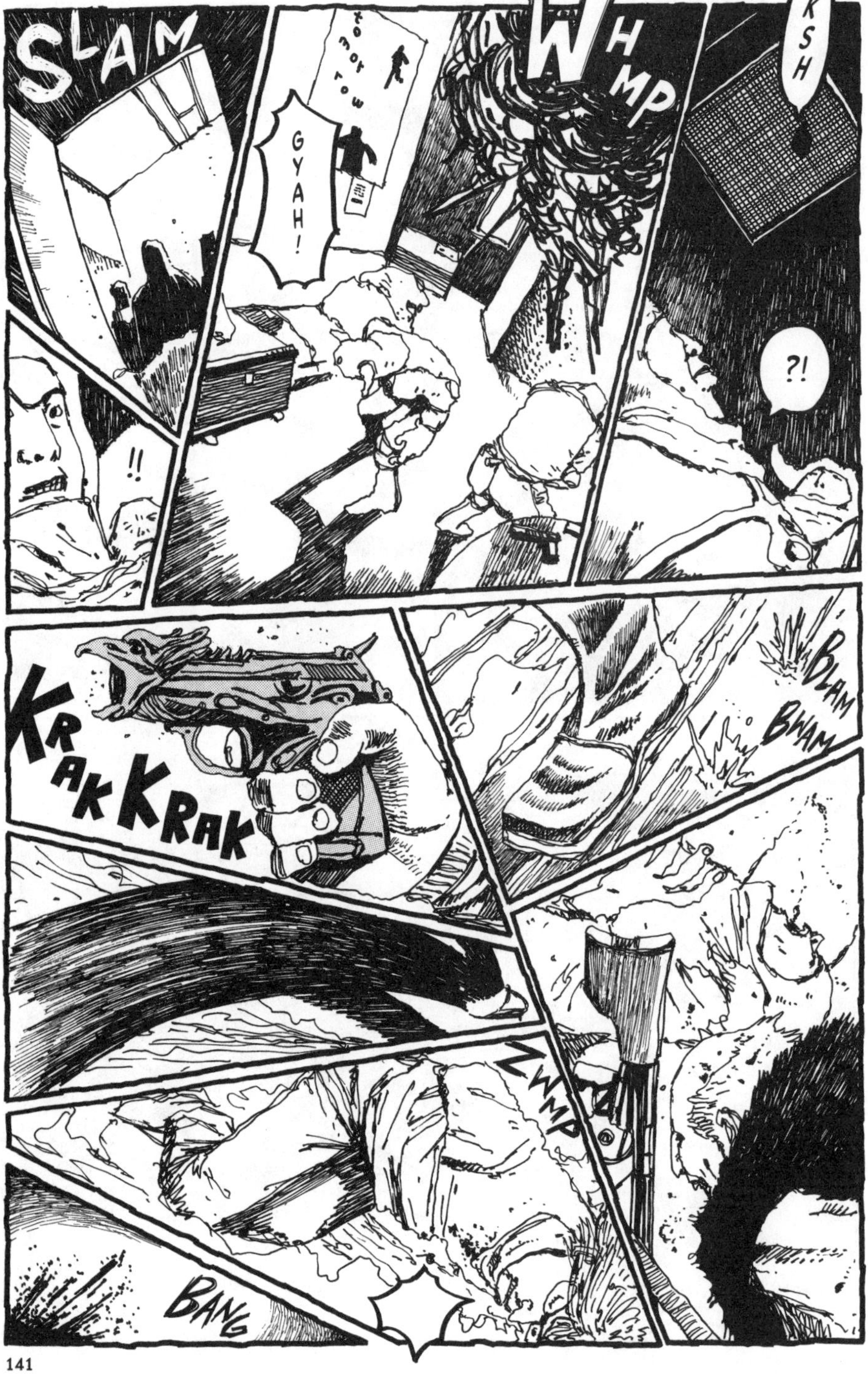
KSH
?!
WHMP
GYAH!
to mor row
SLAM
!!
BLAM
BWAM
KRAK KRAK
ZWMP
BANG

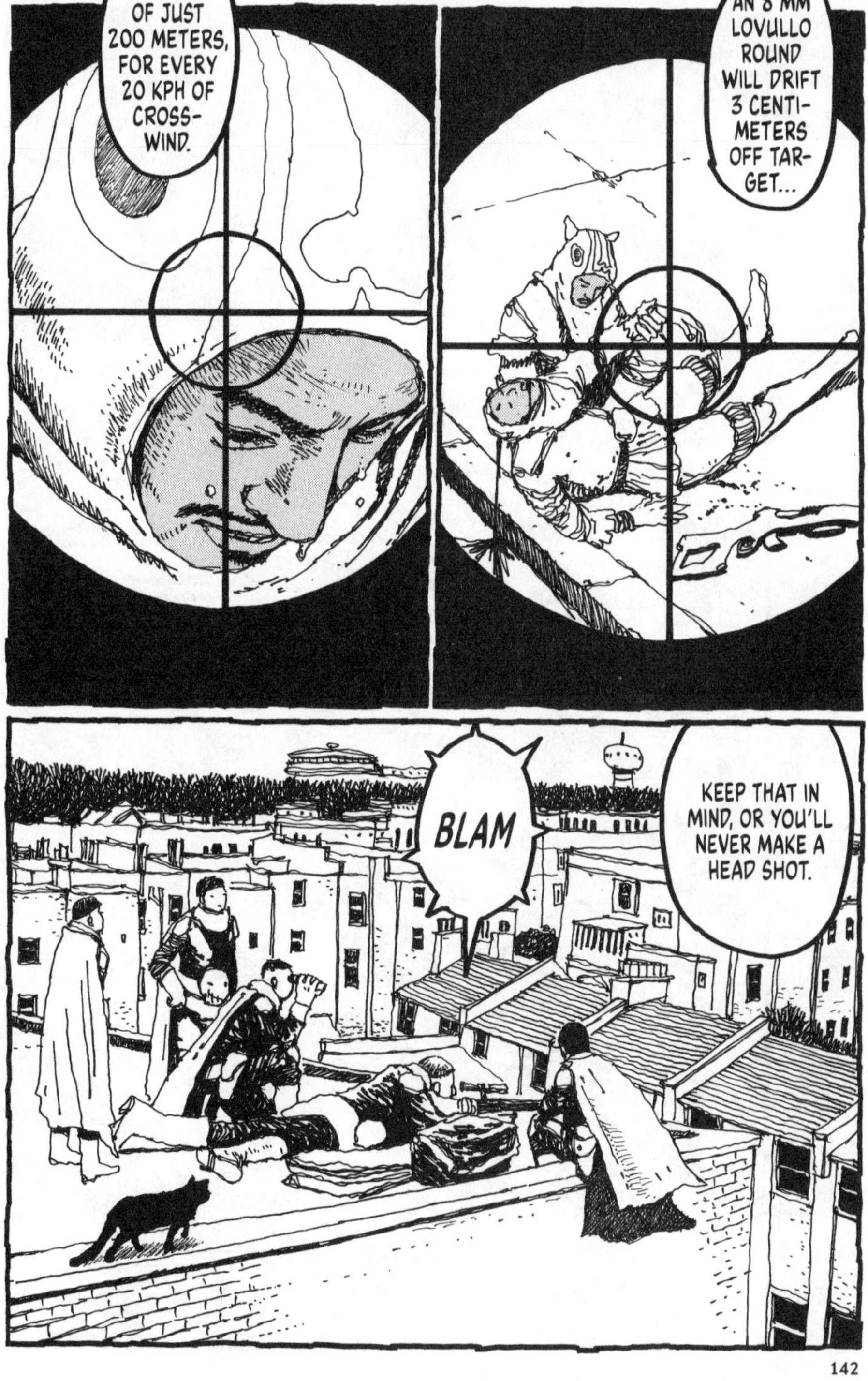
AN 8 MM LOVULLO ROUND WILL DRIFT 3 CENTIMETERS OFF TARGET...
...AT A RANGE OF JUST 200 METERS, FOR EVERY 20 KPH OF CROSSWIND.
KEEP THAT IN MIND, OR YOU'LL NEVER MAKE A HEAD SHOT.
BLAM

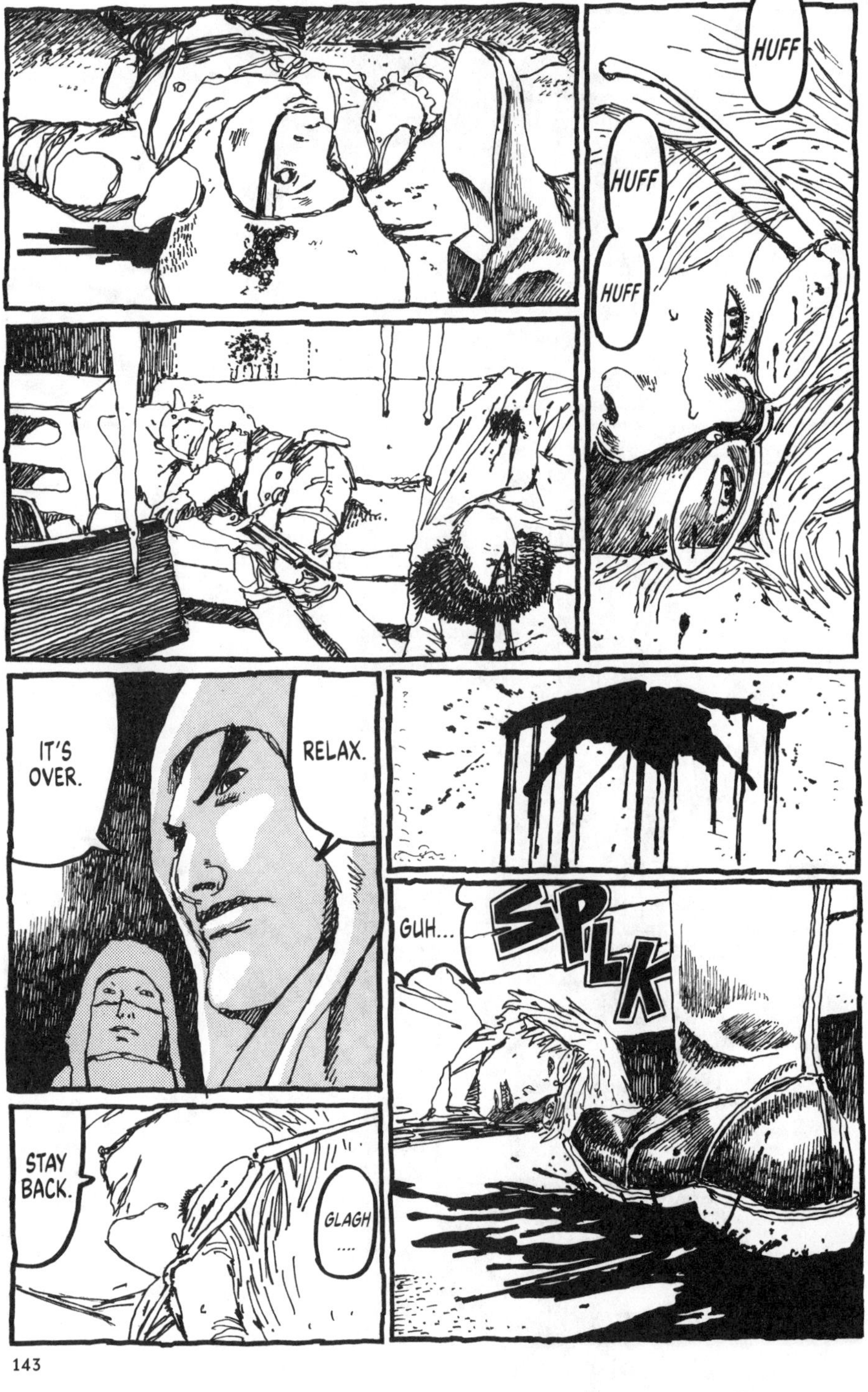
HUFF
HUFF
HUFF
SPLK
GUH...
RELAX.
IT'S OVER.
GLAGH ....
STAY BACK.

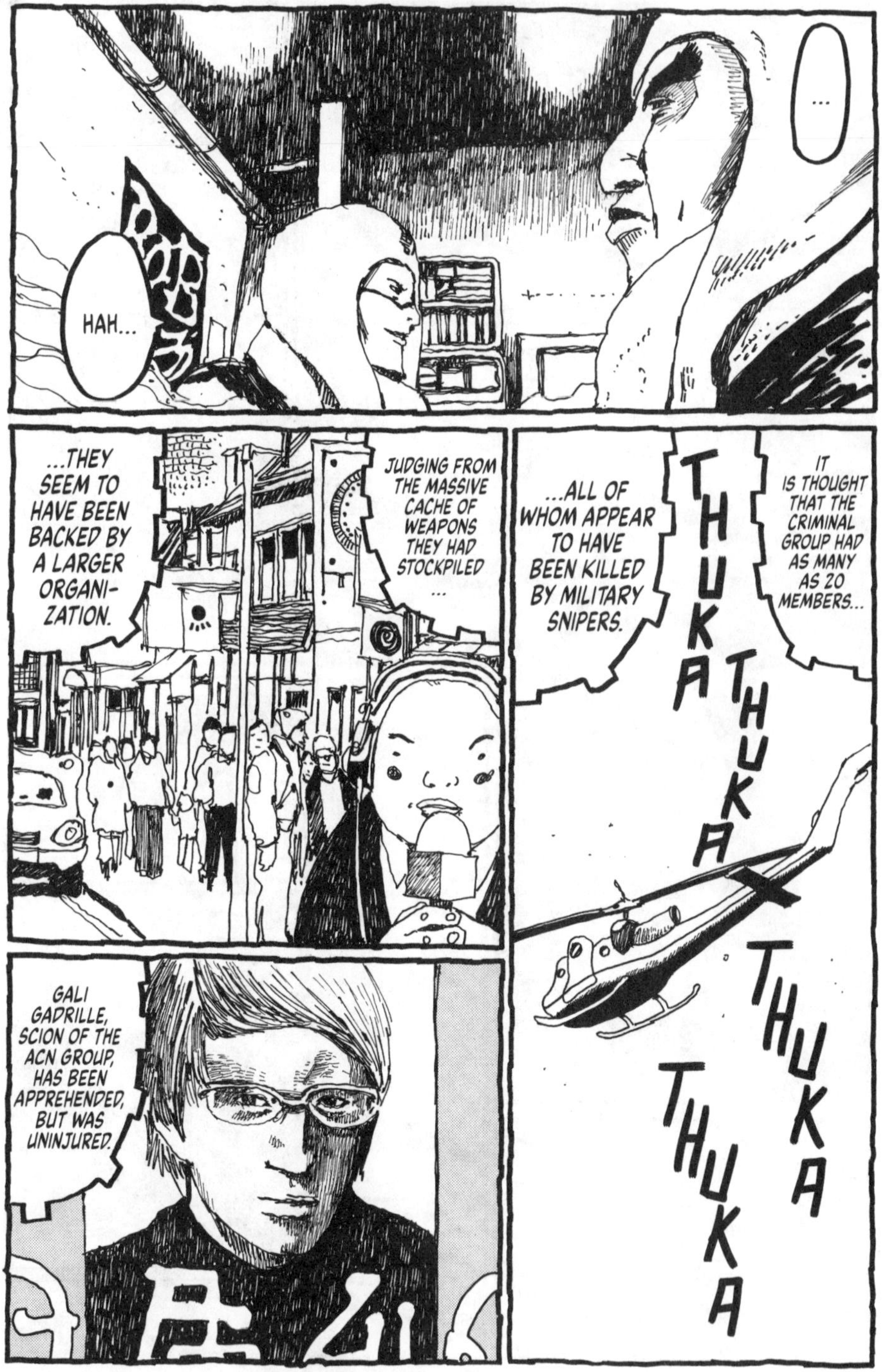
...
HAH...
IT IS THOUGHT THAT THE CRIMINAL GROUP HAD AS MANY AS 20 MEMBERS...
...ALL OF WHOM APPEAR TO HAVE BEEN KILLED BY MILITARY SNIPERS.
THUKA THUKA THUKA THUKA
JUDGING FROM THE MASSIVE CACHE OF WEAPONS THEY HAD STOCKPILED ...
...THEY SEEM TO HAVE BEEN BACKED BY A LARGER ORGANI-ZATION.
GALI GADRILLE, SCION OF THE ACN GROUP, HAS BEEN APPREHENDED, BUT WAS UNINJURED.

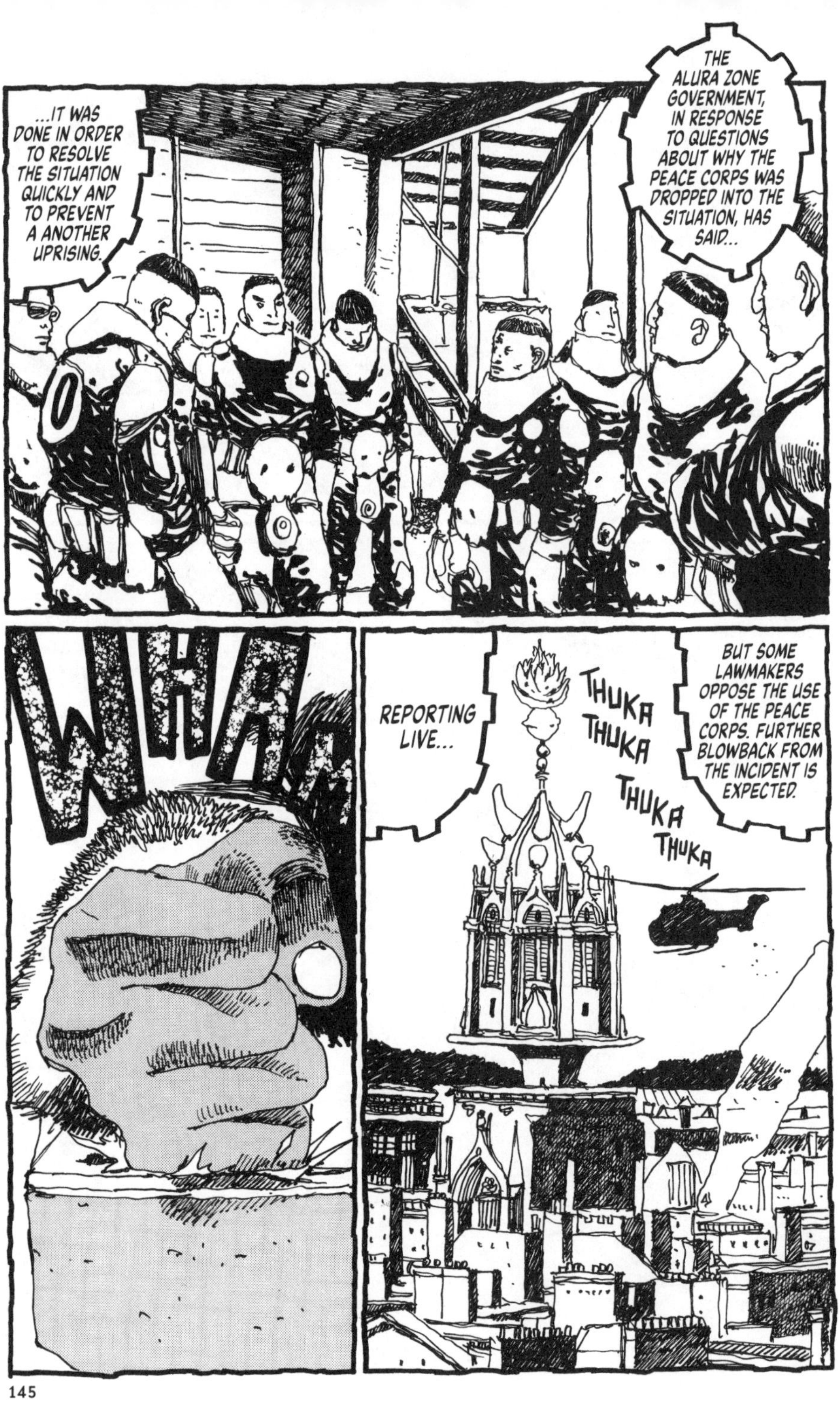
THE ALURA ZONE GOVERNMENT, IN RESPONSE TO QUESTIONS ABOUT WHY THE PEACE CORPS WAS DROPPED INTO THE SITUATION, HAS SAID...
...IT WAS DONE IN ORDER TO RESOLVE THE SITUATION QUICKLY AND TO PREVENT A ANOTHER UPRISING.
BUT SOME LAWMAKERS OPPOSE THE USE OF THE PEACE CORPS. FURTHER BLOWBACK FROM THE INCIDENT IS EXPECTED.
THUKA THUKA THUKA THUKA
REPORTING LIVE...
WHA

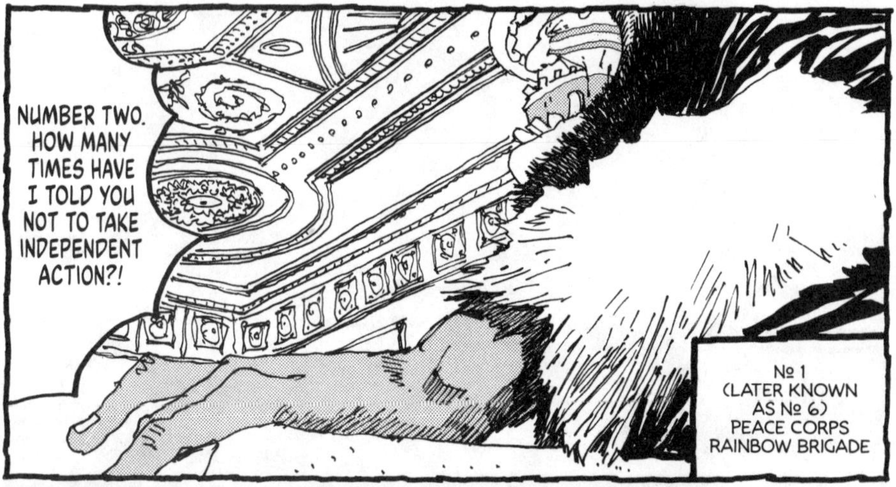
№ 1 (LATER KNOWN AS № 6) PEACE CORPS RAINBOW BRIGADE
NUMBER TWO. HOW MANY TIMES HAVE I TOLD YOU NOT TO TAKE INDEPENDENT ACTION?!
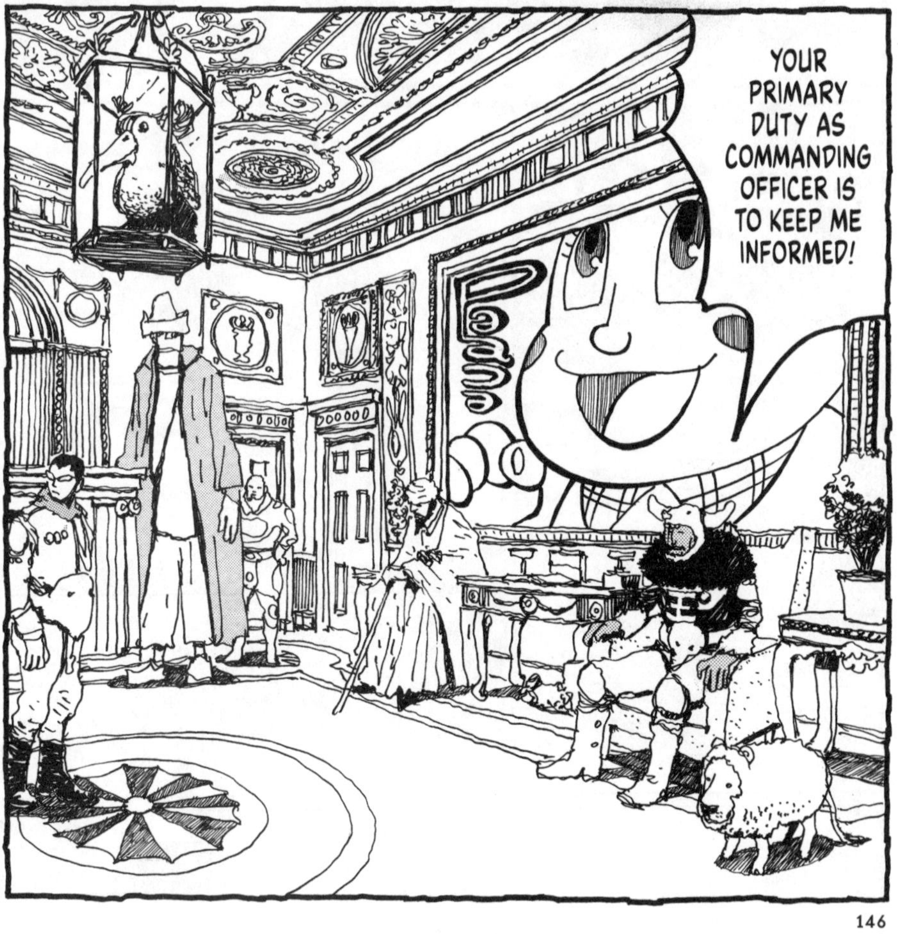
YOUR PRIMARY DUTY AS COMMANDING OFFICER IS TO KEEP ME INFORMED!

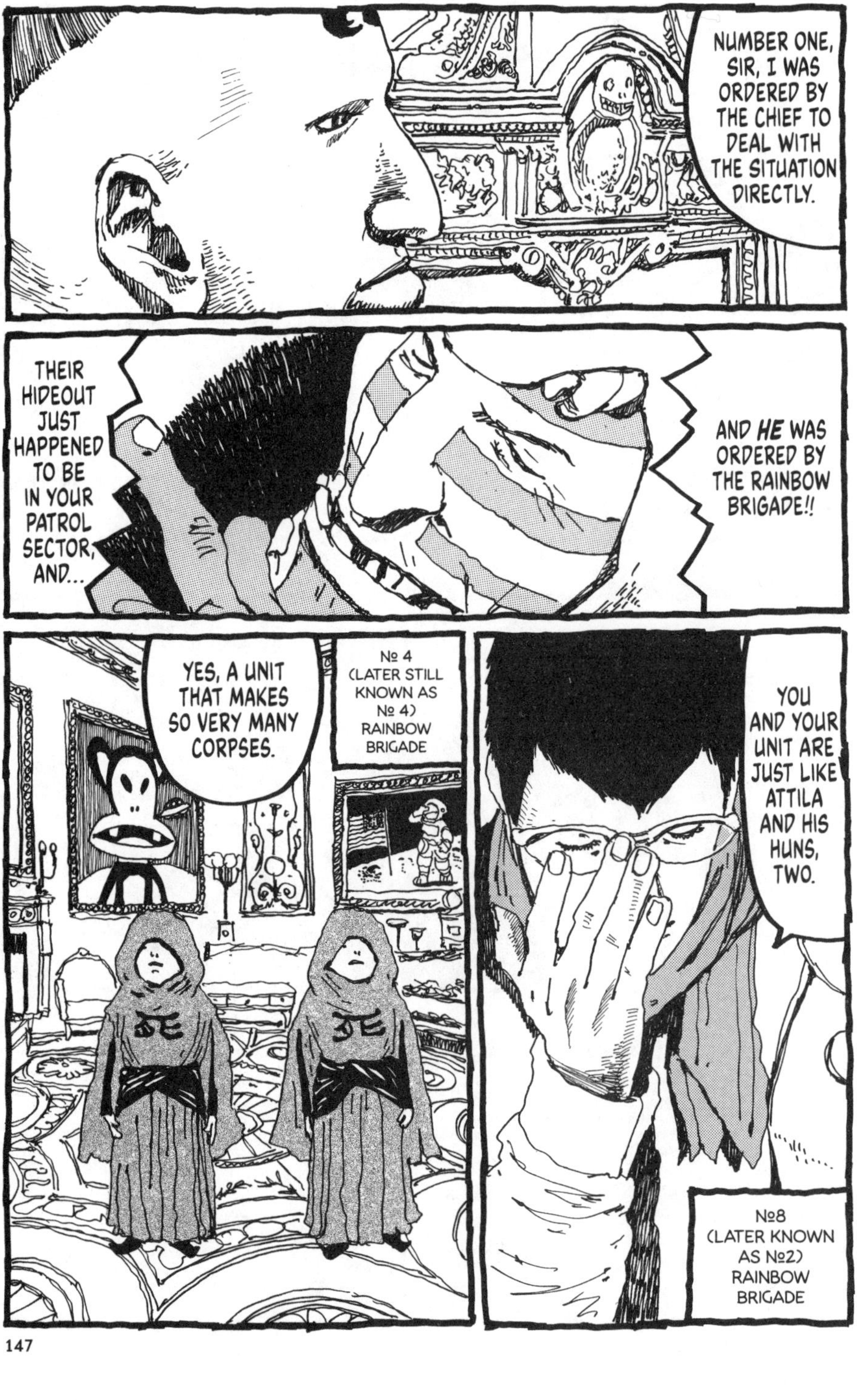
NUMBER ONE, SIR, I WAS ORDERED BY THE CHIEF TO DEAL WITH THE SITUATION DIRECTLY.
AND ***HE*** WAS ORDERED BY THE RAINBOW BRIGADE!!
THEIR HIDEOUT JUST HAPPENED TO BE IN YOUR PATROL SECTOR, AND...
YOU AND YOUR UNIT ARE JUST LIKE ATTILA AND HIS HUNS, TWO.
...
№8 (LATER KNOWN AS №2) RAINBOW BRIGADE
№ 4 (LATER STILL KNOWN AS № 4) RAINBOW BRIGADE
YES, A UNIT THAT MAKES SO VERY MANY CORPSES.

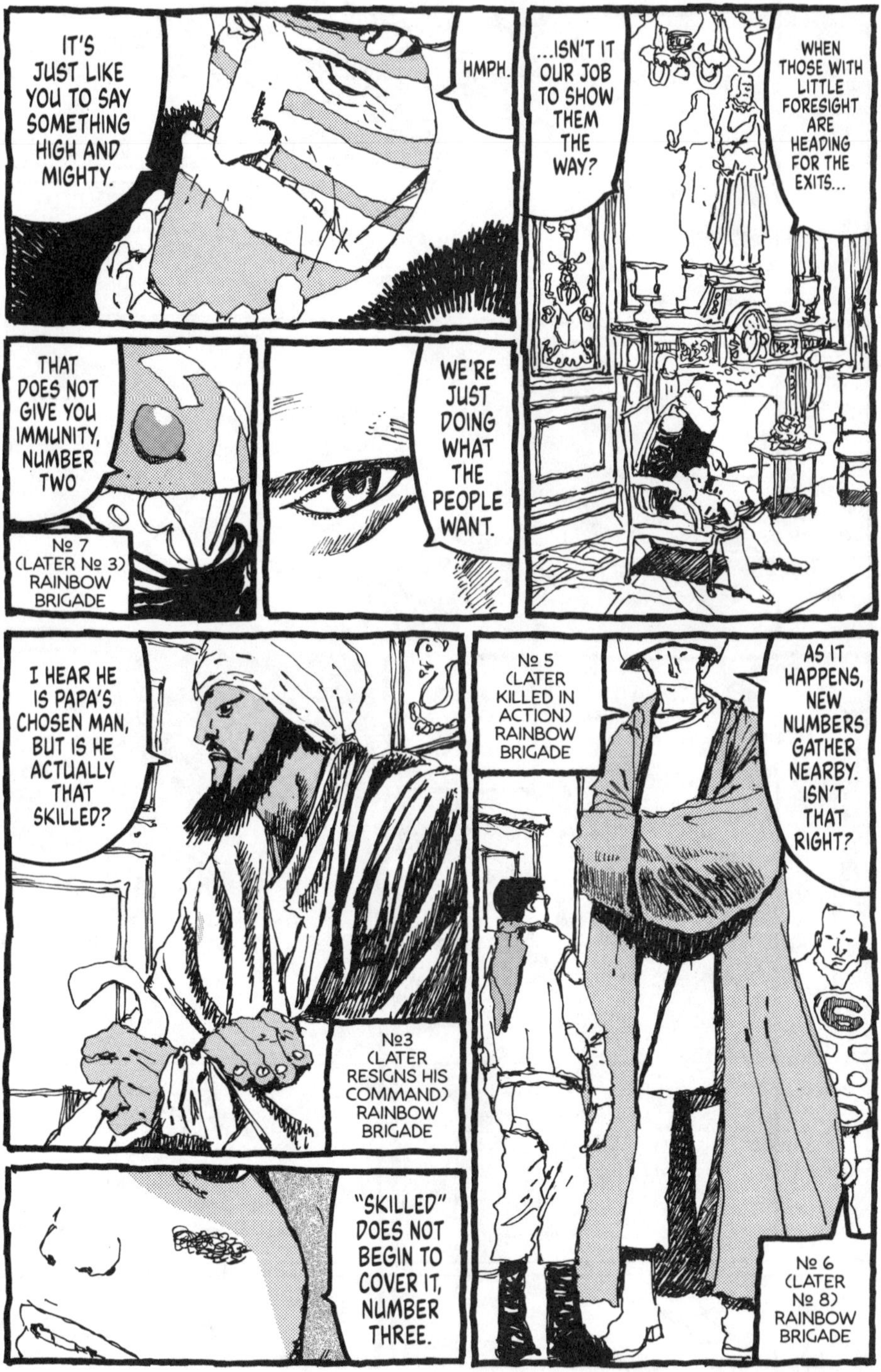
WHEN THOSE WITH LITTLE FORESIGHT ARE HEADING FOR THE EXITS...
...ISN'T IT OUR JOB TO SHOW THEM THE WAY?
IT'S JUST LIKE YOU TO SAY SOMETHING HIGH AND MIGHTY.
HMPH.
WE'RE JUST DOING WHAT THE PEOPLE WANT.
THAT DOES NOT GIVE YOU IMMUNITY, NUMBER TWO
№ 7 (LATER № 3) RAINBOW BRIGADE
AS IT HAPPENS, NEW NUMBERS GATHER NEARBY. ISN'T THAT RIGHT?
№ 5 (LATER KILLED IN ACTION) RAINBOW BRIGADE
№ 6 (LATER № 8) RAINBOW BRIGADE
I HEAR HE IS PAPA'S CHOSEN MAN, BUT IS HE ACTUALLY THAT SKILLED?
№3 (LATER RESIGNS HIS COMMAND) RAINBOW BRIGADE
"SKILLED" DOES NOT BEGIN TO COVER IT, NUMBER THREE.

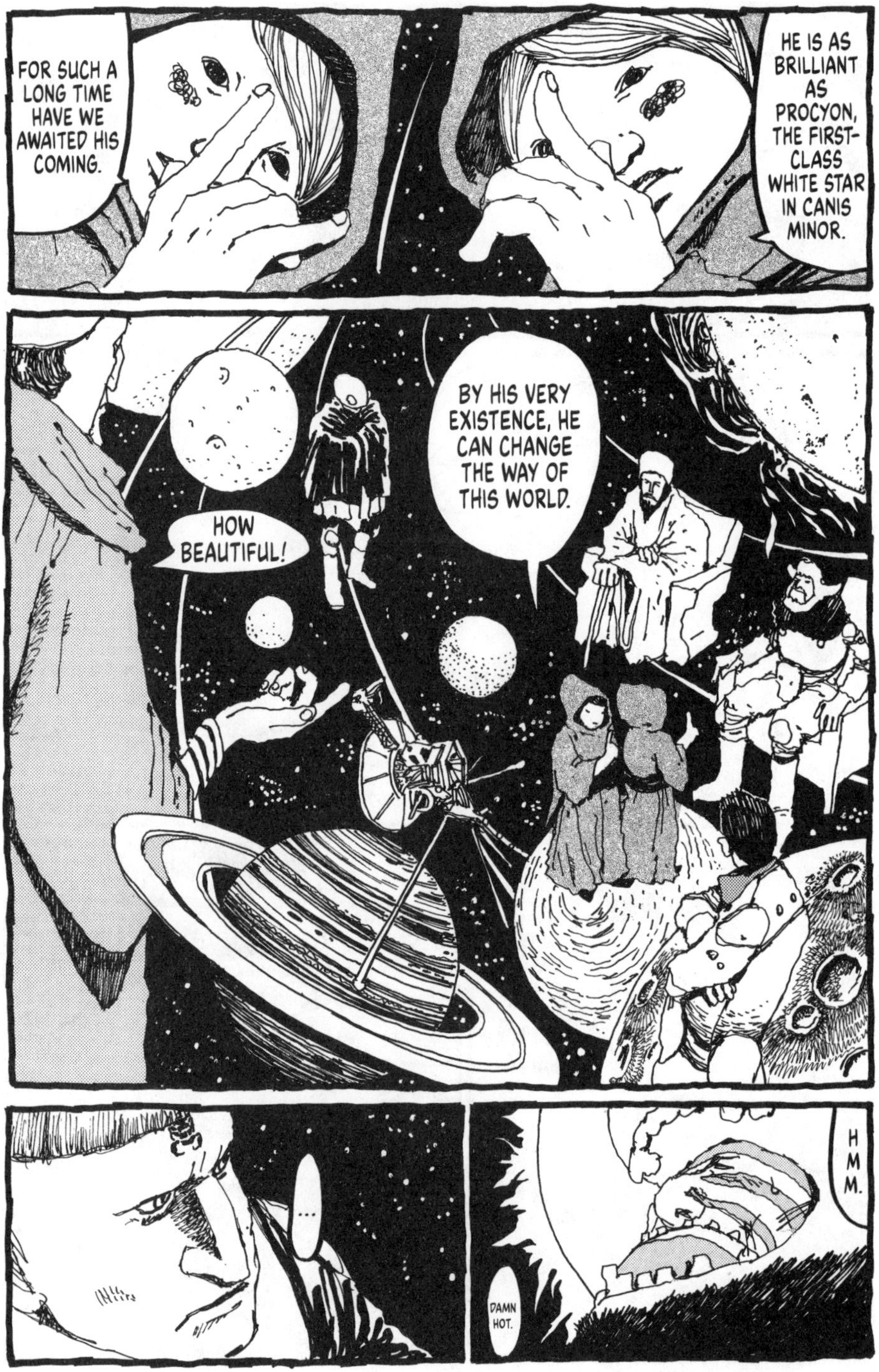
HE IS AS BRILLIANT AS PROCYON, THE FIRST-CLASS WHITE STAR IN CANIS MINOR.
FOR SUCH A LONG TIME HAVE WE AWAITED HIS COMING.
BY HIS VERY EXISTENCE, HE CAN CHANGE THE WAY OF THIS WORLD.
HOW BEAUTIFUL!
HMM.
DAMN HOT.
...

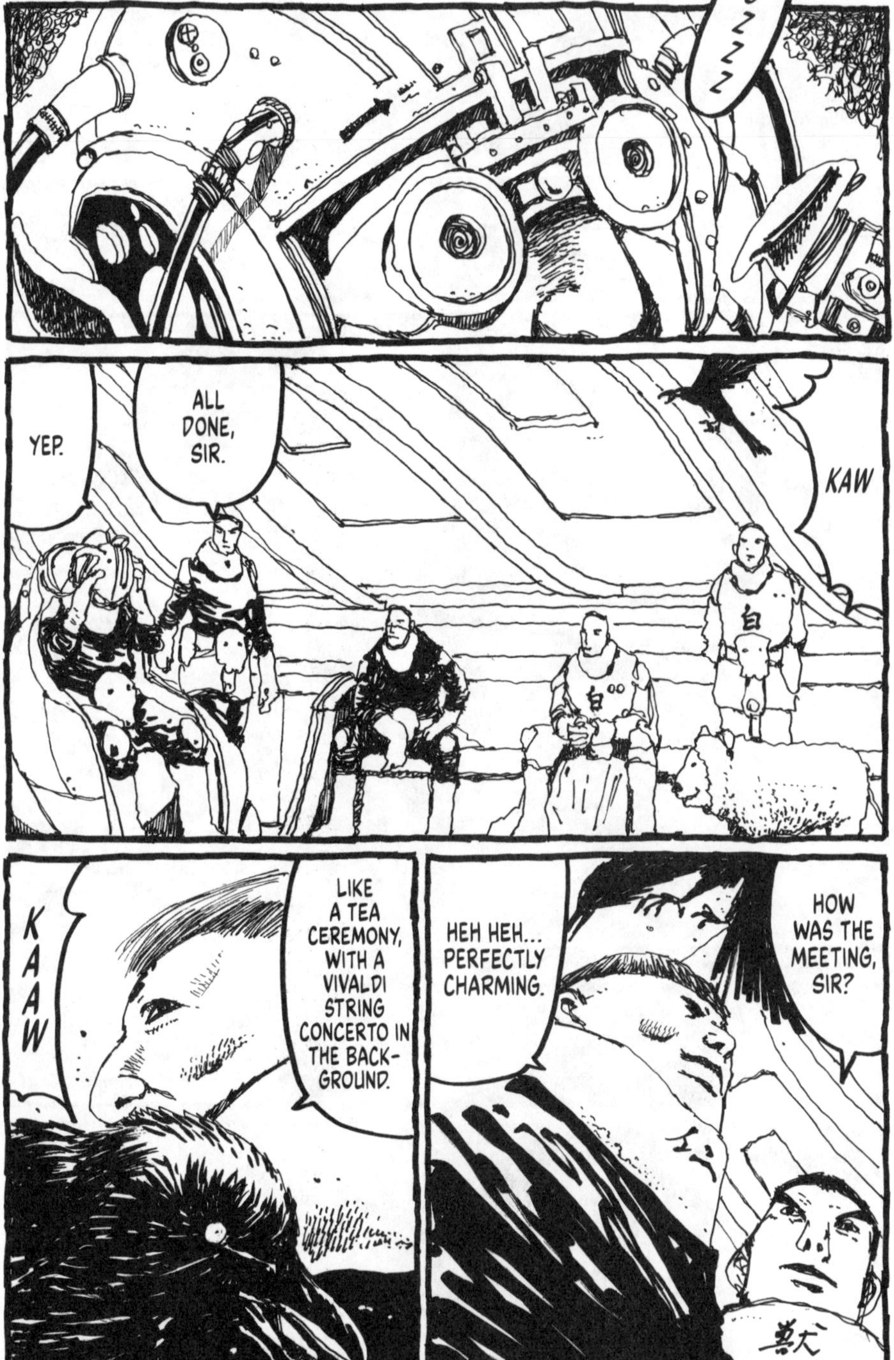
BUZZZ
KAW
ALL DONE, SIR.
YEP.
HOW WAS THE MEETING, SIR?
HEH HEH... PERFECTLY CHARMING.
LIKE A TEA CEREMONY, WITH A VIVALDI STRING CONCERTO IN THE BACK-GROUND.
KAAAW

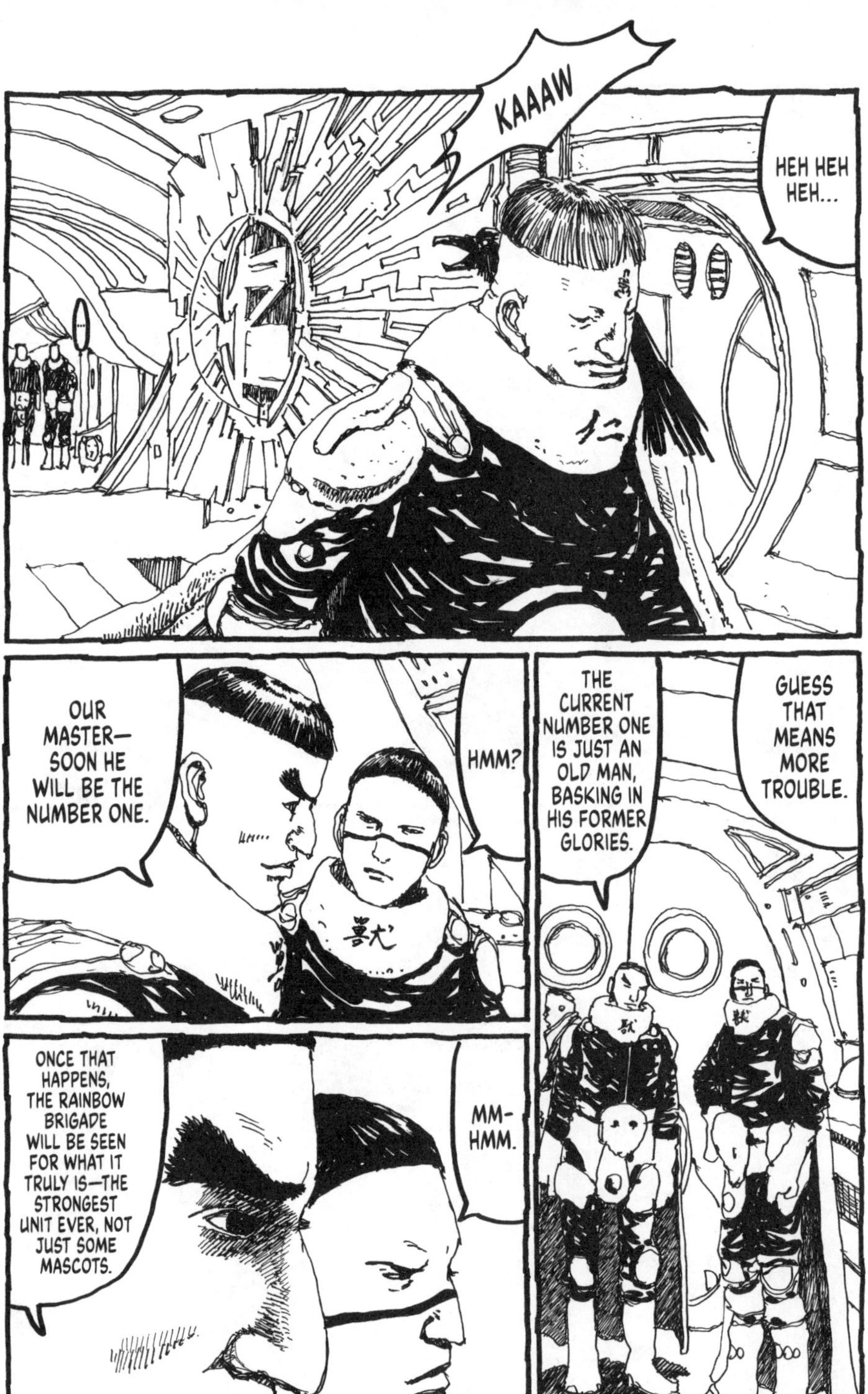
HEH HEH HEH...
KAAAW
GUESS THAT MEANS MORE TROUBLE.
THE CURRENT NUMBER ONE IS JUST AN OLD MAN, BASKING IN HIS FORMER GLORIES.
HMM?
OUR MASTER— SOON HE WILL BE THE NUMBER ONE.
MM-HMM.
ONCE THAT HAPPENS, THE RAINBOW BRIGADE WILL BE SEEN FOR WHAT IT TRULY IS—THE STRONGEST UNIT EVER, NOT JUST SOME MASCOTS.

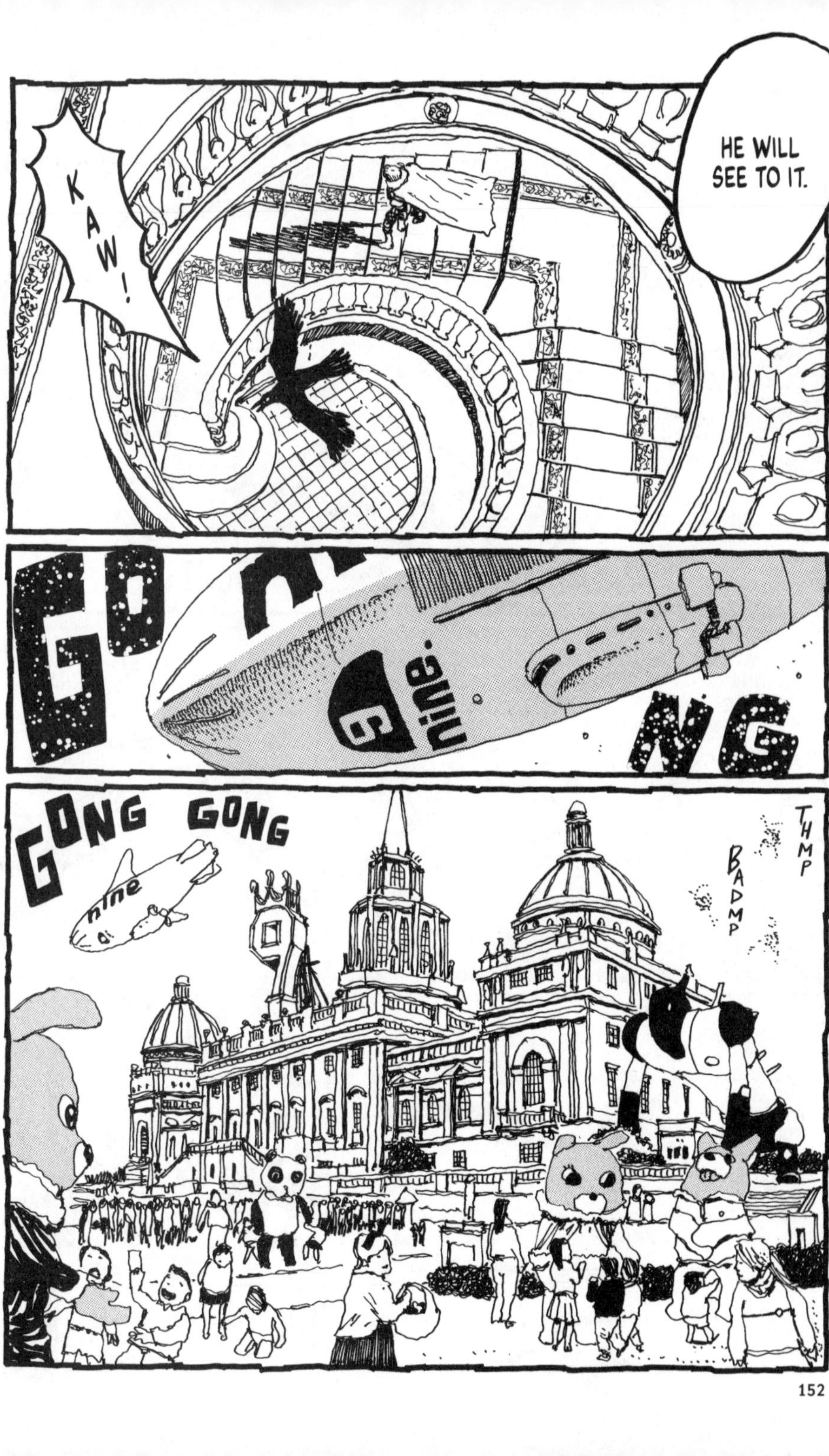
HE WILL SEE TO IT.
KAW!
nine
nine
NG
THMP
BADMP
GONG GONG
nine

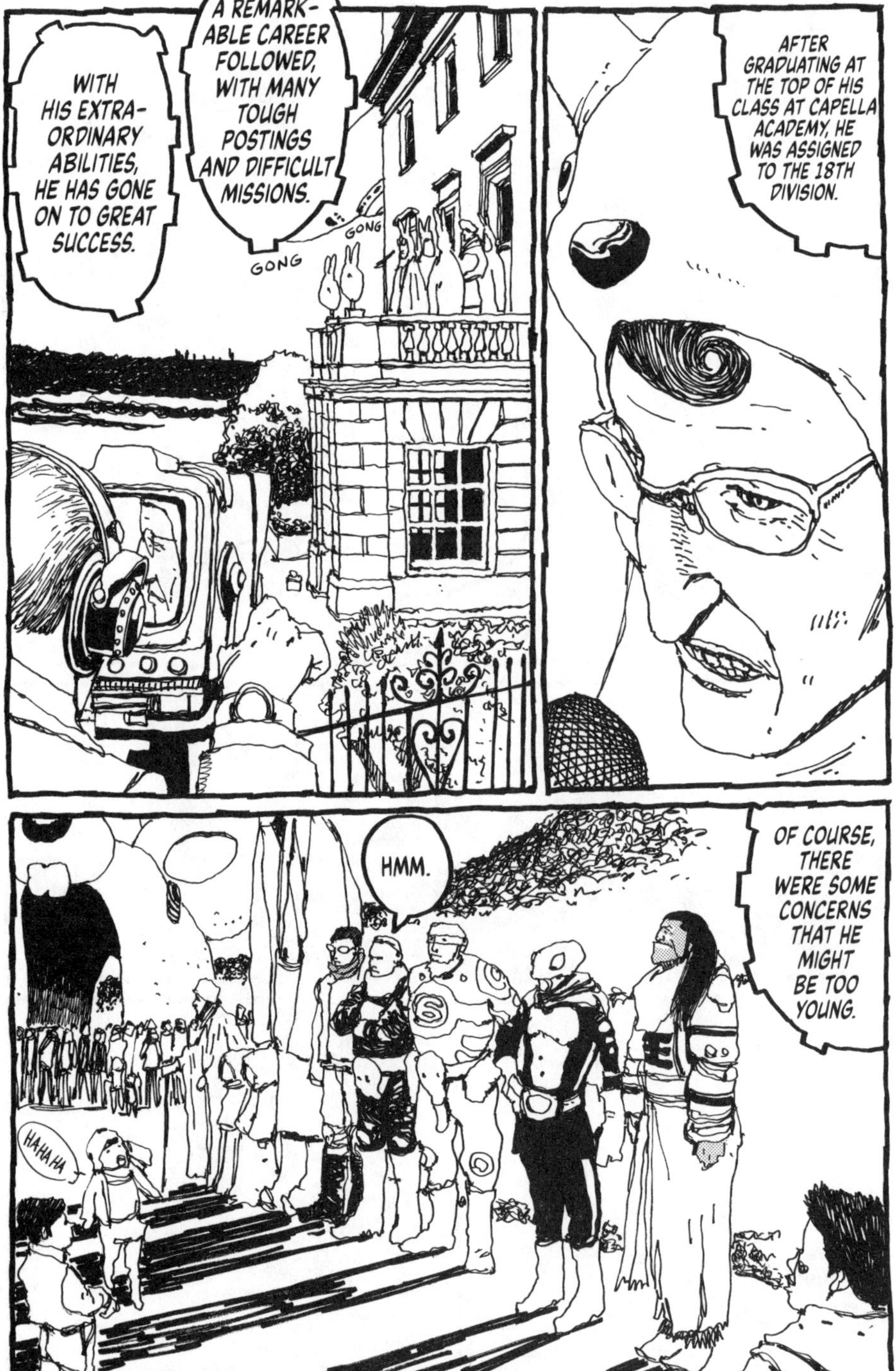
AFTER GRADUATING AT THE TOP OF HIS CLASS AT CAPELLA ACADEMY, HE WAS ASSIGNED TO THE 18TH DIVISION.
A REMARKABLE CAREER FOLLOWED, WITH MANY TOUGH POSTINGS AND DIFFICULT MISSIONS.
WITH HIS EXTRAORDINARY ABILITIES, HE HAS GONE ON TO GREAT SUCCESS.
GONG
GONG
OF COURSE, THERE WERE SOME CONCERNS THAT HE MIGHT BE TOO YOUNG.
HMM.
HAHAHA

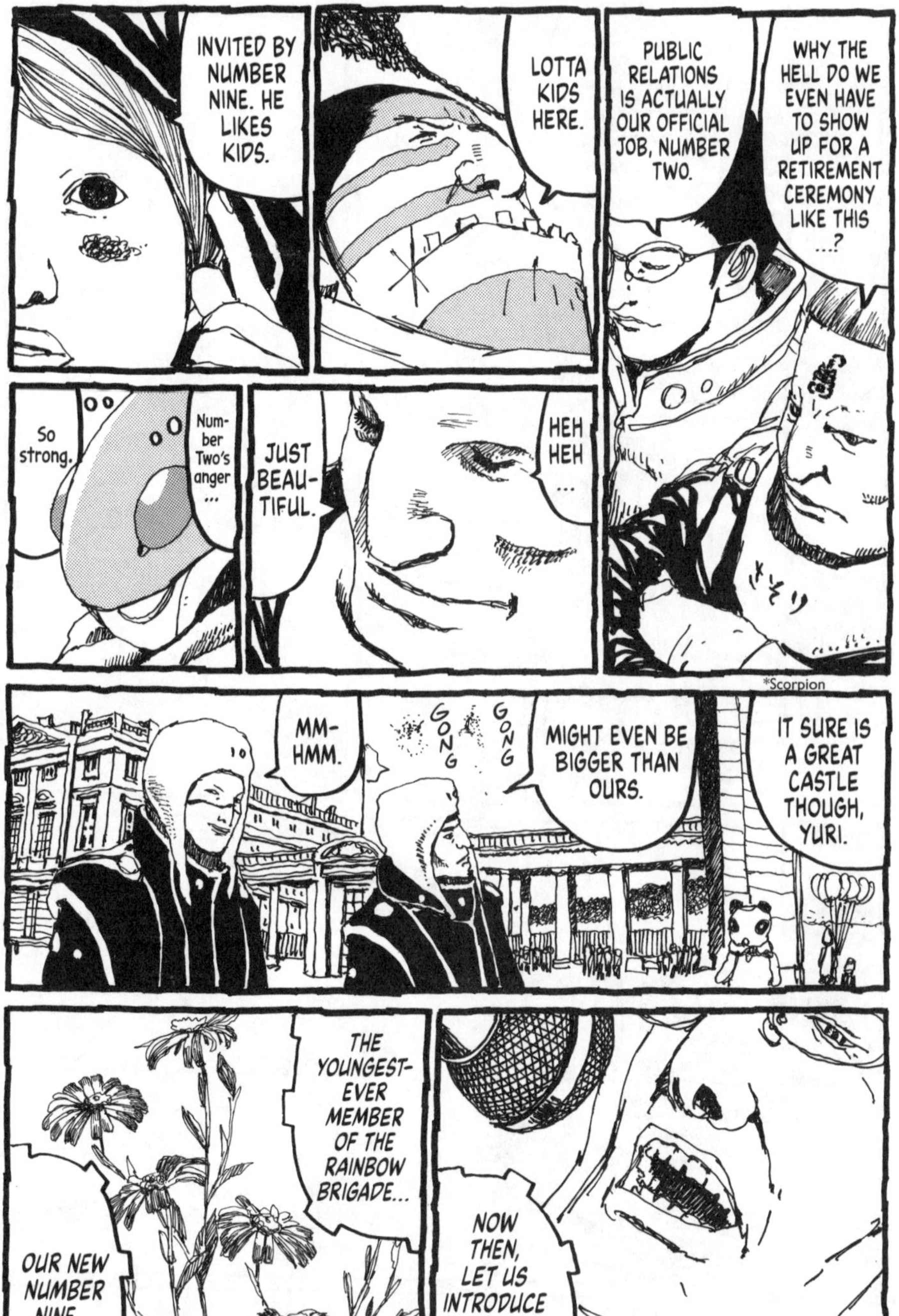
WHY THE HELL DO WE EVEN HAVE TO SHOW UP FOR A RETIREMENT CEREMONY LIKE THIS ...?
PUBLIC RELATIONS IS ACTUALLY OUR OFFICIAL JOB, NUMBER TWO.
さそり
LOTTA KIDS HERE.
INVITED BY NUMBER NINE. HE LIKES KIDS.
HEH HEH ...
JUST BEAU-TIFUL.
Num-ber Two's anger ...
So strong.
*Scorpion
IT SURE IS A GREAT CASTLE THOUGH, YURI.
MIGHT EVEN BE BIGGER THAN OURS.
GONG GONG
MM-HMM.
NOW THEN, LET US INTRODUCE OUR NEW MEMBERS.
THE YOUNGEST-EVER MEMBER OF THE RAINBOW BRIGADE...
OUR NEW NUMBER NINE...

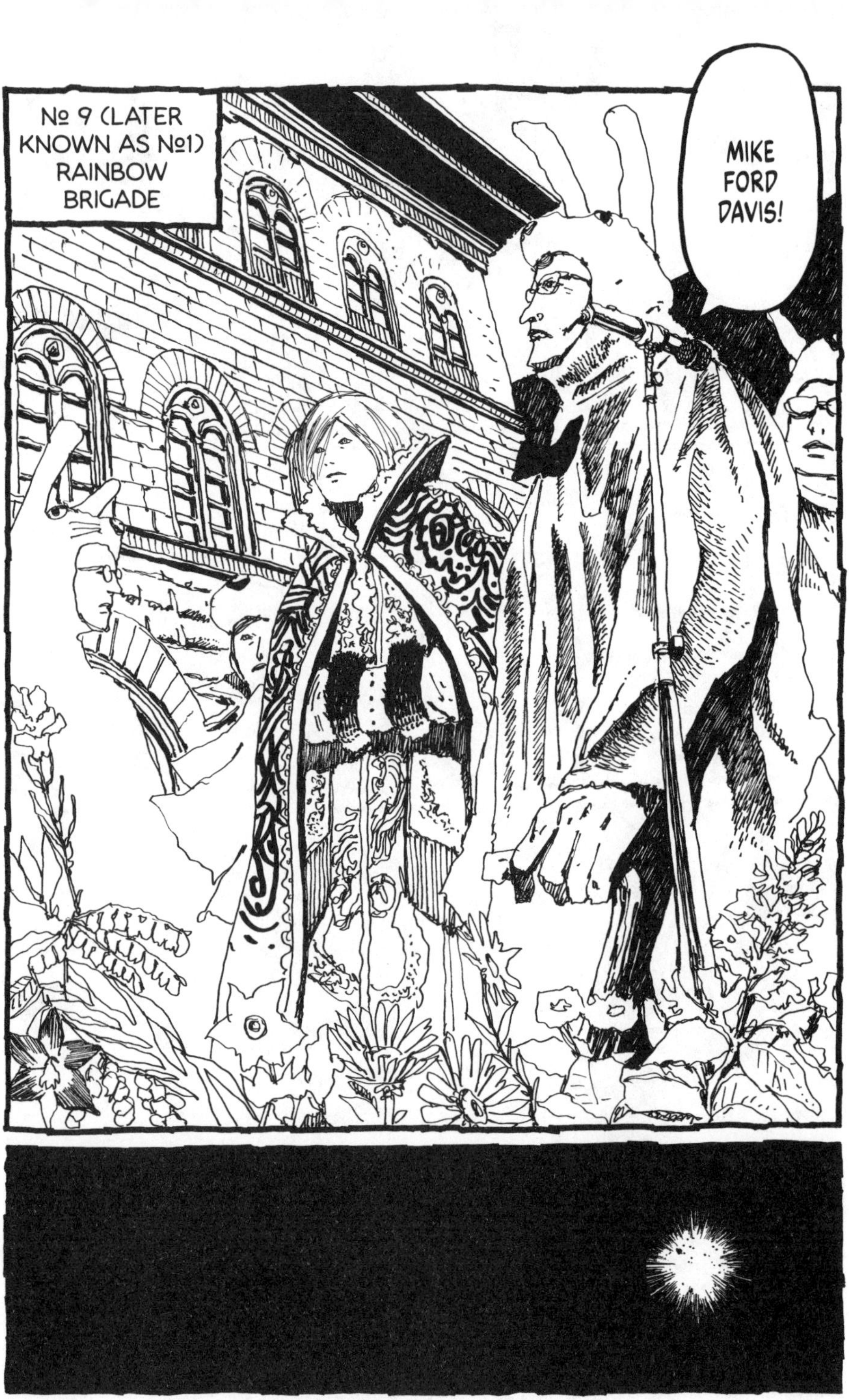
MIKE FORD DAVIS!
№ 9 (LATER KNOWN AS №1) RAINBOW BRIGADE

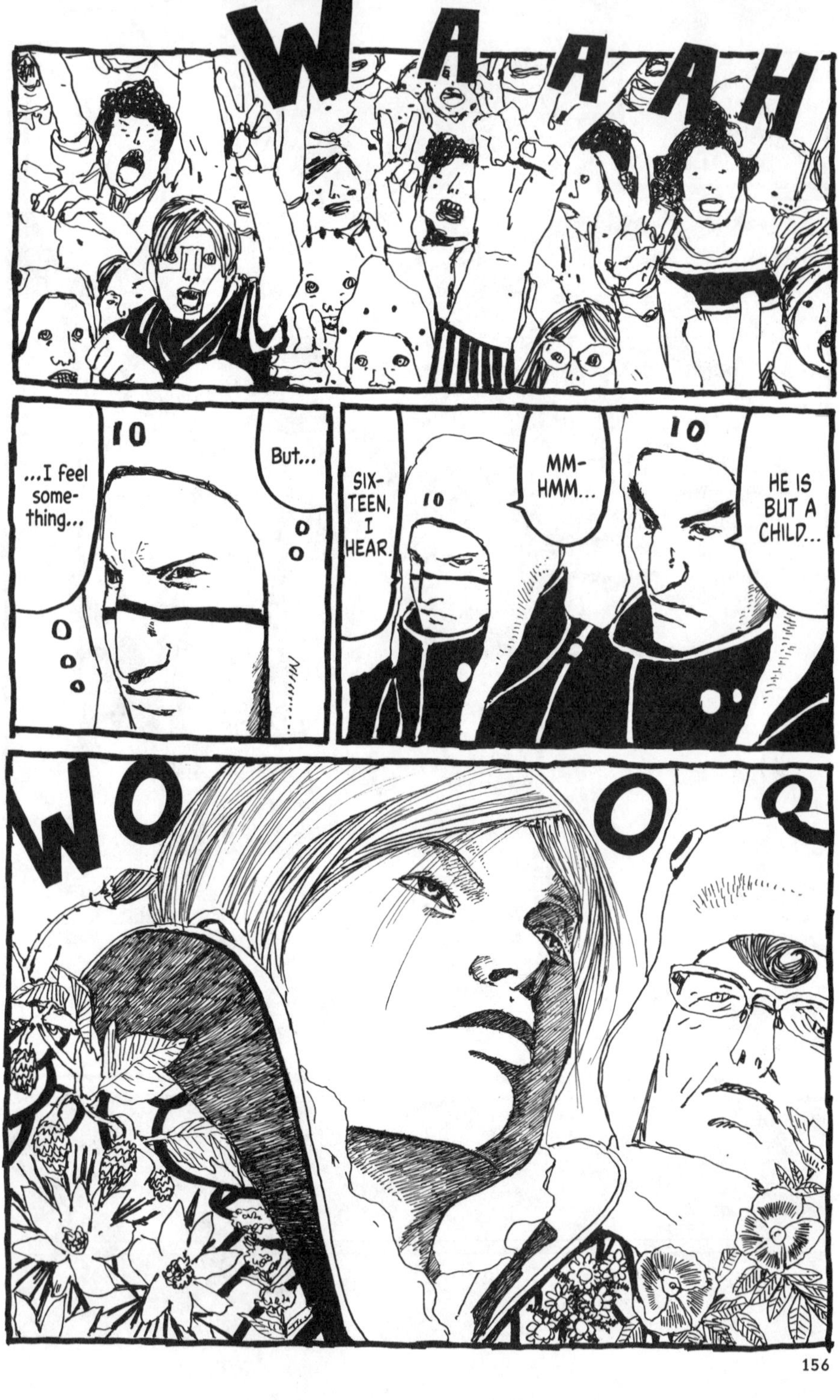
WAAAH
HE IS BUT A CHILD...
MM-HMM...
SIX-TEEN, I HEAR.
But...
...I feel some-thing...
WOOO

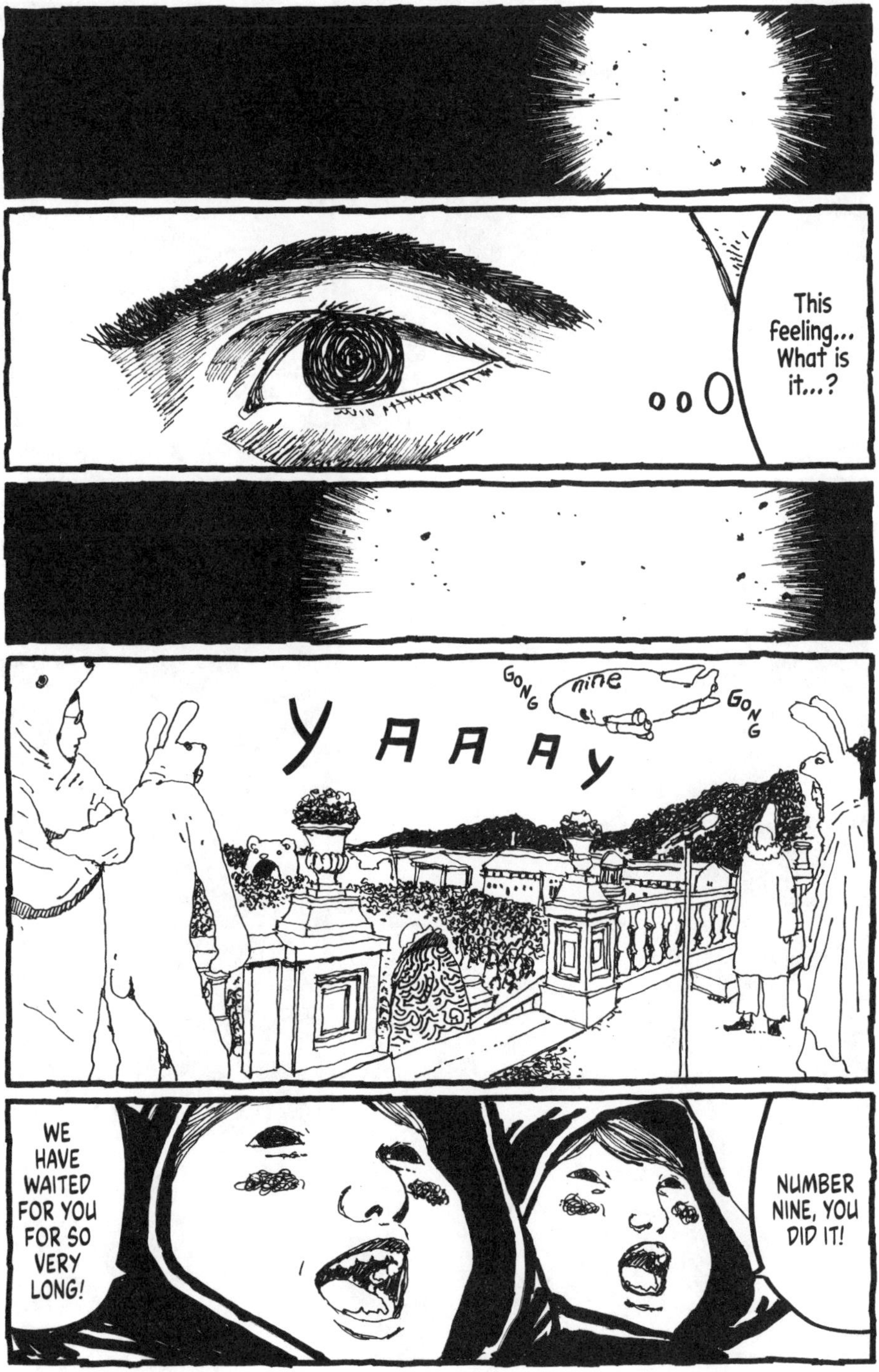
This feeling... What is it...?
GONG
nine
GONG
YAAAY
NUMBER NINE, YOU DID IT!
WE HAVE WAITED FOR YOU FOR SO VERY LONG!

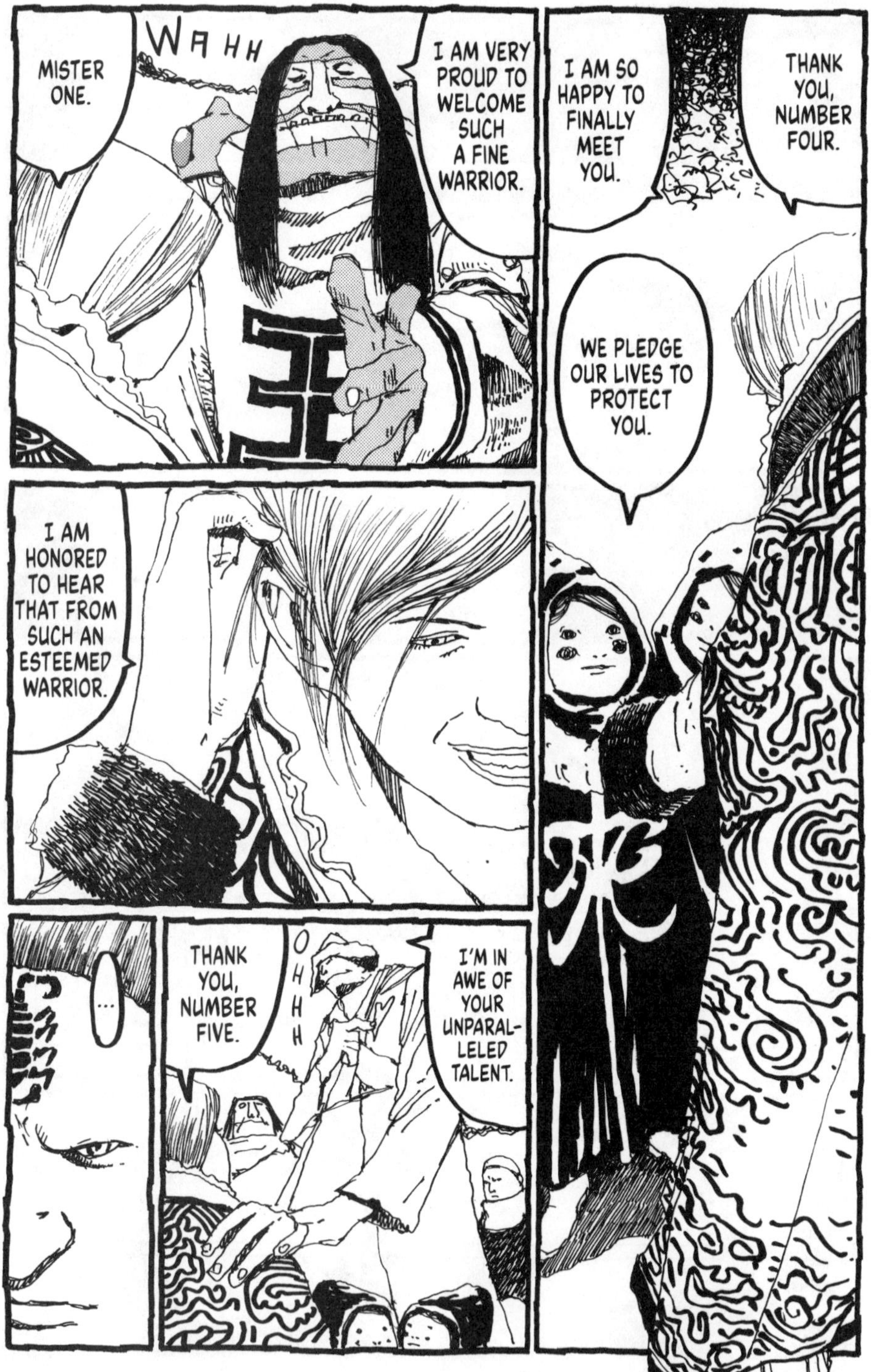
THANK YOU, NUMBER FOUR.
I AM SO HAPPY TO FINALLY MEET YOU.
WE PLEDGE OUR LIVES TO PROTECT YOU.
I AM VERY PROUD TO WELCOME SUCH A FINE WARRIOR.
WAHH
MISTER ONE.
I AM HONORED TO HEAR THAT FROM SUCH AN ESTEEMED WARRIOR.
I'M IN AWE OF YOUR UNPARAL-LELED TALENT.
OHHH
THANK YOU, NUMBER FIVE.
...

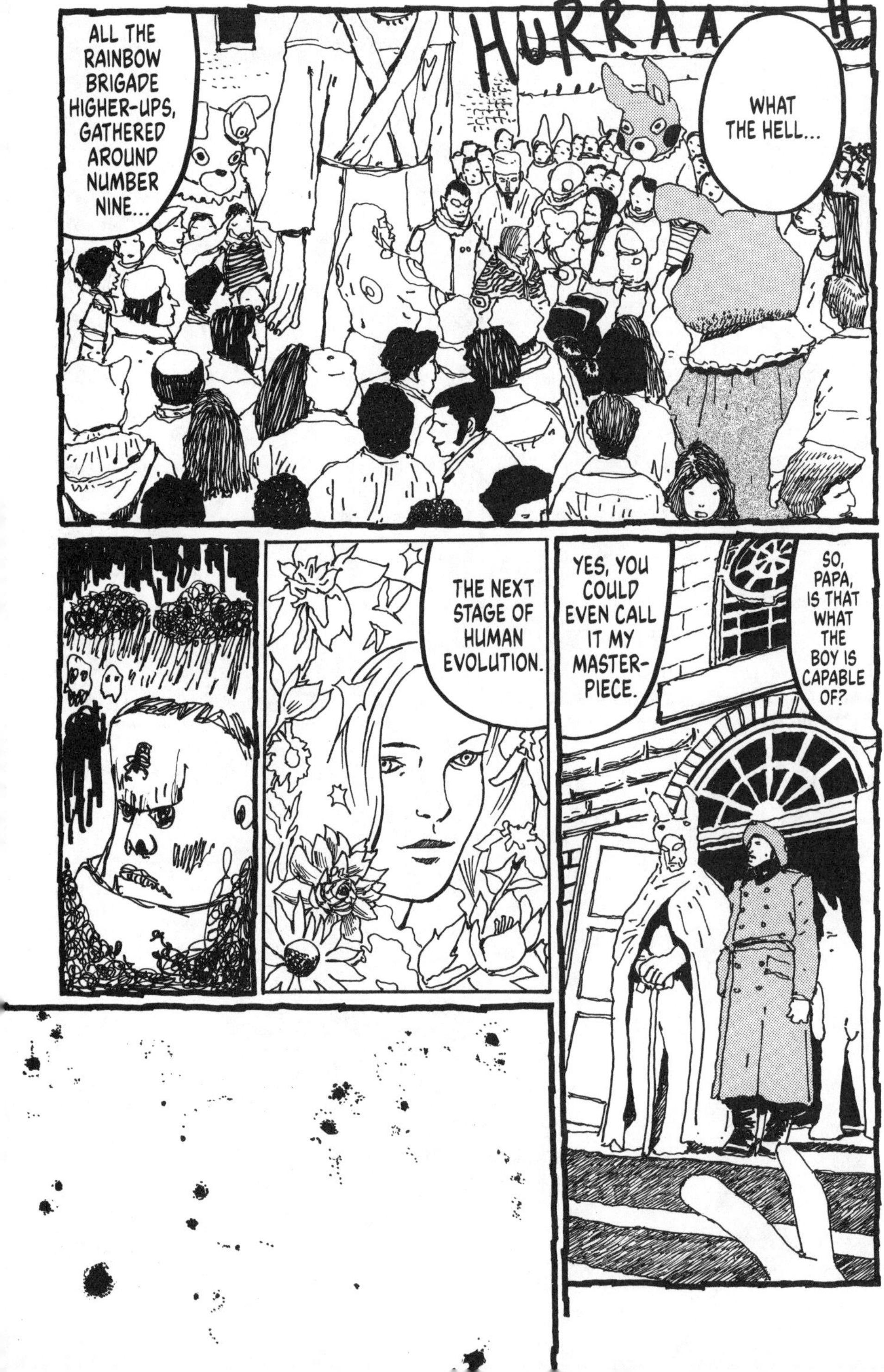
WHAT THE HELL...
HURRAAH
ALL THE RAINBOW BRIGADE HIGHER-UPS, GATHERED AROUND NUMBER NINE...
SO, PAPA, IS THAT WHAT THE BOY IS CAPABLE OF?
YES, YOU COULD EVEN CALL IT MY MASTER-PIECE.
THE NEXT STAGE OF HUMAN EVOLUTION.

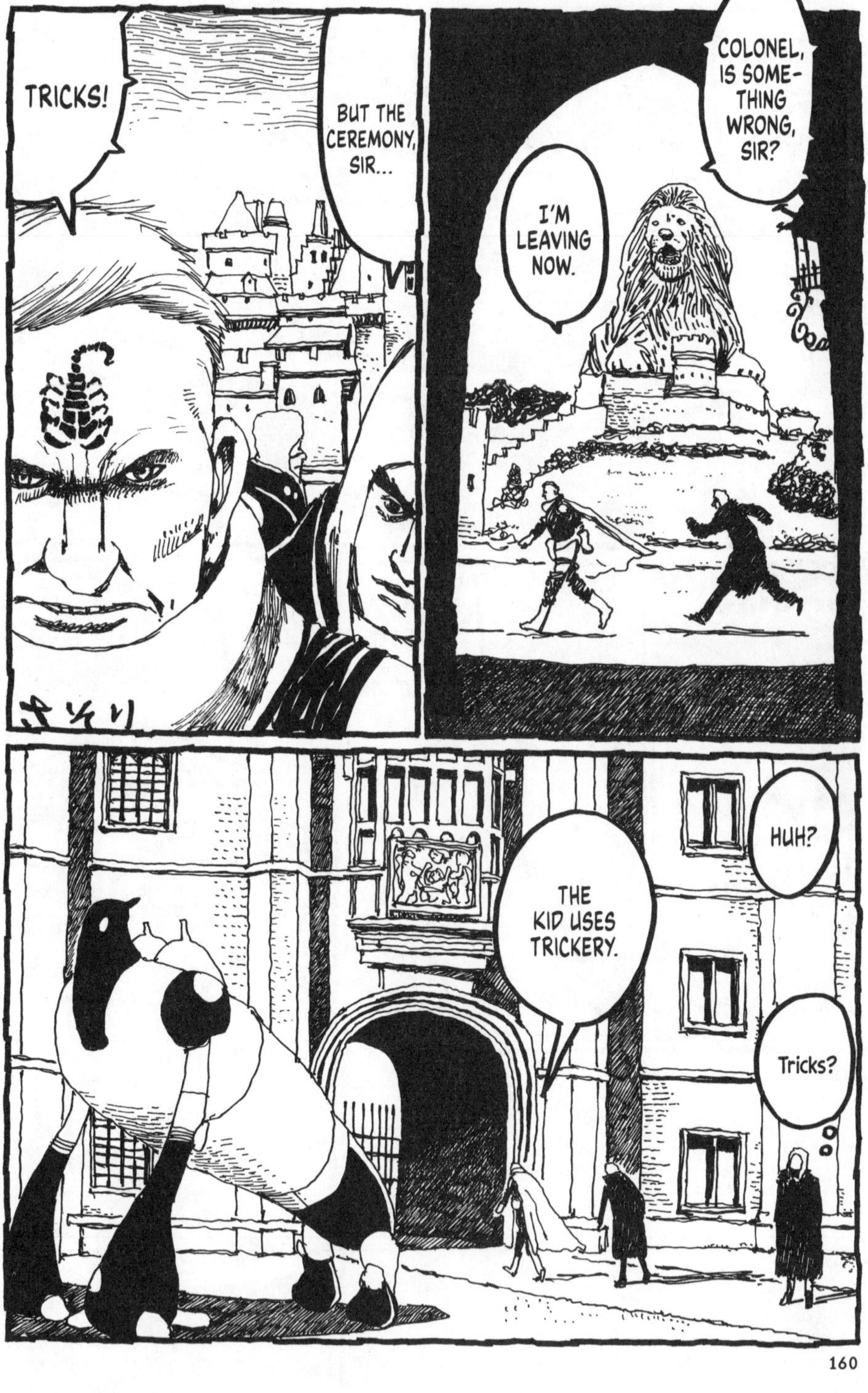
COLONEL, IS SOME-THING WRONG, SIR?
I'M LEAVING NOW.
TRICKS!
BUT THE CEREMONY, SIR...
HUH?
THE KID USES TRICKERY.
Tricks?

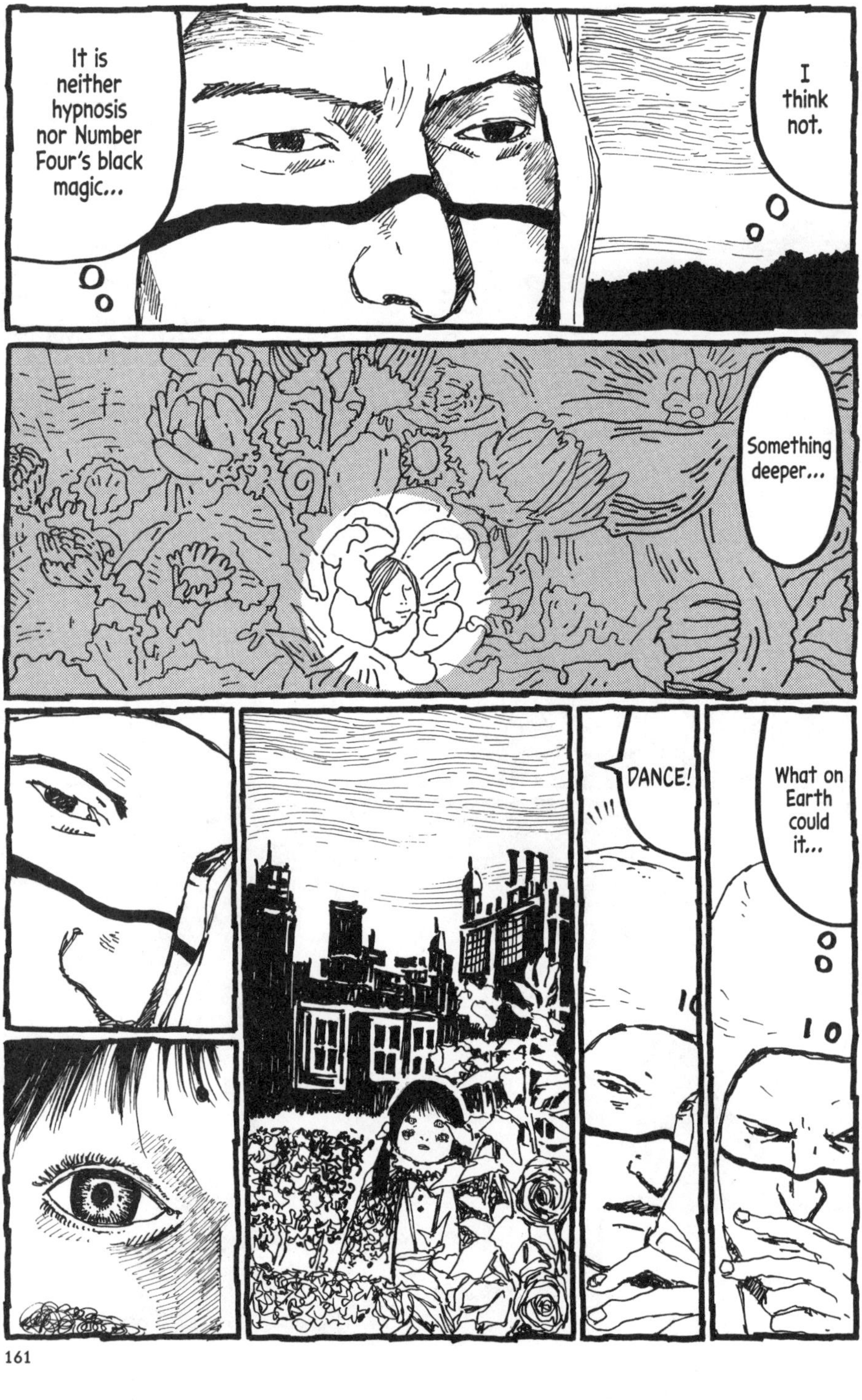
I think not.
It is neither hypnosis nor Number Four's black magic...
Something deeper...
What on Earth could it...
DANCE!

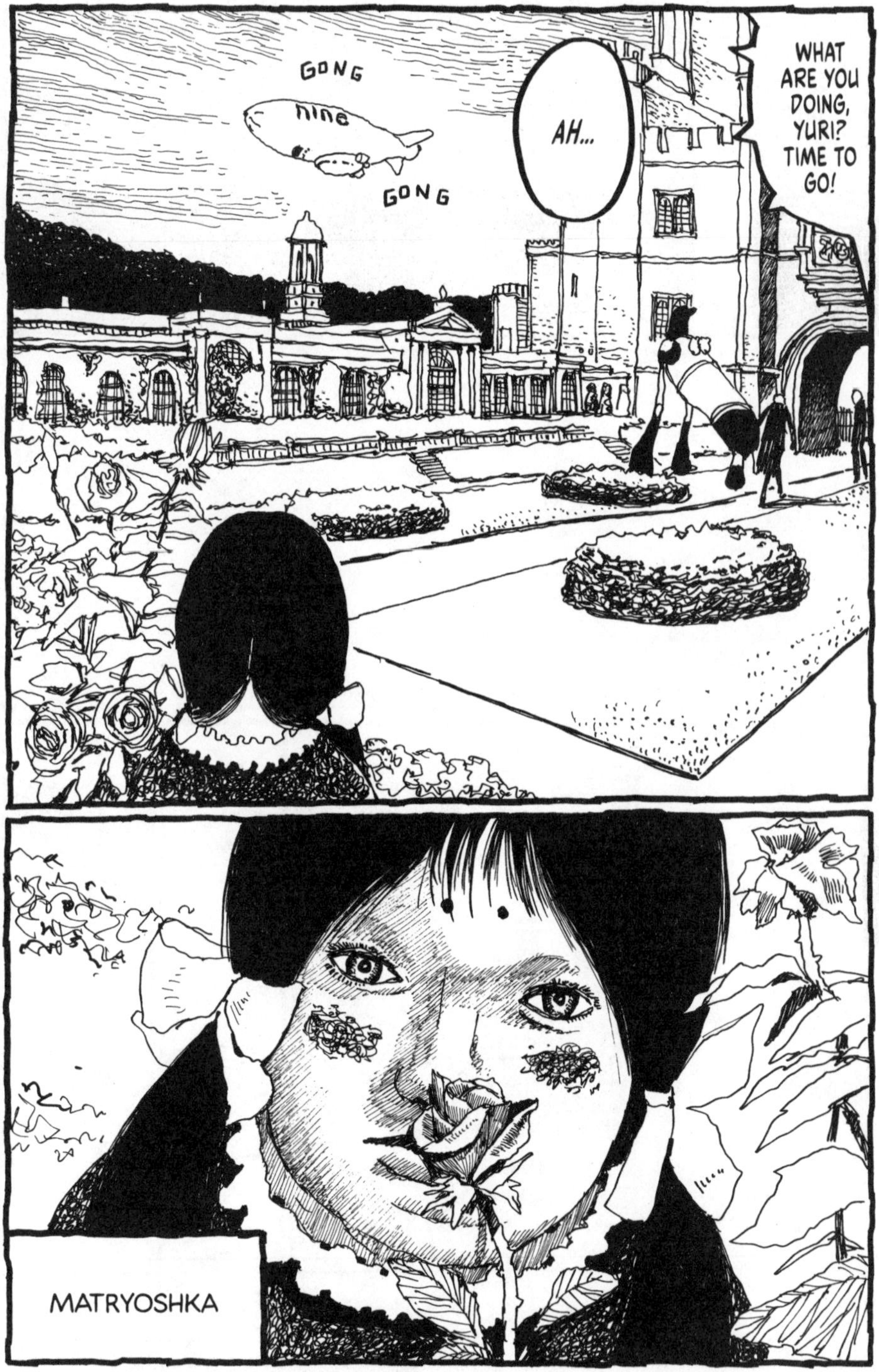
WHAT ARE YOU DOING, YURI? TIME TO GO!
AH...
GONG
nine
GONG
MATRYOSHKA

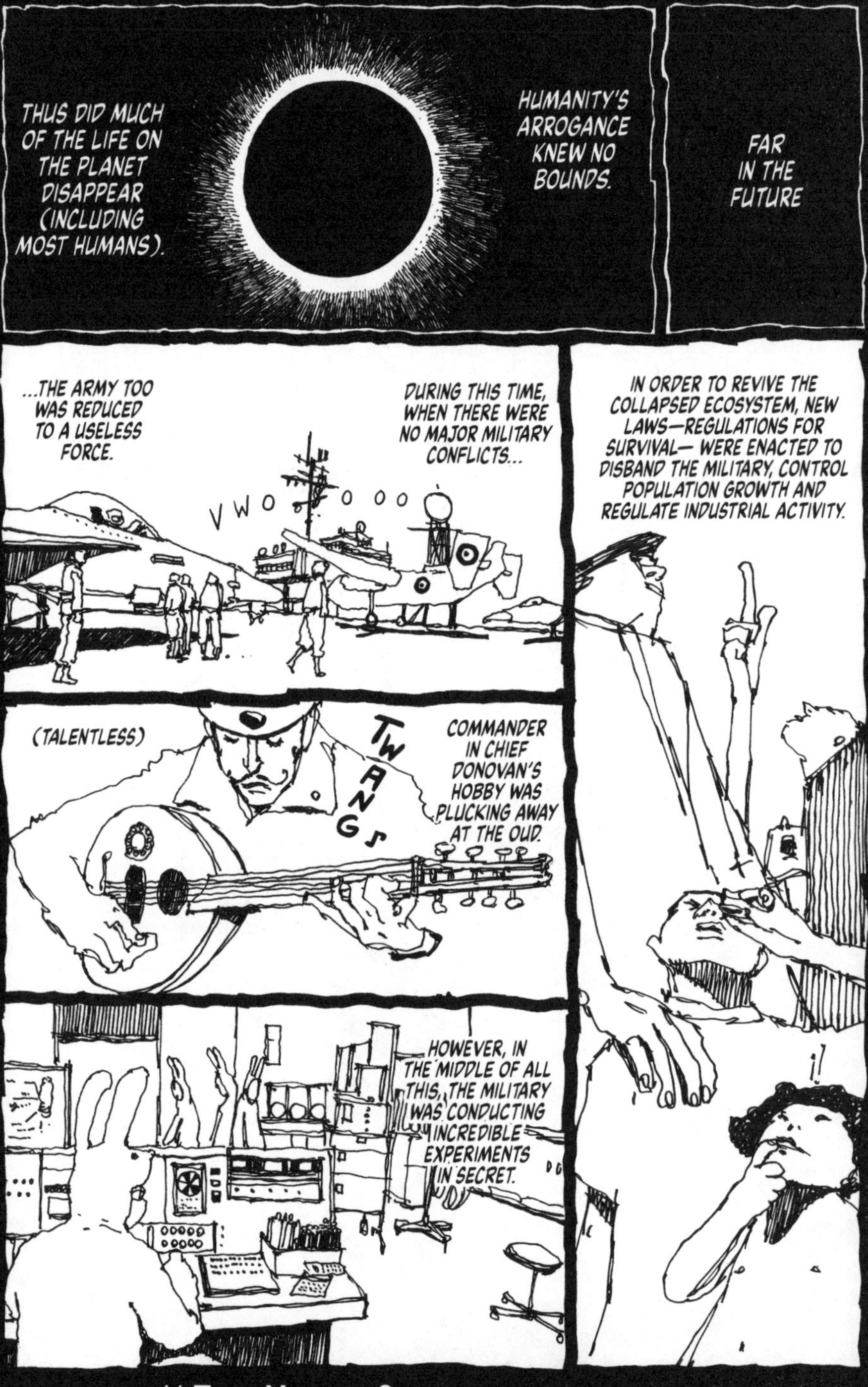
FAR IN THE FUTURE
HUMANITY'S ARROGANCE KNEW NO BOUNDS.
THUS DID MUCH OF THE LIFE ON THE PLANET DISAPPEAR (INCLUDING MOST HUMANS).
IN ORDER TO REVIVE THE COLLAPSED ECOSYSTEM, NEW LAWS—REGULATIONS FOR SURVIVAL— WERE ENACTED TO DISBAND THE MILITARY, CONTROL POPULATION GROWTH AND REGULATE INDUSTRIAL ACTIVITY.
!
DURING THIS TIME, WHEN THERE WERE NO MAJOR MILITARY CONFLICTS...
...THE ARMY TOO WAS REDUCED TO A USELESS FORCE.
VWOOOOO
COMMANDER IN CHIEF DONOVAN'S HOBBY WAS PLUCKING AWAY AT THE OUD.
TWANG
(TALENTLESS)
HOWEVER, IN THE MIDDLE OF ALL THIS, THE MILITARY WAS CONDUCTING INCREDIBLE EXPERIMENTS IN SECRET.

CHAPTER 14 // Ten Years Ago

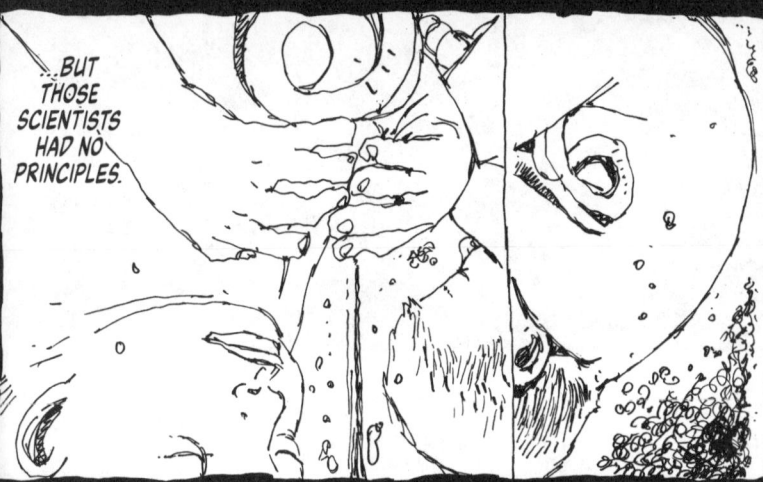

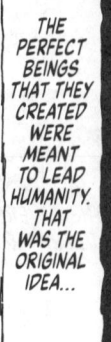

THE PERFECT BEINGS THAT THEY CREATED WERE MEANT TO LEAD HUMANITY. THAT WAS THE ORIGINAL IDEA...
...BUT THOSE SCIENTISTS HAD NO PRINCIPLES.
EVERY EXPERIMENT REFLECTS THE TRUE INTENT OF THOSE WHO DESIGNED IT!!
FRIEDRICH MONTE "PAPA" SIXTH GENERATION
THE BEINGS THEY CREATED WERE FORMED INTO A MILITARY, UNIT—THE PEACE CORPS—AND GIVEN ELITE STATUS.
THE TOP NINE OF THESE TROOPS WERE DUBBED THE RAINBOW BRIGADE. THEY CHOSE TO CALL THEMSELVES BY THEIR GIVEN NUMBERS.
BECAUSE OF THEIR ELITE SOCIAL STATUS, THEIR PRIMARY ROLE WAS TO ACT AS MASCOTS, IMPROVING THE PUBLIC'S NEGATIVE FEELINGS TOWARD THE MILITARY.
(PEACE BOY)
AND THUS, LACKING ANY REAL SPIRIT OF COOPER-ATION...
...INTERNAL TENSIONS INEVITABLY FLARED.

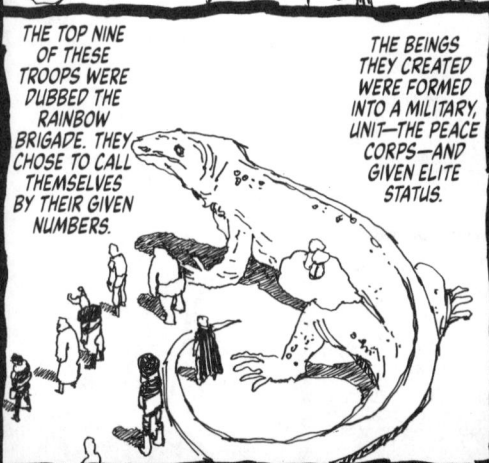

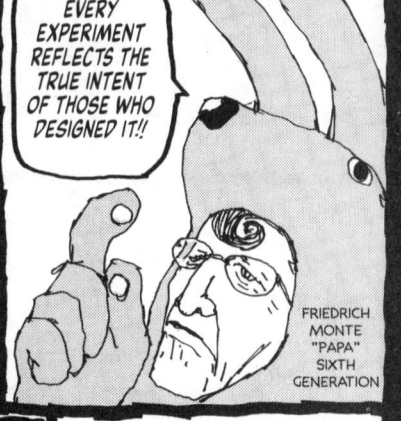

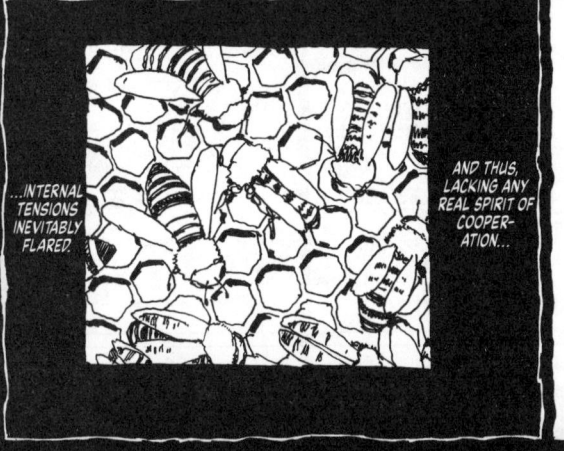

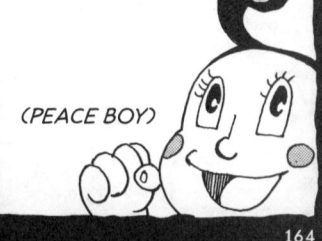

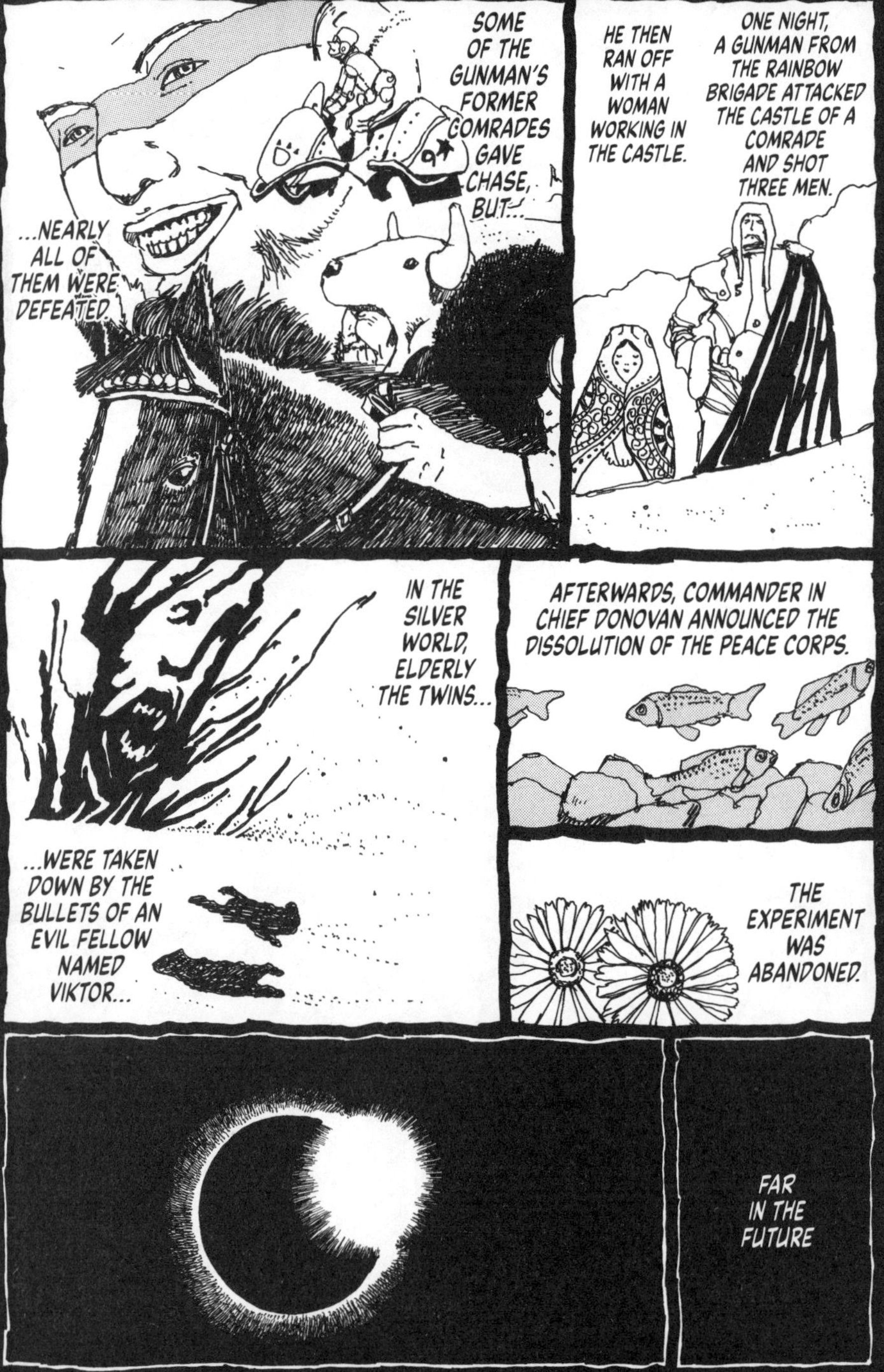
ONE NIGHT, A GUNMAN FROM THE RAINBOW BRIGADE ATTACKED THE CASTLE OF A COMRADE AND SHOT THREE MEN.
HE THEN RAN OFF WITH A WOMAN WORKING IN THE CASTLE.
SOME OF THE GUNMAN'S FORMER COMRADES GAVE CHASE, BUT...
...NEARLY ALL OF THEM WERE DEFEATED.
AFTERWARDS, COMMANDER IN CHIEF DONOVAN ANNOUNCED THE DISSOLUTION OF THE PEACE CORPS.
THE EXPERIMENT WAS ABANDONED.
IN THE SILVER WORLD, ELDERLY THE TWINS...
...WERE TAKEN DOWN BY THE BULLETS OF AN EVIL FELLOW NAMED VIKTOR...
FAR IN THE FUTURE

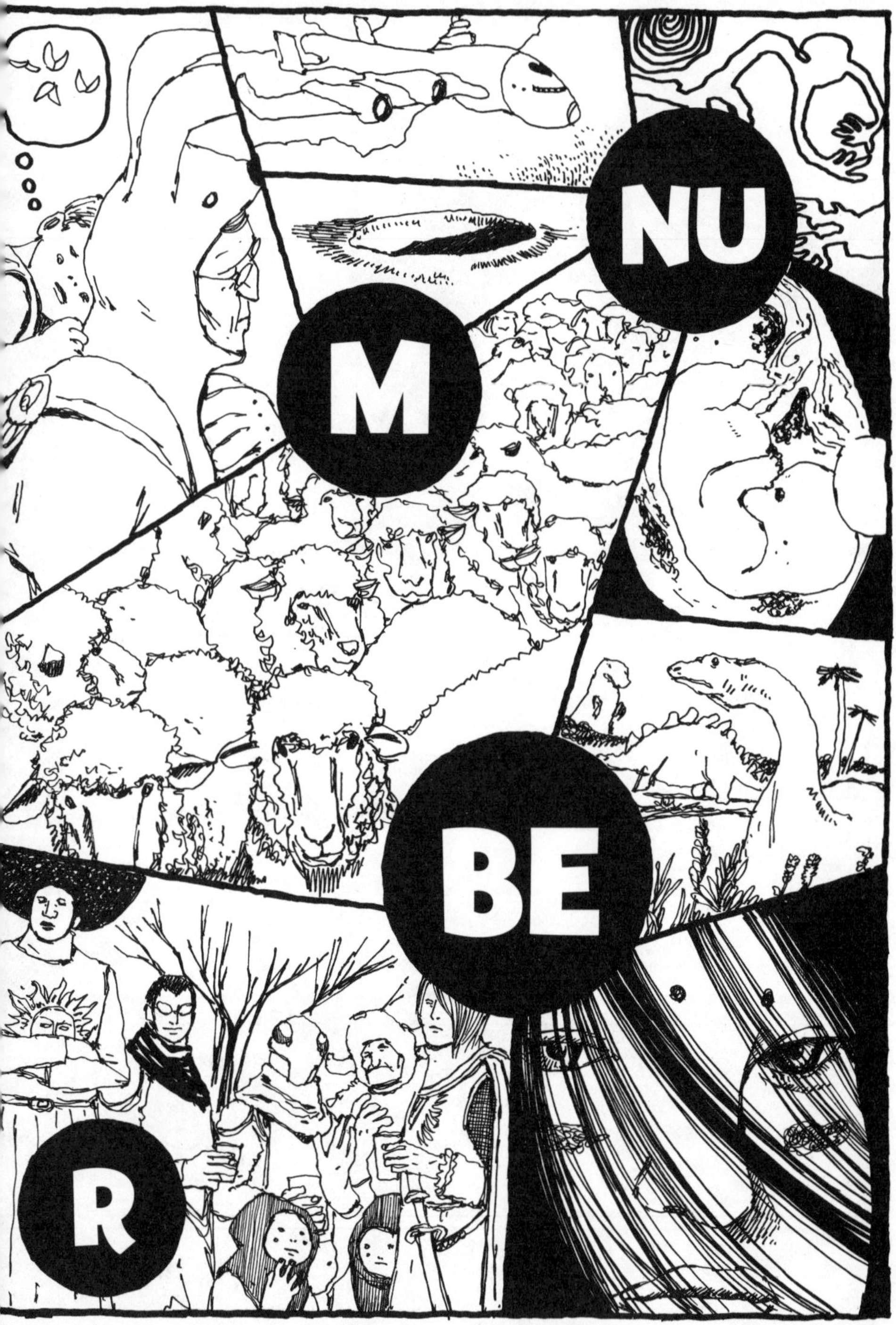
NU
M
BE
R

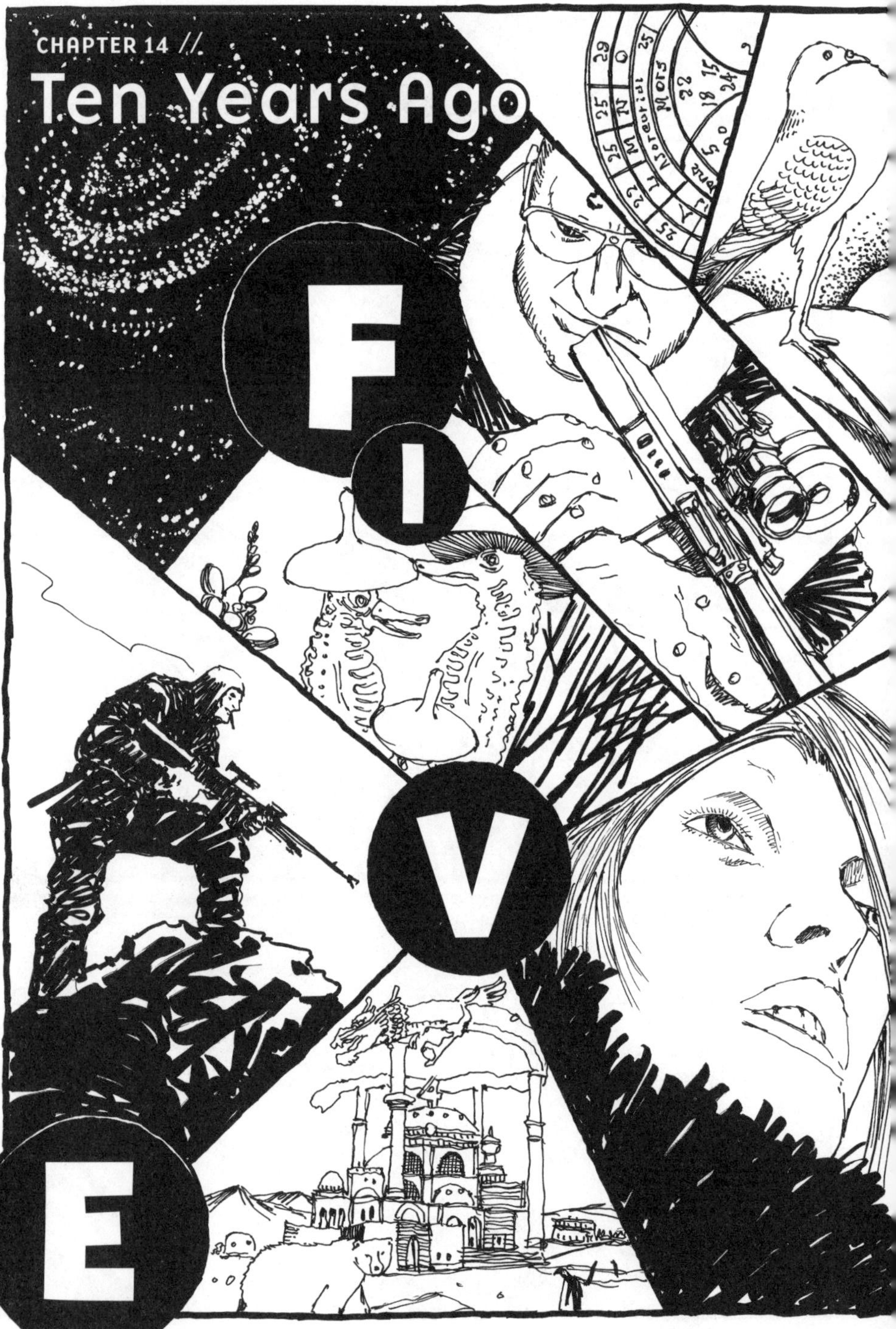
CHAPTER 14 //
Ten Years Ago
F
I
V
E

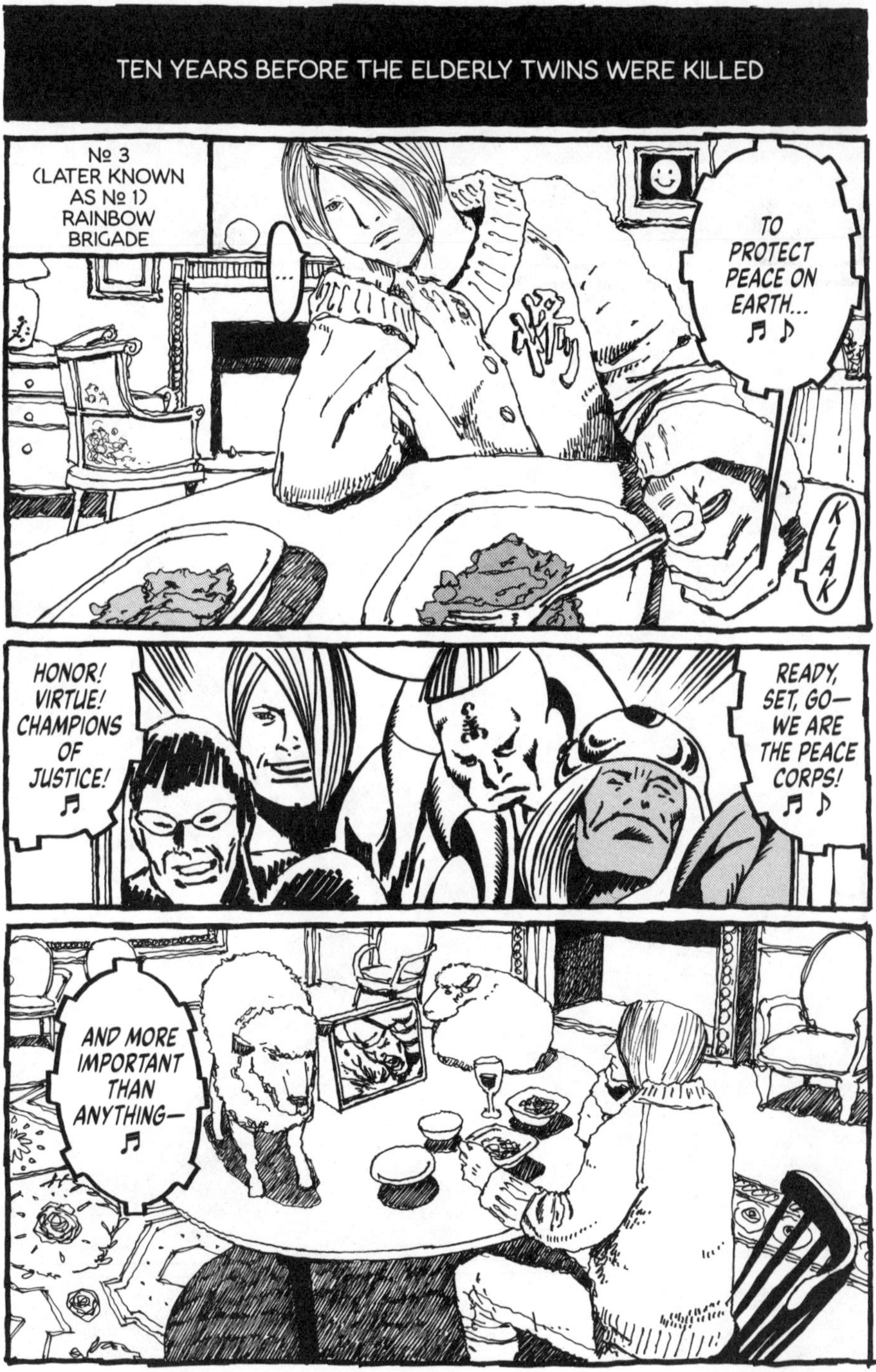
TEN YEARS BEFORE THE ELDERLY TWINS WERE KILLED
TO PROTECT PEACE ON EARTH... ♬ ♪
KLAK
...
№ 3 (LATER KNOWN AS № 1) RAINBOW BRIGADE
READY, SET, GO— WE ARE THE PEACE CORPS! ♬ ♪
HONOR! VIRTUE! CHAMPIONS OF JUSTICE! ♬
AND MORE IMPORTANT THAN ANYTHING— ♬

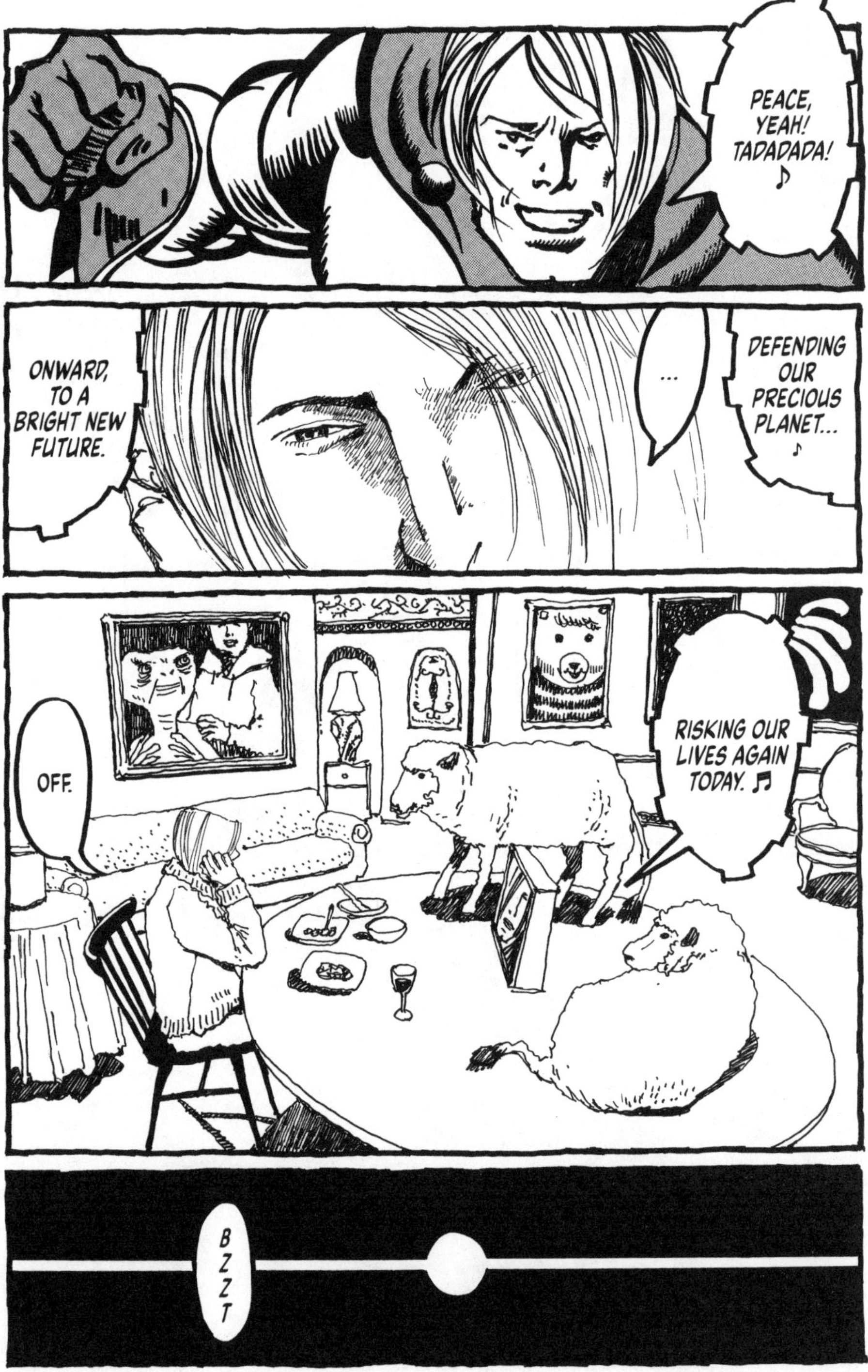
PEACE, YEAH! TADADADA! ♪
DEFENDING OUR PRECIOUS PLANET... ♪
...
ONWARD, TO A BRIGHT NEW FUTURE.
RISKING OUR LIVES AGAIN TODAY. ♫
OFF.
BZZT

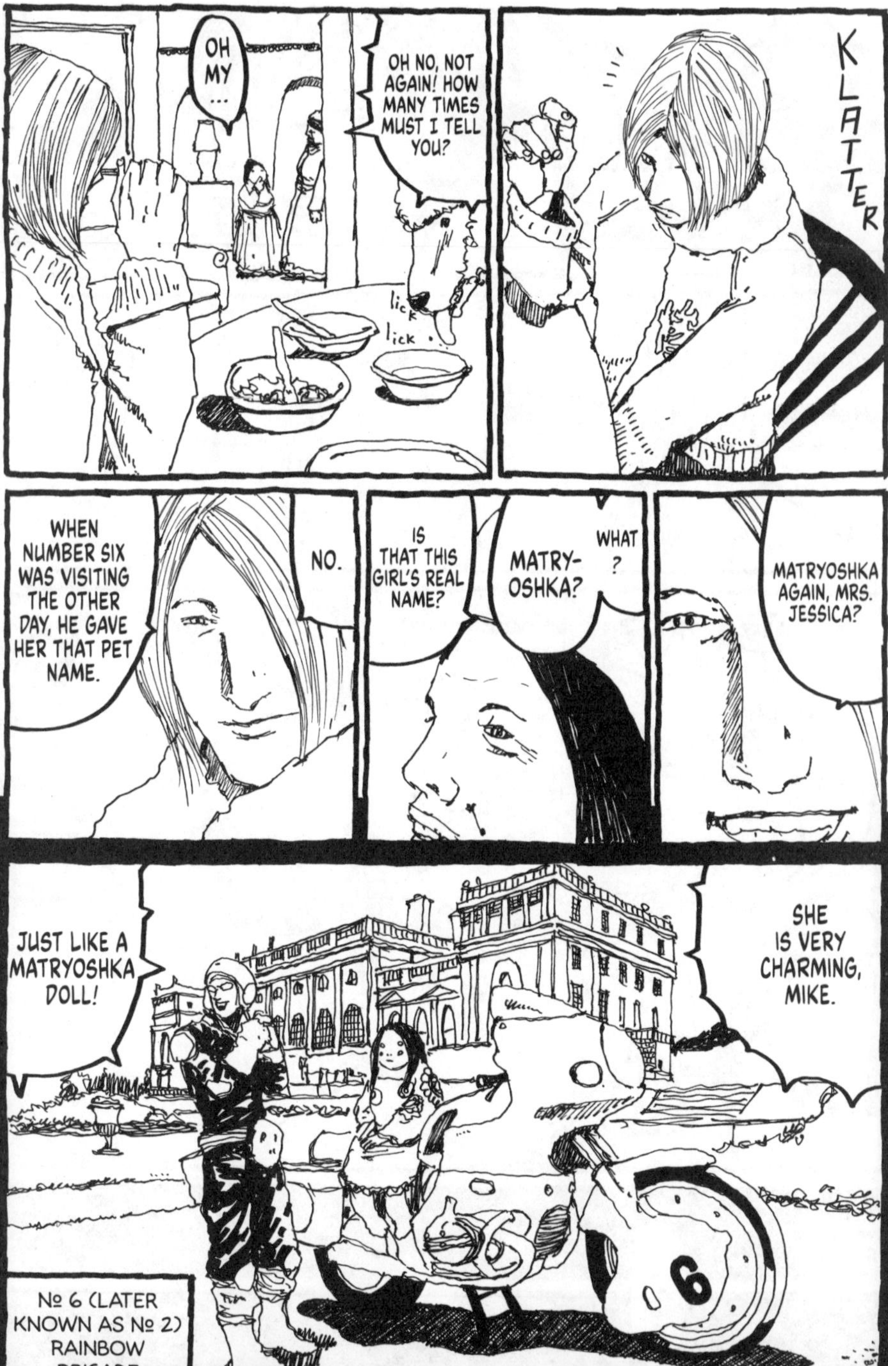
KLATTER
OH NO, NOT AGAIN! HOW MANY TIMES MUST I TELL YOU?
OH MY ...
lick lick
MATRYOSHKA AGAIN, MRS. JESSICA?
WHAT ?
MATRY-OSHKA?
IS THAT THIS GIRL'S REAL NAME?
NO.
WHEN NUMBER SIX WAS VISITING THE OTHER DAY, HE GAVE HER THAT PET NAME.
SHE IS VERY CHARMING, MIKE.
JUST LIKE A MATRYOSHKA DOLL!
№ 6 (LATER KNOWN AS № 2) RAINBOW BRIGADE

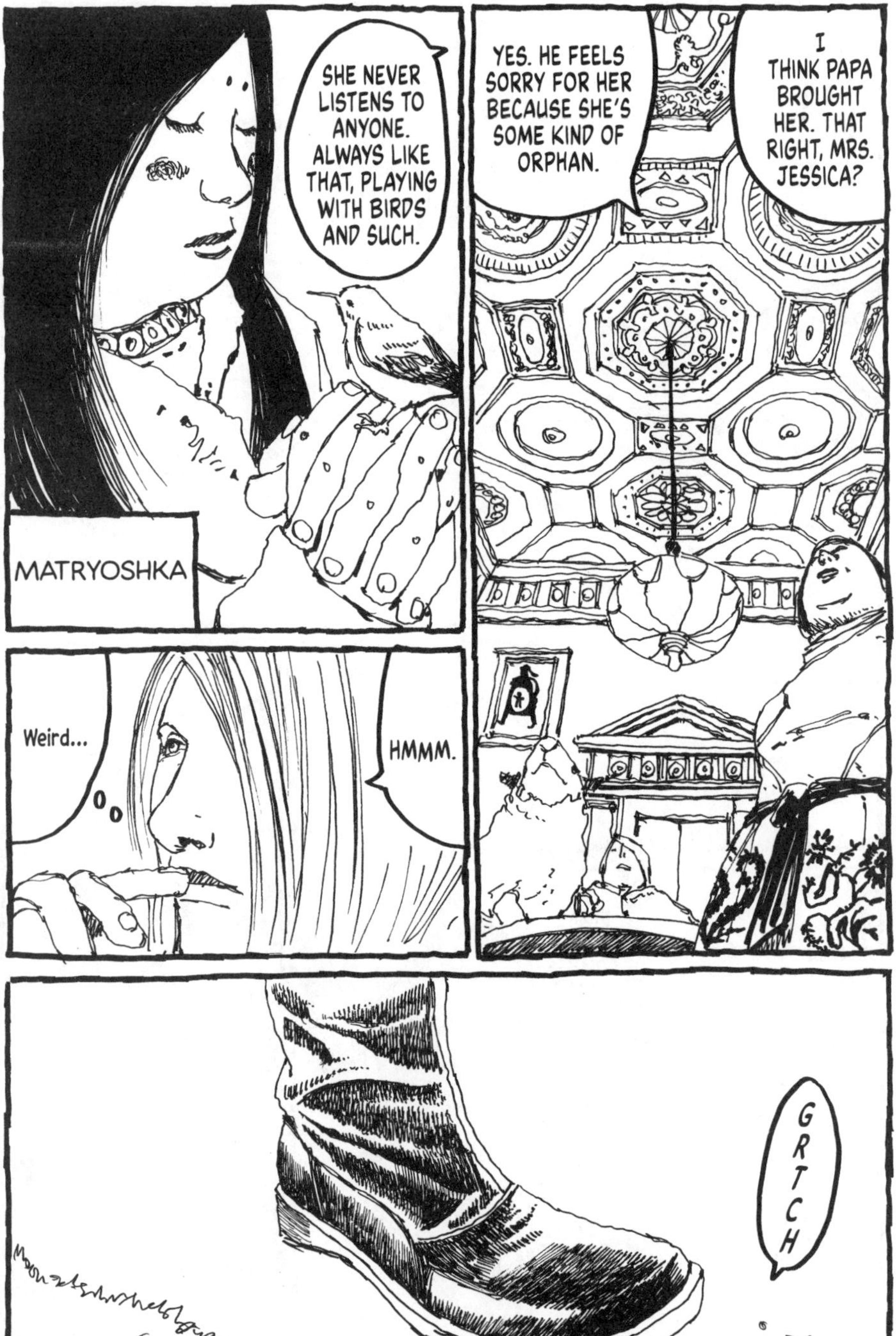
I THINK PAPA BROUGHT HER. THAT RIGHT, MRS. JESSICA?
YES. HE FEELS SORRY FOR HER BECAUSE SHE'S SOME KIND OF ORPHAN.
MATRYOSHKA
SHE NEVER LISTENS TO ANYONE. ALWAYS LIKE THAT, PLAYING WITH BIRDS AND SUCH.
HMMM.
Weird...
GRTCH

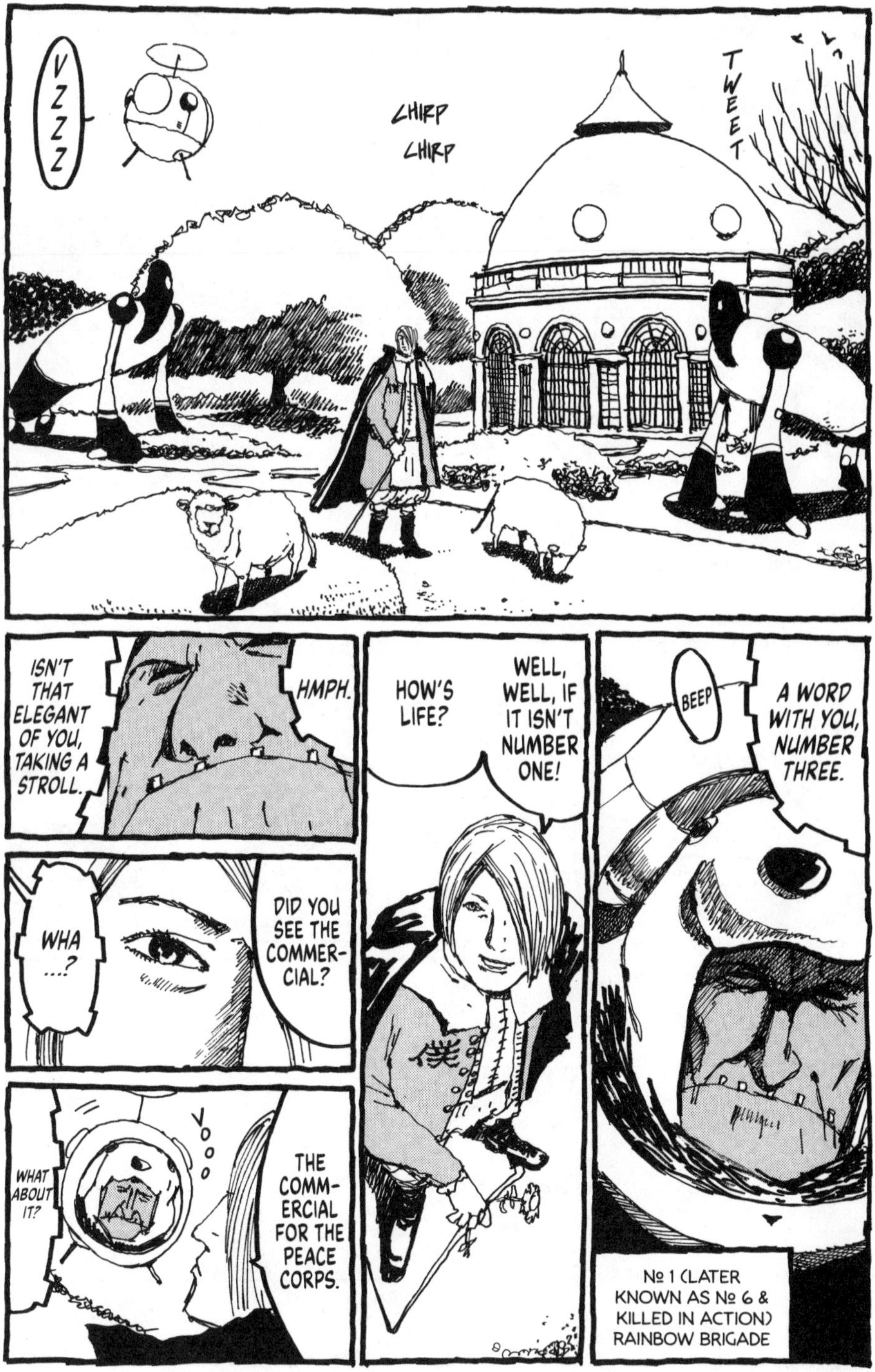
TWEET
CHIRP CHIRP
VZZZ
A WORD WITH YOU, NUMBER THREE.
BEEP
№ 1 (LATER KNOWN AS № 6 & KILLED IN ACTION) RAINBOW BRIGADE
WELL, WELL, IF IT ISN'T NUMBER ONE!
HOW'S LIFE?
HMPH.
ISN'T THAT ELEGANT OF YOU, TAKING A STROLL.
DID YOU SEE THE COMMERCIAL?
WHA ...?
THE COMMERCIAL FOR THE PEACE CORPS.
VOOO
WHAT ABOUT IT?

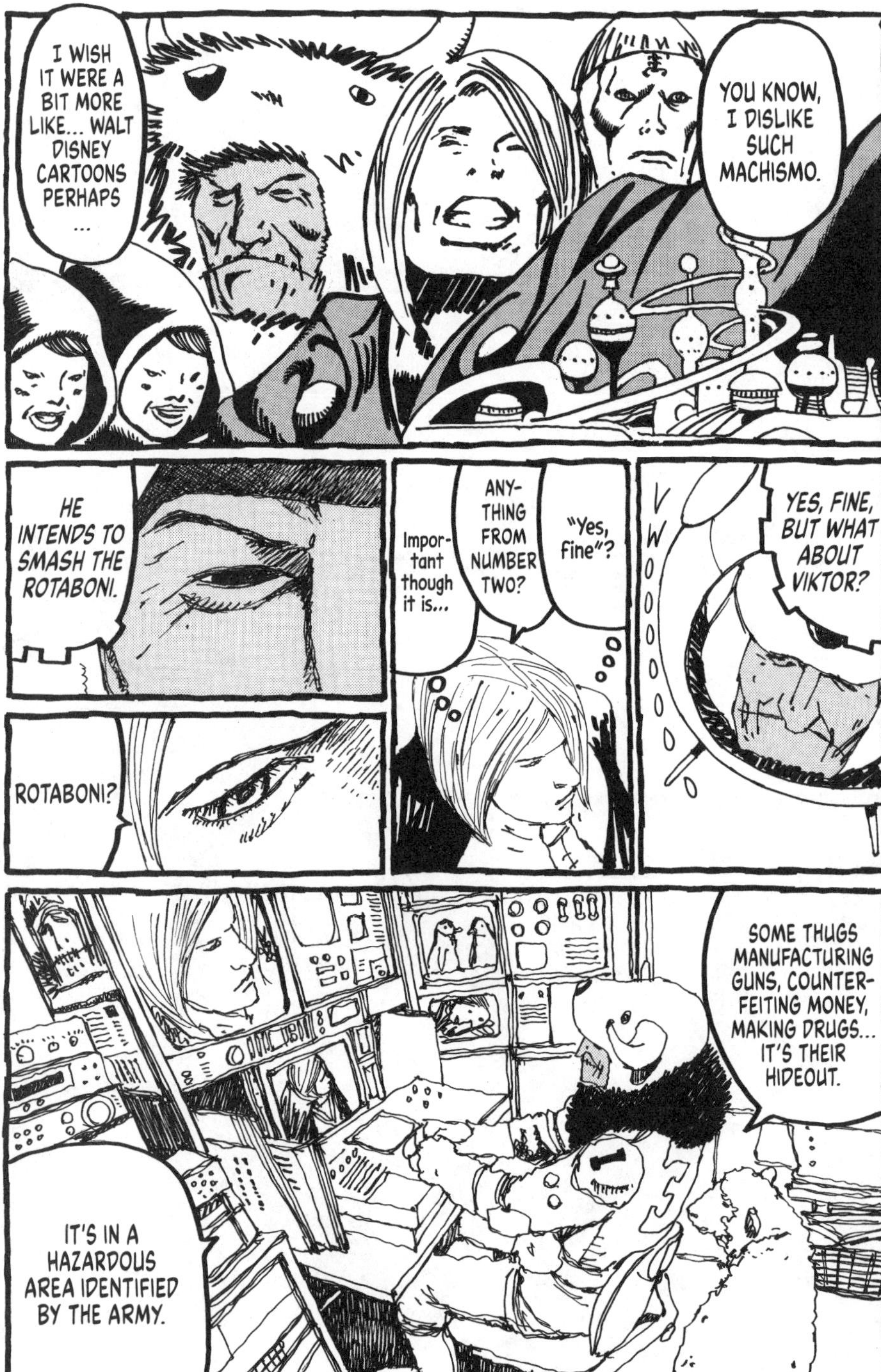
YOU KNOW, I DISLIKE SUCH MACHISMO.
I WISH IT WERE A BIT MORE LIKE... WALT DISNEY CARTOONS PERHAPS ...
YES, FINE, BUT WHAT ABOUT VIKTOR?
VWOOOOOO
"Yes, fine"?
ANYTHING FROM NUMBER TWO?
Important though it is...
HE INTENDS TO SMASH THE ROTABONI.
ROTABONI?
SOME THUGS MANUFACTURING GUNS, COUNTERFEITING MONEY, MAKING DRUGS... IT'S THEIR HIDEOUT.
IT'S IN A HAZARDOUS AREA IDENTIFIED BY THE ARMY.

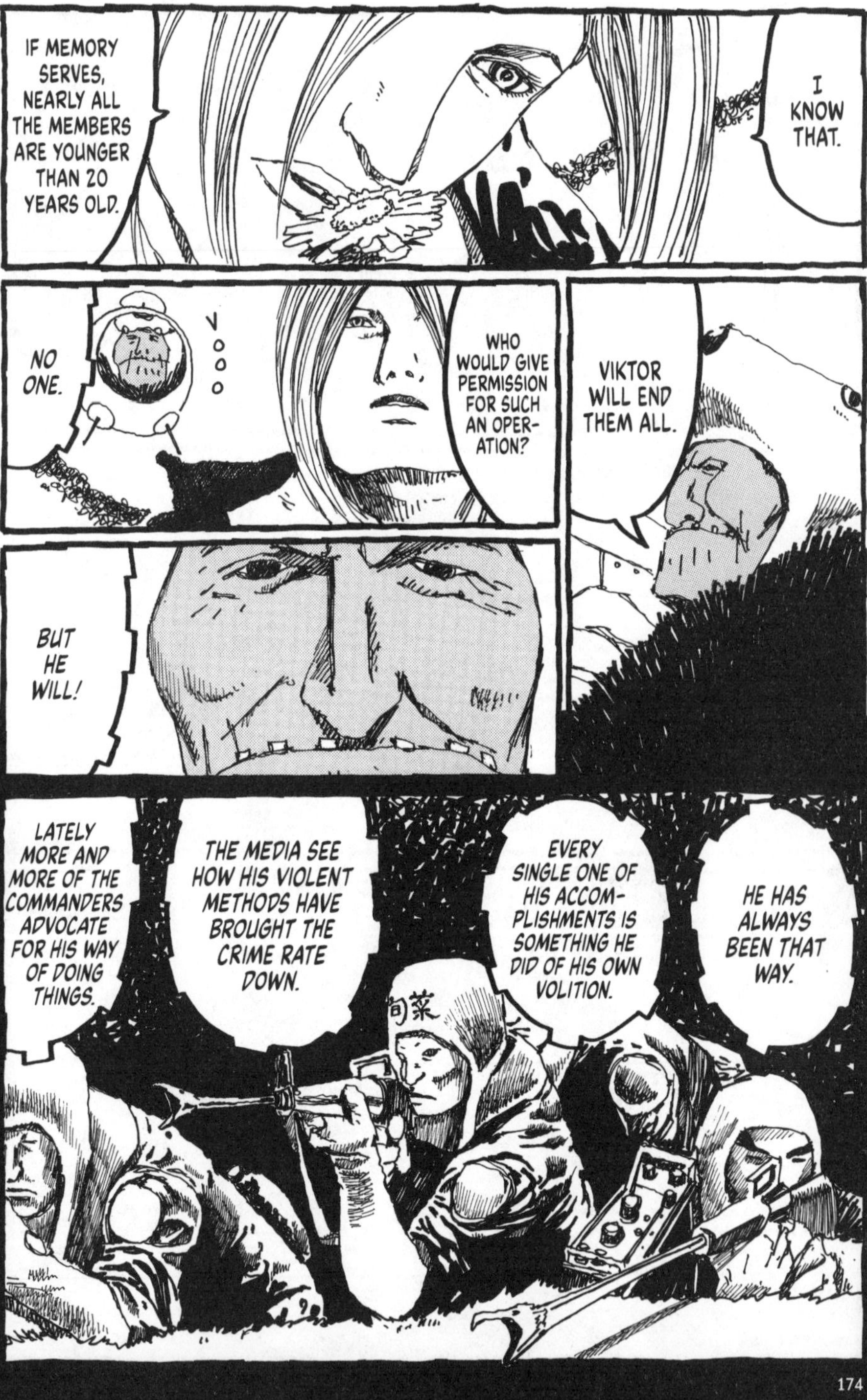
IF MEMORY SERVES, NEARLY ALL THE MEMBERS ARE YOUNGER THAN 20 YEARS OLD.
I KNOW THAT.
VIKTOR WILL END THEM ALL.
WHO WOULD GIVE PERMISSION FOR SUCH AN OPER-ATION?
VOOO
NO ONE.
BUT HE WILL!
LATELY MORE AND MORE OF THE COMMANDERS ADVOCATE FOR HIS WAY OF DOING THINGS.
THE MEDIA SEE HOW HIS VIOLENT METHODS HAVE BROUGHT THE CRIME RATE DOWN.
EVERY SINGLE ONE OF HIS ACCOM-PLISHMENTS IS SOMETHING HE DID OF HIS OWN VOLITION.
HE HAS ALWAYS BEEN THAT WAY.

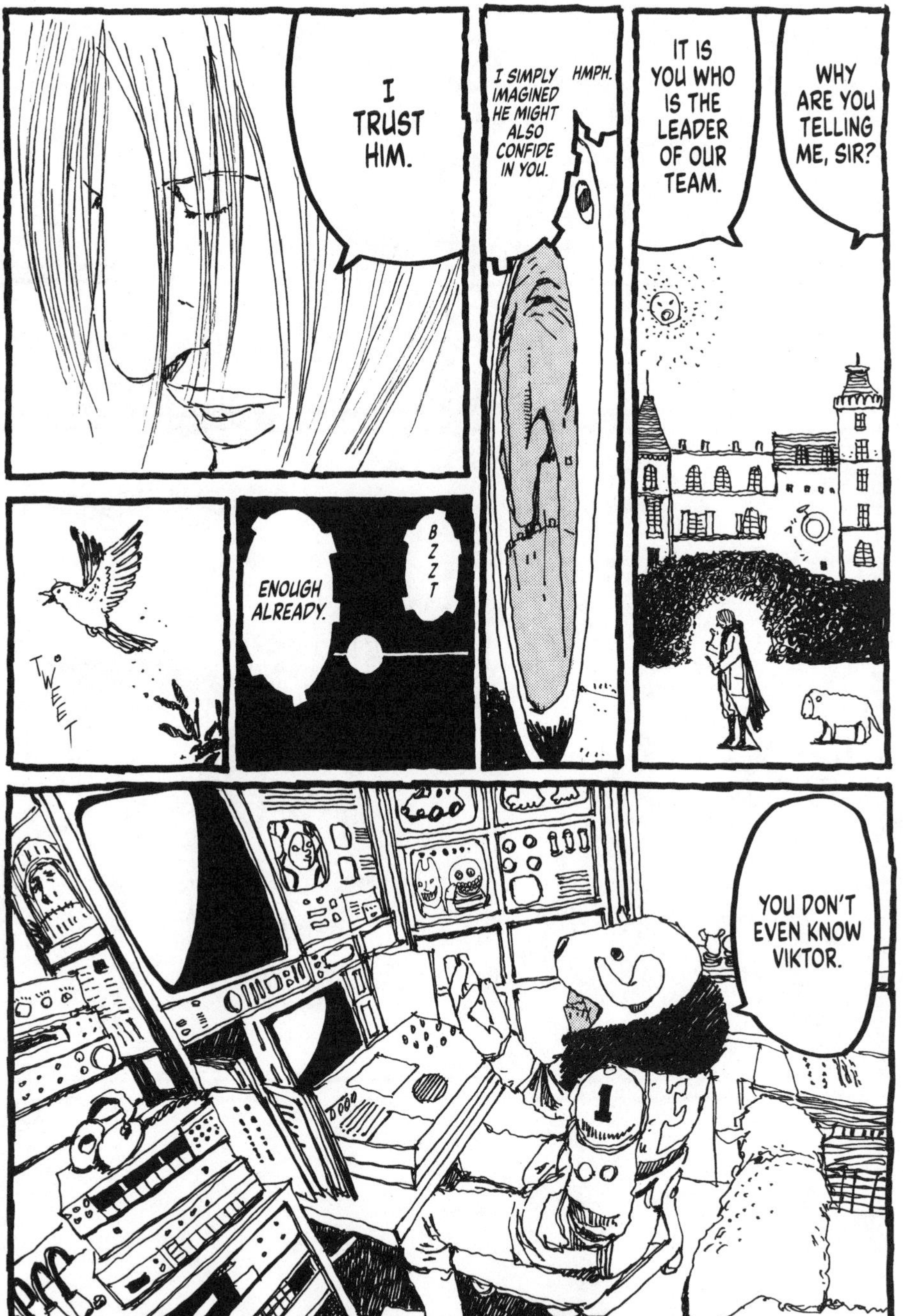
WHY ARE YOU TELLING ME, SIR?
IT IS YOU WHO IS THE LEADER OF OUR TEAM.
HMPH.
I SIMPLY IMAGINED HE MIGHT ALSO CONFIDE IN YOU.
I TRUST HIM.
BZZT
ENOUGH ALREADY.
TWEET
YOU DON'T EVEN KNOW VIKTOR.

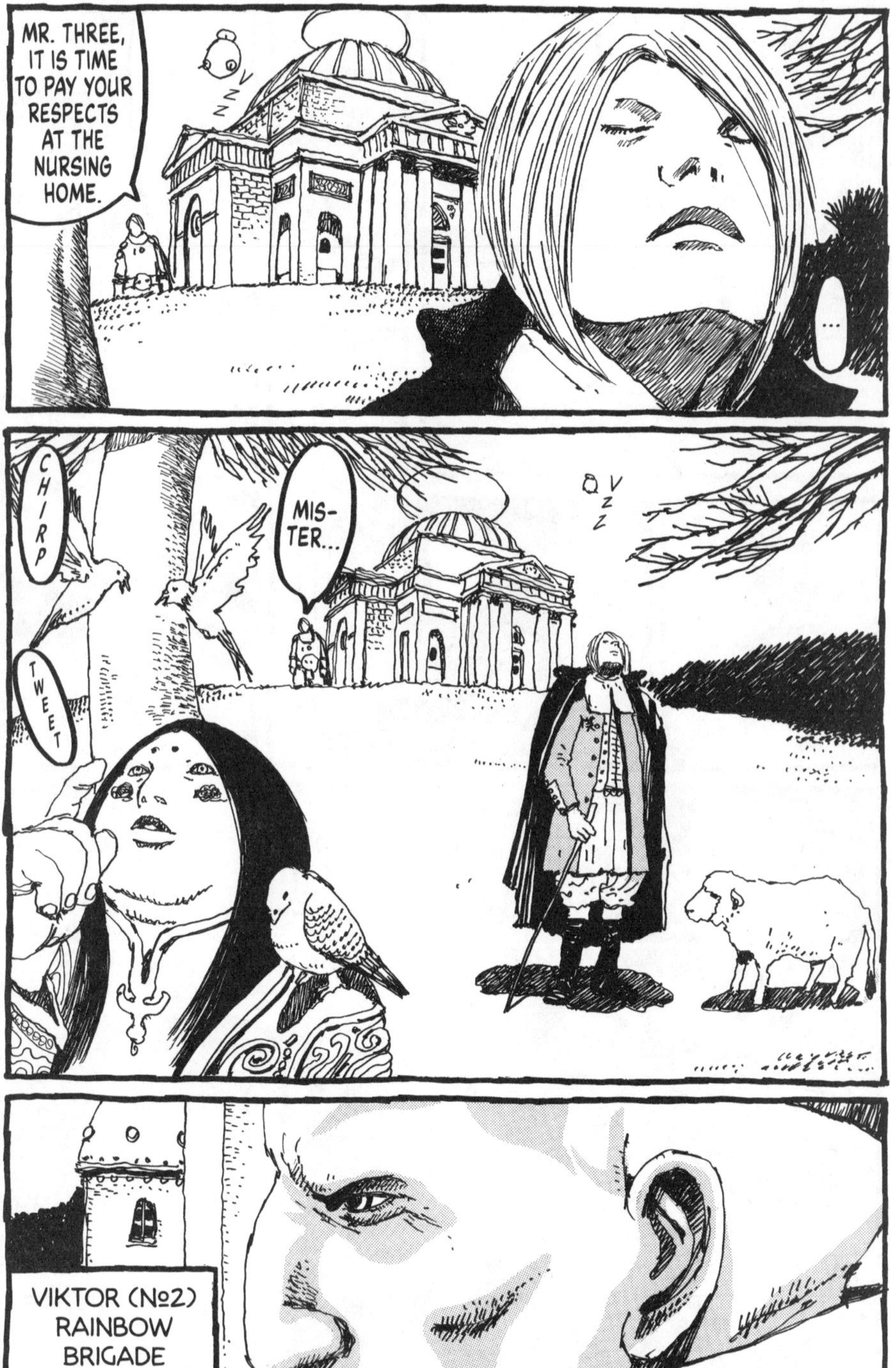
MR. THREE, IT IS TIME TO PAY YOUR RESPECTS AT THE NURSING HOME.
...
MIS-TER...
CHIRP
TWEET
VIKTOR (№2) RAINBOW BRIGADE

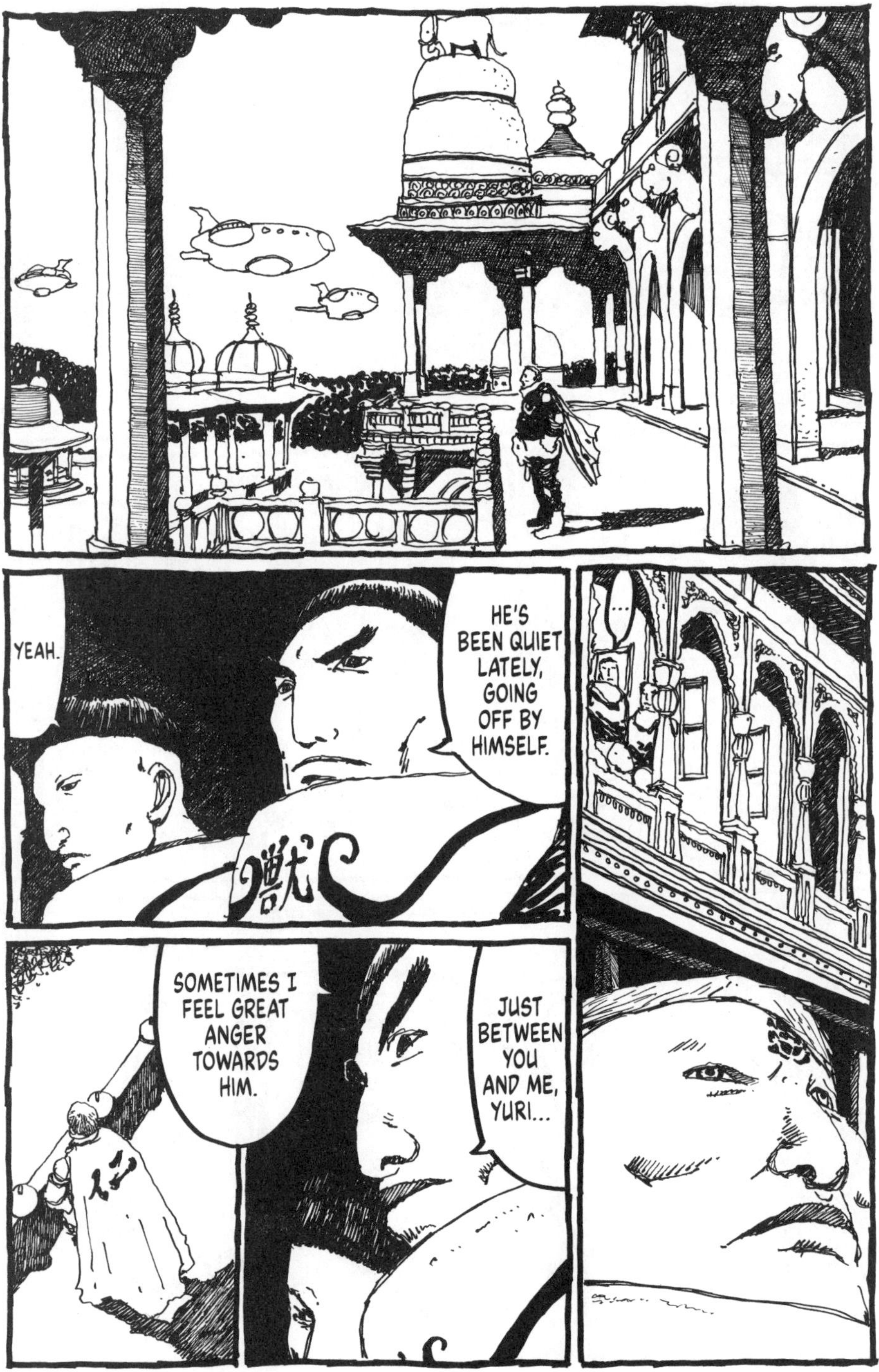
...
HE'S BEEN QUIET LATELY, GOING OFF BY HIMSELF.
YEAH.
JUST BETWEEN YOU AND ME, YURI...
SOMETIMES I FEEL GREAT ANGER TOWARDS HIM.

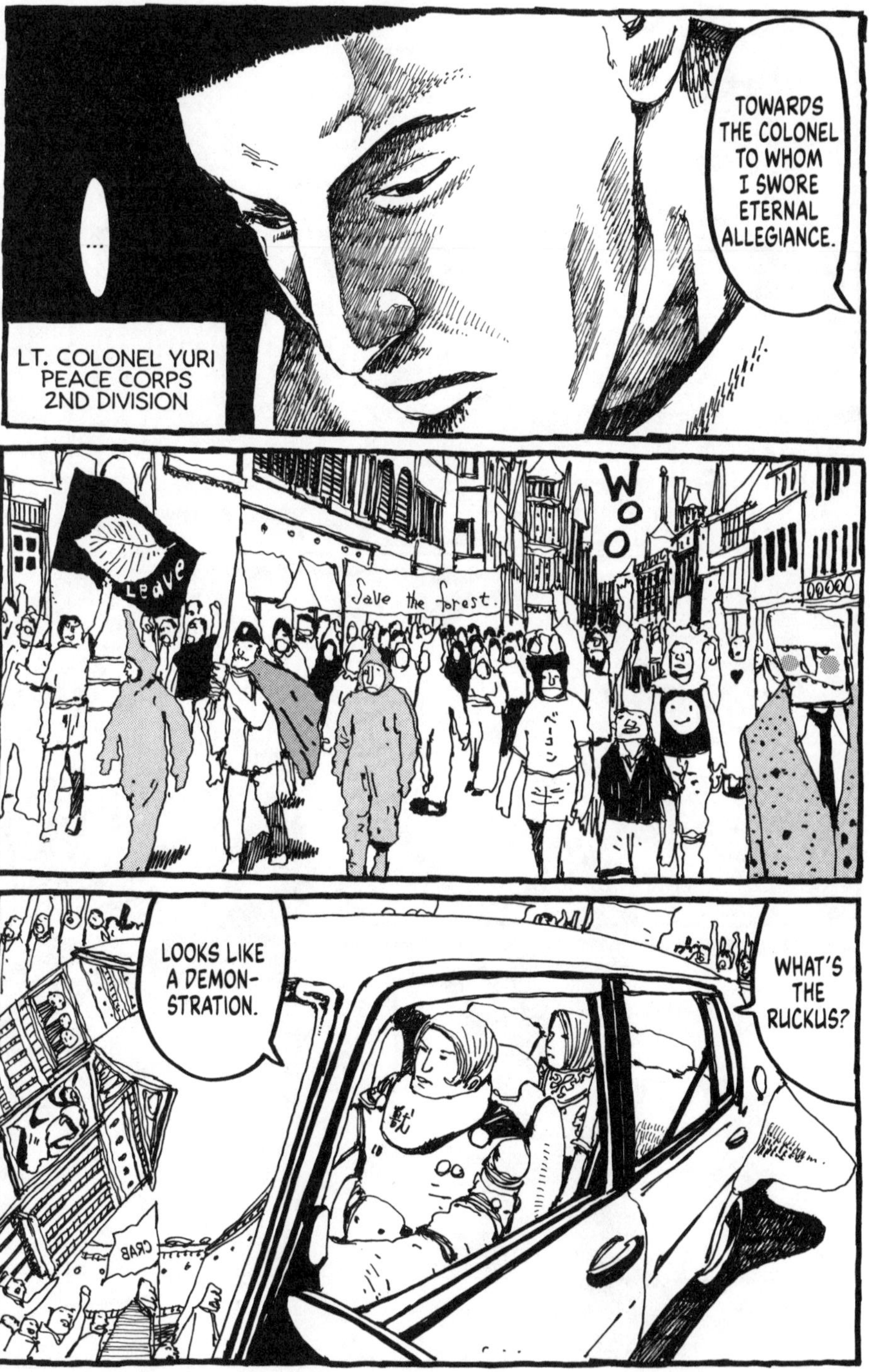
TOWARDS THE COLONEL TO WHOM I SWORE ETERNAL ALLEGIANCE.
...
LT. COLONEL YURI PEACE CORPS 2ND DIVISION
WOO
Leave
Save the forest.
ベーコン
WHAT'S THE RUCKUS?
LOOKS LIKE A DEMON-STRATION.
CRAB

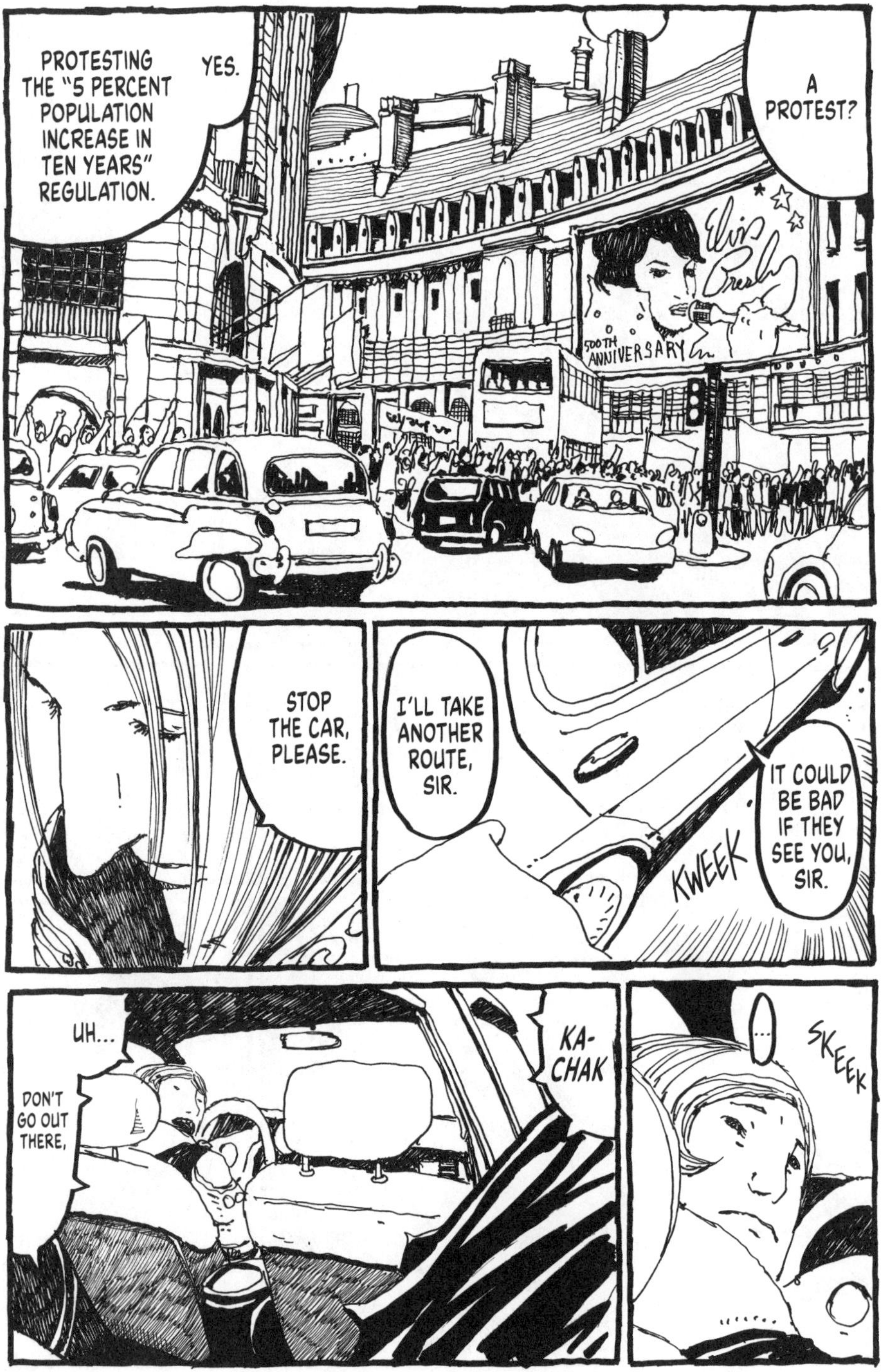
A PROTEST?
YES.
PROTESTING THE "5 PERCENT POPULATION INCREASE IN TEN YEARS" REGULATION.
500TH ANNIVERSARY
I'LL TAKE ANOTHER ROUTE, SIR.
KWEEK
IT COULD BE BAD IF THEY SEE YOU, SIR.
STOP THE CAR, PLEASE.
...
SKEEK
KA-CHAK
UH...
DON'T GO OUT THERE,

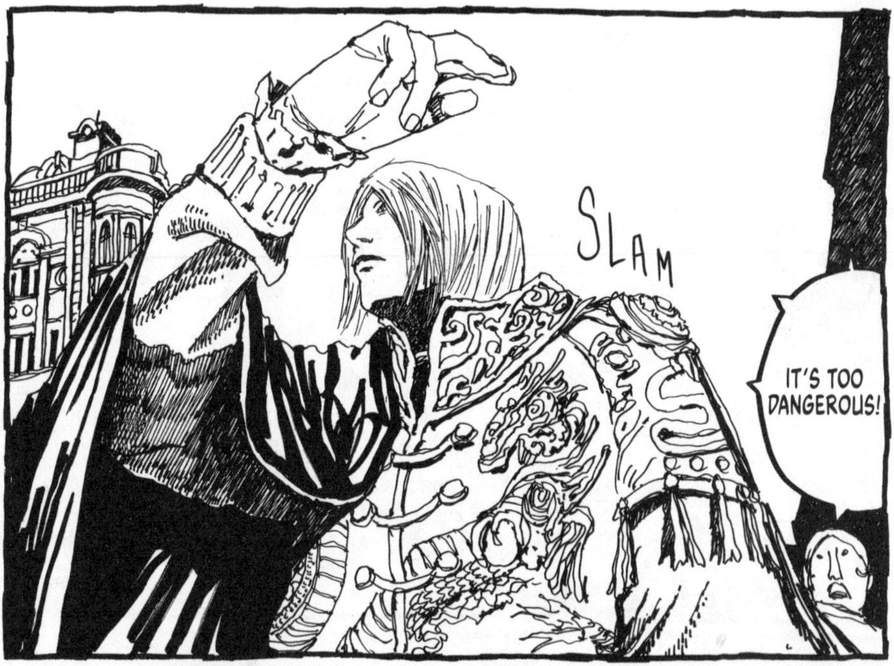
SLAM
IT'S TOO DANGEROUS!
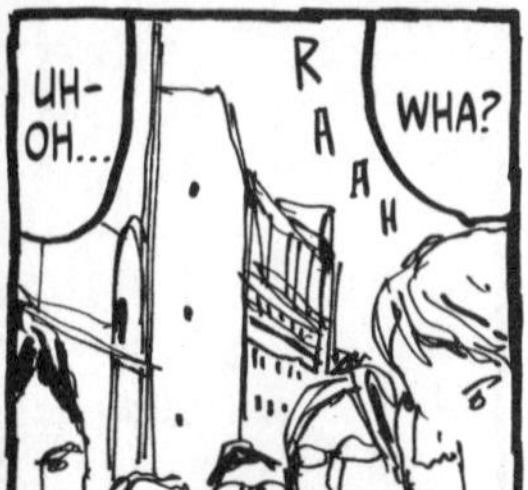
WHA?
RAAH
UH-OH...
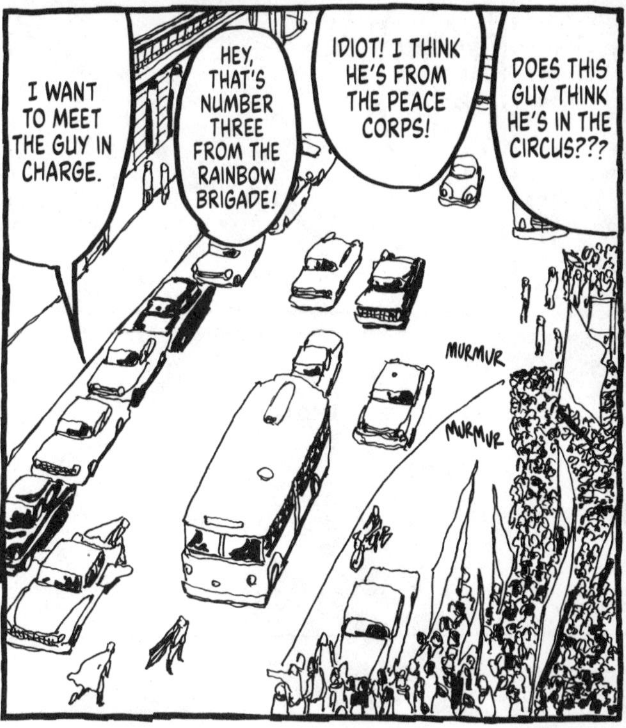
DOES THIS GUY THINK HE'S IN THE CIRCUS???
IDIOT! I THINK HE'S FROM THE PEACE CORPS!
HEY, THAT'S NUMBER THREE FROM THE RAINBOW BRIGADE!
I WANT TO MEET THE GUY IN CHARGE.
MURMUR
MURMUR

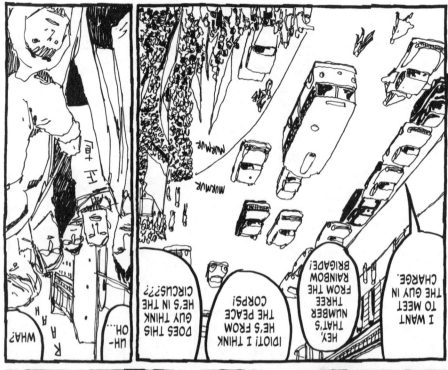

*Guy in charge

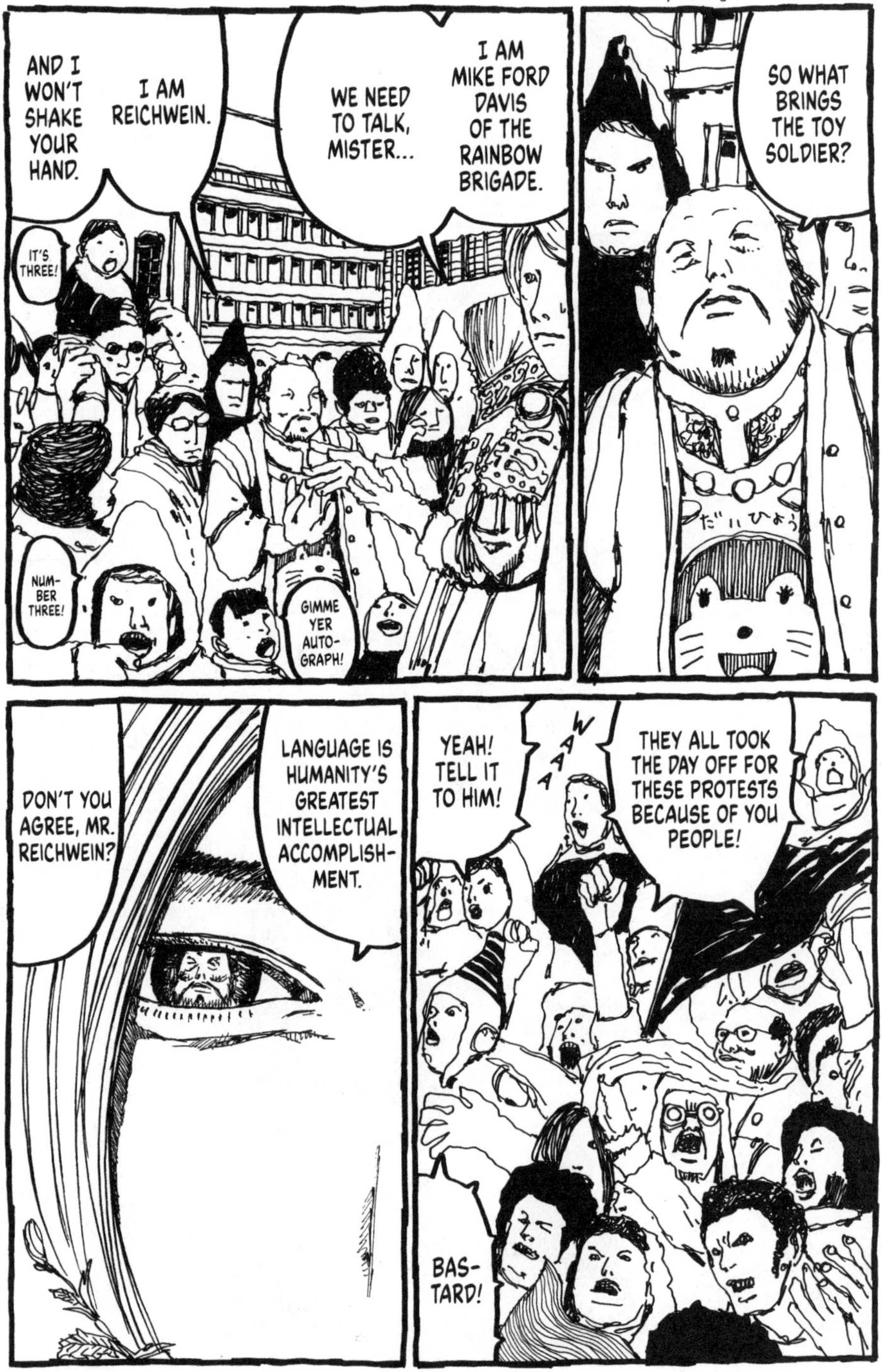
SO WHAT BRINGS THE TOY SOLDIER?
だいひょう
I AM MIKE FORD DAVIS OF THE RAINBOW BRIGADE.
WE NEED TO TALK, MISTER...
I AM REICHWEIN.
AND I WON'T SHAKE YOUR HAND.
IT'S THREE!
NUMBER THREE!
GIMME YER AUTOGRAPH!
THEY ALL TOOK THE DAY OFF FOR THESE PROTESTS BECAUSE OF YOU PEOPLE!
WAAA
YEAH! TELL IT TO HIM!
BASTARD!
LANGUAGE IS HUMANITY'S GREATEST INTELLECTUAL ACCOMPLISHMENT.
DON'T YOU AGREE, MR. REICHWEIN?

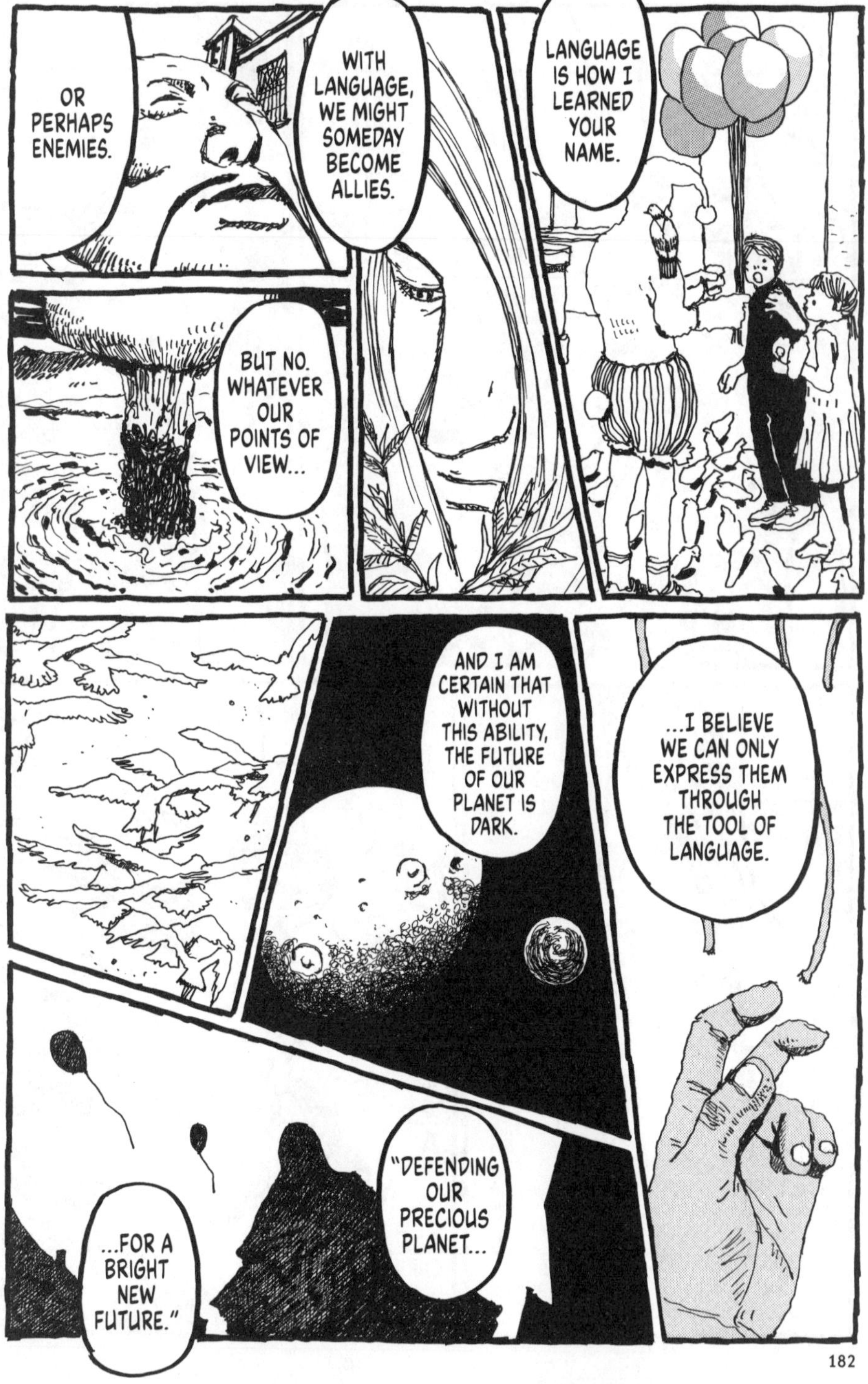
LANGUAGE IS HOW I LEARNED YOUR NAME.
WITH LANGUAGE, WE MIGHT SOMEDAY BECOME ALLIES.
OR PERHAPS ENEMIES.
BUT NO. WHATEVER OUR POINTS OF VIEW...
...I BELIEVE WE CAN ONLY EXPRESS THEM THROUGH THE TOOL OF LANGUAGE.
AND I AM CERTAIN THAT WITHOUT THIS ABILITY, THE FUTURE OF OUR PLANET IS DARK.
"DEFENDING OUR PRECIOUS PLANET...
...FOR A BRIGHT NEW FUTURE."

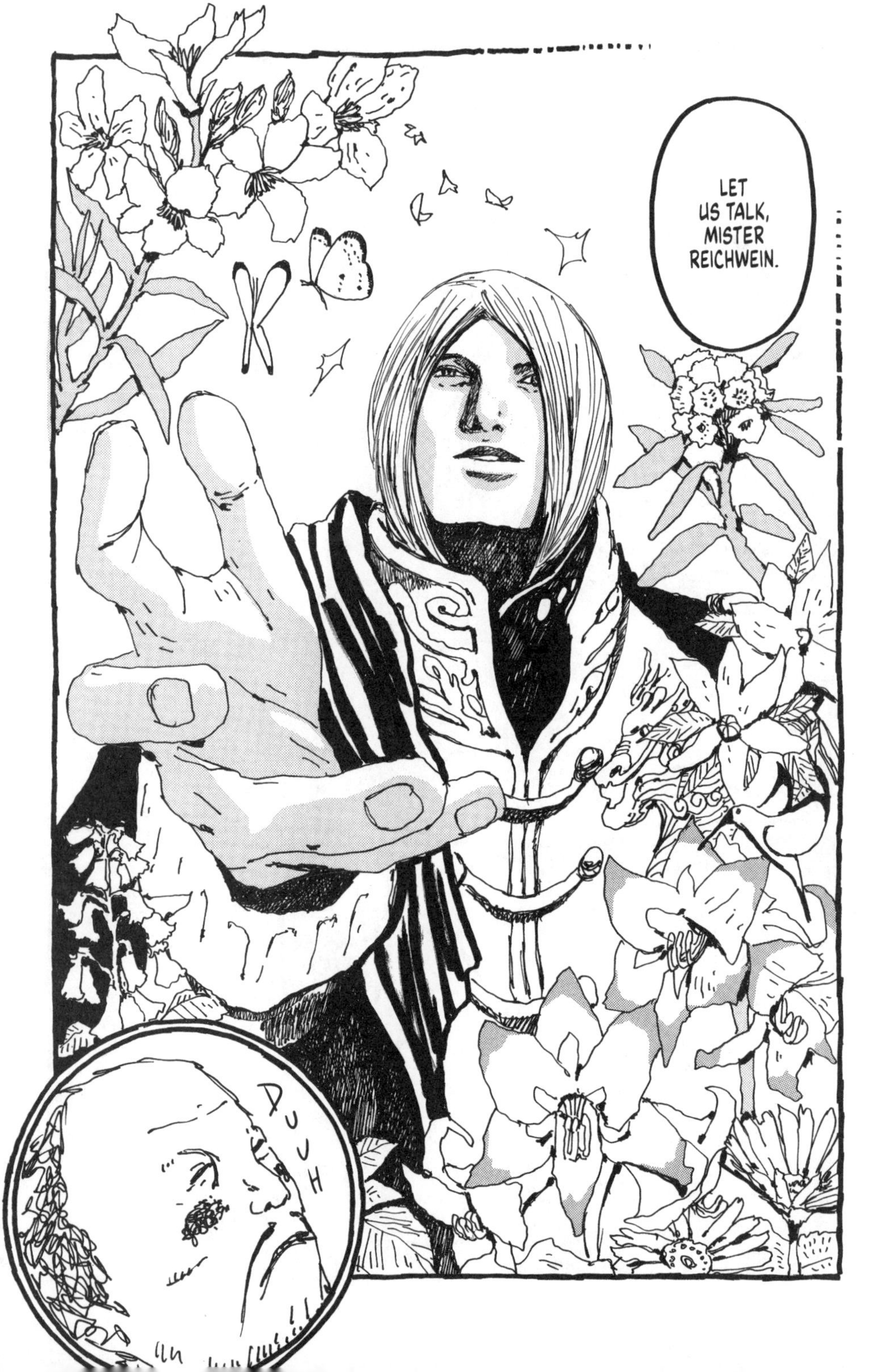
LET US TALK, MISTER REICHWEIN.
DUUH

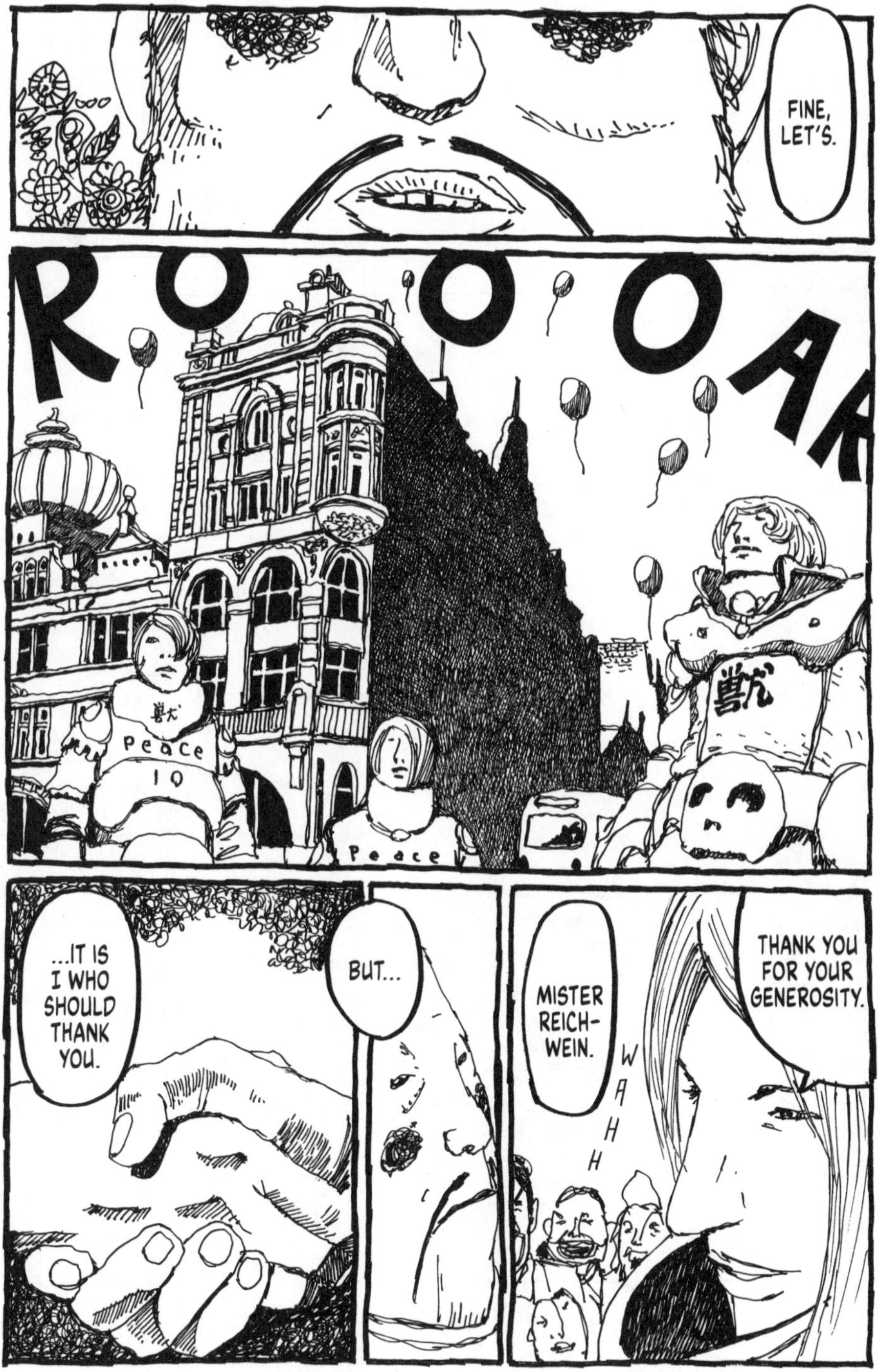
FINE, LET'S.
ROOOAR
獣
peace
10
獣
Peace
THANK YOU FOR YOUR GENEROSITY.
MISTER REICH-WEIN.
WAHHH
BUT...
...IT IS I WHO SHOULD THANK YOU.

VROOOOOOOOOOOO
HEH HEH...
VOOO
"A SAVIOR APPEARS"...? HA HA HA.
FLAP
MAURY Daily
FWAP
WELL, ISN'T THAT SWEET?
"WHAT A WONDERFUL WORLD."

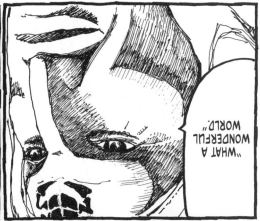

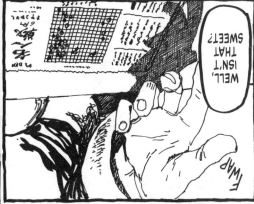

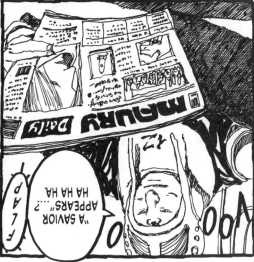

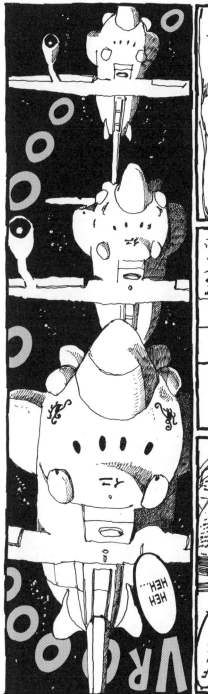

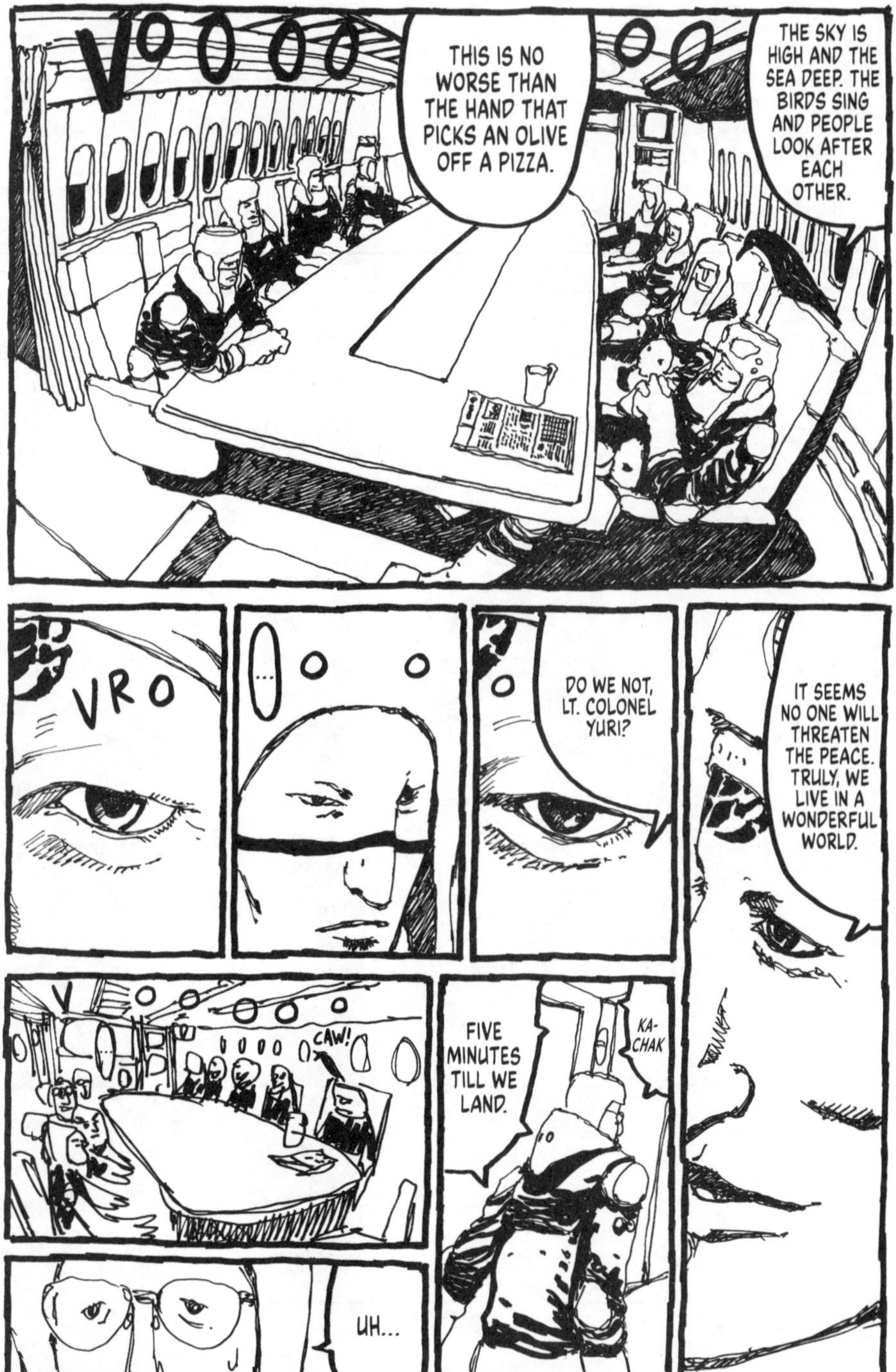
THE SKY IS HIGH AND THE SEA DEEP. THE BIRDS SING AND PEOPLE LOOK AFTER EACH OTHER.
THIS IS NO WORSE THAN THE HAND THAT PICKS AN OLIVE OFF A PIZZA.
VOOOOOO
IT SEEMS NO ONE WILL THREATEN THE PEACE. TRULY, WE LIVE IN A WONDERFUL WORLD.
DO WE NOT, LT. COLONEL YURI?
O
O O
...
VRO
KA-CHAK
FIVE MINUTES TILL WE LAND.
CAW!
VOOOOO
UH...

*Himalayan

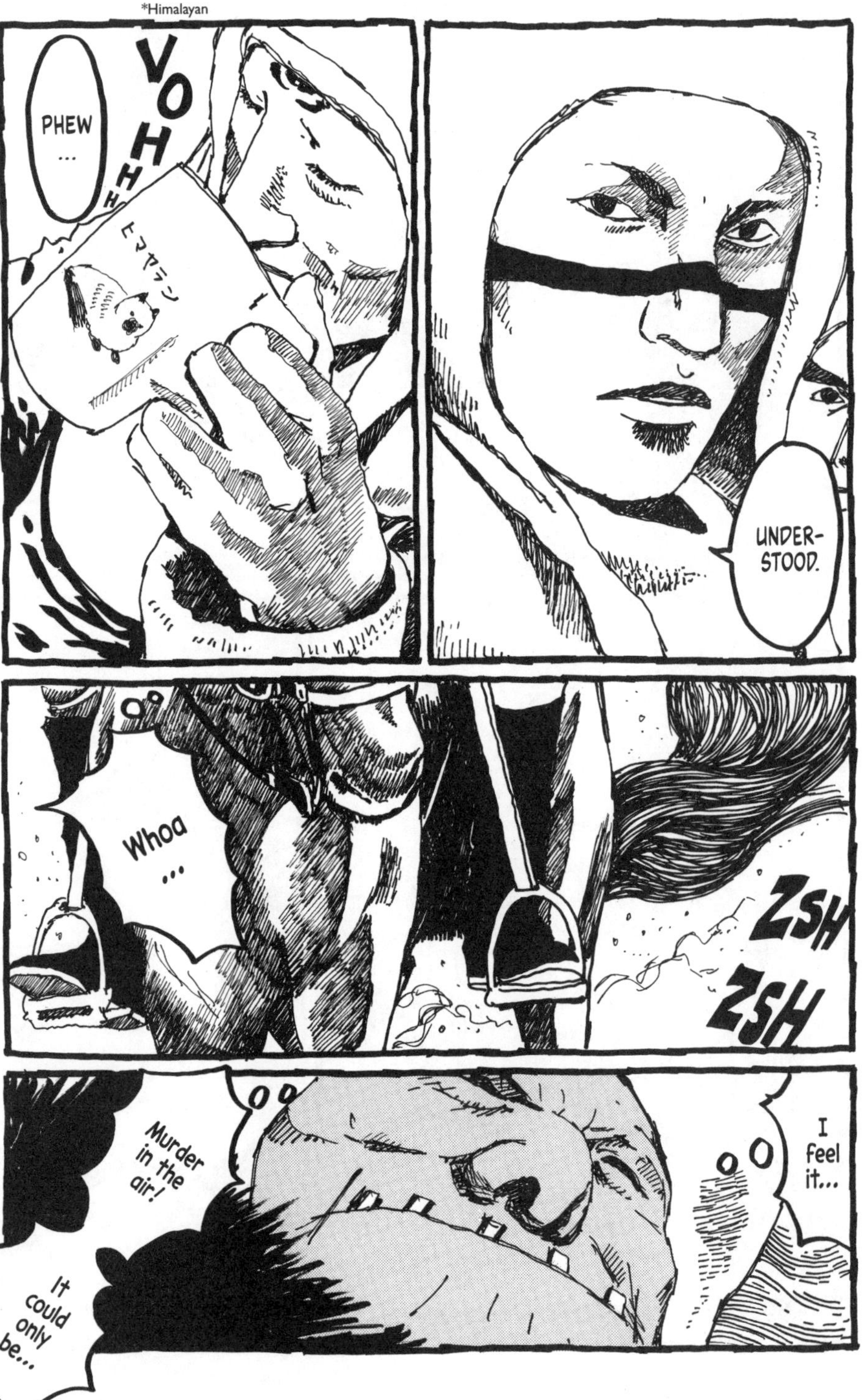
UNDER-STOOD.
VOHHHH
PHEW...
ヒマヤラン
ZSH ZSH
Whoa...
I feel it...
Murder in the air!
It could only be...

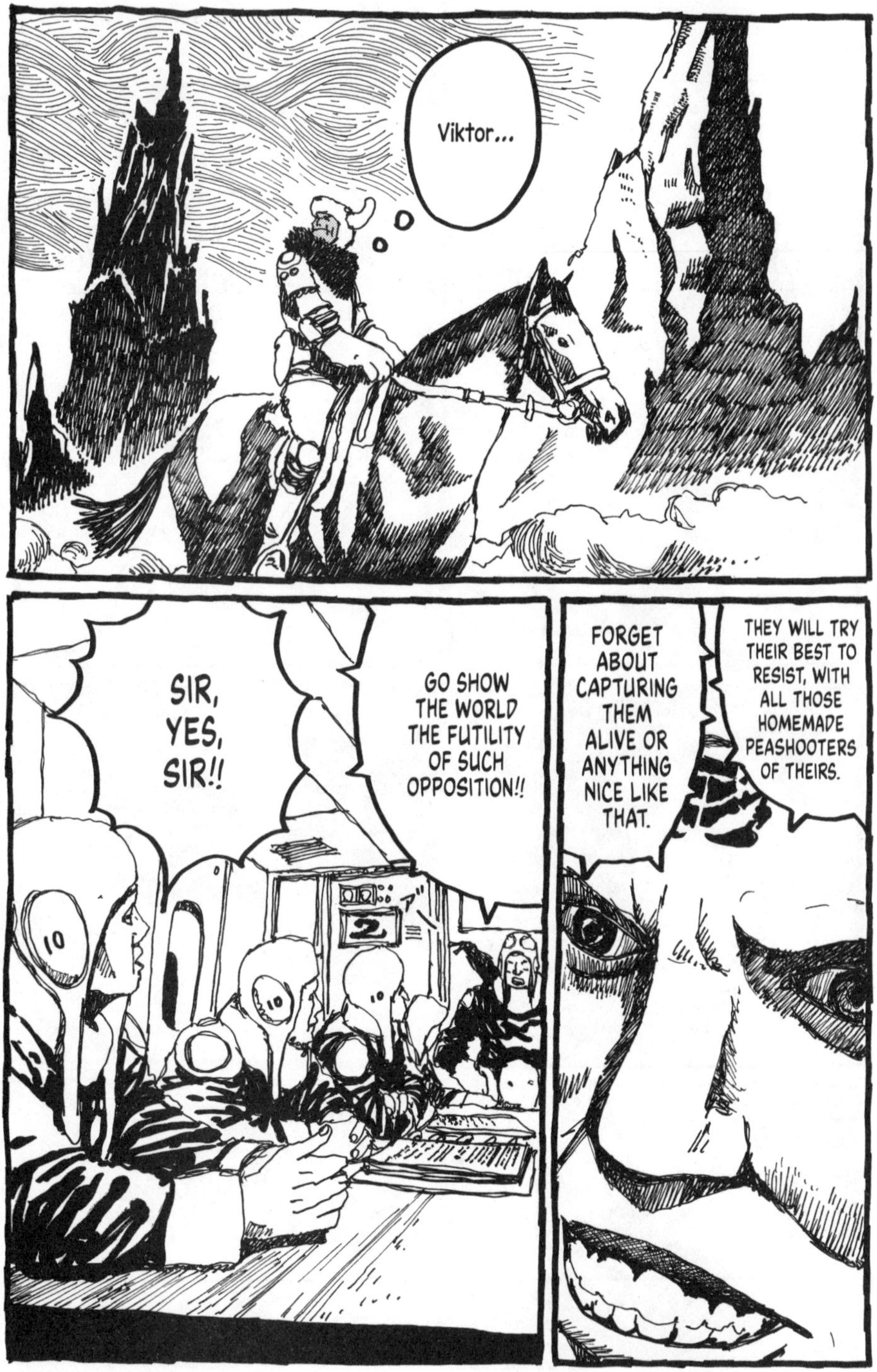
Viktor...
THEY WILL TRY THEIR BEST TO RESIST, WITH ALL THOSE HOMEMADE PEASHOOTERS OF THEIRS.
FORGET ABOUT CAPTURING THEM ALIVE OR ANYTHING NICE LIKE THAT.
GO SHOW THE WORLD THE FUTILITY OF SUCH OPPOSITION!!
SIR, YES, SIR!!

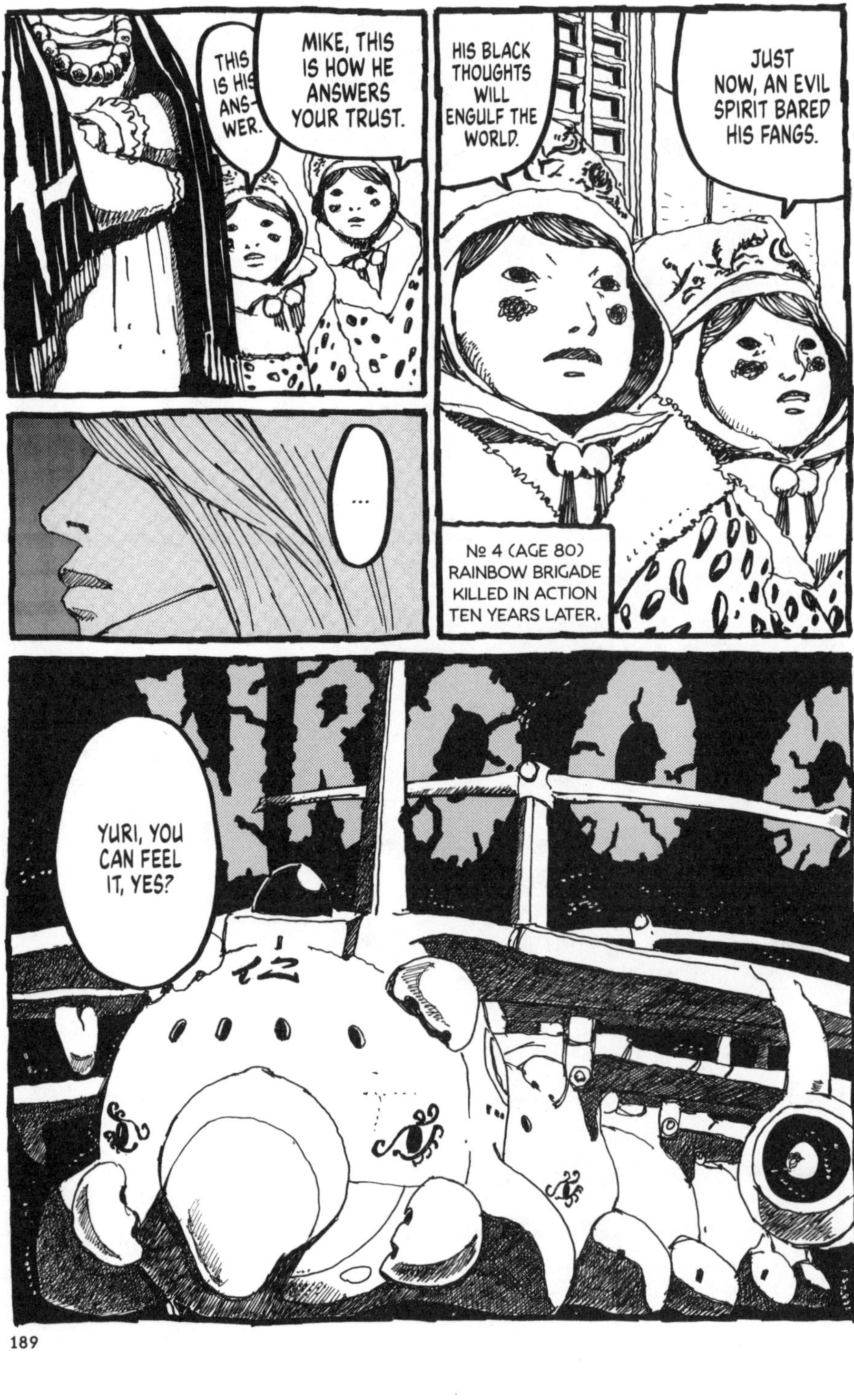
JUST NOW, AN EVIL SPIRIT BARED HIS FANGS.
HIS BLACK THOUGHTS WILL ENGULF THE WORLD.
№ 4 (AGE 80) RAINBOW BRIGADE KILLED IN ACTION TEN YEARS LATER.
MIKE, THIS IS HOW HE ANSWERS YOUR TRUST.
THIS IS HIS ANS- WER.
...
YURI, YOU CAN FEEL IT, YES?

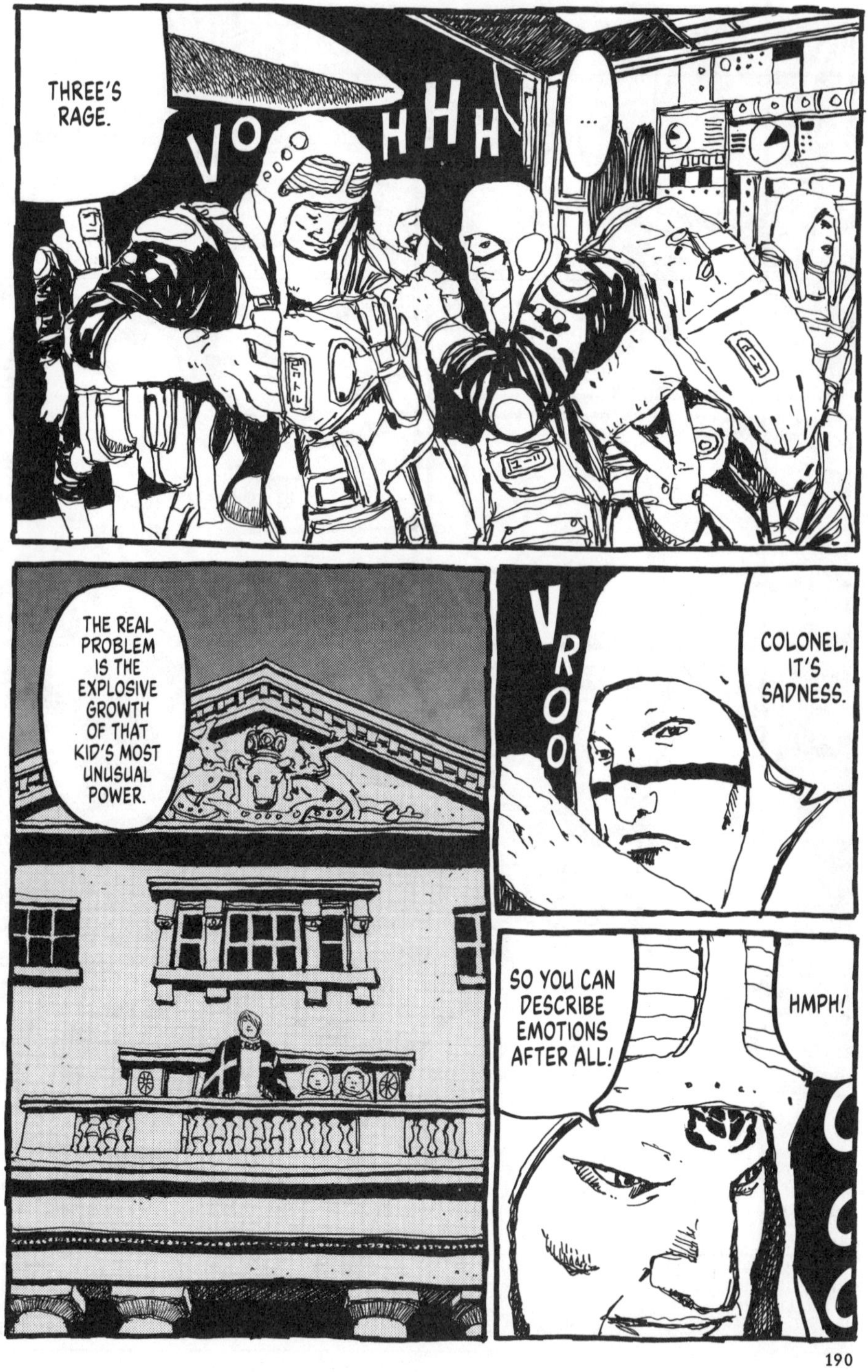
...
VOHHH
THREE'S RAGE.
VROOO
COLONEL, IT'S SADNESS.
HMPH!
SO YOU CAN DESCRIBE EMOTIONS AFTER ALL!
THE REAL PROBLEM IS THE EXPLOSIVE GROWTH OF THAT KID'S MOST UNUSUAL POWER.

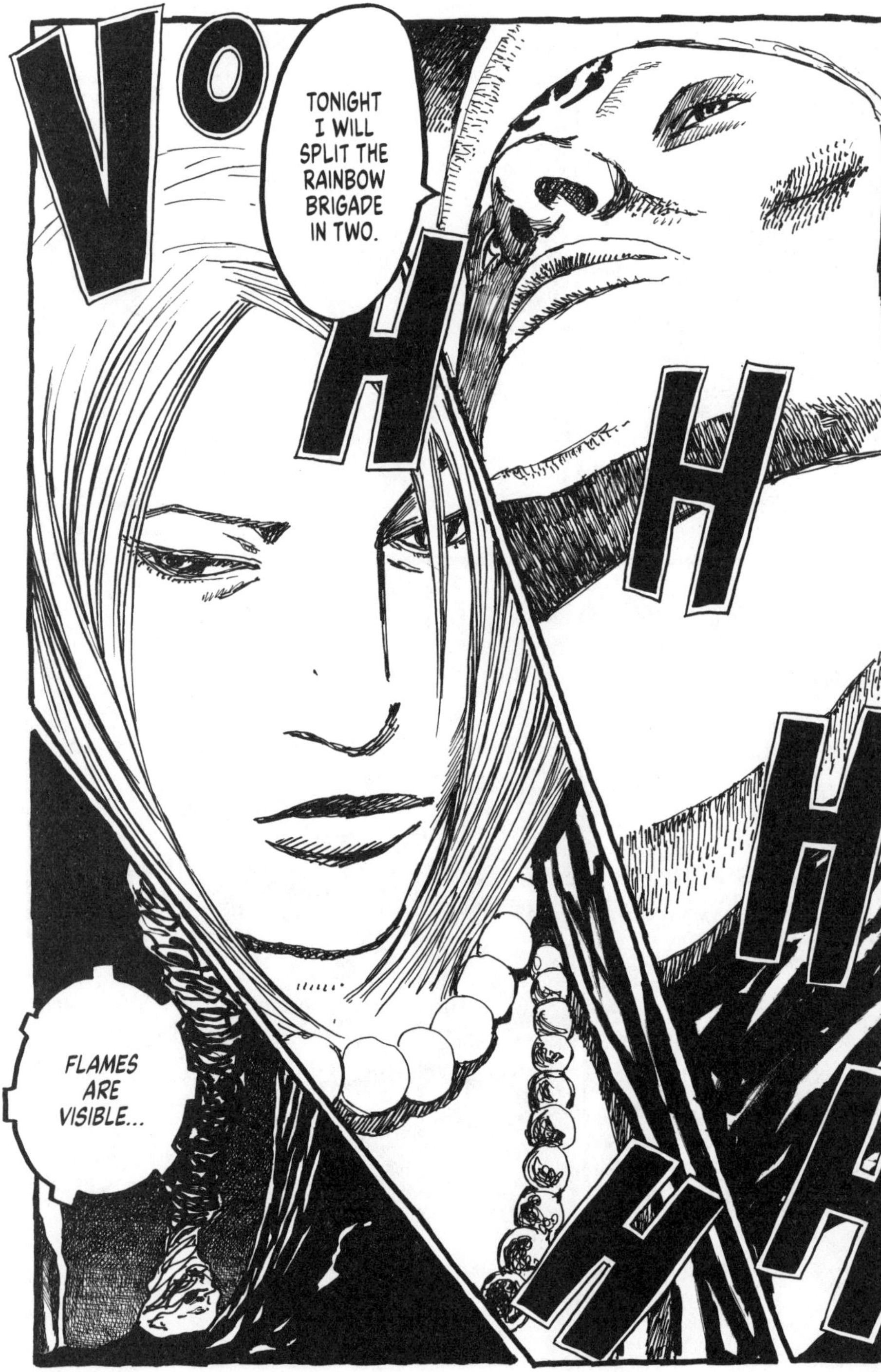
VOHHHHH
TONIGHT I WILL SPLIT THE RAINBOW BRIGADE IN TWO.
FLAMES ARE VISIBLE...

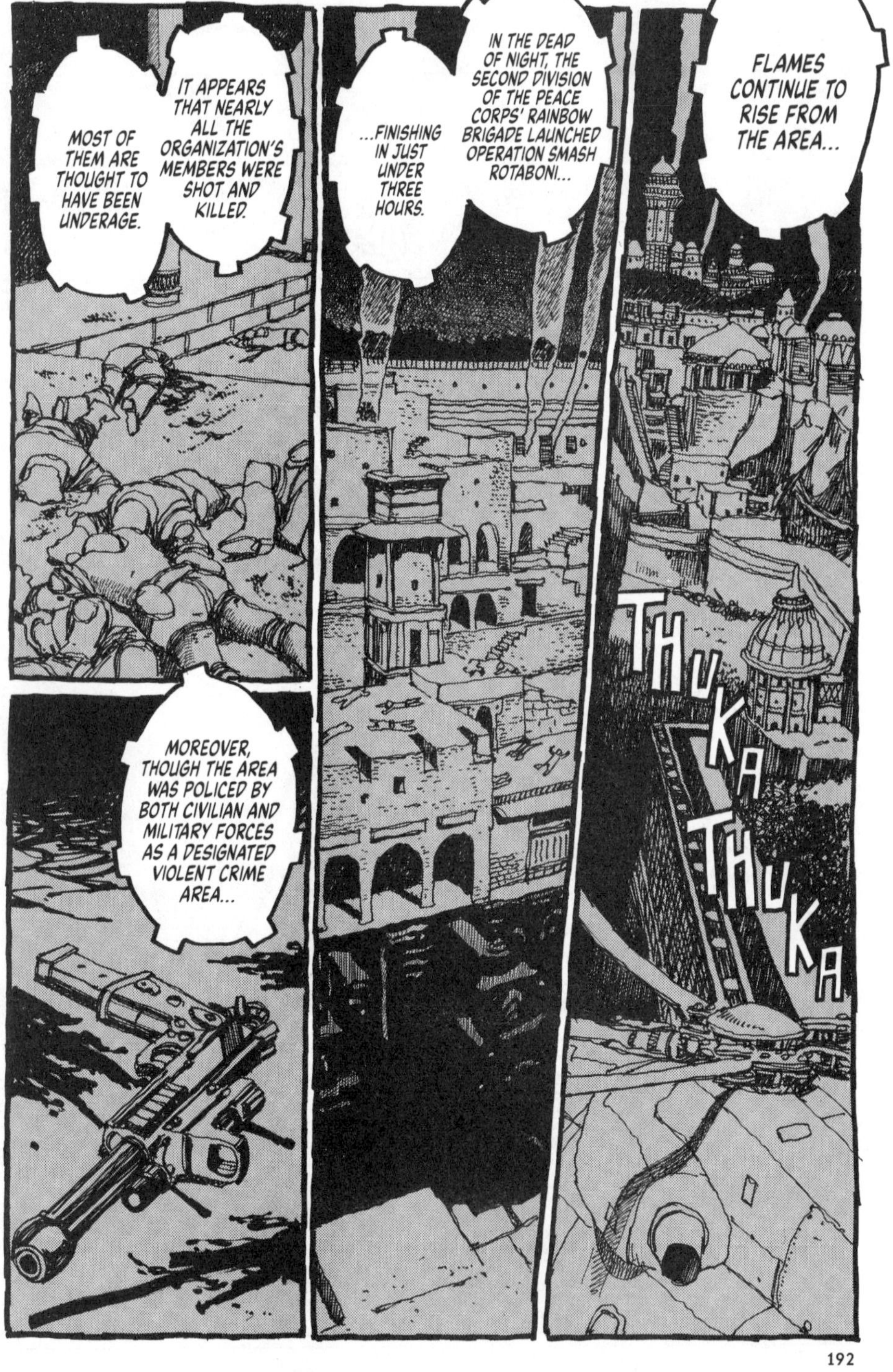
FLAMES CONTINUE TO RISE FROM THE AREA...
THUKA THUKA
IN THE DEAD OF NIGHT, THE SECOND DIVISION OF THE PEACE CORPS' RAINBOW BRIGADE LAUNCHED OPERATION SMASH ROTABONI...
...FINISHING IN JUST UNDER THREE HOURS.
IT APPEARS THAT NEARLY ALL THE ORGANIZATION'S MEMBERS WERE SHOT AND KILLED.
MOST OF THEM ARE THOUGHT TO HAVE BEEN UNDERAGE.
MOREOVER, THOUGH THE AREA WAS POLICED BY BOTH CIVILIAN AND MILITARY FORCES AS A DESIGNATED VIOLENT CRIME AREA...

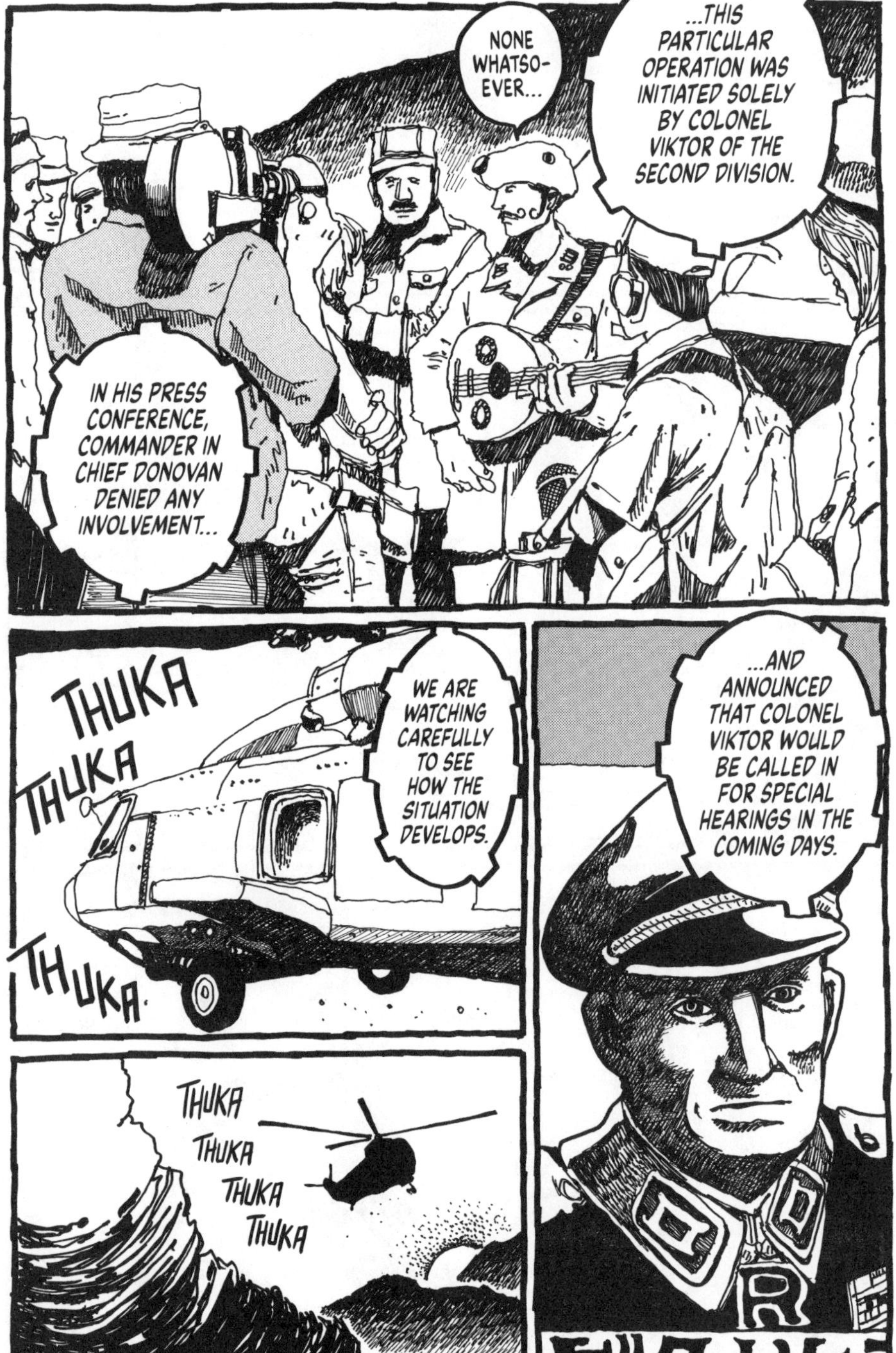
...THIS PARTICULAR OPERATION WAS INITIATED SOLELY BY COLONEL VIKTOR OF THE SECOND DIVISION.
NONE WHATSO-EVER...
IN HIS PRESS CONFERENCE, COMMANDER IN CHIEF DONOVAN DENIED ANY INVOLVEMENT...
...AND ANNOUNCED THAT COLONEL VIKTOR WOULD BE CALLED IN FOR SPECIAL HEARINGS IN THE COMING DAYS.
WE ARE WATCHING CAREFULLY TO SEE HOW THE SITUATION DEVELOPS.
THUKA
THUKA
THUKA
THUKA
THUKA
THUKA
THUKA

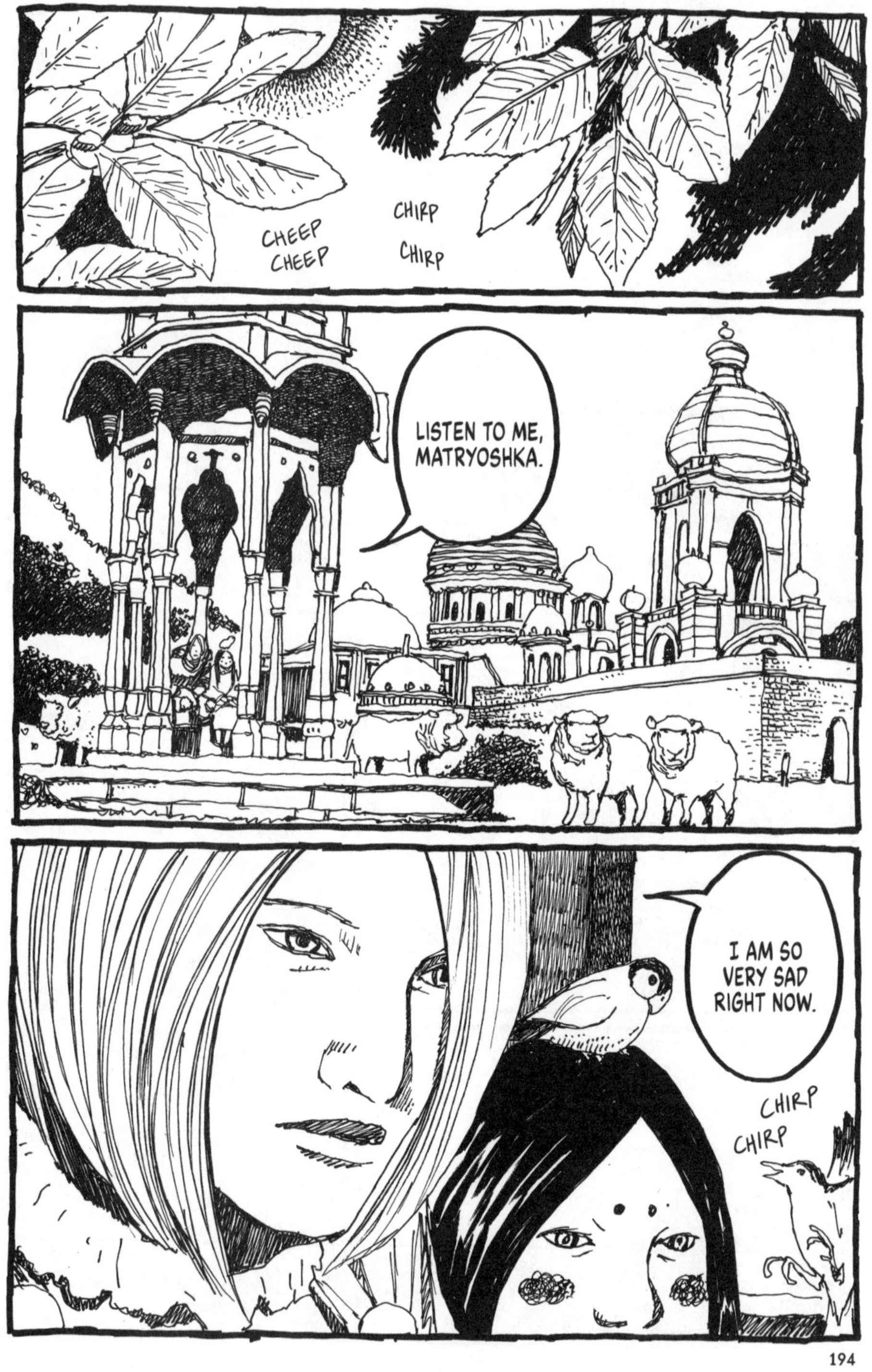
CHIRP
CHIRP
CHEEP
CHEEP
LISTEN TO ME, MATRYOSHKA.
I AM SO VERY SAD RIGHT NOW.
CHIRP
CHIRP

CHAPTER 15 //

Bygone Days

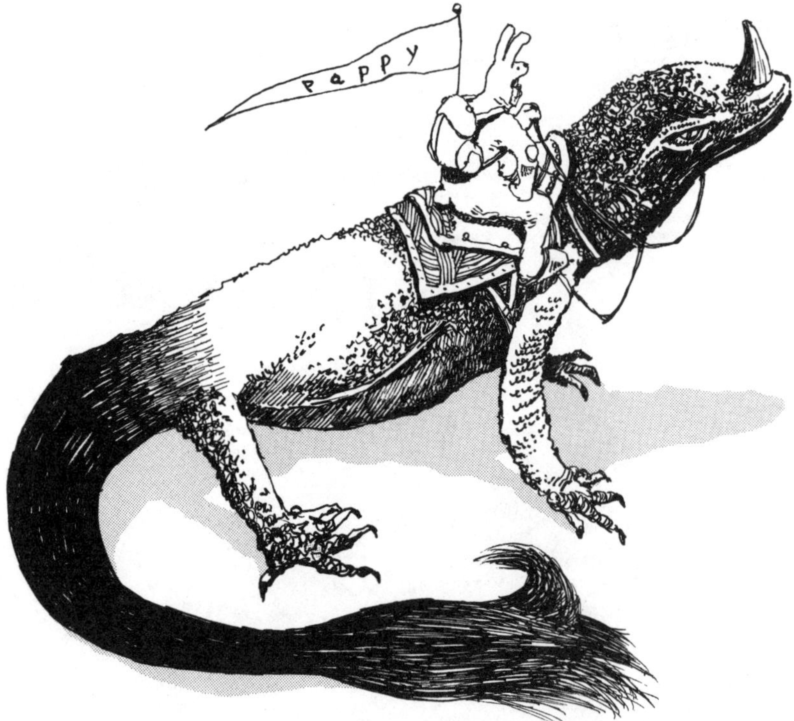

Pappy

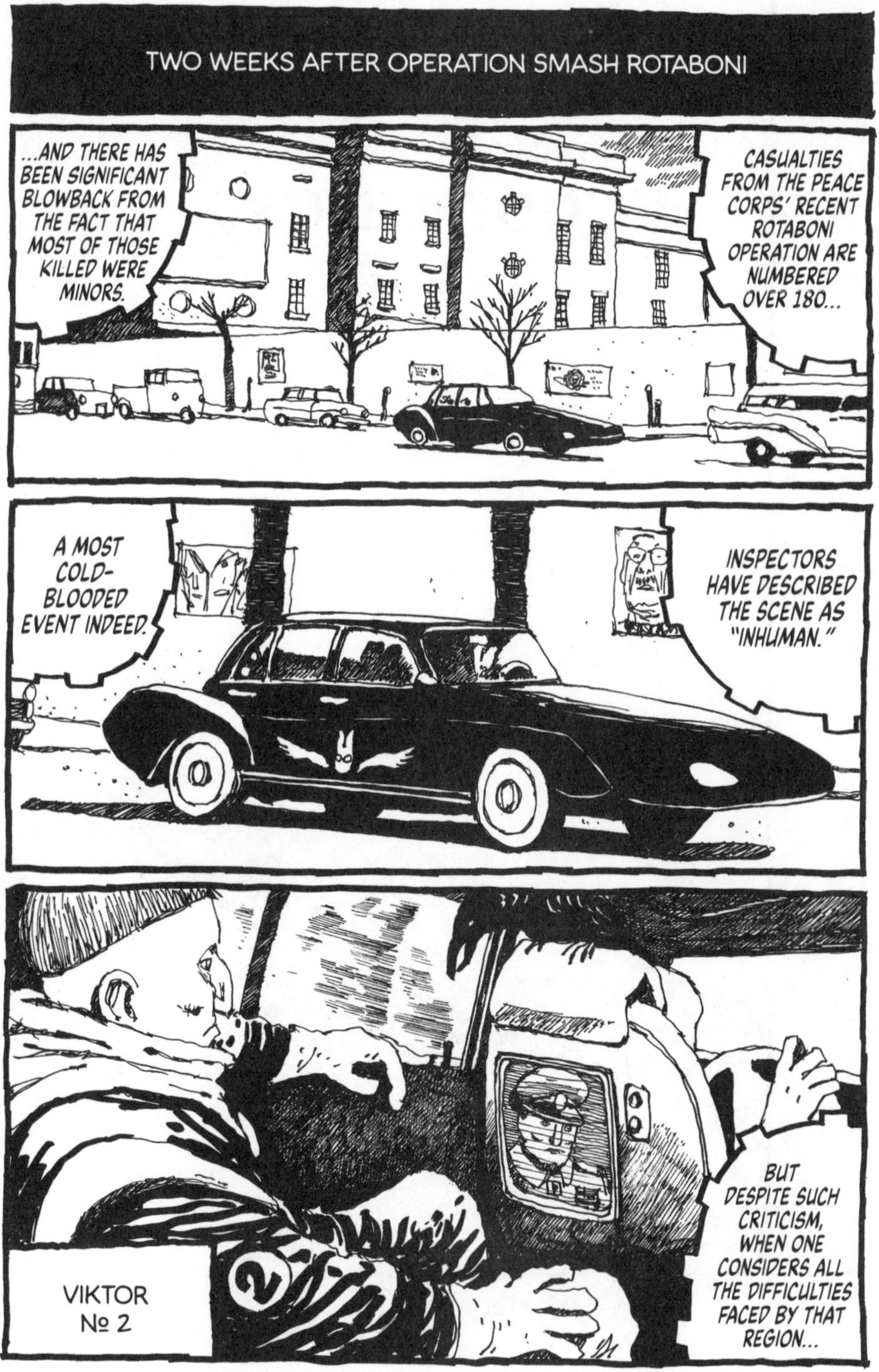
TWO WEEKS AFTER OPERATION SMASH ROTABONI
CASUALTIES FROM THE PEACE CORPS' RECENT ROTABONI OPERATION ARE NUMBERED OVER 180...
...AND THERE HAS BEEN SIGNIFICANT BLOWBACK FROM THE FACT THAT MOST OF THOSE KILLED WERE MINORS.
INSPECTORS HAVE DESCRIBED THE SCENE AS "INHUMAN."
A MOST COLD-BLOODED EVENT INDEED.
BUT DESPITE SUCH CRITICISM, WHEN ONE CONSIDERS ALL THE DIFFICULTIES FACED BY THAT REGION...
VIKTOR
№ 2

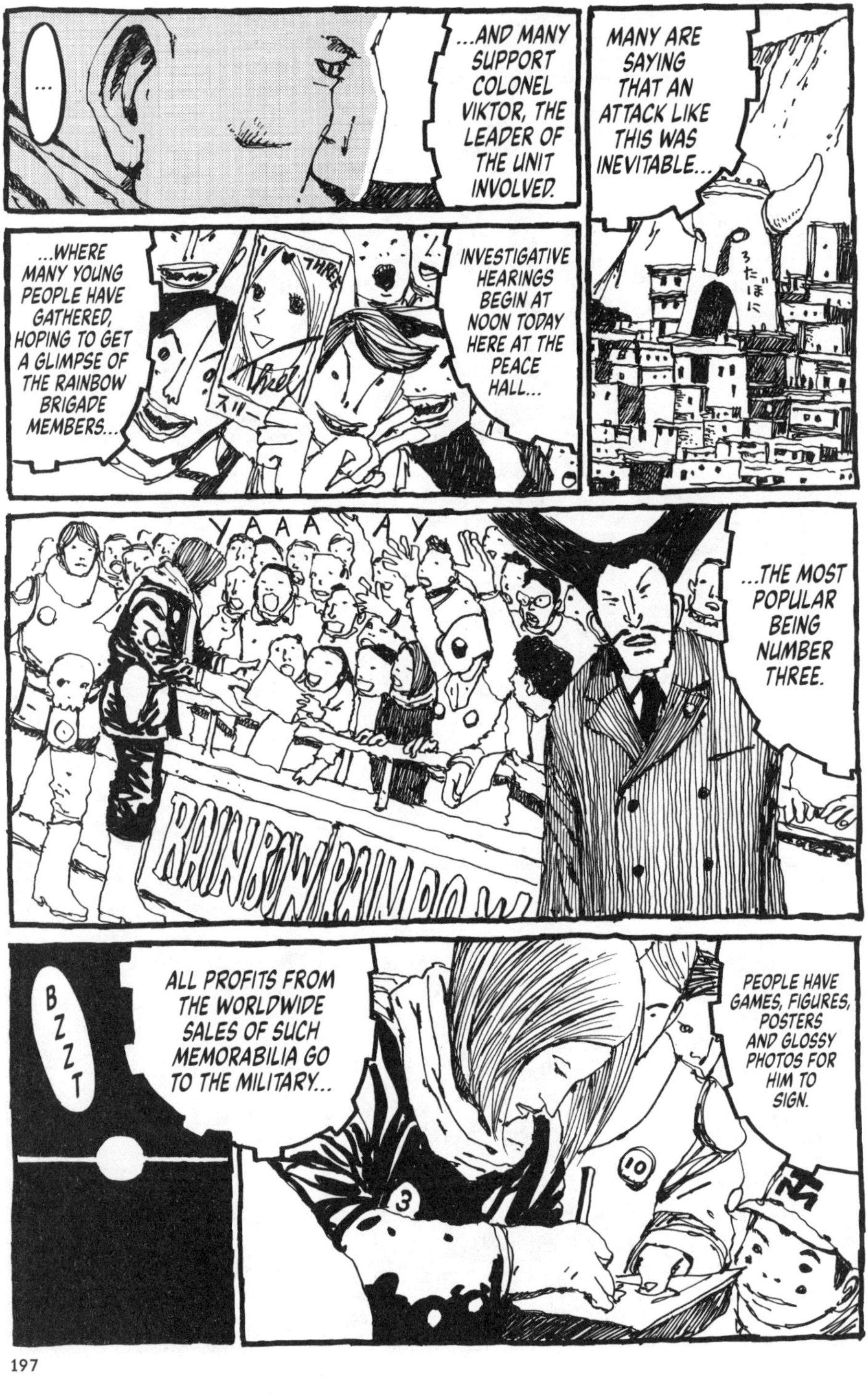
MANY ARE SAYING THAT AN ATTACK LIKE THIS WAS INEVITABLE...
ろたぼに
...AND MANY SUPPORT COLONEL VIKTOR, THE LEADER OF THE UNIT INVOLVED.
...
INVESTIGATIVE HEARINGS BEGIN AT NOON TODAY HERE AT THE PEACE HALL...
...WHERE MANY YOUNG PEOPLE HAVE GATHERED, HOPING TO GET A GLIMPSE OF THE RAINBOW BRIGADE MEMBERS...
THREE
スリー
...THE MOST POPULAR BEING NUMBER THREE.
YAAAAY
RAINBOW RAINBOW
PEOPLE HAVE GAMES, FIGURES, POSTERS AND GLOSSY PHOTOS FOR HIM TO SIGN.
ALL PROFITS FROM THE WORLDWIDE SALES OF SUCH MEMORABILIA GO TO THE MILITARY...
BZZT

*Rotaboni

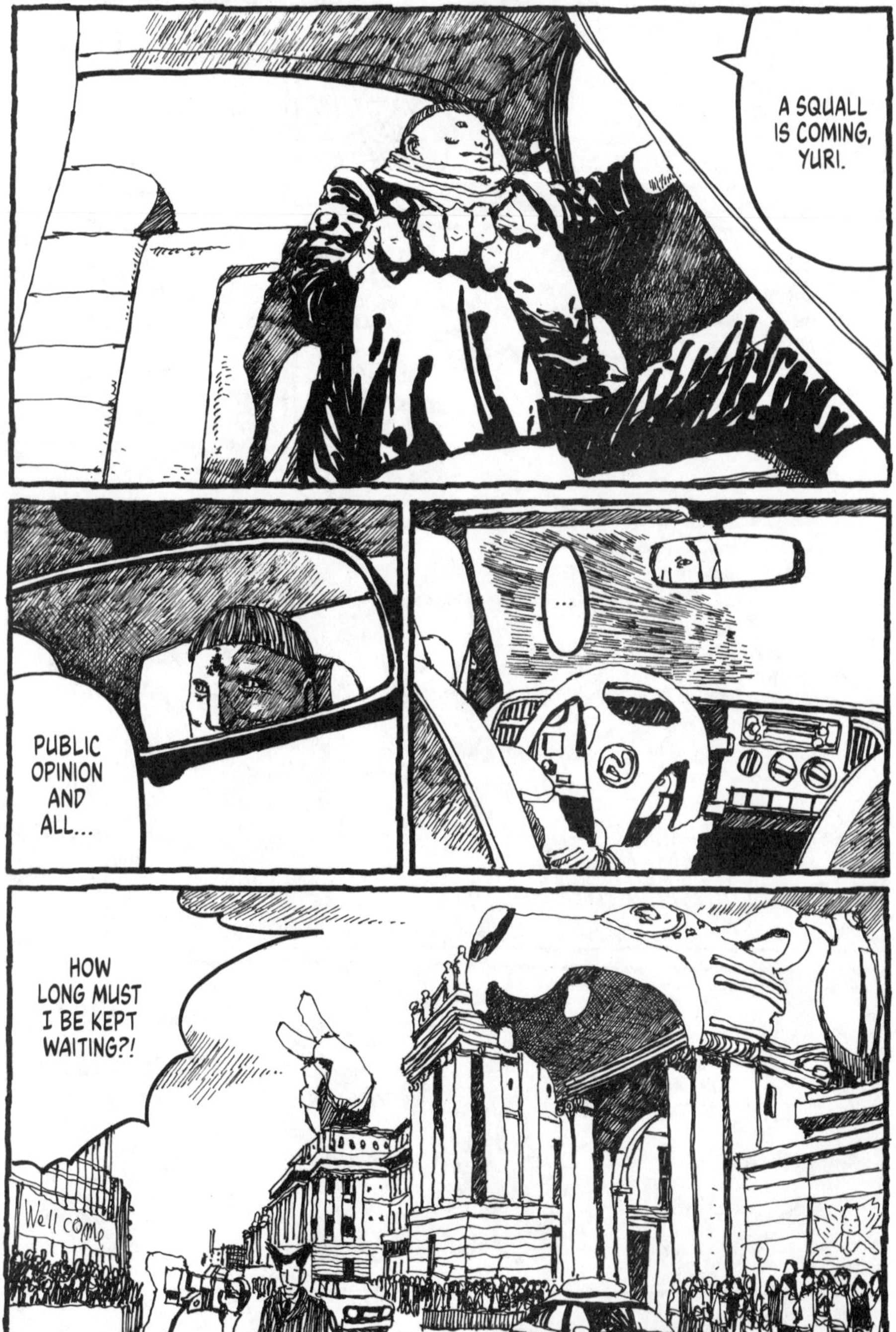
A SQUALL IS COMING, YURI.
...
PUBLIC OPINION AND ALL...
HOW LONG MUST I BE KEPT WAITING?!
Well come

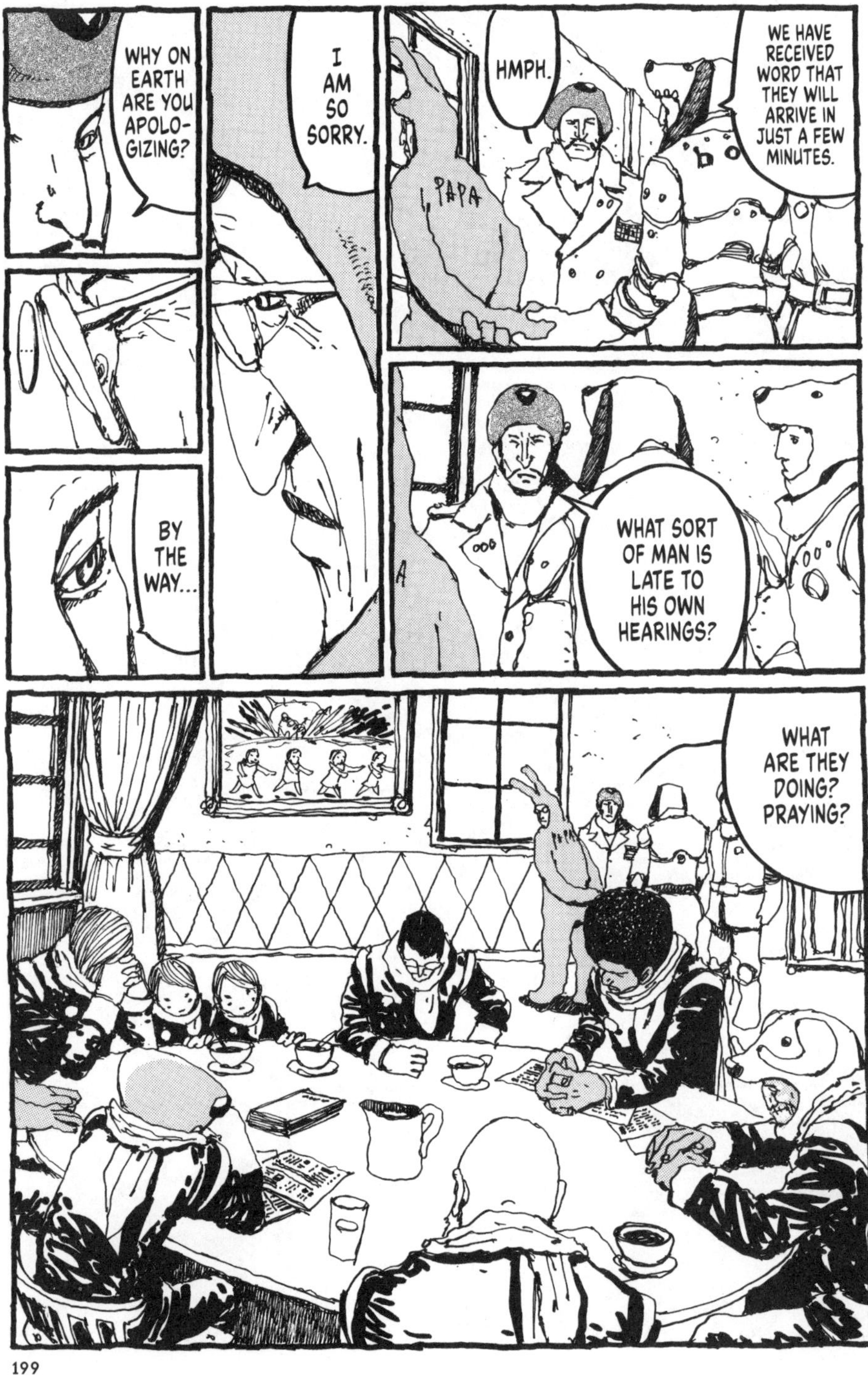
WE HAVE RECEIVED WORD THAT THEY WILL ARRIVE IN JUST A FEW MINUTES.
HMPH.
PAPA
WHAT SORT OF MAN IS LATE TO HIS OWN HEARINGS?
I AM SO SORRY.
WHY ON EARTH ARE YOU APOLO-GIZING?
BY THE WAY...
WHAT ARE THEY DOING? PRAYING?

*Ceramics

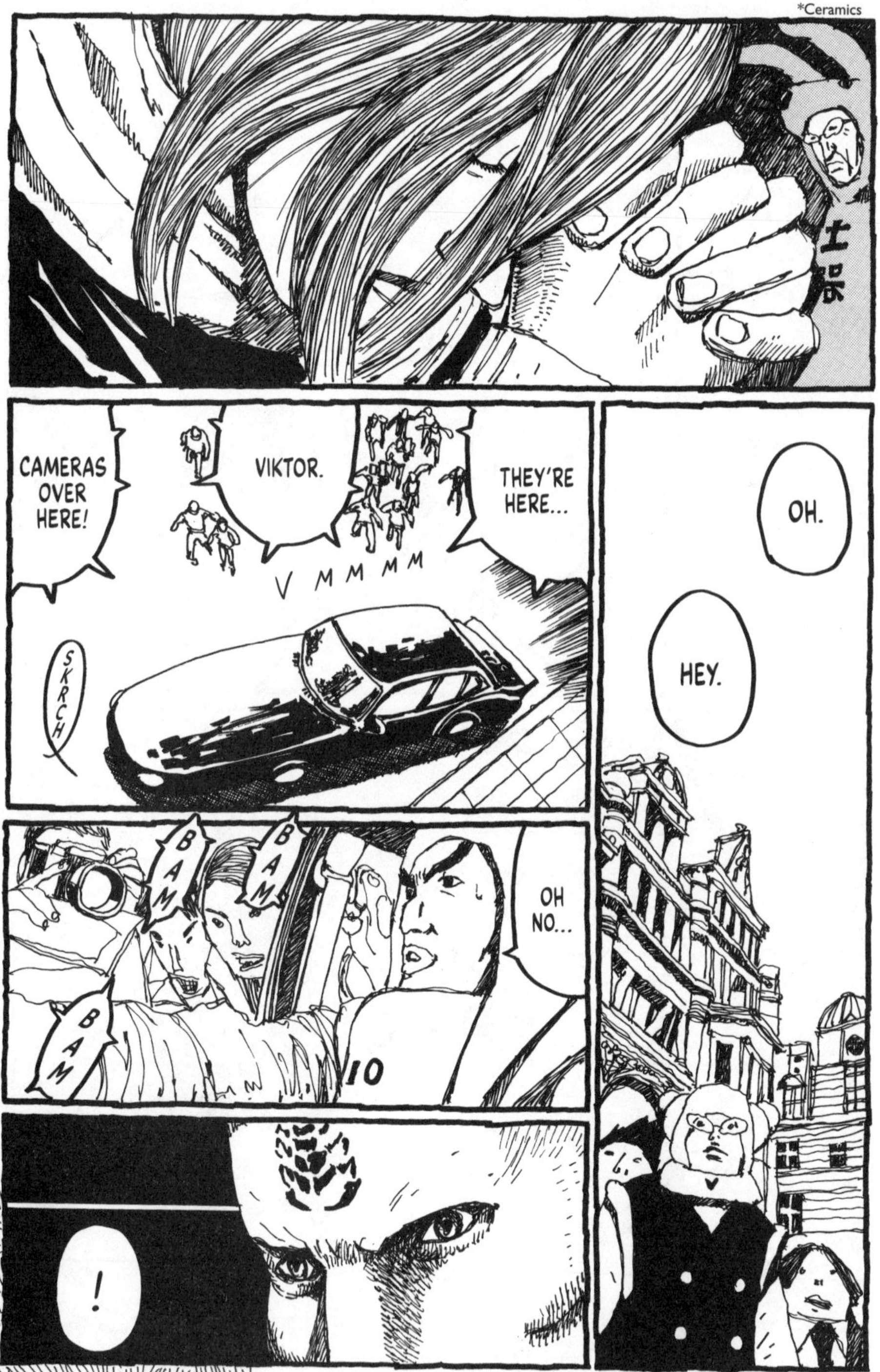

土器
OH.
HEY.
CAMERAS OVER HERE!
VIKTOR.
THEY'RE HERE...
V M M M M M
SKRCH
OH NO...
BAM
BAM
BAM
IO
!

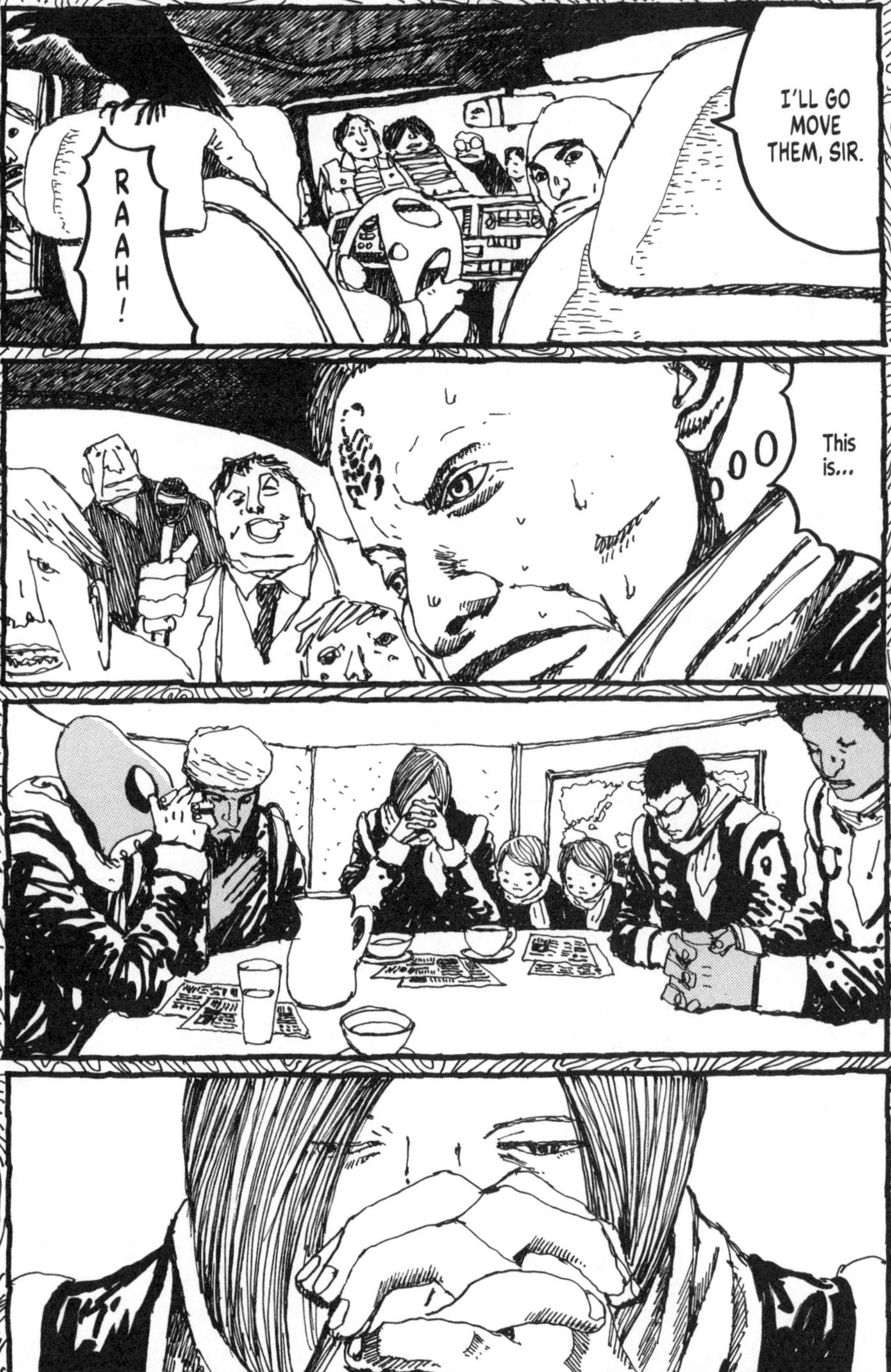
I'LL GO MOVE THEM, SIR.
RAAH!
This is...

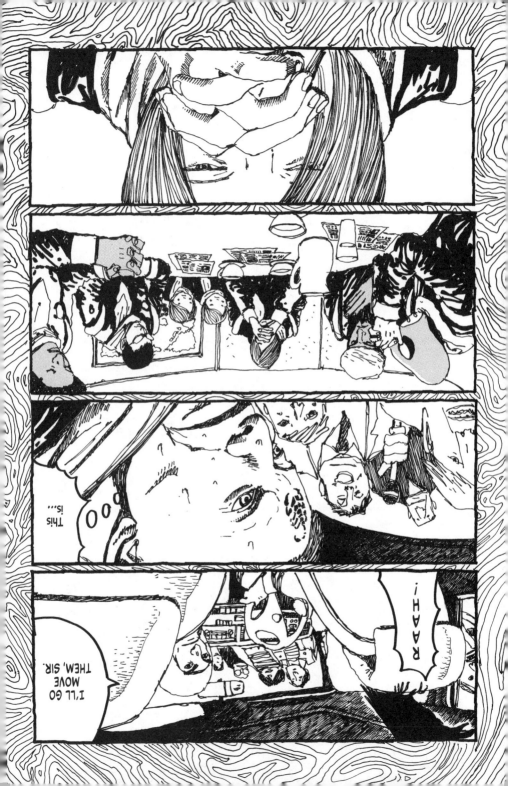

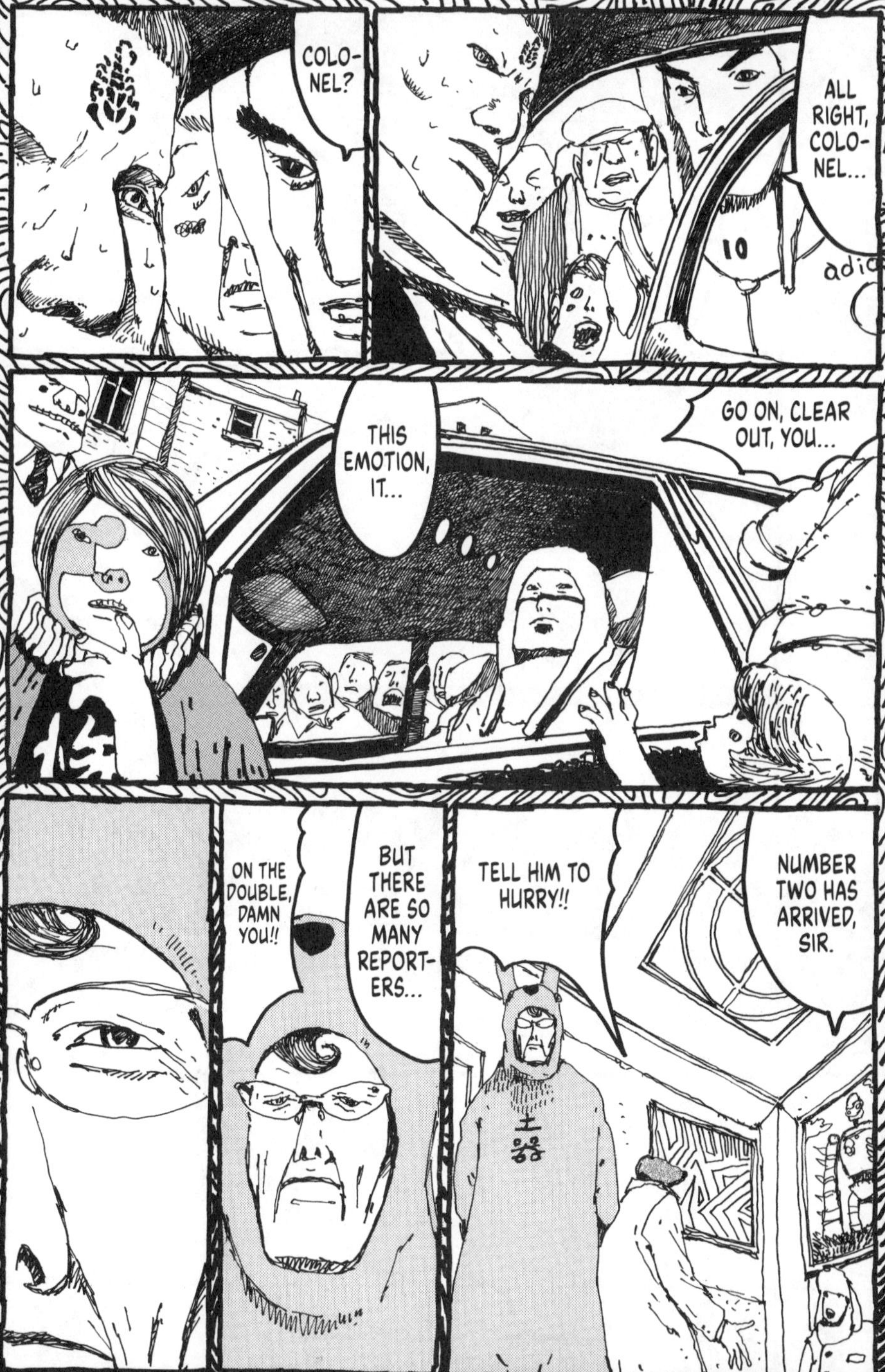
ALL RIGHT, COLO-NEL...
10
adio
COLO-NEL?
GO ON, CLEAR OUT, YOU...
THIS EMOTION, IT...
NUMBER TWO HAS ARRIVED, SIR.
TELL HIM TO HURRY!!
BUT THERE ARE SO MANY REPORT-ERS...
ON THE DOUBLE, DAMN YOU!!

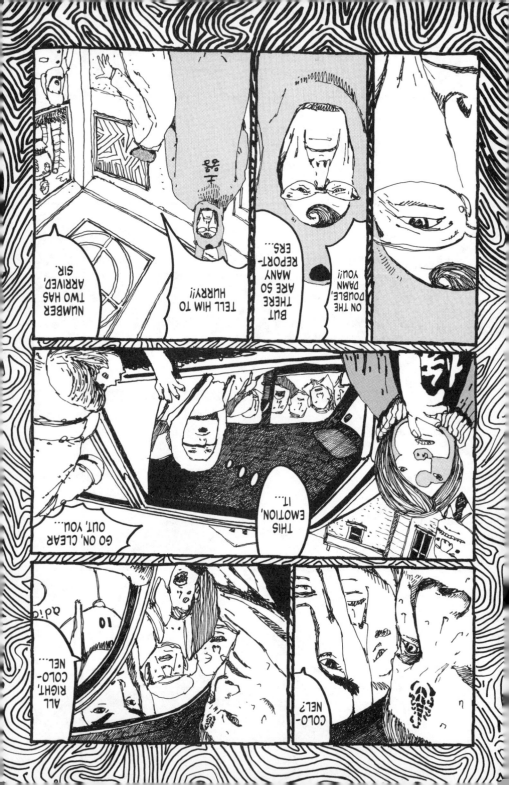

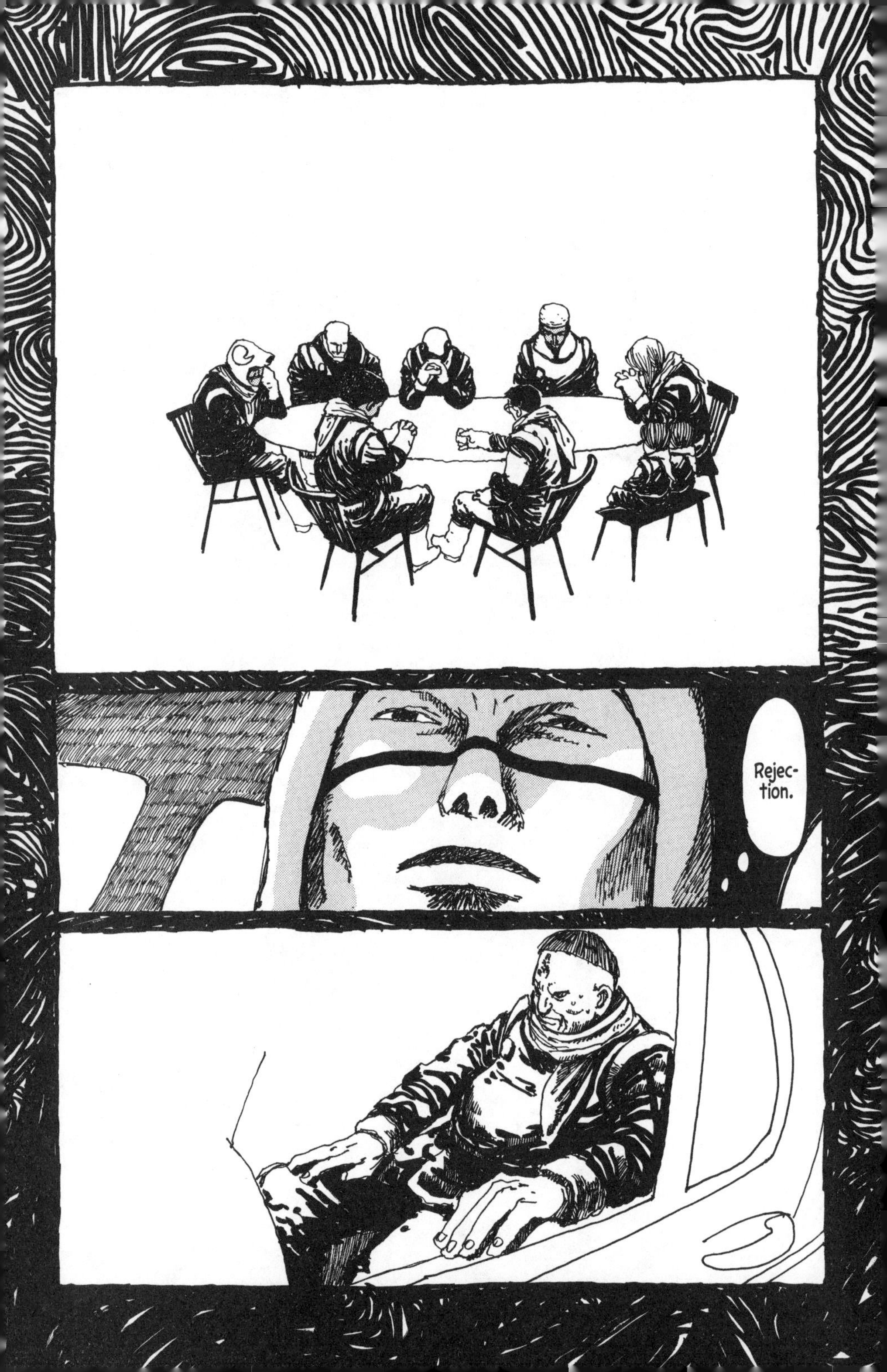
Rejection.

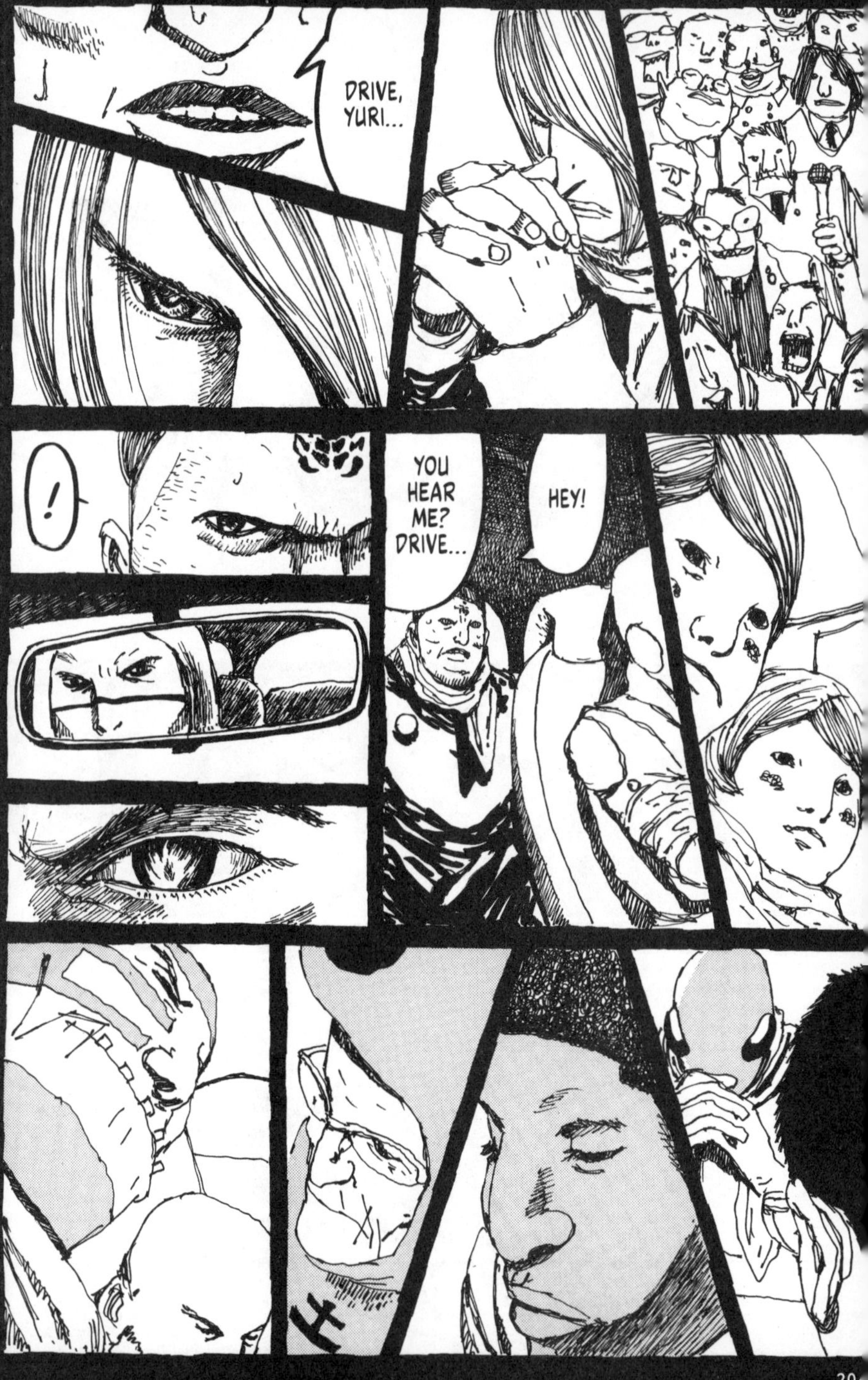
DRIVE, YURI...
!
YOU HEAR ME? DRIVE...
HEY!

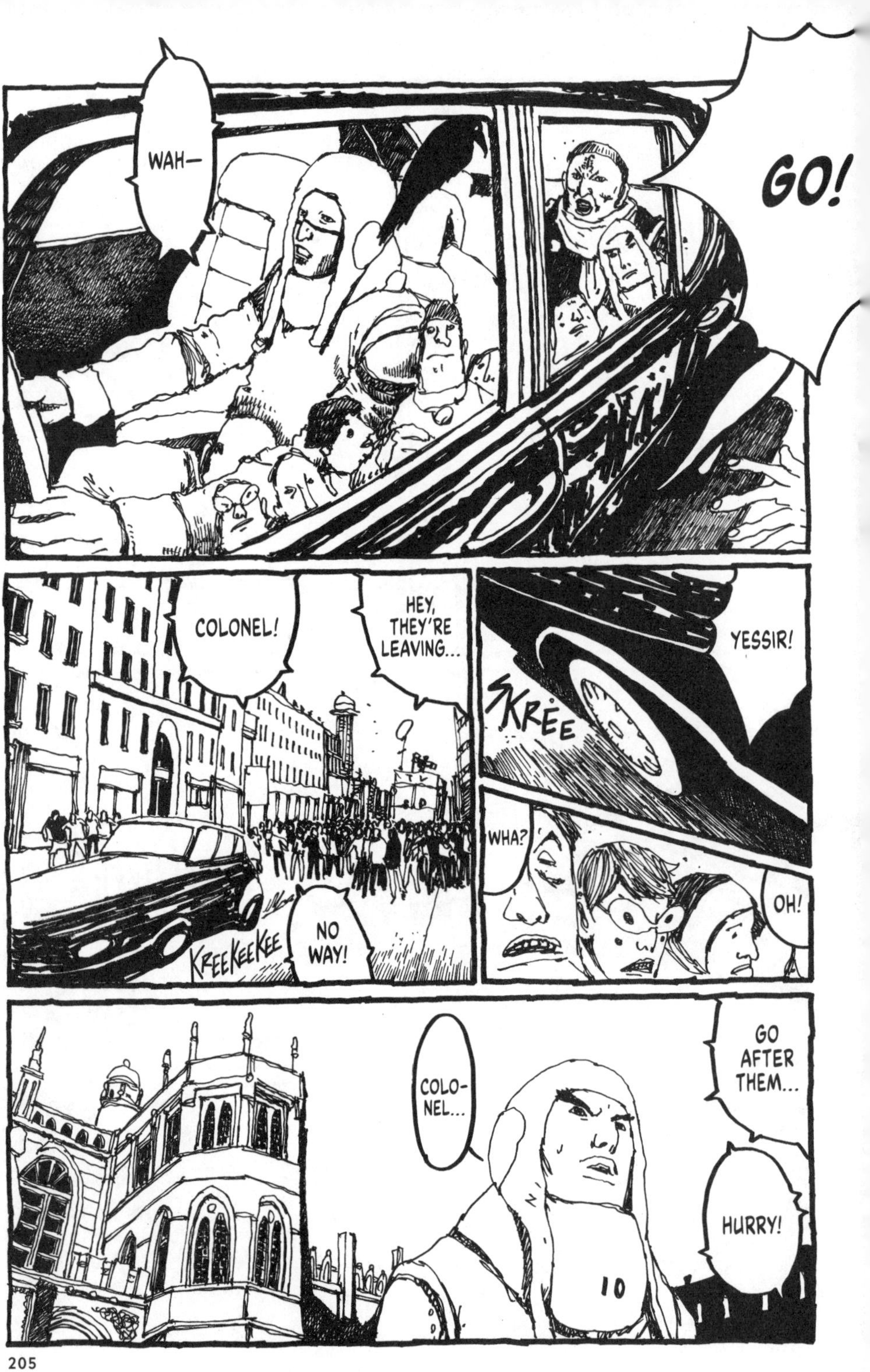
GO!
WAH—
YESSIR!
SKREE
OH!
WHA?
HEY, THEY'RE LEAVING...
COLONEL!
NO WAY!
KREEKEEKEE
GO AFTER THEM...
HURRY!
COLO-NEL...
10

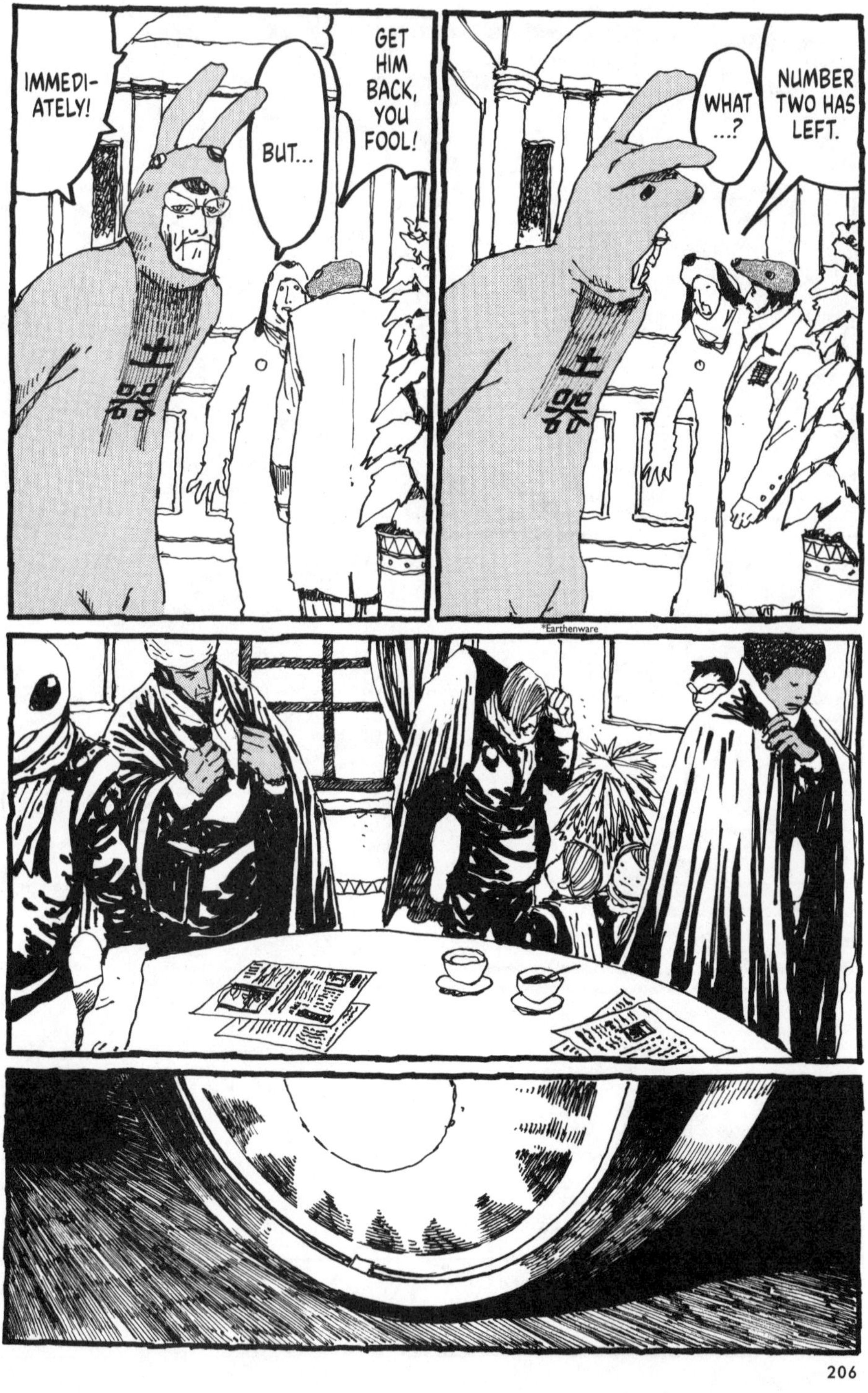
NUMBER TWO HAS LEFT.
WHAT ...?
土器
GET HIM BACK, YOU FOOL!
BUT...
IMMEDI-ATELY!
土器
*Earthenware

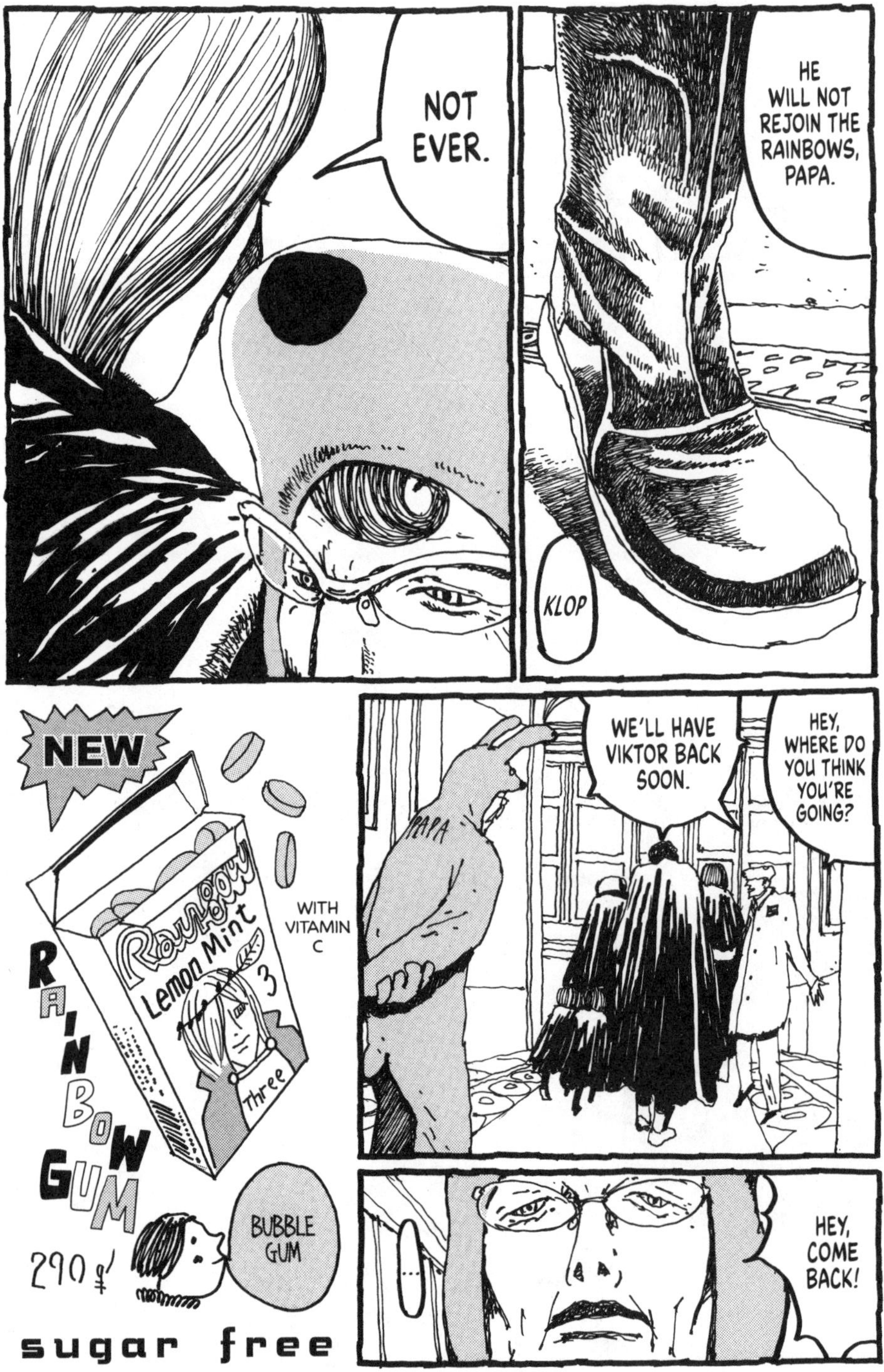
HE WILL NOT REJOIN THE RAINBOWS, PAPA.
KLOP
NOT EVER.
HEY, WHERE DO YOU THINK YOU'RE GOING?
WE'LL HAVE VIKTOR BACK SOON.
HEY, COME BACK!
...
NEW
Rainbow
Lemon Mint
3
Three
WITH VITAMIN C
RAINBOW GUM
290
BUBBLE GUM
sugar free

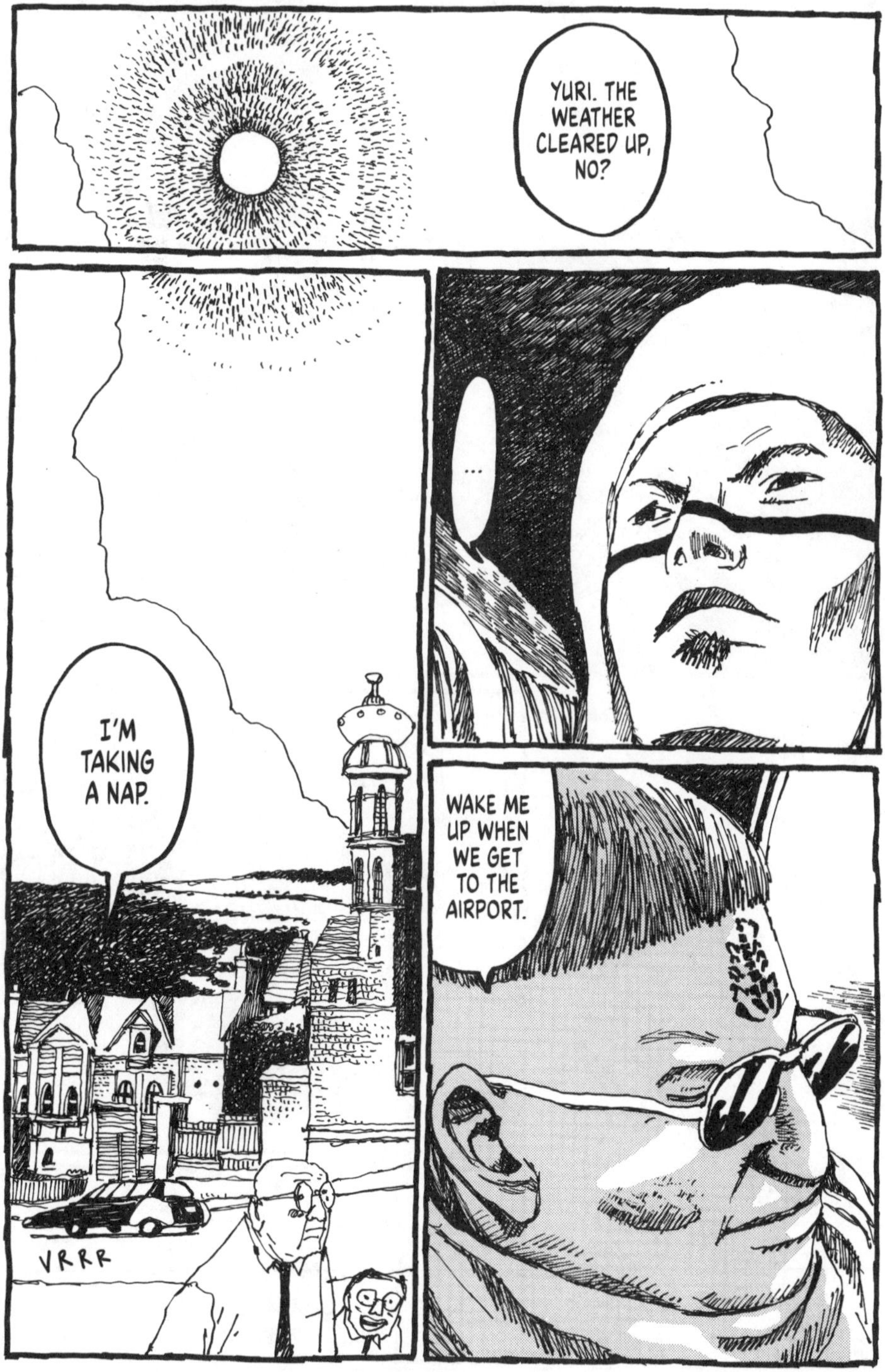
YURI. THE WEATHER CLEARED UP, NO?
...
WAKE ME UP WHEN WE GET TO THE AIRPORT.
I'M TAKING A NAP.
VRRR

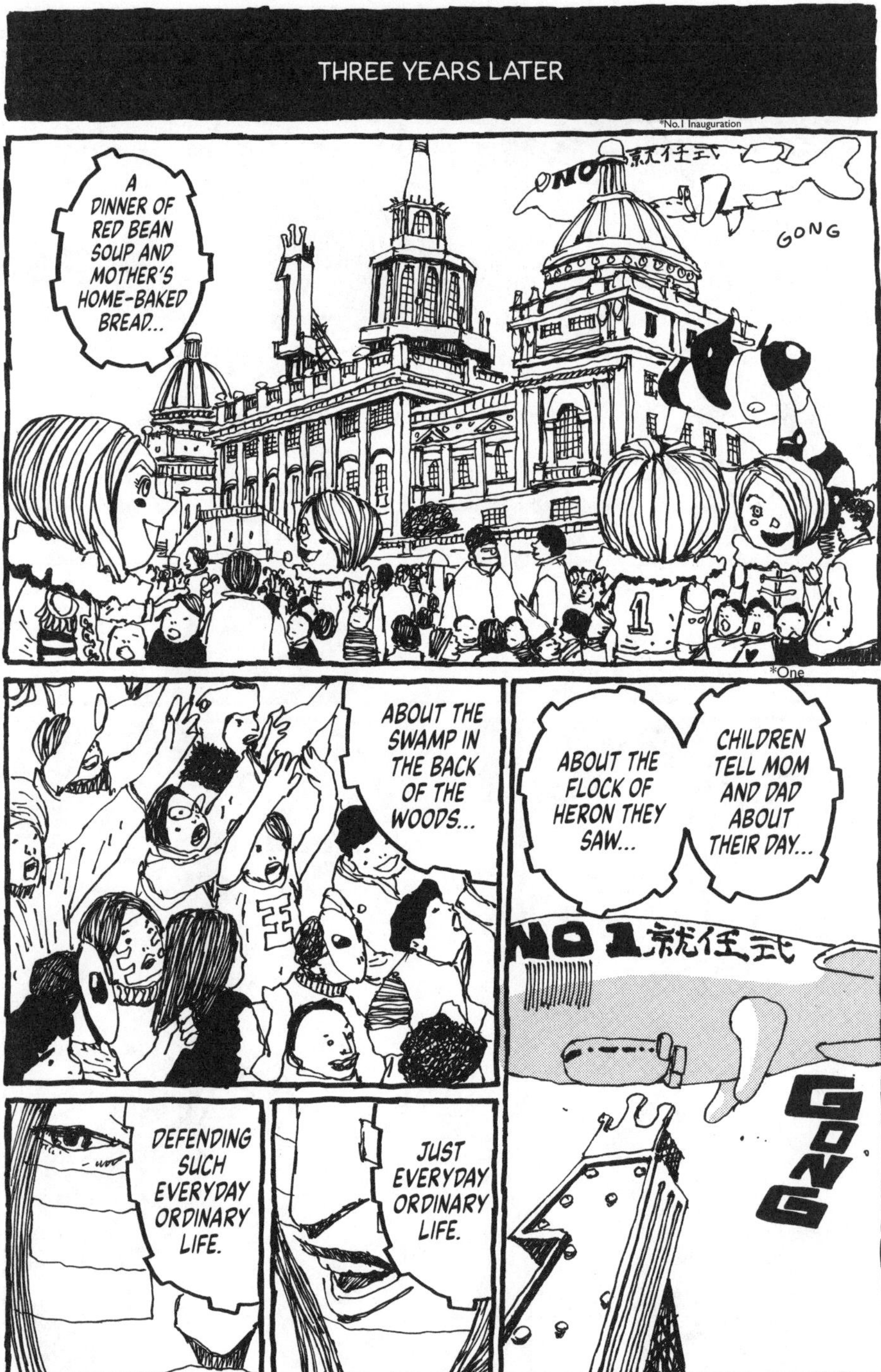
THREE YEARS LATER
*No.1 Inauguration
NO1 就任式
GONG
A DINNER OF RED BEAN SOUP AND MOTHER'S HOME-BAKED BREAD...
1
*One
CHILDREN TELL MOM AND DAD ABOUT THEIR DAY...
ABOUT THE FLOCK OF HERON THEY SAW...
NO1 就任式
GONG
ABOUT THE SWAMP IN THE BACK OF THE WOODS...
JUST EVERYDAY ORDINARY LIFE.
DEFENDING SUCH EVERYDAY ORDINARY LIFE.

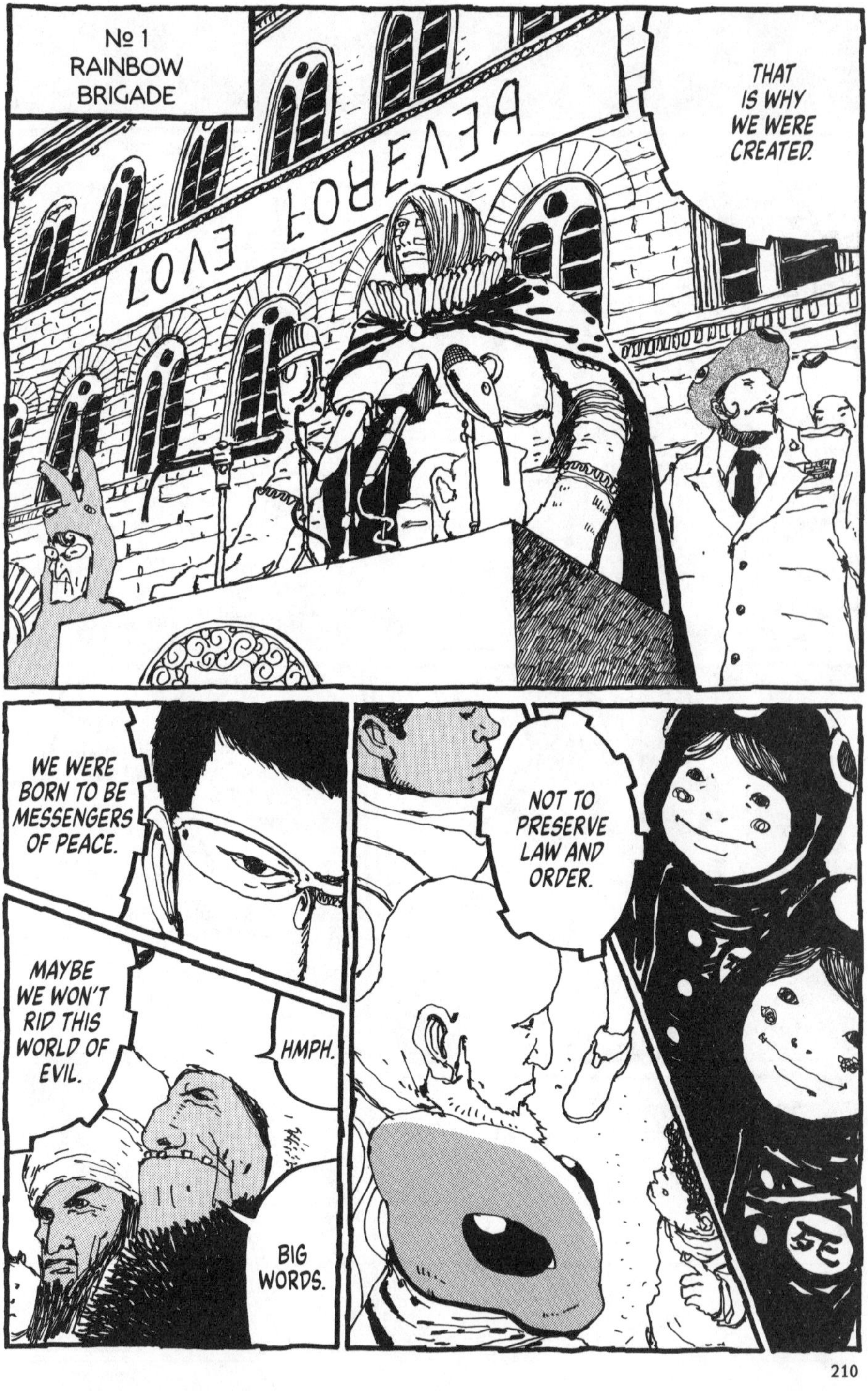
THAT IS WHY WE WERE CREATED.
№ 1 RAINBOW BRIGADE
NOT TO PRESERVE LAW AND ORDER.
WE WERE BORN TO BE MESSENGERS OF PEACE.
MAYBE WE WON'T RID THIS WORLD OF EVIL.
HMPH.
BIG WORDS.

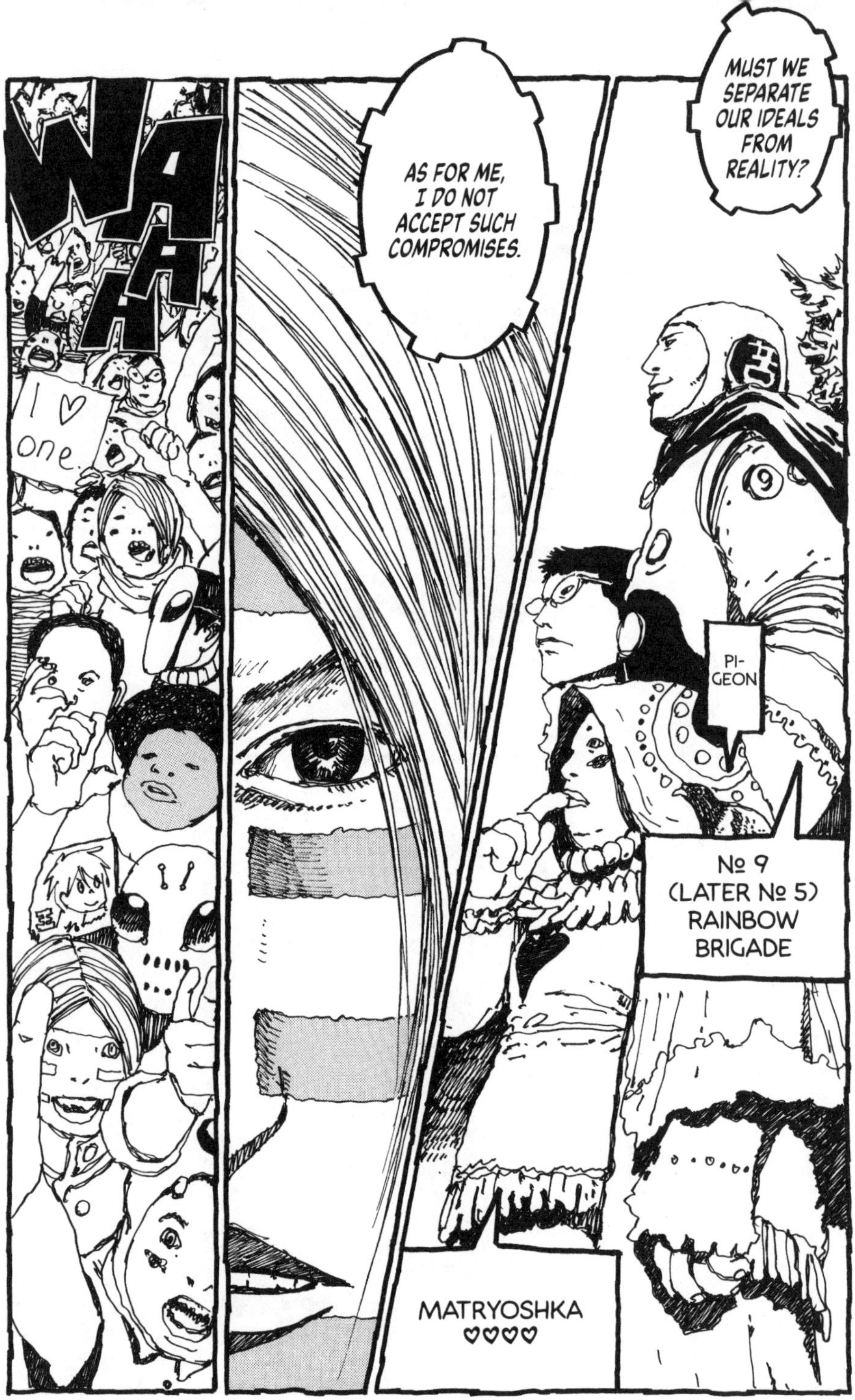
MUST WE SEPARATE OUR IDEALS FROM REALITY?
PI-GEON
№ 9 (LATER № 5) RAINBOW BRIGADE
MATRYOSHKA ♡♡♡♡
AS FOR ME, I DO NOT ACCEPT SUCH COMPROMISES.
WAAAA
I ♡ one.

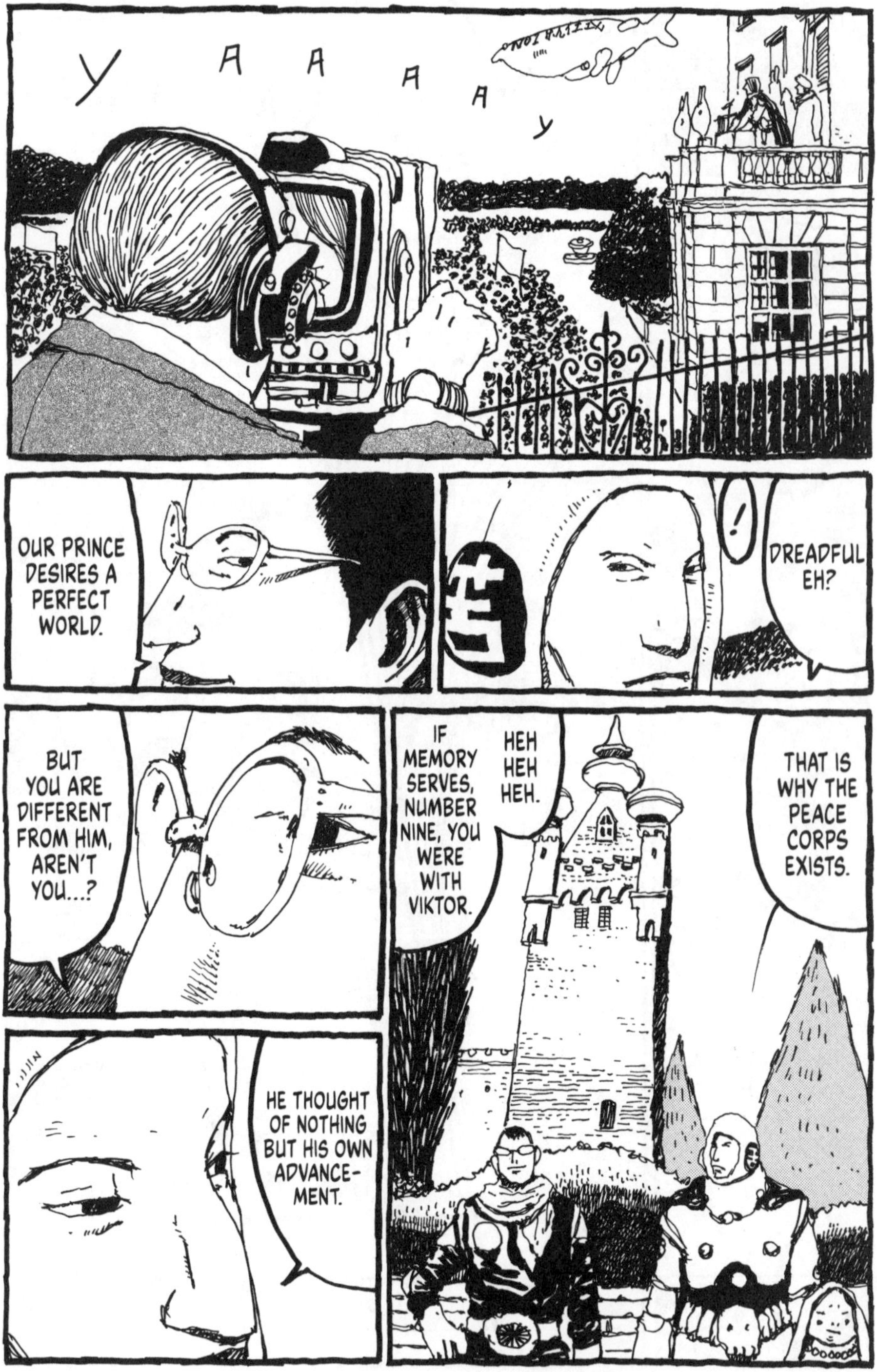
YAAAAY
!
DREADFUL EH?
OUR PRINCE DESIRES A PERFECT WORLD.
THAT IS WHY THE PEACE CORPS EXISTS.
HEH HEH HEH.
IF MEMORY SERVES, NUMBER NINE, YOU WERE WITH VIKTOR.
BUT YOU ARE DIFFERENT FROM HIM, AREN'T YOU...?
HE THOUGHT OF NOTHING BUT HIS OWN ADVANCE-MENT.

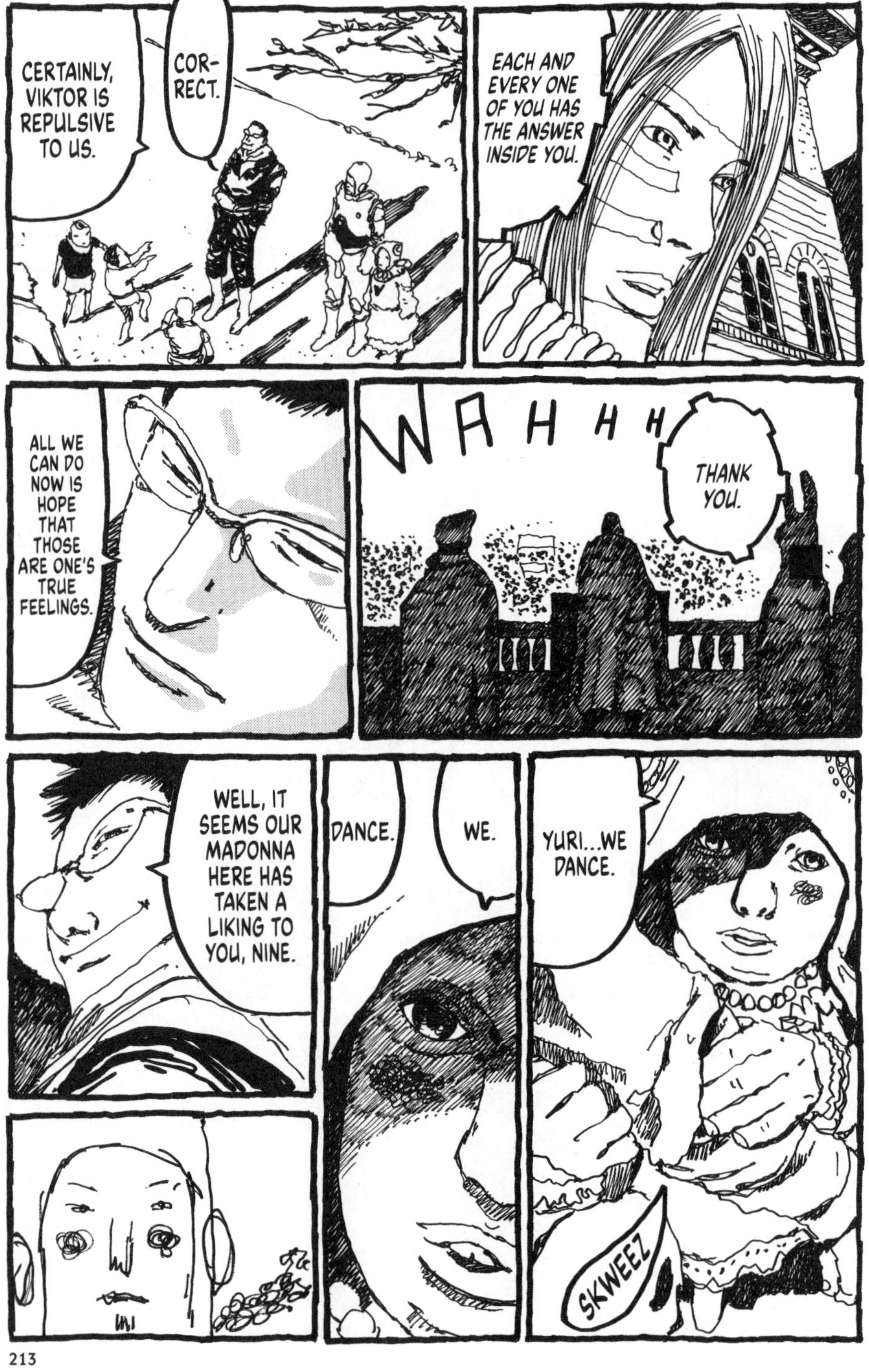
EACH AND EVERY ONE OF YOU HAS THE ANSWER INSIDE YOU.
CERTAINLY, VIKTOR IS REPULSIVE TO US.
COR-RECT.
WAHHH
THANK YOU.
ALL WE CAN DO NOW IS HOPE THAT THOSE ARE ONE'S TRUE FEELINGS.
YURI...WE DANCE.
SKWEEZ
WE.
DANCE.
WELL, IT SEEMS OUR MADONNA HERE HAS TAKEN A LIKING TO YOU, NINE.

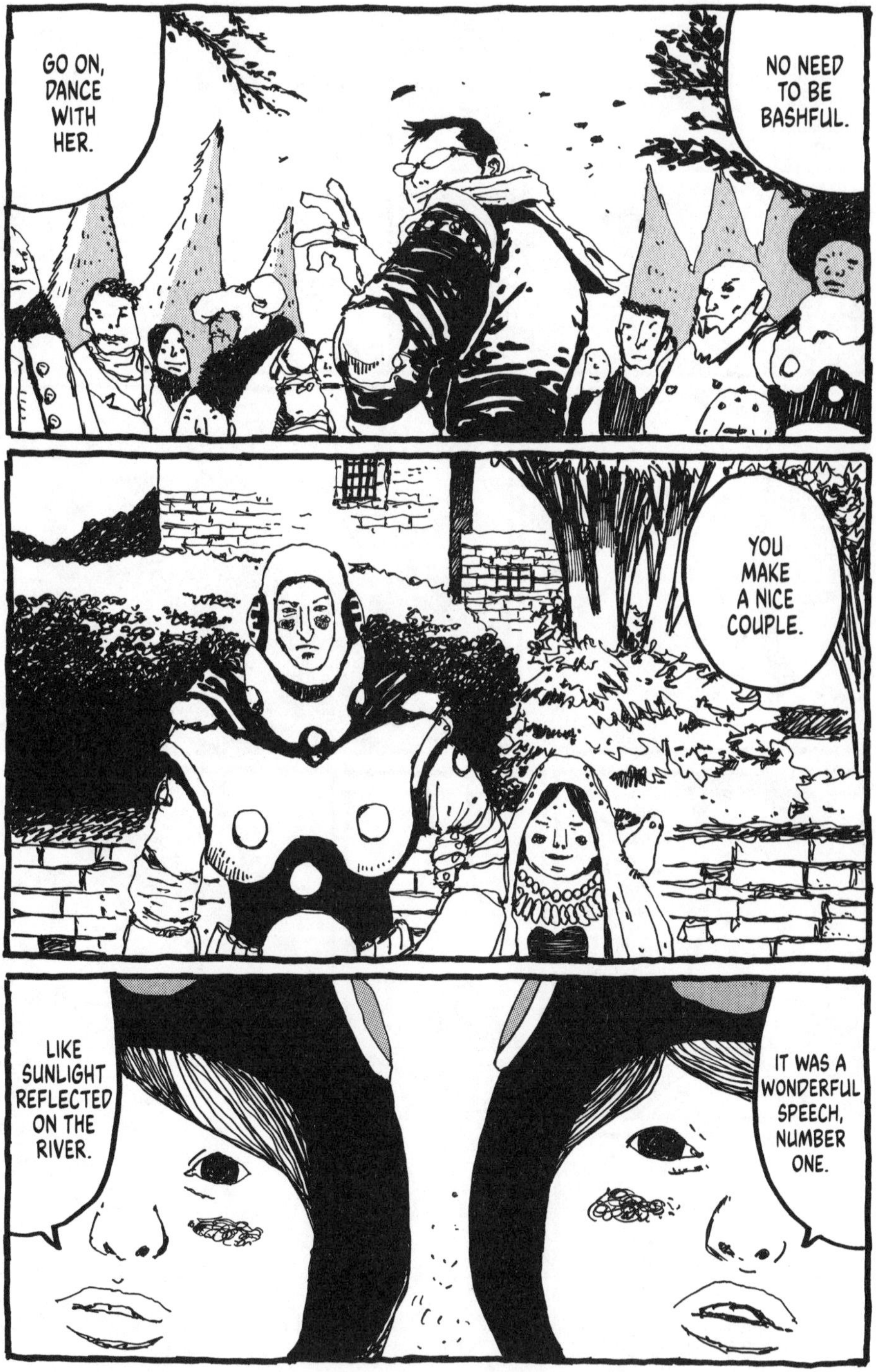
NO NEED TO BE BASHFUL.
GO ON, DANCE WITH HER.
YOU MAKE A NICE COUPLE.
IT WAS A WONDERFUL SPEECH, NUMBER ONE.
LIKE SUNLIGHT REFLECTED ON THE RIVER.

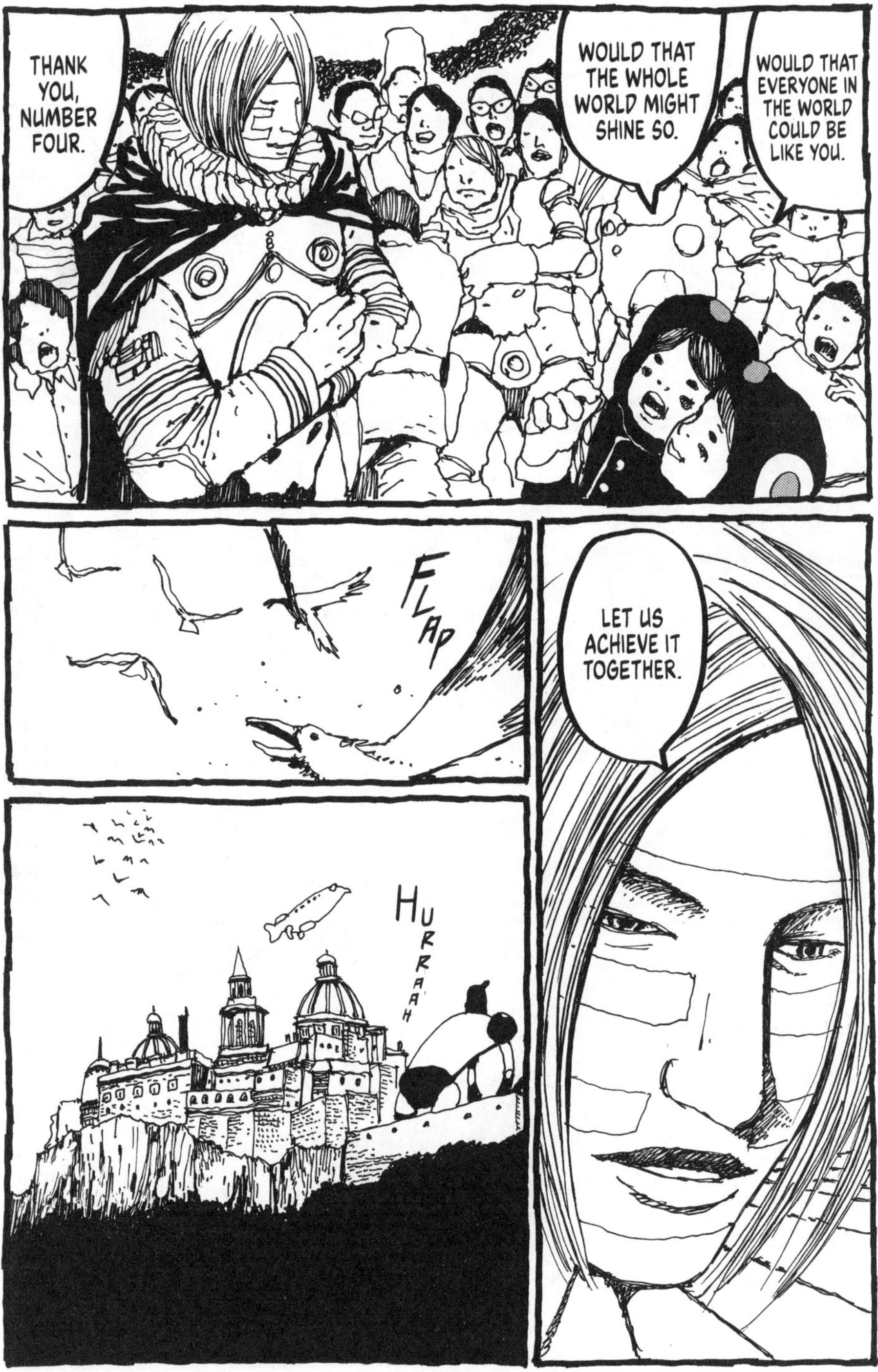
WOULD THAT EVERYONE IN THE WORLD COULD BE LIKE YOU.
WOULD THAT THE WHOLE WORLD MIGHT SHINE SO.
THANK YOU, NUMBER FOUR.
LET US ACHIEVE IT TOGETHER.
FLAP
HURRAAH

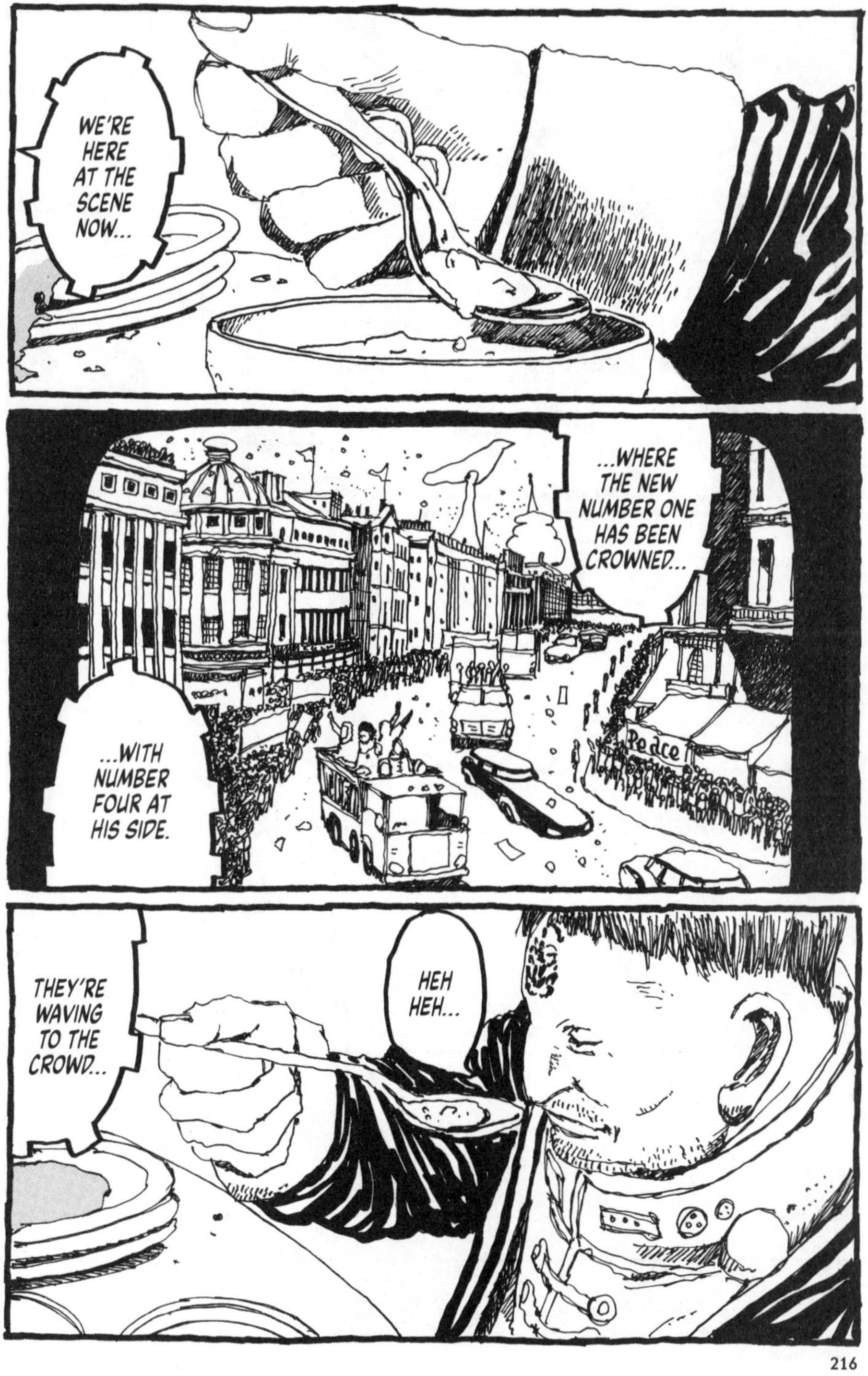
WE'RE HERE AT THE SCENE NOW...
...WHERE THE NEW NUMBER ONE HAS BEEN CROWNED...
Peace
...WITH NUMBER FOUR AT HIS SIDE.
HEH HEH...
THEY'RE WAVING TO THE CROWD...

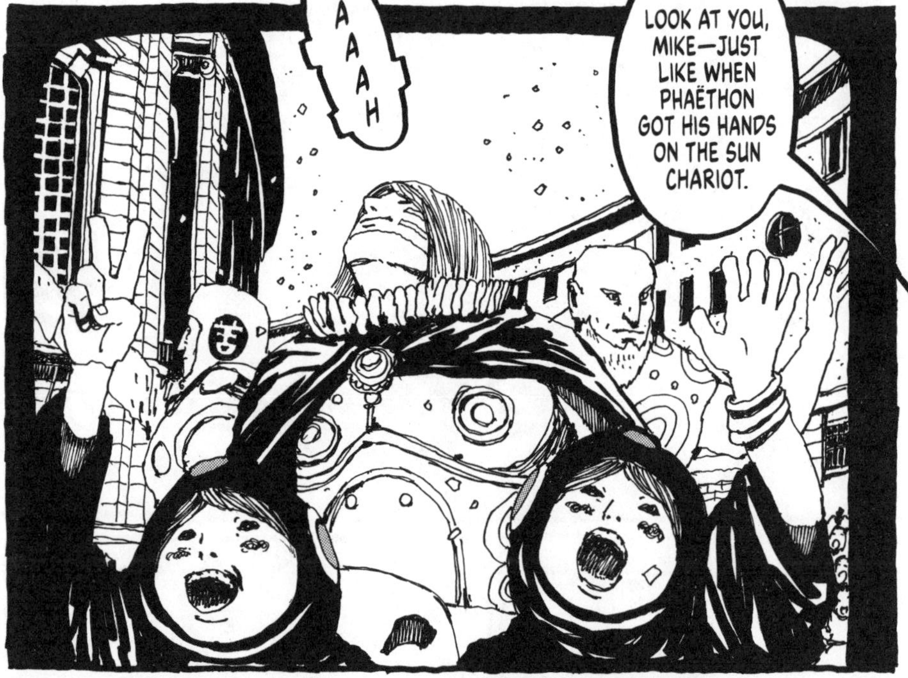
LOOK AT YOU, MIKE—JUST LIKE WHEN PHAËTHON GOT HIS HANDS ON THE SUN CHARIOT.
WAAAH

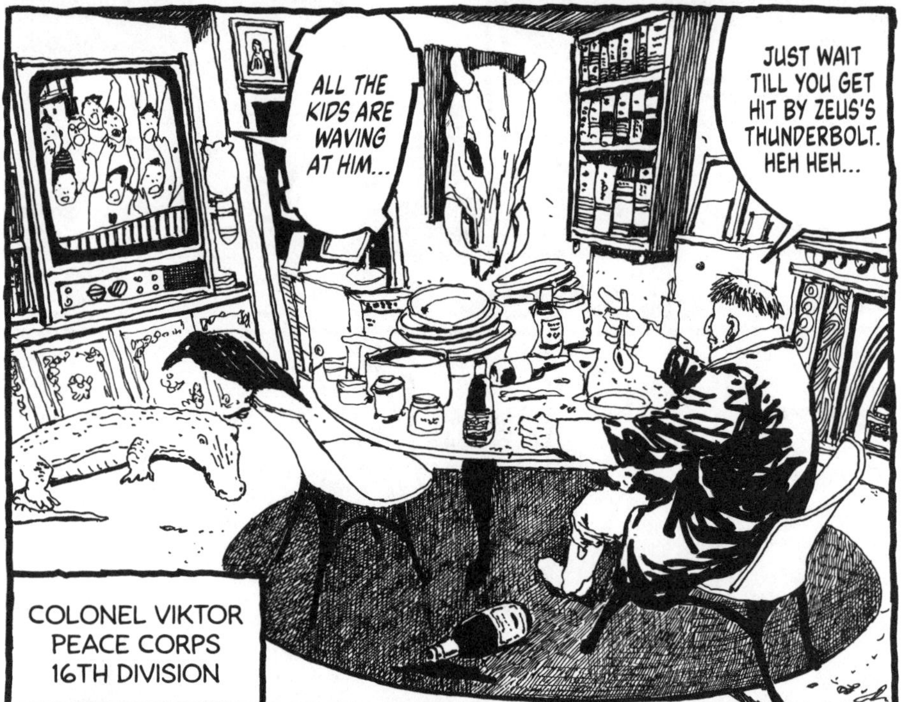
JUST WAIT TILL YOU GET HIT BY ZEUS'S THUNDERBOLT. HEH HEH...
ALL THE KIDS ARE WAVING AT HIM...
COLONEL VIKTOR PEACE CORPS 16TH DIVISION

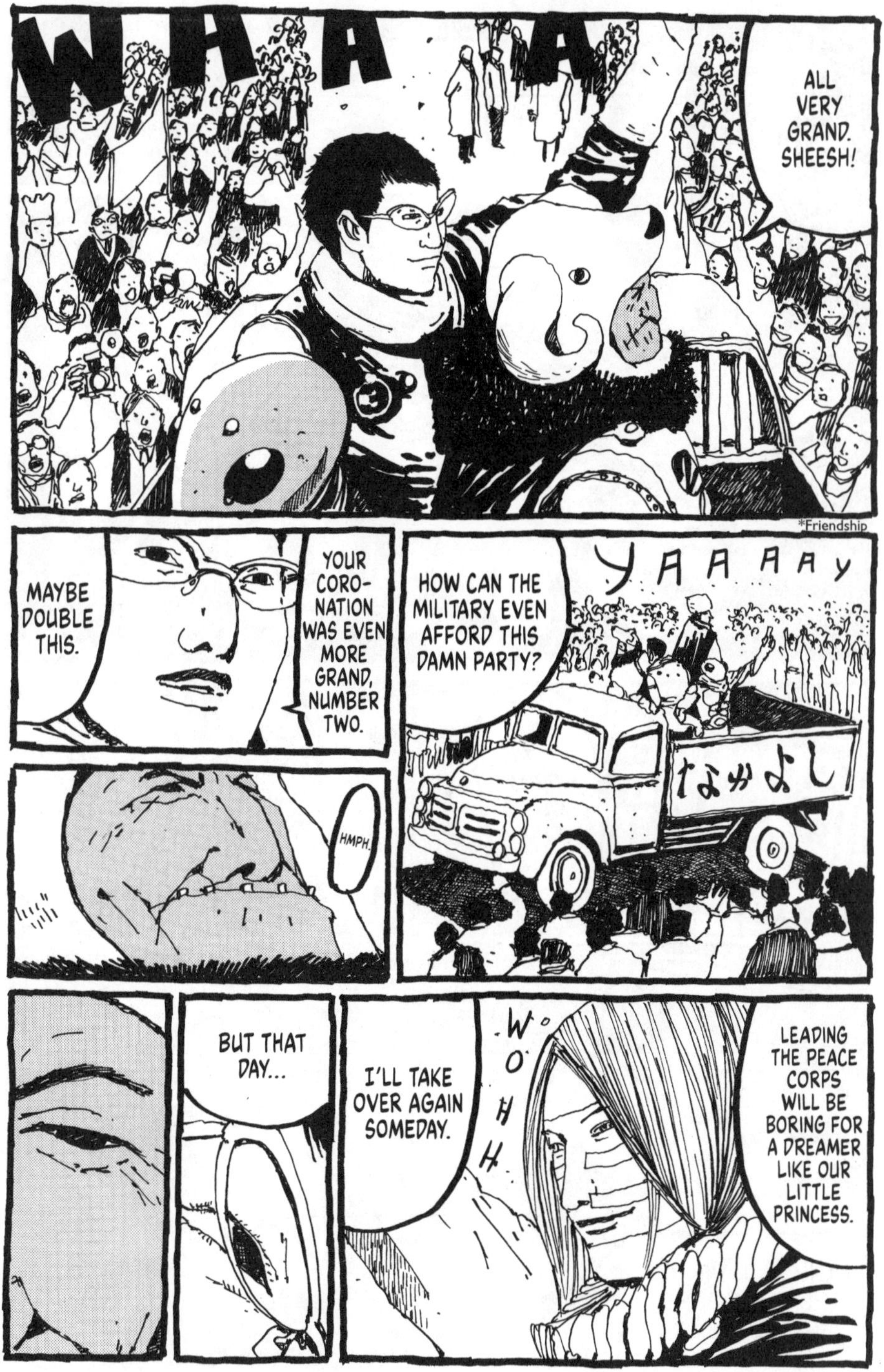
ALL VERY GRAND. SHEESH!
WAAA
YAAAAY
HOW CAN THE MILITARY EVEN AFFORD THIS DAMN PARTY?
なかよし
YOUR CORO-NATION WAS EVEN MORE GRAND, NUMBER TWO.
MAYBE DOUBLE THIS.
HMPH.
LEADING THE PEACE CORPS WILL BE BORING FOR A DREAMER LIKE OUR LITTLE PRINCESS.
WOHH
I'LL TAKE OVER AGAIN SOMEDAY.
BUT THAT DAY...
*Friendship

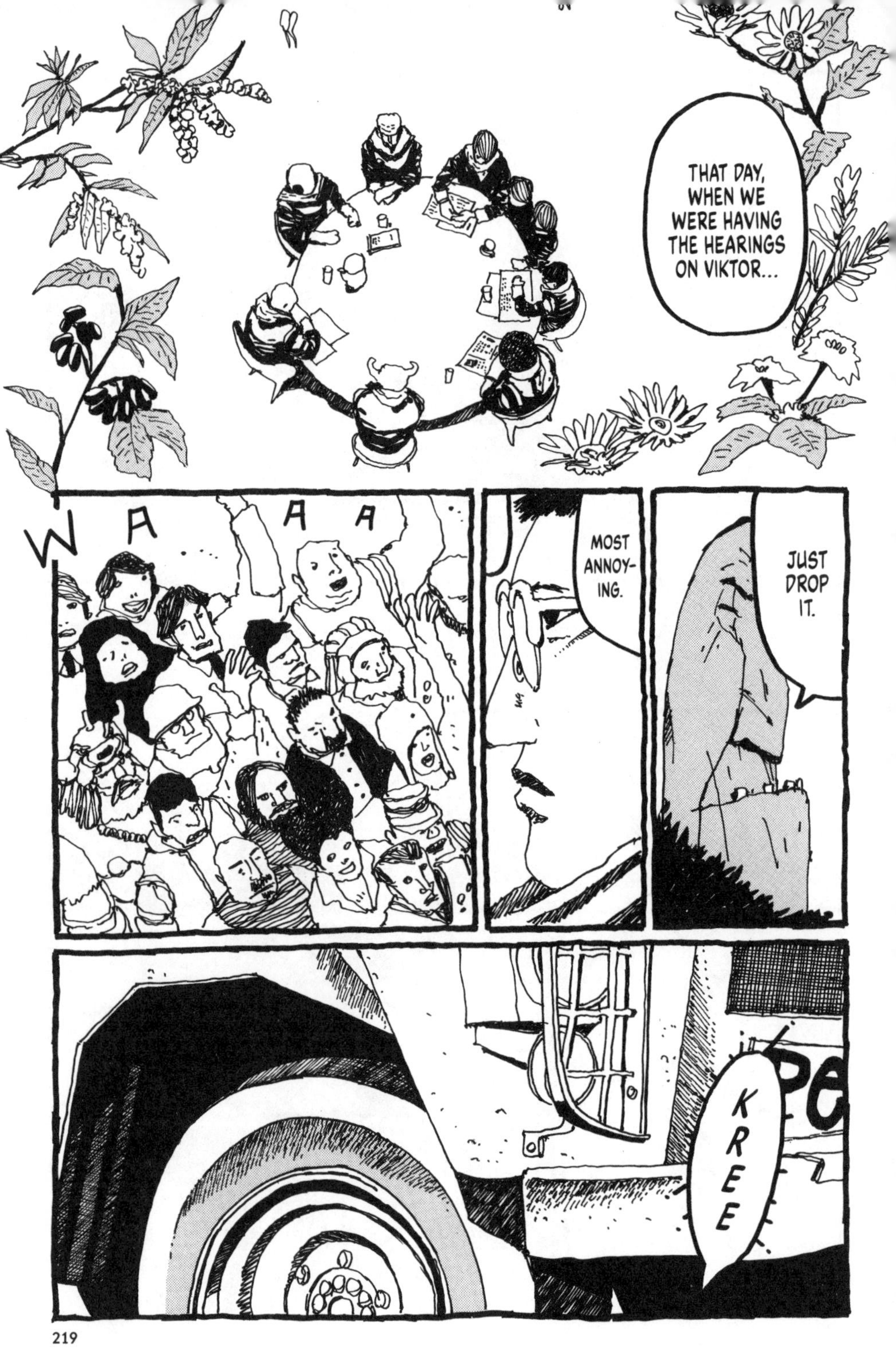
THAT DAY, WHEN WE WERE HAVING THE HEARINGS ON VIKTOR...
JUST DROP IT.
MOST ANNOY-ING.
WAAA
KREE
PE

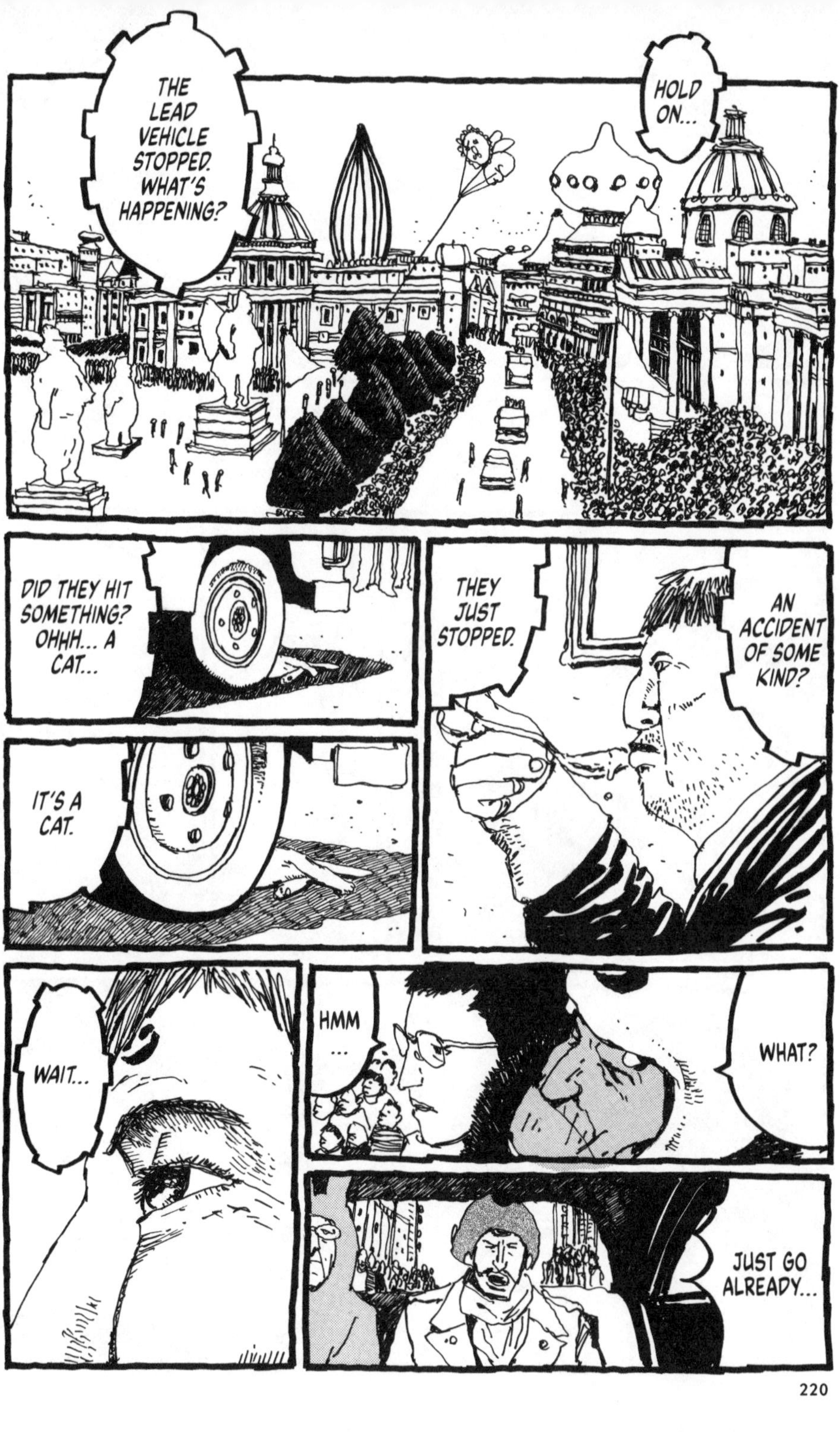
HOLD ON...
THE LEAD VEHICLE STOPPED. WHAT'S HAPPENING?
THEY JUST STOPPED.
AN ACCIDENT OF SOME KIND?
DID THEY HIT SOMETHING? OHHH... A CAT...
IT'S A CAT.
WHAT?
HMM ...
JUST GO ALREADY...
WAIT...

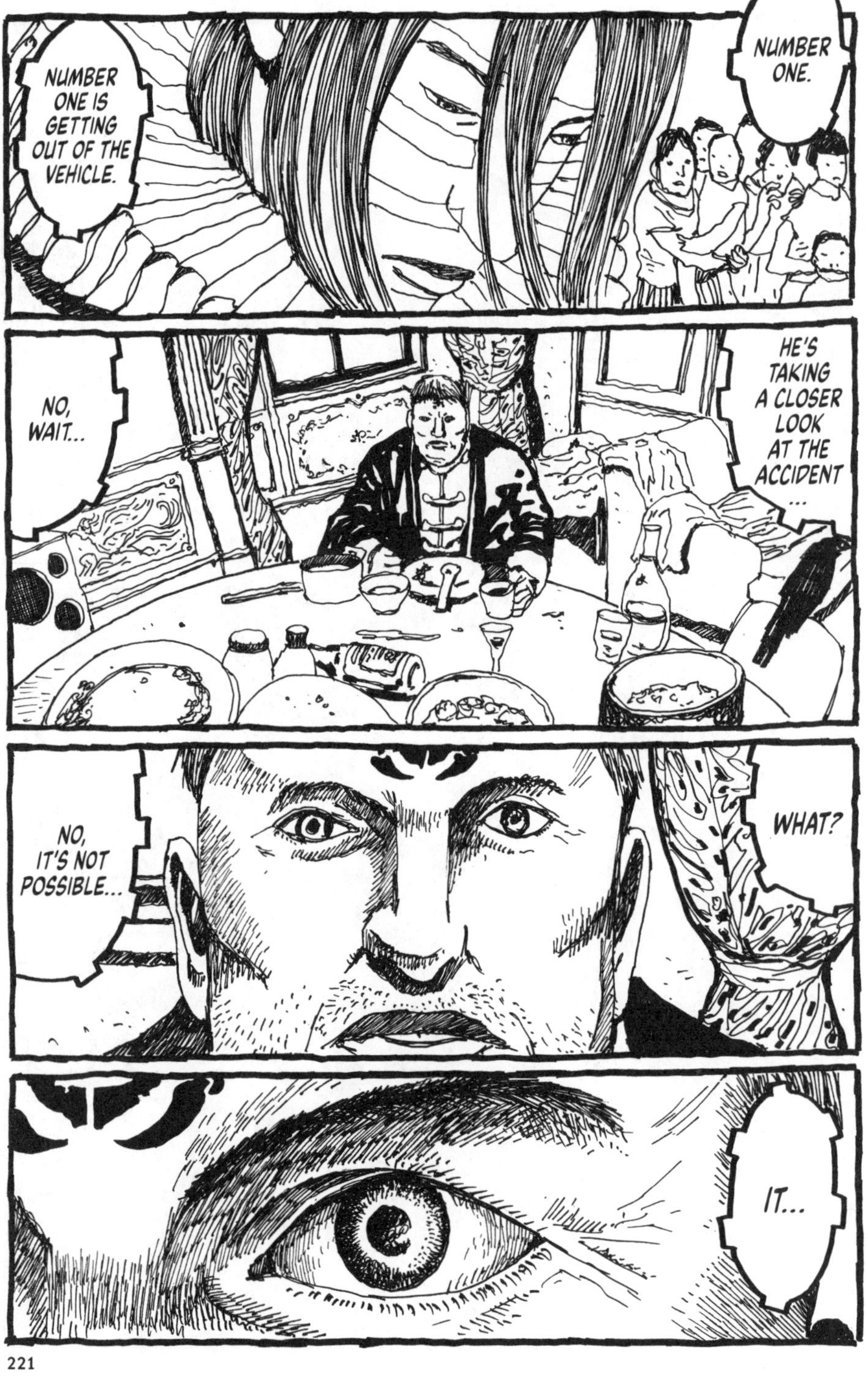
NUMBER ONE.
NUMBER ONE IS GETTING OUT OF THE VEHICLE.
HE'S TAKING A CLOSER LOOK AT THE ACCIDENT ...
NO, WAIT...
WHAT?
NO, IT'S NOT POSSIBLE...
IT...

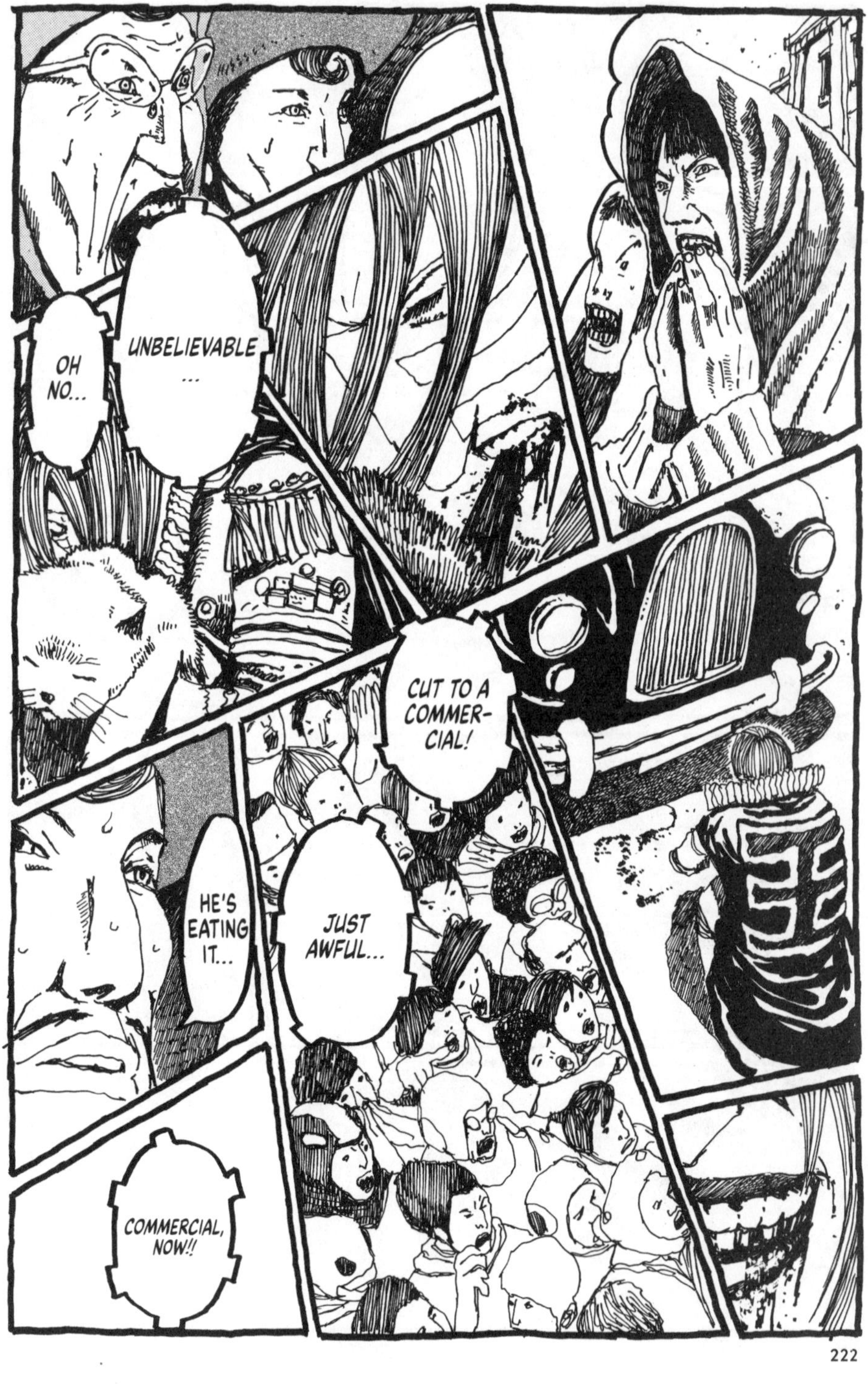
UNBELIEVABLE...
OH NO...
CUT TO A COMMERCIAL!
JUST AWFUL...
HE'S EATING IT...
COMMERCIAL, NOW!!

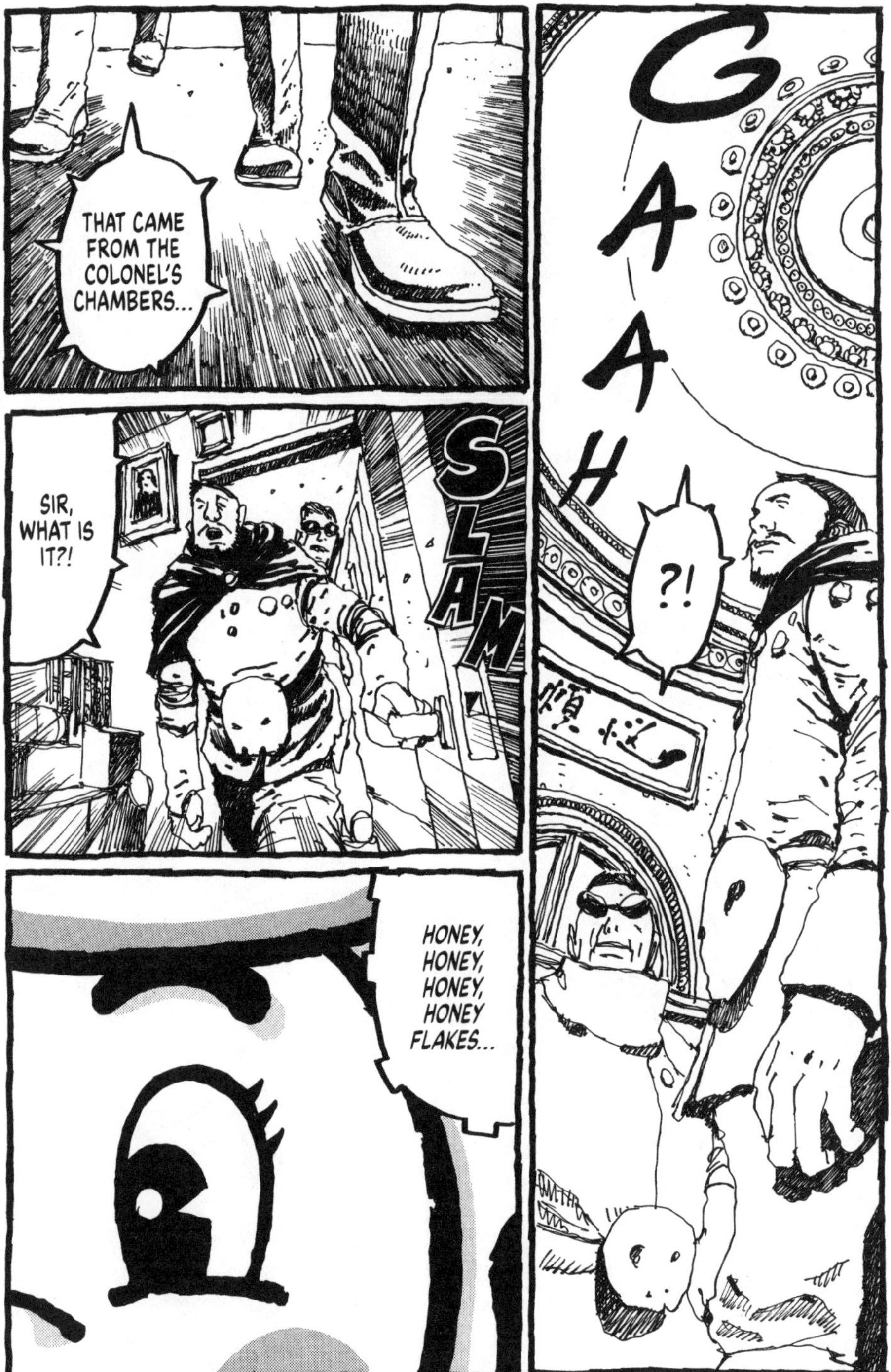
GAAAH
?!
THAT CAME FROM THE COLONEL'S CHAMBERS...
SLAM
SIR, WHAT IS IT?!
HONEY, HONEY, HONEY, HONEY FLAKES...

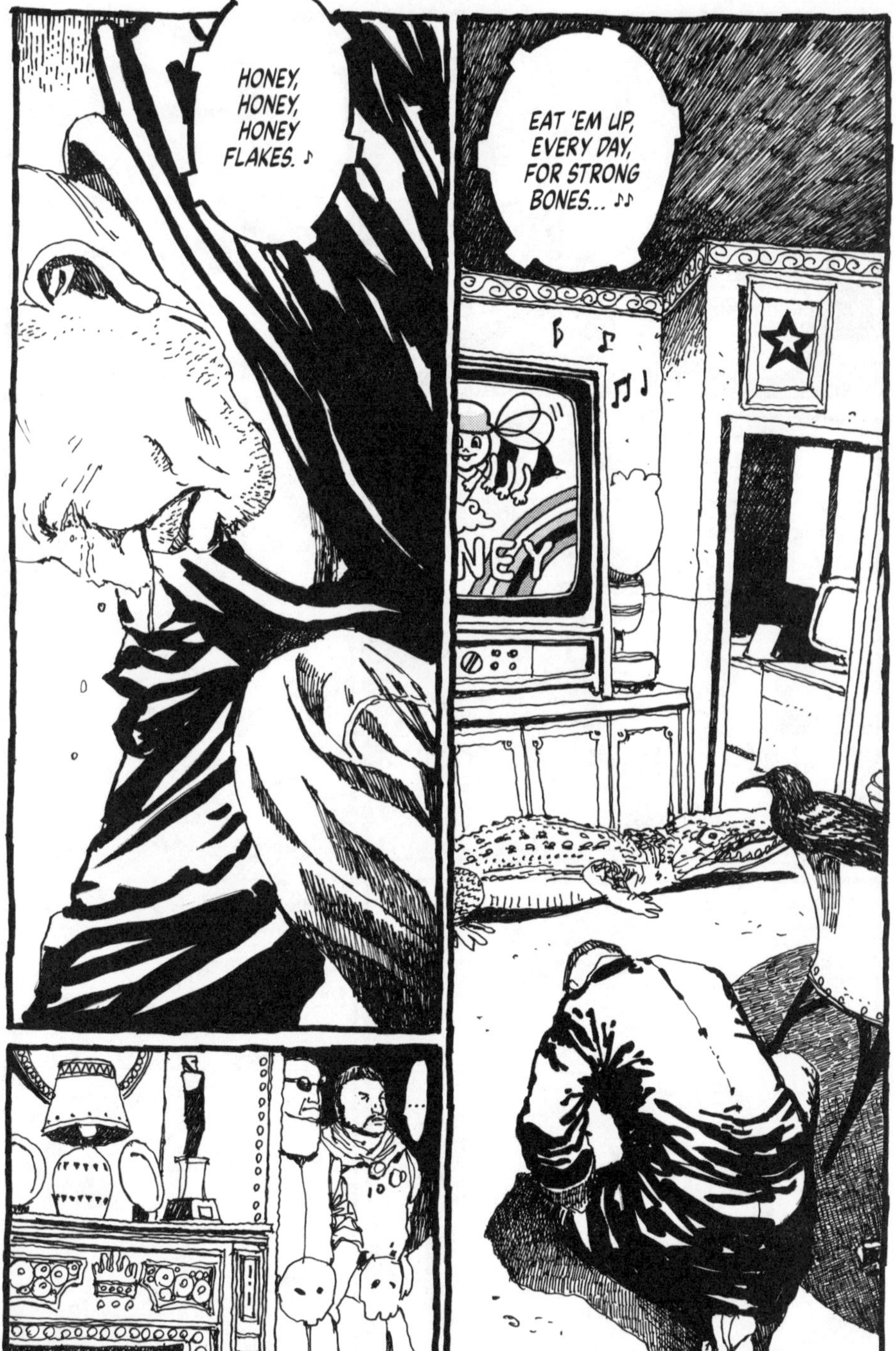
EAT 'EM UP, EVERY DAY, FOR STRONG BONES... ♪♪
NEY
HONEY, HONEY, HONEY FLAKES. ♪
...

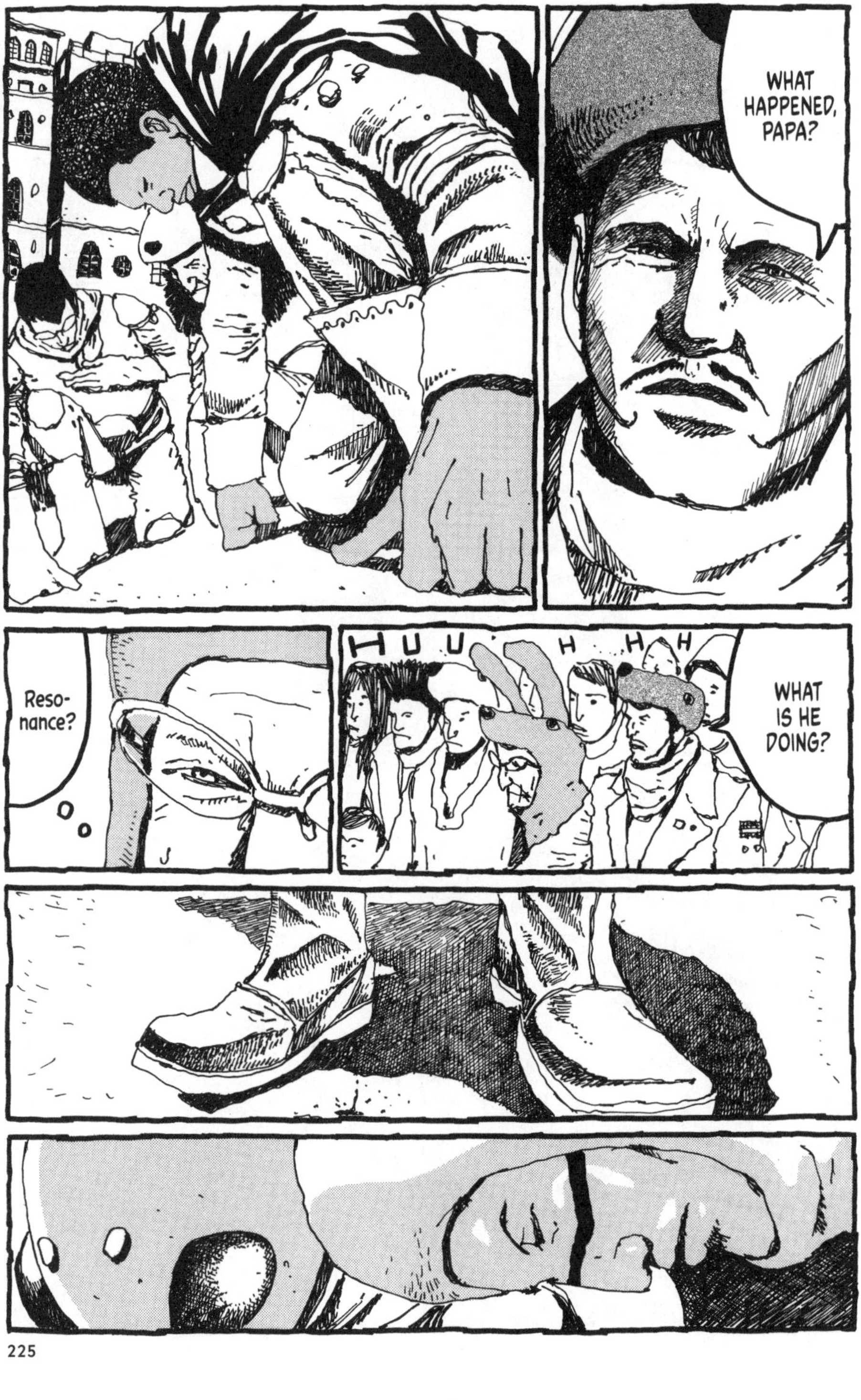
WHAT HAPPENED, PAPA?
HUUHHH
WHAT IS HE DOING?
Reso-nance?

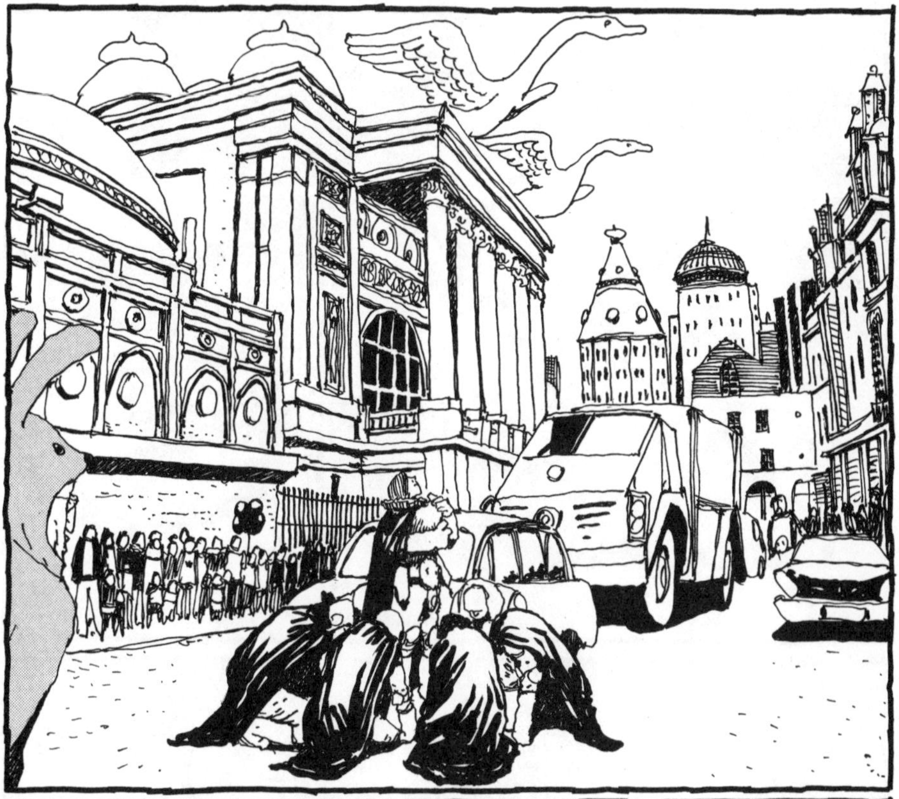

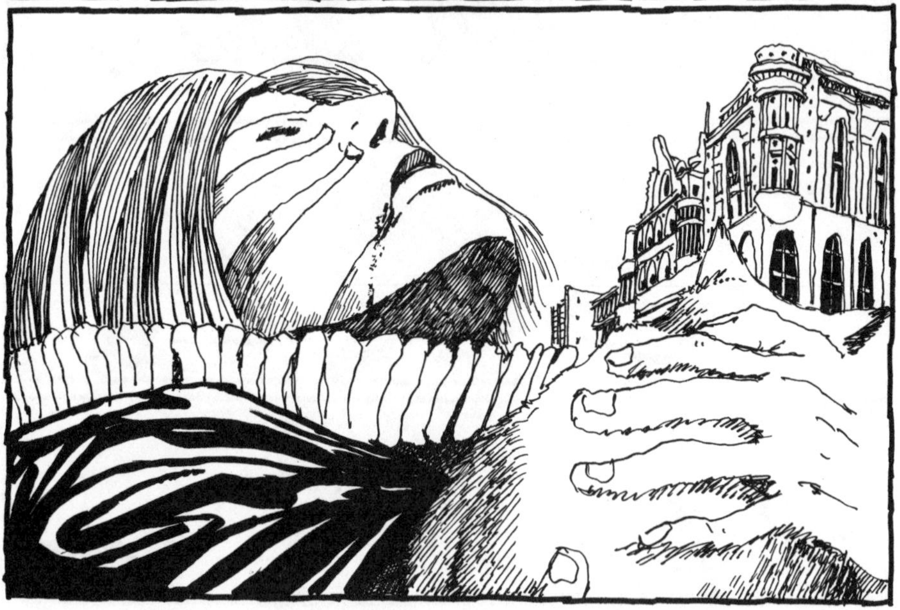

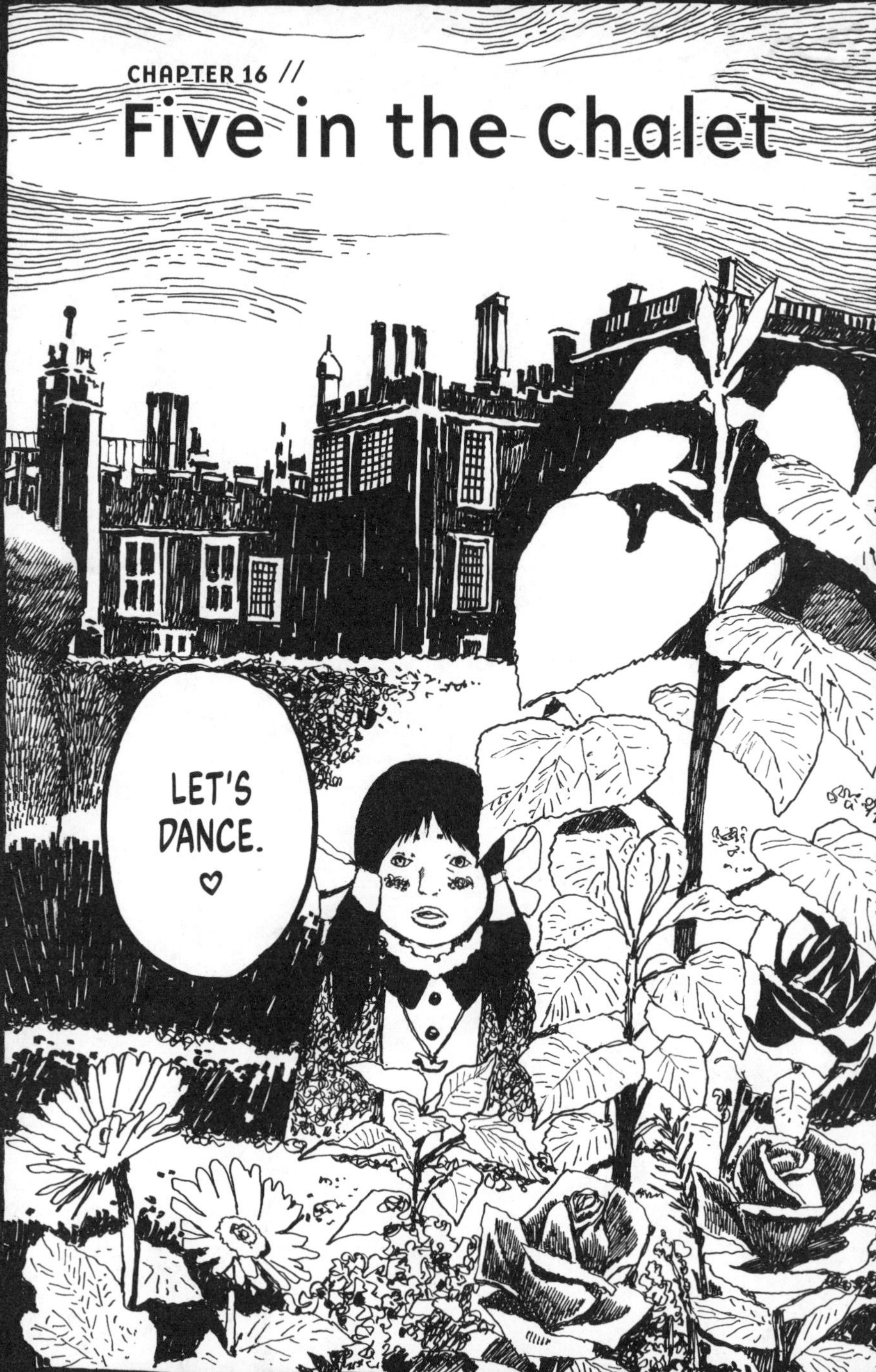
CHAPTER 16 //
Five in the Chalet
LET'S DANCE. ♡

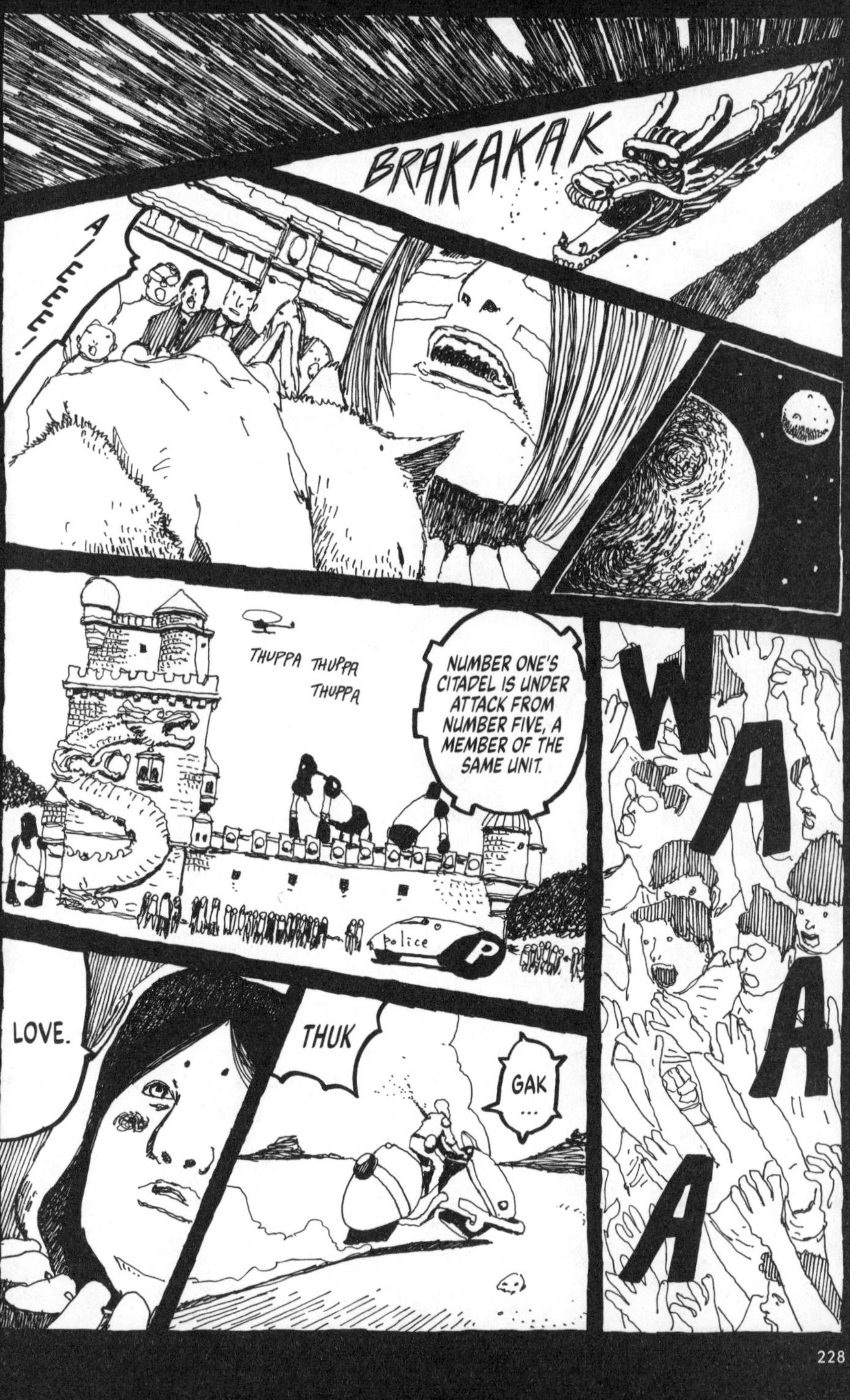
BRAKAKAK
A—EEEE—!
WAAAA
THUPPA THUPPA THUPPA
NUMBER ONE'S CITADEL IS UNDER ATTACK FROM NUMBER FIVE, A MEMBER OF THE SAME UNIT.
police
THUK
GAK ...
LOVE.

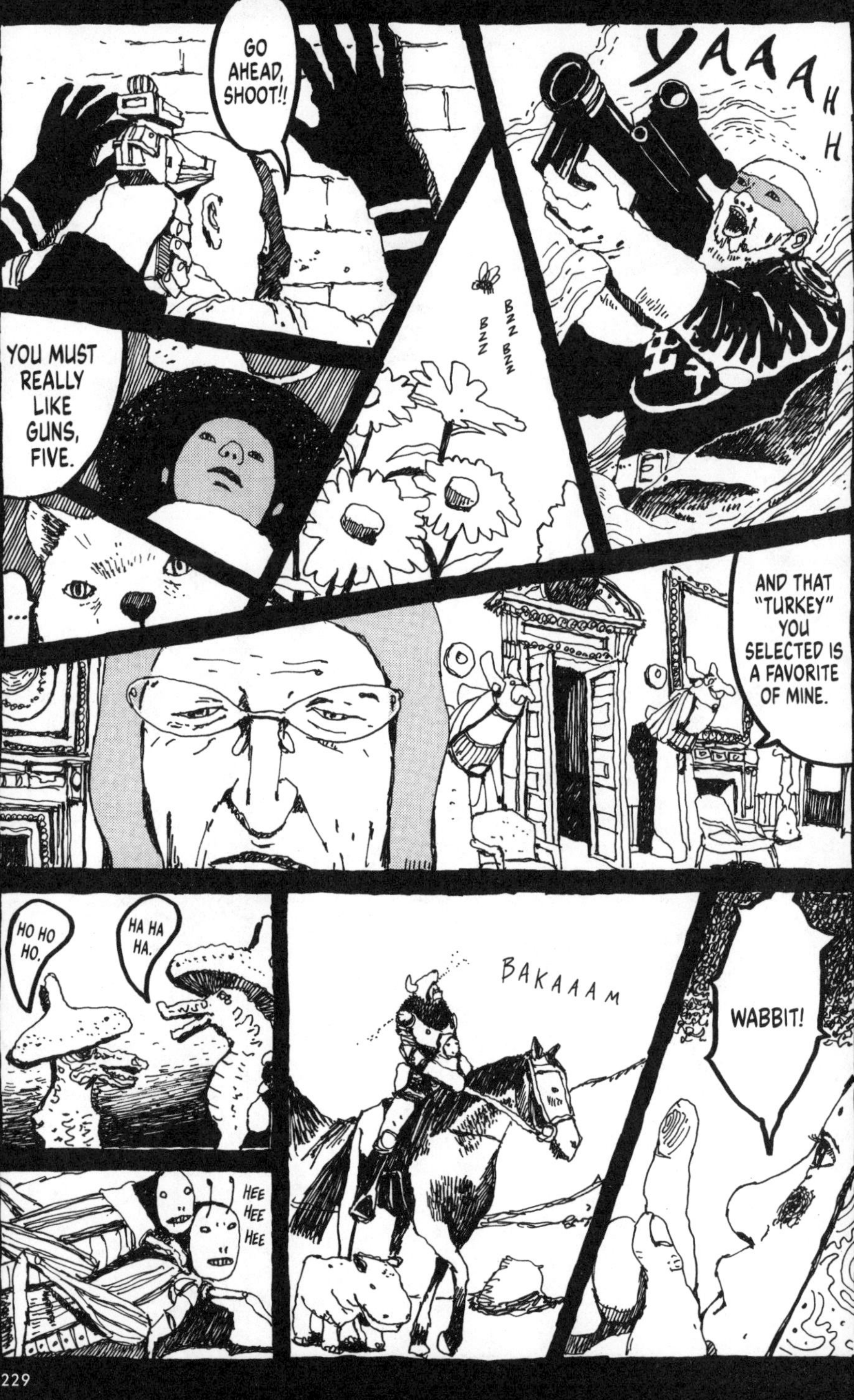
YAAAHHH
BZZ BZZ BZZ
GO AHEAD, SHOOT!!
YOU MUST REALLY LIKE GUNS, FIVE.
AND THAT "TURKEY" YOU SELECTED IS A FAVORITE OF MINE.
WABBIT!
BAKAAAM
HA HA HA.
HO HO HO.
HEE HEE HEE

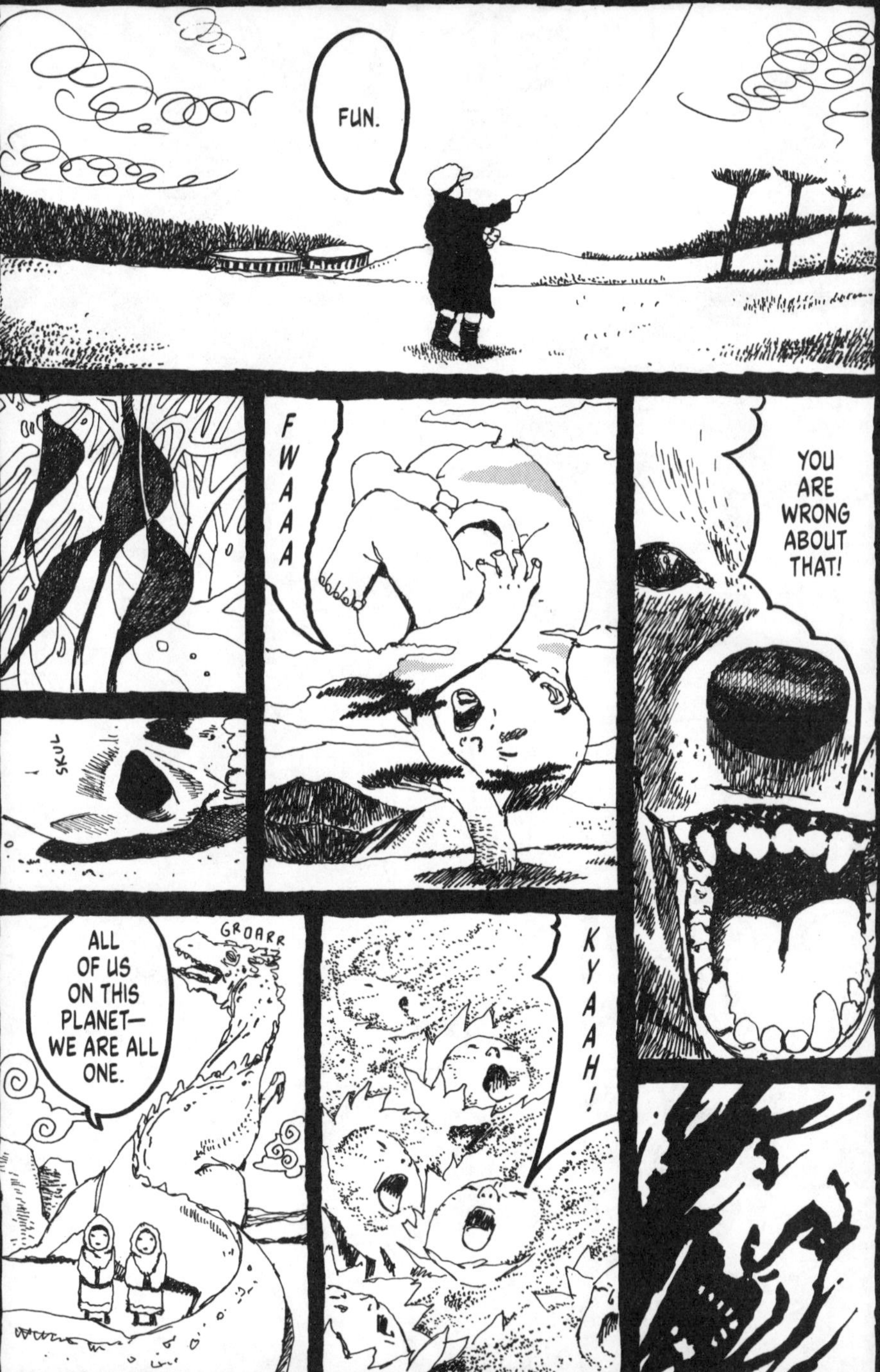
FUN.
YOU ARE WRONG ABOUT THAT!
FWAAAA
SKUL
KYAAAH!
ALL OF US ON THIS PLANET—WE ARE ALL ONE.
GROARR

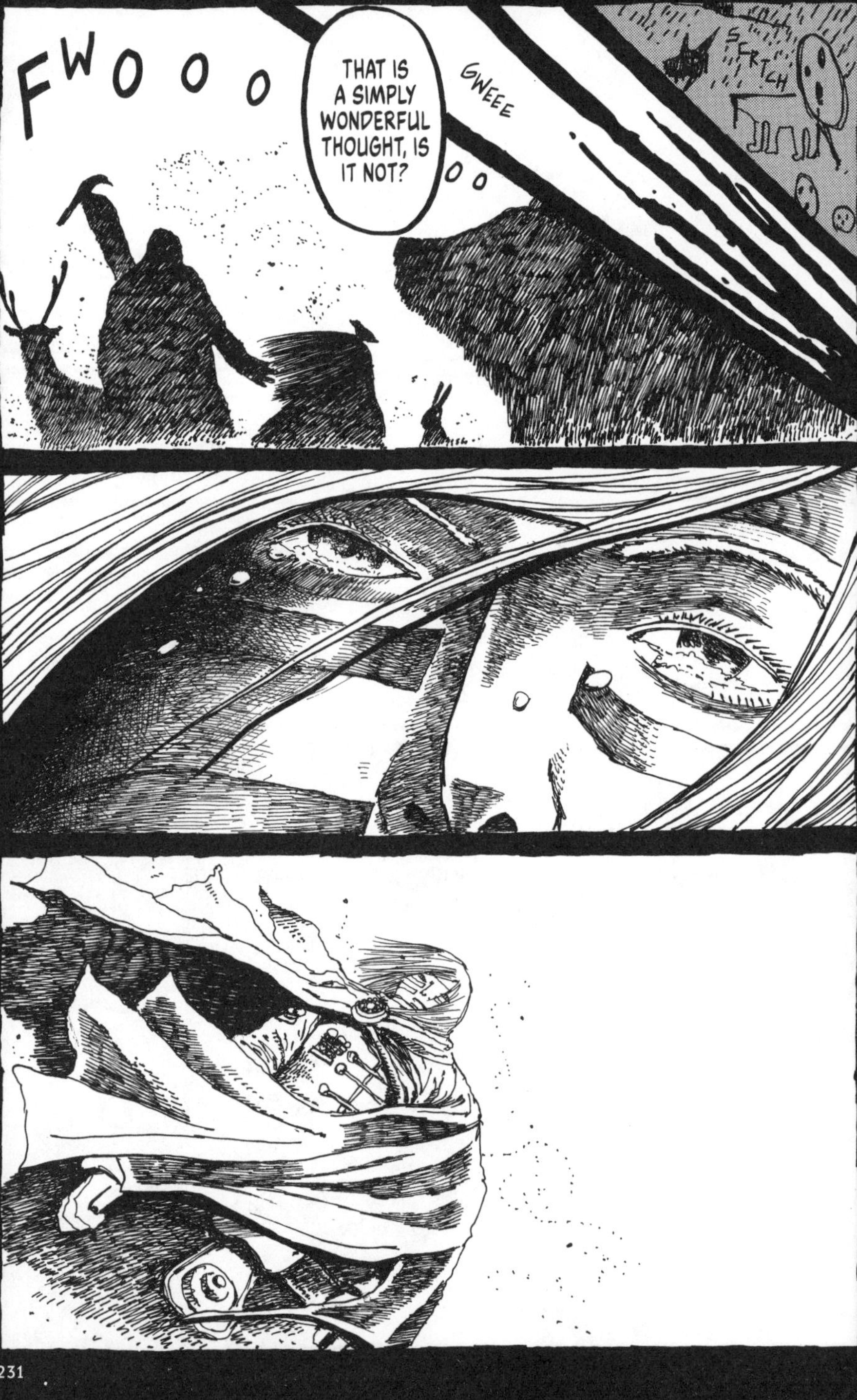
SCRTCH
GWEEE
THAT IS A SIMPLY WONDERFUL THOUGHT, IS IT NOT?
FWOOOOO

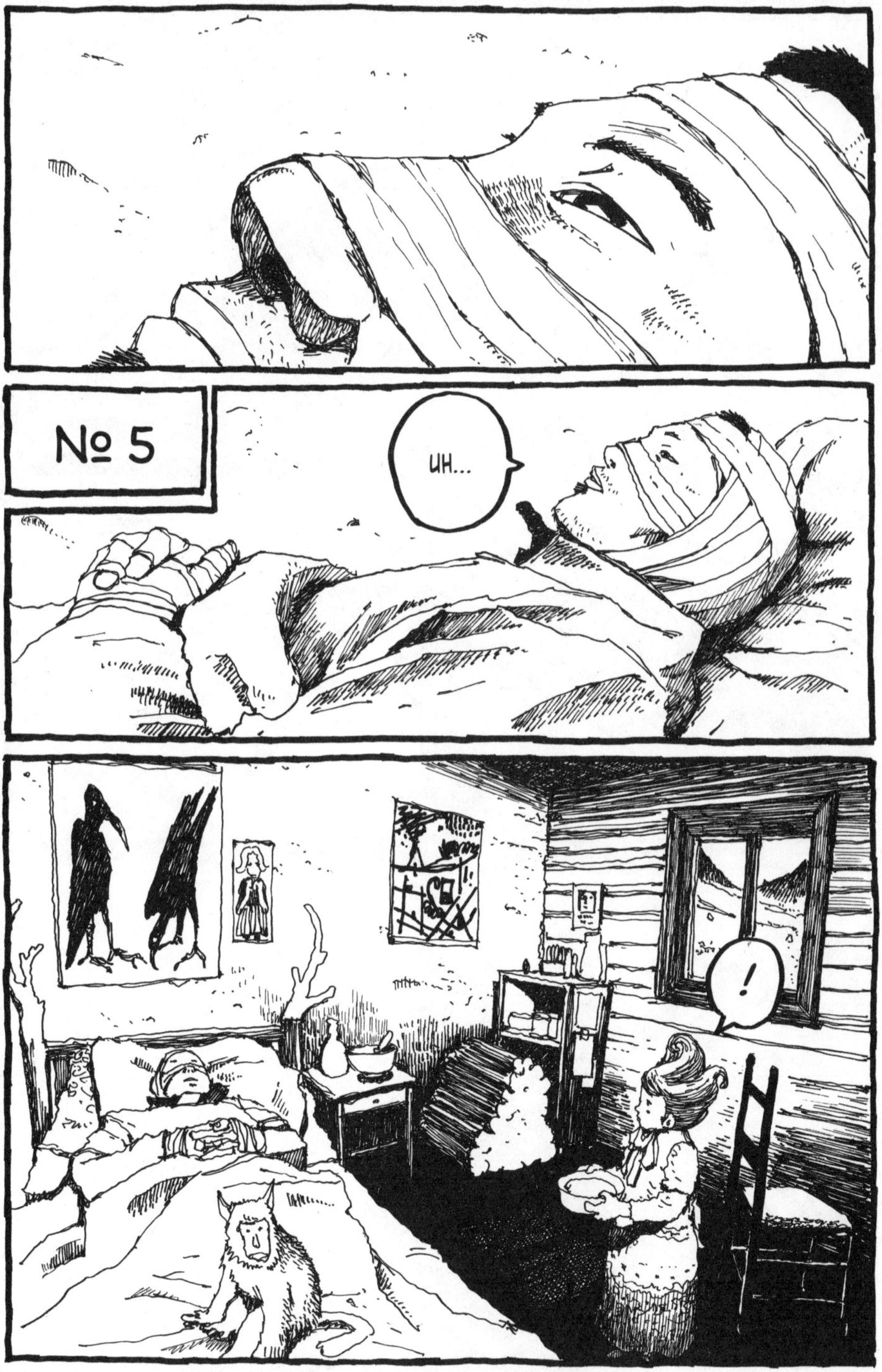
№ 5
UH...
!

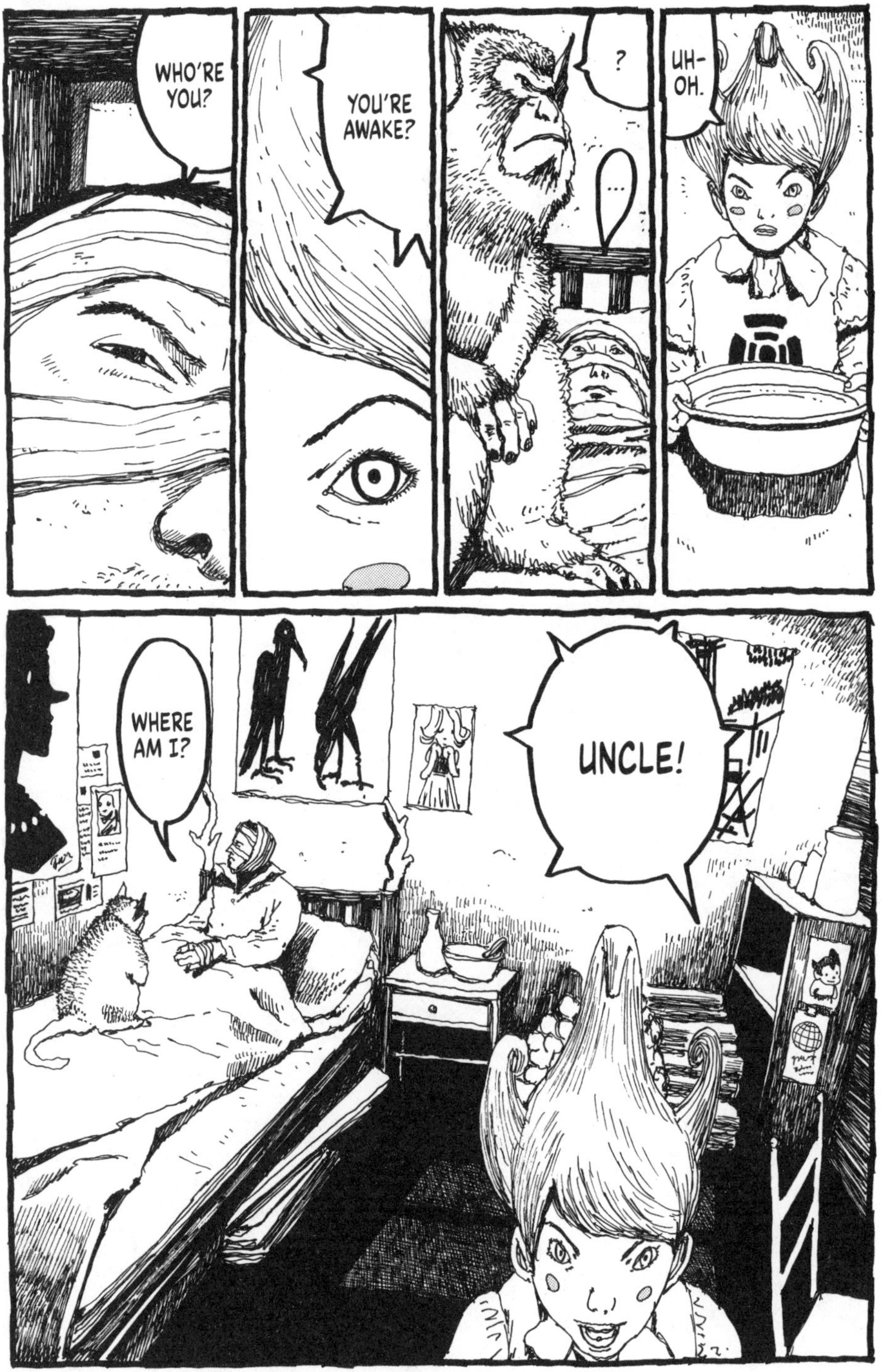
UH-OH.
?
...
YOU'RE AWAKE?
WHO'RE YOU?
UNCLE!
WHERE AM I?

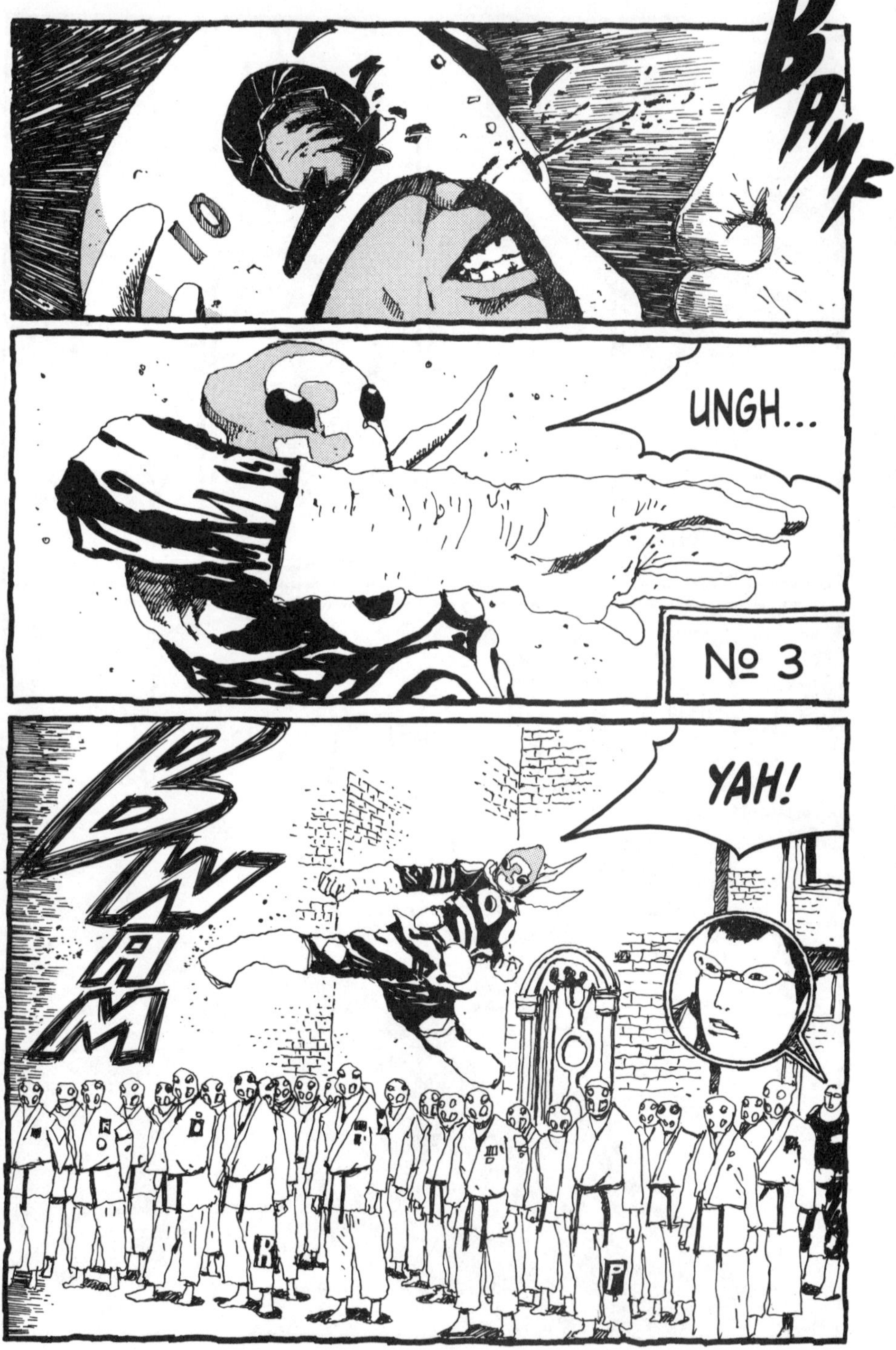
BAMF
UNGH...
№ 3
YAH!
BWRAM

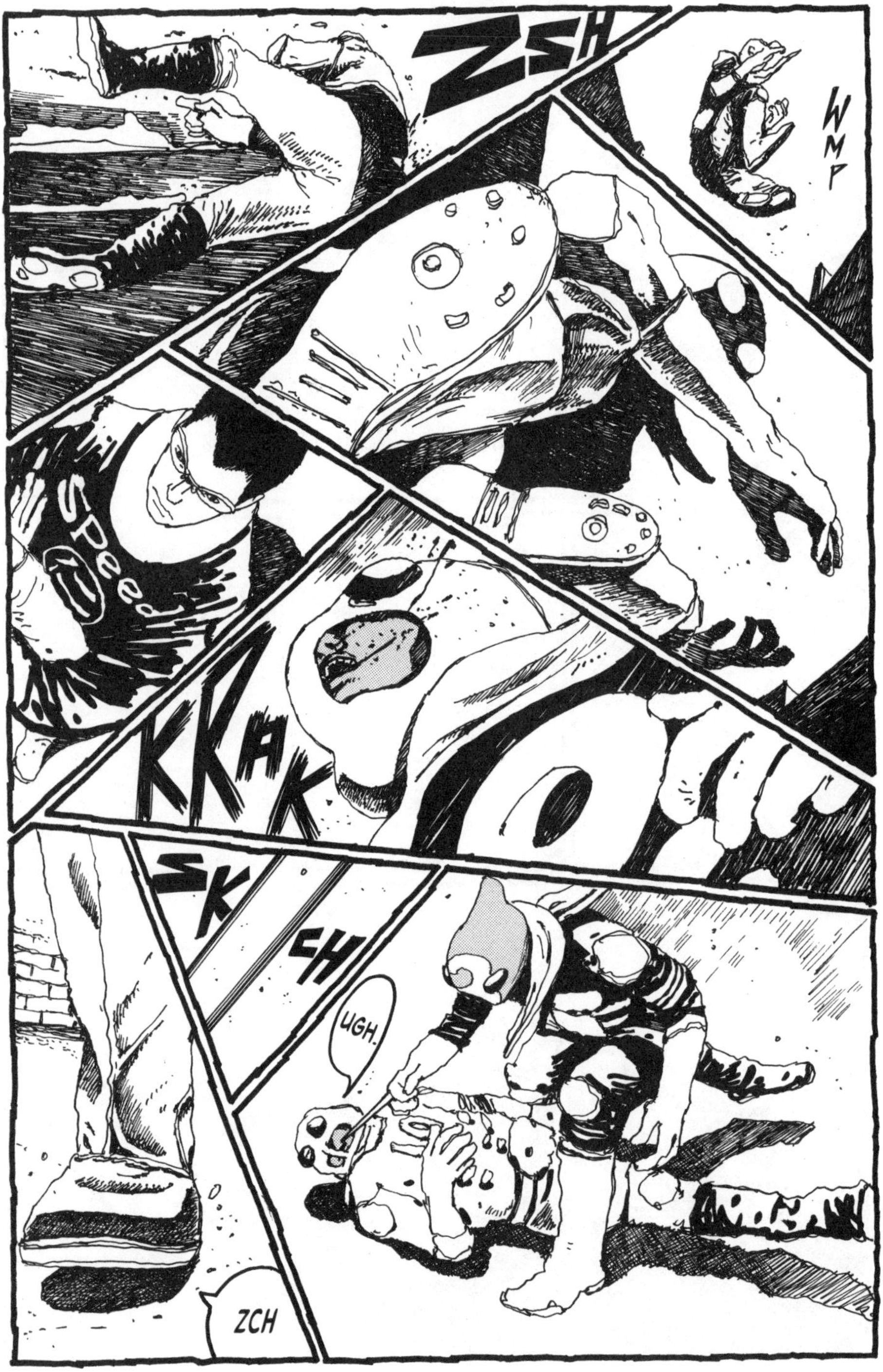

WMP
ZSH
SPEED
KKAK
SK
CH
UGH.
ZCH

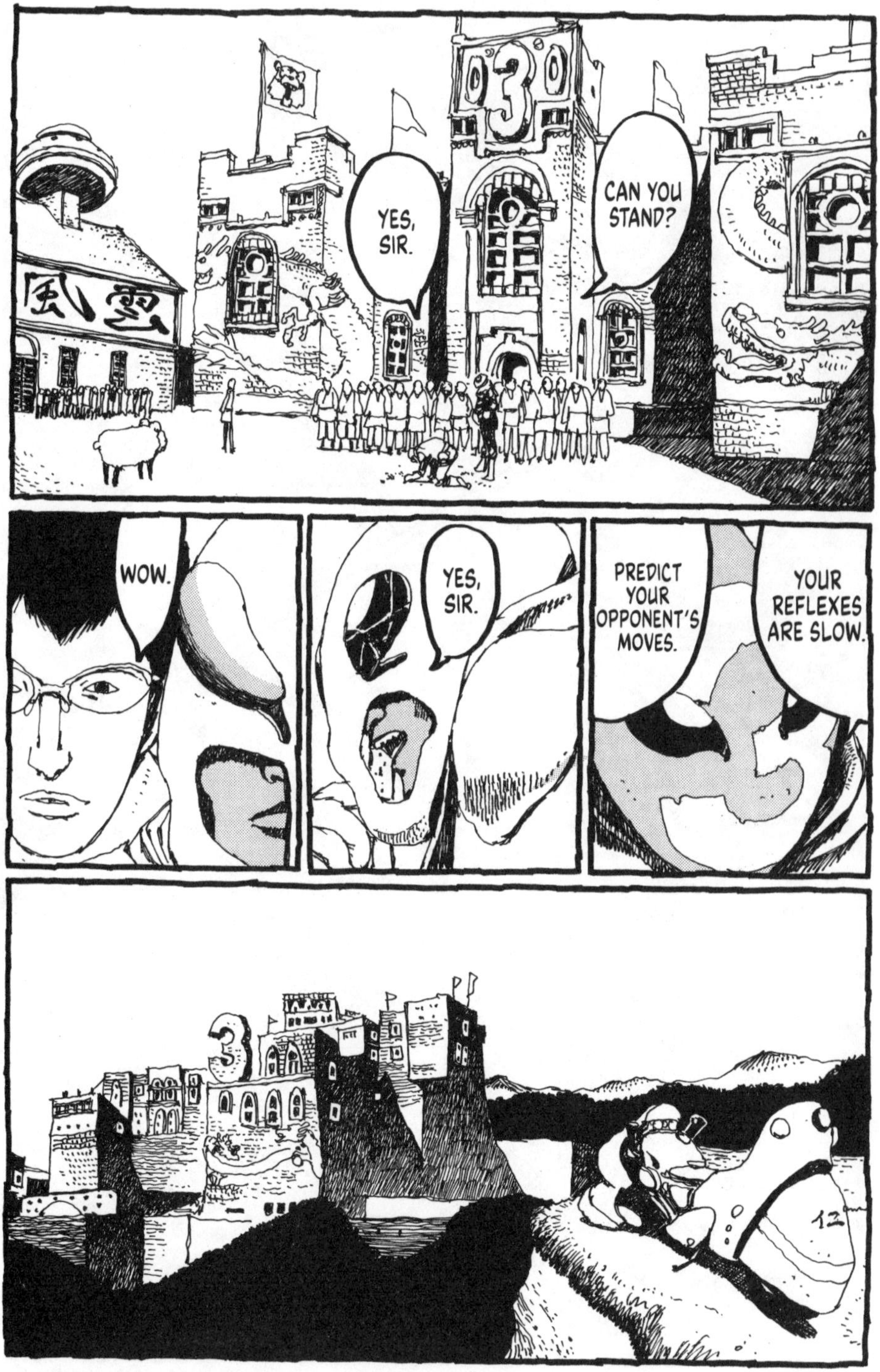
CAN YOU STAND?
YES, SIR.
風雲
YOUR REFLEXES ARE SLOW.
PREDICT YOUR OPPONENT'S MOVES.
YES, SIR.
WOW.

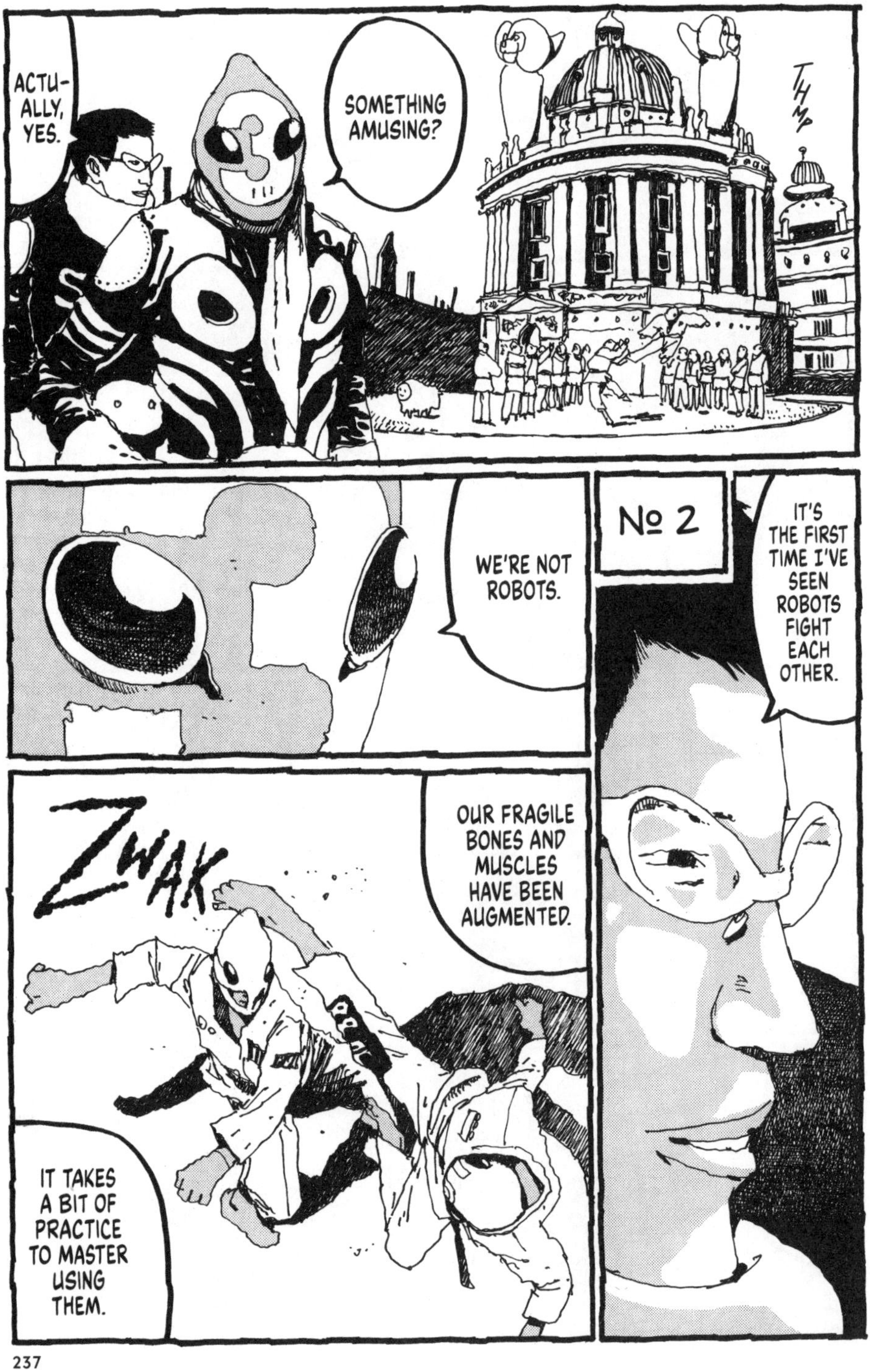
THMP
SOMETHING AMUSING?
ACTU-ALLY, YES.
№ 2
IT'S THE FIRST TIME I'VE SEEN ROBOTS FIGHT EACH OTHER.
WE'RE NOT ROBOTS.
OUR FRAGILE BONES AND MUSCLES HAVE BEEN AUGMENTED.
ZWAK
IT TAKES A BIT OF PRACTICE TO MASTER USING THEM.

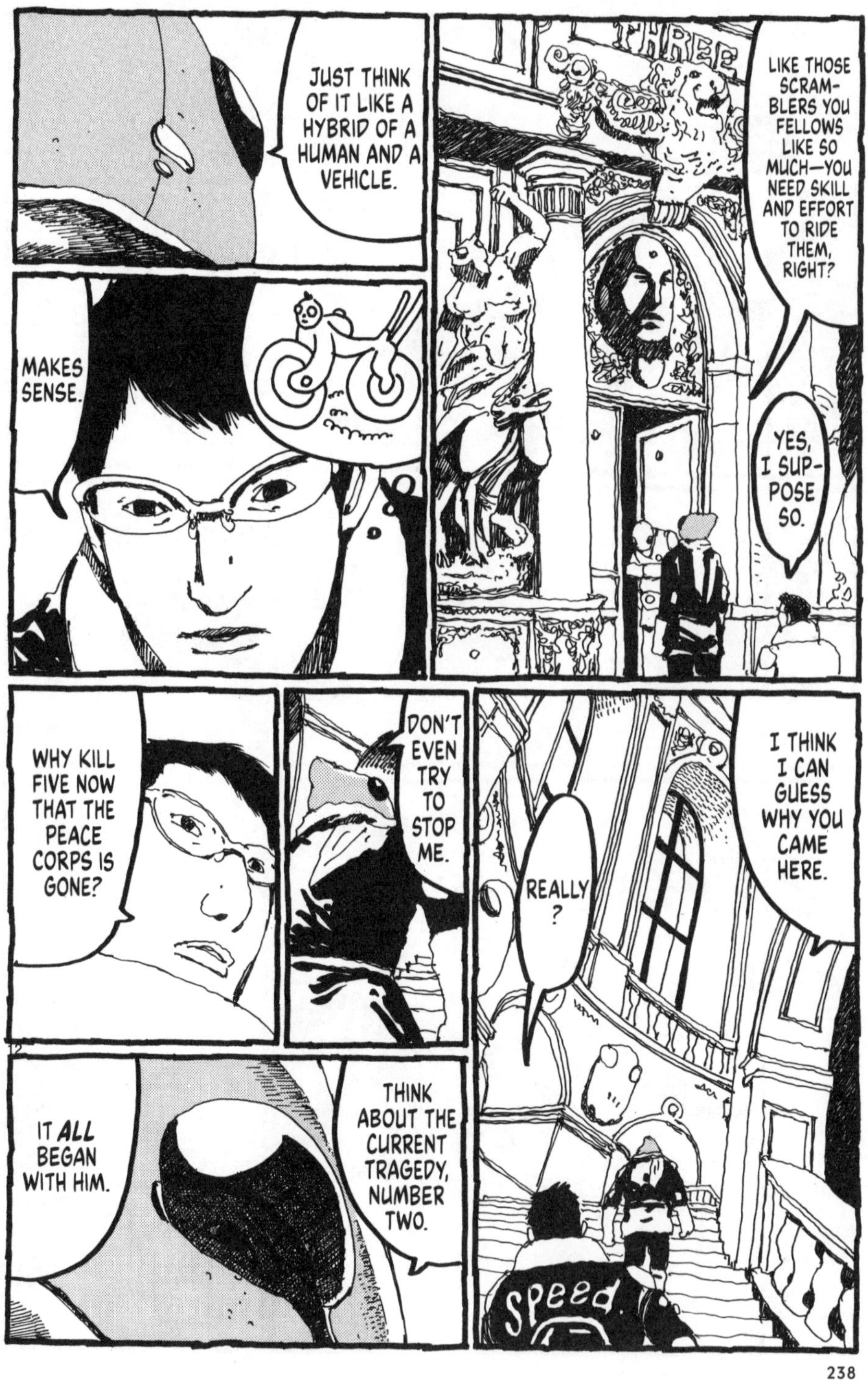
LIKE THOSE SCRAMBLERS YOU FELLOWS LIKE SO MUCH—YOU NEED SKILL AND EFFORT TO RIDE THEM, RIGHT?
YES, I SUPPOSE SO.
JUST THINK OF IT LIKE A HYBRID OF A HUMAN AND A VEHICLE.
MAKES SENSE.
THREE
I THINK I CAN GUESS WHY YOU CAME HERE.
REALLY?
DON'T EVEN TRY TO STOP ME.
WHY KILL FIVE NOW THAT THE PEACE CORPS IS GONE?
THINK ABOUT THE CURRENT TRAGEDY, NUMBER TWO.
IT ***ALL*** BEGAN WITH HIM.
speed

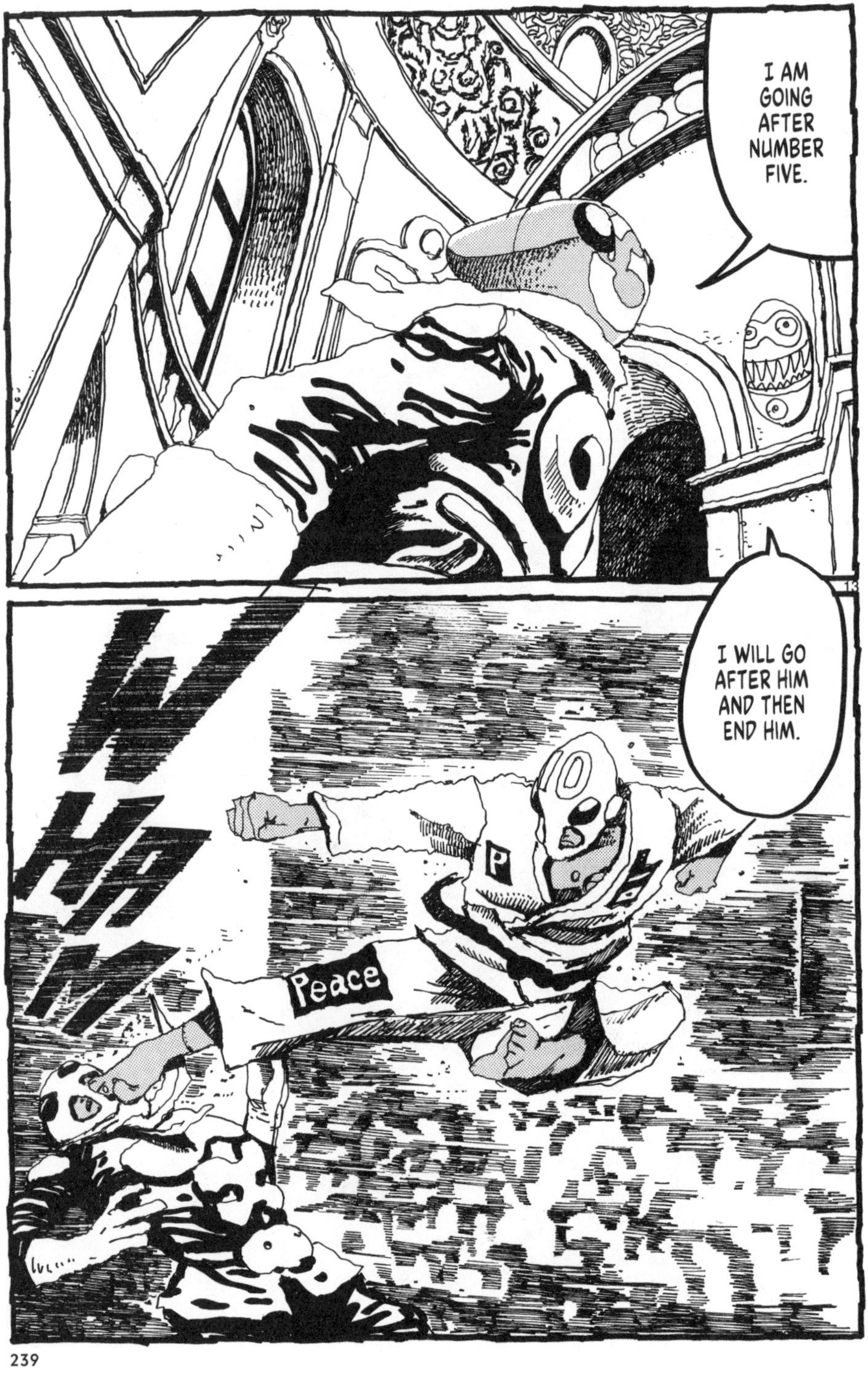
I AM GOING AFTER NUMBER FIVE.
I WILL GO AFTER HIM AND THEN END HIM.
WHAM
Peace
P

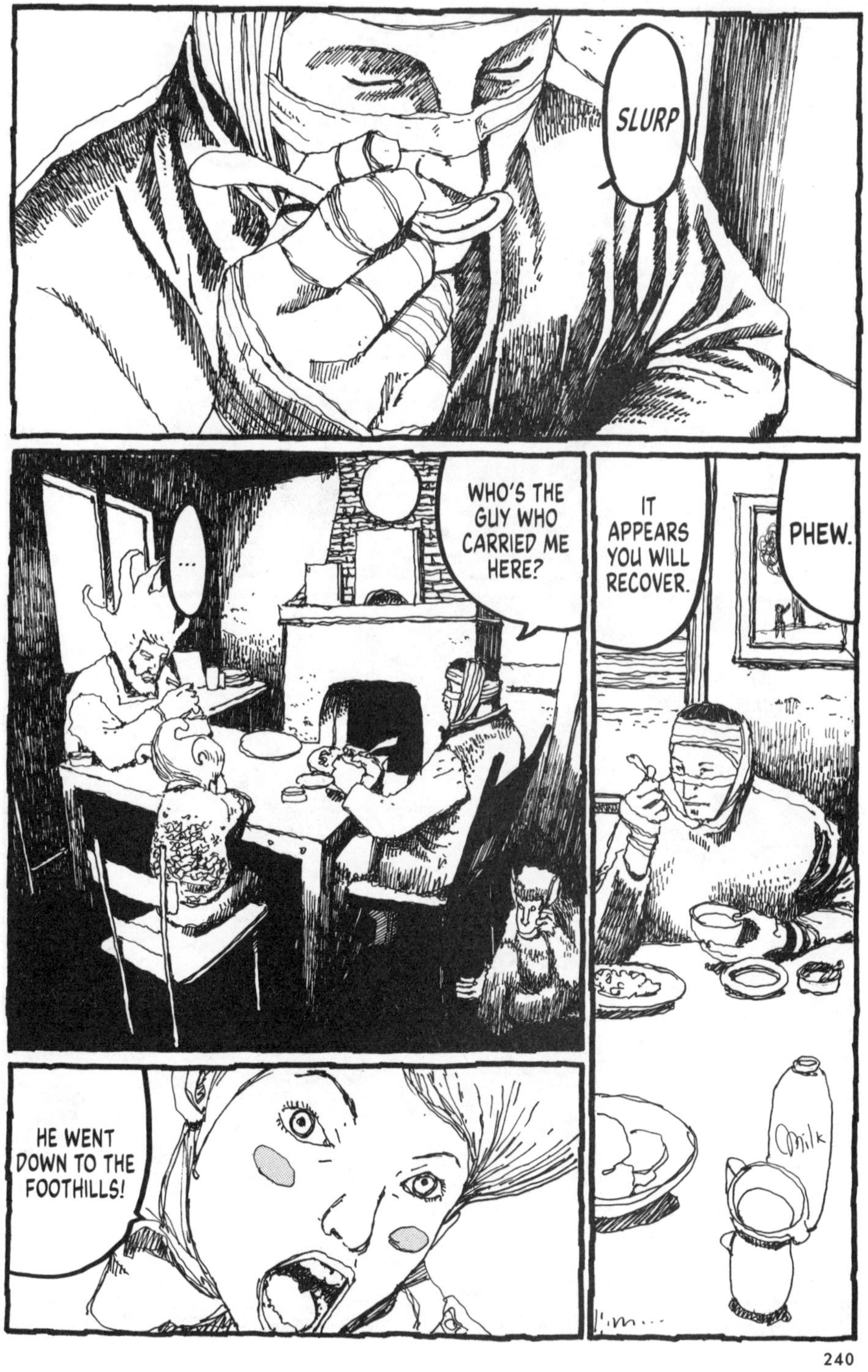
SLURP
PHEW.
IT APPEARS YOU WILL RECOVER.
Milk
I'm...
WHO'S THE GUY WHO CARRIED ME HERE?
...
HE WENT DOWN TO THE FOOTHILLS!

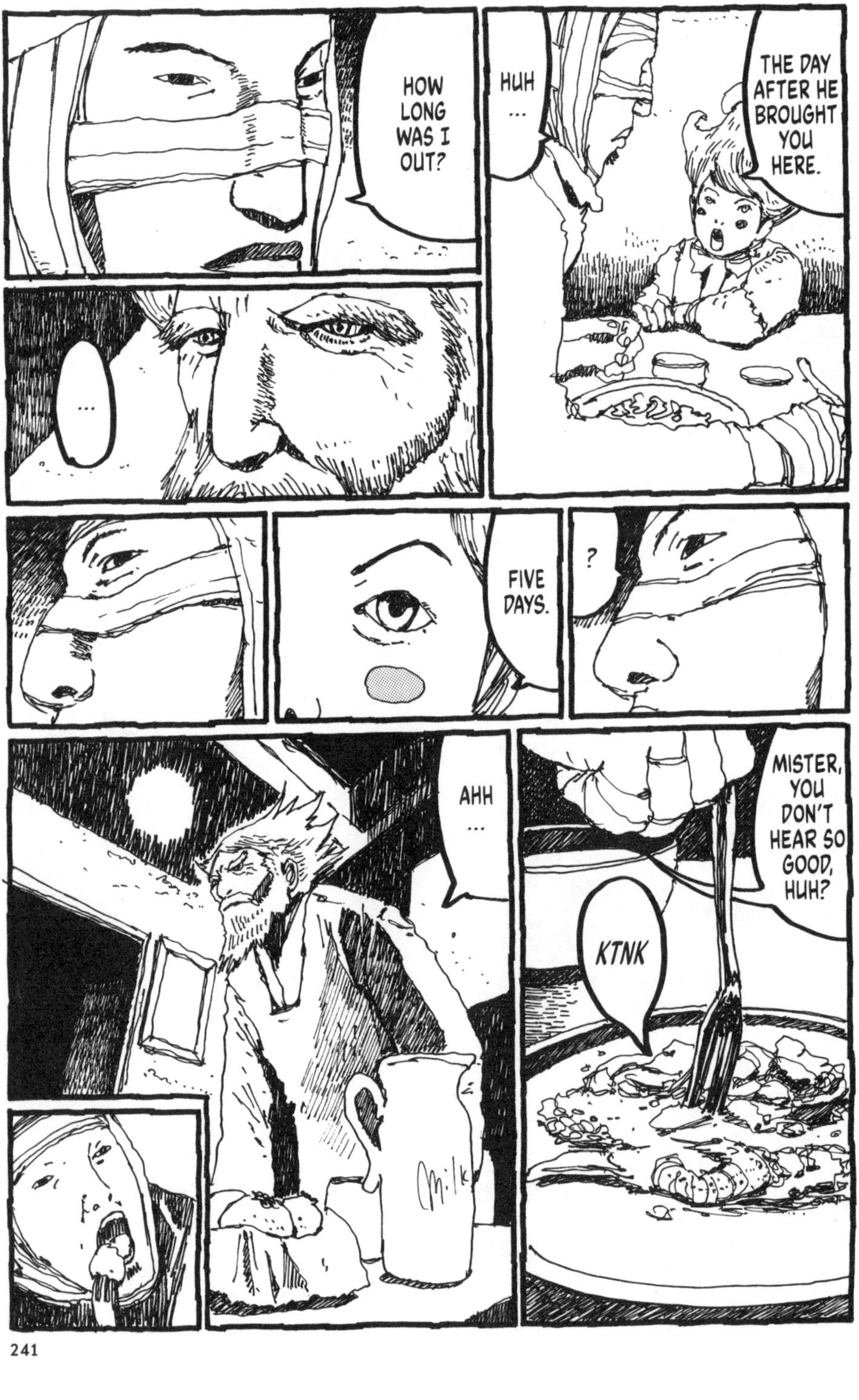
THE DAY AFTER HE BROUGHT YOU HERE.
HUH ...
HOW LONG WAS I OUT?
...
?
FIVE DAYS.
MISTER, YOU DON'T HEAR SO GOOD, HUH?
KTNK
AHH ...

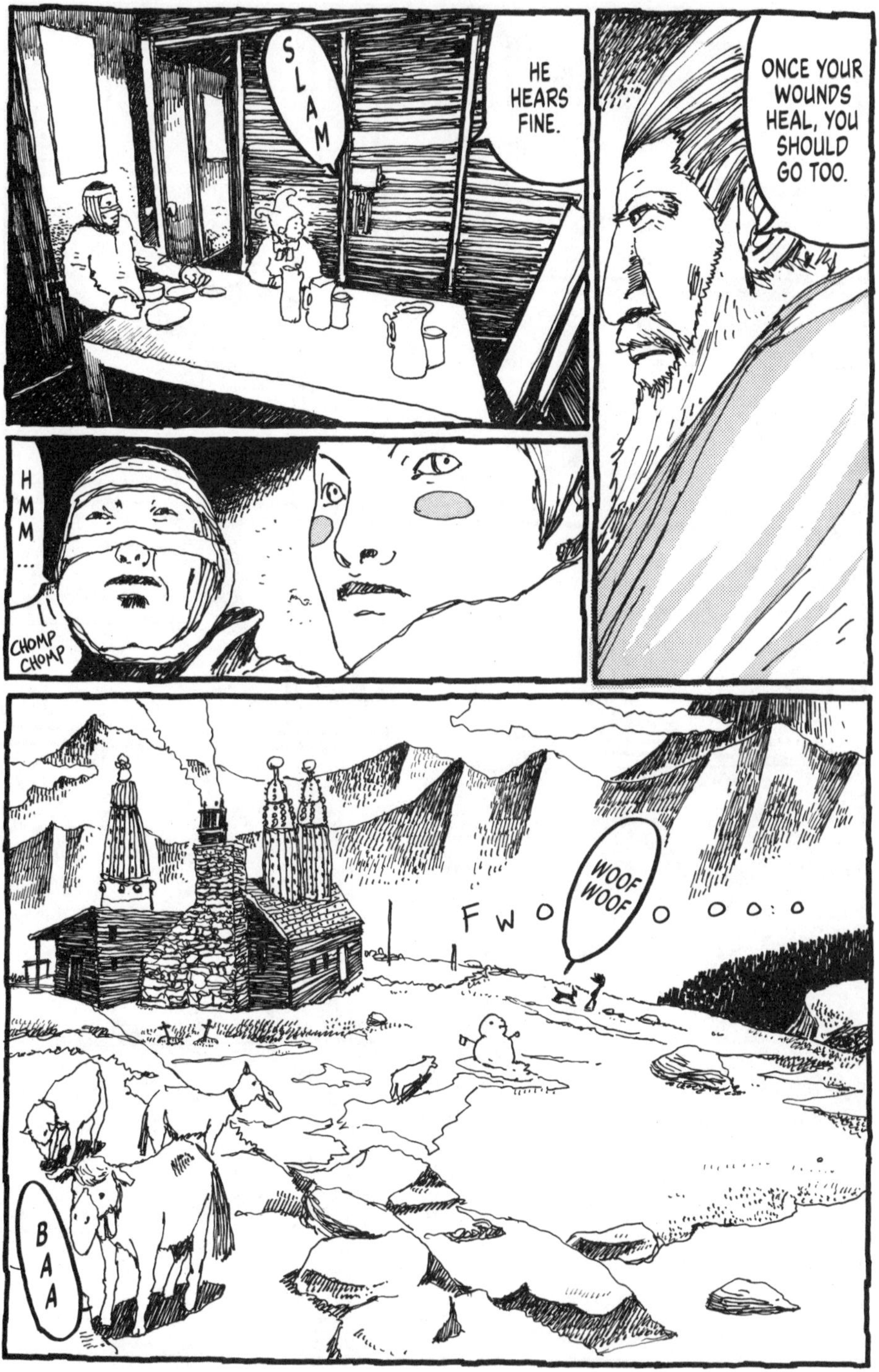
ONCE YOUR WOUNDS HEAL, YOU SHOULD GO TOO.
HE HEARS FINE.
SLAM
HMM...
CHOMP CHOMP
FWOOOOO:O
WOOF WOOF
BAA

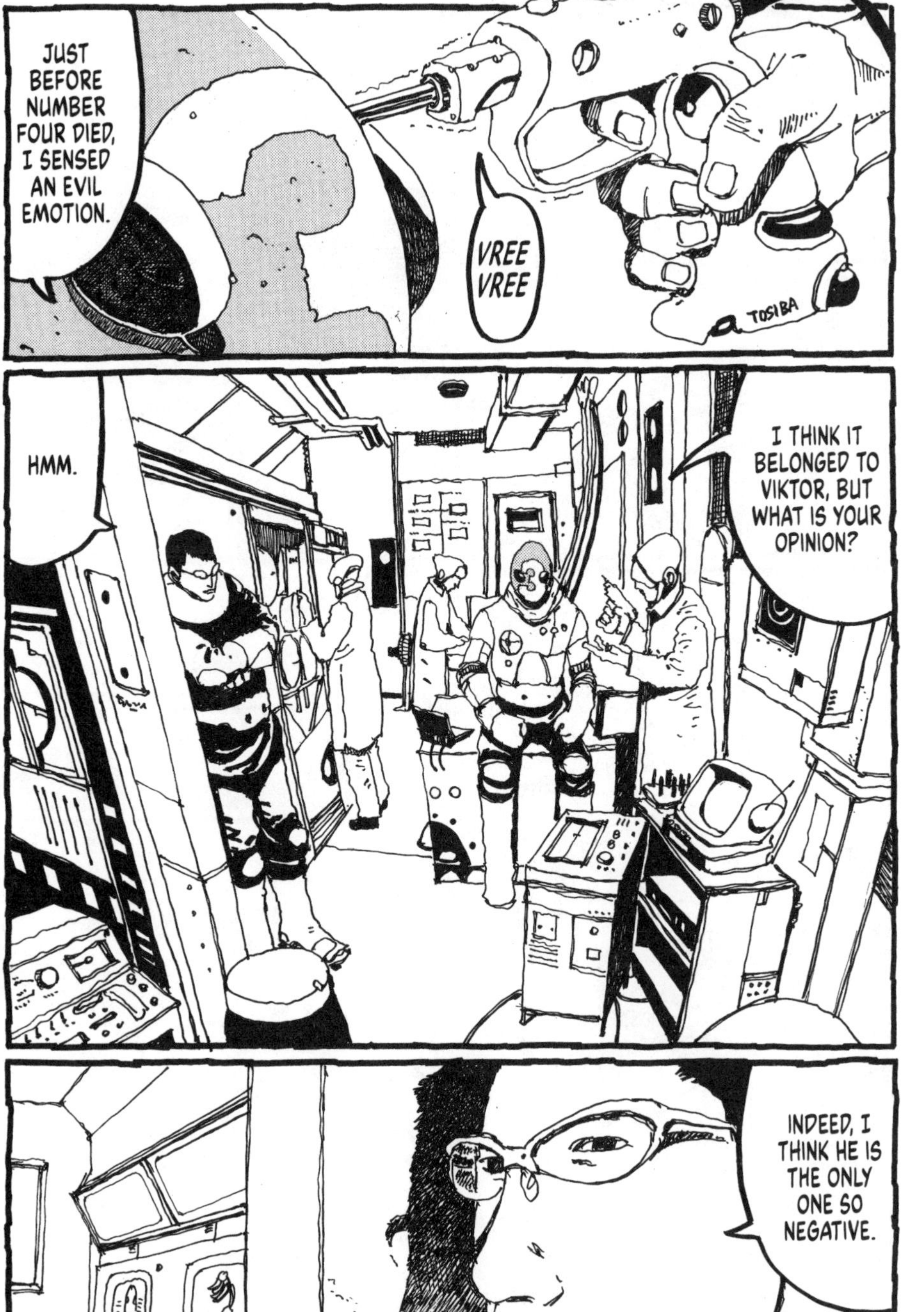
VREE VREE
JUST BEFORE NUMBER FOUR DIED, I SENSED AN EVIL EMOTION.
TOSIBA
I THINK IT BELONGED TO VIKTOR, BUT WHAT IS YOUR OPINION?
HMM.
INDEED, I THINK HE IS THE ONLY ONE SO NEGATIVE.

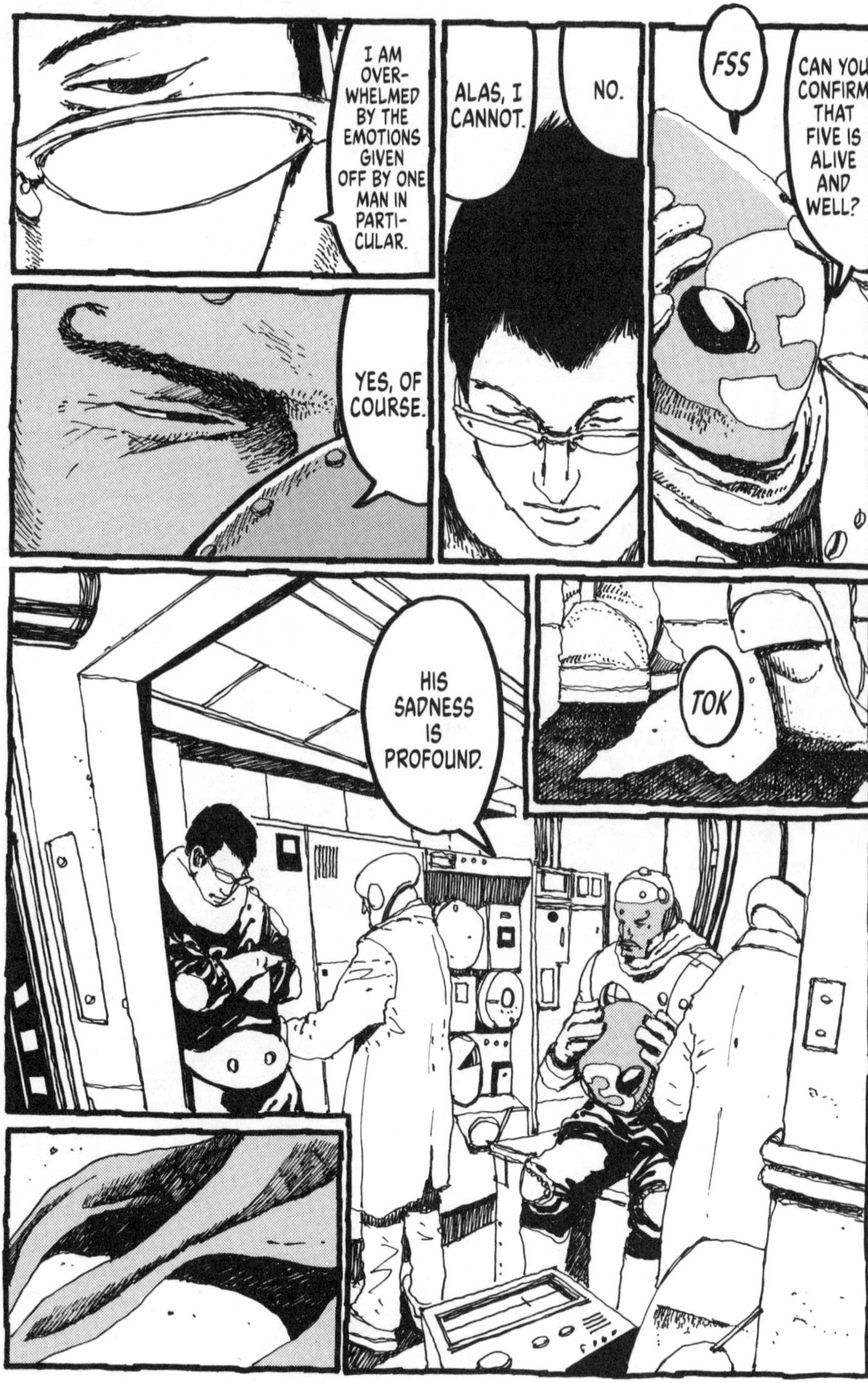
CAN YOU CONFIRM THAT FIVE IS ALIVE AND WELL?
FSS
NO.
ALAS, I CANNOT.
I AM OVERWHELMED BY THE EMOTIONS GIVEN OFF BY ONE MAN IN PARTICULAR.
YES, OF COURSE.
TOK
HIS SADNESS IS PROFOUND.

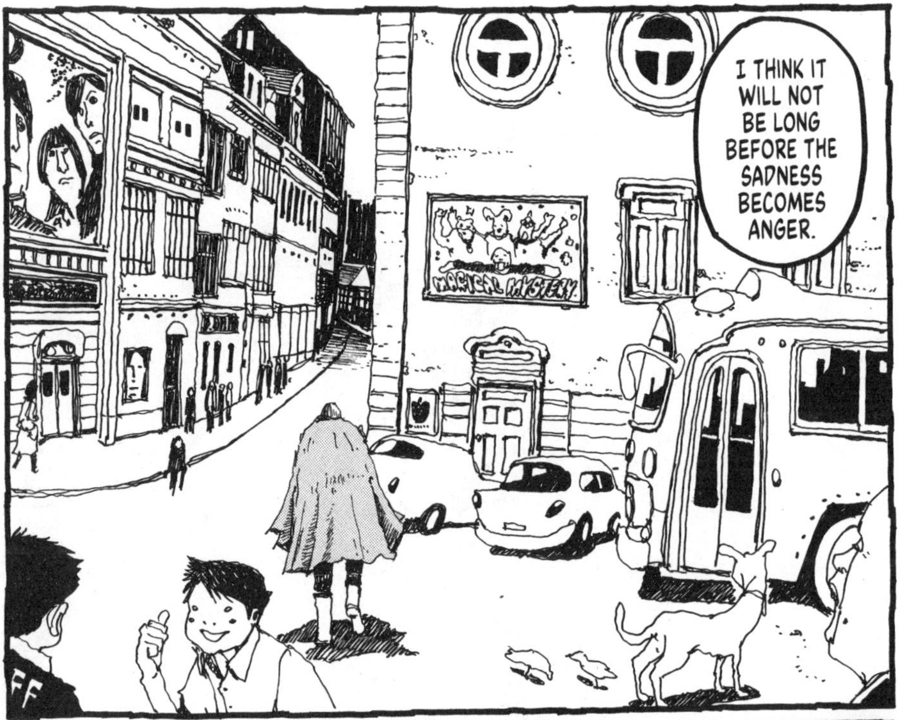
I THINK IT WILL NOT BE LONG BEFORE THE SADNESS BECOMES ANGER.
MAGICAL MYSTERY
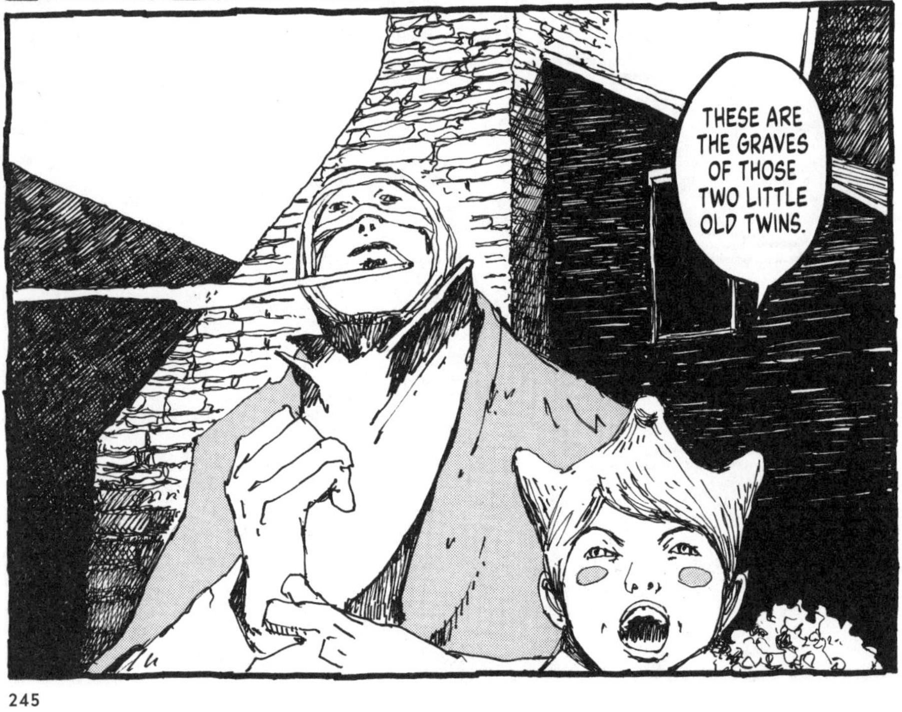
THESE ARE THE GRAVES OF THOSE TWO LITTLE OLD TWINS.

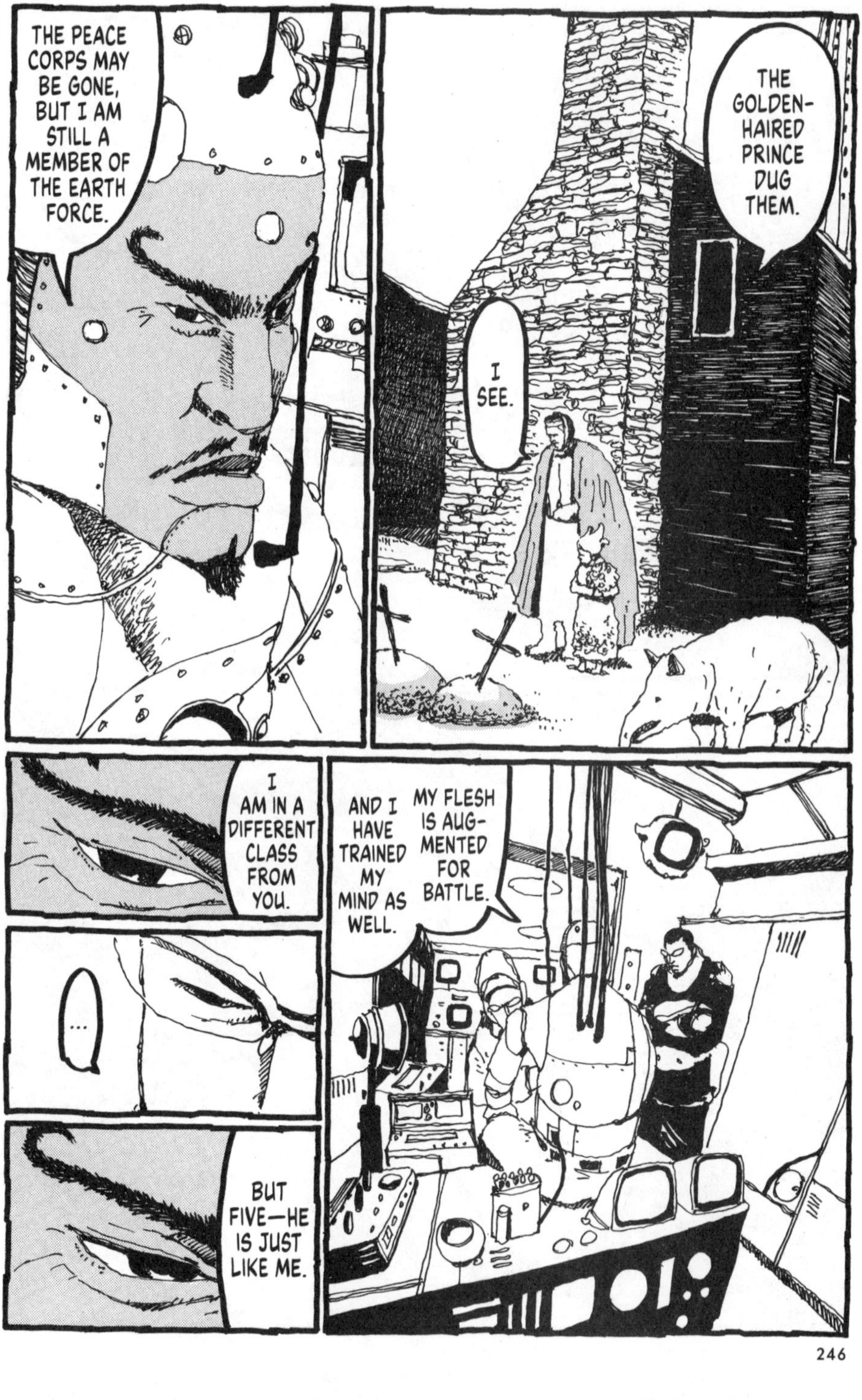
THE GOLDEN-HAIRED PRINCE DUG THEM.
I SEE.
THE PEACE CORPS MAY BE GONE, BUT I AM STILL A MEMBER OF THE EARTH FORCE.
MY FLESH IS AUG-MENTED FOR BATTLE.
AND I HAVE TRAINED MY MIND AS WELL.
I AM IN A DIFFERENT CLASS FROM YOU.
...
BUT FIVE—HE IS JUST LIKE ME.

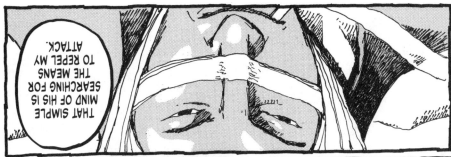

HE ONLY BELIEVES IN VICTORY THROUGH COMBAT.
IF HE IS STILL ALIVE, HE WILL UNDER-STAND MY ANGER NOW.
THAT SIMPLE MIND OF HIS IS SEARCHING FOR THE MEANS TO REPEL MY ATTACK.

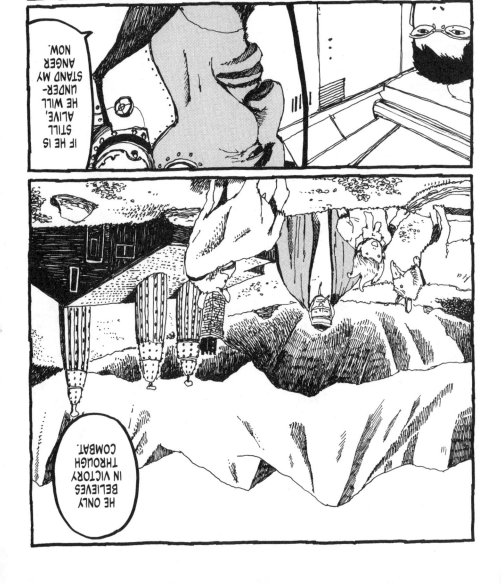

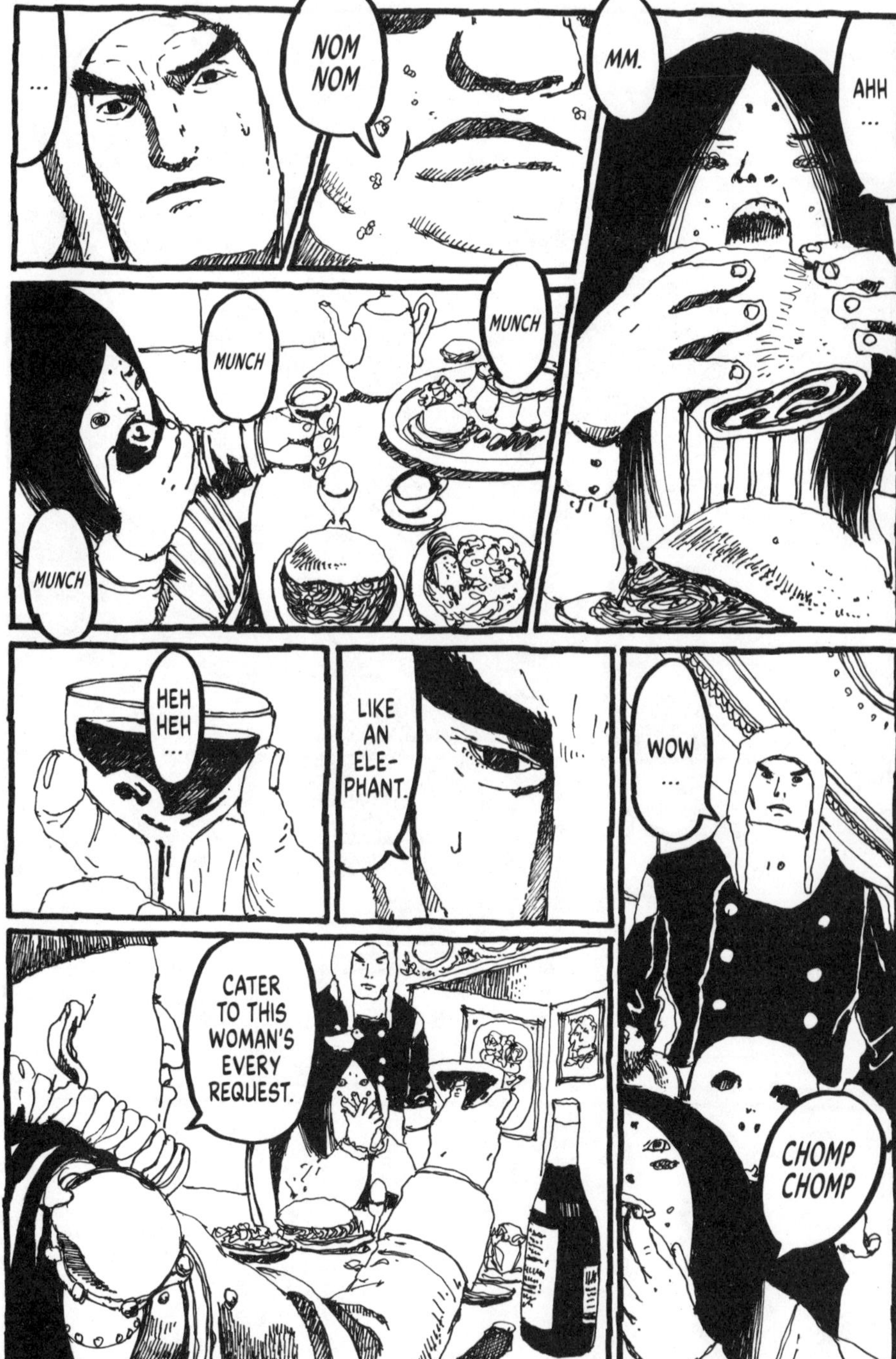
AHH
...
MM.
NOM NOM
...
MUNCH
MUNCH
MUNCH
WOW
...
CHOMP CHOMP
LIKE AN ELE-PHANT.
HEH HEH
...
CATER TO THIS WOMAN'S EVERY REQUEST.

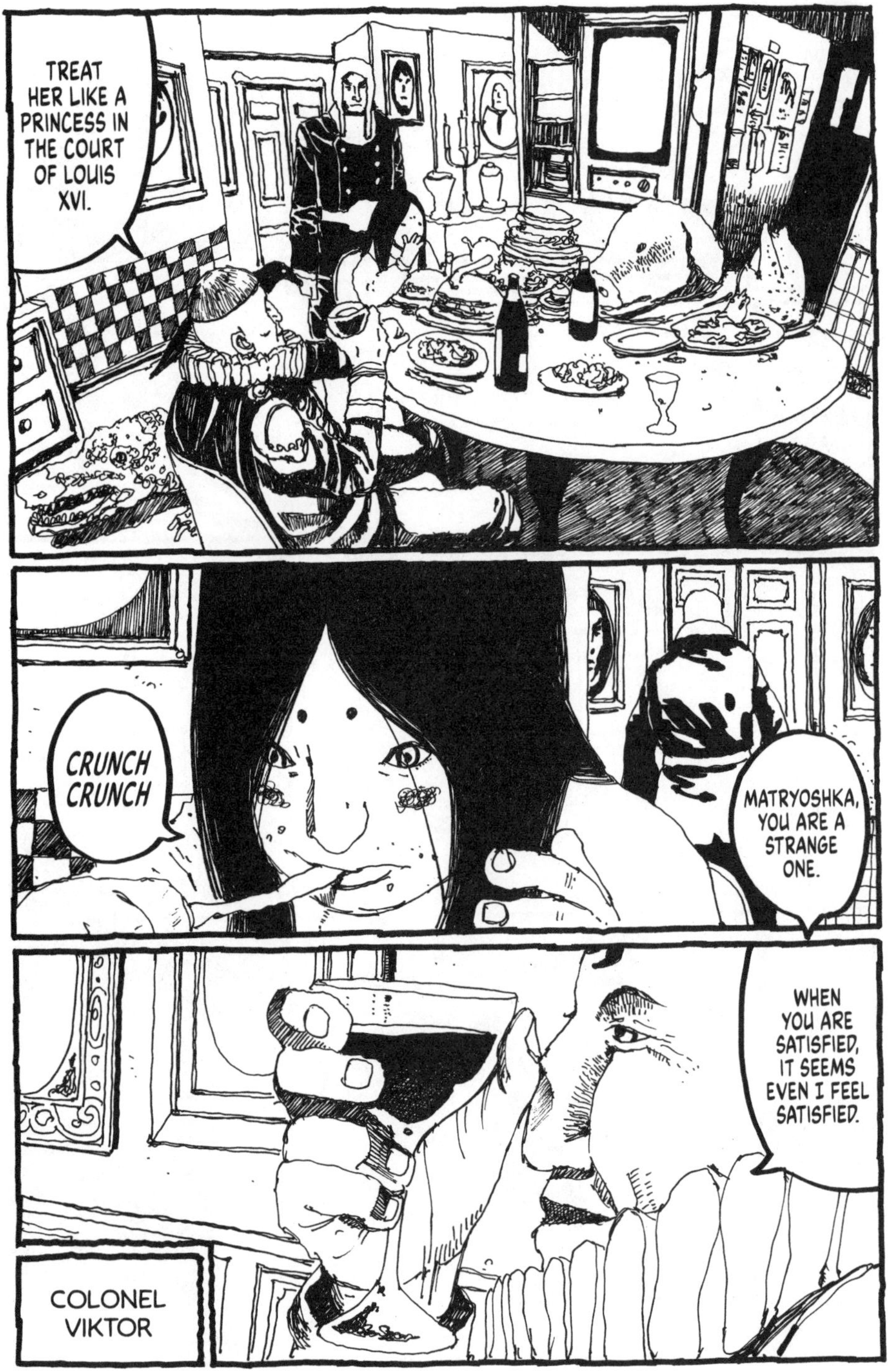
TREAT HER LIKE A PRINCESS IN THE COURT OF LOUIS XVI.
MATRYOSHKA, YOU ARE A STRANGE ONE.
CRUNCH CRUNCH
WHEN YOU ARE SATISFIED, IT SEEMS EVEN I FEEL SATISFIED.
COLONEL VIKTOR

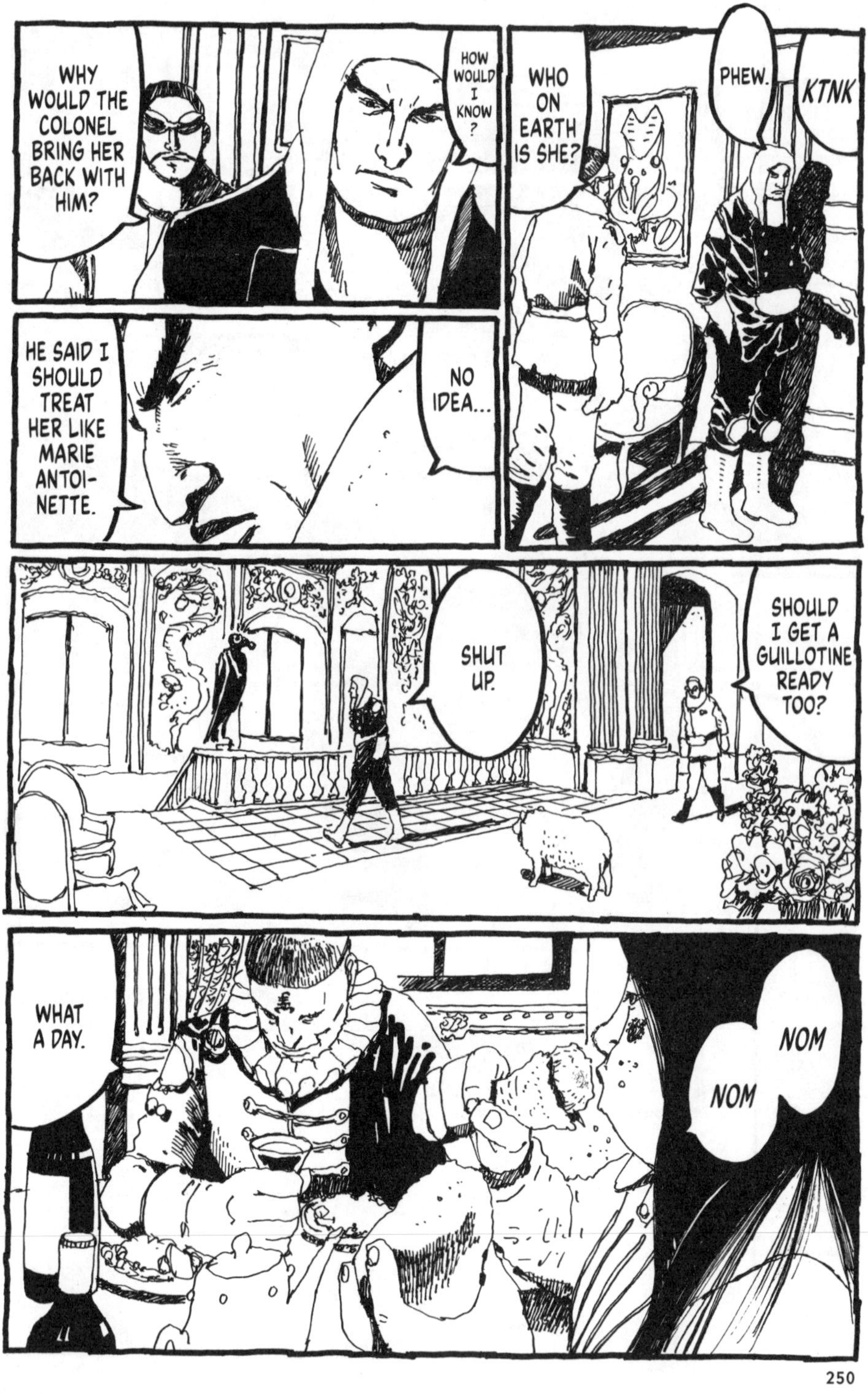
KTNK
PHEW.
WHO ON EARTH IS SHE?
HOW WOULD I KNOW?
WHY WOULD THE COLONEL BRING HER BACK WITH HIM?
NO IDEA...
HE SAID I SHOULD TREAT HER LIKE MARIE ANTOI-NETTE.
SHOULD I GET A GUILLOTINE READY TOO?
SHUT UP.
NOM
NOM
WHAT A DAY.

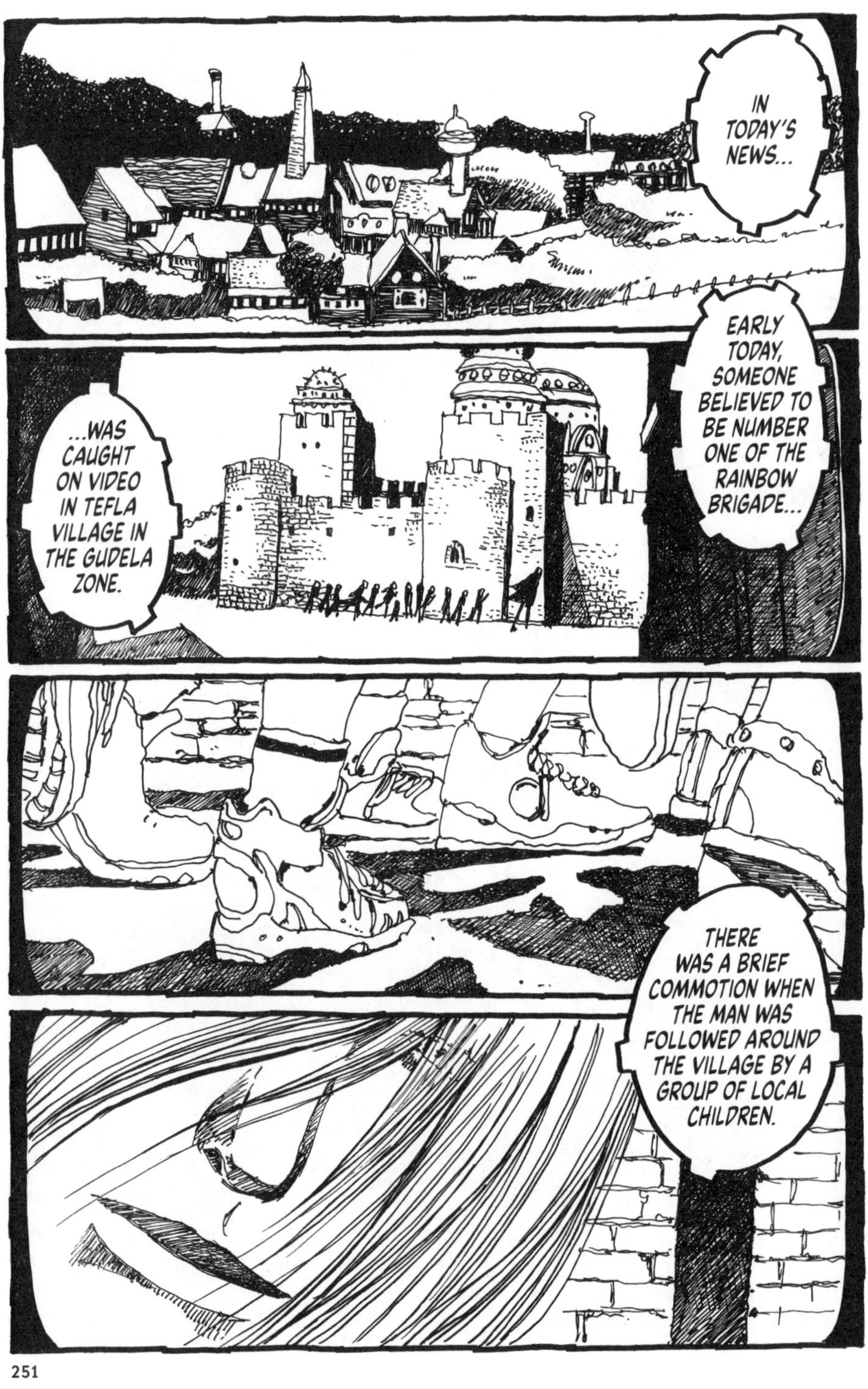
IN TODAY'S NEWS...
EARLY TODAY, SOMEONE BELIEVED TO BE NUMBER ONE OF THE RAINBOW BRIGADE...
...WAS CAUGHT ON VIDEO IN TEFLA VILLAGE IN THE GUDELA ZONE.
THERE WAS A BRIEF COMMOTION WHEN THE MAN WAS FOLLOWED AROUND THE VILLAGE BY A GROUP OF LOCAL CHILDREN.

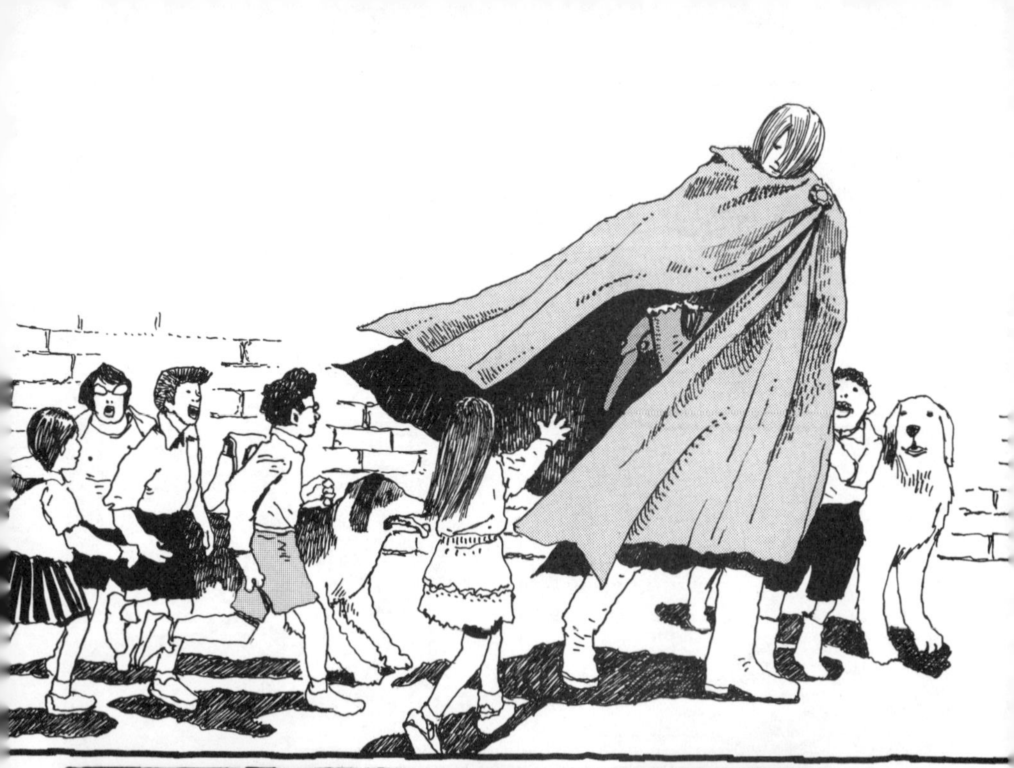

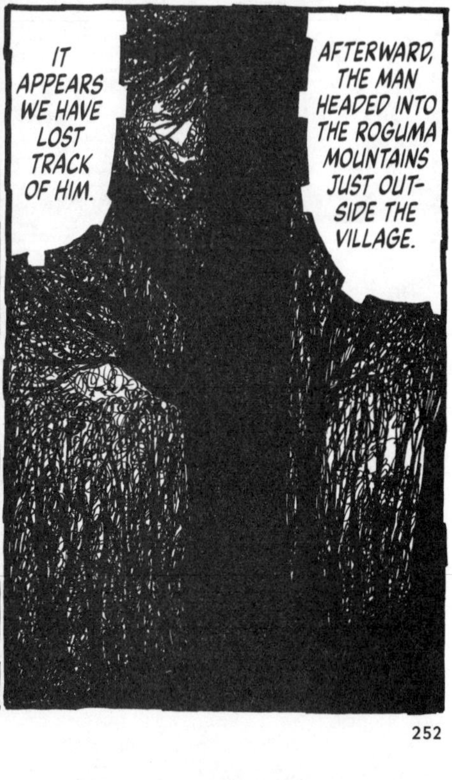
AFTERWARD, THE MAN HEADED INTO THE ROGUMA MOUNTAINS JUST OUT-SIDE THE VILLAGE.
IT APPEARS WE HAVE LOST TRACK OF HIM.

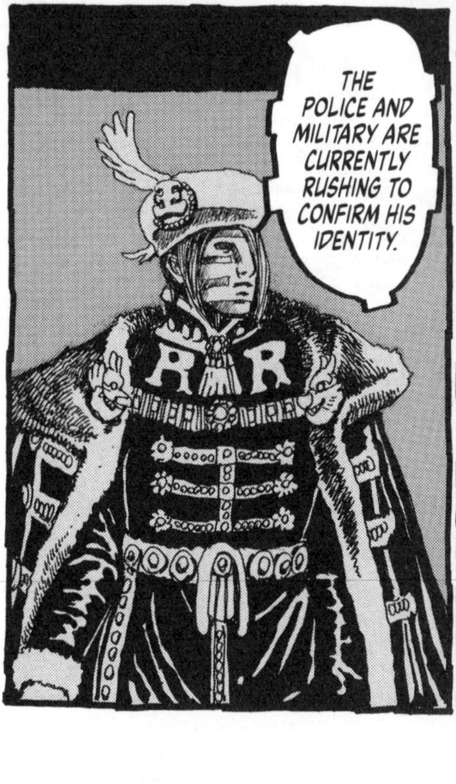
THE POLICE AND MILITARY ARE CURRENTLY RUSHING TO CONFIRM HIS IDENTITY.

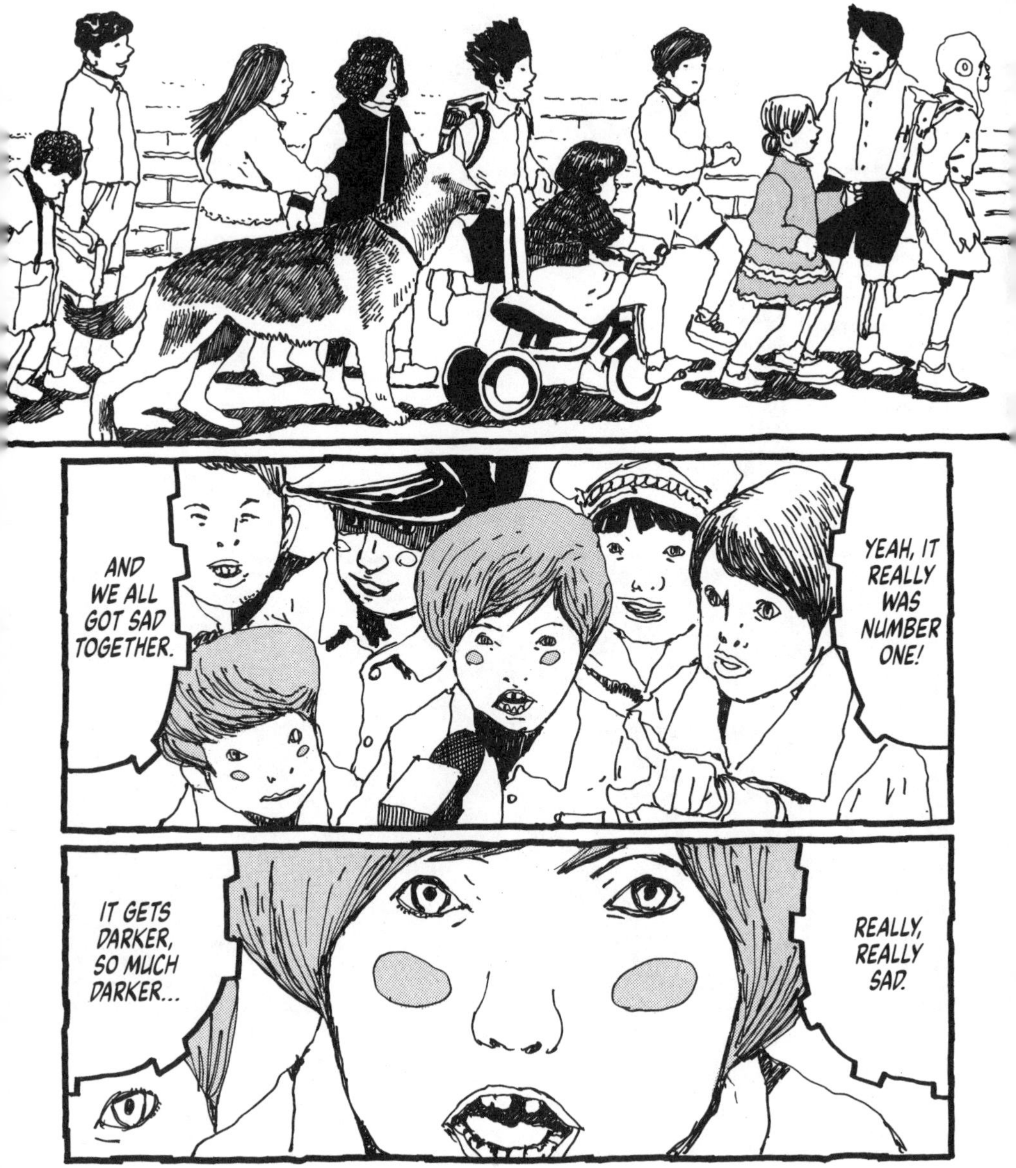
YEAH, IT REALLY WAS NUMBER ONE!
AND WE ALL GOT SAD TOGETHER.
REALLY, REALLY SAD.
IT GETS DARKER, SO MUCH DARKER...

...AND THEN FINALLY YOUR HEART JUST DISAPPEARS.

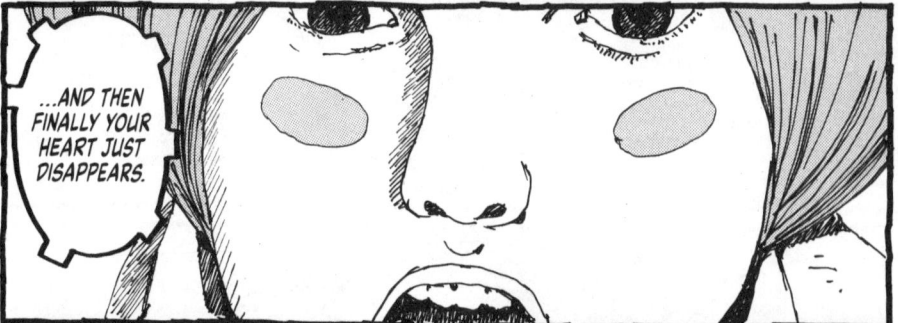

EVERYTHING JUST DISAPPEARS.

No 1

To be continued in volume 3...

TAIYO MATSUMOTO

O is best known to English-reading audiences as the creator of the Eisner Award-winning *Tekkonkinkreet*, which in 2006 was made into an animated feature film of the same name directed by Michael Arias. In 2007, Matsumoto was awarded a Japan Media Arts Festival Excellence Award, and in 2020 he won his second Eisner Award for the English publication of *Cats of the Louvre*.

NOTE: *NO. 5* HAS BEEN PRINTED IN THE ORIGINAL JAPANESE FORMAT IN ORDER TO PRESERVE THE ORIENTATION OF THE ARTWORK.

VOLUME 2 // VIZ SIGNATURE EDITION // Story and Art by TAIYO MATSUMOTO
NUMBER FIVE FUKYUBAN Vol. 2 by Taiyou MATSUMOTO
© 2006 Taiyou MATSUMOTO // All rights reserved. Original Japanese edition published by SHOGAKUKAN. English translation rights in the United States of America, Canada, the United Kingdom, Ireland, Australia and New Zealand arranged with SHOGAKUKAN. // Original Cover Design - Junzi TAKAHASHI

Translation - **MICHAEL ARIAS** // Touch-up Art & Lettering - **DERON BENNETT** // Design - **ADAM GRANO** // Editor - **MIKE MONTESA** // The stories, characters and incidents mentioned in this publication are entirely fictional. // No portion of this book may be reproduced or transmitted in any form or by any means without written permission from the copyright holders.

Printed in Canada // Published by VIZ Media, LLC - P.O. Box 77010 - San Francisco, CA 94107 // 10 9 8 7 6 5 4 3 2 1 // First printing, October 2021

VIZ SIGNATURE
vizsignature.com

VIZ MEDIA
viz.com